THE HAMLYN
CROSSWORD
DICTIONARY

THE HAMLYN
CROSSWORD
DICTIONARY

General Editor, J.M. Bailie

CHANCELLOR
PRESS

This edition first published in 1988 by
The Hamlyn Publishing Group Limited
part of Reed International Books

This 1992 edition published by
Chancellor Press
Michelin House
81 Fulham Road
London SW3 6RB

First published 1932
Revised 1963, 1978

ISBN 1 85152 140 2

Printed in Czechoslovakia

50 861

Contents

Introduction

The Hamlyn Crossword Dictionary is a completely revised edition of the work originally published by C. Arthur Pearson Ltd under the title of the *Complete Crossword Reference Book*. It is the ideal guide for the crossword enthusiast, presenting in a convenient form a collection of over 75,000 carefully selected and classified words which will prove invaluable in solving and compiling crosswords.

It is really very simple to use. In crossword puzzles the number of letters in the required word is known and usually also the subject. The aim of *The Hamlyn Crossword Dictionary* is to enable the reader to quickly find the word he wants. For this reason it has been systematically divided into a number of main subject categories, including *Armed Forces, Business, Professions and Occupations, Geography, Literature and the Arts, Natural History*, and *Science and Technology*, each of which is split up into subdivisions. In these subdivisions all the relevant words will be found under the number of letters required, in lists of words of from two to fifteen (and sometimes more) letters, each list being set out in alphabetical order.

The Hamlyn Crossword Dictionary is not only the indispensable companion for the crossword-puzzle fan but the encyclopedic coverage of its contents makes it a most useful general reference book in addition. Among the many valuable sections in the book are the comprehensive lists of animals, birds, fish, coins, plants, etc., and characters from mythology and literature.

ARMED FORCES
Air force ranks and appellations: British and U.S.

3 AND 4

A.C.2
A.C.1
L.A.C.
W.A.A.F.

5

major (U.S.)
pilot

6

airman
fitter
rigger

7

aviator
captain (U.S.)
colonel (U.S.)
general (U.S.)
private (U.S.)

8

armourer
corporal

mechanic
observer
sergeant

9

air gunner
bomb aimer
drum-major
navigator

10

air marshal
apprentice
balloonist
bombardier (U.S.)
nose gunner
rear gunner
tail gunner

11

aircraftman
belly gunner
second pilot

12

air commodore

group captain
major general (U.S.)
pilot officer

13

flying officer
sergeant major (U.S.)
staff sergeant (U.S.)
wing commander

14

air vice marshal
flight engineer
flight mechanic
flight sergeant
master sergeant (U.S.)
squadron leader
warrant officer

15

air chief marshal
first lieutenant (U.S.)

16

flight lieutenant
second lieutenant (U.S.)

Battles and sieges

3 AND 4

Acre
Aden
Agra
Alma (The)
Amoy
Caen
Gaza
Ivry
Jena
Kut
Laon
Loos
Lys (The)
Maas
Mons
Nile (The)
Taku
Tet
Ulm
Yser (The)
Zama

5

Aisne (The)
Alamo (The)

Arcot
Arras
Basra
Boyne (The)
Cadiz
Cairo
Crécy
Crete
Delhi
El Teb
Eylau
Genoa
Herat
Kabul
Kandy
Liège
Ligny
Maida
Malta
Marne (The)
Meuse
Miami
Narvik
Paris
Pusan
Rhine
Sedan
Selle
Somme (The)

Tagus (The)
Texel (The)
Tours
Valmy
Ypres

6

Actium
Amiens
Arbela
Argaon
Armada (The)
Arnhem
Assaye
Atbara (The)
Bagdad
Barnet
Bataan
Berlin
Burgos
Busaco
Calais
Camden
Cannae
Chusan
Coruña
Dargai

9

Delium
Dunbar
Ferrol
Guarda
Gujrat
Havana
Isonzo (The)
Jattoo
Jhansi
Lutzen
Madras
Madrid
Majuba
Malaga
Manila
Mantua
Midway
Mileto
Minden
Moscow
Nagpur
Naseby
Oporto
Orthez
Ostend
Peking
Plevna
Quebec
Rhodes
Rivoli
Rocroi
Sadowa
Saints (The)
Shiloh
Tarifa
Tobago
Tobruk
Toulon
Tudela
Tugela (The)
Ushant
Verdun
Vienna
Wagram
Warsaw

7

Aboukir
Abu Klea
Alamein
Albuera
Almansa
Almeida
Antwerp
Badajoz
Baghdad
Bapaume
Bautzen
Bousaco
Brienne
Bull Run
Cambrai
Cape Bon
Cassino
Chalons
Coimbra
Colenso
Cordova
Coronel
Corunna
Dresden
Dunkirk
Edghill
El Obeid

Falkirk
Flodden
Granada
Gwalior
Iwo Jima
Jutland
La Hogue
Leipzig
Lemberg
Lepanto
Leuthen
Lucknow
Magdala
Magenta
Marengo
Matapan
Minorca
Moselle
Moskowa (The)
Nations (The)
Newbury
Nivelle (The)
Okinawa
Orleans
Plassey
Poltava
Preston
St. Kitts
St. Lucia
Salerno
Sobraon
Solebay
Vimiera
Vitoria

8

Ardennes
Atlantic (The)
Bastille (The)
Beresina (The)
Blenheim
Bhurtpur
Borodino
Bosworth
Calcutta
Carthage
Cawnpore
Culloden
Edgehill
Flanders
Flushing
Fontenoy
Fort Erie
Hastings
Inkerman
Kandahar
Khartoum
Lake Erie
Le Cateau
Mafeking
Malakoff (The)
Marathon
Maubeuge
Medellin
Messines
Metaurus
Montreal
Navarino
Nieuport
Normandy
Omdurman
Poitiers
Potidaea
Pretoria

Przemysl
St. Mihiel
St. Pierre
Salsette
Saratoga
Spion Kop
Stirling
Suvla Bay
Syracuse
Talavera
Tiberias
Toulouse
Valencia
Waterloo
Yorktown
Zaragoza

9

Agincourt
Algeciras
Balaclava
Belle Isle
Caporetto
Chaeronea
Champagne
Charleroi
Ctesiphon
Dettingen
El Alamein
Falklands (The)
Festubert
Friedland
Gallipoli
Gaugamela
Gibraltar
Hyderabad
Kimberley
Ladysmith
Laing's Nek
Leningrad
Leyte Gulf
Louisburg
Mauritius
Melagnano
Mobile Bay
Oudenarde
Pharsalus
Port Mahon
Ramillies
Rodriguez
Saragossa
St. Quentin
St. Vincent
Salamanca
Sedgemoor
Solferino
Stormberg
Stromboli
Tarragona
Tourcoing
Trafalgar
Vicksburg
Walcheren
Worcester
Zeebrugge

10

Adrianople
Ahmednagar
Alexandria
Appomattox
Austerlitz

Brandywine
Brownstown
Bunker Hill
Camperdown
Chevy-chase
Copenhagen
Corregidor
Dogger Bank
Fort George
Gettysburg
Gravelotte
Guadeloupe
Heligoland
Imjin River
Kut-el-Amara
La Rochelle
Les Saintes
Malplaquet
Martinique
Montevideo
Montfaucon
New Orleans
Nördlingen
Paardeburg
Petersburg
Port Arthur
Porto Praya
Quatre Bras
River Plate
Sevastopol
Shrewsbury
Stalingrad
Tannenberg
Tel-el-Kebir
Tewkesbury
Tinchebray

11

Albuquerque
Bannockburn
Breitenfeld
Chattanooga
Chilianwala
Dardanelles (The)
Dien Bien Phu
Fort Niagara
Guadalcanal
Hohenlinden
Isandhlwana
Jameson Raid (The)
Marston Moor
Pearl Harbor
Philiphaugh
Philippines (The)
Pieter's Hill
Pondicherry
Prestonpans
Quiberon Bay
Rorke's Drift
Schoneveldt
Thermopylae
Ticonderoga

12 AND OVER

Antietam Creek (13)
Battle of Britain (15)
Bloemfontein (12)
Cape St. Vincent (13)
Ciudad Rodrigo (13)
Constantinople (14)

Delville Wood (12)
Falkland Islands (15)
Flodden Field (12)
Lake Champlain (13)
Little Bighorn (12)
Magersfontein (13)

Messines Ridge (13)
Neuve Chapelle (13)
Neville's Cross (13)
Passchendaele (13)
Plains of Abraham (15)
San Sebastian (12)

Seringapatam (12)
Spanish Armada (The) (13)
Stamford Bridge (14)
Trichinopoly (12)
Tsushima Strait (14)
White Mountain (13)

Military ranks and appellations

2 AND 3

A.D.C.
C.O.
C.S.M.
G.I.
N.C.O.
O.C.
R.S.M.
R.T.O.

4

goum
koul
lewa
naik
peon

5

cadet
fifer
Jäger
major
miner
piper
scout
sepoy
sowar
spahi
Tommy
Uhlan

6

batman
bomber
bowman
bugler
cornet
driver
ensign
gunner
Gurkha
hetman
hussar
lancer
marine
ranger
ranker
sapper
sutler
Zouave

7

ancient
captain

colonel
Cossack
dragoon
drummer
estafet
farrier
general
hobbler
hoplite
janizar
jemadar
lancers
marines
marshal
militia
officer
orderly
pikeman
pioneer
private
recruit
redcoat
reserve
saddler
sappers
soldier
subadar
trooper
vedette
veteran
warrior

8

adjutant
armourer
bandsman
cavalier
chasseur
commando
corporal
daffadar
decurion
deserter
doughboy
dragoons
fencible
fugelman
fusilier
havildar
infantry
janizary
Landwehr
marksman
messmate
muleteer
mutineer
partisan
rifleman
risaldar
sentinel
sergeant

spearman
turncoat
waterman

9

beefeater
berserker
brigadier
cannoneer
cannonier
centurion
combatant
commander
conductor
conscript
drum-major
estaffette
field rank
fife-major
fort-major
grenadier
guardsman
guerrilla
Home Guard
irregular
Janissary
lance-naik
man-at-arms
musketeer
paymaster
pensioner
pipe-major
signaller
subaltern
tactician
town-major
trumpeter
tradesman
vexillary
voltigeur
volunteer

10

aide-de-camp
bandmaster
bombardier
campaigner
carabineer
cavalryman
commandant
cuirassier
drummer-boy
file-leader
footguards
halberdier
instructor
Lansquenet
lieutenant
lifeguards

militiaman
other ranks
paratroops
roughrider
strategist

11

arquebusier
artillerist
auxiliaries
bashi-bazook
bersaglieri
condottiere
crack troops
crossbowman
gendarmerie
horse guards
infantryman
Landsknecht
moss-trooper
parachutist
paratrooper
rangefinder
top sergeant
Tommy Atkins

12

armour-bearer
artilleryman
brigade-major
camp-follower
ensign-bearer
field marshal
field officer
horse soldier
jemadar-major
major-general
master gunner
officer cadet
P.T. instructor
Royal Marines
Royal Signals
staff officer
storm-trooper
subadar-major
sub-conductor
territorials

13

army commander
barrack-master
brevet-colonel
bugle-corporal
color-sergeant
corporal-major
dispatch-rider
drill sergeant

11

first sergeant
generalissimo
lance-corporal
lance-daffadar
lance-sergeant
lifeguardsman
light infantry
machine-gunner
marine officer
mounted rifles
prisoner of war
quartermaster
risaldar major
sergeant major
staff-sergeant

14

citizen-soldier
colonel-in-chief
colour-havildar
colour-sergeant
liaison officer
master sergeant
medical officer
military police
orderly officer
provost-marshal
Royal Artillery
Royal Engineers
Royal Tank Corps
second corporal
signals officer

standard bearer
warrant officer

15

adjutant-general
corporal-of-horse
first lieutenant
gentleman-at-arms
honorary colonel
household troops
mounted infantry
orderly corporal
orderly sergeant
ordnance officer
provost sergeant

Military terms (including fortifications)

2–4

aim
ally
ammo
anfo
arm
arms
army
A.W.O.L.
band
base
bawn
belt
berm
blip
camp
defy
draw
duck
duel
dun
fife
file
fire
flag
flak
foe
foot
form
fort
foss
gas
gun
halt
host
hut
jam
jeep
kern
kit
lay
levy
line
loot
man
map
mess
mine
moat
O.C.T.U.
out

pah
park
P.I.A.T.
plan
post
P.O.W.
push
raid
ramp
rank
raze
rear
rout
ruse
sack
sap
shot
slay
slug
spot
spur
star
take
tank
tent
tilt
trap
turn
unit
van
war
ward
wing
zero

5

abort
agent
alarm
alert
annex
A.N.Z.A.C.
armed
armor
array
baton
beret
berme
beset
booty

busby
butts
cadre
cavin
cells
clean
corps
decoy
depot
depth
ditch
dogra
draft
drawn
dress
drill
enemy
enrol
equip
feint
field
fight
flank
flare
foray
fosse
fours
front
gazon
gorge
guard
guide
gurry
herse
horse
khaki
lance
lines
march
medal
mêlée
mount
mufti
onset
order
party
peace
pivot
poilu
pouch
prime
radar

rally
range
ranks
redan
relay
repel
rifle
round
route
royal
sally
salvo
scale
scarp
seize
S.H.A.E.F.
shako
shell
shift
shock
shoot
siege
snipe
sonar
sonic
spoil
squad
staff
stand
storm
strap
talus
T.E.W.T.S.
track
troop
truce
unarm
vexil
wheel
wound
yield

6

abatis
ack-ack
action
affray
allies
ambush
archer

		7	
armour	limber	abattis	gunnery
assail	marker	advance	gun-shot
attack	merlon	aid-post	half-pay
bailey	mining	air-raid	harness
banner	mobile	airlift	holster
barbed	muster	archery	hostage
battle	mutiny	armoury	hostile
beaten	number	arsenal	hutment
billet	obsess	assault	jamming
blinds	occupy	baggage	Kremlin
blow up	oppose	barrack	landing
bonnet	orders	barrage	leaguer
bouche	orgues	basenet	liaison
brevet	outfit	bastion	looting
bunker	parade	battery	lunette
cartel	parley	battled	madrier
castle	parole	besiege	maniple
centre	patrol	bivouac	marquee
charge	pennon	bombard	martial
clayes	permit	brigade	megaton
cohort	picket	bulwark	moineau
colour	plonge	caltrop	mounted
column	pompom	canteen	neutral
combat	pompon	carbine	nuclear
convoy	primer	caserne	on guard
cordon	pursue	cavalry	outpost
corral	raider	chamade	outwing
curfew	ransom	charger	outwork
dagger	rapine	chevron	overawe
débris	rappel	citadel	overrun
decamp	ration	cold war	parados
defeat	ravage	colours	parapet
defend	rebuff	command	pennant
defier	recall	company	phalanx
defile	recoil	conquer	pillbox
deploy	reduce	counter	pitfall
desert	relais	coupure	platoon
detach	relief	crusade	plongée
detail	report	curtain	postern
disarm	resist	debouch	priming
donjon	retake	defence	protect
double	retire	defiant	provost
dugout	review	degrade	prowess
embark	riddle	destroy	pursuit
embody	rideau	détente	quarter
encamp	roster	detrain	rampart
engage	saddle	disband	rations
enlist	salute	dismiss	ravelin
enmity	sconce	dispart	redoubt
ensign	sensor	drawn up	refugee
epaule	signal	draw off	regular
escape	sketch	dungeon	remblai
escarp	sortie	echelon	remount
escort	square	ecoutes	repulse
Fabian	stores	enguard	reserve
fanion	strife	enomoty	retaken
firing	strike	entrain	retreat
fleche	stripe	envelop	reverse
foeman	stroke	environ	Riot Act
forted	subdue	epaulet	salient
fraise	submit	fallout	sand-bag
gabion	supply	fanfare	section
glacis	target	fascine	service
guards	tattoo	fatigue	sniping
guides (the)	thrust	flanker	spurred
guidon	trench	fortify	stand-by
hawhaw	trophy	fortlet	subvert
helmet	umpire	forward	support
hurter	vallum	fourgon	tactics
impact	valour	foxhole	tambour
inroad	victor	fraised	tenable
invade	volley	gallery	tilting
invest	walled	guérite	trailer
inwall	warcry	gunfire	triumph
kitbag	zareba		unarmed
legion	zigzag		uncased

13

uniform
valiant
van-foss
venture
victory
ward off
warfare
wargame
war-hoop
warlike
warpath
warsong
warworn
wheeler
windage
wounded

8

accoutre
advanced
airborne
air force
alarm gun
alliance
armament
armature
armorial
arms race
Army List
baldrick
barbette
barbican
barracks
bartizan
bawdrick
bearskin
billeted
blockade
bull's eye
camisade
camisado
campaign
casemate
casualty
chivalry
civil war
collapse
conquest
cornetcy
crusader
decimate
decisive
defended
defender
defiance
demi-lune
demolish
despatch
detonate
disarray
disenrol
dismount
dispatch
distance
division
doubling
drumhead
duelling
earth-bag
embattle
embodied
enceinte
enfilade
ensigncy

entrench
equipage
escalade
escouade
estacade
eyes left
fastness
field day
fighting
flagpost
flanking
footband
fortress
fourneau
furlough
garrison
gauntlet
gendarme
gonfalon
guerilla
half-moon
hang-fire
hedgehog
herisson
hillfort
horn-work
intrench
invasion
knapsack
last post
lay siege
lay waste
limber up
lodgment
loophole
magazine
majority
Mameluke
mantelet
marching
mark time
matériel
mess bill
militant
military
mobilize
movement
muniment
musketry
mutinous
on parade
on parole
opponent
ordnance
outflank
outguard
outlying
overcome
overkill
palisade
paradrop
passport
password
pavilion
pay corps
pipe-clay
prisoner
punitive
quarters
railhead
ramparts
rear line
rear rank
rearward
recharge
re-embark

re-embody
regiment
remounts
reprisal
resalute
retirade
retrench
reveille
ricochet
rifle-pit
roll-call
sabotage
saboteur
saluting
scout-car
security
sentry-go
services (the)
shabrack
shelling
shooting
shot-belt
siege-war
skirmish
soldiery
spotting
squadron
stampede
standard
star-fort
stockade
stoppage
storming
straddle
strategy
strength
struggle
supplies
support
surprise
surround
sword arm
tactical
tenaille
time-fuse
tortoise
training
transfer
traverse
trooping (the colour)
unallied
unbeaten
unlimber
uprising
valorous
vanguard
vanquish
vexillar
victuals
vigilant
vincible
warfarer
warhorse
warpaint
war-plume
war-whoop
watch-box
wheeling
yeomanry
zero hour

9

aggressor
alarm post

ambuscade
ambuscado
armistice
armouries
army corps
artillery
assailant
atomic war
attrition
ballistic
bandolier
banquette
barricade
barricado
battalion
batteries
battle-cry
beachhead
beleaguer
bellicose
billeting
bodyguard
bombproof
bugle call
bulldozer
cannonade
captaincy
cashiered
cavalcade
ceasefire
challenge
chevalier
colonelcy
comitadji
conqueror
covert-way
crossfire
crown-work
crow's foot
defection
defensive
defiatory
demi-gorge
desertion
devastate
discharge
disembody
disengage
dismantle
earthwork
elevation
embattled
embrasure
encompass
encounter
enfiladed
enrolment
epaulette
equipment
espionage
esplanade
eyes front
eyes right
fencibles
field rank
fire-drill
flagstaff
forage-cap
form fours
fortalice
fortifier
fortilage
fusillade
gabionade
gas attack
gladiator

guardroom	sword-knot	dragonnade	siege-train
guerrilla	taskforce	drawbridge	signal-fire
haversack	tenaillon	embodiment	signalling
heliostat	terrorist	encampment	skirmisher
hersillon	train-band	enfilading	slit trench
homograph	transport	engagement	soldiering
hostility	treachery	engarrison	squad drill
housewife	tricolour	enlistment	state of war
incursion	unbridged	epaulement	sticky bomb
interdict	undaunted	epauletted	stronghold
invalided	undrilled	escalation	subjection
irregular	unguarded	escarpment	subsection
land force	unhostile	expedition	submission
Landsturm	uniformed	fieldworks	submissive
legionary	unopposed	flying camp	subversion
lifeguard	unordered	garrisoned	surrounded
logistics	unscathed	glasshouse	sword-fight
loopholed	unsheathe	ground fire	table money
Luftwaffe	unstormed	guardhouse	terreplein
majorship	unwarlike	hand-to-hand	tirailleur
manoeuvre	unwounded	heliograph	trajectory
mechanist	vigilance	Indian file	triumphant
mercenary	war office	inspection	undecisive
militancy	watchword	investment	undefended
musketoon	Wehrmacht	invincible	unequipped
Mutiny Act	white flag	leadership	unlimbered
objective	withstand	light-armed	unmolested
offensive	zigzagged	light horse	unsheathed
officiate		limited war	vanquisher
onsetting		line of fire	victorious
onslaught	**10**	manoeuvres	volunteers
operation		map-reading	vulnerable
overpower	action left	martial law	war-council
overshoot	aggressive	militarism	watchtower
overthrow	air-defence	musketeers	
overwhelm	ammunition	muster book	
packdrill	annexation	muster roll	**11**
pack train	annihilate	night-watch	
palladium	arbalister	no man's land	action front
parachute	armipotent	nuclear war	action right
predictor	attackable	occupation	aides-de-camp
pregnable	battlement	odd-numbers	assaultable
pressgang	blitzkrieg	operations	barrackroom
projector	blockhouse	opposition	battle-array
promotion	breastwork	outgeneral	battledress
protector	brevet rank	over the top	battlefield
provender	bridgehead	patrolling	battle-royal
rearguard	camel corps	point blank	belligerent
rebellion	camouflage	portcullis	besiegement
reconquer	cantonment	presidiary	bombardment
red ensign	capitulate	prison camp	bridge-train
re-enforce	ceremonial	projectile	bulletproof
refortify	challenger	protection	button-stick
reinforce	color guard	provisions	castellated
rencontre	commandeer	quartering	colour party
reprimand	commissary	quick-march	conquerable
revetment	commission	raking fire	co-operation
revictual	contraband	reconquest	countermine
safeguard	crenulated	recruiting	defenceless
sally-port	dead ground	re-entering	demi-bastion
scrimmage	decampment	regimental	devastation
semaphore	defendable	rencounter	disarmament
sentry-box	defensible	rendezvous	disbandment
sham-fight	defilading	reorganize	disgarrison
slaughter	demobilize	reparation	double-march
slope arms	demolition	resistance	drawn swords
slow-march	deployment	respirator	dress parade
stack arms	desolating	retirement	embarkation
stand-fast	desolation	revolution	emplacement
stand fire	despatches	rifle range	envelopment
stand-firm	detachment	route march	even numbers
stratagem	detonation	sabretache	fatigue duty
strategic	direct fire	sentry beat	firing party
subaltern	dismounted	sentry duty	firing squad
subjugate	dispatches	senty post	flag of truce
surrender	divisional	shell-proof	flying party

15

flying squad
foot-soldier
forced march
forlorn hope
form two deep
fortifiable
generalship
germ warfare
guerilla war
impregnable
indefensive
machicoulis
mobile force
orderly room
penetration
postern gate
present arms
protagonist
range-finder
rank-and-file
reconnoitre
recruitment
redoubtable
review order
royal salute
running-fire
safe conduct
searchlight
shock-troop
skirmishing
smokescreen
stand-to-arms
supply depot
trous-de-loup
trumpet call
unconquered
unfortified
unprotected
unsoldierly
unsupported
vincibility
war memorial

12

advanced base
advance guard
annihilation
anti-aircraft
Bailey bridge
barking-irons
battlemented
bush-fighting
capitulation
civil defence
commissariat
commissioned
conscription
counterguard
countermarch
court-martial
covering fire
demi-distance
disaffection
dropping fire
fatigue party
field colours
field-kitchen
flying column
foot-barracks
garrison town
guerrilla war
headquarters
heavy brigade
hollow square

horse-and-foot
indefensible
indirect fire
intelligence
intrenchment
invulnerable
irresistible
landing party
light brigade
light cavalry
line-of-battle
machicolated
Maltese cross
mobile column
mobilization
outmanoeuvre
platoon drill
plunging fire
protectorate
quarter-guard
remount depot
retrenchment
running fight
ruse-de-guerre
shock tactics
saluting base
shoulder-belt
shoulder-knot
siege tactics
siege warfare
staff college
surveillance
truce-breaker
ungarrisoned
unintrenched
unobstructed
unvanquished
vanquishable
white feather
working party

13

accoutrements
advanced guard
carrier pigeon
cheval-de-frise
circumvallate
co-belligerent
column-of-route
counterattack
counter-parole
counterstoke
disembodiment
encompassment
fatigue parade
field equipage
field of battle
fighting force
flying colours
fortification
guards' brigade
interior lines
invincibility
lorry workshop
machicolation
martello tower
mass formation
mounted police
mushroom cloud
order of battle
ordnance depot
pontoon-bridge
radiolocation
rallying point

re-embarkation
re-enforcement
regular troops
reinforcement
sapper officer
shoulder-strap
splinter-proof
squadron drill
storming-party
strategically
swordsmanship
trench warfare
unarmed combat
unconquerable
unsoldierlike
unsurrendered
urban guerilla
Victoria Cross
vitrified fort
war department

14

ammunition dump
auxiliary force
blockade-runner
castrametation
chevaux-de-frise
demobilization
field allowance
general reserve
mechanized army
military school
miniature-range
medical officer
musketry course
musketry school
nuclear warfare
Pyrrhic victory
reconnaissance
reinforcements
reorganization
standing orders
supreme command
trooping-season
unvanquishable
volunteer force
winter quarters

15

auxiliary forces
casualty station
circumvallation
clearing station
contravallation
counter-approach
discharge papers
dressing-station
flying artillery
guerilla warfare
intrenching tool
invulnerability
married quarters
military academy
military college
military funeral
military railway
non-commissioned
observation post
operation orders
submarine-mining
substantive rank
turning movement

16

Naval (British and U.S.), Fleet Air Arm, Merchant Navy (Merchant Marine) ranks and appellations

4

cook
mate
wren

5

bosun
cadet
diver
middy
pilot

6

cooper
ensign
lascar
marine
master
purser
rating
reefer
seaman
snotty
stoker
topman
writer
yeoman

7

admiral
armorer
artisan
captain
deckboy
fireman
greaser
jack-tar
look-out
messman
recruit
shipman
sideboy
skipper
steward

surgeon
trimmer
wireman

8

armourer
cabinboy
chaplain
coxswain
engineer
flag rank
gun-layer
helmsman
leadsman
messmate
motorman
ship's boy
winchman

9

air-fitter
artificer
boatswain
commander
commodore
cook's mate
donkeyman
engineman
navigator
paymaster
powder-boy
ropemaker
sailmaker
ship's cook
signalman
tugmaster

10

able seaman
apprentice
coastguard
gun captain
instructor
lieutenant
midshipman

range-taker
shipmaster
ship's baker
shipwright
torpedoman
wardmaster

11

air mechanic
branch pilot
chief stoker
electrician
extra master
flag captain
flag officer
foremastman
gunner's mate
leading wren
master's mate
mechanician
port admiral
port officer
post captain
rating pilot
rear-admiral
vice-admiral
watchkeeper

12

boy artificer
cabin steward
chief officer
chief skipper
chief steward
first officer
master-at-arms
master gunner
officers' cook
petty officer
photographer
powder monkey
P.T. instructor
schoolmaster
seaman-bugler
seaman-gunner
second master
senior purser

ship's butcher
ship's caulker
ship's surgeon
supply rating
telegraphist
third officer

13

armourer's mate
captain's clerk
chief armourer
chief engineer
fourth officer
harbourmaster
leading seaman
leading stoker
marine officer
privateersman
quartermaster
quarter rating
radio operator
sailing master
second officer
ship's corporal
signal officer
stern-sheetman
sub-lieutenant
third engineer
torpedo-gunner

14 AND 15

boarding officer
boatswain's mate
first lieutenant
flag-lieutenant
fourth engineer
half-pay officer
leading steward
lieut.-commander
officer's steward
ordinary seaman
rating observer
sailmaker's mate
second engineer
ship's carpenter
torpedo coxswain
warrant officer

Weapons and armour

3 AND 4

ABM
ammo
arm
arms
axe
ball
bill
bola
bolt
bomb
bow

butt
cane
club
colt
dag
dart
dirk
epée
flak
foil
gaff
goad
gun

helm
ICBM
jack
jet
kris
mace
mail
mine
nike
pike
ram
shot
tank

tuck
VTOL
wad
whip
Z-gun

5

A-bomb
aegis
armor
arrow

17

bilbo
birch
clean
crest
estoc
fusee
fusil
grape
H-bomb
hobit
knife
knout
lance
lasso
lathi
Maxim
poker
pouch
rifle
royal
sabre
salvo
shaft
shell
skean
skene
spear
staff
stick
sword
targe
tasse
tawse
visor
vizor

6

ack-ack
air-gun
anlace
armlet
armour
barrel
basnet
bodkin
Bofors
bonnet
buffer
bullet
cannon
carrel
casque
cudgel
cuisse
dagger
dragon
dualin
feltre
glaive
gorget
hanger
helmet
homing
jezail
lariat
lassoo
lorica
mailed
mauser
morion
mortar
musket
muzzle
napalm

petard
pistol
pom-pom
popgun
powder
primer
quarry
rapier
recoil
sallet
saturn
shield
sickle
stylet
swivel
target
tonite
tulwar
umbril
weapon
Webley
zipgun

7

anelace
armbrust
assagai
assegai
ataghan
bar-shot
baslard
bayonet
bazooka
brasset
Bren gun
buckler
carbine
calibre
cordite
couteau
cuirass
curtana
curtein
cutlass
djerrid
dualine
dudgeon
ejector
elf-bolt
espadon
firearm
fire-pot
gantlet
gasmask
greaves
grenade
gunshot
halberd
halbert
handgun
harpoon
hatchet
hauberk
holster
javelin
langrel
longbow
long tom
lyddite
machete
megaton
missile
morglay
murrion

nuclear
oil-bomb
panoply
poitrel
polaris
priming
pole-axe
poniard
quarrel
rabinet
roundel
shotgun
side-arm
sjambok
Skybolt
Sten gun
teargas
torpedo
trident
twibill
vamplet
ventail
warhead
wind-gun

8

arbalist
arquebus
attaghan
balister
ballista
bascinet
basilisk
birdbolt
blowpipe
bludgeon
brassart
broad-axe
Browning
burganet
burgonet
canister
carabine
case-shot
catapult
chamfron
charfron
chausses
claymore
corselet
crossbow
culettes
culverin
damaskin
dynamite
eel-spear
elf-arrow
falchion
falconet
field-gun
firearms
fire-ball
firelock
fireship
gadlings
gauntlet
gavelock
gunsight
half-pike
hand-pike
haquebut
howitzer
jazerant
langrage

Lewis gun
magazine
mangonel
mantelet
Maxim gun
munition
naval gun
oerlikon
ordnance
paravane
paterero
pectoral
pederero
petronel
pistolet
plastron
port-fire
pyroxyle
revolver
ricochet
ringmail
scabbard
scimitar
scorpion
shrapnel
siege-gun
spadroon
spontoon
springal
steam-gun
stiletto
stinkpot
stonebow
tomahawk
Tommy gun
umbriere
vambrace
vamplate
whin-yard
yataghan

9

angel-shot
arquebuse
arrowhead
artillery
aventaile
backpiece
ballistic
bastinado
battleaxe
Blue Water
boar-spear
Bofors gun
bomb-chest
bombshell
boomerang
Brown Bess
brownbill
carronade
cartouche
cartridge
chain-mail
chain-shot
chassepot
columbiad
defoliant
demi-lance
derringer
deterrent
detonator
espringal
face-guard
fish-spear

garde-bras
gelignite
grapeshot
guncotton
gunpowder
habergeon
half-track
hand-staff
headpiece
heavy tank
heelpiece
light tank
matchlock
Mills bomb
munitions
musketoon
needle-gun
poison gas
quaker-gun
shillalah
slow-match
slung-shot
smallarms
smallbore
spring-gun
starshell
stinkbomb
sword-cane
teeth arms
troop ship
truncheon
turret gun
ward staff
welsh-hook
xyloidine
zumbooruk

10

ammunition
arcubalist
battery gun
blind shell
Blue Streak
bowie-knife
brigandine
broadsword
burrel-shot
cannonball
cannon-shot
cataphract
coat armour
coat of mail
cross-arrow
demi-cannon
field-piece
fire-barrel
Gatling gun

grainstaff
harquebuse
knobkerrie
Lee-Enfield
machine-gun
medium tank
Minie rifle
mustard-gas
paixhan-gun
pea-shooter
powder horn
projectile
pyroxyline
recoilless
safety-fuse
six-shooter
sticky bomb
sword-stick
touchpaper

11

antitank gun
armoured car
basket sword
blunderbuss
bow and arrow
breastplate
contact-mine
cruiser tank
Dahlgren gun
depth-charge
grande-garde
gun carriage
gun-howitzer
hand-grenade
harping-iron
Jacob's-staff
Lochaber axe
morning-star
mountain-gun
powder-chest
powder flask
safety-catch
scale-armour
Snider rifle
stern-chaser
Thompson gun

12

Armstrong gun
battering ram
boarding pike
bombing plane
breech-loader
cartridge-box

conventional
cross-bar-shot
demi-culverin
double-charge
flame-thrower
fowling-piece
Lancaster gun
landing craft
Mills grenade
mitrailleuse
muzzle-loader
quarterstaff
rocket-mortar
spigot mortar
Stokes mortar
sword-bayonet
tracer bullet
trench mortar
wheel-lock dag

13

aerial torpedo
armor-piercing
ball-cartridge
cartridge-case
cat-o'-nine-tails
Damocles sword
guided missile
high-explosive
knuckleduster
life preserver
percussion cap
poisoned arrow
scalping-knife
shrapnel shell
sub-machine-gun
submarine-mine
thermonuclear
two-edged sword

14–16

anti-aircraft-gun (15)
armour-piercing (14)
ballistic missile (16)
blank cartridge (a.) (14)
Brennan torpedo (14)
flame-projector (14)
incendiary bomb (a.) (14)
lachrymatory gas (15)
miniature rifle (14)
nitroglycerine (a.) (14)
nuclear weapons (14)
powder-magazine (14)
small-bore rifle (14)

BUSINESS, PROFESSIONS AND OCCUPATIONS
Business, trade and commerce

2 AND 3

A 1
bid
B.O.T.
buy
C.A.
C.O.D.
cut

dun
E.E.C.
fee
F.O.B.
G.N.P.
H.P.
I.O.U.
job
lot

Ltd
net
owe
par
pay
r.d.
rig
S.E.T.
sum

tax
tip
V.A.T.

4

agio
back

19

bail
bank
bear
bill
bond
boom
bull
call
cash
cess
chip
coin
cost
deal
dear
debt
deed
dole
dues
dump
duty
earn
easy
E.F.T.A.
even
fine
firm
fisc
free
fund
gain
G.A.T.T.
gild
gilt
giro
glut
gold
good
hire
idle
I.O.U.S.
kite
lend
levy
lien
loan
long
loss
mart
mint
nett
note
owed
paid
P.A.Y.E.
poll
pool
post
puff
punt
ramp
rate
rent
ring
risk
sale
sell
sink
sold
spot
stag
tare
term
turn
vend
wage

5

agent
angel
asset
at par
audit
award
batch
bears
bid up
block
board
bonds
bonus
brand
bribe
bulls
buyer
buy in
buy up
by-law
cargo
cheap
check
chips
clear
clerk
costs
cover
crash
cycle
debit
draft
entry
ex cap.
ex div.
float
folio
funds
gilts
goods
gross
hedge
'House'
index
issue
labor
lease
limit
money
notes
offer
order
owing
panic
paper
payee
payer
pound
price
proxy
quota
quote
rally
rates
remit
repay
rider
score
scrip
share
shark
short
sight
slump

stock
talon
taxes
teind
tight
tithe
token
trade
trend
trust
usury
value
wages
worth
yield

6

accept
accrue
advice
agency
amount
assets
assign
at cost
avails
bailee
bailor
banker
barter
bearer
borrow
bought
bounce
bounty
bourse
branch
broker
bubble
budget
burden
buying
buy out
by-laws
cartel
cheque
change
charge
client
corner
coupon
credit
crisis
cum. div.
dealer
deal in
debtor
defray
demand
dicker
docket
drawee
drawer
equity
estate
excise
expend
export
factor
figure
fiscal
freeze
godown
growth

hammer
holder
honour
import
in cash
income
in debt
indent
insure
jobber
job lot
labour
ledger
lender
liable
Lloyd's
lock-up
margin
market
mark-up
mature
merger
minute
nem. con.
notice
octroi
office
on call
oncost
option
one off
outbid
outlay
outlet
output
packet
parity
pay-day
paying
pay-off
pay out
pledge
plunge
policy
profit
public
punter
quorum
racket
rating
realty
rebate
recoup
redeem
refund
remedy
rental
rentes
report
resale
retail
return
salary
sample
save up
saving
sell in
sell up
set off
settle
shares
shorts
silver
simony
specie
spiral

spread
staple
stocks
strike
supply
surety
surtax
syndic
tariff
taxman
teller
tender
ticket
tithes
trader
tycoon
unload
unpaid
usance
usurer
valuta
vendor
vendue
volume
wampan
wealth
wind up

7

account
actuary
advance
allonge
annuity
arrears
at sight
auction
auditor
average
backing
bad debt
balance
banking
bargain
bidding
bonanza
bullion
buy back
cambist
capital
cashier
ceiling
certify
charter
company
consols
convert
crossed
customs
cut-rate
damages
day book
dealing
declare
default
deficit
deflate
deposit
douceur
draw out
dumping
duopoly
economy
embargo

endorse
engross
entrust
ex bonus
expense
exploit
exports
factory
failure
fall due
feedback
finance
flutter
forward
freight
funding
futures
gearing
haulage
hedging
holding
imports
imprest
indorse
inflate
in funds
insured
interim
invoice
jobbers
jobbing
kaffirs
killing
lay days
leasing
lending
limited
lockout
lottery
lump sum
manager
mint par
minutes
name day
nest egg
net gain
no funds
on offer
on order
package
partner
payable
pay cash
payment
pay rise
payroll
pay slip
pension
per cent
pre-empt
premium
prepaid
pricing
product
profits
promote
pro rata
pyramid
realize
receipt
reissue
renewal
reserve
returns
revenue
rigging

royalty
salvage
selling
sell-out
service
sold out
solvent
spinoff
squeeze
stipend
storage
subsidy
surplus
swindle
takings
tax free
tonnage
trade in
trading
traffic
trustee
utility
vending
venture
war bond
war loan
warrant
way bill
wound up
write up

8

above par
acceptor
accounts
act of God
after tax
agiotage
amortize
ante-date
appraise
assignee
assigner
auditing
back bond
bailment
bank bill
bankbook
bank giro
bank loan
banknote
bank rate
bankrupt
barratry
basic pay
below par
berthage
blue chip
book debt
borrower
bottomry
business
buying in
carriage
cashbook
cash down
cash sale
clearing
commerce
consumer
contango
contract
creditor
credit to

cum bonus
currency
customer
cut-price
dealings
defrayed
delivery
director
disburse
discount
dividend
drawings
dry goods
earnings
embezzle
employee
employer
emporium
endorsee
endorser
entrepot
equities
estimate
evaluate
exchange
expenses
exporter
ex gratia
ex rights
finances
fine gold
flat rate
gold pool
goodwill
gratuity
hallmark
hammered
hard cash
hard sell
hot money
importer
in arrear
increase
indebted
industry
interest
in the red
investor
lame duck
manifest
mark down
markings
maturing
maturity
merchant
monetary
monopoly
mortgage
net price
novation
on credit
on demand
on strike
operator
ordinary
overhead
overtime
par value
passbook
pin money
poundage
price cut
price war
proceeds
producer
property

21

purchase
quit rent
rack rent
receipts
receiver
recovery
reinvest
reserves
retailer
retainer
scarcity
schedule
security
shipment
sinecure
solvency
spending
spot cash
sterling
straddle
supertax
swindler
takeover
taxation
tax dodge
taxpayer
trade gap
transfer
Treasury
turnover
undercut
unquoted
wage rate
warranty
windfall
write off

9

actuarial
ad valorem
aggregate
allotment
allowance
annuitant
ante-dated
anti-trust
appraisal
appraiser
arbitrage
arrearage
assurance
averaging
bank stock
blank bill
book value
bordereau
borrowing
brokerage
by-product
call money
call price
carry over
certified
chartered
charterer
clearance
closing bid
commodity
cost price
cum rights
death duty
debenture
debit note
deck cargo

deduction
defaulter
deflation
demurrage
depletion
depositor
directors
dishonour
easy money
easy terms
economics
economies
economize
emolument
exchequer
executive
extortion
face value
fair price
fair trade
fiat money
fiduciary
financial
financier
fine paper
firm offer
firm price
first call
first cost
flotation
franchise
free trade
fully paid
garnishee
gilt-edged
going rate
guarantee
guarantor
hard money
import tax
in arrears
incentive
income tax
indemnity
indenture
inflation
insolvent
insurance
inventory
leasehold
liability
liquidate
liquidity
list price
long-dated
mail order
marketing
middleman
mortgagee
mortgagor
near money
negotiate
net income
order book
outgoings
overdraft
overdrawn
overheads
packaging
pari passu
paymaster
pecuniary
petty cash
piecework
portfolio
preferred

price list
price ring
price rise
prime cost
principal
profiteer
promotion
purchaser
put option
quittance
quotation
ratepayer
ready cash
recession
redundant
reflation
reimburse
repayable
repayment
resources
restraint
reversion
royalties
sell short
shift work
short bill
shortfall
short time
sideline
sight bill
sold short
speculate
spot price
stamp duty
statement
stock list
stockpile
subscribe
subsidize
surcharge
syndicate
tax return
ticket day
trade fair
trademark
trade name
tradesman
traveller
treasurer
undersell
unit trust
utilities
valuation
vendition
viability
wage claim
warehouse
wealth tax
wholesale
winding up
work force
work sheet
work study
World Bank

10

acceptance
accountant
account day
accounting
accumulate
active bond
adjustment
advice note

appreciate
assessment
assignment
attachment
auctioneer
automation
average out
bank credit
bank return
bankruptcy
bear market
bearer bond
bill broker
bill of sale
block grant
bondholder
bonus issue
bonus share
bookkeeper
bucket shop
bulk buying
calculator
call option
capitalism
capitalist
capitalize
capitation
chain store
chequebook
closed shop
collateral
colporteur
commercial
commission
compensate
consortium
contraband
conversion
credit bank
credit card
credit note
credit slip
cumulative
defalcator
del credere
depreciate
depression
direct cost
dirty money
drawn bonds
elasticity
encumbered
engrossing
ergonomics
evaluation
excise duty
ex dividend
first offer
fiscal year
fixed charge
fixed costs
fixed price
fixed trust
free market
floor price
forwarding
funded debt
gross value
ground rent
growth area
honorarium
import duty
income bond
industrial
insolvency
instalment

investment
joint stock
lighterage
liquidator
living wage
long period
loss leader
management
marked down
marketable
mass market
mercantile
money order
monopolist
monopolize
moratorium
negotiable
nonpayment
no par value
note of hand
obligation
open cheque
open credit
opening bid
open market
open policy
option rate
overcharge
paper money
pawnbroker
percentage
plough back
pre-emption
preference
prepayment
price index
price level
production
profitable
profits tax
prospector
prospectus
prosperity
prosperous
provide for
purchasing
pure profit
pyramiding
quarter day
ready money
real estate
real income
recompense
redeemable
redemption
redundancy
remittance
remunerate
rock bottom
sales force
scrip issue
second-hand
securities
selling out
settlement
serial bond
share index
short bonds
short-dated
sole agency
speculator
statistics
stockpiles
stock split
subscriber
tape prices

tax evasion
ticker tape
tight money
trade cycle
trade price
trade union
ultra vires
underwrite
unemployed
upset price
wage freeze
Wall Street
wholesaler
working day
work to rule
written off

11

account book
accountancy
acquittance
advance note
advertising
arbitration
asking price
auction ring
auction sale
average bond
bank account
bank balance
bank holiday
bank of issue
bear squeeze
beneficiary
big business
bill of entry
billionaire
bimetallism
black market
blank cheque
bonded goods
bonus scheme
book-keeping
budget price
businessman
capital gain
cash account
central bank
certificate
circulation
commitments
competition
comptometer
commodities
common stock
competitive
consignment
consumption
co-operative
corporation
counterfeit
cum dividend
customs duty
days of grace
defence bond
demand curve
demand draft
deposit rate
deposit slip
devaluation
discounting
dishonoured
distributor
dividend tax

double entry
down payment
economic law
economic man
endorsement
expenditure
fixed assets
fixed charge
fixed income
fluctuation
foreclosure
free on board
freight note
Gresham's Law
gross income
high finance
hypothecate
income stock
indemnified
indirect tax
industrials
job analysis
joint return
legal tender
liquidation
loan capital
manufacture
market overt
market price
mass-produce
merchandise
middle price
millionaire
minimum wage
money-lender
negotiation
net interest
net receipts
open account
option price
outstanding
overpayment
overtrading
package deal
partnership
pay on demand
physiocrats
point of sale
postal order
poverty line
premium bond
price fixing
price freeze
property tax
purchase tax
Queer Street
raw material
realization
reinsurance
reserve bank
revaluation
rights issue
risk capital
safe deposit
sales ledger
savings bank
seigniorage
sell forward
selling day
shareholder
single entry
sinking fund
small trader
sold forward
speculation
stockbroker

stockjobber
stock market
stockpiling
stocktaking
subsistence
supermarket
syndicalism
take-home pay
takeover bid
time deposit
transaction
undercharge
undervalued
underwriter
with profits

12

above the line
account payee
ad valorem tax
amalgamation
amortization
appreciation
assembly line
balance sheet
banker's draft
banker's order
bargain price
below the line
bill of lading
board meeting
Board of Trade
bond creditor
bonded stores
bottomry bond
branch office
bridging loan
buyer's market
callable bond
capital gains
capital goods
capital stock
carrying over
carry-over day
cash and carry
caveat emptor
charter party
clearing bank
closing price
common market
compensation
consumer goods
contract note
cost of living
credit rating
current price
current ratio
customs union
Defence Bonds
denomination
depreciation
differential
direct labour
disbursement
discount rate
disinflation
distribution
Dutch auction
earned income
embezzlement
econometrics
economy drive
entrepreneur
exchange rate

export credit
first refusal
fiscal policy
fixed capital
floating debt
frozen assets
going concern
gold standard
hard currency
hire purchase
indirect cost
interest rate
invoice clerk
irredeemable
joint account
keep accounts
labour market
laissez-faire
life interest
liquid assets
manufacturer
marginal cost
mass-produced
maturity date
mercantilism
merchant bank
mixed economy
monetization
money changer
national bank
national debt
nearest offer
nominal price
nominal value
official list
opening price
overcapacity
pay as you earn
pay in advance
paying-in-slip
policy holder
present worth
price ceiling
price control
price current
price rigging
productivity
profiteering
profit margin
profit motive
profit taking
public sector
rate of growth
raw materials
redeployment
remuneration
remunerative
reserve price
rig the market
rising prices
running costs
sale or return
sales manager
salesmanship
severance pay
share capital
shareholding
sliding scale
social credit
soft currency
specie points
statistician
sterling area
stock in trade
stockjobbery
stockjobbing

surplus value
tax avoidance
tax collector
tax exemption
terms of trade
trade balance
trading stamp
transfer deed
treasury bill
treasury bond
treasury note
trial balance
trustee stock
underwriting
valued policy
welfare state
works council

13

acceptilation
allotment note
appropriation
articled clerk
average clause
backwardation
bank statement
blank transfer
bullion market
business cycle
clearing house
contract curve
credit account
credit control
credit squeeze
crossed cheque
current assets
discount house
dividend yield
dollar premium
Dow-Jones index
exchequer bill
free trade area
futures market
gross receipts
guarantee fund
incomes policy
interim report
issued capital
livery company
Lombard Street
long-dated bill
making-up price
non-cumulative
not negotiable
ordinary share
outside broker
overhead price
paid-up capital
par of exchange
participating
premium income
private sector
profitability
profit sharing
public company
quota sampling
rateable value
sales forecast
settlement day
share transfer
specification
Stock Exchange
switch selling
taxable income

trade discount
value added tax
vendor's shares
wasting assets
wheeler-dealer
works councils

14

account current
advance freight
apprenticeship
balance of trade
bearer security
bill of exchange
blocked account
break-even point
bureau de change
capital account
capital gearing
capitalization
consumer credit
convertibility
corporation tax
current account
current balance
debenture stock
decimalization
deferred rebate
deferred shares
deposit account
discount market
economic growth
featherbedding
fiduciary issue
finance company
floating charge
founders' shares
fringe benefits
full employment
garnishee order
general average
general manager
half-commission
holder for value
holding company
hyperinflation
infrastructure
inscribed stock
invisible trade
joint stock bank
letter of credit
limited company
liquidity ratio
Lloyd's Register
loan conversion
macro-economics
managing agents
market research
micro-economics
monthly account
mortgage broker
new issue market
nominal capital
option dealings
ordinary shares
oversubscribed
preferred stock
progress chaser
promissory note
quality control
random sampling
rate of exchange
rate of interest
receiving order

24

revenue account
short-term gains
social security
superannuation
surrender value
trading account
uberrimae fidei
unearned income
working capital

15

average adjuster
bonded warehouse

building society
capital employed
commission agent
consignment note
dividend warrant
exchange control
ex-gratia payment
foreign exchange
interim dividend
investment trust
labour-intensive
liquidity ratios
marine insurance
nationalization
non-contributory

political science
preference bonds
preference share
preferred shares
preference stock
public ownership
public relations
purchasing power
rationalization
redemption yield
reducing balance
secured creditor
sleeping partner
sterling balance
unissued capital

Journalism, printing and publishing

2

ad
em
en
o.p.
pi
s.c.
w.f.

3

ads
bed
box
cub
cut
die
mat
out
pie
pot
run
set
sub
web

4

back
body
bold
bulk
caps
comp
copy
cyan
dash
demy
edit
etch
face
film
flap
font
grid
lead
limp
news
open
page
pica
puff

pull
quad
ream
ruby
rule
sewn
sink
slug
stet
take
trim
type

5

beard
black
bleed
block
blurb
cameo
canon
caret
cased
chase
chill
cloth
clump
crown
daily
Didot
draft
dummy
flong
folio
forme
fount
gloss
index
leads
libel
linen
litho
metal
pearl
plate
point
print
proof
punch
quire
quote
recto

reset
roman
rough
royal
run-on
scoop
serif
sigla
solid
sorts
spine
stone
story
title
verso
xerox

6

back-up
banner
boards
ceriph
cliché
coated
cock-up
column
delete
editor
flimsy
format
galley
indent
italic
jacket
keep up
layout
leader
linage
lock up
makeup
marked
masked
matrix
minion
morgue
offset
ozalid
punch
quotes
random
review
revise

rotary
screen
serial
series
set-off
sketch
spiked
splash
weekly
weight

7

article
artwork
binding
bled off
brevier
bromide
bumping
capital
caption
cast off
clicker
diamond
display
edition
English
engrave
etching
feature
Fraktur
full out
gravure
gripper
imprint
justify
leading
literal
masking
measure
monthly
mortice
net sale
overrun
overset
preface
prelims
printer
publish
release
reprint
rewrite

25

sits vac
subedit
tabloid
typeset
woodcut

8

art board
ascender
bleeding
boldface
colophon
cut flush
dateline
deadline
designer
endpaper
footnote
fudge box
hairline
halftone
hardback
headband
headline
hot metal
imperial
intaglio
keyboard
linotype
monotype
obituary
paginate
photoset
print run
register
reporter
slipcase
streamer
tailband
turnover
type area
verbatim
vignette
woodpulp

9

art editor
bookplate
bourgeois
box number
brilliant
broadside
casebound
co-edition
collating
columnist
copypaper
copyright
crossword
descender
editorial
exclusive
facsimile
freelance
furniture
idiot tape
laminated
lineblock
lower case
make ready
newspaper
newsprint

nonpareil
overprint
pageproof
paperback
paragraph
photocopy
photostat
pseudonym
publisher
quarterly
sans serif
signature
small pica
stonehand
subeditor
symposium
tear sheet
the morgue
title verso
upper case
watermark
web-offset
woodblock
wrong font

10

assembling
annotation
blockmaker
body matter
broadsheet
casting box
casting-off
catch title
city editor
compositor
copyholder
copytaster
copywriter
dead matter
dirty proof
feuilleton
film critic
four colour
imposition
impression
imprimatur
interleave
journalese
journalism
journalist
lamination
leader page
lithograph
long primer
monochrome
news agency
news editor
nom-de-plume
overmatter
pagination
paraphrase
periodical
plagiarism
press agent
reverse out
separation
short story
stereotype
supplement
syndication
title verso
trade paper
typesetter

typography
vignetting
wrong fount
xerography

11

advance copy
advertising
agony column
circulation
copyfitting
crown octavo
cub reporter
display type
galley proof
great primer
half measure
letterpress
line drawing
lithography
night editor
platemaking
proofreader
running head
section-sewn
unjustified

12

block letters
book reviewer
cross heading
facing matter
feature story
illustration
keep standing
leader writer
London editor
magazine page
perfect bound
sports editor
telegraphese
works manager

13

advertisement
composing room
editor-in-chief
foreign editor
justification
literary agent
photogravure
spiral binding
stop press news
wire stitching

14–16

banner headline (14)
calendered paper (15)
colour separation (16)
dramatic critic (14)
features editor (14)
literary editor (14)
managing editor (14)
offset printing (14)
perfect binding (14)
personal column (14)
photolithography (16)
running headline (15)

archdeacon
archflamen
archimagus
archpriest
areopagite
autocrator
bergmaster
borsholder
bumbailiff
bursarship
camerlengo
carabineer
catechumen
catholicos
censorship
chancellor
chaplaincy
chartulary
chatellany
cimeliarch
cloisterer
cloistress
commandant
commissary
consulship
controller
corporator
corregidor
coryphaeus
councillor
councilman
covenanter
crown agent
czarevitch
dauphiness
deaconship
delegation
designator
dock-master
doorkeeper
enomotarch
enumerator
episcopate
excellency
fire-master
headmaster
heraldship
high master
high priest
Home Office
incumbency
inquisitor
institutor
justiciary
king-at-arms
knighthood
lay brother
legateship
legislator
lieutenant
lower house
mace-bearer
magistracy
magistrate
margravine
marquisate
mayor-elect
midshipman
ministrant
mint-master
monarchism
noblewoman
ochlocracy
officially
oligarchal
opposition

parliament
plutocracy
postmaster
prebendary
presbytery
presidency
proclaimer
procurator
prolocutor
proscriber
proveditor
pursuivant
rectorship
regentship
ringmaster
sachemship
sea captain
sextonship
shrievalty
sign manual
squirehood
squireship
statecraft
state paper
sultanship
suzerainty
tithing-man
unofficial
upper house
vice-consul
vicegerent
vice-master
vice-regent
war council
whiggarchy

11

archdapifer
archduchess
archdukedom
aristocracy
assay-master
autocratrix
burgess-ship
burgomaster
cardinalate
catercousin
chamberlain
chieftaincy
comptroller
corporation
country court
court jester
cross-bearer
crossbowman
crown lawyer
crown prince
diplomatist
directorate
directorial
earl-marshal
ecclesiarch
electorship
executioner
flag officer
functionary
good templar
grand master
grand vizier
gymnasiarch
headborough
intercessor
internuncio
justiceship

landgravine
legislatrix
legislature
lieutenancy
lord provost
marchioness
marshalship
ministerial
monarchical
monseigneur
officialdom
officiating
papal legate
papal nuncio
policewoman
pontificate
pound-keeper
praepositor
premiership
primateship
prince royal
preconsular
proctorship
protocolist
protonotary
provostship
puisne judge
queen-mother
questorship
referendary
school board
senatorship
speakership
squirearchy
stadtholder
stratocracy
subordinate
sword-bearer
tax assessor
tax gatherer
thesmothete
town council
tribuneship
triumvirate
vestry clerk
vice-regency
viceroyalty
viscountess
wreckmaster

12

agent-general
ambassadress
armour-bearer
avant-courier
bound-bailiff
carpet-knight
chairmanship
chief justice
chief of staff
churchwarden
civil servant
civil service
commendatory
commissioner
constabulary
crown-equerry
dictatorship
ecclesiastic
enfranchiser
enthronement
field officer
guardianship
headmistress

heir apparent
House of Lords
inspectorate
internuncius
jack-in-office
laureateship
legislatress
lord-temporal
maid of honour
mastersinger
metropolitan
muster-master
notary-public
office-bearer
parish priest
peace officer
poet laureate
prince-bishop
Privy Council
quaestorship
queen-consort
queen-dowager
queen-regnant
quindecemvir
recordership
remembrancer
sheriff-clerk
staff officer
tax collector
Trinity house
unauthorized
uncovenanted
vicar-general
viscountship
water-bailiff
witenagemote

13

administrator
archidiaconal
archimandrite

archpresbyter
archtreasurer
army commander
barrack-master
borough-master
chieftainship
chorepiscopus
color sergeant
consul-general
count palatine
county council
district judge
generalissimo
grand-seigneur
gubernatorial
high constable
inspectorship
judge-advocate
lord-spiritual
mounted police
parliamentary
prime minister
Prince of Wales
Princess Royal
public trustee
state function
states-general
statesmanship
vice-president
vigintivirate

14

archchancellor
archiepiscopal
auditor-general
chancellorship
chief constable
colour sergeant
crown solicitor
dowager-duchess
lord of the manor

gentleman-usher
high court judge
House of Commons
king's messenger
lord chancellor
lord lieutenant
lords-spiritual
medical officer
parochial board
political agent
provost-marshal
revenue officer
superintendent
town councillor
vicar-apostolic
vice-chancellor

15

advocate-general
archchamberlain
archiepiscopacy
archiepiscopate
astronomer-royal
attorney-general
cabinet minister
chamberlainship
chargé d'affaires
district officer
election auditor
governor-general
heir-presumptive
lords lieutenant
messenger-at-arms
parliamentarian
plenipotentiary
privy councillor
queen's messenger
sheriff's officer
suffragan bishop
surveyor-general
vice-chamberlain
vice-chancellors

People

2 AND 3

A.B.
ace
ass
B.A.
boy
B.Sc.
cad
cit
dab
dad
D.D.
deb
dux
elf
fag
fan
fop
fub
G.I.
gun
guy
hag
ham

kid
imp
kin
lad
lob
M.A.
ma
man
me
men
mob
M.P.
Mr.
Mrs.
mug
N.C.O.
nun
oaf
pa
pal
pet
pig
rat
rip

R.S.M.
she
sir
spy
son
sot
tar
us
wag
we
wit
ye
yob
you

4

ally
aunt
babe
baby
band

bard
bear
beau
bevy
bird
blue
boor
bore
boss
brat
buck
bull
chap
chum
clan
colt
cove
crew
dame
dear
demy
doer
doll
dolt
doxy

drip
duck
dude
dupe
feed
folk
fool
funk
gaby
gang
gawk
girl
goer
goth
grub
gull
haji
heel
heir
herd
hero
hick
hobo
host
idol
jack
jade
jill
jilt
jury
kith
lass
liar
loon
lout
lush
magi
maid
male
mama
mate
mess
mime
minx
miss
mite
mome
monk
muff
mute
mutt
nizy
ogre
papa
peer
peon
prig
rake
roué
runt
sage
salt
sect
seer
self
sept
serf
shot
silk
sire
slut
snob
soak
star
swot
tart

team
them
thug
tike
toff
tony
tool
tory
twin
tyke
tyro
user
vamp
waif
ward
whig
wife
wino
yogi
zany

5

adept
adult
aider
airer
alien
angel
argus
aunty
bairn
beast
being
belle
bigot
biter
black
blade
blood
booby
bride
broad
brute
bully
cadet
carle
cheat
child
choir
chuff
chump
churl
clare
clown
co-aid
couch
crank
crone
crony
crook
crowd
cynic
dandy
darky
decoy
devil
dicer
diver
do-all
donce
donor
doter
dozer

droll
drone
dummy
dunce
duper
dwarf
eater
enemy
exile
extra
fakir
felon
fence
fiend
fifer
filer
firer
flier
flirt
flock
fogey
fraud
freak
freer
gamin
gaper
gazer
genii
ghost
giant
giber
gipsy
giver
goose
grass
groom
guest
guide
hater
heavy
hewer
hider
hiker
hodge
hunks
hussy
idiot
idler
in-law
issue
jingo
joker
Judas
juror
knave
lazar
leper
limey
local
locum
loser
lover
madam
maker
mamma
mater
mimic
minim
minor
miser
moron
mouse
mover
mower
mummy
muser

namer
nanny
Negro
niece
ninny
noddy
nomad
nymph
odist
ogler
owner
pacer
pagan
party
pater
patsy
payee
payer
peach
pigmy
piler
pin-up
piper
porer
poser
posse
proxy
prude
pryer
puker
punch
pupil
puppy
pygmy
quack
queen
queer
racer
raker
raver
rebel
rider
rival
rogue
rough
rover
rower
sahib
saint
saver
scamp
scion
scold
scout
screw
shark
shrew
sider
silly
siren
sizar
skier
snail
sneak
sorry
sower
spark
sport
squab
squaw
staff
stoic
stray
sumph
swain
swell

31

taker
tenor
thief
toady
tommy
toper
toyer
tramp
trier
troop
trull
trump
twins
uncle
urger
vexer
vixen
voter
wader
wench
whoso
widow
wight
wiper
witch
women
wooer
yahoo
yobbo
yokel
youth

6

abaser
abider
abuser
admass
adored
adorer
agnate
albino
allies
alumna
amazon
ambler
angler
apache
auntie
au pair
backer
bandit
bar fly
batman
bayard
beater
beauty
beldam
better
bettor
bibber
bidder
bilker
blacks
blonde
bomber
boozer
bowler
buster
cadger
caller
camper
captor
carper

carver
casual
chaser
client
clique
co-ally
coaxer
codder
codger
co-heir
coolie
copier
co-star
cottar
cotter
cousin
coward
craven
creole
cretin
cueist
damsel
dancer
darner
dauber
debtor
defier
delver
denier
deputy
digger
dipper
dodger
doodle
dotard
double
dragon
drawee
drawer
drazel
driver
drudge
dry-bob
ducker
duffer
dyvour
earwig
egoist
elator
envier
eraser
escort
eunuch
expert
fabler
faggot
family
fanner
father
fawner
feeler
fellow
female
fencer
Fenian
fiancé
fibber
filler
finder
foeman
foiler
forcer
friend
gadder
gaffer
gagger

gainer
gammer
gasbag
genius
gentry
getter
geezer
giglot
gigman
gigolo
gillie
glider
godson
golfer
gossip
granny
grazer
griper
grouch
grower
guiser
guller
gulper
gunman
gunner
gusher
halter
healer
hearer
heater
heaver
hector
hedger
helper
hermit
hinter
hippie
hoaxer
holder
hooter
hopper
howler
hoyden
huffer
humbug
hummer
hunter
hurler
hussar
hymner
iceman
infant
inmate
ironer
jeerer
jerker
jester
Jesuit
jet set
jilter
jogger
jolter
jumper
junior
junker
junkie
keeper
kicker
kidder
killer
kisser
knower
lacker
lagger
lancer
lander

lapper
lasher
lassie
layman
leader
league
leaper
leaser
leaver
lecher
legist
lender
lessee
lessor
letter
lifter
limner
lisper
lister
loafer
lobber
lodger
looker
loonie
looter
lubber
lurker
lyrist
madcap
madman
maiden
maniac
marine
marker
maroon
marrer
martyr
masher
masker
master
matron
medium
melter
member
menial
mentor
mestee
midget
minion
misses
missis
missus
mister
mocker
modist
mohawk
mohock
moiler
monkey
mooter
moppet
mortal
mother
mugger
mulier
mummer
myself
nagger
nation
native
needer
nephew
nipper
nitwit
nobody
nodder

noodle
novice
nudist
ogress
old boy
old man
opener
oracle
orator
orphan
outlaw
pandit
panter
papist
parent
pariah
parter
patron
pauper
pawnee
pawner
paynim
pecker
pedant
peeler
peeper
pelter
penman
penpal
person
piecer
pigeon
pinner
placer
player
poller
Pommie
poseur
poster
pourer
pouter
prater
prayer
preyer
proser
prover
public
puffer
puller
pumper
pundit
punter
puppet
purger
purist
pusher
quaker
quoter
rabbit
rabble
racist
racker
ragtag
raider
railer
rammer
ranter
rapist
rascal
rating
reader
reaper
relict
relier
rhymer
rifter

ringer
rinker
rinser
rioter
ripper
risker
roamer
roarer
rocker
Romany
rookie
rotter
rouser
rubber
ruiner
runner
rusher
rustic
sadist
sailer
santon
savage
savant
scaler
scorer
scouse
scrimp
second
seeker
seizer
selves
sender
senior
sentry
shadow
shaker
shaman
sharer
shaver
sheila
shover
shower
shrimp
sigher
sinner
sipper
sister
sitter
skater
slayer
slicer
slider
sloven
smiler
smiter
smoker
snarer
sniper
snorer
snudge
soaker
solver
sparer
spouse
squire
square
stager
starer
stayer
stoner
stooge
stroke
sucker
suitor
surety
tacker

talker
tartar
tasker
taster
tatler
tearer
teaser
teller
tenant
Teuton
theist
thrall
throng
tilter
toiler
tomboy
tooter
tosser
truant
tutrix
tyrant
umpire
undoer
uniter
urchin
vamper
vandal
vanner
varlet
vendee
vendor
vestal
viator
victim
victor
viewer
Viking
virago
virgin
votary
voyeur
wafter
walker
wanton
warmer
warner
washer
waster
wearer
weeder
weeper
wet-bob
whiner
wincer
winder
winker
winner
wisher
wizard
wittol
worker
worthy
wretch
writer
yapper
yeoman
yonker
zealot
zombie

7

abactor
abetter

abettor
acceder
accuser
adapter
admirer
adviser
agamist
aircrew
also-ran
alumnus
amateur
amorosa
amoroso
anybody
ascetic
assizer
assumer
atheist
athlete
avenger
averter
babbler
ballboy
bastard
batsman
beatnik
bedmate
bedouin
beldame
beloved
best man
bigshot
blabber
blender
boarder
boaster
boggler
bookman
bouncer
bounder
breeder
brother
bucolic
buffoon
bumpkin
bungler
burgher
bushman
bustler
cackler
caitiff
captain
captive
casuist
caveman
changer
chanter
Charlie
charmer
cheater
checker
Chindit
citizen
clapper
cleaver
climber
clipper
clubman
cockney
cognate
colleen
colonel
combine
commons
company
compère

33

comrade	elegist	groupie	knoller
consort	elogist	grouser	know-all
convert	elohist	growler	laggard
convict	empiric	grown-up	landman
copycat	emptier	grubber	laugher
co-rival	enactor	grudger	leaguer
Cossack	endower	grunter	learner
coterie	endurer	guesser	legatee
counter	engager	guildry	liberal
courser	enjoyer	guzzler	limiter
courter	enticer	gymnast	loather
coxcomb	entrant	habitué	lobcock
crawler	epicure	haggler	lookout
creator	erecter	half-wit	lorette
creeper	eremite	handler	lounger
cringer	escapee	has-been	lowbrow
cripple	escaper	hatcher	lunatic
croaker	exactor	haunter	lurcher
crooner	exalter	heathen	magnate
crusher	exciter	heckler	mangler
cry baby	exposer	heiress	manikin
cuckold	failure	hell-hag	mankind
culprit	fair sex	hellier	marcher
curioso	fall-guy	heretic	marplot
cyclist	fanatic	heroine	meddler
dabbler	fancier	hipster	menacer
dabster	fantast	hoarder	mestino
dallier	fascist	hobbler	mestizo
damosel	fathead	homager	milksop
dangler	faulter	hoodlum	mingler
darling	favorer	hostage	minikin
dastard	feaster	hostess	misdoer
dawdler	feoffee	hothead	mobster
daysman	feoffor	huddler	modiste
debaser	fiancée	humbler	monitor
debater	fiddler	hurrier	moulder
defacer	fielder	husband	mounter
defamer	filcher	hustler	mourner
defiler	flapper	hymnist	mouther
defunct	flasher	imagist	mudlark
delator	fleecer	imbiber	mugwump
deluder	floater	impeder	mulatto
denizen	flouter	imposer	mumbler
derider	foister	imputer	Negress
desirer	fondler	inciter	Negrita
devisee	fopling	inducer	nettler
deviser	forager	infidel	nibbler
devisor	founder	infuser	niggard
devotee	freeman	ingrate	niggler
diarist	freezer	inhaler	nithing
dibbler	frisker	injurer	nominee
diehard	frowner	insured	oarsman
dilator	frumper	insurer	obligee
divider	fuddler	invader	obliger
diviner	fumbler	invalid	obligor
dizzard	gabbler	inviter	oddball
doubter	gallant	invoker	offerer
dowager	gambler	jackass	old fogy
dragoon	garbler	jack-tar	old girl
dreader	general	jacobin	old maid
dreamer	gentile	jangler	old salt
drifter	giggler	Jezebel	oppidan
driller	glutton	Joe Soap	opposer
drinker	gobbler	jostler	orderer
droller	goodman	juggler	outcast
drowner	gormand	jumbler	Oxonian
drubber	gossoon	juryman	paddler
dualist	gourmet	juvenal	papoose
dueller	gownman	Kantist	paragon
dullard	grandam	killjoy	partner
dweller	grandma	kindler	parvenu
edifier	grantee	kindred	patcher
egghead	granter	kingpin	patient
egotist	grantor	kinsman	patriot
ejector	grasper	kneeler	Paul Pry
elector	griffin	knocker	peasant

34

peruser	saluter	spurner	usurper
pervert	sandman	spurrer	utopian
piercer	saviour	stabber	utterer
pilgrim	scalder	stand-by	vacuist
pincher	scalper	stand-in	vagrant
pioneer	sceptic	starlet	vampire
plaiter	schemer	starter	vaulter
planner	scholar	stealer	vaunter
playboy	scoffer	stentor	veteran
pleadee	scolder	stepson	villain
pleader	scooper	sticker	villein
pleaser	scorner	stiller	visitor
plenist	scraper	stinger	vouchee
plodder	scraple	stinker	voucher
plotter	scrooge	stinter	voyager
plucker	scroyle	stirrer	vulture
plumper	sculler	stooper	waddler
plunger	seceder	stopper	wagerer
pounder	sectary	strayer	wakener
praiser	securer	striker	waltzer
pranker	seducer	striver	want-wit
presser	seminar	stroker	warbler
pricker	service	student	warlock
prinker	settler	studier	wastrel
private	shammer	stumper	watcher
prodigy	sharker	stylist	waterer
progeny	sharper	subduer	waverer
protégé	shedder	subject	weigher
prowler	shifter	suicide	welcher
puncher	shooter	suspect	wencher
punster	shopper	swagman	whipper
puritan	shouter	swinger	whisker
pursuer	show-off	swearer	widower
puzzler	shutter	sweater	wielder
quaffer	shyster	sweeper	windbag
queller	sibling	swiller	wise guy
querent	skimmer	swimmer	witling
querist	skipper	swinger	witness
quieter	skulker	tarrier	wolf cub
quitter	slacker	tattler	worrier
radical	slammer	taunter	wounder
rambler	slasher	templar	wrapper
ravener	sleeper	tempter	wrecker
reacher	slinger	text-man	wrester
realist	slipper	thinker	wringer
rebuker	slitter	thriver	yielder
reciter	smasher	thrower	younker
recluse	snapper	thumper	Zionist
redhead	snarler	tickler	
redskin	sniffer	tippler	
reducer	snipper	toaster	**8**
referee	snoozer	toddler	
refugee	snorter	tomfool	
refuser	snuffer	toppler	abdicant
refuter	society	tosspot	abductor
regular	soloist	tourist	absentee
relater	someone	trainee	academic
remover	soother	trainer	accepter
renewer	sophist	traitor	achiever
repiner	soprano	treader	adherent
replier	spaniel	treater	adjutant
rescuer	spanker	tricker	adulator
reserve	spanner	trifler	advocate
retaker	speaker	tripper	aesthete
retinue	speeder	trollop	agitator
reverer	speller	trooper	agnostic
reviver	spender	tropist	alarmist
rhymist	spiller	trouper	allottee
riddler	spitter	trudger	allotter
roadhog	spoiler	trustee	alter ego
royalty	sponger	truster	altruist
ruffian	sponsor	tumbler	ancestor
ruffler	sporter	twirler	ancestry
rumbler	spotter	twister	anchoret
runaway	spouter	twitter	antihero
rustler	sprayer	upstart	antipope

35

apostate	combiner	enjoiner	harasser
appellee	commando	enlarger	hardener
appellor	commoner	enricher	harridan
approver	commuter	enslaver	harrower
arranger	complier	ensnarer	hastener
aspirant	computer	ephesian	hazarder
assassin	consumer	erastian	hectorer
assembly	convener	eschewer	hedonist
assertor	conveyer	espouser	helpmate
assignee	coquette	esteemer	helpmeet
assignor	corporal	eulogist	highbrow
assuager	co-surety	euphuist	hijacker
attacker	cottager	Eurasian	hinderer
attestor	courtier	everyman	homicide
audience	co-worker	everyone	honourer
aularian	crackpot	evildoer	hooligan
awakener	creditor	evocator	horseman
bachelor	criminal	examinee	huckster
balancer	customer	examiner	Huguenot
bankrupt	crusader	exceeder	humanist
banterer	dalesman	exceptor	humorist
baritone	daughter	executor	humpback
barrator	deadhead	expiator	idealist
beadsman	deaf-mute	expirant	idolater
beginner	debutant	exploder	idolizer
beguiler	deceased	explorer	idyllist
believer	deceiver	exponent	imaginer
bellower	defector	extender	imbecile
benedict	defender	extoller	imitator
bestower	deferrer	fanfaron	immortal
betrayer	democrat	fatalist	impairer
bigamist	demoniac	favourer	imparter
big noise	departer	feminist	impeller
blackleg	deponent	ferreter	implorer
blazoner	depraver	figurant	impostor
blighter	depriver	finalist	improver
bluecoat	derelict	finisher	impugner
bohemian	deserter	flaunter	inceptor
bookworm	deserver	flincher	incloser
borderer	despiser	folk-hero	indictee
borrower	detainee	follower	indicter
boy scout	detainer	fomenter	indigene
braggart	detector	fondling	inductee
brethren	devourer	foregoer	inductor
brunette	diffuser	foreseer	indulger
busybody	digester	forgiver	infecter
cabalist	diner-out	fourling	inferior
caballer	dirty dog	franklin	inflamer
callgirl	disciple	freedman	informer
canaille	disponee	freshman	initiate
cannibal	disponer	fribbler	innocent
canoeist	disposer	frizzler	inquirer
carouser	disputer	front man	insister
castaway	ditheist	fugitive	insnarer
catamite	diverter	fusilier	inspirer
Catholic	divorcée	futurist	insulter
caviller	divorcer	gadabout	intended
celibate	divulger	galloper	intender
cenobite	do-gooder	gamester	intimate
champion	dogsbody	gaolbird	intruder
chaperon	drencher	garroter	investor
children	dribbler	gatherer	islander
chiliast	drunkard	genearch	jabberer
chuckler	duellist	geometer	jackaroo
cicerone	duettist	getter-on	Jacobite
cicisbeo	dullard	giantess	jailbird
civilian	effector	godchild	Jehovist
claimant	elegiast	goodwife	jingoist
clansman	elevator	gourmand	John Bull
classman	embracer	gownsman	Jonathan
clincher	emigrant	graduate	joy-rider
clodpoll	emulator	grandson	Judaizer
cognizee	enchanter	grisette	juvenile
cognizor	encloser	grumbler	kinsfolk
colonial	enforcer	habitant	lady-love
colonist	enhancer	hanger-on	lame duck

lamenter	numberer	quaverer	scuffler
landsman	numskull	quencher	seafarer
landsmen	nursling	quibbler	searcher
latinist	objector	quidnunc	seconder
launcher	obscurer	quietist	selector
layabout	observer	Quisling	sentinel
lay-clerk	obtainer	rakehell	sergeant
layer-out	obtruder	ransomer	shortner
laywoman	occupant	ratifier	shrieker
legalist	occupier	ravisher	shrimper
levanter	offender	reasoner	shrinker
leveller	old-timer	rebutter	shuffler
libellee	old woman	recaptor	sidekick
libeller	onlooker	receiver	sidesman
liegeman	operator	reckoner	simoniac
linesman	opificer	recliner	simperer
lingerer	opponent	recoiler	skeleton
linguist	oppugner	recorder	sketcher
listener	optimist	recreant	slattern
literate	oratress	redeemer	slugabed
literati	outliver	reformer	sluggard
litigant	outsider	refunder	slyboots
livewire	pacifier	regicide	small fry
logician	pacifist	rejecter	snatcher
loiterer	paleface	rejoicer	snuffler
looker-on	palterer	relapser	sodomite
loyalist	pamperer	relation	softener
luminary	panderer	releasee	softling
lunarian	Papalist	releaser	solecist
lutanist	paramour	reliever	solitary
luxurist	parasite	remarker	somebody
lyricist	parcener	reminder	songster
macaroni	pardoner	remitter	son-in-law
malapert	parodist	renderer	sorcerer
malaprop	partaker	renegade	spinster
maligner	partisan	repealer	spitfire
mandarin	passer-by	repeater	splitter
man-hater	patentee	repeller	spreader
mannikin	pelagian	reporter	springer
marauder	penitent	reprover	sprinter
marksman	perjurer	repulser	squaller
martinet	pesterer	reseizer	squasher
may-queen	pharisee	resenter	squatter
medalist	picaroon	reserver	squeaker
mediator	pilferer	resident	squealer
merryman	pillager	resigner	squeezer
mesmeree	plagiary	resister	squinter
messmate	playgoer	resolver	squireen
mimicker	playmate	resorter	squirter
mislayer	plebeian	restorer	stancher
mistress	poisoner	retarder	stickler
modalist	polluter	retorter	stinkard
modifier	poltroon	returner	stitcher
molester	ponderer	revealer	stowaway
monodist	popinjay	reveller	stranger
monsieur	populace	revenger	stripper
moon-calf	prattler	revolter	stroller
moonling	preparer	rewarder	strutter
moralist	presager	riffraff	stumbler
Moravian	presbyte	rifleman	suborner
motorist	presumer	rigorist	suckling
murderer	prisoner	rodomont	sufferer
murmurer	prize-man	romancer	superior
mutineer	prodigal	Romanist	superman
mutterer	producer	romantic	supposer
namesake	profaner	rotarian	surmiser
narrator	promisee	royalist	survivor
narrower	promiser	runagate	sybarite
naturist	promoter	ruralist	tacksman
neophyte	proposer	saboteur	talesman
nepotist	protégée	satanist	tartuffe
neurotic	provoker	saucebox	taxpayer
new broom	punisher	sciolist	teddy boy
newcomer	purifier	scorcher	teenager
nihilist	Puseyite	scourger	telltale
nuisance	quadroon	scrawler	tenantry

37

testator
theorist
thrasher
threader
thruster
thurifer
thwarter
top brass
torturer
townsman
traditor
traducer
trampler
trappist
trembler
triplets
truckler
truelove
turncoat
twaddler
twitcher
two-timer
underdog
unionist
upholder
upper ten
vagabond
vanguard
vapourer
venturer
verifier
vilifier
villager
violator
visitant
votaress
votarist
wallower
wanderer
wayfarer
waylayer
waymaker
weakener
weanling
welcomer
Wesleyan
wheedler
whistler
whitener
whizz-kid
wiseacre
wonderer
wrangler
wrestler
wriggler
yeomanry
yodeller
yokemate
yourself

9

abecedary
aborigine
absconder
abstainer
academist
accessory
acclaimer
addressee
addresser
admiralty
adulterer
adversary
affirmant

aggressor
alcoholic
analogist
anarchist
anchoress
anchorite
annuitant
apologist
appellant
applauder
applicant
appraiser
arch-enemy
assailant
associate
augmenter
authority
automaton
bacchanal
backbiter
banqueter
barbarian
bargainee
bargainer
battleaxe
bedfellow
bedlamite
beggarman
bel esprit
biblicist
bicyclist
blockhead
bluebeard
blunderer
blusterer
bolsterer
bon vivant
bourgeois
boy friend
bridesman
brigadier
bystander
cabin crew
Calvinist
candidate
canvasser
careerist
carnalist
celebrity
chain-gang
chantress
character
charlatan
charterer
chatterer
chiseller
Christian
churchman
clatterer
clientele
coadjutor
coalition
cocklaird
co-heiress
colleague
collegian
combatant
comforter
commander
committee
committer
committor
commodore
communist
community
compacter

companion
concubine
confessor
confidant
conformer
Confucian
co-nominee
conqueror
conscript
consenter
consignee
consignor
conspirer
constable
consulter
contemner
contender
continuer
contralto
contriver
converter
co-patriot
corrector
corrupter
covergirl
crackshot
creatress
creditrix
cricketer
crookback
cut-throat
daredevil
dark horse
debauchee
débutante
declaimer
declarant
defaulter
defeatist
defendant
defrauder
deliverer
demagogue
demandant
demi-monde
dependant
depositor
depressor
depurator
designate
desperado
despoiler
destinist
destroyer
detractor
dialector
dialogist
disburser
discerner
discloser
disgracer
disguiser
dispeller
disperser
displayer
disprover
disputant
disseizor
dissenter
dissident
disturber
disuniter
divinator
dogmatist
dolly bird
do-nothing

driveller
dyspeptic
early bird
earthling
eccentric
Edwardian
emendator
enchanter
encomiast
energizer
energumen
enfeebler
engrosser
enlivener
entangler
entourage
entreater
epicurean
epileptic
epistoler
evacuator
everybody
exactress
examinant
excusator
executant
executrix
exhauster
exhibiter
exhibitor
exploiter
expositor
expounder
exquisite
extractor
extravert
extrovert
extremist
falsifier
family man
favourite
find-fault
fire-eater
first born
flatterer
flay-flint
fleshling
forbidder
forebears
foreigner
forfeiter
forgetter
formalist
fortifier
forwarder
fossicker
foster-son
foundling
foundress
fratricide
free agent
freelance
free-liver
freemason
fulfiller
furtherer
gainsayer
garnishee
garnisher
garreteer
garrotter
gathering
gentleman
girl guide
Girondist
go-between

godfather
godmother
Gothamite
grandpapa
grandsire
gratifier
great-aunt
greenhorn
grenadier
greybeard
groomsman
groveller
guerrilla
guest star
guineapig
half-breed
half-caste
haranguer
harbinger
harbourer
harnesser
hearkener
hell-hound
highflier
hillbilly
Hottentot
household
housewife
hunchback
hylozoist
hypocrite
ignoramus
immigrant
immolator
impeacher
impleader
inamorata
inamorato
increaser
incurable
indicator
indweller
inebriate
inflicter
informant
infractor
infringer
inhabiter
inheritor
initiator
innovator
in-patient
inscriber
insolvent
instiller
insurgent
intestate
intriguer
introvert
inveigher
inveigler
Jansenist
jay-walker
jitterbug
joculator
joint-heir
journeyer
jovialist
justifier
kidnapper
kinswoman
lackbrain
ladies' man
landowner
law-monger
lay reader

lazybones
libellant
liberator
libertine
lionheart
lip-reader
liturgist
lost sheep
loud-mouth
lowlander
magnifier
makepeace
malthorse
mammonist
mannerist
masochist
matricide
meanderer
medallist
mediatrix
messieurs
Methodist
metrician
middleman
millenary
miscreant
mitigator
moderator
modernist
modulator
monitress
moonraker
moralizer
mortgagee
mortgagor
mortifier
Mrs. Grundy
multitude
muscleman
mutilator
mythmaker
Narcissus
neglecter
neighbour
neogamist
Neptunian
next of kin
nominator
nonentity
non-smoker
nourisher
novitiate
nullifier
numerator
observant
occultist
offspring
old master
oppressor
organizer
ourselves
pacemaker
palaverer
panellist
paralytic
paranymph
parricide
part-owner
passenger
patricide
patroness
peasantry
Pecksniff
peculator
pen-friend
pen-pusher

pensioner
perceiver
perfecter
performer
permitter
personage
personnel
persuader
perturber
perverter
pessimist
pilgarlic
pinchfist
pin-up girl
plaintiff
Platonist
plunderer
plutocrat
plutonist
portioner
possessor
posterity
postponer
postulant
pot-hunter
practiser
precursor
predicant
predictor
preferrer
prelatist
presbyope
presentee
presenter
preserver
pretender
preventer
proceeder
profferer
profiteer
projector
prolonger
promissor
promulger
proselyte
prosodist
protector
protester
protruder
punctuist
purchaser
purloiner
pussyfoot
Quakeress
quickener
rabbinist
racketeer
raconteur
rainmaker
ransacker
rapturist
ratepayer
recipient
recordist
recoveree
recoverer
rectifier
redresser
reflector
refresher
regulator
rehearser
reinsurer
renouncer
renovator
represser

reprobate
requester
respecter
rhymester
ridiculer
ritualist
roisterer
Romanizer
roughneck
routinist
rubrician
ruminator
Samaritan
Sassenach
satellite
satisfier
Saturnist
saunterer
scapegoat
scarecrow
scavenger
schoolboy
scoundrel
scrambler
scratcher
scribbler
scrutator
sea-lawyer
sectarian
separator
serenader
sermonist
sexualist
shaveling
shortener
shoveller
sightseer
simpleton
skin-diver
skinflint
skylarker
slanderer
slobberer
slowcoach
slumberer
smatterer
sniveller
socialist
socialite
sojourner
solicitor
solitaire
son-of-a-gun
sophister
sophomore
spadassin
spectator
Spinozist
spiritist
spokesman
sportsman
sprinkler
sputterer
squabbler
stammerer
stargazer
star pupil
stigmatic
straggler
strangler
stretcher
stripling
strongman
struggler
stutterer
subaltern

39

submitter
subverter
succeeder
successor
succourer
suggester
sundowner
suppliant
supporter
surfeiter
susceptor
suspecter
suspender
sustainer
swaggerer
swallower
sweetener
sycophant
symbolist
syncopist
tactician
Talmudist
targumist
temptress
termagant
terminist
terrorist
testatrix
testifier
theorizer
thickskin
thunderer
toad-eater
tormentor
townsfolk
traitress
trapanner
traveller
traverser
trepanner
tribesman
trickster
trigamist
tritheist
truepenny
underling
unitarian
valentine
venerator
verbalist
versifier
Victorian
vigilante
visionary
volunteer
vulcanist
warmonger
wassailer
whosoever
womanizer
womankind
womenfolk
worldling
wrongdoer
xenophobe
yachtsman
young lady
youngling
youngster

10

aboriginal
aborigines
Abraham man

absolutist
accomplice
admonisher
adulterant
adulteress
adventurer
aficionado
alcoranist
allegorist
alms people
ambidexter
ambodexter
anabaptist
ancestress
anecdotist
anglophile
anglophobe
Anglo-Saxon
antagonist
antecedent
antecessor
antecursor
antichthon
antiscians
apologizer
aristocrat
assemblage
assentient
babe-in-arms
baby-sitter
bamboozler
beautifier
bed-presser
bedswerver
Belgravian
belswagger
benefactor
Benthamite
Bethlemite
better half
big brother
blackamoor
blackguard
black sheep
blasphemer
bobbysoxer
bogtrotter
bold spirit
bootlicker
borstal boy
bridegroom
bridesmaid
bureaucrat
bushranger
campaigner
capitalist
caravanner
card-player
cavalryman
centralist
changeling
chatterbox
chauvinist
cheesecake
churchgoer
Cinderella
clodhopper
cloisterer
cloistress
coadjutant
coadjutrix
cohabitant
coloratura
commonalty
competitor
complainer

confessant
confessary
confidante
considerer
contendent
contestant
controller
co-operator
coparcener
copyholder
co-relation
councillor
counsellor
countryman
crackbrain
cringeling
criticizer
crosspatch
curmudgeon
daggle-tail
daydreamer
day-tripper
declaimant
deforciant
delinquent
demoiselle
depositary
deprecator
depredator
deputation
descendant
diatribist
dilettante
diminisher
directress
discharger
discourser
discoverer
discursist
disheritor
disparager
dispraiser
dispreader
disquieter
dissembler
distracter
distruster
divineress
divisioner
dogmatizer
dominicide
dramatizer
Drawcansir
drug addict
drug pusher
dunderpate
dunderhead
Dutch uncle
dynamitard
early riser
ear-witness
elaborator
electorate
electoress
elucidator
emboldener
empiricist
empoisoner
emulatress
encourager
encroacher
engenderer
Englishman
enigmatist
enthusiast
enumerator

enunciator
epitaphist
epitomizer
equestrian
eternalist
evangelist
exhortator
expatiator
explicator
expurgator
extenuator
extirpator
eye-witness
fabricator
factionist
fagot-voter
fashionist
federalist
fire-raiser
flagellant
flourisher
fly-by-night
footballer
footlicker
forefather
foreleader
foremother
forerunner
forswearer
fosterling
foxhunter
fraternity
freeholder
free-trader
frequenter
fuddy-duddy
fund-holder
fund-raiser
Gasconader
gastronome
gentlefolk
girl friend
glacialist
goal keeper
gold-digger
goodfellow
grandchild
grand juror
grandmamma
grandniece
grand-uncle
grass widow
great-uncle
half-sister
harmonizer
hatchet man
head hunter
heliolater
heresiarch
highjacker
highlander
hitch-hiker
human being
iconoclast
identifier
ideologist
idolatress
impenitent
impoisoner
importuner
imprisoner
incendiary
individual
inhabitant
inheritrix
inquisitor

insinuator
instigator
interceder
interferer
interloper
interposer
intervener
introducer
Ishmaelite
jackadandy
jackanapes
jobbernowl
job-hunter
jolterhead
kith and kin
lady-killer
land-holder
landlubber
languisher
lawbreaker
left-winger
legitimist
liberty man
licentiate
lieutenant
literalist
loggerhead
lotus-eater
lower class
Lychnobite
machinator
magnetizer
maiden aunt
maiden lady
malefactor
malingerer
manoeuvrer
man of straw
married man
marshaller
mastermind
matchmaker
merrymaker
metaphrast
methuselah
middlebrow
militarist
mindreader
misogamist
misogynist
monarchist
moneyed man
monogamist
monologist
monomaniac
monopolist
monotheist
mountebank
mouthpiece
muddied oaf
multiplier
namby-pamby
ne'er-do-well
neutralist
nincompoop
nominalist
non-starter
notability
obstructer
occasioner
old soldier
opinionist
opium-eater
originator
orthoepist
out-patient

overrunner
overturner
painstaker
pall-bearer
panegyrist
paraphrast
past master
patronizer
peacemaker
pedestrian
Peeping Tom
pensionary
persecutor
persifleur
personator
petitioner
phenomenon
philistine
pinchpenny
plagiarist
polo player
polygamist
polyhistor
polytheist
population
positivist
pragmatist
preadamite
procreator
profligate
progenitor
prohibiter
promenader
pronouncer
propagator
prophesier
propounder
proprietor
prosecutor
Protestant
psychopath
pulverizer
pyrrhonist
quarreller
questioner
rabblement
ragamuffin
rascallion
Rechabites
recidivist
reclaimant
recognizer
recognitor
reconciler
reimburser
relinquent
rememberer
reproacher
reprobater
reproducer
republican
repudiator
restrainer
restricter
retributer
reverencer
revivalist
rhapsodist
ringleader
sacrificer
scrapegrace
Scaramouch
schematist
schismatic
scrutineer
secularist

sensualist
separatist
sermonizer
seventh son
shoplifter
shanghaier
sinecurist
slammerkin
smart aleck
snuff-taker
solemnizer
solicitant
solifidian
solitarian
son and heir
songstress
soothsayer
Sorbonnist
speculator
spoilsport
squanderer
starveling
stepfather
stepmother
stepsister
stimulator
stipulator
strategist
street arab
strokesman
subscriber
substitute
subtracter
sugar daddy
supplanter
supplicant
suppressor
surmounter
suscipient
sweetheart
sworn enemy
syllogizer
syncopater
syncretist
synonymist
tale-bearer
tale-teller
tantalizer
taskmaster
tea-drinker
televiewer
temporalty
temporizer
tenderfoot
tenderling
textualist
textuarist
themselves
thickskull
third party
threatener
timeserver
tramontane
transferee
transferer
transmuter
trespasser
troglodyte
troubadour
tub-thumper
tweedledee
tweedledum
tuft-hunter
unbeliever
undertaker
unemployed

upper class
upper crust
utopianist
vacillator
vanquished
vanquisher
Vaticanist
vegetarian
vindicator
voluptuary
wallflower
well-wisher
white friar
whomsoever
widow-maker
wine-bibber
wirepuller
withdrawer
withholder
woman-hater
worshipper
yoke-fellow
young blood
yourselves

11

abbreviator
abecedarian
academician
accompanier
accumulator
adventuress
animal lover
aristocracy
association
bandy-player
beauty queen
belligerent
beneficiary
Bible reader
bibliolater
bibliophile
bird's-nester
blackmailer
bloodsucker
blue-eyed boy
blunderhead
bourgeoisie
braggadocio
breadwinner
brotherhood
calumniator
catabaptist
cave-dweller
centenarian
chance-comer
cheer leader
cheese parer
chucklehead
clairvoyant
coalitioner
cognoscenti
co-inheritor
collitigant
commentator
complainant
condisciple
confamiliar
confiscator
conjecturer
connoisseur
conspirator
constituent
continuator

41

contributor
co-ordinator
deliberator
denominator
denunciator
depopulator
depreciator
detractress
devotionist
dilapidator
diluvialist
dipsomaniac
discipliner
discourager
dishonourer
dissentient
dissertator
distributor
disunionist
doctrinaire
domestician
double agent
draggle-tail
dram-drinker
drug peddler
eager beaver
electioneer
emancipator
embellisher
embroiderer
enchantress
encounterer
endeavourer
enlightener
enlisted man
enterpriser
entertainer
epigenesist
epistolizer
equilibrist
equivocator
establisher
euphemerist
exaggerator
exasperater
father-in-law
fault-finder
femme fatale
fifth column
fighting man
first cousin
flat dweller
flying squad
foot soldier
forestaller
foster-child
francophile
francophobe
freethinker
frothblower
fustilarian
galley slave
gallows bird
gatecrasher
gentlefolks
gentlewoman
ginger group
god-daughter
gormandizer
grandfather
grandmother
grandnephew
grandparent
gull-catcher
guttersnipe
half brother

hard drinker
harum-scarum
helping hand
high society
hobbledehoy
holder-forth
homo sapiens
hyperbolist
hypercritic
ideopraxist
imperialist
inaugurator
infantryman
inhabitress
inheritress
interceptor
intercessor
interrupter
interviewer
intimidater
joint-tenant
knucklehead
leaseholder
libertarian
lickspittle
lilliputian
littérateur
living image
lycanthrope
manipulator
marrying-man
masquerader
materialist
matinee idol
maxim-monger
merry Andrew
metaphorist
middle class
millenarian
millionaire
misanthrope
misbeliever
misinformer
monopolizer
moonlighter
mother-in-law
mountaineer
mouth-friend
Mrs. Malaprop
name dropper
nationalist
necessarian
neutralizer
night-walker
nondescript
non-resident
nosey-parker
opportunist
owner-driver
pacificator
panic-monger
parishioner
participant
pearly queen
pedobaptist
peripatetic
perpetrator
personality
perturbator
phenomenist
philosopher
physicalist
predecessor
prize-winner
probabilist
probationer

prodigal son
proletarian
proletariat
promulgator
propitiator
prosecutrix
protagonist
protectress
protestator
Punchinello
punctualist
purgatorian
questionist
rank and file
rapscallion
rationalist
reactionary
recommender
recompenser
religionist
replenisher
reprehender
resuscitant
reversioner
right-winger
Rosicrucian
royal family
rugby player
sabbatarian
sacrilegist
sans-culotte
scaremonger
scatterling
scoutmaster
scripturist
scrutinizer
search party
shareholder
simple Simon
singularist
sister-in-law
sleepwalker
spectatress
speculatist
speech-maker
speed-skater
spendthrift
spindlelegs
stepbrother
stockholder
stonewaller
stool pigeon
story teller
stump-orator
subordinate
suffragette
surrenderee
surrenderer
sword player
sworn friend
sympathizer
systematist
system-maker
tautologist
teetotaller
teleologist
telepathist
thanksgiver
theosophist
time-pleaser
Tommy Atkins
torch-bearer
town-dweller
traditioner
transmitter
trencherman

trend setter
undersigned
undervaluer
undesirable
Walter Mitty
war criminal
wastethrift
weathercock
wholehogger
withstander

12

abolitionist
acquaintance
advance party
antediluvian
anticourtier
appropriator
artful dodger
assassinator
awkard squad
bachelor girl
backwoodsman
barber-monger
benefactress
bible-thumper
bibliomaniac
blood brother
bluestocking
bond-creditor
bottle-friend
brother-in-law
bounty hunter
carpet-knight
chief mourner
church-member
coalitionist
collaborator
Colonel Blimp
commiserator
committeeman
communicator
competitress
complimenter
compossessor
conservative
consignatory
conquistador
contemplator
contemporary
controverter
convalescent
conventicler
conventioner
convivialist
co-respondent
corporealist
cosmopolitan
defectionist
demimondaine
demonstrator
determinator
dialectician
disciplinant
discommender
discontinuer
disenchanter
disorganizer
dispossessor
disseminator
doppelgänger
double-dealer
eavesdropper

educationist
elocutionist
encumbrancer
enfranchiser
equestrienne
exclusionist
excursionist
exhibitioner
experimenter
expostulator
exserviceman
extemporizer
extensionist
exterminator
extinguisher
featherbrain
filibusterer
firstnighter
foster father
foster mother
foster parent
foster sister
foundationer
gastronomist
gesticulator
globe-trotter
gospel-gossip
grey eminence
guest speaker
hair-splitter
headshrinker
heir-apparent
holidaymaker
humanitarian
impersonator
impoverisher
improvisator
inseparables
intellectual
intercipient
interlocutor
intermeddler
intermediary
interpolator
interrogator
investigator
irregularist
kleptomaniac
knight-errant
landed gentry
leading light
legacy-hunter
letter-writer
longshoreman
lounge lizard
mademoiselle
man-about-town
married woman
melancholist
mercurialist
mezzo soprano
misconstruer
misinformant
modest violet
morris dancer
natural child
near relation
neoplatonist
noctambulist
nonagenarian
obscurantist
octogenarian
old gentleman
pantophagist
participator
peace-breaker

penitentiary
perambulator
peregrinator
persona grata
philosophist
pillion-rider
poor relation
postdiluvian
postgraduate
pot-companion
precipitator
prevaricator
primogenitor
proprietress
proselytizer
public figure
quater-cousin
recriminator
redemptioner
relinquisher
remonstrator
residentiary
resolutioner
resuscitator
roller-skater
rolling stone
salvationist
scatterbrain
schoolfellow
second cousin
second fiddle
sequestrator
sexagenarian
significator
single person
sister-german
sole occupant
somnambulist
somniloquist
spiritualist
spirit-rapper
stepdaughter
stormtrooper
straightener
street-urchin
stuffed shirt
sub-committee
sublapsarian
subpurchaser
Sunday driver
swashbuckler
sworn enemies
systematizer
system-monger
tennis player
testificator
theologaster
transgressor
transmigrant
transvestite
troublemaker
truce-breaker
truncheoneer
ugly customer
ugly duckling
ultramontane
undermanager
unemployable
universalist
velocipedist
versificator
village idiot
way passenger
wicket keeper
wool gatherer
working class

13

adminiculator
administrator
anagrammatist
Anglo-American
Anglo-Catholic
annexationist
anthropophagi
antisocialist
apothegmatist
bibliophilist
blood relation
brother-german
bureaucratist
castle-builder
chamber-fellow
comprovincial
conceptualist
concessionist
conspiratress
conventionist
co-religionist
correspondent
daughter-in-law
deck passenger
deuterogamist
devotionalist
discriminator
distinguisher
exhibitionist
experimentist
fashion-monger
first offender
foot passenger
fortune-hunter
foster brother
fresh-air fiend
grand-daughter
hard bargainer
high churchman
hypochondriac
immaterialist
irreligionist
Job's comforter
laughing stock
life-annuitant
machiavellian
millennialist
miracle-monger
miracle-worker
misanthropist
mischief-maker
multiplicator
necessitarian
nonconformist
paterfamilias
perfectionist
philhellenist
philosophizer
predestinator
protectionist
proverbialist
reprobationer
revolutionary
sophisticator
speed merchant
spindleshanks
spiritualizer
state criminal
state prisoner
strike-breaker
tranquillizer
transmigrator
undergraduate
understrapper

43

14

antiaristocrat
armchair critic
billiard-player
corpuscularian
destructionist
disciplinarian
disenchantress
foster daughter
galactophagist
good-for-nothing
grammaticaster
ichthyophagist
improvisatrice
indifferentist
latitudinarian
ministerialist
misinterpreter
obstructionist
paragrammatist
philanthropist

procrastinator
prognosticator
progressionist
prohibitionist
promise-breaker
psilanthropist
quadragenarian
quodlibetarian
requisitionist
restorationist
sabbath-breaker
sacramentarian
sensationalist
sentimentalist
septuagenarian
skittles-player
squandermaniac
stamp-collector
superior person
tatterdemalion
trencher-friend
ultramontanist

undergraduette
valetudinarian
waifs-and-strays
weather prophet
whippersnapper

15

antitrinitarian
autograph hunter
circumnavigator
constitutionist
conversationist
emancipationist
experimentalist
heir-presumptive
insurrectionary
insurrectionist
intellectualist
supernaturalist
Tom, Dick, and Harry

Professions, occupations, trades, etc.

2–4

alma
ayah
babu
bard
boss
char
chef
cook
crew
diva
doc
don
dyer
gang
G.P.
gyp
hack
hand
head
herd
hind
lead
magi
maid
mate
mime
M.D.
M.O.
P.A.
page
peon
P.M.
poet
pro
P.R.O.
rep
ryot
seer
serf
spy
syce
thug
tout
vet
ward
whip

5

actor
ad-man
agent
augur
avoué
baker
bonze
boots
bosun
caddy
choir
clerk
clown
coach
comic
crier
crimp
curer
daily
egger
envoy
extra
fakir
fence
fifer
filer
finer
flier
gager
gipsy
gluer
groom
guard
guide
guild
hakim
harpy
helot
hirer
hiver
hoppo
lamia
leech
luter
mason
medic

miner
navvy
nurse
oiler
owler
pilot
piper
plyer
pupil
quack
quill
rabbi
rater
reeve
runer
scout
sewer
shoer
slave
smith
sower
staff
sweep
tamer
tawer
taxer
thief
tiler
tuner
tutor
tyler
usher
valet
viner

6

airman
archer
artist
aurist
author
bagman
bailee
bailer

bailor
balker
bandit
banker
barber
bargee
barker
barman
batman
bearer
beggar
binder
boffin
bookie
bowman
brewer
broker
bugler
burler
bursar
busker
butler
cabbie
cabman
calker
canner
carman
carter
carver
casual
censor
clergy
cleric
codist
coiner
comber
conder
con man
coolie
cooper
copper
co-star
coster
cowboy
cowman
critic
cutler
cutter

dacoit	medico	singer	actuary
dancer	mender	sircar	alewife
dealer	menial	skivvy	almoner
digger	mentor	slater	alnagar
docker	mercer	slaver	alnager
doctor	milker	slavey	analyst
dowser	miller	sleuth	ancient
draper	minter	snarer	apposer
drawer	monger	socman	Arabist
driver	morisk	sorter	arbiter
drover	mummer	souter	artisan
editor	mumper	spicer	artiste
fabler	mystic	squire	assayer
factor	nailer	stager	assizer
farmer	notary	stoker	assured
fellah	nurser	storer	assurer
feller	oboist	sutler	auditor
fictor	oilman	tabler	aviator
fisher	orator	tailor	awarder
fitter	ostler	tamper	bailiff
flayer	packer	tanner	bandman
forger	parson	tasker	barmaid
fowler	pastor	taster	bedeman
framer	patrol	teller	bellboy
fuller	pavier	termer	bellhop
gaffer	pavior	tester	birdman
ganger	pedant	tiller	blaster
gaoler	pedlar	tinker	blender
gaucho	penman	tinman	boatman
gauger	picker	tinner	bondman
gigolo	pieman	toller	bookman
gilder	pirate	touter	bottler
gillie	pitman	toyman	brigand
glazer	plater	tracer	builder
glover	player	trader	burglar
graver	porter	troupe	butcher
grocer	potboy	tubman	buttons
guider	potter	turner	callboy
guidon	priest	tycoon	cambist
gunman	pruner	typist	carrier
gunner	purser	usurer	caseman
harper	querry	vacher	cashier
hatter	rabbin	valuer	cateran
hawker	ragman	vamper	caterer
healer	ranger	vanman	caulker
heaver	ratter	vassal	cellist
hodman	reader	vender	chanter
hooper	reaper	vendor	chapman
horner	reaver	verger	chemist
hosier	rector	verser	chorist
hunter	regent	viewer	cleaner
intern	relief	waiter	clicker
issuer	renter	walker	clippie
jailer	rigger	waller	co-agent
jailor	ringer	warden	coalman
jobber	robber	warder	cobbler
jockey	roofer	warper	cockler
joiner	rooter	washer	collier
jowter	sacker	weaver	co-pilot
jurist	sailor	weeder	copyist
keeler	salter	welder	coroner
keeper	salvor	whaler	corsair
killer	sapper	worker	counsel
lackey	sartor	wright	courier
lander	sawyer	writer	cowherd
lascar	scribe		cowpoke
lawyer	sea-dog		crofter
lector	sealer		cropper
lender	seaman	**7**	curator
loader	seiner		currier
logman	seizor	abacist	custode
lumper	seller	abigail	danseur
magian	server	acolyte	dentist
marker	setter	acolyth	dialist
master	sexton	acrobat	dietist
matron	shroff	actress	ditcher

dominie	marbler	spotter	boxmaker
doorman	marcher	stainer	brewster
dragman	mariner	stamper	broacher
drapier	marshal	stapler	busheler
drawboy	matador	statist	cabin boy
drayman	matelot	steerer	cellarer
dredger	mealman	steward	ceramist
dresser	meatman	surgeon	chandler
drogman	metayer	swabber	choirboy
drummer	metrist	sweeper	co-author
dustman	midwife	taborer	ciderist
famulus	milkman	tallier	claqueur
farrier	modiste	tapster	clothier
fascist	moneyer	taxi-man	coachman
faunist	monitor	teacher	codifier
fiddler	mootman	tipster	coistril
fireman	moulder	tracker	collator
fish-fag	newsboy	trainer	comedian
flesher	oculist	trapper	compiler
florist	officer	trawler	composer
flunkey	orderer	trimmer	conclave
flutist	orderly	trucker	conjurer
footboy	packman	trustee	conveyor
footman	pageboy	tumbler	coryphée
footpad	painter	turnkey	courtier
foreman	palmist	vintner	cow-leech
founder	pantler	violist	coxswain
friseur	peddler	wagoner	croupier
frogman	pianist	waister	cutpurse
fueller	picador	warrior	dairyman
furrier	planner	waterer	danseuse
gateman	planter	webster	deckhand
girdler	pleader	weigher	defender
glazier	plumber	wheeler	designer
gleaner	poacher	whetter	director
gleeman	poetess	wireman	dog-leech
glosser	postboy	woodman	domestic
graffer	postman	woolman	doughboy
grafter	presser	workman	dragoman
grainer	prestor	wrapper	druggist
granger	printer		editress
grantee	puddler		educator
grantor	rancher	**8**	embalmer
grazier	realtor		emissary
grinder	refiner	adscript	employee
gymnast	riveter	aeronaut	employer
hackler	roadman	algerine	engineer
harpist	roaster	analyser	engraver
haulier	rustler	annalist	enroller
helotry	sacrist	aphorist	epic poet
herbist	saddler	apjarist	essayist
herdman	sampler	apron-man	essoiner
heritor	samurai	arborist	exorcist
higgler	scourer	armourer	explorer
hogherd	scraper	armorist	exporter
hostler	servant	arrester	fabulist
indexer	settler	arrestor	factotum
inlayer	sharper	assessor	falconer
ironist	shearer	attorney	famulist
janitor	shipper	bagmaker	farmhand
juggler	shopboy	bagpiper	ferryman
junkman	shopman	ballader	figurant
juryman	showman	bandsman	filmstar
keelman	shunter	bargeman	finisher
knacker	silkman	bearherd	fishwife
knitter	simpler	bearward	flatfoot
laborer	skinner	bedesman	flautist
laceman	skipper	bedmaker	fletcher
linkboy	slipper	bit-maker	fodderer
linkman	smelter	bleacher	forester
lockman	snipper	boatsman	forgeman
lombard	socager	bondmaid	fugleman
mailman	soldier	bondsman	gangster
maltman	soloist	boniface	gardener
manager	spencer	botanist	gavelman
46 mangler	spinner	bowmaker	gendarme

glassman
goatherd
godsmith
gossiper
governor
guardian
gunsmith
hammerer
handmaid
handyman
hatmaker
haymaker
headsman
head cook
helmsman
henchman
herdsman
hired man
hireling
histrion
home help
hotelier
houseboy
huckster
huntsman
importer
improver
inkmaker
inventor
japanner
jet pilot
jeweller
jongleur
kipperer
labourer
landgirl
landlady
landlord
lapidary
larcener
larderer
leadsman
lecturer
linesman
lumberer
magician
magister
maltster
masseuse
measurer
mechanic
medalist
melodist
mercator
merchant
messager
metal-man
milkmaid
millgirl
millhand
milliner
minister
minstrel
mistress
modeller
muleteer
muralist
musician
neatherd
newshawk
novelist
onion-man
operator
optician
ordainer
ordinand

organist
outrider
overseer
pargeter
parodist
penmaker
perfumer
peterman
pewterer
picaroon
picklock
pinmaker
plagiary
plougher
polisher
portress
postiler
potmaker
preacher
prefacer
preluder
pressman
probator
procurer
promoter
prompter
prosaist
provider
psalmist
publican
pugilist
purveyor
quarrier
raftsman
ranchero
rapperee
receiver
regrater
relessee
relessor
repairer
reporter
resetter
restorer
retailer
retainer
reviewer
rewriter
rivetter
romancer
rugmaker
rumourer
salesman
satirist
sawbones
scullion
sculptor
seamster
sea-rover
seasoner
seedsman
sempster
servitor
shearman
shepherd
ship's boy
shipmate
shopgirl
showgirl
sidesman
simplist
sketcher
smuggler
soldiery
spaceman.
spearman

speedcop
spurrier
starcher
stitcher
stockman
storeman
stripper
strummer
stuntman
supplier
surveyor
swindler
tabourer
tallyman
taverner
teamster
thatcher
thespian
thresher
tin miner
tinsmith
torturer
toymaker
tripeman
truckman
turncock
turnspit
tutoress
unionist
valuator
vintager
virtuoso
vocalist
volumist
waitress
walker-on
wardress
warrener
watchman
waterman
wet nurse
whaleman
whitener
whitster
wigmaker
winnower
wool-dyer
workfolk
workhand
wrestler

9

alchemist
alluminor
anatomist
annotator
announcer
arbitress
arborator
archeress
architect
archivist
art critic
art dealer
artificer
astronaut
attendant
authoress
balladist
ballerina
bank agent
barrister
barrow boy

beefeater
beekeeper
beemaster
berserker
biologist
boanerges
boatswain
bodyguard
boilerman
bondslave
bondwoman
bookmaker
bootblack
bootmaker
buccaneer
bus driver
burnisher
cab driver
café owner
cameraman
car driver
caretaker
carpenter
casemaker
catechist
cellarman
charwoman
chauffeur
cheapjack
chorister
clarifier
clergyman
clinician
clogmaker
coalminer
coalowner
collector
columnist
colourist
comprador
concierge
conductor
conserver
cosmonaut
cost clerk
costumier
courtesan
couturier
cowfeeder
cowkeeper
cracksman
craftsman
crayonist
critickin
cymbalist
dactypist
daily help
dairymaid
decorator
decretist
desk clerk
detective
dice-maker
die-sinker
dietetist
dietitian
directrix
dispenser
dissector
distiller
doctoress
draftsman
dramatist
drawlatch
drum major
drum-maker

47

drysalter
ecologist
embezzler
enameller
engineman
engrosser
epitomist
errand boy
estimator
examinant
excavator
excerptor
exchanger
executive
exercitor
exciseman
exorciser
eye doctor
fabricant
fashioner
felt-maker
figurante
financier
film actor
film extra
film-maker
fire-eater
fish-curer
fisherman
fish-woman
flag-maker
flax-wench
flyfisher
freelance
freighter
fripperer
fruiterer
furbisher
furnisher
galvanist
gasfitter
gazetteer
gem-cutter
geologist
gladiator
gluemaker
goldsmith
gondolier
gospeller
governess
groundman
guardsman
guerrilla
guitarist
gun-runner
harlequin
harmonist
harpooner
harvester
Hellenist
herbalist
herbarian
herborist
herb-woman
hired hand
hired help
homeopath
historian
hog-ringer
hop-picker
hosteller
housemaid
housewife
hygienist
hypnotist
incumbent

ingrafter
innholder
innkeeper
inscriber
inspector
intendant
ironsmith
itinerant
jack-smith
job-master
kennel-man
lacemaker
lacquerer
lady's maid
lampooner
land agent
landreeve
larcenist
launderer
laundress
law writer
legionary
librarian
linotyper
liontamer
liveryman
loan agent
lockmaker
locksmith
log-roller
lumberman
machinist
magnetist
majordomo
male model
male nurse
man-at-arms
mannequin
mechanic
medallist
memoirist
mendicant
mercenary
mesmerist
messenger
metallist
metrician
middleman
mill-owner
modelgirl
mortician
muffin-man
musketeer
musketoon
myologist
navigator
negotiant
neologian
neologist
newsagent
nursemaid
odd job man
office boy
operative
orchestra
ordinator
osteopath
otologist
outfitter
pantaloon
pasquiler
paymaster
pedagogue
performer
physician
physicist

pitsawyer
planisher
plasterer
ploughboy
ploughman
pluralist
poetaster
pointsman
policeman
pontonier
pop artist
porteress
portrayer
portreeve
postilion
postwoman
poulterer
practiser
precentor
predicant
preceptor
prelector
priestess
privateer
professor
profilist
provedore
publicist
publisher
pulpiteer
puppeteer
pythoness
qualifier
quarryman
quirister
racketeer
railmaker
recruiter
reformist
rehearser
ribbonman
roadmaker
romancist
ropemaker
roundsman
ruddleman
rum-runner
sacristan
safemaker
sailmaker
scarifier
scavenger
scenarist
scholiast
schoolman
scientist
scrivener
scytheman
sea-robber
secretary
ship's mate
shipowner
shoeblack
shoemaker
sightsman
signalman
sinologue
soapmaker
solicitor
sonneteer
sopranist
sorceress
soubrette
space crew
spiderman
stableboy

stableman
stagehand
stationer
stay-maker
steersman
stevedore
subeditor
subworker
succentor
sur-master
swan-upper
swineherd
switchman
swordsman
syndicate
synoptist
tablemaid
tactician
tailoress
teataster
tentmaker
test pilot
therapist
theurgist
throwster
timberman
toolsmith
town clerk
towncrier
tire-woman
tradesman
tragedian
traveller
treasurer
trepanner
tributary
trumpeter
tympanist
usherette
varnisher
versifier
vetturino
vexillary
violinist
volcanist
voltigeur
wadsetter
warrantee
warranter
washerman
waxworker
whitester
winemaker
wood-reeve
workwoman
zookeeper
zoologist
zootomist

10

able seaman
accomptant
accoucheur
accountant
acolothist
advertiser
aerologist
agrologist
agronomist
air hostess
air steward
algebraist
amanuensis
apothecary

apple-woman
apprentice
arbalister
arbitrator
astrologer
astronomer
atmologist
auctioneer
audit clerk
ballet girl
balloonist
ballplayer
bandmaster
bank robber
baseballer
bassoonist
beadswoman
beautician
bell-hanger
bell-ringer
bibliopole
bill-broker
billposter
biochemist
biographer
blacksmith
bladesmith
blockmaker
bluejacket
bombardier
bondswoman
bonesetter
bookbinder
bookholder
bookkeeper
bookseller
bootlegger
bricklayer
brickmaker
brushmaker
bureaucrat
butterwife
caravaneer
career girl
cartoonist
cartwright
cash-keeper
cat breeder
cat burglar
ceramicist
chair-maker
chargehand
charioteer
chirurgeon
chorus girl
chronicler
chucker-out
circuiteer
claim agent
clapper boy
clockmaker
clog dancer
cloth maker
coachmaker
coal-backer
coal-fitter
coalheaver
coal-master
co-assessor
coastguard
collocutor
colloquist
colporteur
comedienne
compositor
compounder

concordist
contractor
controller
copyholder
copywriter
cordwainer
cotton lord
counsellor
crow-keeper
cultivator
customs man
cytologist
delineator
directress
disc jockey
discounter
discoverer
dishwasher
dispatcher
distrainer
distrainor
dockmaster
dog breeder
dog-fancier
doorkeeper
dramaturge
dressmaker
drummer-boy
dry cleaner
emblazoner
emboweller
enamellist
ephemerist
epitaphist
epitomizer
evangelist
examinator
explorator
eye-servant
fell-monger
fictionist
file-cutter
filibuster
film editor
firemaster
fire-worker
fishmonger
flight crew
flowergirl
fluvialist
folk-dancer
folk-singer
forecaster
frame-maker
freebooter
fund raiser
fustianist
gamekeeper
game warden
geisha girl
gear-cutter
geneticist
geographer
glee-singer
glossarist
glue-boiler
gold-beater
gold-digger
gold-washer
governante
grammarian
gunslinger
hackney-man
hall porter
handmaiden
harvestman

hatcheller
head porter
head waiter
hierophant
highwayman
horn player
horologist
horsecoper
horse-leech
house agent
huckstress
husbandman
inoculator
institutor
instructor
interagent
ironmonger
ironworker
journalist
journeyman
lady doctor
land holder
land jobber
land waiter
land worker
laundryman
law officer
legislator
librettist
lighterman
lime-burner
linotypist
liquidator
lobsterman
lock-keeper
lumberjack
magistrate
management
manageress
manicurist
manservant
matchmaker
meat-hawker
medical man
militiaman
millwright
mineralist
ministress
mintmaster
missionary
moonshiner
naturalist
nautch girl
negotiator
news editor
newscaster
newsvendor
newswriter
night nurse
nosologist
nurseryman
obituarist
oil painter
orchardist
osteologer
overlooker
panegyrist
pantrymaid
park-keeper
park-ranger
pasquilant
pastry-cook
pathfinder
pawnbroker
pearl-diver
pediatrist

pedicurist
peltmonger
penologist
perruquier
pharmacist
philologer
piano tuner
pickpocket
platelayer
playwright
politician
portionist
postillion
postmaster
prescriber
prima donna
private eye
procurator
programmer
pronouncer
proprietor
prospector
protractor
proveditor
puncturist
pyrologist
quiz-master
railwayman
rat-catcher
recitalist
researcher
ringmaster
roadmender
ropedancer
roughrider
safeblower
sales force
saleswoman
schoolmarm
scrutineer
sculptress
sea-captain
seamstress
second mate
seminarist
serving-man
sexologist
ship-broker
ship-holder
shipmaster
shipwright
shopfitter
shopkeeper
shopwalker
signwriter
silentiary
silk-mercer
silk-weaver
sinologist
skirmisher
slop seller
sneak thief
soap-boiler
specialist
staff nurse
steersmate
stewardess
stipulator
stocktaker
stone-borer
stonemason
strategist
street-ward
supercargo
superviser
surcharger

49

surface-man
swan-keeper
symphonist
tally clerk
taskmaster
taxi-dancer
taxi-driver
tea-blender
tea planter
technician
technocrat
theogonist
theologian
theologist
threnodist
timekeeper
tractarian
trade union
traffic cop
trafficker
tram-driver
transactor
translator
trawlerman
treasuress
troubadour
typesetter
undertaker
veterinary
victualler
vinegrower
vivandiere
vocabulist
wage-earner
wainwright
warrioress
watchmaker
waterguard
wharfinger
wholesaler
whitesmith
winegrower
wine-waiter
wireworker
woodcarver
woodcutter
wood-monger
woodworker
wool-carder
wool-comber
wool-driver
wool-grower
wool-sorter
wool-trader
wool-winder
wool-worker
work-fellow
working man
workmaster
work people
yardmaster
zinc-worker
zoographer
zymologist

11

accompanist
accoucheuse
acoustician
adjudicator
allopathist
annunciator

antiquarian
apple-grower
arbitratrix
army officer
arquebusier
artillerist
audio typist
auscultator
bag-snatcher
ballad-maker
bank cashier
bank manager
bargemaster
basketmaker
batti-wallah
battologist
beachcomber
bell-founder
Benedictine
bill-sticker
bird-catcher
bird-fancier
bird-watcher
boatbuilder
body servant
boilermaker
boilersmith
bondservant
boot-catcher
broadcaster
bullfighter
businessman
butter-woman
candlemaker
car salesman
cattle thief
cat's-meat-man
chair-mender
chalk-cutter
chambermaid
chiffonnier
chirologist
chiromancer
chiropodist
choirmaster
chronologer
cinder-wench
cinder-woman
clock-setter
cloth-worker
coal-whipper
coffin-maker
cognoscente
collar-maker
common-crier
condisciple
condottiere
conductress
confederate
congressman
consecrator
conservator
constituent
conveyancer
coppersmith
cosmogonist
cosmologist
crane driver
crimewriter
cub reporter
cypher clerk
day-labourer
delivery man
demographer
dispensator
draughtsman

duty officer
electrician
emblematist
embroiderer
entertainer
estate agent
ethnologist
etymologist
executioner
extortioner
face-painter
factory hand
faith healer
fancy-monger
field worker
figure-maker
filing clerk
finestiller
fire brigade
fire insurer
flax-dresser
flesh-monger
fourbisseur
fringe-maker
fruit picker
funambulist
galley-slave
genealogist
ghostwriter
glass-bender
glass-blower
glass-cutter
glass-worker
grass-cutter
grave-digger
greengrocer
haberdasher
hagiologist
hairdresser
hair stylist
hardwareman
harvest lord
head foreman
head workman
hedge-priest
hedge-writer
hierologist
histologist
horse doctor
horse jockey
horse-keeper
horse trader
hospitaller
hotel-keeper
housekeeper
housemaster
housemother
hymnologist
illuminator
illusionist
illustrator
infantryman
institutist
interpreter
interviewer
iron-founder
ivory-carver
ivory-turner
ivory-worker
kennelmaid
kitchenmaid
lamplighter
land steward
laundrymaid
leading lady
ledger clerk

lifeboatman
lightkeeper
linen draper
lithologist
lithotomist
lorry driver
madrigalist
maidservant
mammalogist
master baker
mechanician
medicine man
merchantman
memorialist
metal worker
miniaturist
money-broker
money-lender
monographer
mule-spinner
music critic
music master
myographist
mysteriarch
mythologist
necrologist
necromancer
needlewoman
neurologist
neurotomist
night porter
night sister
nightworker
nomenclator
numismatist
office staff
onion-seller
opera singer
ophiologist
orientalist
orthopedist
osteologist
pamphleteer
panel-beater
pantomimist
paperhanger
parish clerk
parlourmaid
pathologist
pattenmaker
pearlfisher
penny-a-liner
petrologist
pettifogger
philatelist
philologist
piece worker
phytologist
phonologist
polyphonist
pork butcher
portraitist
preceptress
print-seller
probationer
promulgator
proofreader
property man
proprietrix
quacksalver
questionary
radiologist
rag merchant
representer
republisher
rhetorician

12

roadsweeper
safebreaker
sandwich man
Sanscritist
saxophonist
scoutmaster
scrapdealer
scrip-holder
secret agent
seditionary
servant girl
serving-maid
share-broker
sheepfarmer
shepherdess
shipbreaker
shipbuilder
ship's master
shopsteward
silk-thrower
silversmith
slaughterer
slave-driver
slave-holder
smallholder
sociologist
stage-driver
stage-player
stake-holder
steeplejack
stereotyper
stipendiary
stockbroker
stockjobber
stonecutter
storekeeper
stripteaser
sundriesman
system-maker
taxidermist
telegrapher
telephonist
ticket agent
toastmaster
tobacconist
tooth-drawer
topographer
torch-bearer
town planner
toxophilite
tragedienne
train-bearer
transcriber
transporter
travel agent
type-founder
typographer
underbearer
underletter
underwriter
upholsterer
versemonger
vine-dresser
waiting-maid
washerwoman
watchkeeper
water-doctor
water-gilder
wax-chandler
wheel-cutter
wheelwright
whitewasher
witch-doctor
wool-stapler
xylophonist
zoographist

accordionist
actor manager
ambulance man
anaesthetist
animalculist
archeologist
artilleryman
artist's model
bagpipe-maker
ballad singer
ballet dancer
ballet master
bantamweight
bellows-maker
bibliologist
bibliopegist
bibliopolist
body-snatcher
booking clerk
bus conductor
cabinet-maker
calligrapher
caricaturist
carpet-bagger
carpet-fitter
cartographer
cataclysmist
cerographist
cheesemonger
chief cashier
chimney-sweep
chiropractor
chronologist
churchwarden
circuit rider
civil servant
clarinettist
clerk of works
cloth-shearer
coach-builder
coleopterist
commissioner
conchologist
confectioner
corn chandler
cosmographer
costermonger
crafts-master
craniologist
cryptogamist
dance hostess
deep-sea diver
demonologist
demonstrator
dendrologist
dramaturgist
ecclesiastic
Egyptologist
elecutionist
engastrimuth
engine-driver
entomologist
entomotomist
entrepreneur
escapologist
ethnographer
experimenter
family doctor
farm labourer
film director
film producer
first officer
flying doctor
footplateman

geometrician
geriatrician
glass-grinder
glossologist
greasemonkey
guild brother
gymnosophist
gynecologist
hagiographer
haliographer
harness-maker
head gardener
headshrinker
homeopathist
horse-breaker
horse-courser
horse-knacker
hotel manager
housebreaker
housepainter
house steward
house surgeon
hydrographer
hydropathist
hypothecator
immunologist
impropriator
instructress
invoice clerk
jerry-builder
joint-trustee
jurisconsult
juvenile lead
king's counsel
knife-grinder
knife-thrower
labouring man
land surveyor
lath-splitter
leader-writer
legal adviser
lexicologist
lithographer
longshoreman
loss adjuster
lumber-dealer
maitre d'hotel
make-up artist
malacologist
man of letters
manual worker
manufacturer
mass producer
meat-salesman
mezzo soprano
metallurgist
microscopist
mineralogist
miscellanist
money-changer
monographist
morris-dancer
mosaic-artist
mosaic-worker
mythographer
newspaperman
notary public
nutritionist
obstetrician
office junior
oneirocritic
orchestrator
organ-builder
organ-grinder
orthodontist
orthographer

ovariotomist
paper-stainer
pattern-maker
pediatrician
phonographer
photographer
phrenologist
physiologist
plant manager
ploughwright
plumber's mate
plyer-for-hire
postmistress
practitioner
press officer
prestigiator
prison warder
prize-fighter
professional
propagandist
proprietress
psychiatrist
psychologist
publicity man
pupil-teacher
puppet-player
pyrotechnist
quarry master
racing driver
radiographer
receptionist
remembrancer
restaurateur
riding-master
right-hand man
rubber-grader
sales manager
scene-painter
scene-shifter
schoolmaster
screenwriter
scriptwriter
scullery-maid
seafaring man
seed-merchant
seismologist
sharecropper
sharpshooter
ship chandler
ship's husband
shoe-repairer
silver-beater
slaughterman
snake-charmer
social worker
soil mechanic
special agent
speechwriter
spice-blender
sportscaster
sportswriter
stage manager
statistician
steel erector
stenographer
stonebreaker
stonedresser
stonesquarer
street-trader
street-walker
sugar-refiner
tax-collector
technologist
telegraph boy
telegraphist
test engineer

therapeutist
thief-catcher
ticket-porter
timber trader
toll-gatherer
tourist agent
toxicologist
tradespeople
transplanter
trichologist
undermanager
underservant
veterinarian
waiting-woman
water diviner
warehouseman
wine merchant
wood-engraver
woollen-draper
works manager
zincographer

13

administrator
agriculturist
antique dealer
arachnologist
archaeologist
arithmetician
articled clerk
Assyriologist
barber-surgeon
bibliographer
calico-printer
campanologist
cartographist
chartographer
chicken-farmer
chirographist
choreographer
chronographer
civil engineer
clearstarcher
coffee-planter
cometographer
contrabandist
contortionist
cotton-spinner
counter-caster
counterfeiter
cranioscopist
cryptographer
dancing master
deipnosophist
dermatologist
diagnostician
diamond-cutter
draughtswoman
drawing-master
dress designer
drill sergeant
electroplater
electrotypist
emigrationist
encyclopedist
entozoologist
epigrammatist
estate manager
exhibitionist
family butcher
fencing-master
fortune-teller

freight-broker
galvanologist
game-preserver
gastriloquist
glossographer
glyphographer
ground-bailiff
gynaecologist
harbour master
hieroglyphist
horse-milliner
hospital nurse
ichthyologist
industrialist
intelligencer
joint-executor
letter-carrier
letter-founder
lexicographer
lighthouse-man
maid-of-all-work
master-builder
master mariner
mathematician
melodramatist
metaphysician
meteorologist
metoposcopist
music mistress
night-watchman
old-clothes-man
ornithologist
orthographist
park attendant
periodicalist
pharmaceutist
physiognomist
physiographer
posture-master
poultry farmer
privateersman
process-server
psalmographer
psychoanalyst
pteridologist
public speaker
queen's counsel
racing-tipster
revolutionary
revolutionist
rubber-planter
sailing master
schoolteacher
science master
shop assistant
silk-throwster
singing-master
station-master
stenographist
stereoscopist
stethoscopist
street-sweeper
sub-contractor
superintender
supernumerary
thaumaturgist
thimble-rigger
toll collector
trade unionist
tram conductor
tramcar-driver
ventriloquist
violoncellist
window-cleaner
window-dresser
writing-master

14

administratrix
anthropologist
autobiographer
bacteriologist
ballet mistress
billiard-marker
billiard-player
chamber-counsel
chimney-sweeper
citizen-soldier
classics master
colour sergeant
commissionaire
dancing partner
discount-broker
educationalist
ecclesiologist
encyclopaedist
exchange-broker
grammaticaster
handicraftsman
heresiographer
horticulturist
house decorator
house furnisher
language master
leather-dresser
manual labourer
market-gardener
medical officer
merchant-tailor
miscellanarian
money-scrivener
mother-superior
music publisher
naval pensioner
painter-stainer
pharmacologist
pneumatologist
psalmographist
reception clerk
representative
schoolmistress
ship's-carpenter
siderographist
spectacle-maker
spectroscopist
superintendent
systems analyst
tallow chandler
water-colourist
weather prophet

15

arboriculturist
assistant master
Bow Street runner
crossing-sweeper
crustaceologist
dancing mistress
diamond merchant
domestic servant
forwarding agent
gentleman-farmer
hackney coachman
heart specialist
helminthologist
hierogrammatist
historiographer
instrumentalist
insurance broker

jack-of-all-trades	portrait-painter	scripture-reader
musical director	professional man	sleeping partner
numismatologist	programme seller	stretcher-bearer
ophthalmologist	provision dealer	ticket collector
palaeontologist	railway engineer	tightrope walker
platform-speaker	resurrectionist	tonsorial artist

DOMESTIC
Clothes and materials

3

alb
bag
bib
boa
bra
cap
fez
fur
hat
hem
jam
kid
lap
mac
net
PVC
rag
rep
sox
tie
wig
zip

4

band
belt
boot
brim
cape
clog
coat
coif
cony
cope
cowl
cuff
down
drag
duck
duds
felt
frog
garb
gear
gimp
gown
gros
haik
hide
hood
hose
jute
képi
kilt
lace
lamé
lawn

leno
maud
maxi
mesh
mini
mink
mitt
moff
muff
mule
mull
pelt
poke
repp
robe
ruff
sack
sari
sash
shag
shoe
silk
slip
sock
spur
stud
suit
tapa
toga
togs
tutu
vamp
veil
vest
wool
wrap

5

abaya
amice
amict
apron
baize
batik
beige
benjy
beret
bezan
boots
braid
budge
busby
capoc
caxon
chaps
cloak
clogs
cloth

clout
crape
crash
crêpe
denim
dhoti
dicky
dress
drill
ephod
ermin
fanon
fichu
finos
floss
frill
frock
gauze
get-up
glove
gunny
habit
haick
heels
inkle
jabot
jasey
jeans
jippo
jupon
jussi
khaki
lacet
lapel
Levis
linen
lisle
middy
mitre
mitts
moiré
mufti
nylon
orlon
orris
pants
parka
plaid
pleat
plume
plush
pumps
quoif
rayon
romal
ruche
sable
sabot
sagum
satin
scarf

serge
shako
shawl
shift
shirt
skirt
slops
smock
snood
spats
stays
stock
stola
stole
stuff
suede
surah
tabby
tails
tammy
toile
topee
toque
train
trews
tulle
tunic
tweed
twill
vamps
V-neck
voile
weeds

6

alpaca
angola
angora
anorak
aridas
baftas
banian
barret
basque
beaver
bengal
berlin
bikini
biggin
blazer
blouse
boater
bob-wig
bodice
bolero
bonnet
bonten
bootee

53

bouclé
bowler
bow tie
braces
briefs
brogan
brogue
buckle
burlap
buskin
bustle
button
byssus
cabeca
caftan
calash
calico
camlet
canvas
capoch
capote
chintz
cloche
coatee
collar
collet
corset
cossas
cotton
cravat
crepon
cyprus
dacron
damask
diadem
diaper
dickey
dimity
dirndl
dolman
domino
dornic
dorsel
dowlas
duffel
ear-cap
edging
ermine
fabric
fag-end
faille
fedora
ferret
fibule
flares
fleece
foxfur
frieze
fringe
gaiter
garter
girdle
guimpe
gurrah
gusset
hankie
helmet
humbum
insole
jacket
jerkin
jersey
joseph
jumper
juppon
kaftan

kersey
kimono
kirtle
lappet
lining
linsey
livery
madras
mantle
mantua
marmot
merino
mitten
mobcap
mohair
moreen
mundil
muslin
nutria
nylons
panama
patten
peltry
peplum
peruke
pleats
pompon
poncho
pongee
poplin
puttee
PVC mac
raglan
ratine
reefer
riband
ribbon
rigout
rochet
ruffle
russet
samite
sandal
sarong
sateen
sendal
sequin
serape
sheath
shoddy
shorts
slacks
sleeve
smalls
soneri
stamin
sunhat
tabard
taminy
tartan
ticken
tights
tippet
tissue
tobine
toison
top-hat
toquet
torque
toupee
toupet
tricot
trilby
trunks
T-shirt
tucker

turban
tussah
tuxedo
tweeds
ulster
velure
velvet
visite
waders
wampum
weeper
whites
wimple
wincey
woolly
zonnar

7

abb wool
acrilan
anarak
anorak
apparel
art-silk
bandana
bandeau
batiste
bay-yarn
beveren
biretta
blanket
blucher
bocking
bottine
brocade
brogans
buckram
burnous
bycoket
byssine
calotte
camblet
cambric
capuche
cantoon
cassock
casuals
challis
chamois
chapeau
chemise
chenille
chimere
chlamys
chopine
chrisom
civvies
clobber
clothes
coating
cockade
coronet
corsage
costume
cow-hide
crochet
crounet
cut-away
delaine
doeskin
dogskin
dollman
dornock
doublet

drabbet
drawers
drip-dry
egrette
epaulet
ermelin
fallals
falsies
felt hat
felting
filibeg
flannel
flat hat
floroon
flounce
foulard
frislet
frounce
fur coat
fustian
gaiters
galloon
gantlet
garment
gaskins
genappe
gingham
grogram
grogan
guipure
G-string
gymslip
handbag
hat-band
hessian
hoggers
hogskin
holland
homburg
hosiery
jaconet
lasting
latchet
layette
leather
legging
leghorn
leotard
loafers
lockram
Mae West
malines
maniple
mantlet
matting
mechlin
minever
miniver
montero
morocco
muffler
nacarat
nankeen
necktie
nightie
oilskin
organza
orleans
orphrey
overall
paisley
paletot
pallium
panties
parasol
partlet

pattens
pelisse
periwig
petasus
pigskin
pugaree
purflew
puttees
pyjamas
raiment
rompers
rosette
sacking
sarsnet
satinet
scarlet
singlet
slip-ons
slipper
spencer
sporran
stammel
stetson
suiting
sunsuit
surcoat
surtout
sweater
tabaret
tabinet
taffeta
taffety
tatting
ticking
tiffany
top coat
top-knot
tricorn
tunicle
turn-ups
tussore
twinset
uniform
vandyke
velours
vesting
vesture
webbing
wellies
wetsuit
whittle
wiggery
woollen
worsted
yashmak

8

aigrette
appliqué
babouche
baffetas
baldrick
barathea
barracan
bathrobe
baudekin
bearskin
bed linen
bedsocks
biggonet
blancard
bloomers
bluchers

boat-neck
body-belt
bombasin
bonelace
bootikin
bottines
breeches
brocatel
brodekin
buckskin
Burberry
burnoose
bycocket
camisole
cardigan
carlisle
cashmere
Celanese
chagreen
chaperon
chasuble
chausses
chaussure
chenille
chesible
cloaking
cloth cap
clothing
coiffure
collaret
corduroy
cordwain
corporal
corselet
cracowes
cretonne
culottes
dagswain
deerskin
diamanté
dress tie
drilling
dungaree
earmuffs
ensemble
Fair Isle
fatigues
fillibeg
fingroms
flannels
florence
fontange
footwear
frilling
frippery
frontlet
froufrou
furbelow
gabarage
galoshes
gambeson
gambroon
gauntlet
glad rags
gold lamé
gossamer
gumboots
gymshoes
half-hose
headband
hipsters
homespun
jackboot
Jacquard
jodhpurs
jump suit

kerchief
knickers
knitwear
lambskin
leggings
lingerie
mantelet
mantilla
material
moccasin
moleskin
moquette
muffetee
muslinet
musquash
nainsook
neckband
négligée
nightcap
oilcloth
opera hat
organdie
osnaburg
overalls
overcoat
overshoe
paduasoy
pelerine
piccadil
pinafore
playsuit
plumelet
polo-neck
ponyskin
prunella
prunello
pullover
raincoat
rose-knot
sandshoe
sarcanet
sealskin
scapular
shagreen
shalloon
Shantung
sheeting
shirring
shirting
shoelace
shot silk
skiboots
skipants
skullcap
slippers
smocking
sneakers
snoeshoe
sombrero
stitchel
stocking
straw hat
sundress
sunshade
surplice
swanskin
swimsuit
tabbinet
taglioni
tailcoat
tapestry
tarboosh
tarlatan
terai-hat
Terylene
Thai silk

trimming
trousers
two-piece
umbrella
valentia
vallancy
vestment
wardrobe
woollens
wristlet

9

alice band
astrakhan
baby linen
balaclava
bandolier
beachwear
bedjacket
billycock
blond lace
blue jeans
bombazine
bowler hat
brassiere
broadbrim
bushshirt
calamanco
camelhair
caparison
cassimere
cerecloth
chantilly
clump boot
cocked hat
comforter
Courtelle
crinoline
Cuban heel
dalmatica
décolleté
dog collar
dress coat
dress suit
duffle bag
dungarees
epaulette
fermillet
fingering
fleshings
flipflops
floss silk
forage cap
frockcoat
full dress
full skirt
fur collar
gaberdine
galoshes
gambadoes
garibaldi
gauntlets
georgette
Glengarry
greatcoat
grosgrain
haircloth
hairshift
hairpiece
headdress
headscarf
high heels
hoop skirt
horsehair

55

housecoat
huckaback
Inverness
jack boots
jockey cap
justi-coat
kid gloves
knee socks
lambswool
levantine
linen mesh
loincloth
longcloth
long dress
long skirt
long socks
millinery
miniskirt
moiré silk
nightgown
nightwear
neckcloth
organzine
overdress
overshoes
panama hat
pantalets
pantaloon
paramatta
patchwork
pea jacket
peaked cap
percaline
petticoat
pina cloth
pixie hood
plimsolls
plus-fours
point lace
polonaise
pourpoint
polyester
press stud
quoiffure
redingote
round-neck
sackcloth
sack dress
safety pin
sailcloth
sailor cap
sailor hat
sanbenito
satinette
scapulary
school cap
scoop-neck
separates
sharkskin
sheepskin
shovel hat
shower cap
silk serge
sloppy joe
slouch hat
snowshoes
sou'wester
spun rayon
stockings
stomacher
strapless
strouding
suede coat
sunbonnet
swansdown
56 sweatband

sword belt
tarpaulin
towelling
track suit
trilby hat
trousseau
underwear
velveteen
vestments
waistband
waistcoat
wedge heel
wide-awake
wristband
zucchetto

10

angora wool
ankle socks
balbriggan
ballet shoe
bathing cap
beaverteen
Berlin wool
bishop's-cap
blanketing
bobbin lace
bobbysocks
boiler suit
bombazette
broadcloth
brocatello
bushjacket
buttonhole
canonicals
cassinette
chatelaine
chemisette
chinchilla
court dress
court shoes
coverchief
crepe soles
cricket cap
cummerbund
diving suit
drainpipes
dress shoes
embroidery
epauletted
Eton collar
Eton jacket
fancy dress
fearnought
feather boa
florentine
foot mantle
foresleeve
fustanella
gold thread
grass cloth
grass skirt
habiliment
halterneck
Havana pelt
hodden-gray
hodden-grey
horsecloth
Irish linen
jersey silk
jersey wool
kerseymere
khaki drill
lounge suit

mackintosh
mess jacket
middy skirt
mock velvet
mousseline
needlecord
new clothes
nightdress
nightshirt
old clothes
opera cloak
overblouse
Oxford bags
pantaloons
party dress
persiennes
piccadilly
pillow lace
pilot-cloth
pith helmet
plastic mac
print dress
rabbitskin
riding-hood
roquelaure
sailorsuit
scratch wig
seersucker
shoebuckle
shoe string
slingbacks
sportscoat
suspenders
tablecloth
table linen
thrown silk
trench coat
trousering
turtle-neck
tussah silk
underpants
waterproof
windjammer
wing collar
wraparound

11

Aran sweater
battledress
bellbottoms
best clothes
black patent
candystripe
canvas shoes
cap and bells
cheesecloth
clodhoppers
cloth-of-gold
crash-helmet
deerstalker
diving dress
Dolly Varden
dreadnought
farthingale
flannelette
flared skirt
football cap
hammer cloth
hand-me-downs
Harris tweed
herringbone
Honiton lace
Kendal green
leather coat

leatherette
leopardskin
mechlin lace
morning coat
mortarboard
neckerchief
nettlecloth
Norfolk suit
panty girdle
Phrygian cap
pilot jacket
pinstripes
ready-to-wear
regimentals
riding habit
shoe leather
shoulder bag
slumberwear
stiff collar
stockinette
suede jacket
tam-o'-shanter
tennis dress
tennis skirt
torchon lace
trencher cap
trouser suit
tussore silk
watered silk
wellingtons
widow's weeds
windcheater
yachting cap

12

antigropelos
asbestos suit
bathing dress
billycock hat
body stocking
bolting cloth
business suit
cardinal's hat
cavalry twill
chastity belt
collar and tie
college scarf
crêpe-de-chine
dinner jacket
divided skirt
donkey jacket
dress clothes
dressing gown
Easter bonnet
evening dress
football boots
galligaskins
handkerchief
Indian cotton
knee breeches
leather skirt
lumber jacket
moiré antique
monkey jacket
morning dress
plain clothes
pleated skirt
service dress
shirtwaister
sleeping suit
sportsjacket
underclothes
wedding dress
Welsh flannel

13

Anthony Eden
Bermuda shorts
cashmere shawl
chinchilla fur
football scarf
leather jacket
Norfolk jacket
patent leather
pinafore dress
platform soles
Russia leather

spatterdashes
swaddling band
underclothing

14

artificial silk
bathing costume
chamois leather
Fair Isle jumper
knickerbockers
Morocco leather

riding breeches
Shetland jumper
shoulder strap
swaddling cloth
undress uniform

15

maribou feathers
mourning clothes
ostrich feathers
tarpaulin jacket

Dances

3
bop
hop
jig

4
ball
jive
jota
juba
kolo
reel

5
bebop
caper
fling
mambo
polka
rondo
rumba
samba
tango
twist
valse
waltz

6
bolero
boston
bourée

cancan
cha-cha
chassé
corant
colipee
gallop
minuet
morisk
morris
pavane
redowa
shimmy
valeta

7
beguine
coranto
fox-trot
gavotte
lancers
la volta
madison
mazurka
morisco
one-step
rondeau
two-step

8
bunny-hug
cake-walk
capriole
chaconne
cotillon

courante
danseuse
fandango
galliard
habanera
hornpipe
hulahula
huy-de-guy
rigadoon
saraband
tap-dance

9
arabesque
barndance
bossa nova
cha-cha-cha
clog dance
écossaise
farandole
folkdance
gallopade
jitterbug
paso doble
Paul Jones
pirouette
polonaise
poussette
quadrille
rock 'n' roll

10
boston reel
charleston

hey-de-guize
pooka-pooka
saltarello
strathspey
sword-dance
tambourine
tarantella
torch dance
turkey-trot
tripudiary

11
contra-dance
jolly miller
morris dance
rock and roll
square-dance
varsovienne

12
country dance
maypole dance
palais-glide
state-lancers
tripudiation

13
eightsome reel
Helston flurry
Highland fling

Drinks (wines, spirits, non-alcoholic beverages, etc.)

3
ale
bub
cha
flx
gin
kir
nog
rum
rye

tea

4
arak
asti
bass
beer
bock
bols

cola
fizz
flip
grog
hock
kava
marc
mead
mild
milk
moët

mumm
ouzo
port
raki
reid
rosé
sack
sake
saki
stum
tent

wine
wort

5

arack
ayala
bohea
broth
bumbo
byrrh
capri
chica
cider
cocoa
congo
cream
daisy
hooch
hyson
Irish
irroy
julep
kvass
lager
Maçon
Médoc
mobby
morat
negus
noyau
padra
pekoe
perry
plonk
punch
purre
quass
shrub
sirop
smash
stout
tafia
toddy
Tokay
tonic
vichy
winox

6

alegar
arrack
Barsac
Beaune
bitter
Bovril
brandy
bubbly
canary
cassis
caudle
claret
coffee
Cognac
Cooper
egg-nog
elixir
geneva
Gibson
gimlet
grappa
Graves
junora

kirsch
kummel
liquor
Lisbon
Malaga
masdeu
mastic
muscat
oolong
perkin
Pernod
pimint
pontac
porter
posset
poteen
ptisan
pulque
rickey
Saumur
Scotch
shandy
sherry
spirit
squash
stingo
Strega
swipes
volnay
wherry
whisky

7

alcohol
ale-gill
alicant
aquavit
bitters
bourbon
Campari
catawba
Chablis
Chandon
Chianti
cobbler
cordial
curaçao
egg-flip
Falerno
gin fizz
gin sour
hock-clip
koumiss
liqueur
low-wine
mace ale
Madeira
Malmsey
Marsala
martini
Moselle
Orvieto
pale ale
perrier
pink gin
Pomerol
Pommard
Pommery
Pouilly
pulchra
ratafia
red wine
retsina
samshoo

sherbet
sloe-gin
spirits
stinger
tequila
tintara
twankay
vibrona
vouvray
whiskey

8

absinthe
Advocaat
alkermes
anisette
aperitif
Assam tea
bees'-wing
beverage
block tea
bock-beer
Bordeaux
brick tea
Burgundy
charneco
China tea
cider cup
ciderkin
Clicquot
coca-cola
cocktail
Drambuie
dry wines
Dubonnet
eau-de-vie
espresso
florence
gin-sling
green tea
Guinness
highball
Hollands
Horlick's
hydromel
lemonade
montilla
muscadel
muscatel
nightcap
oopak tea
padra tea
pekoe tea
pilsener
Pol Roger
pouchong
prasites
punt y mes
ramboose
red biddy
red wines
roederer
ruby port
rum-punch
rum-shrub
St. Julien
sangaree
Sauterne
schnapps
sillabub
skim-milk
souchong
sour milk
syllabub

tia maria
verjuice
vermouth
vin blanc
wish-wash

9

altar wine
angostura
Anjou wine
applejack
aqua vitae
barley-pop
birch wine
bitter ale
black beer
Bollinger
brut wines
Ceylon tea
champagne
chocolate
claret cup
Cointreau
copa de oro
cuba libre
elder wine
Falernian
ginger-ale
ginger-pop
grenadine
gunpowder
Hall's wine
hermitage
Heidsieck
hippocras
iced water
Indian tea
lager beer
limejuice
Manhattan
metheglin
milk-punch
mint julep
mulled ale
muscadine
oolong-tea
orangeade
orange-gin
St. Emilion
St. Raphael
salutaris
Scotch ale
slivovitz
small-beer
soda water
soft drink
still-hock
sundowner
tarragona
tawny port
white lady
white port
white wine
Wincarnis

10

Beaujolais
bitter beer
black-strap
bloody mary
café-au-lait
calcavella

cappuccino
chartreuse
clary-water
constantia
dry martini
frontiniac
genevrette
ginger beer
ginger wine
goldwasser
horse's neck
iced drinks
Jamaica rum
lime-squash
malt liquor
malted milk
malt whisky
maraschino
Mateus Rosé
mickey finn
Moselle cup
mulled wine
Munich beer
pale sherry
raisin wine
Rhine wines
Rhône wines
rye whiskey
sack posset
shandygaff
soft drinks
spruce beer
still wines
sweet wines
tanglefoot
tonic water
usquebaugh
twankay tea
vichy water
white capri
white wines

11

aguardiente
amontillado
apollinaris
apple brandy
barley broth
barleywater
benedictine
black velvet
Bristol milk
cider-brandy
citron water

Courvoisier
cowslip wine
dry monopole
Irish coffee
Irish whisky
John Collins
lemon squash
montefiasco
mountain-dew
Niersteiner
orange-pekoe
peach brandy
Plymouth gin
potash water
pouchong tea
Saint Julien
scuppernong
soda and milk
souchong tea
spring water
tomato juice
vin de Graves
vintage wine

12

champagne cup
cherry brandy
crème de cacao
crême-de-menthe
Cyprus sherry
Fernet-Branca
ginger brandy
Grand Marnier
ice-cream soda
India pale ale
Irish whiskey
kirschwasser
Malvern water
mulled claret
old fashioned
orange brandy
orange squash
peach bitters
Perrier-Jouet
red wine punch
Rhenish wines
Saint Emilion
Saint Raphael
sarsaparilla
Scotch whisky
seltzer water
still Moselle
treacle water
vin ordinaire

13

aërated waters
aperitif wines
apricot brandy
bijou cocktail
bronx cocktail
Château-Lafite
Contrexéville
dandelion wine
Darjeeling tea
Falernian wine
ginger cordial
Liebfraumilch
liqueur brandy
liqueur whisky
mineral waters
orange bitters
pink champagne
planters' punch
prairie oyster
seidlitz water
sherry cobbler
sparkling hock
sparkling wine
Touraine wines
Veuve Clicquot

14

bamboo-cocktail
blended whiskey
champagne cider
champagne punch
Château-Margaux
French vermouth
Johannisberger
Moët and Chandon
Piper-Heidsieck
Rob Roy cocktail
sparkling-wines
vermouth cassis
white wine punch

15

cascade-cocktail
champagne-cognac
duchess-cocktail
green chartreuse
Italian vermouth
martini-cocktail
sacramental wine
sparkling waters
tintara burgundy

Food

3 AND **4**

bap
bean
beef
bran
bun
cake
cate
chop
curd
Edam
egg

fare
fat
fish
flan
fool
fowl
game
ghee
grub
ham
hare
hash
herb

ice
jam
jowl
junk
kale
lamb
lard
lean
loaf
loin
lung
meat
milk

mint
mush
oxo
pâté
pie
pork
puff
rice
rob
roe
roll
roux
rusk

59

sago
snow
soup
soy
stew
suet
tart
veal
whey
yolk

5

aioli
aspic
bacon
blood
bombe
brawn
bread
brose
broth
candy
chili
clove
cream
crêpe
crust
curds
curry
dough
dulse
filet
flour
fruit
fudge
gigot
glaze
Gouda
gravy
gruel
gumbo
heart
honey
icing
jelly
joint
juice
kebab
liver
lunch
manna
melba
melts
mince
mocha
pasta
pasty
patty
pilaf
pilau
pilaw
pilta
pizza
prune
pulse
roast
salad
salmi
sauce
scone
skirt
snack
syrup
spice

steak
stock
sugar
sweet
syrup
taffy
tansy
toast
tripe
viand
wafer
yeast

6

almond
batter
biffin
blintz
bonbon
Bovril
brains
brunch
burger
butter
canapé
casein
caviar
cheese
collop
comfit
congee
cookie
crowdy
crumbs
cutlet
dainty
dinner
eclair
eggnog
entrée
faggot
fillet
flitch
fodder
fondue
fumado
gammon
garlic
gâteau
ginger
grease
greens
grouse
haggis
hot dog
hot-pot
humbug
hummus
jujube
jumble
junket
kelkel
kidney
leaven
lights
mousse
muffin
mutton
noodle
nougat
noyeau
nut oil
oliver
omelet

oxtail
paella
panada
pastry
pepper
pickle
pilaff
pillau
polony
posset
potage
potato
quiche
rabbit
ragout
raisin
rasher
relish
salami
sea-pie
simnel
sorbet
sowens
sponge
sundae
supper
sweets
tiffin
tit-bit
toffee
tongue
trifle
viands
waffle
walnut
yogurt

7

bannock
banquet
bath bun
beef tea
biltong
biscuit
blossom
borscht
bouilli
brisket
broiler
brownie
calipee
caramel
catchup
caviare
cheddar
chicken
chicory
chowder
chutney
cobloaf
compote
confect
corn cob
cracker
crumpet
currant
custard
dariole
dessert
fig cake
fritter
galette
game pie
gelatin

giblets
glucose
goulash
gristle
gruyère
haricot
houmous
jam roll
jam tart
ketchup
lasagne
Marmite
meat pie
mustard
oatcake
oatmeal
pancake
paprika
pickles
plum jam
plum pie
popcorn
potargo
pottage
poultry
praline
pretzel
pudding
ramekin
rarebit
ravioli
rhubarb
rice bun
risotto
rissole
sapsago
sausage
saveloy
savoury
seafood
sherbet
sirloin
soufflé
Stilton
strudel
succado
sucrose
tapioca
tartlet
teacake
treacle
truffle
venison
vinegar

8

allspice
aperitif
apple jam
apple pie
bath chap
béchamel
biscotin
bouillon
chestnut
chop suey
chow mien
coleslaw
confetti
conserve
consommé
couscous
cracknel
cream bun

cross bun
dainties
date roll
déjeuner
delicacy
dog's-meat
doughnut
dripping
dumpling
fishmeal
flapjack
flummery
frumenty
frosting
fruit pie
hardbake
hazelnut
hotchpot
hung beef
ice cream
iced cake
Julienne
kedgeree
lamb chop
loblolly
lollipop
luncheon
macaroni
macaroon
marzipan
meatball
meringue
mince pie
mishmash
molasses
mushroom
olive oil
omelette
parmesan
pemmican
porridge
preserve
racahout
raisinée
rice cake
rollmops
roly poly
ryebread
salad oil
salpicon
salt fish
salt junk
salt pork
sandwich
seedcake
skim milk
slapjack
soda cake
sparerib
squab pie
steak pie
stuffing
turnover
undercut
victuals
whitepot

9

antipasti
appetizer
arrowroot
beefsteak
breakfast
bridecake

bubblegum
cassareep
casserole
cassonade
chipolata
chocolate
chump-chop
comfiture
condiment
confiture
corn bread
corn salad
crackling
cream cake
croquette
Easter egg
entremets
forcemeat
fricassee
fried eggs
fried fish
fruit cake
fruit tart
galantine
Genoa cake
giblet pie
gravy soup
hamburger
hard sauce
honeycomb
Irish stew
lemon curd
loafsugar
lobscouse
lump sugar
macedoine
margarine
marmalade
mincemeat
mint sauce
mutton ham
mutton pie
nutriment
pigeon pie
potato pie
potpourri
pound cake
puff paste
raised pie
schnitzel
scotch egg
seasoning
shellfish
shortcake
sour cream
sourdough
spaghetti
stirabout
succotash
sugarloaf
sugar-plum
sweetmeat
swiss roll
tipsy cake
vegetable
white meat
whole meal
wild honey

10

apple sauce
apricot jam
bath oliver

beefburger
bêche-de-mer
blancmange
blanquette
Bombay duck
bosh butter
breadstuff
bridescake
brown bread
buttermilk
cannelloni
capillaire
cheesecake
chelsea bun
comestible
confection
corned beef
cornflakes
cottage pie
currant bun
delicacies
dog biscuit
estouffade
fig pudding
flesh broth
frangipane
French loaf
fricandeau
fruit salad
giblet soup
ginger cake
girdle cake
gloucester
gorgonzola
grape sugar
ground rice
guava jelly
ham and eggs
hodge-podge
hotch-potch
ice pudding
indian corn
jugged hare
lamb cutlet
maple sugar
marrow bone
mayonnaise
minced meat
mock turtle
mutton chop
pepper cake
peppermint
poached egg
potted fish
potted meat
pudding pie
puff pastry
raisin loaf
rhubarb pie
rolled oats
saccharine
salmagundi
salt butter
sauerkraut
shortbread
shortcrust
simnel cake
sponge cake
stale bread
stewed meat
sugar candy
sustenance
sweetbread
tea biscuit
temse bread
tenderloin

tinned food
turtle soup
vermicelli
water gruel
white bread
white sauce

11

baked Alaska
Banbury cake
barley sugar
bonne bouche
cassava cake
chiffon cake
cream cheese
curry powder
frankfurter
French bread
gingerbread
golden syrup
green turtle
griddle cake
ham sandwich
hors d'oeuvre
hot cross bun
iron rations
jam sandwich
meat biscuit
meat pudding
medlar jelly
milk pudding
olla podrida
oyster patty
peppermints
plum pudding
raisin bread
refreshment
rice biscuit
rice pudding
sago pudding
sausage roll
short pastry
stewed fruit
suet pudding
tagliatelle
wedding cake
Welsh mutton
Welsh rabbit
wheaten loaf
wine biscuit

12

apple fritter
birthday cake
burnt almonds
butterscotch
chip potatoes
clotted cream
Cornish pasty
corn-on-the-cob
curds and whey
Danish pastry
dunmow flitch
eggs and bacon
finnan haddie
guarana-bread
hasty pudding
Julienne soup
liver sausage
lobster patty
maid of honour
marshmallow

61

merry thought
mullagatawny
mulligatawny
nutmeg butter
peanut butter
pease pudding
plum porridge
pumpernickel
quartern loaf
refreshments
shepherd's pie
ship's biscuit
steak pudding
sweet and sour
tripe de roche
Welsh rarebit

13

apple dumpling
béchamel sauce
bouillabaisse
cheddar cheese

chili con carne
Christmas cake
confectionery
cottage cheese
custard-coffin
flitch of bacon
German sausage
gigot de mouton
ginger pudding
gruyère cheese
Oxford sausage
roll and butter
salad dressing
scotch collops
sirloin of beef
sponge pudding
Stilton cheese
veal-and-ham pie

14

almond hardbake
apple charlotte

bologna sausage
bread and butter
bread and cheese
caramel custard
charlotte russe
haunch of mutton
household bread
mashed potatoes
mock-turtle soup
parmesan cheese
saddle of mutton
toasted teacake
turkish delight
wholemeal bread

15

bakewell pudding
black-cap pudding
bubble and squeak
chocolate éclair
Devonshire cream
haunch of venison

Furniture, fittings, and personal effects
See also **Kitchen utensils and requisites.**

3

bag
bar
bed
bin
can
cot
fan
hod
ink
mat
nib
nog
pad
ped
pen
pew
pin
rug
urn
vat

4

ambo
bath
bowl
bunk
butt
case
cask
cist
comb
cott
crib
desk
door
etui
form
gong
hi-fi
lamp

mull
oven
poke
rack
sack
safe
seal
seat
sofa
tank
tape
till
trap
tray
trug
vase
wick

5

apron
arras
basin
bench
besom
bidet
blind
board
broom
chair
chest
china
cigar
clock
cloth
coign
couch
cover
crate
creel
crock
cruet
cruse

diota
divan
doily
dosel
doser
duvet
flask
flisk
glass
globe
grill
guard
jesse
joram
jorum
label
laver
leash
light
linen
mural
paper
paten
patin
piano
pouch
purse
quill
quilt
radio
razor
scrip
shade
shelf
skeel
slate
spill
stand
stool
stoup
strop
suite
swing
table

tache
tapis
tongs
tools
torch
towel
traps
trunk
twine
vesta
watch

6

air-bed
ash-bin
ash-can
awning
basket
beaker
bicker
bucket
bunker
bureau
camera
carafe
carboy
carpet
carver
casket
castor
cheval
chowry
coffer
consol
cooker
cradle
day-bed
dishes
dosser
drapet
drawer
duster

fender
fly-net
forfex
fridge
geyser
goblet
goglet
hamper
hat-box
hearth
heater
hookah
hoppet
hussif
ink-pot
ice-box
ladder
keeler
kit-bag
kurkee
locker
log bin
loofah
mangle
mirror
mobile
napery
napkin
needle
noggin
oilcan
pallet
patera
patine
pelmet
pencil
piggin
pillow
plaque
pomade
posnet
pottle
pouffe
punkah
punnet
red ink
rocker
saddle
salver
scales
sconce
scovel
screen
settee
settle
shovel
shower
siphon
sponge
starch
string
syphon
tablet
teapot
tea set
tea urn
thread
throne
tiller
tin box
tinder
toy box
trevet
tripod
trivet
trophy

tureen
valise
wallet
window
wisket
zip-bag

7

adaptor
aerator
amphora
andiron
armoire
ash-tray
baggage
bath mat
bathtub
bedding
beeswax
bellows
blanket
blotter
bolster
brasier
brazier
broiler
bunk bed
cabinet
camp bed
canteen
chalice
chamois
chopper
cistern
cobiron
coir-mat
commode
compact
costrel
counter
cue-rack
cutlery
curtain
cushion
door-mat
down-bed
drapery
dresser
drugget
dustbin
dust-pan
epergne
flacket
flasket
fly-rail
fuse-box
gas-fire
gas ring
goggles
griddle
hair-oil
hammock
hassock
hip bath
holdall
horn-cup
ink-horn
knocker
lagging
lantern
lectern
lighter
matches
matting

monocle
netsuke
oil-lamp
ottoman
padlock
pannier
percher
pianino
pianola
picture
pillion
pin-case
playpen
pomatum
pottager
pot-hook
roaster
rundlet
rush-mat
saccule
sadiron
samovar
sampler
sand-box
satchel
scraper
shelves
shoebox
show-box
skimmer
soap-box
sofa-bed
steamer
stopper
stopple
syringe
tallboy
tambour
tankard
tea-cosy
tea-tray
tent-bed
thermos
thimble
tin-case
toaster
tobacco
tool kit
trammel
trolley
truckle
tumbler
tun-dish
valance
wardian
wash-tub
what-not
whisket
wine-bag
woodcut
work-bag
workbox
wringer
yule-log

8

ale bench
angel bed
armchair
banister
barbecue
bassinet
bed cover
bed linen

bed quilt
bedstaff
bedstead
bed-straw
bird-bath
bird-cage
bookcase
bookends
borachio
camp-bath
card-case
cashbook
cathedra
causeuse
cellaret
chair-bed
chattels
clay pipe
coat-hook
colander
coverlet
crockery
cupboard
curtains
cuspidor
decanter
demi-john
ditty-box
dog-chain
doorbell
doorknob
door-step
egg-timer
endirons
eyeglass
fauteuil
field-bed
firewood
flock-bed
fly paper
foot-bath
fuse wire
gallipot
gasalier
handbell
hangings
hat-brush
hatstand
heirloom
hip flask
holdfast
inkstand
jalousie
knapsack
lamp-wick
lanthorn
latchkey
linoleum
lipstick
loo table
love seat
matchbox
mattress
nail-file
note-book
oak chest
oilcloth
ornament
penknife
pianette
pipe-rack
postcard
press-bed
quill-pen
radiator
reticule

63

road-book
saddlery
scissors
sea chest
shoehorn
shoelace
show-case
sink unit
sitz-bath
slop bowl
slop pail
snuffbox
snuffers
soap dish
speculum
spittoon
stair-rod
standish
steel pen
suitcase
sun-blind
table-mat
tabouret
tantalus
tape-line
tapestry
tea-board
tea-caddy
tea-chest
tea-cloth
tea-table
trencher
tridarne
triptych
tweezers
umbrella
vestiary
vestuary
wall-safe
wardrobe
watch-key
water-can
water-pot
water tap
wax cloth
wax light
wineskin
wireless

9

barometer
bathtowel
bedspread
black-jack
bookshelf
book-stand
boot-brush
bric-à-brac
cakestand
camp-chair
camp-stool
cane-chair
cantharus
card-table
carpet-bag
carpeting
case-knife
casserole
china bowl
chinaware
cigarette
clack-dish
clasplock
club chair

coffee-cup
coffee-pot
comb-brush
container
corkscrew
crumb-tray
cullender
cushionet
davenport
deck chair
devonport
directory
dishcloth
dish-clout
dish-cover
dog-basket
dog-collar
dog-kennel
dust-brush
dust-sheet
Dutch oven
easy chair
egg boiler
eiderdown
equipment
face towel
faldstool
fire-board
fire-brush
fire-grate
fire-guard
fire-irons
fireplace
fish-knife
fish-plate
flower-pot
food-mixer
foot-board
footstool
frying-pan
gas-burner
gas-cooker
gas-geyser
girandole
gold-plate
gout-stool
hairbrush
hair tonic
hall table
hand-towel
haversack
high chair
horsewhip
housewife
ink-bottle
ink-holder
inventory
jack-towel
jewel case
kitchener
lamp-shade
lampstand
letter-box
light bulb
loving-cup
marquetry
master-key
mouse-trap
muffineer
music book
nail brush
newspaper
nick-nacks
nipperkin
notepaper
ornaments

paillasse
palliasse
paper clip
paper-rack
parchment
pepper-pot
perdonium
pewter pot
pier-glass
pier-table
piggy-bank
plate-rack
porringer
portfolio
port glass
pot-hanger
pot-pourri
pounce-box
powder-box
punchbowl
punkah-fan
quail-pipe
radiogram
rush-light
safety-pin
scrutoire
secretary
serviette
shakedown
shoe-brush
shower-cap
sideboard
side-light
side-table
slop-basin
spin-drier
sponge-bag
sprinkler
stair rods
stamp-case
steel wool
stopwatch
string-box
sword-cane
table bell
table hook
table lamp
tableware
tea-kettle
telephone
timepiece
timetable
tinder-box
tin-opener
toothpick
underfelt
vanity-box
wall-clock
wallpaper
wall-light
wash-basin
wash-board
wash-stand
water-butt
water-tank
wax candle
wax polish
window-box
wine glass
work table

10

air-cushion
alarm clock

alarm watch
bedclothes
biscuit-box
boot polish
broomstick
brown paper
buck-basket
cabbage net
calefactor
candelabra
canterbury
ceiling fan
chandelier
chessboard
chiffonier
chopsticks
clamp-irons
clothes peg
clothes pin
coal bucket
coal bunker
coat hanger
crumb-brush
crumb cloth
curtain rod
dandy-brush
deep-freeze
disfurnish
dishwasher
down pillow
dumb-waiter
elbow-chair
escritoire
featherbed
finger-bowl
fire-basket
fire-bucket
fire-escape
firescreen
fire-shovel
fish-basket
fish-carver
fish-kettle
fish-trowel
flesh-brush
floor-cloth
flower-bowl
fly-catcher
fly-swotter
foot-warmer
fourposter
garbage-can
gas-bracket
gas-lighter
gramophone
grand piano
hair lotion
hair pomade
jardinière
knife-board
langsettle
lead pencil
letter-rack
loose cover
marking ink
musical box
music-stand
music-stool
napkin ring
needle-book
needle-case
needlework
night-light
nutcracker
opera glass
overmantel

pack-saddle
pack-thread
paper-knife
paper-stand
pencil-case
peppermill
persian mat
persian rug
pewter dish
photograph
pianoforte
piano stool
pile carpet
pillowcase
pillowslip
pincushion
plate-glass
pocket-book
prayer-book
rattan-cane
razor-strop
riding-whip
rolling-pin
saddle-bags
salt-cellar
scatter rug
sealing-wax
secretaire
shower-bath
soda syphon
spectacles
spirit lamp
stamp-album
stationery
step-ladder
strip light
tablecloth
table linen
tablespoon
television
time-keeper
time-switch
tobacco-jar
toilet roll
toothbrush
toothpaste
truckle-bed
trug-basket
trundlebed
typewriter
upholstery
vapour-bath
warming-pan
wash basket
wassail-cup
watch-chain
watch-glass
watch-guard
watch-light
watch-stand
window-seat
wine-bottle
wine-cooler
work basket
wrist-watch

11

account book
address book
airing horse
alarm clock
alarum watch
attaché case
basket chair

bed-hangings
billiard-cue
bolster-case
book matches
boot-scraper
braising-pan
butter-print
butter-stamp
button-stick
candelabrum
candlestick
centrepiece
chafing-dish
cheese board
cheval-glass
chiffonnier
clothes-hook
clothes-line
coal-scuttle
coffee table
coir-matting
counterpane
curtain hook
curtain rail
curtain ring
despatch-box
dining-table
dinner-table
dispatch-box
dredging-box
dripping-pan
Dutch carpet
finger-glass
fire-lighter
first-aid box
floor polish
flour-dredge
footcushion
foot-scraper
fountain-pen
gaming-table
garden chair
hearth brush
knick-knacks
lamp-chimney
leather case
linen basket
minute glass
minute watch
mosquito-net
nut-crackers
ormolu clock
paper-basket
paperweight
picture-rail
pipe-lighter
pocket flask
pocket-glass
pocket-knife
porridge-pot
portmanteau
primus stove
pumice-stone
reading lamp
roll-top desk
saddle-cloth
safety-razor
scuttle-cask
shopping bag
siphon-stand
slate-pencil
stair-carpet
straw pillow
syphon-stand
table napkin
table-runner

tape-measure
tea-canister
thermometer
tin-lined box
tissue paper
tobacco pipe
toilet-cover
toilet-table
tooth-powder
vacuum flask
vinaigrette
waffle-irons
washing line
wash-leather
wassail-bowl
waste-basket
water heater
watering-can
watering-pot
window blind
writing-desk

12

adhesive tape
antimacassar
bedside light
bedside table
blotting book
bottle-opener
bucking stool
camp-bedstead
candleholder
candle-sconce
carpet beater
chaise longue
chesterfield
churchwarden
clothes-brush
clothes drier
clothes-horse
console table
cottage piano
cup and saucer
despatch-case
dessert-spoon
dispatch-case
dressing-case
drinking-horn
Dutch dresser
electric bulb
electric fire
electric iron
electric lamp
fan regulator
field-glasses
fish-strainer
flour-dredger
flower-basket
folding stool
gate-leg table
gladstone bag
hot-water tank
hubble-bubble
ironing board
ironing table
judgment-seat
kitchen table
kneehole desk
knife-cleaner
looking-glass
lucifer match
nail-scissors
nutmeg-grater
opera-glasses

packing cloth
packing paper
packing sheet
paraffin lamp
picnic basket
picnic hamper
playing cards
porridge-bowl
postage stamp
reading glass
record-player
refrigerator
roasting-jack
rocking chair
rocking horse
standard lamp
straw bolster
sweating-bath
table lighter
table service
tallow-candle
tape recorder
thermos flask
tin-lined case
toasting fork
tobacco pouch
toilette case
trestle table
turkey carpet
visitors' book
upright piano
walking-staff
walking stick
washing board
water pitcher
Welsh dresser
wicker basket
Windsor chair
wine decanter
writing table
writing paper

13

billiard balls
billiard table
blotting paper
carpet sweeper
chopping block
chopping knife
cribbage board
dressing-table
electric clock
electric stove
feather pillow
feeding bottle
filing cabinet
florence flask
folding screen
medicine glass
netting needle
newspaper rack
packing needle
persian blinds
persian carpet
petrol-lighter
ping-pong table
quizzing-glass
razor-stropper
roulette table
sewing-machine
smoothing-iron
sounding-board
straw mattress
styptic pencil

65

turnover table
umbrella stand
vacuum cleaner
visiting-cards
washhand-stand
window curtain
witney blanket

14

anglepoise lamp
billiard marker
chamber-hanging

chest-of-drawers
cocktail-shaker
eiderdown quilt
electric cooker
electric geyser
electric kettle
feather bolster
glove-stretcher
hot water bottle
kitchen dresser
meerschaum pipe
tobacco stopper
Venetian blinds
washing machine

15

electric blanket
feather mattress
garden furniture
gate-legged table
Japanese lantern
knitting needles
mosquito curtain
pestle and mortar
photograph album
photograph frame
pneumatic pillow

Games, sports and pastimes

3

ace
art
bat
bet
bob
bow
box
bye
cue
cup
die
fun
gym
hux
lap
l.b.w.
lie
lob
lov
nap
oar
out
pam
peg
put
rod
set
ski
sod
tag
taw
tig
tir
top
toy
win
won

4

arts
bait
ball
bias
bite
boat
brag
club
crib
dice
dive
draw

epée
faro
foil
fore
foul
gala
game
goal
golf
grab
hunt
jack
jazz
judo
king
knar
knur
love
ludo
luge
main
mate
meet
mime
miss
mora
Oaks
odds
pace
pawn
play
polo
pool
punt
quiz
race
ride
ring
rink
ruff
shot
sice
side
skip
slam
slip
snap
solo
spar
suit
swim
team
toss
tote
trap

trey
trip
trot
turf
vole
volt
walk
whip
wide
xyst
yoga
yo-yo

5

amuse
arena
baign
bails
bandy
basto
batik
bingo
bogey
boule
bowls
boxer
caddy
capot
cards
chase
cheat
chess
clubs
dance
darts
Derby
deuce
dicer
diver
dormy
drama
drawn
drive
dummy
extra
field
fives
fluke
glaze
hobby
joker
joust
kayle

kendo
knave
lasso
links
lists
loser
lotto
lucky
match
mount
music
ombre
opera
paced
pacer
party
pitch
point
poker
prize
queen
quits
racer
rafia
reins
relay
revel
rider
rifle
rodeo
rugby
rummy
samba
score
skate
skier
slice
slide
slosh
spade
spoon
sport
spurt
stalk
start
stump
stunt
swing
throw
touch
track
train
trial
trump
vault

veney
wager
whist
yacht

6

aikido
archer
ballet
banker
basset
battue
bewits
bowler
bowman
boxing
bridge
casino
cinque
cobnut
cockal
course
crafts
crambo
crease
crochet
cup tie
dealer
defeat
discus
diving
domino
driver
dyeing
ecarté
euchre
falcon
finish
fluker
flying
gambit
gamble
gammon
gillie
gobang
go-kart
googly
gully
gymnic
hazard
header
hiking
hockey
hunter
hurdle
huxing
jetton
jigger
jockey
karate
kicker
knight
kung-fu
lariat
leg-bye
loader
lobber
manege
marker
mashie
masque
maying
no-ball
not-out

outing
outrun
pacing
paddle
peg-top
pelota
piquet
pistol
player
poetry
punter
putter
puzzle
quoits
rabbit
racing
racket
raffle
rattle
recite
record
revoke
riddle
riding
rowing
rubber
rugger
runner
scorer
second
see-saw
shinny
shinty
single
skater
skiing
slalom
slider
soccer
soirée
squash
stroke
stumps
T'ai chi
tarocs
tenace
tennis
tierce
tip-cat
toss-up
travel
trophy
umpire
unfair
venery
victor
vigaro
wicket
winner
xystos
yorker

7

agonism
agonist
allonge
amateur
ambs-ace
ames-ace
angling
archery
athlete
auction
average

bathing
batsman
batting
beagles
benefit
bezique
bicycle
boating
bone ace
bowling
bran-pie
bruiser
canasta
carving
cassino
century
charade
checker
chicane
codille
collage
concert
contest
cookery
cooking
cooncan
cricket
croquet
curling
cycling
cyclist
dancing
diabolo
dice-box
discard
doddart
doubles
drawing
dribble
driving
etching
fencing
fielder
fishery
fishing
fluking
forward
fowling
fox hunt
gambler
glasses
glazing
gliding
golf bag
gunning
gymnast
hunting
hurling
innings
joy-ride
ju-jitsu
jumping
keep fit
last lap
leaping
loggats
lottery
love all
love set
low bell
macramé
mahjong
marbles
may-pole
misdeal
montant

mosaics
netball
oarsman
oarsmen
off-side
old-maid
outdoor
outride
pageant
pallone
pastime
pat ball
picquet
pitcher
play day
playing
pontoon
pottery
potting
primero
pushpin
putting
rackets
reading
referee
regatta
reversi
rinking
roadhog
running
sailing
saltant
scooter
scoring
scratch
sculler
sea trip
shuffle
singing
singles
skating
ski jump
sliding
snooker
St. Leger
stadium
starter
sub-aqua
surfing
tilting
tinchel
tombola
top spin
tourney
trained
trainer
trapeze
'vantage
vaulter
wagerer
walking
wargame
weaving
weights
whip top
winning
wrestle
writing

8

all-fours
antiques
appliqué
aquatics

67

baccarat
baseball
boat race
boundary
canoeing
carnival
carolina
catapult
ceramics
champion
charades
cheating
chessmen
climbing
commerce
contract
counters
coursing
cribbage
cup final
dead heat
deck golf
dominoes
doublets
drag-hunt
draughts
duelling
eurythme
eventing
exercise
face card
fair play
falconry
fielding
flat race
football
foot race
forfeits
fox chase
full back
game laws
gin rummy
goal line
golf ball
golf club
gymkhana
handball
handicap
harriers
high jump
hurdling
jiu-jitsu
jousting
juggling
knitting
korfball
lacrosse
leapfrog
long jump
long stop
love game
lucky-dip
marathon
may games
motoring
movement
natation
ninepins
olympiad
olympics
out-field
outsider
painting
palestra
pall-mall
patience

ping-pong
pole jump
pony race
pope Joan
printing
proverbs
pugilism
pugilist
pyramids
quatorze
racquets
rambling
roulette
rounders
sack race
sculling
sculpture
shooting
sing-song
skipping
skittles
sledding
softball
somerset
spadille
sparring
sporting
stalking
stumping
swimming
teamwork
teetotum
third-man
tiny golf
toboggan
training
tray-trip
trial run
tricycle
trotting
tumbling
turf club
umpiring
vaulting
vauntlay
walkover
wall-game
woodwork
yachting

9

advantage
adventure
agonistes
agonistic
amusement
archeress
athletics
aunt-sally
babyhouse
badminton
bagatelle
ball games
bandalore
bicycling
bilboquet
billiards
bob cherry
breakdown
broad jump
bull board
bull feast
bullfight
camelling

challenge
checkmate
cherry pit
chicanery
clock golf
close time
cockfight
cockmatch
conqueror
court-card
cricketer
cup winner
deck games
decoy duck
dirt track
dog racing
drawn game
dumbbells
embrocado
engraving
entertain
equitancy
fairy tale
fancy ball
fish spear
frivolity
gardening
gate money
goal posts
golf clubs
grand slam
gymnasium
gymnastic
hatha yoga
hopscotch
horseplay
horserace
ice hockey
joy riding
lampadist
lob bowler
make merry
marooning
marquetry
megaphone
merrimake
merriment
merriness
motorboat
newmarket
night club
nine holes
novelette
overmatch
pacemaker
pageantry
palestric
palmistry
pedalling
philately
plaything
pole vault
prize-ring
programme
promenade
racehorse
racestand
reception
relay race
repasture
revelment
revel rout
river trip
rolly poly
scorching
scorecard

scrapbook
showplace
shrimping
ski runner
skylarker
sleighing
smock race
solitaire
spectacle
sportsman
springing
square-leg
stalemate
stool ball
stopwatch
storybook
stroke oar
summerset
symposiac
symposium
tablegame
tabletalk
test match
tie dyeing
tip and run
torch race
touch line
trap stick
trial game
trial race
trump card
untrained
victoress
vingt-et-un
wandering
water jump
water polo
whipper-in
whirligig
whistling
woodcraft
wrestling
yacht-race
yachtsman

10

acrobatics
agonistics
agonothete
backgammon
ballooning
basket-ball
bat-fowling
battledoor
battledore
bear garden
blind harry
challenger
chessboard
collecting
competitor
conundrums
cover-point
cricket-bat
cup-and-ball
deck quoits
deck tennis
derby sweep
doll's house
dumb crambo
eel fishing
embroidery
enamelling
equitation

fancy dress
fast bowler
feathering
feuilleton
field games
fishing net
fishing rod
fisticuffs
fives court
flat racing
flop-dragon
fly-fishing
fox-hunting
goalkeeper
goalkicker
grandstand
greasy pole
groundbait
gymnastics
handspring
handy-dandy
hippodrome
hobby horse
hockey ball
hockey club
hotcockles
hucklebone
humming-top
hunting box
hurdle race
ice dancing
ice sailing
ice skating
kettle pins
lace making
lampadrome
landing net
lansquenet
lawn tennis
ledger line
lob bowling
masquerade
midget golf
Monte Carlo
needlework
opposition
palestrian
pancratist
pancratium
paper chase
pony racing
pot hunting
prison base
prize fight
racecourse
raceground
recreation
relaxation
riding pony
riding whip
rollicking
rotary club
roundabout
rowing club
saturnalia
scoreboard
scratch man
sea bathing
shovepenny
shuffle cap
silk screen
ski running
skylarking
slow bowler
snapdragon
somersault

stirrup cup
strokesman
surf riding
sweepstake
switchback
table bowls
tap dancing
tarantella
tauromachy
team spirit
tennis ball
thimblerig
tomfoolery
tournament
travelling
trial match
trick track
tricycling
victorious
volley ball
weighing-in
whirlabout
word making

11

agonistical
athleticism
barley-brake
bear baiting
bull baiting
bumblepuppy
calligraphy
chariot race
chess player
competition
competitive
county match
cricket ball
croquet ball
deck cricket
Derby winner
dicing house
disportment
diving board
fast bowling
field sports
fishing line
five hundred
flaconnade
fleet-footed
fluking-iron
folk dancers
free fishery
garden party
general post
grand circle
grass skiing
gymnasiarch
hang gliding
happy family
heavyweight
hide-and-seek
high jumping
high pitched
hockey stick
horse racing
horse riding
hunt counter
hunting horn
ice yachting
indian clubs
inter-county
lawn bowling
lightweight

lithography
long jumping
magic square
make-believe
masquerader
merrymaking
minute watch
oarsmanship
open-air life
picnic party
pillow fight
pole jumping
prawning net
prize giving
prizewinner
promenading
protagonist
public stand
regatta card
riding horse
river sports
rouge-et-noir
rough riding
sand sailing
schottische
shovel board
show jumping
shuttlecock
sightseeing
single stick
skateboard
skating club
skating rink
skittle pool
slot machine
slow bowling
snowballing
soap bubbles
span-counter
spelling bee
springboard
stirrup lamp
stonewaller
summersault
sweepstakes
sword player
table tennis
tale telling
tennis court
tent pegging
theatre-goer
tobogganing
top-spinning
totalisator
toxophilite
trap-and-ball
trick riding
trolmydames
trout-stream
uncontested
unexercised
water skiing
whipping-top
wild fowling
winning crew
winning side
winning team
wood cutting
world record
yacht racing

12

bantamweight
billiard ball

bird's nesting
bobsleighing
bowling alley
brass rubbing
bullfighting
butterfly net
calisthenics
championship
club swinging
cockfighting
competitress
consequences
cricket match
curling stone
deer stalking
draughtboard
drinking bout
field glasses
figure skater
first-nighter
flower making
glass blowing
googly bowler
hoodman-blind
horsemanship
housewarming
hunting-horse
huntsmanship
jigsaw puzzle
losing hazard
magic lantern
marathon race
marking board
medicine ball
merry-go-round
miss milligan
mixed bathing
mixed doubles
nimble footed
novel reading
obstacle race
Olympic games
opera glasses
parallel bars
parlour games
pitch-and-toss
pleasure trip
point-to-point
pole vaulting
professional
prize fighter
prize winning
pyrotechnics
Pythian games
racing stable
rock climbing
roller skater
rope climbing
rope spinning
rope throwing
sand yachting
scotch-hopper
shrimping net
skipping rope
skittle alley
speed skating
starting post
state lottery
steeplechase
stilt walking
stirrup strap
storytelling
swimming gala
table croquet
table turning
tennis player

69

tennis racket
theatre-going
thoroughbred
tiddley-winks
tittle-tattle
wicket keeper
winning horse
winter sports

13

alectoromachy
alectryomachy
aquatic sports
auction bridge
ballad singing
blindman's buff
bubble blowing
camera obscura
Christmas tree
chuck farthing
cribbage board
cricket ground
cricket stumps
croquet mallet
deck billiards
divertisement
double or quits
entertainment
featherweight
figure skating
fishing tackle
googly-bowling
ground-angling
hare-and-hounds
horizontal bar
international
Isthmian games

jigsaw puzzles
jollification
machine junket
model yachting
motor cruising
musical chairs
Olympian games
parlour tricks
pillion riding
prisoner's base
prize fighting
record breaker
roller skating
roulette table
speed merchant
spirit rapping
sportsmanship
squash rackets
stalking horse
starting point
steeplechaser
sword fighting
ten-pin bowling
track and field
vantage ground
vaulting horse
victor ludorum
weight lifting
wicket keeping
winning hazard

14

all-in wrestling
billiard marker
billiard player
bladder angling

children's party
coin collecting
contract bridge
discus-throwing
divertissement
double patience
downhill skiing
driving licence
ducks-and-drakes
hunt-the-slipper
hunt-the-thimble
long-arm balance
mountaineering
record breaking
rubicon bezique
shove-halfpenny
steeplechasing
thimblerigging
weight training

15

ballroom dancing
cinderella dance
consolation race
crossword puzzle
Derby sweepstake
dirt track racing
greyhound racing
javelin throwing
king-of-the-castle
Old English bowls
public enclosure
short-arm balance
stamp collecting
talking pictures
three-legged race
unsportsmanlike
youth hostelling

Jewellery, gems, etc.

3 AND 4

bead
clip
gaud
gem
jade
jet
onyx
opal
ring
ruby
sard
stud
torc

5

agate
aglet
amber
badge
beads
beryl
bezel
bijou
brait
bugle
cameo

carat
clasp
coral
crown
ivory
jewel
lapis
links
nacre
paste
pearl
tiara
topaz
watch

6

albert
amulet
anklet
armlet
augite
bangle
bauble
brooch
diadem
enamel
fibula
garnet

gewgaw
iolite
ligure
locket
olivet
pearls
pyrope
quartz
signet
sphere
spinel
telesm
tiepin
torque
turkis
wampum
zircon

7

abraxas
adamant
annulet
armilla
asteria
axinite
cat's eye
chaplet
coronet

crystal
diamond
eardrop
earring
emerald
espinel
euclase
faceted
filigree
jacinth
jewelry
olivine
pendant
peridot
regalia
ringlet
rubicel
sardine
sardius
sceptre
smaragd
spangle
telesia
trinket

8

adularia
aigrette

amethyst
armillet
carcanet
cardiace
corundum
diopside
hallmark
hyacinth
intaglio
liginite
necklace
pectoral
rock ruby
sapphire
sardonyx
scarf-pin
shirt-pin
sunstone

9

balas ruby
black onyx
black opal
breast-pin
brilliant
carbuncle
carnelian
cornelian
cufflinks
foil-stone
gold watch
jadestone
jewellery

marcasite
medallion
moonstone
morganite
moss-agate
paillette
phenacite
press stud
pyreneite
seed pearl
starstone
thumbring
trinketry
turquoise

10

adderstone
amber beads
andalusite
aquamarine
black pearl
bloodstone
chalcedony
chrysolite
coral beads
glass beads
madrepearl
Mocha stone
rhinestone
signet ring
topazolite
tourmaline
watch-chain

watchstrap
water opal
wristwatch

11

aiguillette
alexandrite
bostrychite
cameo brooch
chalcedonyx
chrysoberyl
chrysophrase
colophonite
crocidolite
lapis lazuli
slave bangle
wedding-ring

12 AND OVER

bead necklace (12)
chain bracelet (13)
coral necklace (13)
crystal necklace (15)
engagement ring (14)
eternity ring (12)
link bracelet (12)
mother-of-pearl (13)
mourning brooch (14)
mourning ring (13)
pearl necklace (13)
precious stone (13)

Kitchen utensils and requisites

3

bin
can
cup
hob
jar
jug
lid
mop
mug
pan
pot
tap
tin
tub
urn

4

bowl
coal
cosy
dish
ewer
fork
grid
hook
iron
lard
oven
pail
peel

rack
salt
sink
soap
soda
spit
suet
trap
tray

5

airer
basin
besom
broom
broth
brush
caddy
china
cover
crock
cruet
doily
dough
drier
flour
glass
grate
grill
gruel
hatch
herbs

jelly
joint
knife
ladle
match
mixer
mould
paste
plate
poker
range
sauce
scoop
shelf
sieve
spice
spoon
steel
stock
stove
sugar
table
timer
tongs
towel
whisk
wiper
yeast

6

ash-pan
beaker

beater
boiler
bottle
bucket
burner
butter
candle
carver
caster
cooker
cupful
drawer
duster
eggbox
eggcup
fender
filter
flagon
funnel
gas-jet
geyser
grater
grease
haybox
heater
ice-box
jugful
juicer
kettle
larder
mangle
mincer
pantry
pastry

71

pepper
pickle
polish
pot-lid
recipe
salver
saucer
scales
shovel
sifter
skewer
slicer
starch
tea-cup
tea-pot
tea-urn
trivet
tureen
vessel

7

basting
blender
bluebag
broiler
butlery
cake-tin
cambrel
canteen
chopper
coal-bin
coal-box
cuisine
cutlery
dishmat
dishmop
drainer
dresser
dust-bin
dust-pan
freezer
griller
grinder
infuser
kneader
kneeler
milk-jug
panikin
pie-dish
pitcher
platter
potager
sapples
saltbox
scuttle
seether
skillet
spatula
steamer
stew-pan

tea-cosy
tea-tray
terrine
toaster
tumbler
vinegar
wash-tub

8

bread bin
canister
cauldron
clapdish
colander
covercle
cream-jug
crockery
cupboard
dish rack
egg-slice
eggspoon
eggwhisk
fish fork
flan ring
flat-iron
gas stove
gridiron
hotplate
matchbox
meatsafe
oilcloth
oilstove
patty pan
saucepan
scissors
shoe box
slop bowl
stockpot
strainer
tea caddy
teacloth
teaplate
teaspoon
water jug

9

can opener
casserole
chinaware
coffee-cup
coffee pot
corkscrew
crumb tray
dishcloth
dish cover
egg beater
egg boiler
firegrate

fire-irons
fireplace
fish-knife
fish-plate
fish-slice
flue brush
frying-pan
gas burner
gas cooker
gas geyser
gravy boat
muffineer
pepper-box
pepper-pot
plate-rack
porringer
slop basin
soupspoon
sugar bowl
tea kettle
tin opener
wineglass

10

apple corer
biscuit box
bread board
bread knife
broomstick
butter dish
coffee mill
cook's knife
dishwasher
egg poacher
fish carver
fish kettle
floor cloth
flour crock
gas lighter
ice freezer
jelly mould
knife board
liquidizer
milk boiler
pan scourer
pepper mill
percolator
rolling pin
rotisserie
salamander
salt cellar
tablecloth
tablespoon
waffle iron

11

baking sheet
bread grater

butter knife
coalscuttle
dinner plate
dripping pan
flour dredge
meat chopper
paring knife
porridge pot
pudding bowl
sugar dredge
tea canister
water filter

12

breakfast-cup
carving knife
dessertspoon
double boiler
fishstrainer
flour dredger
hot cupboard
ironing board
kitchen range
knife cleaner
knife machine
measuring cup
nutmeg grater
porridge bowl
potato masher
potato peeler
pudding basin
pudding cloth
refrigerator
thermos flask
toasting fork

13

chopping board
coffee grinder
lemon squeezer
saucepan brush
water softener

14

crockery washer
fuelless cooker
galvanized pail
knife sharpener
mincing machine
pressure cooker
scrubbing brush

15

vegetable cutter

EDUCATION
Educational terms

3

cap
C.S.E.
D.E.S.

don
fag
G.C.E.
gyp
Pop

4

bump
crib
dean

demy
digs
exam
form
gate

gown
hall
head
hood
I.L.E.A.
poly
swot
term
test

5

backs
bedel
class
coach
gaudy
grant
house
lines
pupil
scout
sizar
study
tawse
tutor

6

A-level
beadle
bodley
bursar
course
day boy
degree
eights
fellow
Hilary
incept
locals
locker
master
matron
O-level
optime
reader
rector
school
sconce
senate
tripos
warden

7

academy
battels
Bodley's
bull-dog

burgess
bursary
captain
college
crammer
diploma
dominie
faculty
gestalt
head boy
honours
lecture
monitor
nursery
prefect
proctor
project
provost
reading
scholar
seminar
smalls
student
teacher
teach-in
the high
torpids
tuition

8

academic
ad eundem
backward
emeritus
encaenia
examinee
famulist
graduate
guidance
head girl
homework
learning
lecturer
little-go
manciple
May races
mistress
red-brick
research
roll-call
semester
seminary
send down
statutes
textbook
tuck-shop
tutorial
vacation
viva voce
wrangler

9

art master
art school
bilateral
classroom
collegian
day school
dormitory
great hall
pedagogue
playgroup
preceptor
prelector
president
principal
professor
refectory
registrar
scale post
scholarly
schoolboy
selection
speech day
streaming
sub-rector
trimester

10

blackboard
chancellor
collegiate
commonroom
day release
dining-hall
eleven-plus
exhibition
extra-mural
fellowship
fives court
form-master
illiteracy
imposition
instructor
laboratory
sabbatical
schooldays
schoolgirl
schoolmarm
schoolmate
schoolroom
school year
Sheldonian
university

11

convocation
examination

games master
head teacher
holiday task
housemaster
matriculate
mortarboard
music master
polytechnic
responsions
scholarship
school hours

12

aptitude test
exhibitioner
headmistress
kindergarten
master of arts
night-classes
public orator
pupil-teacher
schoolfellow
schoolmaster
Sunday school

13

adult learning
co-educational
comprehension
comprehensive
doctor of music
grammar school
matriculation
mature student
schoolteacher
science master
supply teacher
undergraduate
vice-principal

14

bachelor of arts
common entrance
junior wrangler
language master
Open University
schoolmistress
senior wrangler
vice-chancellor

15

doctor of science
master of science
school inspector
secondary modern

Oxford and Cambridge colleges

(C.) = Cambridge; (m.) = mixed;
(O.) = Oxford; (p.p.h.) = permanent private hall; (w.) = women.

3 – 5

B.N.C. (O.) (Brasenose)
Caius (C.) (Gonville and)

Clare (C.) (m)
Hall (C.) (Trinity Hall)
House (O.) (Christ Church)
Jesus (C. and O.)

Keble (O.)
King's (C.) (m)
New (O.)
Oriel (O.)

6

Darwin (C.) (m)
Exeter (O.)
Girton (C.) (w)
Merton (O.)
New Hall (C.) (w.)
Queens' (C. and O.)
Selwyn (C.) (m)
Wadham (O.)

7

Balliol (O.)
Christ's (C.)
Downing (C.)
Linacre (O.)
Lincoln (O.)
New Hall (C.) (w)
Newnham (C.) (w)
St. Anne's (O.)
St. Cross (O.)
St. Hugh's (O.) (w)
St. John's (C. and O.)
Trinity (C. and O.)
Wolfson (C. and O.)

8

All Souls (O.)
Emmanuel (C.)
Hertford (O.)
Magdalen (O.)
Nuffield (O.)
Pembroke (C. and O.)
St. Hilda's (O.) (w)
St. Peter's (O.)

9 AND 10

Brasenose (O.) (9)
Churchill (C.) (m) (9)
Clare Hall (C.) (m) (9)
Greyfriars (O.) (p.p.h.) (10)
Hughes Hall (C.) (w) (10)
Magdalene (C.) (9)
Mansfield (O.) (p.p.h.) (9)
Peterhouse (C.) (10)
St. Antony's (O.) (9)
Saint Hugh's (O.) (w) (10)
Saint John's (C. and O.) (10)
Somerville (O.) (w) (10)
University (O.) (10)
Worcester (O.) (9)

11 AND 12

Campion Hall (O.) (p.p.h.) (11)
Christ Church (O.) (12)
Fitzwilliam (C.) (11)
Regent's Park (O.) (p.p.h.) (11)
St. Benet's Hall (O.) (p.p.h.) (12)
St. Catharine's (C.) (12)
St. Catherine's (O.) (12)
St. Edmund Hall (O.) (12)
Saint Hilda's (O.) (w) (11)
Saint Peter's (O.) (11)
Sidney Sussex (C.) (m) (12)
Trinity Hall (C.) (11)

13 AND OVER

Corpus Christi (C. and O.) (13)
Gonville and Caius (C.) (16)
Lady Margaret Hall (O.) (w) (16)
Lucy Cavendish (C.) (w) (13)
Saint Benet's Hall (O.)
   (p.p.h.) (15)
Saint Catharine's (C.) (15)
Saint Catherine's (O.) (15)
Saint Edmund Hall (O.) (15)
St. Edmund's House (C.) (14)

Some boys' schools

(c.) = "College", as distinct from "School," in title.

4 – 6

Dover (c.) (5)
Durham (6)
Eltham (c.) (6)
Epsom (c.) (5)
Eton (c.) (4)
Exeter (6)
Fettes (c.) (6)
Harrow (6)
Leys (The) (4)
Oakham (6)
Oundle (6)
Radley (c.) (6)
Repton (6)
Rugby (5)
St. Bees (6)
Stowe (5)
Trent (c.) (5)

7

Bedales
Bedford
Bloxham
Clifton (c.)
Dulwich (c.)
Felsted
Lancing (c.)
Loretto
Malvern (c.)
Mercers'
Oratory

Rossall
St. Paul's
Taunton
The Leys
Warwick

8

Abingdon
Ardingly (c.)
Beaumont (c.)
Blue Coat
Brighton (c.)
Denstone (c.)
Downside
Highgate
Mill Hill
St. Albans
St. Olave's
Sedbergh
Whitgift

9

Blundell's
Bradfield (c.)
Bryanston
Cranbrook
Cranleigh
Dean Close
Liverpool (c.)
Sherborne

Tonbridge
Uppingham
Wakefield

10

Ampleforth (c.)
Birkenhead
Bromsgrove
Cheltenham (c.)
Eastbourne (c.)
Haileybury (c.)
Royal Naval (c.)
Shrewsbury
Stonyhurst (c.)
Summerhill
Wellington (c.)
Winchester (c.)

11

Berkhamsted
Eton College
Framlingham (c.)
Giggleswick
Gordonstoun
Leatherhead
   (St. John's)
Marlborough (c.)
Westminster

12

Charterhouse
City of London
King's College (School)
Monkton Combe

13

Bedford Modern
Bedford School
Wolverhampton

14

Blue Coat School
Hurstpierpoint (c.)
Wellingborough

15

Christ's Hospital
Imperial Service (c.)
King's, Canterbury
Magdalen College
   (School)
Merchant Taylors'

FAMOUS PEOPLE
Admirals

3 – 5

Anson (Lord)
Bacon
Blake
Boyle
Brand
Brock
Broke
Byng
Cowan
Dewar
Dewey
Drake
Field
Hawke
Hood (Lord)
Hope
Howes (Lord)
James
Jones
Keith
Kerr
Keyes (Lord)
Mahan
May
Milne
Moore
Noble
Rooke
Scott
Sims
Stark
Togo
Tovey
Tromp
Tryon

6

Beatty (Lord)
Bridge
Brueys
Calder
Colomb
Darlan
Duncan
Fisher (Lord)
Fraser
Horton
Howard (Lord)
Jerram

Jervis
Keppel
Madden
Nelson (Lord)
Nimitz
Oliver
Parker
Popham
Porter
Ramsay
Rawson
Rodney (Lord)
Rupert (Prince)
Ruyter
Scheel
Scheer
Shovel

7

Burnaby
Burnett
Dampier
de Chair
Doenitz
Exmouth (Lord)
Hopkins
Jackson
Markham
Rainier
Raleigh
Ronarch
Seymour
Sturdee
von Spee
Watkins

8

Berkeley
Boscawen
Caldwell
Cochrane (Lord)
Cockburn
Colville
Craddock
Custance
de Robeck
de Ruyter
Fanshawe
Farragut

Jellicoe (Lord)
Mark Kerr
Muselier
Richmond
Saunders
Saumarez
Tyrwhitt
Villaret
van Tromp
Yamamoto

9

Albemarle
Arbuthnot
Beresford (Lord)
Callaghan
Chatfield (Lord)
Duckworth
Effingham
Fremantle
St. Vincent (Lord)
von Hipper
Warrender

10

Codrington
Cunningham
Evan-Thomas
Kempenfelt
Mountevans (Lord)
Somerville
Troubridge
Villeneuve
von Tirpitz

11 AND 12

Collingwood (11)
Culme-Seymour (12)
Elphinstone (11)
Mountbatten (Lord) (11)
Wester-Wemyss (Lord) (12)

13 AND OVER

Cork and Orrery (Lord) (13)
Rozhdestvensky (14)

Celebrities
1. The World of Entertainment: theatre, opera, ballet, films, the circus, television, radio, music (classical, jazz, folk, pop, etc.).

3 AND 4

Baez, Joan
Bass, Alfie
Bilk, Acker
Bron, Eleanor
Cash, Johnny
Coco (the clown)
Cole, George

Cole, Nat King
Cook, Peter
Day, Doris
Day, Robin
Dean, James
Dors, Diana
Ford, John
Fury, Billy
Getz, Stan

Gish, Lillian
Hall, Henry
Hall, Sir Peter
Hess, Dame Myra
Hope, Bob
Joad, Prof. Cyril
John, Elton
Kean, Edmund
Kerr, Deborah

Lean, David
Lee, Christopher
Lee, Peggy
Lunt, Alfred
Lynn, Vera
Marx brothers
Monk, Thelonious
More, Kenneth
Muir, Frank

75

Nunn, Trevor
Peck, Gregory
Piaf, Edith
Ray, Satyajit
Reed, Carol
Reid, Beryl
Rix, Brian
Ross, Annie
Sim, Alistair
Swan, Donald
Tati, Jacques
Took, Barrie
Tree, Sir Herbert
Wise, Ernie
Wise, Robert
Wood, Sir Henry
York, Michael
York, Susannah

5

Adler, Larry
Allen, Chesney
Allen, Dave
Arden, John
Askey, Arthur
Baker, Dame Janet
Baker, Richard
Baker, Sir Stanley
Basie, Count
Bates, Alan
Benny, Jack
Black, Cilla
Blair, David
Boult, Sir Adrian
Bowie, David
Brain, Dennis
Bream, Julian
Brice, Fanny
Brook, Peter
Bryan, Dora
Clark, Lord
Clark, Petula
Cooke, Alistair
Costa, Sam
Cukor, George
Davis, Bette
Davis, Colin
Davis, Miles
Davis, Sammy
Dench, Judi
Dolan, Anton
Dyall, Valentine
Dylan, Bob
Evans, Dame Edith
Faith, Adam
Felix, Julie
Finch, Peter
Flynn, Errol
Fonda, Henry
Fonda, Jane
Frost, David
Gable, Clark
Gabor, Zsa Zsa
Garbo, Greta
Gigli, Beniamino
Gobbi, Tito
Gould, Elliot
Grade, Lord
Grant, Cary
Greco, Juliette
Green, Hughie
Haley, Bill
Handl, Irene
Hines, Earl

Holly, Buddy
Horne, Kenneth
Horne, Lena
James, Sid
Jones, Tom
Kazan, Elia
Kelly, Barbara
Kelly, Grace
Kempe, Rudolf
Korda, Alexander
La Rue, Danny
Leigh, Vivien
Lloyd, Harold
Losey, Joseph
Magee, Patrick
Marks, Alfred
Mason, James
Melba, Dame Nellie
Melly, George
Miles, Sir Bernard
Mills, Bertram
Mills, Mrs
Moore, Dudley
Moore, Gerald
Mount, Peggy
Negus, Arthur
Niven, David
Ogdon, John
Pears, Peter
Quinn, Anthony
Reith, Lord
Scott, Terry
Smith, Bessie
Smith, Maggie
Somes, Michael
Sousa, John
Starr, Ringo
Stern, Isaac
Swann, Sir Michael
Sykes, Eric
Tatum, Art
Teyte, Dame Maggie
Terry, Ellen
Tynan, Kenneth
Wayne, John
Welch, Raquel
Welsh, Alex
Worth, Irene

6

Adrian, Max
Ashton, Sir Frederick
Bacall, Lauren
Barber, Chris
Bardot, Brigitte
Barnet, Lady (Isobel)
Barnum, P. T.
Bassey, Shirley
Baylis, Lilian
Bechet, Sidney
Bogart, Humphrey
Boulez, Pierre
Braden, Bernard
Brando, Marlon
Burney, Fanny
Burton, Richard
Callas, Maria
Caruso, Enrico
Casals, Pablo
Cleese, John
Colyer, Ken
Cooper, Gary
Curran, Sir Charles
Curzon, Clifford

Cusack, Cyril
Cushing, Peter
de Sica, Vittorio
Disney, Walt
Dowell, Anthony
Duncan, Isadora
Fields, Gracie
Fields, W. C.
Finney, Albert
Greene, Sir Hugh
Garson, Greer
Godard, Jean-Luc
Goring, Marius
Groves, Sir Charles
Harlow, Jean
Heston, Charlton
Hiller, Dame Wendy
Hobson, Harold
Howard, Frankie
Irving, Sir Henry
Jacobs, David
Jagger, Mick
Joplin, Scott
Keaton, Buster
Kemble, Fanny
Kramer, Stanley
Lennon, John
Lidell, Alvar
Lillie, Beatrice
Miller, Glenn
Miller, Jonathan
Mingus, Charlie
Monroe, Marilyn
Moreau, Jeanne
Morley, Robert
Morton, Jelly Roll
Mostel, Zero
Nerina, Nadia
Newman, Nanette
Newman, Paul
Norden, Dennis
Oliver, King
O'Toole, Peter
Parker, Charlie
Parker, Dorothy
Powell, Dilys
Previn, André
Quayle, Anthony
Renoir, Jean
Robson, Dame Flora
Rogers, Ginger
Rooney, Mickey
Savile, Jimmy
Seegar, Peggy
Seegar, Pete
Sibley, Antoinette
Sinden, Donald
Snagge, John
Talbot, Godfrey
Tauber, Richard
Taylor, Elizabeth
Temple, Shirley
Waller, Fats
Waring, Eddie
Warner brothers
Warner, David
Welles, Orson
Wilder, Billy
Wilder, Gene
Wolfit, Sir Donald

7

Andrews, Eamonn
Andrews, Julie

Astaire, Fred
Baillie, Isobel
Beecham, Sir Thomas
Bennett, Alan
Bennett, Jill
Bentine, Michael
Bentley, Dick
Bergman, Ingmar
Bergman, Ingrid
Blondin, Charles
Bogarde, Dirk
Brubeck, Dave
Chaplin, Sir Charles
Chester, Charlie
Cocteau, Jean
Collins, Judy
Connery, Sean
Corbett, Harry
Donegan, Lonnie
Donovan
Dougall, Robert
Douglas, Kirk
Edwards, Jimmy
Feldman, Marty
Fellini, Federico
Ferrier, Kathleen
Fonteyn, Dame Margot
Freeman, John
Garland, Judy
Garnett, Alf
Garrick, David
Gielgud, Sir John
Goldwyn, Sam
Goosens, Léon
Goodman, Benny
Guiffre, Jimmy
Guthrie, Sir Tyrone
Guthrie, Woody
Hammond, Joan
Hancock, Sheila
Hancock, Tony
Handley, Tommy
Harding, Gilbert
Hawkins, Jack
Hendrix, Jimi
Hepburn, Audrey
Hepburn, Katherine
Hoffman, Dustin
Holiday, Billie
Hopkins, Antony
Houdini, Harry
Jackson, Glenda
Jackson, Michael
Jacques, Hattie
Karloff, Boris
Kendall, Kenneth
Kennedy, Ludovic
Kubrick, Stanley
Lympany, Moira
MacColl, Ewan
Markova, Alicia
Menuhin, Yehudi
Montand, Yves
Monteux, Pierre
Murdoch, Richard
Novello, Ivor
Nureyev, Rudolph
Olivier, Lord
Pavlova, Anna
Pickles, Wilfred
Rambert, Dame Marie
Rantzen, Esther
Redford, Robert
Richard, Cliff
Roberts, Rachel
Rodgers, Richard

Rushton, William
Russell, Jane
Russell, Ken
Sargent, Sir Malcolm
Secombe, Harry
Sellers, Peter
Seymour, Lynn
Shankar, Ravi
Shearer, Moira
Sherrin, Ned
Siddons, Mrs Sarah
Simmons, Jean
Sinatra, Frank
Stevans, Cat
Stewart, James
Swanson, Gloria
Ulanova, Galina
Ustinov, Peter
Vaughan, Frankie
Vaughan, Sarah
Whicker, Alan
Wheldon, Huw
Withers, Googie

8

Anderson, Lindsay
Anderson, Marian
Ashcroft, Dame Peggy
Beerbohm, Sir Max
Brambell, Wilfred
Bygraves, Max
Campbell, Mrs Pat
Chisholm, George
Christie, Julie
Clements, Sir John
Coltrane, John
de Valois, Dame Ninette
Dietrich, Marlene
Dimbleby, Richard
Eastwood, Clint
Flanagan, Bud
Flanders, Michael
Fletcher, Cyril
Grenfell, Joyce
Guinness, Sir Alec
Harrison, George
Harrison, Rex
Helpmann, Sir Robert
Hoffnung, Gerard
Holloway, Stanley
Horowitz, Vladimir
Laughton, Charles
Lawrence, Gertrude
Liberace
Matthews, Jessie
Milligan, Spike
Mitchell, Joni
Mulligan, Gerry
Nijinski, Vaslav
Oistrakh, David
Oistrakh, Igor
Paganini, Niccolò
Pickford, Mary
Polanski, Roman
Redgrave, Sir Michael
Redgrave, Vanessa
Robinson, Edward G.
Robinson, Eric
Robinson, Robert
Scofield, Paul
Stephens, Robert
Streeter, Fred
Truffaut, François
Visconti, Luchino

Williams, Andy
Williams, John
Williams, Kenneth
Zeppelin, Led

9

Antonioni, Michelangelo
Armstrong, Louis
Ashkenazy, Vladimir
Barenboim, Daniel
Barrymore, John
Belafonte, Harry
Bernhardt, Sarah
Brannigan, Owen
Cardinale, Claudia
Chevalier, Maurice
Christoff, Boris
Courtenay, Tom
Dankworth, John
Davenport, Bob
Diaghilev, Serge
Ellington, Duke
Gillespie, Dizzy
Grisewood, Freddy
Engelmann, Franklin
Fairbanks, Douglas
Hampshire, Susan
Hitchcock, Alfred
Humphries, Barry
Klemperer, Otto
Leadbelly
Lyttelton, Humphrey
McCartney, Paul
Monkhouse, Bob
Morecombe, Eric
Pleasance, Donald
Plowright, Joan
Preminger, Otto
Reinhardt, Django
Reinhardt, Max
Sternberg, Joseph von
Streisand, Barbra
Thorndike, Dame Sybil

10

Barbirolli, Sir John
Eisenstein, Sergei
Fitzgerald, Ella
Littlewood, Joan
Michelmore, Cliff
Muggeridge, Malcolm
Richardson, Sir Ralph
Rubinstein, Artur
Rutherford, Dame Margaret
Sutherland, Joan

11 AND OVER

Attenborough, David (12)
Attenborough, Sir Richard
 (12)
Beiderbecke, Bix (11)
Chipperfield, Mary (12)
Fischer-Dieskau, Dietrich
 (14)
Granville-Barker, Harley
 (15)
Hammerstein, Oscar (11)
Springfield, Dusty (11)
Stradivarius, Antonio (12)
Terry-Thomas (11)

77

2. Sports and Games

ath. = athletics; *box.* = boxing; *crc.* = cricket; *fb.* = football; *gf* = golf;
gym. = gymnastics; *hr.* = horseracing; *mr.* = motor-racing;
mt. = mountaineering; *sj.* = showjumping; *sw.* = swimming; *ten.* = tennis;
yt. = yachting

3 AND 4

Ali, Muhammed *box.*
Amis, Dennis, *crc.*
Ashe, Arthur *ten.*
Best, George *fb.*
Borg, Bjorn *ten.*
Clay, Cassius *box.*
Cobb, Ty *baseball*
Endo, Yukio *gym.*
Fox, Uffa *yt.*
Hill, Graham *mr.*
Hoad, Lew *ten.*
Hunt, James *mr.*
Hunt, Sir John *mt.*
John, Barry *rugby*
Kim, Nellie *gym.*
King, Billie Jean *ten.*
Law, Denis *fb.*
Lock, Tony *crc.*
May, Peter *crc.*
Moss, Stirling *mr.*
Read, Phil *motor-cycling*
Ruth, 'Babe' *baseball*
Snow, John *crc.*
Wade, Virginia *ten.*
Webb, Capt. M. *sw.*

5

Banks, Gordon *fb.*
Brown, Joe *mt.*
Bueno, Maria *ten.*
Busby, Sir Matthew *fb.*
Clark, Jim *mr.*
Close, Brian *crc.*
Court, Margaret *ten.*
Curry, John *skating*
Davis, Joe, *billiards*
Evans, Godfrey *crc.*
Evert, Chris *ten.*
Grace, Dr W. G. *crc.*
Greig, Tony *crc.*
Hobbs, Sir John *crc.*
Hogan, Ben *gf*
Irwin, Hale *gf*
Jones, Ann *ten.*
Keino, Kip *ath.*
Knott, Alan *crc.*
Kodes, J. *ten.*
Laker, Jim *crc.*
Lauda, Niki *mr.*
Laver, Rod *ten.*
Lloyd, Clive *crc.*
Louis, Joe *box.*
Moore, Ann *sj.*
Moore, Bobby *fb.*
Perry, Fred, *ten.*
Pirie, Gordon *ath.*
Revie, Don *fb.*
Roche, Tony *ten.*
Scott, Sheila *aviation*
Sloan, James *hr.*
Smith, Harvey *sj.*
Smith, Stan *ten.*
Spitz, Mark *sw.*
Wills, Helen *ten.*

6

Barker, Sue *ten.*
Bedser, Alec *crc.*
Benaud, Richard *crc.*
Broome, David *sj.*
Bugner, Joe *box.*
Casals, Rosemary *ten.*
Cooper, Henry *box.*
Dexter, Ted *crc.*
Drobny, Jaroslav *ten.*
Edrich, John *crc.*
Fangio, Juan *mr.*
Foster, Brendan *ath.*
Fraser, Dawn *sw.*
Gibson, Althea *ten.*
Hutton, Sir Len *crc.*
Kanhai, Rohan *crc.*
Keegan, Kevin *fb.*
Korbut, Olga *gym.*
Lillee, Dennis *crc.*
Liston, Sonny *box.*
Merckx, Eddy *cycling*
Palmer, Arnold *gf*
Peters, Mary *ath.*
Player, Gary *gf*
Ramsey, Sir Alf *fb.*
Sobers, Sir Gary *crc.*
Smythe, Pat *sj.*
Stolle, Fred *ten.*
Taylor, Roger *ten.*
Thoeni, G. *skiing*
Titmus, Fred *crc.*
Turpin, Randolph *box.*
Wilkie, David *sw.*

7

Boycott, Geoffrey *crc.*
Brabham, Jack *mr.*
Bradman, Sir Don *crc.*
Compton, Dennis *crc.*
Connors, Jimmy *ten.*
Cowdrey, Colin *crc.*
Dempsey, Jack *box.*
Elliott, Herb *ath.*
Emerson, Roy *ten.*
Ferrari, Enzio *mr.*
Fischer, Bobby *chess*
Foreman, George *box.*
Frazier, Joe *box.*
Greaves, Jimmy *fb.*
Hillary, Sir Edmund *mt.*
Hopkins, Thelma *ath, hockey*
Jacklin, Tony *gf*
Johnson, Amy *aviation*
Mottram, Buster *ten.*
Nastase, Ilie *ten.*
Piggott, Lester *hr.*
Spassky, Boris *chess*
Stewart, Jackie *mr.*
Surtees, John *mr.*
Tabarly, Eric *yt.*
Tensing, Sherpa *mt.*
Thomson, Jeff *crc.*
Trevino, Lee *gf*

8

Brinkley, Brian *sw.*
Chappell, Greg *crc.*
Chappell, Ian *crc.*
Charlton, Bobby *fb.*
Charlton, Jack *fb.*
Comaneci, Nadia *gym.*
Connolly, Maureen *ten.*
Cordobés, El *bullfighting*
Cousteau, Jacques-Yves *diving*
Docherty, Tommy *fb.*
Elvstrom, Paul *yt.*
Gligorić, Svetozar *chess*
Graveney, Tom *crc.*
Latynina, Larissa *gym.*
Marciano, Rocky *box.*
Matthews, Sir Stanley *fb.*
McClaren, Bruce *mr.*
Mortimer, Angela *ten.*
Newcombe, John *ten.*
Nicklaus, Jack *gf*
Phillips, Capt. Mark *sj.*
Richards, Sir Gordon *hr.*
Rosewall, Ken *ten.*
Weiskopf, Tom *gf*

9

Bannister, Dr Roger *ath.*
Bonington, Chris *mt.*
D'Oliveira, Basil *crc.*
Goolagong, Evonne *ten.*
Johansson, Ingomar *box.*
Lindbergh, Charles *aviation*
Patterson, Floyd *box.*
Pattisson, Rodney *yt.*
Underwood, Derek *crc.*

10 AND OVER

Barrington, Jonah *squash* (10)
Blanchflower, Danny *fb.* (12)
Capablanca, José *chess* (10)
Chichester, Sir Francis *yt.* (10)
Constantine, Sir Leary *crc.* (11)
Fittipaldi, Emerson *mr.* (10)
Fredericks, Roy *crc.* (10)
Illingworth, Ray *crc.* (11)
Lonsbrough, Anita *sw.* (10)
Oosterhuis, Peter *gf* (10)
Schockemohle, Alwin *sj.* (12)
Turischeva, Ludmila *gym.* (10)
Weissmuller, Johnny *sw.* (11)

Trueman, Freddie *crc.*
Worrell, Sir Frank *crc.*

3. Other prominent people

3 AND 4

Beit, Alfred (S. African financier)
Cid, The (Spanish hero)
Eddy, Mrs Mary Baker (U.S. founder of Christian Science)
Fox, George (Eng. preacher)
Fry, Elizabeth (Eng. social reformer)
Hus, Jan (Bohemian religious reformer)
Hall, Marshall (Eng. physiologist)
Hill, Octavia (Eng. social reformer)
Hill, Sir Rowland (Eng. pioneer in postal services)
Jung, Carl Gustav (Swiss psychoanalyst)
Kant, Immanuel (Ger. philosopher)
Kidd, Capt. William (Sc. pirate)
Knox, John (Sc.religious reformer)
Kun, Bela (Communist leader in Hungary)
Lee, Ann (Eng. founder of Society of Shakers)
Low, David (N.Z.-born cartoonist)
Luce, Henry Robinson (U.S. publisher)
Marx, Karl (Ger. Socialist)
Mond, Ludwig (Ger.-born chemist)
Penn, William (Eng. Quaker, founder of Pennsylvania)
Polo, Marco (It. explorer)
Salk, Jonas Edward (U.S. scientist)

5

Acton, John Dalberg, Lord (Eng. historian)
Adams, Henry (U.S. historian)
Adler, Alfred (Austrian psychologist)
Amati, Nicolò (Italian violin-maker)
Astor, John Jacob (U.S. millionaire)
Astor, Nancy, Viscountess (first woman in Br. House of Commons)
Bacon, Roger (philosopher)
Baird, John Logie (Sc. pioneer in TV)
Banks, Sir Joseph (Eng. naturalist)
Barth, Karl (Swiss theologian)
Booth, William (founder of the Salvation Army)
Botha, General Louis (Boer leader)

Clive, Robert (Indian Empire pioneer)
Freud, Sigmund (Austrian pioneer psychoanalyst)
'Grock' (Adrien Wettach) (Swiss clown)
Hegel, Georg Wilhelm Friedrich (Ger. philosopher)
Herzl, Theodor (Hung.-born founder of Zionism)
Karsh, Yousuf (Armenian-born photographer)
Keble, John (Eng. divine)
Zeiss, Carl (Ger. optical instrument maker)

6

Alcock, Sir John William (pioneer aviator)
Attila (King of the Huns)
Barker, Sir Herbert Atkinson (Eng. specialist in manipulative surgery)
Baruch, Bernard Mannes (U.S. financier)
Besant, Mrs Anne (Eng. theosophist)
Boehme, Jakob (Ger. theosophist)
Butler, Mrs Josephine (Eng. social reformer)
Calvin, John (Fr. theologian)
Capone, Al (U.S. gangster)
Caslon, William (Eng. typefounder)
Cavell, Nurse Edith (Eng. patriot)
Caxton, William (first Eng. printer)
Cicero, Marcus Tullius (Roman statesman and writer)
Diesel, Rudolf (Ger. engineer)
Dunant, Henri (Swiss founder of International Red Cross)
Euclid (Greek mathematician)
Fokker, Anton (Dutch aviation pioneer)
Graham, Billy (U.S. evangelist)
Halley, Edmond (Eng. astronomer)
Hearst, William Randolph (U.S. newspaper publisher)
Keynes, John Maynard (Eng. economist)
Luther, Martin (Ger. church reformer)
Mellon, Andrew William (U.S. financier)
Mesmer, Friedrich Franz (Ger. hypnotist)

Morgan, John Pierpont (U.S. financier)
Petrie, William Flinders (Eng. archaeologist)
Planck, Max (Ger. physicist – formulated quantum theory)
Stopes, Dr Marie (Eng. pioneer in family planning)
Tagore, Rabindrath (Indian poet and philosopher)
Turpin, Dick (Eng. highwayman)
Wesley, John (founder of Methodism)
Wright, Orville (U.S. pioneer aviator)
Wright, Wilbur (U.S. pioneer aviator)
Wyclif, John (Eng. religious reformer)

7

Abelard, Peter (Fr. philosopher)
Aga Khan (Ismaili leader)
Atatürk, Kemal (Turkish soldier and statesmen)
Bleriot, Louis (Fr. aviator)
Blondin, Charles (Fr. acrobat)
Boyd-Orr, John, Baron (Sc. nutritionist)
Buchman, Frank (U.S. founder of Moral Rearmament)
Cassini, Giovanni Domenico (It. astronomer)
Celsius, Anders (Sw. inventor of Centigrade thermomenter)
Ehrlich, Paul (Ger. bacteriologist)
Erasmus, Desiderius (Dutch religious reformer and theologian)
Haeckel, Ernest Heinrich (Ger. naturalist)
Houdini, Harry (Erich Weiss) (Hung.-born magician and conjurer)
Leblanc, Nicolas (Fr. chemist)
Linacre, Thomas (Eng. founder of Royal College of Physicians)
Lumière, August and Louis (Fr. pioneers of cinematography)
MacEwen, Sir William (Sc. surgeon)
Scribner, Charles (U.S. publisher)
Spinoza, Benedict (Dutch philosopher)
Steiner, Rudolf (Hung.-born philosopher and educationalist)

Tussaud, Mme Marie
(Swiss-born modeller in
wax)

8

Avicenna (Arab
philosopher)
Bancroft, George (U.S.
historian)
Berkeley, George (Irish
philosopher)
Carnegie, Andrew (Sc.-born
philanthropist)
Earheart, Amelia (U.S.
aviator)
Grimaldi, Joseph (Eng.
clown)
Larousse, Pierre Athanase
(Fr. encyclopaedist)
Mercator, Geradus (Flemish
geographer)
Negretti, Enrico (It.-born
instrument-maker)
Nuffield, William Richard
Morris, Viscount (motor
manufacturer and
philanthropist)
Sheraton, Thomas (Eng.
cabinet-maker)
Wedgwood, Josiah (Eng.
potter)

9

Arbuthnot, Alexander
(printer of first bible,
1579, in Scotland)
Aristotle (Greek
philosopher)
Arkwright, Sir Richard
(inventor)
Blackwell, Dr. Elisabeth
(first Eng. registered
woman doctor)

Blavatsky, Madame Helena
(Russian-born
theosophist)
Courtauld, Samuel (Eng.
silk manufacturer)
Descartes, René (Fr.
philospher)
Gutenberg, Johannes (Ger.
founder of western
printing)
Heidegger, Martin (Ger.
philosopher)
Macgregor, Rober ('Rob
Roy') (Sc. rebel)
Nietzsche, Friedrich (Ger.
philosopher)
Pankhurst, Mrs. Emmeline
(Eng. suffragette leader)

10

Bernadotte, Jean Baptiste
(Fr. general and king of
Sweden)
Cagliostro, Alessandro
(Guiseppe Balsamo) (It.
alchemist)
Flammarion, Camille (Fr.
astronomer)
Guggenhiem, Meyer (U.S.
financier)
Macpherson, Aimée Semple
(U.S. evangelist)
Max-Müller, Friedrich
(Ger.-born philologist and
orientalist)
Montessori, Maria (It.
founder of Montessori
educational method).
Rothermere, Harold Sidney
Harmsworth, Viscount
(Eng. newspaper
publisher)
Rothschild, Meyer Amshel
(Ger. financier)
Rutherford, Daniel (Sc.
discoverer of nitrogen)

Schweitzer, Dr. Albert
(Alsatian musician and
medical missionary)
Stradivari, Antonio (It.
violin-maker)
Swedenborg, Emanuel (Sw.
theologian)
Vanderbilt, Cornelius (U.S.
financier)

11

Beaverbrook, William
Maxwell Aitken, 1st
Baron (Canadian-born
newspaper publisher)
Chippendale, Thomas (Eng.
furniture designer)
Hippocrates (Greek
physician)
Machiavelli (It. political
reformer)
Nightingale, Florence (Eng.
pioneer in training
nurses)
Northcliffe, Alfred
Harmsworth, Viscount
(Irish-born newspaper
owner)
Shaftesbury, Anthony
Ashley Cooper, 7th Earl
(Eng. philanthropist)
Wilberforce, Samuel (Eng.
divine)
Wilberforce, William (Eng.
abolitionist)

12

Krishnamurti, Jiddu
(Indian mystic)
Schopenhauer, Arthur (Ger.
philosopher)
Wittgenstein, Ludwig
(Austrian-born
philosopher)

Explorers

3 AND 4

Back
Beke
Bird
Byrd
Cam
Cook
Diaz
Gama
Gann
Hore
Leif
Park
Polo
Rae
Ross (Sir John)
Rut

5

Anson (Lord George)
Baker

Brown (Lady)
Bruce (General)
Burke
Cabot
Clark
Davis
Drake (Sir Francis)
Dyatt
Dyott (Commander)
Evans (Capt.)
Fuchs
Gomez
Hanno
Hedin
Lewis
Mosto
Nares (Sir George)
Necho
Nuyts
Oates (Capt.)
Ojeda
Parry (Admiral)
Peary (Admiral)

Penny (Capt.)
Prado
Scott (Capt.)
Smith (Capt.)
Speke (Capt.)
Terry
Welzl
Wills

6

Andrée
Austin (Capt.)
Baffin
Balboa
Barnes
Barrow (Sir John)
Bellot
Bering
Burton (Sir Richard)
Cabral
Conway (Sir Martin)

Cortes
Da Gama
de Soto
Dr. Gann
Duguid
Duluth
Eannes
Forbes (Rosita)
Fraser
Hanway
Hartog
Hedges
Henday
Hobson
Hudson
Hurley (Capt.)
Joliet
Kellas
Landor
Marcks
Mawson
Morton
Nansen
Nobile (General)
Osborn
Philby
Philip
Pocok (Capt.)
Siemel
Smythe
Tasman
Thomas (Bertram)
Torres
Treatt

7

Abruzzi
Almeida
Behring
Belzoni
Bullock
Cameron
Cartier
Charcot
Colbeck
Dampier (William)
de Ojeda
de Piano
de Prado (Albert)
de Windt
Doughty
Fawcett (Col.)
Francke
Fremont
Gilbert
Hawkins (Sir John)
Hillary (Sir Edmund)
Houtman
John Rae
Kearton
Kellett (Capt.)
Kennedy (William)
Kosloff
La Salle
McClure (Sir Robert)
Markham (Albert)
Mendana
Pizzaro
Raleigh (Sir Walter)
Shippee (Robert)
Stanley (Sir H. M.)
Stewart (Capt.)
Tristam

Tweedie (Mrs.)
Watkins
Wegener
Wilkins
Workman

8

Agricola
Amundsen
Bee-Mason
Champion
Clifford
Columbus
Coronado
de Torres
Diego Cam
Etherton
Filchner
Flinders
Franklin (Sir John)
Grenfell
Hovgaard
Humboldt
Jan Welzl
Johansen
Johnston
Kingsley
Lawrence.
McGovern
Magellan
Ommanney
Radisson
Sverdrup
Thompson (David)
Vespucci
William (Sir Hubert)

9

Africanus
Cadamosto
Champlain
Cockerill
de Almeida
de Filippi
de Houtman
de Mendana
Emin Pasha
Frobisher (Sir Martin)
Gonsalvez
Grenville
Jenkinson
John Cabot
John Davis
John Smith (Capt.)
Kropotkin (Prince)
Lancaster
Mackenzie
M'Clintock
Marco Polo
Mrs. Marcks
Mungo Park
Sven Hedin
Vancouver
Van Diemen
Velasquez

10

Abel Tasman
Bransfield
Chancellor

Clapperton
Diego Gomez
Dirk Hartog
Dr. McGovern
Eric the Red
Herjulfson
Inglefield
Kohl-Larsen
Leichhardt
Leigh Smith
Lewis Cabot
McClintock
Mandeville
Prjevalsky
Richardson (Sir James)
Schliemann
Shackleton
Stefansson
Thomas Gann
Willoughby (Sir Hugh)

11

Admiral Byrd
Albuquerque
Captain Bird
Captain Cook
Court-Treatt
Dr. Sven Hedin
Dyhrenfurth
Jean Charcot
Kingdon-Ward
La Vérendrye
Leif Ericson
Livingstone
Nuno Tristam
Pieter Nuyts
Prince Henry
Roger Pocock
Vasco da Gama

12

Bougainville
Cabeza de Vaca
Cressy-Marcks (Mrs.)
Friar Oderico
Nordenskjöld
Piano Carpini
St. John Philby
Sascha Siemel
Savage Landor
Younghusband

13

Bellinghausen
Cherry Kearton
de Albuquerque
Hunter Workman
Louis de Torres
Richmond Brown (Lady)

14

Antam Gonsalvez
Bullock-Workman
Diego Velasquez
Fridtjof Nansen
Pierre de Brazza
Sebastian Cabot

81

Generals, field marshals, air marshals, etc.

3 – 5

Adam
Baird
Blood
Bols
Botha
Bruce
Byng
Clark
Clive
Condé
Craig
Dawes
Dayan
de Wet
Duff
Dyer
Foch
Giap
Gort
Gough
Grant
Haig
Hart
Horne
Ismay
Jacob
Jodl
Junot
Lee
Leese
Maude
Milne
Model
Monro
Moore
Munro
Murat
Neill
Ney
Nye
Paget
Parma
Patch
Peck
Pile
Raban
Robb
Saxe
Shea
Slim
Smuts
Soult
Sulla
Tojo
Tully
Weeks
White
Wolfe
Wood

6

Barrow
Buller
Butler
Caesar
Capper
Creagh
Crerar
Cronje
Daxout
Douglas
Dundas
Eugene
French
Giraud
Gordon
Göring
Graham
Harris
Hunter
Joffre
Keitel
Koniev
Mangin
Marius
Moltke
Murray
Napier
Newall
Outram
Patton
Pétain
Plumer
Pompey
Portal
Raglan
Rommel
Rundle
Rupert (Prince)
Scipio
Spaatz
Tedder
Trajan
Wilson
Zhukov

7

Allenby
Blücher
Bradley
Cadorna
Capello
Dempsey
Fairfax
Gamelin
Gaselee
Gatacre
Gonzalo

Gourand
Haldane
Joubert
Leclerc
Lyautey
McMahon
MacMunn
Masséna
Maurice
Maxwell
Methuen
Mortier
Nivelle
O'Connor
Roberts
Salmond
Sherman
Simpson
Stewart
Turenne
Weygand
Wingate

8

Birdwood
Brancker
Browning
Campbell
Chetwode
Cromwell
De Gaulle
Freyberg
Galliéni
Gleichen
Hamilton
Hannibal
Havelock
Ironside
Lockhart
Napoleon
Pershing
Radetsky
Saunders
Skobelev
Townsend
Urquhart
von Bülow
von Kluck
Wolseley

9

Alexander
Berthelot
Boulanger
Cambridge
Chermside
Connaught

Dundonald
Garibaldi
Harington
Higginson
Kitchener
Lyttelton
Ludendorf
Macdonald
Miltiades
Nicholson
Rawlinson
Robertson
Trenchard
Wellesley
Willcocks

10

Alanbrooke
Auchinleck
Bernadotte
Chelmsford
Cornwallis
Eisenhower
Falkenhayn
Hindenburg
Kesselring
Kuropatkin
Montgomery
Voroshilov
Wellington

11

Abercrombie
Baden-Powell
Brackenbury
de Castelnau
Marlborough
Ochterlonie
Strathnairn
Wallenstein

12 AND 13

Hunter-Weston (12)
Smith-Dorrien (12)
von Mackensen (12)
von Rundstedt (12)
Younghusband (12)

14 AND 15

Forestier-Walker (15)
Garnet-Wolseley (14)
Napier of Magdala (15)

Politicians and statesmen:
a selection

3 AND 4

Amin
Blum

Burr
Cato
Chou

Clay
Foot
Fox

Grey
Hess
Hull

Meir
Pitt
Pym
Rhee
Root
Rusk
Tito

5

Banda
Benés
Bevan
Bevin
Burke
Ciano
Cleon
Desai
Hiero
Hoare
Hoxha
Husak
Jagan
Kadar
Laval
Lenin
Marat
Nehru
Perón
Sadat
Simon
Smith
Smuts
Solon

6

Bhutto
Borgia
Brandt
Caesar
Castro
Cavour
Chiang
Cobden
Cripps

Cromer
Curzon
Danton
Dubcek
Dulles
Franco
Gadafy
Gandhi
Hitler
Horthy
Kaunda
Mobutu
Mosley
Nasser
Pétain
Powell
Rhodes
Samuel
Stalin

7

Acheson
Allende
Batista
Bolivar
Bormann
Giscard
Gomulka
Halifax
Hampden
Himmler
Kennedy
Kosygin
Kreisky
Lumumba
Masaryk
Menzies
Mintoff
Molotov
Nkrumah
Nyerere
Parnell
Pearson
Ptolemy
Redmond
Reynaud

Salazar
Sukarno
Trotsky
Trudeau
Vorster
Webster

8

Adenauer
Augustus
Ayub Khan
Bismarck
Brezhnev
Bulganin
Cromwell
Daladier
De Gaulle
De Valera
Dollfuss
Duvalier
Goebbels
Hamilton
Kenyatta
Lycurgus
Makarios
Montfort
Morrison
Napoleon
O'Higgins
Pericles
Pinochet
Podgorny
Pompidou
Ulbricht
Verwoerd
Welensky

9

Alexander
Ben Gurion
Bonaparte
Bourguiba
Chou En-Lai
Churchill

Clarendon
Dionysius
Garibaldi
Ho Chi Minh
Mussolini
Richelieu
Salisbury
Strafford

10

Buonaparte
Clemenceau
Hindenburg
Khrushchev
Lee Kuan-Yew
Mao Tse-Tung
Metternich
Ribbentrop
Sekou Touré
Talleyrand

11

Boumédienne
Castlereagh
Chamberlain
Cleisthenes
Robespierre
Shaftesbury

12

Bandaranaike
Hammarskjöld
Kemal Atatürk
Mendès-France
Themistocles

13 AND OVER

Chiang Kai-Shek (13)
Giscard d'Estaing (15)
Hailé Selassié (13)

Presidents of the United States

4 AND 5

Adams, John
Adams, John Quincy
Ford, Gerald
Grant, Ulysses S.
Hayes, Rutherford B.
Nixon, Richard M.
Polk, James K.
Taft, William
Tyler, John

6

Arthur, Chester A.
Carter, Jimmy
Hoover, Herbert
Munroe, James
Pierce, Franklin
Taylor, Zachary

Truman, Harry
Wilson, Woodrow

7

Harding, Warren G.
Jackson, Andrew
Johnson, Andrew
Johnson, Lyndon B.
Kennedy, John F.
Lincoln, Abraham
Madison, James

8

Buchanan, James
Coolidge, Calvin

Fillmore, Millard
Garfield, James A.
Harrison, Benjamin
Harrison, William
McKinley, William
Van Buren, Martin

9

Cleveland, Grover
Jefferson, Thomas
Roosevelt, Franklin D.
Roosevelt, Theodore

10

Eisenhower, Dwight
Washington, George

83

Prime ministers of Great Britain

4 AND 5

Bute, Lord
Derby, Lord
Eden, Sir Anthony
Grey, Lord
Heath, Edward
North, Lord
Peel, Sir Robert
Pitt, William (the Younger)

6

Attlee, Clement
Pelham, Henry
Wilson, Sir Harold

7

Asquith, Herbert
Baldwin, Stanley
Balfour, Arthur
Canning, George
Chatham, Lord (Wm Pitt
  the Elder)

Grafton, Duke of
Russell, Lord John
Walpole, Sir Robert

8

Aberdeen, Lord
Bonar Law, Andrew
Disraeli, Benjamin
Goderich, Lord
Perceval, Spencer
Portland, Duke of
Rosebery, Lord

9

Addington, Henry
Callaghan, James
Churchill, Sir Winston
Gladstone, William
Grenville, George
Grenville, Lord
Liverpool, Lord
MacDonald, Ramsay

Macmillan, Harold
Melbourne, Lord
Newcastle, Duke of
Salisbury, Marquis of
Shelburne, Lord

10

Devonshire, Duke of
Palmerston, Lord
Rockingham, Marquis of
Wellington, Duke of
Wilmington, Lord

11 AND OVER

Beaconsfield, Lord (12)
Campbell-Bannerman, Sir
  Henry (17)
Chamberlain, Neville (11)
Douglas-Home, Sir Alec (11)
Lloyd George, David (11)

Scientists and engineers

3 AND 4

Aird
Ball
Bell
Bohr
Bose
Coué
Davy
Ford
Gall
Gibb
Gold
Hahn
Hale
Hero
Hess
Howe
Koch
Low
Ohm
Paré
Ray
Reed
Swan
Watt
Wren

5

Bacon
Banks
Barry
Boole
Boyle
Bragg
Brahe
Crick

Curie
Debye
Ewing
Fermi
Galen
Gamow
Gauss
Haber
Henri
Hertz
Hooke
Jacob
Jeans
Joule
Klein
Krebs
Lodge
Maxim
Monod
Morse
Pauli
Pliny
Segrè
Smith
Volta
White

6

Ampère
Brunel
Bunsen
Calvin
Cardew
Dalton
Darwin
Dawson
Edison

Euclid
Froude
Fulton
Halley
Harvey
Hubble
Hughes
Hutton
Huxley
Jenner
Kekulé
Kelvin
Kepler
Kuiper
Liebig
Lister
Mendel
Morgan
Napier
Nernst
Newton
Pascal
Pavlov
Planck
Ramsay
Rennie
Roscoe
Stokes
Thales
Watson

7

Andrews
Banting
Charles
Compton
Coulomb

Coulson
Crookes
Daimler
Da Vinci
Doppler
Faraday
Fleming
Galileo
Galvani
Huggins
Huygins
Kendrew
Lamarck
Lockyer
Lorentz
Marconi
Maxwell
Medawar
Moseley
Newmann
Pasteur
Pauling
Piccard
Ptolemy
Röntgen
Rumford
Seaborg
Siemens
Thomson
Tyndall
Virchow
Wallace
Whitney

8

Agricola
Bessemer

Blackett	Roentgen	Eddington	Heisenberg
Chadwick	Thompson	Fibonnaci	Hipparchus
Crompton	Van Allen	Gay-Lussac	Paracelsus
De Forest	Van't Hoff	Heaviside	Rutherford
Einstein	Zeppelin	Kirchhoff	Stephenson
Foucault		Lankester	Torricelli
Franklin		Mendeleev	
Goodyear	**9**	Michelson	
Harrison		Priestley	**11** AND OVER
Herschel	Aristotle		
Humboldt	Armstrong		Grosseteste (11)
Lawrence	Arrhenius	**10**	Le Chatelier (11)
Linnaeus	Becquerel		Leeuwenhoek (11)
Malpighi	Bernoulli	Archimedes	Oppenheimer (11)
Mercator	Cavendish	Cannizzaro	Schrödinger (11)
Millikan	De Broglie	Copernicus	Szent-Györgyi (12)
Rayleigh	Descartes	Fahrenheit	Van der Waals (11)

GEOGRAPHY
References for geographical lists

Adr.	Adriatic Sea	Eth. Ethiopia
Aeg.	Aegean Sea	Eur. Europe
Af.	Africa	Fin. Finland
Afghan.	Afghanistan	Fr. France
Alg.	Algeria	Ger. Germany
Am.	America	Gr. Greece
Antarc.	Antarctic (Ocean)	Him. Himalayas
Arab.	Arabia	Hung. Hungary
	Arabian Sea	Ind. India
Arc.	Arctic (Ocean)	Indian Ocean
Arg.	Argentina	Indo. Indonesia
Asia M.	Asia Minor	Ire. Ireland
Atl.	Atlantic Ocean	Republic of
Aust.	Austria	Ireland
Austral.	Australia	Isr. Israel
Balt.	Baltic (Sea)	It. Italy
Bangla.	Bangladesh	Jap. Japan
Belg.	Belgium	Jord. Jordan
Boliv.	Bolivia	Malag. Rep. Malagasy
Braz.	Brazil	Republic
Bulg.	Bulgaria	Malay. Malaysia
C.Am.	Central America	Med. Mediterranean (Sea)
Can.	Canada	Mex. Mexico
Cen. Af. Rep.	Central	Mon. Mongolia
	African	Moroc. Morocco
	Republic	Moz. Mozambique
Ch. Is.	Channel Islands	N.Af North Africa
Cors.	Corsica	N.Am. North America
Cze.	Czechoslovakia	Nep. Nepal
Den.	Denmark	N. Guin. New Guinea
E. Af.	East Africa	Neth. Netherlands
E. Ger.	East Germany	N.I. Northern Ireland
E.I.	East Indies	Nig. Nigeria
Eng.	England	Nor. Norway

N.Z.	New Zealand
Pac.	Pacific Ocean
Pak.	Pakistan
Papua	Papua New Guinea
P.D.R. Yemen	People's
	Democratic Republic of
	Yemen
Philip.	Philippines
Pol.	Poland
Port.	Portugal
Pyr.	Pyrenees
Rom.	Romania
S.A.	South Africa
S.Am.	South America
Sard.	Sardinia
Saudi	Saudi Arabia
Scot.	Scotland
Sib.	Siberia
Sic.	Sicily
Sp.	Spain
Sri	Sri Lanka
Swed.	Sweden
Swit.	Switzerland
Thai.	Thailand
Tanz.	Tanzania
Tas.	Tasmania
Turk.	Turkey
Venez.	Venezuela
Viet.	Vietnam
W.Af.	West Africa
W.Ger.	West Germany
W.I.	West Indies
Yug.	Yugoslavia

Bays, bights, firths, gulfs, sea lochs, loughs, and harbours
B. = Bay. Bi. = Bight. F. = Firth. Fi. = Fiord. G. = Gulf.
Har. = Harbour. L. = Loch (Scottish). Lou = Lough (Irish.) S. = Sea.

2 – 4
Acre, B. of (Isr.)
Aden, G. of (Arab.)
Awe, L. (Scot.)
Clew, B. (Ire.)
Ewe, L. (Scot.)
Fyne, L. (Scot.)

Gilp, L. (Scot.)
Goil, L. (Scot.)
Kiel, B. (Ger.)
Long, L. (Scot.)
Luce, B. (Scot.)
Lyme B. (Eng.)
Ob, G. of (U.S.S.R.)

Riga, G. of (U.S.S.R.)
Siam, G. of (Asia)
Suez, G. of (Red S.)
Tay, F. of (Scot.)
Tees, B. (Eng.)
Tor B. (Eng.)
Wash, The (Eng.)

5
Aqaba, G. of (Arab.)
Algoa B. (S.A.)
Benin, Bi. of (W.Af.)
Blind B. (N.Z.)
Broom, L. (Scot.)

85

Chi-Li, G. of (China)
Clyde, F. of (Scot.)
Cutch, G. of (Ind.)
Enard B. (Scot.)
Evans B. (N.Z.)
False B. (S.A.)
Forth, F. of (Scot.)
Foyle, Lou. (Ire.)
Fundy, B. of (Can.)
Genoa, G. of (It.)
Hawke B. (N.Z.)
Izmir, G. of (Turk.)
James B. (Can.)
Leven, L. (Scot.)
Lions, G. of (Med.)
Lorne, F. of (Scot.)
Moray F. (Scot.)
Otago Har. (N.Z.)
Papua, G. of (N. Guin.)
Paria, G. of (S. Am.)
Table B. (S.A.)
Tunis, G. of (N.Af.)

6

Aegina, G. of (Gr.)
Aylort, L. (Scot.)
Baffin B. (Can.)
Bantry B. (Ire.)
Bengal, B. of (Ind.)
Biafra, Bi. of (W. Af.)
Biscay, B. of (Fr.)
Botany B. (Austral.)
Broken B. (Austral.)
Cambay, G. of (Ind.)
Cloudy B. (N.Z.)
Colwyn B. (Wales)
Danzig, G. of (Pol.)
Darien, G. of (S. Am.)
Denial B. (Austral.)
Dingle B. (Ire.)
Drake's B. (U.S.A.)
Dublin B. (Ire.)
Galway B. (Ire.)
Guinea, G. of (W.Af.)
Hervey B. (Austral.)
Hudson B. (Can.)
Ijssel S. (Neth.)
Linnhe, L. (Scot.)
Lübeck B. (Ger.)
Manaar, G. of (Ind.)
Mexico, G. of (Mex.)
Mounts B. (Eng.)
Naples, B. of (It.)
Panama, G. of (C. Am.)
Plenty, B. of (N.Z.)
St. Malo, G. of (Fr.)
Sharks B. (Austral.)
Smyrna, G. of (Turk.)
Solway F. (Scot.)
Sunart, L. (Scot.)
Swilly, Lou. (Ire.)
Sydney Har. (Austral.)
Tasman B. (N.Z.)

Tonkin, G. of (S. China S.)
Venice, G. of (It.)
Walvis B. (S.A.)
Zuider S. (Neth.)

7

Aboukir B. (Med.)
Argolis, G. of (Gr.)
Baffin's B. (Can.)
Belfast Lou. (N.I.)
Boothia, G. of (Can.)
Bothnia, G. of (Swed.)
Bustard B. (Austral.)
Chaleur B. (Can.)
Delagoa B. (S.A.)
Donegal B. (Ire.)
Dornoch F. (Scot.)
Dundalk B. (Scot.)
Finland, G. of (U.S.S.R.)
Fortune B. (Can.)
Halifax B. (Austral.)
Hudson's B. (Can.)
Kaipara Har. (N.Z.)
Lepanto, G. of (Gr.)
Moreton B. (Austral.)
Pe-Chi-Li, G. of (China)
Pegasus B. (N.Z.)
Persian B. (Asia)
Salerno, G. of (It.)
Snizort, L. (Scot.)
Taranto, G. of (It.)
Tarbert, L. (Scot.)
Trieste, G. of (Adr.)
Trinity B. (Can.)
Volcano B. (Jap.)

8

Cagliari, G. of (It.)
Campeche, B. of (Mex.)
Cardigan B. (Wales)
Cromarty F. (Scot.)
Delaware B. (U.S.A.)
Georgian B. (Can.)
Hammamet, G. of (N. Af.)
Hang-Chow B. (China)
Honduras, G. of (C. Am.)
Liau-Tung, G. of (China)
Martaban, G. of (Burma)
Pentland F. (Scot.)
Plymouth Har. (Eng.)
Portland B. (Austral.)
Portland Har. (Eng.)
Quiberon B. (Fr.)
Salonika, G. of (Gr.)
San Jorge, G. of (S. Am.)
San Pablo B. (U.S.A.)
Spencer's G. (Austral.)
Thailand, G. of (Asia)
Tongking, G. of(S. China S.)
Tremadoc B. (Wales)
Weymouth Bay (Eng.)

9

Admiralty B. (N.Z.)
Broughton B. (Austral.)
Buzzard's B. (U.S.A.)
Cambridge G. (Austral.)
Discovery B. (Austral.)
Encounter B. (Austral.)
Frobisher B. (Can.)
Galveston B. (U.S.A.)
Geographe B. (Austral.)
Hermitage B. (Can.)
Inverness F. (Scot.)
Mackenzie B. (Can.)
Morecambe B. (Eng.)
Notre Dame B. (Can.)
Placentia B. (Can.)
St. Bride's B. (Wales)
St. George's B. (Can.)
St. George's B. (S. Am.)
Saint Malo, G. of (Fr.)
San Matias, G. of (S. Am.)
St. Vincent G. (Austral.)
Van Diemen G. (Austral.)
Venezuela, G. of (S. Am.)

10 AND OVER

Barnstaple B. (Eng.) (10)
Bridgewater B. (Eng.) (11)
California, G. of (Mex.) (10)
Canterbury Bi. (N.Z.) (10)
Carmarthen B. (Wales) (10)
Carpentaria, G. of(Austral.)
  (11)
Chesapeake B. (U.S.A.) (10)
Christiania Fi. (Nor.) (11)
Conception B. (Can.) (10)
Great Australian Bi.
  (Austral.) (15)
Heligoland B. (Ger.) (10)
Pomeranian B. (Baltic S.)
  (10)
Port Jackson B. (Austral.)
  (11)
Port Philip B. (Austral.) (10)
Portsmouth Har. (Eng.) (10)
Princess Charlotte B.
  (Austral.) (17)
Ringkøbing Fi. (Den.) (1)
Robin Hood's B. (Eng.) (10)
Saint Bride's B. (Wales) (11)
St. Lawrence, G. of (Can.)
  (10)
Saint Lawrence, G. of(Can.)
  (13)
Saint Vincent, G. of
  (Austral.) (12)
San Francisco B. (U.S.A.)
  (12)
Southampton Water (Eng.)
  (16)
Tehuantepec, G. of (Mex.)
  (12)

Capes, headlands, points, etc.

C. = Cape.   Hd. = Head, or Headland.   N. = Ness.   Pt. = Point.

3 AND 4

Aird Pt. (Scot.)
Ann, C. (U.S.A.)

Ayre Pt. (Eng.)
Baba, C. (Turk.)
Bon, C. (N. Af.)
Busa, C. (Crete)

Cod, C. (U.S.A.)
Cruz, C. (S. Am.)
East C. (N.Z.)
East Pt. (Can.)

Farr Pt. (Scot.)
Fear, C. (U.S.A.)
Fife N. (Scot.)
Fogo, C. (Can.)

Frio, C. (Braz.)
Frio, C. (W. Af.)
Hoe Pt. (Scot.)
Horn, C. (S. Am.)
Howe, C. (Austral.)
Icy C. (Can.)
King, C. (Jap.)
Krio, C. (Crete)
Loop Hd. (Ire.)
May, C. (U.S.A.)
Nao, C. (It.)
Naze (The) (Eng.)
Naze (The) (Nor.)
Nord, C. (Nor.)
Noss Hd. (Scot.)
Nun, C. (W. Af.)
Race, C. (Can.)
Roxo, C. (Can.)
Sima, C. (Jap.)
Slea Hd. (Ire.)
Soya, C. (Jap.)
Sur Pt. (S. Am.)
Toe Hd. (Scot.)
Turn N. (Scot.)
York, C. (Austral.)

5

Adieu, C. (Austral.)
Amber, C. (E. Af.)
Aniva, C. (U.S.S.R.)
Bauer, C. (Austral.)
Brims N. (Scot.)
Byron, C. (Austral.)
Clark Pt. (Can.)
Clare, C. (Ire.)
Corso, C. (Cors.)
Creus, C. (Sp.)
Dunge N. (Eng.)
Gallo, C. (Gr.)
Gaspé, C. (Can.)
Lopez, C. (W. Af.)
Malia, C. (Gr.)
Mirik, C. (W. Af.)
Negro, C. (W. Af.)
North C. (N.Z.)
North C. (Nor.)
Orme's Hd. (Wales)
Otway, C. (Austral.)
Quoin Pt. (S.A.)
Roray Hd. (Scot.)
Sable, C. (Can.)
Sable, C. (U.S.A.)
Sandy C. (Austral.)
San Ho, C. (Viet.)
Sheep Hd. (Ire.)
Slade Pt. (Austral.)
Sleat Pt. (Scot.)
Slyne Hd. (Ire.)
South C. (China)
Spurn Hd. (Eng.)
Start Pt. (Eng.)
Tavoy Pt. (Burma)
Troup Hd. (Scot.)
Verde, C. (W. Af.)
Wiles, C. (Austral.)
Worms Hd. (Wales)
Wrath, C. (Scot.)
Yakan, C. (Sib.)

6

Andres Pt. (S. Am.)
Bantam, C. (Indo.)

Barren, C. (Austral.)
Beachy Hd. (Eng.)
Blanco, C. (N. Af.)
Blanco, C. (S. Am.)
Branco, C. (S. Am.)
Breton, C. (Can.)
Buddon N. (Scot.)
Burrow Hd. (Scot.)
Burrow Pt. (Scot.)
Carmel, C. (Isr.)
Castle Pt. (N.Z.)
Comino, C. (Sard.)
Cuvier, C. (Austral.)
De Gata, C. (Spain)
De Roca, C. (Port)
Dodman Pt. (Eng.)
Dunnet Hd. (Scot.)
Egmont, C. (N.Z.)
Formby Hd. (Eng.)
Friars Pt. (U.S.A.)
Galley Hd. (Ire.)
Gallon Hd. (Scot.)
Glossa, C. (Turk.)
Lizard (The) (Eng.)
Orford N. (Eng.)
Palmas, C. (W. Af.)
Prawle Pt. (Eng.)
Recife, C. (S.A.)
Rhynns Pt. (Scot.)
St. Abb's Hd. (Scot.)
St. Bees Hd. (Eng.)
St. Mary, C. (Can.)
St. Paul, C. (W. Af.)
Sambro, C. (Can.)
Sanaig Pt. (Scot.)
Sidero, C. (Crete)
Sorell, C. (Austral.)
Tarbat, N. (Scot.)
Tarifa, C. (Sp.)
Tolsta Hd. (Scot.)
Wad Nun, C. (N. Af.)
Whiten Hd. (Scot.)
Yerimo, C. (Jap.)

7

Agulhas, C. (S.A.)
Arisaig Pt. (Scot.)
Bengore Hd. (N.I.)
Bismark, C. (Green.)
Bizzuto, C. (It.)
Blanche, C. (Austral.)
Charles, C. (U.S.A.)
Clogher Hd. (Ire.)
Colonna, C. (Gr.)
Comorin, C. (Ind.)
De Palos, C. (Sp.)
De Penas, C. (Sp.)
De Sines, C. (Port.)
Formosa, C. (W. Af.)
Gregory, C. (Can.)
Gris-Nez, C. (Fr.)
Haytian, C. (W.I.)
Icy Cape (Can.)
Kataska, C. (Jap.)
Kennedy, C. (U.S.A.)
La Hague, C. (Fr.)
Leeuwin, C. (Austral.)
Matapan, C. (Gr.)
Milazzo, C. (Sic.)
Mondego, C. (Port)
Mumbles Hd. (Wales)
Needles, The (Eng.)
Negrais, C. (Burma)
Orlando, C. (Sic.)

Ortegal, C. (Sp.)
Rattray Hd. (Scot.)
Romania, C. (Malay.)
Runaway, C. (N.Z.)
St. Lucia, C. (S.A.)
San Blas, C. (U.S.A.)
São Tomé, C. (Braz.)
Spartel, C. (N. Af.)
Strathy Pt. (Scot.)
Tegupan Pt. (Mex.)
Teulada, C. (Sard.)
The Horn (S. Am.)
The Naze (Eng.)
The Naze (Nor.)
Toe Head (Scot.)
Upstart, C. (Austral.)
Vincent, C. (U.S.A.)
Yang-tsi, C. (China)

8

Bathurst, C. (Can.)
Cambodia Pt. (Thai.)
East Cape (N.Z.)
Espichel, C. (Port.)
Fairhead, C. (N.I.)
Farewell, C. (Green.)
Farewell, C. (N.Z.)
Fife Ness (Scot.)
Flattery, C. (U.S.A.)
Foreland (The) (Eng.)
Gallinas Pt. (S. Am.)
Good Hope, C. of (S.A.)
Greenore Pt. (Ire.)
Hangklip, C. (S.A.)
Hartland Pt. (Eng.)
Hatteras, C. (U.S.A.)
Kaliakra, C. (Bulg.)
Kinnaird Hd. (Scot.)
Land's End (Eng.)
Loop Head (Ire.)
Maranhao, C. (Braz.)
Melville, C. (Austral.)
Palliser, C. (N.Z.)
Palmyras Pt. (Ind.)
Patience, C. (Jap.)
St. Albans Hd. (Eng.)
St. David's Hd. (Wales)
St George, C. (Can.)
St. Gowan's Hd. (Wales)
San Diego, C. (S. Am.)
San Lucas, C. (Mex.)
São Roque, C. (Braz.)
Sidmouth, C. (Austral.)
Slea Head (Ire.)
Sordwana Pt. (S.A.)
Strumble Hd. (Wales)
Sumburgh Hd. (Scot.)
Sur Point (U.S.A.)
Thorsden, C. (Arc.)
Turn Ness (Scot.)
Vaticano, C. (It.)

9

Bonàvista, C. (Can.)
Brims Ness (Scot.)
Canaveral, C. (U.S.A.)
Carvoeira, C. (Port.)
Claremont Pt. (Austral.)
De Talbert Pt. (Fr.)
Dungeness (Eng.)
East Point (Can.)
Esquimaux, C. (Can.)

87

Farr Point (Scot.)
Girardeau, C. (U.S.A.)
Granitola, C. (Sic.)
Guardafin, C. (E. Af.)
Inishowen Hd. (Ire.)
Mendocino, C. (U.S.A.)
Murchison, C. (Can.)
Nash Point (Wales)
North Cape (N.Z.)
North Cape (Nor.)
Ormes Head (Wales)
Roray Head (Scot.)
Saint Abbs Hd. (Scot.)
Saint Bees Hd. (Eng.)
St. Francis, C. (Can.)
Saint Mary, C. (Can.)
Saint Paul, C. (W. Af.)
St. Vincent, C. (Port.)
Sand Patch Pt. (Austral.)
Sandy Cape (Austral.)
Sandy Cape (Tas.)
Santo Vito, C. (Sic.)
Sheep Head (Ire.)
Slyne Head (Ire.)
South Cape (China)
Spurn Head (Eng.)
Streedagh Pt. (Ire.)
The Lizard (Eng.)
Trafalgar, C. (Sp.)
Troup Head (Scot.)
Vaternish Pt. (Scot.)
Worms Head (Wales)

10

Beachy Head (Eng.)
Breakheart Pt. (Can.)
Buddon Ness (Scot.)
Burrow Head (Scot.)
Clark Point (Can.)
Conception Pt. (U.S.A.)
Duncansbay Hd. (Scot.)
Dunnet Head (Scot.)
Finisterre, C. (Sp.)
Galley Head (Ire.)
Gallon Head (Scot.)

Great Ormes Hd. (Wales)
Greenstone Pt. (Scot.)
Orford Ness (Eng.)
Palmerston, C. (Austral.)
Quoin Point (S.A.)
Rayes Point (S. Am.)
Saint Lucia, C. (S.A.)
St. Margaret Pt. (Can.)
St. Matthieu Pt. (Fr.)
San Antonio Pt. (Mex.)
San Lorenzo, C. (S. Am.)
Santa Maria, C. (Port.)
Selsey Bill (Eng.)
Slade Point (Austral.)
Sleat Point (Scot.)
Snettisham Pt. (Can.)
Start Point (Eng.)
Tarbat Ness (Scot.)
Tavoy Point (Burma)
The Needles (Eng.)
Tolsta Head (Scot.)
Walsingham, C. (Can.)
Washington, C. (Arc.)
Whiten Head (Scot.)

11

Andres Point (S. Am.)
Bengore Head (N.I.)
Bridgewater, C. (Austral.)
Castle Point (N.Z.)
Catastrophe, C. (Austral.)
Clogher Head (Ire.)
De San Adrian, C. (Sp.)
Dodman Point (Eng.)
Downpatrick Hd. (N.I.)
Flamborough Hd. (Eng.)
Friars Point (U.S.A.)
Little Ormes Hd. (Wales)
Lizard Point (Eng.)
Mumbles Head (Wales)
Murraysburg, C. (S.A.)
Prawle Point (Eng.)
Rattray Head (Scot.)
Rhynns Point (Scot.)
Saint Albans Hd. (Eng.)

Saint David's Hd. (Wales)
Saint Gilda's Pt. (Fr.)
Saint Gowan's Hd. (Wales)
Sanaig Point (Scot.)
The Foreland (Eng.)
Three Points, C. (W. Af.)
Tribulation, C. (Austral.)

12 AND OVER

Ardnamurchan Pt. (Scot.) (12)
Arisaig Point (Scot.) (12)
Breakheart Point (Can.) (15)
Cape of Good Hope (S.A.) (14)
Cayenne Point (E. Af.) (12)
Claremont Point (Austral.) (14)
Conception Point (U.S.A.) (15)
Downpatrick Head (N.I.) (15)
Duncansbay Head (Scot.) (14)
Flamborough Head (Eng.) (15)
Gracias a Dios, C. (C. Am.) (12)
Inishowen Head (Ire.) (13)
North Foreland (Eng.) (13)
Northumberland, C. (Austral.) (14)
Palmuras Point (Ind.) (13)
Portland Bill (Eng.) (12)
Saint Margaret Pt. (Can.) (13)
Sand Patch Point (Austral.) (14)
San Francisco, C. (S. Am.) (12)
Strumble Head (Wales) (12)
Sumburgh Head (Scot.) (12)
Tegupan Point (Mex.) (12)
Vaternish Point (Scot.) (14)

Capital cities of the world

3 AND 4

Aden (P.D.R. Yemen)
Apia (W. Samoa)
Bern (Swit.)
Bonn (W. Ger.)
Doha (Qatar)
Lima (Peru)
Lomé (Togo)
Male (Maldives)
Oslo (Nor.)
Rome (It.)
San'a (Yemen)
Suva (Fiji)

5

Accra (Ghana)
Agana (Guam)
Ajman (Ajman)
Amman (Jordan)

Berne (Swit.)
Cairo (Egypt)
Dacca (Bangla.)
Dakar (Senegal)
Dubai (Dubai)
Hanoi (N. Viet.)
Kabul (Afghan.)
Lagos (Nig.)
La Paz (Boliv.)
Macao (Macao)
Paris (Fr.)
Praia (Cape Verde Is.)
Quito (Ecuador)
Rabat (Moroc.)
Sanaa (Yemen)
Seoul (S. Korea)
Sofia (Bulg.)
Sucre (Boliv.)
Tokyo (Jap.)
Tunis (Tunisia)
Vaduz (Liechtenstein)
Zomba (Malawi)

6

Ankara (Turk.)
Athens (Gr.)
Bagdad (Iraq)
Bamako (Mali)
Bangui (Cen. Af. Rep.)
Banjul (Gambia)
Beirut (Lebanon)
Belice } (Belice)
Belize }
Bissau (Guinea - Bissau)
Bogotá (Colombia)
Brunei (Brunei)
Dublin (Ire.)
Habana } (Cuba)
Havana }
Kigali (Rwanda)
Kuwait (Kuwait)
Lisbon (Port.)
London (U.K.)
Luanda (Angola)

Lusaka (Zambia)
Madrid (Sp.)
Malabo (Equatorial Guinea)
Manama (Bahrain)
Maputo (Mozambique)
Maseru (Lesotho)
Masqat (Oman)
Mexico (Mexico)
Monaco (Monaco)
Moroni (Comoro Is.)
Moscow (U.S.S.R.)
Muscat (Oman)
Nassau (Bahamas)
Niamey (Niger)
Ottawa (Can.)
Panama (Panama)
Peking (China)
Prague (Cze.)
Riyadh (Saudi)
Roseau (Dominica)
Saigon (S. Viet.)
Taipei (Taiwan)
Tehran (Iran)
Thimbu }
Thimpu } (Bhutan)
Tirana (Albania)
Vienna (Aust.)
Warsaw (Pol.)

7

Abidjan (Ivory Coast)
Algiers (Alg.)
Andorra (Andorra)
Baghdad (Iraq)
Bangkok (Thai.)
Caracas (Venez.)
Colombo (Sri)
Conakry (Guinea)
Cotonou (Benin)
Douglas (Isle of Man)
El Aaiun (W. Sahara)
Gangtok (Sikkim)
Jakarta (Indo.)
Kampala (Uganda)
Managua (Nicaragua)
Mbabane (Swaziland)
Nairobi (Kenya)
Nicosia (Cyprus)
Rangoon (Burma)
St. John's (Antigua)
San José (Costa Rica)
São Tomé (São Tomé and
   Principé)
Sharjah (Sharjah)
Stanley (Falkland Is.)
Tripoli (Libya)
Valetta (Malta)
Vatican (Vatican)
Yaoundé (Cameroun)

8

Abu Dhabi (Abu Dhabi)
Asunción (Paraguay)
Belgrade (Yug.)
Brasilia (Braz.)
Brussels (Belg.)
Budapest (Hung.)
Canberra (Austral.)
Cape Town (S.A.)
Castries (St. Lucia)
Damascus (Syria)
Djibouti (Djibouti)
Freetown (Sierra Leone)
Fujairah (Fujairah)
Gaborone (Botswana)
Hamilton (Bermuda)
Helsinki (Fin.)
Katmandu (Nep.)
Khartoum (Sudan)
Kingston (Jamaica)
Kinshasa (Zaïre)
Lilongwe (Malawi)
Monrovia (Liberia)
N'Djamena (Chad)
New Delhi (Ind.)
Plymouth (Montserrat)
Pretoria (S.A.)
St. Helier (Jersey)
Santiago (Chile)
Valletta (Malta)
Victoria (Hong Kong)
Victoria (Seychelles)
Windhoek (Namibia)

9

Amsterdam (Neth.)
Bucharest (Rom.)
Bujumbura (Burundi)
Edinburgh (Scot.)
Gaberones (Botswana)
Grand Turk (Turks and
   Caicos Is.)
Guatemala (Guatemala)
Islamabad (Pak.)
Jamestown (St. Helena)
Jerusalem (Isr.)
Kingstown (St. Vincent)
Mogadishu (Somalia)
Nukualofa (Tonga)
Phnom Penh (Cambodia)
Port Louis (Mauritius)
Porto Novo (Benin)
Pyongyang (N. Korea)
Reykjavik (Iceland)
St. George's (Grenada)
Salisbury (Rhodesia)

San Marino (San Marino)
Singapore (Singapore)
Stockholm (Swed.)
Ulan Bator (Mon.)
Vientiane (Laos)

10

Addis Ababa (Eth.)
Basseterre (St. Christopher-
   Nevis-Anguilla)
Bridgetown (Barbados)
Copenhagen (Den.)
East Berlin (E. Ger.)
Georgetown (Cayman Is.)
Georgetown (Guyana)
Kuwait City (Kuwait)
Libreville (Gabon)
Luxembourg (Luxembourg)
Mexico City (Mexico)
Montevideo (Uruguay)
Nouakchott (Mauritania)
Ougadougou (Upper Volta)
Paramaribo (Surinam)
Quezon City (Philip.)
Tananarive (Malag. Rep.)
Washington (U.S.A.)
Wellington (N.Z.)

11 AND OVER

Brazzaville (Congo) (11)
Buenos Aires (Arg.) (11)
Dar es Salaam (Tanz.) (11)
Guatemala City
   (Guatemala) (13)
Kuala Lumpur (Malay.) (11)
Luang Prabang (Laos) (12)
Medina as-Shaab (P.D.R.
   Yemen) (13)
Port-au-Prince (Haiti) (12)
Port Moresby (Papua) (11)
Port of Spain (Trinidad and
   Tobago) (11)
Ras al-Khaimah (Ras
   al-Khaimah) (12)
St. Peter Port (Guernsey)
   (11)
San Salvador (El Salvador)
   (11)
Santa Isabel (Equatorial
   Guinea) (11)
Santo Domingo (Dominican
   Rep.) (12)
Tegucigalpa (Honduras)
   (11)
Uaboe District (Nauru) (13)
Umm al-Qaiwain (Umm
   al-Qaiwain) (12)
Vatican City (Vatican) (11)

Channels, passages, sounds, and straits

Ch. = Channel.   P. = Passage.   Sd. = Sound.   St.(s). = Strait(s).

Note.—The land references are to give a general idea as to location.

3 AND 4

Bass St. (Austral.)
Coll, P. of (Scot.)
Cook St. (N.Z.)

Fox Ch. (Can.)
Jura Sd. (Scot.)
Mona P. (W.I.)
Nore (The) (Eng.)
Palk St. (Ind.)

5

Cabot St. (Can.)
Davis St. (Can.)
Dover, Sts. of (Eng.)

Downs (The) (Eng.)
Korea St. (Jap.)
Menai Sts. (Wales)
Minch (The) (Scot.)
North Ch. (Scot.)
Ormuz, St. of (Iran)
Puget Sd. (U.S.A.)
Sleat, Sd. of (Scot.)
Smith Sd. (Can.)
Sound (The) (Swed.)
Sunda, St. of (E.I.)

Formosa St. (China)
Foveaux St. (N.Z.)
Georgia, St. of (Can.)
Le Maire St. (S. Am.)
Malacca St. (Malaya)
Messina, St. of (It.)
Molucca P. (E.I.)
Otranto, St. of (It.)
Pamlico Sd. (U.S.A.)
The Nore (Eng.)
Yucatan Ch. (Mex.)

The Solent (Eng.)
Van Diemen St. (Jap.)

10

Dogger Bank (N. Sea)
Golden Gate (U.S.A.)
Golden Horn (Turk.)
Kilbrennan Sd. (Scot.)
King George Sd. (Austral.)
Little Belt (The) (Den.)
Mozambique Ch. (E. Af.)

6

Achill Sd. (Ire.)
Barrow St. (Can.)
Bering St. (Pac.)
Denmark St. (Green.)
Harris, St. of (Scot.)
Hecate St. (Can.)
Hudson St. (Can.)
Nootka Sd. (Can.)
Panama Canal (C. Am.)
Queen's Ch. (Austral.)
Solent (The) (Eng.)
Torres St. (Austral.)
Tromso Sd. (Nor.)

8

Cattegat (The) (Den.)
Colonsay, P. of (Scot.)
Kattegat (The) (Den.)
Magellan St. (S. Am.)
Plymouth Sd. (Eng.)
Spithead (Eng.)
The Downs (Eng.)
The Minch (Scot.)
The Sound (Swed.)
Windward P. (W.I.)

11 AND OVER

Bab-el-Mandeb St. (Red S.)
  (11)
Caledonian Canal (Scot.)
  (15)
Dardanelles (The) (Turk.)
  (11)
Goodwin Sands (Eng.) (12)
Hampton Roads (U.S.A.)
  (12)
Northumberland St. (Can.)
  (14)
Pas de Calais (Fr.) (11)
Queen Charlotte Sd. (Can.)
  (14)
Saint George's Ch. (Eng.)
  (12)
The Bosphorus (Turk.) (12)
The Dardanelles (Turk.)
  (14)
The Great Belt (Den.) (12)
The Little Belt (Den.) (13)

9

Bonifacio, St. of (Med.)
Bosphorus (The) (Turk.)
Gibraltar, Sts. of (Spain)
Great Belt (The) (Den.)
Lancaster Sd. (Can.)
St. George's Ch. (Eng.)
Scapa Flow (Scot.)
Skagerrak (Nor. and Den.)
Suez Canal (Af.)

7

Behring St. (Sib.)
Bristol Ch. (Eng.)
Cuillin Sd. (Scot.)
Dolphin St. (Can.)
English Ch. (Eng.)
Florida St. (U.S.A.)

Counties: United Kingdom and Republic of Ireland

(E.) = England.   (Ire.) = Republic of Ireland.   (N.I.) = Northern Ireland.   (S.) = Scotland.   (W.) = Wales.

Note.—As the names of some counties are commonly used in shortened form, both full and shortened names are given in this list. It also includes county names no longer officially in use.

3 AND 4

Avon (E.)
Ayr (S.)
Beds (E.)
Bute (S.)
Cork (Ire.)
Down (N.I.)
Fife (S.)
Kent (E.)
Leix (Ire.)
Mayo (Ire.)
Oxon (E.)
Ross (S.)
York (E.)

5

Angus (S.)
Banff (S.)
Berks (E.)

Bucks (E.)
Cavan (Ire.)
Clare (Ire.)
Clwyd (W.)
Derby (E.)
Devon (E.)
Dyfed (W.)
Elgin (S.)
Essex (E.)
Flint (W.)
Gwent (W.)
Hants (E.)
Herts (E.)
Hunts (E.)
Kerry (Ire.)
Lancs (E.)
Meath (Ire.)
Moray (S.)
Nairn (S.)
Notts (E.)
Perth (S.)
Powys (W.)
Salop (E.)

Sligo (Ire.)
Wilts (E.)

6

Antrim (N.I.)
Argyll (S.)
Armagh (N.I.)
Brecon (W.)
Carlow (Ire.)
Dorset (E.)
Dublin (Ire.)
Durham (E.)
Forfar (S.)
Galway (Ire.)
Lanark (S.)
London (E.)
Offaly (Ire.)
Orkney (S.)
Oxford (E.)
Radnor (W.)
Staffs (E.)

Surrey (E.)
Sussex (E.)
Tyrone (N.I.)

7

Bedford (E.)
Berwick (S.)
Cumbria (E.)
Denbigh (W.)
Donegal (Ire.)
Dundalk (Ire.)
Gwynedd (W.)
Kildare (Ire.)
Kinross (S.)
Leitrim (Ire.)
Lincoln (E.)
Norfolk (E.)
Peebles (S.)
Renfrew (S.)
Rutland (E.)
Selkirk (S.)

Suffolk (E.)
Warwick (E.)
Wexford (Ire.)
Wicklow (Ire.)
Wigtown (S.)

8

Aberdeen (S.)
Anglesey (W.)
Ayrshire (S.)
Cardigan (W.)
Cheshire (E.)
Cornwall (E.)
Cromarty (S.)
Dumfries (S.)
Hereford (E.)
Hertford (E.)
Kilkenny (Ire.)
Limerick (Ire.)
Longford (Ire.)
Monaghan (Ire.)
Monmouth (E.)
Pembroke (W.)
Roxburgh (S.)
Somerset (E.)
Stafford (E.)
Stirling (S.)

9

Berkshire (E.)
Caithness (S.)
Cambridge (E.)
Cleveland (E.)
Connaught (Ire.)
Dunbarton (S.)
Edinburgh (S.)
Fermanagh (N.I.)
Glamorgan (W.)
Hampshire (E.)
Inverness (S.)
Leicester (E.)
Merioneth (W.)
Middlesex (E.)
Northants (E.)
Roscommon (Ire.)
Tipperary (Ire.)
Waterford (Ire.)

Westmeath (Ire.)
Wiltshire (E.)
Worcester (E.)
Yorkshire (E.)

10

Banffshire (S.)
Buckingham (E.)
Caernarvon (W.)
Carmarthen (W.)
Cumberland (E.)
Derbyshire (E.)
Devonshire (E.)
East Sussex (E.)
Flintshire (W.)
Gloucester (E.)
Haddington (S.)
Humberside (E.)
Huntingdon (E.)
Kincardine (S.)
Lancashire (E.)
Linlithgow (S.)
Merseyside (E.)
Midlothian (S.)
Montgomery (W.)
Nottingham (E.)
Perthshire (S.)
Shropshire (E.)
Sutherland (S.)
West Sussex (E.)

11 AND 12

Argyllshire (S.) (11)
Bedfordshire (E.) (12)
Berwickshire (S.) (12)
Clackmannan (S.) (11)
Denbighshire (W.) (12)
Dorsetshire (E.) (11)
East Lothian (S.) (11)
Forfarshire (S.) (11)
Isle of Wight (E.) (11)
King's County (Ire.) (11)
Lanarkshire (S.) (11)
Lincolnshire (E.) (12)
Londonderry (N.I.) (11)
Mid Glamorgan (W.) (12)
Northampton (E.) (11)

Oxfordshire (E.) (11)
Queen's County (Ire.) (12)
Radnorshire (W.) (11)
Renfrewshire (S.) (12)
Rutlandshire (E.) (12)
Tyne and Wear (E.) (11)
Warwickshire (E.) (12)
West Lothian (S.) (11)
West Midlands (E.) (12)
Westmorland (E.) (11)

13 AND 14

Aberdeenshire (S.) (13)
Brecknockshire (W.) (14)
Cambridgeshire (E.) (14)
Cardiganshire (W.) (13)
Dunbartonshire (S.) (14)
Dumfriesshire (S.) (13)
Glamorganshire (W.) (14)
Herefordshire (E.) (13)
Hertfordshire (E.) (13)
Inverness-shire (S.) (14)
Kircudbright (S.) (13)
Leicestershire (E.) (14)
Merionethshire (W.) (14)
Monmouthshire (E.) (13)
Northumberland (E.) (14)
North Yorkshire (E.) (14)
Pembrokeshire (W.) (13)
Somersetshire (E.) (13)
South Glamorgan (W.) (14)
South Yorkshire (E.) (14)
Staffordshire (E.) (13)
West Glamorgan (W.) (13)
West Yorkshire (E.) (13)
Worcestershire (E.) (14)

15 AND 16

Buckinghamshire (E.) (15)
Caenarvonshire (W.) (15)
Carmarthenshire (W.) (15)
Gloucestershire (E.) (15)
Huntingdonshire (E.) (15)
Montgomeryshire (W.) (15)
Northamptonshire (E.) (16)
Nottinghamshire (E.) (15)
Ross and Cromarty (S.) (15)

Countries and continents

Note.—This list includes names of former countries.

3 AND 4

Anam (Asia)
Asia
Bali (Asia)
Chad (Af.)
Cuba (W.I.)
D.D.R. (E. Ger.)
Eire (Eur.)
Fiji (S. Pac.)
G.D.R. (E. Ger.)
Guam (Pac.)
Iran (Asia)
Iraq (Asia)
Java (Asia)
Laos (Asia)
Mali (Af.)

Nejd (Asia)
Oman (Asia)
Peru (S. Am.)
Siam (Asia)
Togo (Af.)
U.A.R. (Af.)
U.S.A. (N. Am.)
U.S.S.R. (Asia, Eur.)

5

Annam (Asia)
Benin (Af.)
Burma (Asia)
Chile (S. Am.)
China (Asia)

Congo (Af.)
Corea (Asia)
Egypt (Af.)
Fiume (Eur.)
Gando (Af.)
Ghana (Af.)
Haiti (W.I.)
India (Asia)
Italy (Eur.)
Japan (Asia)
Kandy (Asia)
Kenya (Af.)
Khmer (Asia)
Korea (Asia)
Libya (Af.)
Lydia (Asia)
Malta (Med.)

Natal (Af.)
Nauru (Pac.)
Nepal (Asia)
Niger (Af.)
Papua (E.I.)
Qatar (Asia)
Spain (Eur.)
Sudan (Af.)
Syria (Asia)
Tchad (Af.)
Texas (N. Am.)
Tibet (Asia)
Timor (E.I.)
Tonga (Pac.)
Tunis (Af.)
Wales (Eur.)
Yemen (Asia)
Zaïre (Af.)

6

Africa
Angola (Af.)
Arabia (Asia)
Azores (Atl.)
Belice⎫
Belize⎬(C. Am.)
Bhutan (Asia)
Brazil (S. Am.)
Brunei (E.I.)
Canada (N. Am.)
Ceylon (Asia)
Cyprus (Med.)
Epirus (Eur.)
Europe
France (Eur.)
Gambia (Af.)
Greece (Eur.)
Guinea (Af.)
Guyana (S. Am.)
Hawaii (Pac.)
Israel (Asia)
Johore (Asia)
Jordan (Asia)
Kuwait (Asia)
Latvia (Eur.)
Malawi (Af.)
Malaya (Asia)
Mexico (N. Am.)
Monaco (Eur.)
Muscat (Asia)
Norway (Eur.)
Panama (S. Am.)
Persia (Asia)
Poland (Eur.)
Ruanda (Af.)
Russia (Eur., Asia)
Rwanda (Af.)
Serbia ⎫
Servia ⎬(Eur.)
Sicily (Eur.)
Sikkim (Asia)
Soudan (Af.)
Sweden (Eur.)
Taiwan (Asia)
Tobago (W.I.)
Turkey (Eur., Asia)
Ulster (Eur.)
Uganda (Af.)
Urundi (Af.)
Zambia (Af.)

7

Albania (Eur.)
Algeria (Af.)
Andorra (Eur.)
Antigua (W.I.)
America
Armenia (Asia)
Ashanti (Af.)
Assyria (Asia)
Austria (Eur.)
Bahamas (W.I.)
Bahrain (Arab.)
Bavaria (Eur.)
Belgium (Eur.)
Bermuda (Atl.)
Bohemia (Eur.)
Bolivia (S. Am.)
Britain (Eur.)
Burundi (Af.)
Croatia (Eur.)
Dahomey (Af.)
Denmark (Eur.)
Ecuador (S. Am.)
England (Eur.)
Eritrea (Af.)
Estonia (Eur.)
Faeroes (Atl.)
Finland (Eur.)
Formosa (Asia)
Germany (Eur.)
Grenada (W.I.)
Holland (Eur.)
Hungary (Eur.)
Iceland (Eur.)
Ireland (Eur.)
Jamaica (W.I.)
Lebanon (Asia)
Lesotho (Af.)
Liberia (Af.)
Livonia (Eur.)
Macedon (Eur.)
Morocco (Af.)
Namibia (Af.)
Nigeria (Af.)
Prussia (Eur.)
Romania ⎫
Rumania ⎬(Eur.)
St. Kitts (W.I.)
São Tomé (Atl.)
Sarawak (Asia)
Senegal (Af.)
Somalia (Af.)
Sumatra (E.I.)
Sumeria (Asia)
Surinam (S. Am.)
Tangier (Af.)
Tartary (Asia)
Tripoli (Af.)
Tunisia (Af.)
Ukraine (Eur.)
Uruguay (S. Am.)
Vatican (Eur.)
Vietnam (Asia)

8

Barbados (W.I.)
Botswana (Af.)
Bulgaria (Eur.)
Burgundy (Eur.)
Cambodia (Asia)
Cameroun (Af.)
Colombia (S. Am.)
Djibouti (Af.)

Dominica (W.I.)
Ethiopia (Af.)
Honduras (S. Am.)
Hong Kong (Asia)
Malagasy (Af.)
Malaysia (Asia)
Maldives (Ind.)
Mongolia (Asia)
Pakistan (Asia)
Paraguay (S. Am.)
Portugal (Eur.)
Rhodesia (Af.)
Roumania (Eur.)
St. Helena (Atl.)
Salvador (C. Am.)
Sardinia (Med.)
Scotland (Eur.)
Sri Lanka (Asia)
Tanzania (Af.)
Tasmania (Austral.)
Thailand (Asia)
Togoland (Af.)
Trinidad (W.I.)
Zanzibar (Af.)
Zimbabwe (Af.)
Zululand (Af.)

9

Abyssinia (Af.)
Argentina (S. Am.)
Argentine, The (S. Am.)
Australia
Babylonia (Asia)
Caledonia (Eur.)
Cameroons (Af.)
Costa Rica (C. Am.)
Gibraltar (Eur.)
Greenland (Arc.)
Guatemala (C. Am.)
Hindustan (Asia)
Indochina (Asia)
Indonesia (E.I.)
Lithuania (Eur.)
Luxemburg (Eur.)
Macedonia (Eur.)
Manchuria (Asia)
Mauritius (Ind.)
New Guinea (E.I.)
Nicaragua (C. Am.)
Nyasaland (Af.)
Palestine (Asia)
Pondoland (Af.)
San Marino (Eur.)
Singapore (Asia)
Swaziland (Af.)
The Gambia (Af.)
Transvaal (Af.)
Venezuela (S. Am.)

10

Antarctica
Bangladesh (Asia)
Basutoland (Af.)
California (N. Am.)
Cape Colony (Af.)
Damaraland (Af.)
El Salvador (C. Am.)
Ivory Coast (Af.)
Luxembourg (Eur.)
Madagascar (Af.)

Mauretania ⎱ (Af.)
Mauritania ⎰

Montenegro (Eur.)
Montserrat (W.I.)
Mozambique (Af.)
New Zealand (Pac.)
North Korea (Asia)
Seychelles (Ind.)
Shan States (Asia)
Somaliland (Af.)
South Korea (Asia)
South Yemen (Asia)
Tanganyika (Af.)
Upper Volta (Af.)
Yugoslavia (Eur.)

11

Afghanistan (Asia)
Australasia
Baluchistan (Asia)
Cochin China (Asia)
Cook Islands (Pac.)
Dutch Guiana (S. Am.)
East Germany (Eur.)
French Congo (Af.)
Malay States (Asia)
Mashonaland (Af.)
Mesopotamia (Asia)
Namaqualand (Af.)
Netherlands (Eur.)
New Hebrides (Pac.)
Philippines (Asia)
Saudi Arabia (Asia)
Sierra Leone (Af.)
South Africa
Soviet Union (Asia, Eur.)
Switzerland (Eur.)
Transjordan (Asia)
Vatican City (Eur.)
West Germany (Eur.)

12

Bechuanaland (Af.)
Belgian Congo (Af.)
Cocos Islands (Ind.)
Faroe Islands (Atl.)
French Guiana (S. Am.)
Great Britain (Eur.)
Guinea-Bissau (Af.)
Indian Empire (Asia)
Matabeleland (Af.)
Newfoundland (N. Am.)
North America
North Vietnam (Asia)
Ruanda-Urundi (Af.)
South America
South Vietnam (Asia)
The Argentine (S. Am.)
United States (N. Am.)

13

Afars and Issas (Af.)
Barbary States (Af.)
Cayman Islands (W.I.)
Comoro Islands (Af.)
Khmer Republic (Asia)
Liechtenstein (Eur.)
Norfolk Island (Pac.)
Trucial States (Asia)
United Kingdom (Eur.)

14

Cape of Good Hope (Af.)
Congo Free State (Af.)
Czechoslovakia (Eur.)
Gilbert Islands (Pac.)
Irish Free State (Eur.)

Maldive Islands (Ind.)
Mariana Islands (Pac.)
Papua-New Guinea (E.I.)
Pitcairn Island (Pac.)
Society Islands (Pac.)
Solomon Islands (Pac.)

15

British Honduras (C. Am.)
Caroline Islands (Pac.)
Christmas Island (Pac.)
Falkland Islands (Atl.)
Holy Roman Empire (Eur.)
Northern Nigeria (Af.)
Northern Ireland (Eur.)
Orange Free State (Af.)
Southern Nigeria (Af.)
South-West Africa (Af.)

16 AND OVER

Cape Verde Islands (Af.)
(16)
Congolese Republic (Af.)
(17)
Dominican Republic (W.I.)
(17)
Equatorial Guinea (Af.) (16)
Malagasy Republic (Af.)
(16)
São Tomé and Principé (Af.)
(18)
United Arab Emirates
(Asia) (18)
United Arab Republic (Af.,
Asia) (18)
Vatican City State (Eur.)
(16)

Geographical terms

3	cape	lock	wadi
	city	marl	weir
ait	comb	mead	west
alp	cove	mere	wind
bay	crag	mesa	wold
ben	croy	moor	wood
bog	dale	mull	wynd
cay	dell	naze	zone
col	dene	ness	
cwm	dike	pass	**5**
dam	doab	peak	
fen	dune	pole	abyss
lea	east	pond	alley
map	eyot	port	atlas
sea	ford	race	atoll
tor	glen	reef	bayou
voe	gulf	rill	bight
	hill	road	brook
4	holm	rock	canal
	holt	sike	chart
aber	inch	spit	chasm
bank	isle	sudd	chine
beck	lake	syke	cliff
berg	land	tarn	clime
bill	lane	town	coast
burn	loam	tump	combe
	loch	vale	

creek
crest
croft
delta
donga
downs
drift
duchy
fault
field
fiord
fjord
firth
fleet
ghaut
glade
globe
gorge
grove
haven
heath
hithe
hurst
hythe
inlet
islet
karoo
kloof
kopje
knoll
lande
llano
loess
lough
marsh
mound
mount
mouth
north
oasis
ocean
plain
point
polar
poles
reach
ridge
river
sands
scarp
shelf
shire
shoal
shore
slade
sound
south
state
swale
swamp
swang
sward
weald

6

alpine
arctic
boreal
canton
canyon
circar
clough
colony
colure

common
county
cranny
crater
defile
desert
dingle
divide
domain
empery
empire
eyalet
forest
geyser
glacis
hamlet
harbor
inland
inning
island
isobar
jungle
lagoon
maidan
meadow
morass
nullah
orient
pampas
parish
polder
rapids
ravine
region
riding
rillet
runlet
runnel
seaway
sierra
skerry
spinny
steppe
strait
strath
stream
street
suburb
summit
talook
tropic
tundra
upland
valley
warren

7

airport
austral
bogland
channel
clachan
commune
compass
contour
country
cutting
deltaic
drought
eastern
enclave
eparchy
equator
estuary

euripus
exclave
georama
glacier
habitat
harbour
highway
hillock
hilltop
hommock
hornito
hummock
hundred
iceberg
ice-floe
insular
isthmus
kingdom
lakelet
lowland
midland
new town
oceanic
plateau
polders
prairie
rivulet
rosland
satrapy
savanna
seaport
seaside
spurway
straits
thicket
torrent
tropics
village
volcano
western

8

affluent
alluvial
alluvium
altitude
brooklet
cantonal
cataract
crevasse
currents
district
dominion
downland
easterly
eastward
eminence
eminency
environs
foreland
frontier
headland
highland
high road
hillside
home-park
interior
isthmian
landmark
latitude
littoral
lowlands
mainland
midlands

moorland
mountain
neap-tide
northern
occident
oriental
post-town
province
quagmire
republic
salt lake
seaboard
seacoast
seashore
sheading
snow-line
southern
sub-polar
toparchy
township
tropical
volcanic
westerly
westward
wild land
woodland

9

antarctic
antipodal
antipodes
backwater
backwoods
cadastral
capricorn
catchment
cisalpine
coastline
continent
coral reef
fleet-dike
foothills
heathland
highlands
landslide
longitude
marshland
monticule
north-east
northerly
northward
north-west
peninsula
precipice
rockbound
salt-marsh
sandbanks
shore-line
south-east
southerly
southmost
southward
south-west
stewartry
streamlet
sub-alpine
tableland
territory
tetrarchy
trade wind
tributary
wapentake
waterfall
watershed

waterside
westwards

10

co-latitude
county town
equatorial
escarpment
fluviatile
frigid zone
garden city
geographer
Gulf Stream
hemisphere
interfluve
land-locked
margravate
market town
meridional
metropolis
mountainet
no-man's-land
occidental
palatinate
peninsular
plantation
polar-angle
population
presidency

projection
promontory
quicksands
sandy beach
south downs
spring tide
table-shore
tidal creek
torrid zone
water table
wilderness

11

archipelago
bergschrund
circumpolar
cisatlantic
continental
conurbation
coral island
countryside
equinoctial
morningland
mountainous
northwardly
polar circle
polar region
river course
septentrion
subtropical

territorial
tetrarchate
tidal waters
transalpine
transmarine
trout stream
ultramarine
watercourse

12

equatorially
landgraviate
magnetic pole
northeastern
northwestern
principality
protectorate
southeastern
southernmost
southwestern
stratosphere
ultramontane
virgin forest

13

deltafication
extratropical
intertropical

magnetic north
Mediterranean
mother country
neighbourhood
northeasterly
northeastward
northwesterly
northwestward
polar distance
septentrional
southeasterly
southeastward
southwesterly
southwestward
temperate zone
transatlantic
virgin country
watering place

14 AND 15

acclimatization (15)
circummeridian (14)
circumnavigate (14)
irrigation canal (15)
magnetic equator (15)
Mercator's chart (14)
north frigid zone (15)
south frigid zone (15)
tropic of cancer (14)

Islands

Arch. = Archipelago   I. = Island.   Is. = Islands.   (v.) = volcanic.

2 – 4

Adi (Pac.)
Amoy (China)
Aran (Ire.)
Arru Is. (Indo.)
Bali (Indo.)
Bay Is. (C. Am.)
Bere (Ire.)
Bua (Adr.)
Buru (Indo.)
Bute (Scot.)
Ceos (Gr.)
Coll (Scot.)
Cook Is. (Pac.)
Cuba (W.I.)
Dago (Fin.)
Dogs, I. of (Eng.)
Eigg (Scot.)
Elba (Med.)
Ewe (Scot.)
Farn Is. (Eng.)
Faro (Balt.)
Fiji Is. (Pac.)
Fohr (Ger.)
Gozo (Med.)
Guam (Pac.)
Hall Is. (Pac.)
Herm (Ch. Is.)
High I. (Ire.)
Holy I. (Scot.)
Hoy (Scot.)
Idra (Gr.)
Iona (Scot.)
Java (Indo.)
Jura (Scot.)

Kei Is. (Indo.)
Long I. (U.S.A.)
Low Arch. (Pac.)
Man, I. of (Eng.)
May, I. of (Scot.)
Milo (Gr.)
Moen (Den.)
Muck (Scot.)
Mull, I. of (Scot.)
Oahu (Pac.)
Paxo (Gr.)
Rat Is. (Pac.)
Ré (Fr.)
Rum (Scot.)
Saba (W.I.)
Sark (Ch. Is.)
Scio (Gr.)
Skye (Scot.)
Sulu Is. (Indo.)
Sylt (Ger.)
Syra (Gr.)
Tory (Ire.)
Ulva (Scot.)
Unst (Scot.)
Uist (Scot.)
Yap (Pac.)
Yell (Scot.)
Yezo (Jap.)
Zea (Gr.)
Zebu (Indo.)

5

Abaco (W.I.)
Aland Is. (Balt.)

Albay (Indo.)
Arran (Scot.)
Banca (Malay)
Banda (Indo.)
Banks (S. Pac.)
Barra (Heb.)
Bonin Is. (Pac.)
Caldy (Wales)
Canna (Scot.)
Capri (It.)
Ceram (Indo.)
Cheja (Korea)
Chios (Gr.)
Clare (Ire.)
Clear (Ire.)
Cocos Is. (Ind.)
Corfu (Gr.)
Corvo (Atl.)
Crete (Med.)
Dabaz (Scot.)
Delos (Gr.)
Disco (Arc.)
Disko (Arc.)
Eagle I. (Ire.)
Ellis (U.S.A.)
Farne Is. (Eng.)
Fayal (Atl.)
Ferro (Atl.)
Foula (Scot.)
Funen (Den.)
Goree (Atl.)
Gozzo (Med.)
Haiti (W.I.)
Hart's I. (U.S.A.)
Hatia (Ind.)
Hondo (Jap.)

Hydra (Gr.)
Ibiza (Med.)
Inyak (S.A.)
Islay (Scot.)
Ivica (Med.)
Lewis (Scot.)
Leyte (Philip.)
Lissa (Adr.)
Lobos Is. (S. Am.)
Lundy I. (Eng.)
Luzon (Philip.)
Malta (Med.)
Matsu (China)
Melos (Gr.)
Milos (Gr.)
Nauru (Pac.)
Naxos (Gr.)
Nevis (W.I.)
Oesel (Balt.)
Ormuz (Iran)
Papua (E.I.)
Paros (Gr.)
Parry Is. (Arc.)
Pearl Is. (Pac.)
Pelew Is. (E.I.)
Pelew Is. (Pac.)
Pemba (Af.)
Perim (Af.)
Pines, I. of (Pac. and W.I.)
Pinos (S. Am.)
Rhode I. (U.S.A.)
Rugen (Ger.)
Sable I. (Can.)
Samoa (Pac.)
Samos (Gr.)
Skyro (Gr.)

Spice Is. (Indo.)
Sunda Is. (Indo.)
Texel (Neth.)
Timor (Malay)
Tiree (Scot.)
Tonga (Pac.)
Turk's I. (W.I.)
Voorn (Neth.)
Wight, I. of (Eng.)
Zante (Gr.)

6

Achill (Ire.)
Aegina (Gr.)
Albany (Austral.)
Anamba Is. (Indo.)
Andros (Gr.)
Azores (Atl.)
Baffin (Can.)
Bahama Is. (W.I.)
Banana Is. (Atl.)
Bissao (Atl.)
Borkum (Ger.)
Borneo (Indo.)
Bounty Is. (N.Z.)
Brazza (Adr.)
Burray (Scot.)
Caicos Is. (W.I.)
Calamo (Gr.)
Candia (Med.)
Canary Is. (Atl.)
Cayman Is. (W.I.)
Cerigo (Med.)
Cherso (It.)
Chiloe (S. Am.)
Chusan (China)
Comoro Is. (Af.)
Crozet Is. (Ind.)
Cyprus (Med.)
Dursey (Ire.)
Easter I. (Pac.)
Ellice Is. (Pac.)
Euboea (Aeg.)
Faeroes (Atl.)
Flores (Atl.)
Flores (Indo.)
Gilolo (Indo.)
Gomera (Can.)
Hainan (China)
Harris (Scot.)
Hawaii (Pac.)
Honshu (Jap.)
Imbros (Aeg.)
Inagua (W.I.)
Ionian Is. (Med.)
Ischia (It.)
Ithaca (Med.)
Iturup (Jap.)
Jaluit (Pac.)
Jersey (Ch. Is.)
Jethou (Ch. Is.)
Kishni (Iran)
Kodiak (Pac.)
Kurile Is. (Pac.)
Kyushu (Jap.)
Labuan (Malay.)
Lambay (Ire.)
Lemnos (Aeg.)
Lerins Is. (Fr.)
Lesbos (Aeg.)
Lesina (Adr.)
Limmos (Aeg.)
Lipari Is. (Med.)
Lombok (Malay)

Marajo (S. Am.)
Marken (Neth.)
Negros (Indo.)
Oleron (Fr.)
Orkney Is. (Scot.)
Patmos (Med.)
Penang (Malay)
Philae (Nile)
Pomona (Scot.)
Puffin I. (Wales)
Quemoy (China)
Rhodes (Med.)
Robben (S. A.)
Rottum (Neth.)
St. John (W.I.)
St. Paul (Ind.)
Samsoe (Den.)
Sangir Is. (Indo.)
Savage I. (Pac.)
Scarba (Scot.)
Scilly Is. (Eng.)
Sicily (Med.)
Staffa (Scot.)
Staten I. (U.S.A.)
Stroma (Scot.)
Tahiti (Pac.)
Taiwan (China)
Thanet, I. of (Eng.)
Tholen (Neth.)
Tobago (W.I.)
Trömso (Nor.)
Tubugi Is. (Pac.)
Usedom (Ger.)
Ushant (Fr.)
Vaigen (Indo.)
Virgin Is. (W.I.)

7

Aegades Is. (Med.)
Aeolian Is. (v.) (Med.)
Amboina (Indo.)
Ameland (Neth.)
Andaman Is. (Ind.)
Antigua (W.I.)
Bahamas (W.I.)
Bahrain Is. (Arab.)
Balleny Is. (Antarc.)
Behring Is. (Pac.)
Bermuda (Atl.)
Bernera (Scot.)
Bourbon (Ind.)
Cabrera (Med.)
Capraja (Med.)
Caprera (Med.)
Celebes (Indo.)
Channel Is. (Eng.)
Chatham Is. (Pac.)
Chincha Is. (S. Am.)
Corisco (Af.)
Corsica (Med.)
Cumbrae (Scot.)
Curaçao (W.I.)
Curzola (Adr.)
Dampier Is. (Austral.)
Dinding Is. (Malay.)
Diomede Is. (Arc.)
Domingo (W.I.)
Falster (Balt.)
Fanning (Pac.)
Fehmeru (Balt.)
Flannan Is. (Scot.)
Formosa (China)
Frisian Is. (Neth.)
Gambier Is. (Pac.)

Gilbert Is. (Pac.)
Gotland (Balt.)
Grenada (W.I.)
Hayling I. (Eng.)
Iceland (v.) (Atl.)
Ichaboe (Af.)
Ireland
Jamaica (W.I.)
Johanna (Af.)
Kamaran (Red S.)
Kandava (Pac.)
Keeling Is. (Ind.)
Kolonev (Rus.)
Laaland (Den.)
Leeward Is. (W.I.)
Liakhov Is. (Arc.)
Lofoten Is. (Nor.)
Loo Choo Is. (China)
Loyalty Is. (Pac.)
Madeira (Atl.)
Mageroe (Arc.)
Majorca (Med.)
Maldive Is. (Ind.)
Massowa (Red S.)
Mayotte (Af.)
Minicoy (Ind.)
Minorca (Sp.)
Molokai (Pac.)
Molucca Is. (Indo.)
Mombasa (Af.)
Mykonos (Gr.)
Nicobar Is. (Ind.)
Norfolk I. (Austral.)
Nossi Be (v.) (Af.)
Oceania (Pac.)
Orkneys (Scot.)
Phoenix Is. (Pac.)
Portsea I. (Eng.)
Princes Is. (Turk.)
Purbeck, I. of (Eng.)
Rathlin (N.I.)
Reunion (Ind.)
Roanoke (U.S.A.)
Rockall (Atl.)
Rotumah (Pac.)
St. Agnes (Eng.)
St. Kilda (Scot.)
St. Kitts (Pac.)
St. Lucia (W.I.)
St. Marie (Af.)
Salamis (Gr.)
São Tomé (Af.)
Sheppey, I. of (Eng.)
Sherbro (Af.)
Shikoka (Jap.)
Society Is. (Pac.)
Socotra (Ind.)
Solomon Is. (Pac.)
Stewart I. (N.Z.)
Sumatra (Indo.)
Sumbawa (Indo.)
Tenedos (Med.)
Ternate (Indo.)
Tortola (W.I.)
Tortuga (W.I.)
Tuamotu (Pac.)
Watling I. (W.I.)
Whalsay (Scot.)

8

Alderney (Ch. Is.)
Aleutian Is. (Pac.)
Amirante Is. (Ind.)
Andamans (Ind.)

Anglesey (Wales)
Antilles Is. (W.I.)
Aucklands Is. (N.Z.)
Balearic Is. (Med.)
Barbados (Is.) (W.I.)
Bermudas (Is.) (Atl.)
Berneray (Scot.)
Billiton (Indo.)
Bismark Arch. (Pac.)
Bissagos Is. (Af.)
Bornholm (Balt.)
Campbell (N.Z.)
Canaries (Atl.)
Caribbee Is. (W.I.)
Caroline Is. (Pac.)
Colonsay (Scot.)
Copeland Is. (Ire.)
Cyclades Is. (Gr.)
Desertas (Atl.)
Desirade (W.I.)
Dominica (W.I.)
Fair Isle (Scot.)
Falkland Is. (Atl.)
Flinders (Austral.)
Friendly Is. (Pac.)
Furneaux Is. (Austral.)
Guernsey (Ch. Is.)
Hebrides (Scot.)
Hokkaido (Jap.)
Hong Kong (China)
Inchcolm (Scot.)
Jan Mayen (Arc.)
Kangaroo Is. (Austral.)
Kermadec Is. (Pac.)
Krakatoa (v.) (Indo.)
Ladrones (Pac.)
Leucadia (Med.)
Lord Howe Is. (Austral.)
Magdalen Is. (Can.)
Malicolo (Pac.)
Mallorca (Med.)
Manihiki Is. (Pac.)
Marianne Is. (Pac.)
Marshall Is. (Pac.)
Melville (Am. and Austral.)
Mindanao (Philip.)
Miquelon (Can.)
Mitylene (Gr.)
Moluccas (Indo.)
Otaheite (Pac.)
Pitcairn Is. (Pac.)
Portland, I. of (Eng.)
Pribilof Is. (Pac.)
Pribylov Is. (Pac.)
Quelpart (Korea)
Rothesay (Scot.)
St. Helena (Atl.)
St. Martin (W.I.)
St. Thomas (Af. and W.I.)
Sakhalin (U.S.S.R.)
Salsette (Ind.)
Sandwich Is. (Pac.)
Scillies (Eng.)
Sri Lanka (Asia)
Shetland Is. (Scot.)
Starbuck (Pac.)
Tasmania (Austral.)
Thousand Is. (N. Am.)
Thursday I. (Austral.)
Tortugas Is. (U.S.A.)
Trinidad (W.I.)
Unalaska (U.S.A.)
Valentia (Ire.)
Victoria (Can.)
Viti-Levu (Fiji)
Vlieland (Neth.)

Windward Is. (W.I.)
Zanzibar (Af.)

9

Admiralty Is. (Pac.)
Anticosti (Can.)
Arranmore (Ire.)
Ascension (Atl.)
Belle Isle (Fr.)
Beverland (Neth.)
Buccaneer Arch. (Ind.)
Cape Verde Is. (Atl.)
Cerigotto (Med.)
Christmas I. (Pac. and Ind.)
Dordrecht (Neth.)
Elephanta (Ind.)
Eleuthera (W.I.)
Ellesmere (N. Am.)
Erromanga (Scot.)
Falklands (Atl.)
Galapagos Is. (v.) (Pac.)
Greenland (Arc.)
Halmahera (Indo.)
Inchkeith (Scot.)
Inishturk (Ire.)
Isle of Man (Eng.)
Isle of May (Scot.)
Lampedusa (Med.)
Langeland (Den.)
Louisiade Arch (E.I.)
Manhattan (U.S.A.)
Margarita (W.I.)
Marquesas Is. (Pac.)
Mauritius (Ind.)
Melanesia (Pac.)
Nantucket (U.S.A.)
Negropont (Gr.)
New Guinea (E.I.)
Norderney (Ger.)
Polynesia (Pac.)
Porto Rico (W.I.)
Raratonga (Pac.)
Rodrigues (Ind.)
Saghalien (U.S.S.R.)
Saint John (W.I.)
St. Michael (Atl.)
St. Nicolas (Atl.)
Saint Paul (Ind.)
St. Vincent (W.I.)
Santa Cruz (W.I.)
Santorini (v) (Gr.)
Sardinia (Med.)
Scarpanto (Med.)
Shetlands (Scot.)
Singapore (Asia)
Stromboli (v.) (Med.)
Teneriffe (Atl.)
Timor Laut Is. (Pac.)
Vancouver (Can.)
Vanua Levu (Fiji)
Walcheren (Neth.)
Wellesley Is. (Austral.)

10

Ailsa Craig (Scot.)
Bay Islands (C. Am.)
Calamianes (Indo.)
Cape Barren I. (Austral.)
Cape Breton I. (Can.)
Cephalonia (Gr.)
Dirk Hartog (Austral.)
Dodecanese (Med.)

Fernando Po (Af.)
Formentera (Med.)
Fortune Bay I. (Can.)
Friendlies (Pac.)
Grenadines (W.I.)
Guadeloupe (W.I.)
Heligoland (N. Sea)
Holy Island (Scot.)
Inchgarvie (Scot.)
Inishshark (Ire.)
Isle of Dogs (Eng.)
Isle of Skye (Scot.)
Isle of Mull (Scot.)
Kuria Muria Is. (Arab.)
Laccadives (Arab.)
Long Island (U.S.A.)
Madagascar (Af.)
Manitoulin Is. (Pac.)
Martinique (W.I.)
Micronesia (Pac.)
Montserrat (W.I.)
Navigators' I. (Pac.)
New Britain (Pac.)
New Siberia (Arc.)
New Zealand (Pac.)
North Devon (Arc.)
Nova Zembla (Arc.)
Philippine Is. (Asia)
Puerto Rico (W.I.)
Rat Islands (Pac.)
Ronaldshay (Scot.)
Saint Agnes (Eng.)
Saint Kilda (Scot.)
Saint Kitts (W.I.)
Saint Lucia (W.I.)
Saint Marie (Af.)
Sandlewood I. (Malay.)
Seychelles (Ind.)
Skerryvore (Scot.)
West Indies (Atl.)

11

Cook Islands (Pac.)
Eagle Island (Ire.)
Grand Canary (Atl.)
Guadalcanal (Pac.)
Hall Islands (Pac.)
Hart's Island (U.S.A.)
Isle of Pines (Pac. and W.I.)
Isle of Wight (Eng.)
Isola Grossa (Adr.)
Lindisfarne (Scot.)
Lundy Island (Eng.)
Mascarenene Is. (Ind.)
Monte Cristo (It.)
New Hebrides (Pac.)
North Island (N.Z.)
Pantellaria (Med.)
Philippines (Asia)
Rhode Island (U.S.A.)
Sable Island (Can.)
Saint Helena (Atl.)
Saint Martin (W.I.)
Saint Thomas (W.I.)
Scilly Isles (Eng.)
Southampton (Can.)
South Island (N.Z.)
Spitsbergen (Arc.)

12

Baffin Island (N. Am.)
Bougainville (Pac.)

British Isles
Easter Island (Pac.)
Great Britain (U.K.)
Great Cumbrae (Scot.)
Inaccessible I. (Atl.)
Isle of Thanet (Eng.)
Mariagalante (W.I.)
Melville Land (Arc.)
New Caledonia (Pac.)
Newfoundland (Can.)
Novaya Zemlya (Arc.)
Prince Albert (Can.)
Prince Edward I. (Can.)
Puffin Island (Wales)
Saint Michael (Atl.)
Saint Nicolas (Atl.)
Saint Vincent (W.I.)
Savage Island (Pac.)

South Georgia (Atl.)
Staten Island (U.S.A.)
Turks' Islands (W.I.)

13 AND OVER

D'Entrecastreaux Is.
(Austral.) (15)
Isle of Portland (Eng.) (14)
Isle of Purbeck (Eng.) (13)
Isle of Sheppey (Eng.) (13)
Juan Fernandez (Pac.) (13)
Kerguelen Land (Pac.) (13)
Little Cumbrae (Scot.) (13)
Martha's Vineyard (U.S.A.)
(15)

Norfolk Island (Pac.) (13)
North Somerset (Arc.) (14)
Prince of Wales I. (Malay.)
(13)
Queen Charlotte Is. (Can.)
(14)
St. Bartholomew (W.I.) (13)
St. Christopher (W.I.) (13)
South Shetlands (Atl.) (14)
Stewart Island (N.Z.) (13)
Thursday Island (Austral.)
(14)
Tierra del Fuego (Chile) (14)
Tristan da Cunha (Atl.) (14)
Watling Island (Atl.) (13)
West Spitsbergen (Arc.) (15)

Lakes, inland lochs, etc.

3 AND 4

Aral (U.S.S.R.)
Ard (Scot.)
Awe (Scot.)
Bala (Wales)
Bay (Phil.)
Bear (U.S.A.)
Biwa (Jap.)
Chad (Af.)
Como (It.)
Derg (Ire.)
Dore (Can.)
Earn (Scot.)
Eil (Scot.)
Erie (Can and U.S.A.)
Erne (N.I.)
Ewe (Scot.)
Eyre (Austral.)
Ha Ha (Can.)
Iseo (It.)
Key (Ire.)
Kivu (Af.)
Mead (U.S.A.)
Ness (Scot.)
Oahu (N.Z.)
Ree (Ire.)
Ryan (Scot.)
Sego (U.S.S.R.)
Shin (Scot.)
Tana (Eth.)
Tay (Scot.)
Thun (Swit.)
Utah (U.S.A.)
Van (Turk.)
Voil (Scot.)
Zug (Swit.)

5

Abaya (Eth.)
Allen (Ire.)
Baker (Can.)
Camm (Can.)
Elton (U.S.S.R.)
Enara (Fin.)
Etive (Scot.)
Frome (Austral.)
Garda (It.)
Garry (Can.)
Ghana (Can.)

Hamun (Afghan.)
Honey (U.S.A.)
Huron (Can. and U.S.A.)
Ilmen (U.S.S.R.)
Kossu (Af.)
Leven (Scot.)
Lochy (Scot.)
Loyal (Scot.)
Malar (Swed.)
Maree (Scot.)
Minto (Can.)
Mjøsa (Nor.)
Moero (Af.)
Morar (Scot.)
Mweru (Af.)
Neagh (N.I.)
Moore (Austral.)
Nevis (Scot.)
Nyasa (Af.)
Onega (U.S.S.R.)
Payne (Can.)
Rainy (Can.)
Shiel (Scot.)
Talka (Can.)
Taupo (N.Z.)
Tsano (Eth.)
Tumba (Af.)
Urmia (Iran)
Volta (Ghana)
Wener (Swed.)
Yssel (Neth.)

6

Albert (Af.)
Arkaig (Scot.)
Assynt (Scot.)
Austin (Austral.)
Baikal (Sib.)
Buloke (Austral.)
Chilka (Ind.)
Edward (Af.)
Ennell (Ire.)
Geneva (Swit.)
George (Af. and Austral.)
Indian (U.S.A.)
Itasca (U.S.A.)
Kariba (Af.)
Khanka (Asia)
Ladoga (U.S.S.R.)

Lomond (Scot.)
Lugano (Swit.)
Mahood (Can.)
Malawi (Af.)
Nasser (Egypt)
Oneida (U.S.A.)
Peipus (U.S.S.R.)
Placid (U.S.A.)
Quoich (Scot.)
Rideau (Can.)
Rudolf (Af.)
St. John (Can.)
Shasta (U.S.A.)
Shirwa (Af.)
Simcoe (Can.)
Stuart (Can.)
Te Anau (N.Z.)
Tuz Gol (Turk.)
Vanern (Swed.)
Viedma (S. Am.)
Vyrnwy (Wales)
Wanaka (N.Z.)
Wenham (U.S.A.)
Wetter (Swed.)
Zürich (Swit.)

7

Abitibi (Can.)
Balaton (Hung.)
Balkash (Asia)
Benmore (N.Z.)
Blanche (Austral.)
Caillou (U.S.A.)
Caspian (Asia)
Chapala (Mex.)
Dead Sea (Asia)
Etawney (Can.)
Fannich (Scot.)
Galilee (Asia)
Hirakud (Ind.)
Hjelmar (Swed.)
Idi Amin (Af.)
Katrine (Scot.)
Koko Nor (China)
Lachine (Can.)
Leopold (Af.)
Loch Eil (Scot.)
Loch Tay (Scot.)
Lucerne (Swit.)

Muskoka (Can.)
Nipigon (Can.)
Okhrida (Turk.)
Ontario (Can. and U.S.A.)
Perugia (It.)
Quesnal (Can.)
Rannoch (Scot.)
Rosseau (Can.)
Rybinsk (U.S.S.R.)
Seistan (Afghan.)
Sempach (Swit.)
Sheelin (Ire.)
Tarbert (Scot.)
Texcoco (Mex.)
Tezcuco (Mex.)
Torrens (Austral.)
Tyrrell (Austral.)

8

Akamyara (Af.)
Balkhash (Asia)
Bear Lake (U.S.A.)
Chowilla (Austral.)
Cooroong (Austral.)
Drummond (U.S.A.)
Gairdner (Austral.)
Grasmere (Eng.)
Hirfanli (Turk.)
Humboldt (Austral.)
Issyk-Kul (Asia)
Kakhovka (U.S.S.R.)
Kawarthi (Can.)
Kootenay (Can.)
La Crosse (U.S.A.)
Loch Ness (Scot.)
Loch Ryan (Scot.)
Luichart (Scot.)
Maggiore (It.)
Manipuri (N.Z.)
Manitoba (Can.)
Mareotis (Egypt)
Menteith (Scot.)
Menzaleh (Egypt)
Michigan (U.S.A.)

Reindeer (Can.)
Seaforth (Scot.)
Sese Soko (Af.)
Stefanie (Af.)
Superior (U.S.A.)
Tarawera (N.Z.)
Titicaca (Peru)
Tungting (China)
Victoria (Af.)
Wakatipu (N.Z.)
Winnipeg (Can.)
Xaltocan (Mex.)

9

Argentino (S. Am.)
Athabaska (Can.)
Bangweolo (Af.)
Champlain (N. Am.)
Constance (Swit.)
Ennerdale (Eng.)
Eucumbene (Austral.)
Great Bear (Can.)
Great Salt (U.S.A.)
Hindmarsh (Austral.)
Honey Lake (U.S.A.)
Killarney (Ire.)
Kuibyshev (U.S.S.R.)
Lochinvar (Scot.)
Loch Leven (Scot.)
Loch Maree (Scot.)
Loch Nevis (Scot.)
Maracaibo (Venez.)
Maravilla (S. Am.)
Neuchâtel (Swit.)
Nicaragua (Am.)
Nipissing (Can.)
Playgreen (Can.)
Tengri-Nor (Tibet)
Thirlmere (Eng.)
Trasimeno (It.)
Ullswater (Eng.)
Wastwater (Eng.)
Wollaston (Can.)
Yssel Lake (Neth.)

10

Brokopondo (S. Am.)
Great Slave (Can.)
Hawes Water (Eng.)
Ijsselmeer (Neth.)
Indian Lake (U.S.A.)
Lackawanna (U.S.A.)
Loch Lomond (Scot.)
Lough Neagh (N.I.)
Michikamau (Can.)
Mistassini (Can.)
Roguaguado (Boliv.)
Rotomahana (N.Z.)
Rydal Water (Eng.)
Serpentine (Eng.)
Tanganyika (Af.)
Windermere (Eng.)
Xochimilco (Mex.)

11 AND OVER

Albert Edward Nyanza (Af.)
  (18)
Albert Nyanza (Af.) (12)
Bitter Lakes (Egypt) (11)
Cabora Bassa (Af.) (11)
Coniston Water (Eng.) (13)
Derwentwater (Eng.) (12)
Diefenbaker (Can.) (11)
Grand Coulee (U.S.A.) (11)
Great Salt Lake (U.S.A.) (13)
Great Slave Lake (Can.) (14)
Lake of the Woods (Can. and
  U.S.A.) (14)
Lesser Slave Lake (Can.) (15)
Loch Katrine (Scot.) (11)
Loch Tarbert (Scot.) (11)
Pontchatrain (U.S.A.) (12)
The Cooroong (Austral.) (11)
Timiskaming (Can.) (11)
Victoria Nyanza (Af.) (14)
Virginia Water (Eng.) (13)
Winnipegosis (Can.) (12)
Yellowstone (U.S.A.) (11)

Mountains

H. = Hill. Hs. = Hills. M. = "Mountain," commonly used *after* name. Ms. = Mountains. Mt = "Mount," "Monte," or "Mont," commonly used *before* name. (v.) = volcanic.

2–4

Abu, Mt. (Ind.)
Aboo, Mt. (Ind.)
Alps Ms. (Eur.)
Blue Ms. (Austral. and
  U.S.A.)
Caha Ms. (Ire.)
Cook M. (N.Z.)
Ebal, Mt. (Jord.)
Elk Ms. (U.S.A.)
Etna, Mt. (v.) (Sic.)
Fuji, Mt. (v.) (Jap.)
Harz Ms. (Ger.)
Ida, Mt. (Crete)
Iron M. (U.S.A.)
Jura Ms. (Eur.)
K2 (Him.)
Kea (v.) (Hawaii)
Kibo, Mt. (Tanz.)
Kong Ms. (Af.)

Naga Hs. (Ind.)
Qara Ms. (Arab.)
Rigi, Mt. (Swit.)
Rosa, Mt. (Alps)
Ural Ms. (U.S.S.R.)
Zug M. (Ger.)

5

Adams M. (U.S.A.)
Altai Ms. (Him.)
Andes Ms. (S. Am.)
Athos, Mt. (Gr.)
Atlas Ms. (Af.)
Baker (v.) (U.S.A.)
Barry Ms. (Austral.)
Black Ms. (U.S.A. and
  Wales)
Blanc, Mt. (Alps)
Brown M. (N. Am.)

Cenis, Mt. (Alps)
Eiger (Swit.)
Djaja, Mt. (Indo.)
Downs, The (Hs.) (Eng.)
Ghats, The (Ms.) (Ind.)
Green Ms. (U.S.A.)
Hecla (v.) (Iceland)
Kamet, Mt. (Him.)
Kenia, Mt. (E. Af.)
Kenya, Mt. (E. Af.)
Logan, Mt. (Yukon)
Maipu (v.) (Arg.)
Mönch, (Swit.)
Ochil Hs. (Scot.)
Ophir, M. (Malay.)
Overo (v.) (S. Am.)
Pelée (v.) (W.I.)
Rocky Ms. (N. Am.)
Sinai, Mt. (Arab.)
Table M. (S.A.)
Tabor, Mt. (Isr.)

Vinta, Mt. (U.S.A.)
White, Ms. (U.S.A.)
Wolds, The (Hs.) (Eng.)

6

Ararat, Mt. (Turk.)
Averno, Mt. (v.) (It.)
Balkan Ms. (Eur.)
Beluha (Him.)
Bogong, Mt. (Austral.)
Carmel, Mt. (Isr.)
Darwin, Mt. (S. Am.)
Elbruz (U.S.S.R.)
Erebus (v.) (Antarc.)
Galtee Ms. (Ire.)
Hayden, Mt. (U.S.A.)
Hermon, Mt. (Asia)
Hooker, M. (Can.)
Hoosac Ms. (U.S.A.)
Juncal (v.) (S. Am.)
Kazbek, Mt. (U.S.S.R.)
Lennox Hs. (Scot.)
Lhotse, Mt. (Him.)
Makalu, Mt. (Him.)
Masaya (v.) (C. Am.)
Mendip Hs. (Eng.)
Mourne Ms. (Ire.)
Nelson, Mt. (Tas.)
Nuptse, Mt. (Him.)
Olives, Mt. of (Isr.)
Pamirs (Asia)
Pindus Ms. (Gr.)
Robson (Can.)
Sahama (v.) (S. Am.)
Sangay (v.) (S. Am.)
Scafel, Mt. (Eng.)
Sidlaw Hs. (Scot.)
Sorata (2 Ms.) (S. Am.)
Taunus Ms. (Ger.)
Terror (v.) (Antarc.)
Tolima (v.) (S. Am.)
Vosges Ms. (Fr.)

7

Balkans Ms. (Eur.)
Ben More (Scot.)
Bernima, Mt. (Alps)
Big Horn Ms. (U.S.A.)
Bow Fell Mt. (Eng.)
Brocken, Mt. (Ger.)
Cascade Ms. (N. Am.)
Cazambe, Mt. (S. Am.)
Cheviot Hs. (Eng.)
Dapsang, Mt. (Him.)
Darling, Mt. (Austral.)
El Potra, Mt. (S. Am.)
Everest, Mt. (Him.)
Hoffman, Mt. (U.S.A.)
Illampa, Mt. (Boliv.)
Jaintia Ms. (Assam)
Jonsong, Mt. (Him.)
Jorullo (v.) (Mex.)
Kilauea (v.) (Pac.)
La Pelée (v.) (W.I.)
Lebanon, Mt. (Leb.)
Lookout M. (U.S.A.)
Malvern Hs. (Eng.)
Mamturk Ms. (Ire.)
Mendips Hs. (Eng.)
Milanji, Mt. (Af.)
Miltsin, Mt. (Af.)
M'Kinley (Alaska)

Nilgiri Hs. (Ind.)
Pennine Ms. (Eng.)
Peteroa (v.) (S. Am.)
Pilatus, Mt. (Swit.)
Orizaba (Mex.)
Quizapu (v.) (S. Am.)
Rainier, Mt. (U.S.A.)
Rhodope, Mt. (Turk.)
Rockies Ms. (N. Am.)
Roraima, Mt. (S. Am.)
Ruahine, Mt. (N.Z.)
San José (v.) (S. Am.)
San Juan Ms. (U.S.A.)
Simplon, Mt. (Swit.)
Siwalik Hs. (Ind.)
Skiddaw, Mt. (Eng.)
Snowdon, Mt. (Wales)
St. Elias, Mt. (Can. and Gr.)
Sudetes Ms. (Eur.)
Tomboro (v.) (Jap.)
Vindhya Ms. (Ind.)
Vulcano (v.) (It.)
Wenchow, Mt. (China)
Whitney, Mt. (U.S.A.)

8

Anapurna (Him.)
Aravalli Ms. (Ind.)
Auvergne Ms. (Fr.)
Ben Nevis (Scot.)
Ben Venue (Scot.)
Ben Wyvis (Scot.)
Ben-y-Gloe (Scot.)
Catskill Ms. (U.S.S.A.)
Caucasus Ms. (Eur.)
Cheviots (Hs.) (Eng.)
Chiltern Hs. (Eng.)
Cotopaxi (v.) (Ecuad.)
Cotswold Hs. (Eng.)
Demavend, Mt. (Iran)
Edgehill (H.) (Eng.)
Estrelle, Mt. (Port.)
Flinders Ms. (Austral.)
Fujiyama (v.) (Jap.)
Goatfell, Mt. (Scot.)
Haramokh, Mt. (Him.)
Hualalai (v.) (Pac.)
Illimani, Mt. (Bol.)
Jungfrau, Mt. (Swit.)
Katahdin, Mt. (U.S.A.)
Kinabalu (v.) (Born.)
Koh-i-Baba (Afghan.)
Krakatoa (v.) (Indo.)
Kuenluiv Ms. (Asia)
McKinley, Mt. (Alaska)
Moorfoot Hs. (Scot.)
Mulhacén, Mt. (Sp.)
Nilgiris Hs. (Ind.)
Pennines (Hs.) (Eng.)
Pentland Hs. (Scot.)
Preseley Ms. (Wales)
Pyrenees Ms. (Eur.)
Quantock Hs. (Eng.)
Rajmahal Hs. (Ind.)
Rushmore, Mt. (U.S.A.)
Scawfell, Mt. (Eng.)
Snaefell, Mt. (I. of Man)
Sulaiman, Ms. (Ind.)
Tarawera, Mt. (N.Z.)
The Downs (Hs.) (Eng.)
The Ghats (Ms.) (Ind.)
The Wolds (Hs.) (Eng.)
Tien Shan Ms. (Asia)
Townsend, Mt. (Austral.)

Vesuvius (v.) (It.)
Wrangell, Mt. (Can.)
Yablonoi Ms. (Asia)

9

Aconcagua (v.) (Arg.)
Adam's Peak (Sri)
Allegheny Ms. (U.S.A.)
Annapurna (Him.)
Apennines (It.)
Ben Lawers (Scot.)
Ben Lomond (Scot.)
Black Dome Mt. (U.S.A.)
Blue Ridge Ms. (U.S.A.)
Breithorn (Alps)
Cairntoul (Scot.)
Carstensz (Indo.)
Chilterns (Hs.) (Eng.)
Chumalari, Mt. (Him.)
Communism (U.S.S.R.)
Cotswolds (Hs.) (Eng.)
Cuchullin Hs. (Skye)
Dardistan, Mt. (Ind.)
Faucilles Ms. (Fr.)
Grampians (Ms.) (Scot.)
Helvellyn, Mt. (Eng.)
Himalayas (Ms.) (Asia)
Hindu-Kush Ms. (Asia)
Itaculomi, Mt. (S. Am.)
Karakoram, Mt. (Asia)
Koseiusko, Mt. (Austral.)
Lafayette, Mt. (U.S.A.)
Las Yeguas (v.) (Chile)
Lenin Peak (U.S.S.R.)
Licancaur, Mt. (Chile)
Liverpool (Austral.)
Maladetta, Mt. (Pyr.)
Mont Blanc (Alps)
Mont Cenis (Alps)
Mont Perdu (Pyr.)
Monte Rosa (Alps)
Naga Hills (Ind.)
Parnassus, Mt. (Gr.)
Pic du Midi (Pyr.)
Pike's Peak (U.S.A.)
Rakaposhi (Him.)
Ruwenzori Ms. (Uganda and
  Zaïre)
Solfatara (v.) (It.)
St. Bernard (Pass) (Swit.)
St. Gothard, Mt. (Swit.)
Stromboli (v.) (Med.)
Thian-Shan Ms. (Asia)
Tongariro (v.) (N.Z.)
Tupungato (v.) (S. Am.)
Wind River Ms. (U.S.A.)

10

Adirondack Ms (U.S.A.)
Ben Macdhui (Scot.)
Cairngorms (Scot.)
Cantabrian Ms. (Sp.)
Carpathian Ms. (Eur.)
Cedar Berge, Mt. (S.A.)
Chimborazo (v.) (Ecuad.)
Chumallari, Mt. (Him.)
Dent du Midi (Swit.)
Dhaulagiri, Mt. (Him.)
Diablerets, Mt. (Swit.)
Erzgebirge (Ger.)
Graian Alps (Eur.)
Khyber Pass (Afghan., Pak.)

Koshtan Tau (U.S.S.R.)
Kuh-i-Taftan (v.) (Iran)
Kwathlamba, Mt. (S.A.)
Lammermuir Hs. (Scot.)
Laurentian Ms. (Can.)
Matterhorn, The (Alps)
Moel Fammau, Mt. (Wales)
Monte Corno (It.)
Nanga-Devi (Him.)
Ochil Hills (Scot.)
Pinlimmon, Mt. (Wales)
Saint Elias (Can. and Gr.)
Wellington, Mt. (Tas.)
Wetterhorn, The (Swit.)

11

Appalachian Ms. (U.S.A.)
Bernese Alps (Swit.)
Carpathians (Ms.) (Eur.)
Citlaltepec, Mt. (Mex.)
Descapezado (v.) (Chile)
Dinaric Alps (Eur.)
Drachenfels, Mt. (Ger.)
Drakensberg Ms. (S.A.)
Drakenstein, Mt. (S.A.)
Hochstetter, Mt. (N.Z.)
Kilimanjaro, Mt. (Tanz.)
La Sonfrière (v.) (W.I.)
Lennox Hills (Scot.)
Livingstone Ms. (Af.)

Mendip Hills (Eng.)
Nanga Parbat (Him.)
Ortler Spitz (Aust.)
Owen Stanley Ms. (Papua)
Pennine Alps (Eur.)
Schreckhorn (Swit.)
Sidlow Hills (Scot.)
Sierra Madre Ms. (Mex.)
Splugen Pass (Swit.)
Stelvio Pass (It.)
Swabian Alps (Ger.)
Vatnajökull (Iceland)

12

Bougainville, Mt. (Papua)
Cheviot Hills (Eng.)
Godwin Austen, Mt. (Him.)
Ingleborough, Mt. (Eng.)
Jaintia Hills (Ind.)
Kanchenjunga, Mt. (Him.)
Kinchinjunga, Mt. (Him.)
Llullaillaco (v.) Chile
Malvern Hills (Eng.)
Maritime Alps (Fr., It.)
Nilgiri Hills (Ind.)
Peak District (Eng.)
Popocatepetl (v.) (Mex.)
Roncesvalles (v.) (Pyr.)
Saint Gothard, Mt. (Swit.)
Schiehallion, Mt. (Scot.)

Sierra Morena, Mt. (Sp.)
Sierra Nevada Ms. (Sp.)
Siwalik Hills (Ind.)
Tinguiririca (v.) (Chile)
Zoutpansberg, Mt. (S.A.)

13 AND OVER

Black Dome Peak (U.S.A. (13)
Carrantuohill, Mt. (Ire.) (13)
Chiltern Hills (Eng.) (13)
Cotswold Hills (Eng.) (13)
Fichtelgebirge (Ger.) (14)
Finsteraahorn, Mt. (Swit.) (13)
Grossglockner, Mt. (Alps) (13)
Knockmealdown, Mt. (Ire.) (13)
Mont Aux Sources (Lesotho) (14)
Mount of Olives (Isr.) (13)
Pentland Hills (Scot.) (13)
Pidurutalagala (Sri) (14)
Riesengebirge Ms. (Eur.) (13)
Skaptarjökull (v.) Iceland (13)
Table Mountain (S.A.) (13)
Tabor Mountain (Isr.) (13)

Oceans and seas

3 AND 4

Aral S. (U.S.S.R.)
Azov, S. of (U.S.S.R.)
Dead S. (Jord., Isr.)
Java S. (Indo.)
Kara S. (U.S.S.R.)
Red S. (Egypt, Arab.)
Ross S. (Antarc.)
Sava S. (Indo.)
Sulu S. (Philip.)

5

Banda S. (Indo.)
Black S. (Eur., Turk.)
Ceram S. (Indo.)
China S. (China)
Coral S. (Indo.)
Irish S. (Brit. Isles)
Japan, S. of (Jap.)
Malay S. (Malay.)
North S. (Eur.)
Timor S. (Indo.)
White S. (U.S.S.R.)

6

Aegean S. (Gr., Turk.)
Arctic O.

Baltic S. (N. Eur.)
Bering S. (Pac.)
Flores S. (Indo.)
Gaelic S. (Brit. Isles)
Indian O.
Ionian S. (Gr.)
Laptev S. (U.S.S.R.)
Scotia S. (Antarc.)
Tasman S. (Austral.)
Yellow S. (China)

7

Andaman S. (Indo.)
Arabian S. (Ind.)
Arafura S. (Austral.)
Barents S. (U.S.S.R.)
Behring S. (Pac.)
Caspian S. (U.S.S.R., Iran)
Celebes S. (Indo.)
Marmora, S. of (Turk.)
Molucca S. (Indo.)
Okhotsk, S. of (U.S.S.R.)
Pacific O.
Weddell S. (Antarc.)

8

Adriatic S. (Med.)
Amundsen S. (Antarc.)

Atlantic O.
Beaufort S. (Can.)
Ligurian S. (It.)
Macassar S. (Indo.)
McKinley S. (Green.)
Sargasso S. (Atl.)

9

Antarctic O.
Caribbean S. (Am.)
East China S. (China)
Greenland S. (Green.)
Norwegian S. (Nor.)
Zuider Zee }
Zuyder Zee } (Neth.)

10 AND OVER

Bellingshausen S. (Antarc.) (13)
East Siberian S. (U.S.S.R.) (12)
King Haakon VIII S. (Antarc.) (14)
Mediterranean S. (Eur., Af.) (13)
South China S. (China) (10)
Tyrrhenian S. (W. Med. (10)

101

Ports

3 AND 4

Acre (Isr.)
Aden (P.D.R. Yemen)
Akko (Isr.)
Amoy (China)
Baku (U.S.S.R.)
Bar (Yug.)
Bari (It.)
Cebu (Philip.)
Cobh (Ire.)
Cork (Ire.)
Elat (Isr.)
Erie (U.S.A.)
Hull (Eng.)
Ilo (Peru)
Kiel (W. Ger.)
Kobe (Jap.)
Okha (U.S.S.R.)
Oran (Alg.)
Oslo (Nor.)
Para (Braz.)
Pula (Yug.)
Riga (U.S.S.R.)
Safi (Moroc.)
Suez (Egypt)
Tain (Scot.)
Tema (Ghana)
Wick (Scot.)

5

Akyab (Burma)
Arica (Chile)
Basra (Iraq)
Beira (Moz.)
Belem (Braz.)
Brest (Fr.)
Cadiz (Fr.)
Canea (Gr.)
Ceuta (Moroc.)
Colon (Panama)
Corfu (Gr.)
Dakar (Senegal)
Delft (Neth.)
Dover (Eng.)
Eilat (Isr.)
Emden (W. Ger.)
Gaeta (It.)
Galle (Sri.)
Genoa (It.)
Haifa (Isr.)
Havre (Le) (Fr.)
Izmir (Turk.)
Kerch (U.S.S.R.)
Kochi (Jap.)
Kotor (Yug.)
Lagos (Nig.)
Leith (Scot.)
Lulea (Swed.)
Malmö (Swed.)
Mocha (Yemen)
Osaka (Jap.)
Ostia (It.)
Palma (Sp.)
Palos (Sp.)
Pusan (S. Korea)
Rabat (Moroc.)
Reval (U.S.S.R.)
Scapa (Scot.)
Trani (It.)

Varna (Bulg.)
Wisby (Swed.)
Yalta (U.S.S.R.)
Ystad (Swed.)

6

Agadir (Moroc.)
Ahmedi (Yemen)
Ancona (It.)
Ashdod (Isr.)
Balboa (Panama)
Bastia (Cors.)
Beirut (Lebanon)
Bergen (Nor.)
Bilbao (Sp.)
Bombay (Ind.)
Bremen (W. Ger.)
Calais (Fr.)
Callao (Peru)
Cannes (Fr.)
Chalna (Pak.)
Chefoo (China)
Cochin (Ind.)
Danzig (Pol.)
Dieppe (Fr.)
Douala (Cameroun)
Dunbar (Scot.)
Dundee (Scot.)
Durban (S.A.)
F'derik (Mauritania)
Ferrol (Sp.)
Gdansk (Pol.)
Gdynia (Pol.)
Haldia (Ind.)
Hankow (China)
Hobart (Tas.)
Izmail (U.S.S.R.)
Jeddah (Saudi)
Kalmar (Swed.)
Kandla (Ind.)
Kuwait (Kuwait)
Larvik (Nor.)
Lisbon (Port.)
Lobito (Angola)
London (Eng.)
Madras (Ind.)
Malaga (Sp.)
Manila (Philip.)
Matadi (Zaïre)
Mtwara (Tanz.)
Naples (It.)
Narvik (Nor.)
Nelson (N.Z.)
Odense (Den.)
Odessa (U.S.S.R.)
Oporto (Port.)
Ostend (Belg.)
Padang (Indo.)
Patras (Gr.)
Penang (Malay.)
Ramsey (I. of Man)
Recife (Braz.)
Rhodes (Gr.)
Rijeka (Yug.)
Santos (Braz.)
Sittwe (Burma)
Skikda (Alg.)
Smyrna (Turk.)
Suakin (Sudan)
Swatow (China)

Sydney (Austral.)
Tainan (Taiwan)
Tetuán (Moroc.)
Toulon (Fr.)
Tromsó (Nor.)
Venice (It.)
Weihai (China)
Wismar (E. Ger.)

7

Aalborg (Den.)
Abidjan (Ivory Coast)
Ajaccio (Cors.)
Algiers (Alg.)
Antwerp (Belg.)
Bangkok (Thai.)
Belfast (N.I.)
Bushire (Iran)
Cardiff (Wales)
Cattaro (Yug.)
Cayenne (Fr. Guiana)
Chatham (Eng.)
Colombo (Sri)
Corunna (Sp.)
Cotonou (Benin)
Dampier (Austral.)
Detroit (U.S.A.)
Donegal (Ire.)
Dundalk (Ire.)
Dunkirk (Fr.)
Foochow (China)
Funchal (Sp.)
Geelong (Austral.)
Grimsby (Eng.)
Guaymas (Mex.)
Halifax (Can.)
Hamburg (W. Ger.)
Harwich (Eng.)
Hodeida (Yemen)
Horsens (Den.)
Houston (U.S.A.)
Jakarta (Indo.)
Karachi (Pak.)
Keelung (Taiwan)
Kitimat (Can.)
La Plata (Arg.)
Larnaca (Cyprus)
Leghorn (It.)
Le Havre (Fr.)
Marsala (It.)
Melilla (Moroc.)
Messina (It.)
Mogador (Moroc.)
Mombasa (Kenya)
New York (U.S.A.)
Norfolk (U.S.A.)
Okhotsk (U.S.S.R.)
Palermo (It.)
Piraeus (Gr.)
Rangoon (Burma)
Rostock (E. Ger.)
Salerno (It.)
San Juan (Puerto Rico)
Seattle (U.S.A.)
Stettin (Pol.)
Swansea (Wales)
Tallinn (U.S.S.R.)
Tangier (Moroc.)
Tilbury (Eng.)
Tobarao (Braz.)

Trapani (It.)
Trieste (It.)
Tripoli (Libya)
Yingkow (China)
Youghal (Ire.)

8

Abu Dhabi
Adelaide (Austral.)
Alicante (Sp.)
Arrecife (Sp.)
Auckland (N.Z.)
Benghazi (Libya)
Bordeaux (Fr.)
Boulogne (Fr.)
Brindisi (It.)
Brisbane (Austral.)
Budapest (Hung.)
Calcutta (Ind.)
Cape Town (S.A.)
Cocanada (Ind.)
Coquimbo (Chile)
Cuxhaven (W. Ger.)
Damietta (Egypt)
Djibouti (Djibouti)
Dunleary (Ire.)
Elsinore (Den.)
Europort (Neth.)
Falmouth (Eng.)
Flushing (Neth.)
Freetown (Sierra Leone)
Gisborne (N.Z.)
Göteborg (Swed.)
Greenock (Scot.)
Hakodate (Jap.)
Halmstad (Swed.)
Helsinki (Fin.)
Holyhead (Wales)
Honfleur (Fr.)
Hong Kong
Honolulu (Hawaii)
Istanbul (Turk.)
Kakinada (Ind.)
Kingston (Jam.)
La Guaira (Venez.)
La Coruña (Sp.)
Llanelli (Wales)
Macassar (Indo.)
Makassar (Indo.)
Matarini (Peru)
Montreal (Can.)
Moulmein (Burma)
Nagasaki (Jap.)
Nakhodka (U.S.S.R.)
Navarino (Gr.)
Newhaven (Eng.)
New Haven (U.S.A.)
Nyköping (Swed.)
Paradeep (Indo.)
Pechenga (U.S.S.R.)
Pembroke (Wales)
Penzance (Eng.)
Plymouth (Eng.)
Portland (Eng.)
Port Said (Egypt)
St. Helier (Ch. Is.)
Sandwich (Eng.)
Szczecin (Pol.)
Shanghai (China)
Taganrog (U.S.S.R.)

Takoradi (Ghana)
Tamatave (Malag. Rep.)
Tientsin (China)
Tiksi Bay (U.S.S.R.)
Vera Cruz (Mex.)
Weymouth (Eng.)
Yokohama (Jap.)

9

Algeciras (Sp.)
Amsterdam (Neth.)
Archangel (U.S.S.R.)
Ardrossan (Scot.)
Avonmouth (Eng.)
Baltimore (U.S.A.)
Barcelona (Sp.)
Cartagena (Sp. and
   Colombia)
Cherbourg (Fr.)
Churchill (Can.)
Cristobal (Panama)
Devonport (Eng.)
Dubrovnik (Yug.)
Esquimalt (Can.)
Essaouira (Moroc.)
Flensburg (W. Ger.)
Fos-sur-Mer (Fr.)
Fremantle (Austral.)
Galveston (U.S.A.)
Gibraltar (Med.)
Gravesend (Eng.)
Guayaquil (Equador)
Helsingör (Den.)
Hiroshima (Jap.)
Kagoshima (Jap.)
Kaohsiung (Taiwan)
King's Lynn (Eng.)
Kolobrzeg (Pol.)
Las Palmas (Sp.)
Leningrad (U.S.S.R.)
Liverpool (Eng.)
Lyttelton (N.Z.)
Mbuji-Mayi (Zaïre)
Melbourne (Austral.)
Mossel Bay (S.A.)
Nantucket (U.S.A.
Newcastle (Eng. and
   Austral.)
Owen Sound (Can.)
Port Arzew (Alg.)
Pensacola (U.S.A.)
Port Klang (Malay.)
Port Louis (Mauritius)
Portmadoc (Wales)
Port Mahon (Sp.)

Port Natal (S.A.)
Porto Novo (Benin)
Port Royal (Jam.)
Port Sudan (Sudan)
Rotterdam (Neth.)
Scapa Flow (Scot.)
Sheerness (Eng.)
Singapore
Stavangar (Nor.)
Stockholm (Swed.)
Stornaway (Scot.)
Trondheim (Nor.)
Vancouver (Can.)
Zeebrugge (Belg.)

10

Alexandria (Egypt)
Barnstaple (Eng.)
Bridgeport (U.S.A.)
Casablanca (Moroc.)
Charleston (U.S.A.)
Chittagong (Ind.)
Colchester (Eng.)
Constantsa (Rom.)
Copenhagen (Den.)
East London (S.A.)
Felixstowe (Eng.)
Folkestone (Eng.)
George Town (Malay.)
Gothenburg (Swed.)
Hammerfest (Nor.)
Hartlepool (Eng.)
Hermopolis (Gr.)
Jersey City (U.S.A.)
La Rochelle (Fr.)
Los Angeles (U.S.A.)
Marseilles (Fr.)
Montego Bay (Jam.)
Montevideo (Uruguay)
New Bedford (U.S.A.)
New Orleans (U.S.A.)
Nouadhibou (Mauretania)
Pernambuco (Braz.)
Perth Amboy (U.S.A.)
Port Arthur (China)
Portsmouth (Eng. and
   U.S.A.)
Rock Harbour (U.S.A.)
San Juan Bay (Peru)
Simonstown (S.A.)
Sunderland (Eng.)
Teignmouth (Eng.)
Travemünde (W. Ger.)
Vlissingen (Neth.)
Whitstable (Eng.)

11

Bremerhaven (W. Ger.)
Buenos Aires (Arg.)
Christiana (Nor.)
Cinque Ports (Eng.)
Dar es Salaam (Tanz.)
Dun Laoghaire (Ire.)
Grangemouth (Scot.)
Helsingborg (Swed.)
Hermoupolis (Gr.)
Masulipatam (Ind.)
Pearl Harbor (Hawaii)
Pondicherry (Ind.)
Port Glasgow (Scot.)
Port Jackson (Austral.)
Port Moresby (Papua)
Port of Spain (Trinidad)
Richard's Bay (S.A.)
Saint Helier (Ch. Is.)
St. Peter Port (Ch. Is.)
Shimonoseki (Jap.)
Southampton (Eng.)
Three Rivers (Can.)
Trincomalee (Ind.)
Vladivostok (U.S.S.R.)

12

Barranquilla (Colombia)
Buenaventura (Colombia)
Kotakinabalu (Malay.)
Masulipatnam (Ind.)
Mina al-Ahmadi (Kuwait)
Milford Haven (Wales)
North Shields (Eng.)
Port Adelaide (Austral.)
Port Harcourt (Nig.)
Port Sunlight (Eng.)
Puerto Hierro (Venez.)
Rio de Janeiro (Braz.)
San Francisco (U.S.A.)

13 AND 14

Christiansund (Nor.) (13)
Constantinople (Turk.) (14)
Frederikshavn (Den.) (13)
Middlesbrough (Eng.) (13)
Mina Hassan Tani (Moroc.) (14)
Petropavlovsk (U.S.S.R.) (13)
Port Elizabeth (S.A.) (13)
Puerto Cabello (Venez.) (13)
Santiago de Cuba (Cuba) (14)
Wilhelmshaven (W. Ger.) (13)

Provinces, cantons, districts, regions, dependent states, etc.

3 AND 4

Ain (Fr.)
Aube (Fr.)
Aude (Fr.)
Bari (It.)
Bern (Swit.)
Cher (Fr.)
Diu (Ind.)
Eure (Fr.)
Fars (Iran)

Gard (Fr.)
Gaza (Isr.)
Gers (Fr.)
Goa (Ind.)
Ica (Peru)
Iowa (U.S.A.)
Jaen (Sp.)
Jura (Fr.)
Kano (Nig.)
Kum (Iran)
Leon (Sp.)

Lima (Peru)
Lot (Fr.)
Lugo (Sp.)
Nord (Fr.)
Ohio (U.S.A.)
Oise (Fr.)
Orne (Fr.)
Oudh (Ind.)
Pale (The) (Ire.)
Para (Braz.)
Pegu (Burma)

Pisa (It.)
Rome (It.)
Saar (Ger.)
Sind (Pak.)
Sus (Moroc.)
Tarn (Fr.)
Uri (Swit.)
Utah (U.S.A.)
Var (Fr.)
Vaud (Swit.)
Zug (Swit.)

103

5

Achin (Indo.)
Adana (Turk.)
Aisne (Fr.)
Anjou (Fr.)
Assam (Ind.)
Baden (Ger.)
Bahia (Braz.)
Banat (Eur.)
Basel (Swit.)
Béarn (Fr.)
Beira (Port.)
Berne (Swit.)
Berry (Fr.)
Bihar (Ind.)
Cadiz (Sp.)
Ceara (Braz.)
Doubs (Fr.)
Drome (Fr.)
Eifel (Ger.)
Eupen (Belg.)
Fayum (Egypt)
Genoa (It.)
Goiás (Braz.)
Hamar (Nor.)
Hejaz (Saudi)
Herat (Afghan.)
Hesse (Ger.)
Honan (China)
Hopeh (China)
Hunan (China)
Hupeh (China)
Idaho (U.S.A.)
Indre (Fr.)
Isère (Fr.)
Judea (Asia)
Jujuy (Arg.)
Kansu (China)
Khiva (Asia)
Kirin (China)
Kwara (Nig.)
Lagos (Nig.)
La Paz (Boliv.)
Lecce (It.)
Liège (Belg.)
Loire (Fr.)
Lucca (It.)
Maine (U.S.A. and Fr.)
Marne (Fr.)
Meuse (Fr.)
Milan (It.)
Morea (Gr.)
Namur (Belg.)
Nubia (Sudan)
Ojaca (Mex.)
Oruro (Boliv.)
Otago (N.Z.)
Padua (It.)
Parma (It.)
Pavia (It.)
Perak (Malay.)
Posen (Pol.)
Rhône (Fr.)
R.S.F.S.R. (U.S.S.R.)
Sabah (Malay.)
Sahel (Af.)
Salta (Arg.)
Savoy (It.)
Seine (Fr.)
Simla (Ind.)
Sivas (Turk.)
Somme (Fr.)
Surat (Ind.)
Tacna (Chile)
Tavoy (Burma)

Tepic (Mex.)
Terai (Ind.)
Texas (U.S.A.)
Tibet (China)
Tigre (Eth.)
Tokay (Hung.)
Tomsk (U.S.S.R.)
Tyrol (Aust.)
Vizeu (Port.)
Weald (The) (Eng.)
Yonne (Fr.)
Yukon (Can.)

6

Aargau (Swit.)
Alaska (U.S.A.)
Alisco (Mex.)
Allier (Fr.)
Alsace (Fr.)
Anhwei (China)
Apulia (It.)
Aragon (Sp.)
Ariège (Fr.)
Artois (Fr.)
Bashan (Asia)
Basque Prov.
Bengal (Ind.)
Bergen (Nor.)
Biscay (Sp.)
Bombay (Ind.)
Bosnia (Yug.)
Cachar (Ind.)
Creuse (Fr.)
Crimea (U.S.S.R.)
Dakota (U.S.A.)
Darfur (Sudan)
Emilia (It.)
Epirus (Gr.)
Faenza (It.)
Fukien (China)
Geneva (Swit.)
Gerona (Sp.)
Ghilan (Iran)
Glarus (Swit.)
Guiana (S. Am.)
Hawaii (U.S.A.)
Hedjaz (Saudi)
Huelva (Sp.)
Huesca (Sp.)
Iloilo (Philip.)
Johore (Ind.)
Judaea (Asia)
Kansas (U.S.A.)
Karroo (S.A.)
Kaspan (Iran)
Kerala (Ind.)
Kerman (Iran)
Kielce (Pol.)
Ladakh (Ind.)
Landes (Fr.)
Latium (It.)
Latvia (U.S.S.R.)
Lerida (Sp.)
Levant (Asia)
Loiret (Fr.)
Loreto (Port.)
Lozère (Fr.)
Lublin (Pol.)
Madras (Ind.)
Málaga (Sp.)
Manche (Fr.)
Mantua (It.)
Marico (S.A.)
Mercia (Eng.)

Mergui (Burma)
Modena (It.)
Molise (It.)
Murcia (Sp.)
Mysore (Ind.)
Nelson (N.Z.)
Nevada (U.S.A.)
Nièvre (Fr.)
Novara (It.)
Oaxaca (Mex.)
Oregon (U.S.A.)
Orense (Sp.)
Orissa (Ind.)
Oviedo (Sp.)
Pahang (Malay.)
Pampas (S. Am.)
Paraná (Braz.)
Poitou (Fr.)
Potosi (Boliv.)
Punjab (Ind. and Pak.)
Quebec (Can.)
Rivers (Nig.)
Sahara (Af.)
St. Gall (Swit.)
Sarthe (Fr.)
Saxony (Ger.)
Scania (Swed.)
Schwyz (Swit.)
Scinde (Ind.)
Serbia (Yug.)
Shansi (China)
Shensi (China)
Sicily (It.)
Sokoto (Nig.)
Sonora (Mex.)
Soudan (Af.)
Styria (Aust.)
Swabia (Ger.)
Sylhet (Ind.)
Thrace (Gr.)
Ticino (Swit.)
Toledo (Sp.)
Tromsø (Nor.)
Ulster (N.I.)
Umbria (It.)
Upsala (Swed.)
Valais (Swit.)
Vendée (Fr.)
Veneto (It.)
Viborg (Den.)
Vienne (Fr.)
Vosges (Fr.)
Wessex (Eng.)
Yunnan (China)
Zamora (Sp.)
Zurich (Swit.)

7

Abruzzi (It.)
Alabama (U.S.A.)
Alagoas (Braz.)
Alberta (Can.)
Algarve (Port.)
Almeria (Sp.)
Antwerp (Belg.)
Arizona (U.S.A.)
Armenia (U.S.S.R.)
Aveyron (Fr.)
Bavaria (Ger.)
Bohemia (Cze.)
Bokhara (Asia)
Brabant (Belg.)
Caceres (Sp.)
Castile (Sp.)

Chiapas (Mex.)
Corrèze (Fr.)
Côte-d'Or (Fr.)
Croatia (Yug.)
Drenthe (Neth.)
Durango (Mex.)
Eritrea (Eth.)
Estonia (U.S.S.R.)
Ferrara (It.)
Finmark (Nor.)
Florida (U.S.A.)
Galicia (Pol. and Sp.)
Galilee (Isr.)
Gascony (Fr.)
Georgia (U.S.S.R. and
    U.S.A.)
Granada (Sp.)
Grisons (Swit.)
Guienne (Fr.)
Gujarat (Ind.)
Hanover (Ger.)
Haryana (Ind.)
Hérault (Fr.)
Hidalgo (Mex.)
Holland (Neth.)
Huanuco (Peru)
Indiana (U.S.A.)
Iquique (Chile)
Jalisco (Mex.)
Jutland (Den.)
Karelia (U.S.S.R.)
Kashmir (Ind. and Pak.)
Kiangsi (China)
Lapland (Eur.)
Leghorn (It.)
Liguria (It.)
Limburg (Neth.)
Linares (Chile)
Logroño (Sp.)
Lucerne (Swit.)
Malacca (Malay.)
Manipur (Ind.)
Marches (It.)
Mayenne (Fr.)
Mendoza (Arg.)
Montana (U.S.A.)
Moravia (Cze.)
Munster (Ire.)
Navarre (Sp.)
New York (U.S.A.)
Ontario (Can.)
Orléans (Fr.)
Paraíba (Braz.)
Perugia (It.)
Picardy (Fr.)
Potenza (It.)
Prussia (Ger.)
Ravenna (It.)
Riviera (The) (Fr., It.)
Samaria (Asia)
Santa Fé (Arg.)
Sarawak (Malay.)
Segovia (Sp.)
Sennaar (Sudan)
Sergipe (Braz.)
Seville (Sp.)
Siberia (U.S.S.R.)
Silesia (Pol.)
Simaloa (Mex.)
Sondrio (It.)
Tabasco (Mex.)
Tafilet (Moroc.)
Tanjore (Ind.)
Teheran (Iran)
Thurgau (Swit.)
Tripura (Ind.)

Tucuman (Arg.)
Tuscany (It.)
Ukraine (U.S.S.R.)
Utrecht (Neth.)
Venetia (It.)
Vermont (U.S.A.)
Waldeck (Ger.)
Western (Nig.)
Wyoming (U.S.A.)
Yucatan (Mex.)
Zealand ⎱
Zeeland ⎰ (Neth.)

8

Alentejo (Port.)
Alicante (Sp.)
Amazonas (Braz.)
Anatolia (Turk.)
Ardennes (Fr.)
Arkansas (U.S.A.)
Asturias (Sp.)
Auckland (N.Z.)
Brittany (Fr.)
Bukovina (Eur.)
Burgundy (Fr.)
Calabria (It.)
Calvados (Fr.)
Campania (It.)
Campeche (Mex.)
Carniola (Aust.)
Carolina (U.S.A.)
Caucasia (U.S.S.R.)
Charente (Fr.)
Chekiang (China)
Coahuila (Mex.)
Colorado (U.S.A.)
Columbia (U.S.A.)
Dalmatia (Yug.)
Dauphiné (Fr.)
Delaware (U.S.A.)
Dordogne (Fr.)
Ferghana (Turk.)
Flanders (Belg.)
Florence (It.)
Fribourg (Swit.)
Girgenti (It.)
Gothland (Swed.)
Guerrero (Mex.)
Hainault (Belg.)
Hannover (Ger.)
Haut Rhin (Fr.)
Hawke Bay (N.Z.)
Holstein (Ger.)
Illinois (U.S.A.)
Kandahar (Afghan.)
Kentucky (U.S.A.)
Kirgizia (U.S.S.R.)
Korassan (Iran)
Kordofan (Sudan)
Kweichow (China)
Labrador (Can.)
Leinster (Ire.)
Liaoning (China)
Limousin (Fr.)
Lombardy (It.)
Lorraine (Fr.)
Lothians (The) (Scot.)
Lowlands (Scot.)
Luristan (Iran)
Lyonnais (Fr.)
Macerata (It.)
Manitoba (Can.)
Maranhao (Braz.)
Maryland (U.S.A.)

Michigan (U.S.A.)
Missouri (U.S.A.)
Moldavia (Rom. and
    U.S.S.R.)
Mongolia (China and
    U.S.S.R.)
Morbihan (Fr.)
Nagaland (Ind.)
Nebraska (U.S.A.)
Normandy (Fr.)
Norrland (Swed.)
Oberland (Swit.)
Oklahoma (U.S.A.)
Palencia (Sp.)
Parahiba (Braz.)
Peshawar (Ind.)
Piacenza (It.)
Piedmont (It.)
Provence (Fr.)
Roumelia (Turk.)
Ruthenia (Eur.)
Saarland (Ger.)
Salonika (Gr.)
Salzburg (Aust.)
Sardinia (It.)
Shantung (China)
Sinkiang (China)
Slavonia (Eur.)
Slovakia (Cze.)
Slovenia (Yug.)
Syracuse (It.)
Szechwan (China)
Taranaki (N.Z.)
Tarapaca (Chile)
Thessaly (Gr.)
Tlaxcala (Mex.)
Tongking (Asia)
Trentino (It.)
Tsinghai (China)
Valdivia (Chile)
Valencia (Sp.)
Vaucluse (Fr.)
Vera Cruz (Mex.)
Victoria (Austral.)
Virginia (U.S.A.)
Wallonia (Belg.)
Westland (N.Z.)
Wimmeria (Austral.)

9

Alto Adige (It.)
Andalusia (Sp.)
Appenzell (Swit.)
Aquitaine (Fr.)
Asia Minor (Asia)
Astrakhan (U.S.S.R.)
Carinthia (Aust.)
Catalonia (Sp.)
Champagne (Fr.)
Chihuahua (Mex.)
Connaught (Ire.)
Dakahlieh (Egypt)
Entre Rios (Arg.)
Franconia (Ger.)
Friesland (Neth.)
Groningen (Neth.)
Guipuzcoa (Sp.)
Hadramaut (Arab.)
Highlands (Scot.)
Kamchatka (U.S.S.R.)
Karnataka (Ind.)
Khuzestan (Iran)
Kwangtung (China)
Languedoc (Fr.)

105

Linköping (Swed.)
Lithuania (U.S.S.R.)
Louisiana (U.S.A.)
Macedonia (Gr.)
Meghalaya (Ind.)
Melanesia (Pac.)
Michoacan (Mex.)
Minnesota (U.S.A.)
Neuchâtel (Swit.)
New Forest (Eng.)
New Jersey (U.S.A.)
New Mexico (U.S.A.)
Nivernais (Fr.)
Nuevo Leon (Mex.)
Oedenburg (Hung.)
Oldenburg (Ger.)
Overyssel (Neth.)
Palestine (Asia)
Patagonia (S. Am.)
Polynesia (Pac.)
Pomerania (Ger. and Pol.)
Potteries (The) (Eng.)
Queretaro (Mex.)
Rajasthan (Ind.)
Rajputana (Ind.)
Rhineland (Ger.)
Saint Gall (Swit.)
Salamanca (Sp.)
Samarkand (Asia)
Saragossa (Sp.)
Schleswig (Ger.)
Southland (N.Z.)
Tamil Nadu (Ind.)
Tarragona (Sp.)
Tennessee (U.S.A.)
Thayetmyo (Burma)
Thuringia (Ger.)
Transvaal (S.A.)
Trebizond (Turk.)
Trondheim (Nor.)
Turkestan (Asia)
Turkistan (Asia)
Turkmenia (Asia)
Villareal (Port.)
Wallachia (Rom.)
Wisconsin (U.S.A.)
Zacatecas (Mex.)

10

Adrianople (Turk.)
Azerbaijan (U.S.S.R.)
Bafffinland (Can.)
Basilicata (It.)
Belorussia (U.S.S.R.)
Bessarabia (U.S.S.R.)
Burgenland (Aust.)
California (U.S.A.)
Canterbury (N.Z.)
East Africa
East Anglia (Eng.)
Eure-et-Loir (Fr.)
Gelderland (Neth.)
Griqualand (S.A.)
Guanajuato (Mex.)
Haute-Loire (Fr.)
Haute-Marne (Fr.)
Haute-Saône (Fr.)
Kazakhstan (U.S.S.R.)
Kermanshah (Iran)
Lambayeque (Peru)
Loir-et-Cher (Fr.)
Mazandaran (Iran)
Micronesia (Pac.)
Mid-Western (Nig.)

Montenegro (Yug.)
New Castile (Sp.)
Nova Scotia (Can.)
Old Castile (Sp.)
Overijssel (Neth.)
Palatinate (Ger.)
Pernambuco (Braz.)
Pontevedra (Sp.)
Queensland (Austral.)
Rawalpindi (Pak.)
Rohilkhand (Ind.)
Roussillon (Fr.)
Senegambia (Af.)
Slave Coast (Af.)
Tamaulipas (Mex.)
Tavastehus (Fin.)
Tenasserim (Burma)
Valladolid (Sp.)
Valparaiso (Chile)
Vorarlberg (Aust.)
Washington (U.S.A.)
Waziristan (Pak.)
West Africa
West Bengal (Ind.)
West Indies (Carib.)
Westphalia (Ger.)

11

Baluchistan (Pak.)
Bourbonnais (Fr.)
Brandenburg (Ger.)
Byelorussia (U.S.S.R.)
Connecticut (U.S.A.)
Côtes-du-Nord (Fr.)
East-Central (Nig.)
Estremadura (Port. and Sp.)
Great Karroo (S.A.)
Guadalajara (Sp.)
Guelderland (Neth.)
Hautes-Alpes (Fr.)
Haute-Savoie (Fr.)
Haute-Vienne (Fr.)
Herzegovina (Yug.)
Hesse-Nassau (Ger.)
Île-de-France (Fr.)
Lower Saxony (Ger.)
Maharashtra (Ind.)
Matto Grosso (Braz.)
Mecklenburg (Ger.)
Minas Gerais (Braz.)
Mississippi (U.S.A.)
North Africa
North Dakota (U.S.A.)
Northumbria (Eng.)
Pas de Calais (Fr.)
Peloponnese (Gr.)
Quintana Roo (Mex.)
Rhode Island (U.S.A.)
Schwarzwald (Ger.)
South Dakota (U.S.A.)
Sudetenland (Ger.)
The Lothians (Scot.)
Unterwalden (Swit.)
Uzbekhistan (U.S.S.R.)
Valle d'Aosta (It.)
West Prussia (Pol.)
White Russia (U.S.S.P.)
Württemberg (Ger.)

12

Benue-Plateau (Nig.)
British Isles (Eur.)

Franche-Comté (Fr.)
Haute-Garonne (Fr.)
Heilungkiang (China)
Hohenzollern (Ger.)
Huancavelica (Peru)
Indre-et-Loire (Fr.)
Latin America
Little Russia (U.S.S.R.)
Lot-et-Garonne (Fr.)
Lower Austria (Aust.)
New Brunswick (Can.)
Newfoundland (Can.)
New Hampshire (U.S.A.)
North Brabant (Neth.)
North-Central (Nig.)
North-Eastern (Nig.)
North Holland (Neth.)
North-Western (Nig.)
Pennsylvania (U.S.A.)
Rio de Janeiro (Braz.)
Saskatchewan (Can.)
Schaffhausen (Swit.)
Schleswig-Holstein (Ger.)
Seine-et-Marne (Fr.)
South-Eastern (Nig.)
South Holland (Neth.)
Tadzhikistan (U.S.S.R.)
The Potteries (Eng.)
Transylvania (Rom.)
Turkmenistan (U.S.S.R.)
Upper Austria (Aust.)
Uttar Pradesh (Ind.)
West Virginia (U.S.A.)

13

Andhra Pradesh (Ind.)
Canary Islands (Sp.)
Christiansand (Nor.)
Emilia-Romagna (It.)
Espirito Santo (Braz.)
Ille-et-Vilaine (Fr.)
Inner Mongolia (China)
Madhya Pradesh (Ind.)
Massachusetts (U.S.A.)
New South Wales (Austral.)
North Carolina (U.S.A.)
Outer Mongolia (U.S.S.R.)
Rhondda Valley (Wales)
Romney Marshes (Eng.)
San Luis Potosi (Mex.)
Santa Catarina (Braz.)
Saxe-Altenberg (Ger.)
Saxe-Meiningen (Ger.)
South Carolina (U.S.A.)
Tarn-et-Garonne (Fr.)
Transbaikalia (U.S.S.R.)
Witwatersrand (S.A.)

14 AND OVER

Alpes-Maritimes (Fr.) (14)
Alsace-Lorraine (Fr.) (14)
Baden-Württemberg (Ger.)
    (16)
Baltic Provinces (U.S.S.R.)
    (15)
Basque Provinces (Sp.) (14)
Bihar and Orissa (Ind.) (14)
British Columbia (Can.) (15)
Central America (14)
Channel Islands (U.K.) (14)
District of Columbia
    (U.S.A.) (18)

106

Entre-Douro-e-Minho (Port.) (16)
Griqualand West (S.A.) (14)
Hautes-Pyrénées (Fr.) (14)
Himachal Pradesh (Ind.) (15)
Loire-Atlantique (Fr.) (15)
Lower California (Mex.) (15)
Northern Ireland (U.K.) (15)
North Rhine-Westphalia (Ger.) (20)
North-West Frontier (Pak.) (17)
Orange Free State (S.A.) (15)
Rhenish Prussia (Ger.) (14)
Rio Grande do Sul (Braz.) (14)
Santa Catharina (Braz.) (14)
Saxe-Coburg-Gotha (Ger.) (15)
Schaumberg-Lippe (Ger.) (15)
South Australia (Austral.) (14)
Southern Africa (14)
United Provinces (Ind.) (15)
Western Australia (Austral.) (16)

Rivers

R. = River, and is inserted where "River" commonly follows the name.

1–3

Aar (Swit.)
Ain (Fr.)
Aln (Eng.)
Axe (Eng.)
Bug (Pol., U.S.S.R.)
Cam (Eng.)
Dee (Eng.)
Don (Scot.)
Ems (Ger.)
Esk (Scot.)
Exe (Eng.)
Fal (Eng.)
Fly (Papua)
Hex R. (S.A.)
Hsi (China)
Hue (Asia)
Ili (Asia)
Ill (Fr.)
Inn (Aust.)
Ket (Sib.)
Kur (U.S.S.R.)
Kwa (Af.)
Lea (Eng.)
Lee (Ire.)
Lek (Neth.)
Lot (Fr.)
Lys (Fr. and Belg.)
Nen (Eng.)
Ob (Sib.)
Oka (U.S.S.R.)
Po (It.)
Red R. (U.S.A.)
Rur (Eur.)
Rye (Eng.)
Sid (Eng.)
Sow (Eng.)
Syr (U.S.S.R.)
Taw (Eng.)
Tay (Scot.)
Tom (Sib.)
Ure (Eng.)
Usa (U.S.S.R.)
Usk (Wales)
Var (Fr.)
Wey (Eng.)
Wye (Eng.)
Wye (Wales)
Y (Neth.)
Yeo (Eng.)
Zab (Turk.)

4

Adda (It.)
Adur (Eng.)
Aire (Eng.)
Aire (Scot.)
Alma (U.S.S.R.)
Amur (Asia)
Anio (It.)
Arno (It.)
Arun (Eng.)
Avon (Eng.)
Bann (N.I.)
Beas (Ind.)
Bure (Eng.)
Cart (Scot.)
Cher (Fr.)
Cole (Eng.)
Coln (Eng.)
Dart (Eng.)
Doon (Scot.)
Dora (It.)
Dove (Eng.)
Duna (U.S.S.R.)
Earn (Scot.)
Ebro (Sp.)
Eden (Eng.)
Eden (Scot.)
Elbe (Ger.)
Enns (Aust.)
Erne (Ire.)
Fall (U.S.A.)
Geba (W. Af.)
Gila (U.S.A.)
Gota (Swed.)
Ha Ha (Can.)
Isar (Ger.)
Isis (Eng.)
Juba (E. Af.)
Kama (U.S.S.R.)
Kusi (Ind.)
Lahn (Ger.)
Lech (Ger.)
Lena (Sib.)
Loir (Fr.)
Lune (Eng.)
Lynd (Austral.)
Maas (Neth.)
Main (Ger.)
Main (Ire.)
Mole (Eng.)
Mooi (S. A.)
Naze (Eng.)
Neva (U.S.S.R.)
Nida (U.S.S.R.)
Nile (Af.)
Nith (Scot.)
Oder (Cze., E. Ger., Pol.)
Ohio (U.S.A.)
Oise (Fr.)
Ouse (Eng.)
Oxus (Asia)
Peel (Austral.)
Peel (Can.)
Pina (U.S.S.R.)
Prah (Af.)
Ravi (Ind.)
Rede (Eng.)
Roer (Eur.)
Ruhr (Ger.)
Saar (Fr., Ger.)
Salt R. (U.S.A.)
Save (Fr.)
Spey (Scot.)
Styr (Spain)
Suck (Ire.)
Suir (Ire.)
Swan (Austral.)
Taff (Wales)
Tana (E. Af.)
Tara (Sib.)
Tarn (Fr.)
Tawe (Wales)
Tees (Eng.)
Test (Eng.)
Thur (Swit.)
Tons (Ind.)
Towy (Wales)
Tyne (Eng.)
Umea (Swed.)
Ural (U.S.S.R.)
Vaal (S. Af.)
Vire (Fr.)
Waag (Hung.)
Waal (Neth.)
Wash (Eng.)
Wear (Eng.)
Yana (Sib.)
Yare (Eng.)

5

Abana (Syr.)
Adige (It.)
Adour (Fr.)
Agout (Fr.)
Aisne (Fr.)
Alice (Austral.)
Allan (Scot.)
Allen (Scot.)
Aller (Ger.)
Annan (Scot.)
Avoca (Austral.)
Benue (W. Af.)
Black R. (U.S.A.)
Blood R. (S. A.)
Bober (Ger.)
Bogie (Scot.)
Boyne (Ire.)
Brent (Eng.)
Bride (Ire.)
Camel (Eng.)
Clyde (Scot.)
Colne (Eng.)
Congo (Af.)
Desna (U.S.S.R.)
Devon (Scot.)
Douro (Port., Sp.)
Dovey (Wales)
Drave (Hung.)
Drina (Yug.)
Eider (Ger.)
Etive (Scot.)
Feale (Ire.)
Forth (Scot.)
Foyle (Ire.)
Frome (Eng.)
Gogra (Ind.)
Green R. (U.S.A.)
Gumti (Ind.)
Habra (N. Af.)
Havel (Ger.)
Huang (China)
Hugli (Ind.)
Hunza (Ind.)
Ikopa (E. Af.)
Indus (Ind.)
Isère (Fr.)
Ishim (U.S.S.R.)
James R. (U.S.A.)
Jelum (Ind.)
Jumna (Ind.)
Kabul R. (Afghan.)
Kafue (Af.)
Karun (Iran.)
Katun (Sib.)
Koros (Hung.)
Kowie (S.A.)
Kuram (Afghan.)
Lagan (N. Ire.)
Lenea (U.S.S.R.)
Leven (Scot.)
Liard (Can.)
Loire (Fr.)
Marne (Fr.)
Maroo (Rom.)
Memel (Ger.)
Menam (China)
Meuse (Belg.)
Miami (U.S.A.)
Minho (Port. and Sp.)
Moose (Can.)
Neath (Wales)
Neuse (U.S.A.)
Niger (Af.)
Oglio (It.)
Onega (U.S.S.R.)
Otter (Eng.)
Peace R. (Can.)
Pecos (U.S.A.)

Pei Ho (China)
Perak (Malay.)
Plate (S. Am.)
Pruth (Rom.)
Purus (S. Am.)
Rance (Fr.)
Reuss (Swit.)
Rhine
   (Ger., Neth., Swit.)
Rhone (Fr., Swit.)
Saale (Ger.)
Saone (Fr.)
Seine (Fr.)
Shari (E. Af.)
Sheaf (Eng.)
Shiel (Scot.)
Shire (Af.)
Snake R. (U.S.A.)
Somme (Fr.)
Spree (Ger.)
Stolp (U.S.S.R.)
Stour (Eng.)
Sugar (U.S.A.)
Sulir (Swit.)
Swale (Eng.)
Tagus (Port.)
Tamar (Eng.)
Tapti (Ind.)
Tarim (China)
Teffe (S. Am.)
Teifi (Wales)
Teign (Eng.)
Teith (Scot.)
Temes (Hung.)
Tiber (It.)
Tisza (Hung.)
Traun (Aust.)
Trent (Can.)
Trent (Eng.)
Tweed (Scot.)
Usuri (Asia)
Volga (U.S.S.R.)
Volta (W. Af.)
Warta (Pol.)
Welle (Af.)
Werra (Ger.)
Weser (Ger.)
Xiugo (S. Am.)
Yonne (Fr.)
Yssel (Neth.)
Yukon (Can.)
Zaïre (Af.)
Zenta (Hung.)

6

Agogno (It.)
Aguada (Sp.)
Alagon (Sp.)
Albany (Can.)
Albert (Austral.)
Allier (Fr.)
Amazon (S. Am.)
Angara (U.S.S.R.)
Arinos (S. Am.)
Atbara (Af.)
Barrow (Ire.)
Barwon (Austral.)
Beauly (Scot.)
Bolsas (Mex.)
Brazos (U.S.A.)
Buller (N.Z.)
Calder (Eng.)

Canton R. (China)
Caroni (S. Am.)
Carron (Scot.)
Chenab (Ind.)
Coquet (Eng.)
Crouch (Eng.)
Danube (Eur.)
Dihong (Ind.)
Draava (Hung.)
Elster (Ger.)
Foyers (Scot.)
Fraser (Can.)
French (Can.)
Gambia (Af.)
Gandak (Ind.)
Ganges (Ind.)
Grande (S. Am.)
Grande (U.S.A., Mex.)
Grande (W. Af.)
Hamble (Eng.)
Hawash (E. Af.)
Hudson (U.S.A.)
Humber (Eng.)
Irtish (U.S.S.R.)
Irwell (Eng.)
Itchen (Eng.)
Japura (Braz.)
Jhelum (Ind.)
Jordan
   (Isr., Jord., Syria)
Kagera (Af.)
Kaveri (Ind.)
Kennet (Eng.)
Komati (E. Af.)
Kwanza (W. Af.)
Lehigh (U.S.A.)
Leitha (Hung.)
Liffey (Ire.)
Loddon (Eng.)
Loddon (Austral.)
Lomami (Af.)
Medina (Eng.)
Medway (Eng.)
Mekong (Asia)
Mersey (Eng.)
Mincio (It.)
Mobile (U.S.A.)
Modder R. (S.A.)
Mohawk (U.S.A.)
Moldau (Cze.)
Monnow (Eng.)
Morava (Cze.)
Moskva (U.S.S.R.)
Murray R. (Austral.)
Neckar (Ger.)
Neisse (Ger.)
Nelson (Can.)
Neutra (Hung.)
Niemen (U.S.S.R.)
Ogowai (Af.)
Oneida (U.S.A.)
Orange (S.A.)
Orwell (Eng.)
Ottawa (Can.)
Paraná (S. Am.)
Parima (Braz.)
Parret (Eng.)
Platte (U.S.A.)
Porali (Ind.)
Pungwe (E. Af.)
Pungwe (S.A.)
Racket (U.S.A.)
Ribble (Eng.)
Roding (Eng.)
Rother (Eng.)
Rovuma (E. Af.)

Rufiji (E. Af.)
Sabine (U.S.A.)
Sarthe (Fr.)
St. Paul (W. Af.)
Salwin (Burma)
Sambre (Belg., Fr.)
Santee (U.S.A.)
Scioto (U.S.A.)
Seneca (U.S.A.)
Sereth (Rom.)
Severn (Can.)
Severn (Eng., Wales)
Slaney (Ire.)
Stroma (Balkans)
Sunday (S.A.)
Sutlej (Ind.)
Sutluj (Ind.)
Swilly (Ire.)
Tamega (Port.)
Tanaro (It.)
Teviot (Scot.)
Thames (Can.)
Thames (Eng.)
Thames (N.Z.)
Theiss (Hung.)
Ticino (Swit.)
Tigris (Iraq., Turk.)
Tormes (Sp.)
Tornio (Fin.)
Tugela (S.A.)
Tummel (Scot.)
Ubangi (Af.)
Viatka (U.S.S.R.)
Vienne (Fr.)
Vltava (Cze.)
Wabash (U.S.A.)
Waihou (N.Z.)
Wandle (Eng.)
Warthe (Pol.)
Weaver (Eng.)
Wensum (Eng.)
Wharfe (Eng.)
Wipper (Ger.)
Witham (Eng.)
Yarrow (Scot.)
Yavari (S. Am.)
Yellow R. (China)
Zarang (Iran)
Zontag (S.A.)

7

Abitibi (Can.)
Alabama (U.S.A.)
Big Blue R. (U.S.A.)
Buffalo (S.A.)
Calabar (Af.)
Catawba (U.S.A.)
Cauvery (Ind.)
Chambal (Ind.)
Chelmer (Eng.)
Chumbal (Ind.)
Darling (Austral.)
Derwent (Eng.)
Deveron (Scot.)
Dnieper (U.S.S.R.)
Dunajec (Pol.)
Durance (Fr.)
Ettrick (Scot.)
Feather (U.S.A.)
Fitzroy (Austral.)
Gamtoos (S.A.)
Garonne (Fr.)

Gauritz (S.A.)
Genesee (U.S.A.)
Gilbert (Austral.)
Glenelg (Austral.)
Glommen (Nor.)
Guapore (S. Am.)
Heri Rud (Afghan.)
Hoang Ho (China)
Hooghli (Ind.)
Hwangho (China)
Juniata (U.S.A.)
Kanawha (Ind.)
Kubango (Af.)
Lachlan (Austral.)
La Plata (S. Am.)
Limpopo (S.A.)
Lualaba (Af.)
Luangwa (Af.)
Lugendi (Af.)
Madeira (S. Am.)
Marañón (S. Am.)
Maritza (Gr.)
Mattawa (Can.)
Mayenne (Fr.)
Meklong (Thail.)
Moselle (Eur.)
Muluyar (N. Af.)
Murghab (Afghan.)
Narbuda (Ind.)
Niagara (N. Am.)
Niagara (U.S.A.)
Olifant (S.A.)
Orinoco (S. Am.)
Orontes (Syria)
Paraıba (S. Am.)
Paraná (Braz.)
Parsnip (Can.)
Passaic (U.S.A.)
Pechora (U.S.S.R)
Potomac (U.S.A.)
Rubicon (It.)
San Juan (S. Am.)
Sankuru (Af.)
St. Johns (U.S.A.)
Salween (Burma)
Schelde (Belg., Neth.)
Scheldt (Belg., Neth.)
Selenga (Asia)
Semliki (Af.)
Senegal (Af.)
Shannon (Ire.)
Spokane (U.S.A.)
Sungari (Asia)
Surinam (S. Am.)
Suwanee (U.S.A.)
Tampico (Mex.)
Tapajos (S. Am.)
Thomson (Austral.)
Tobique (Can.)
Torridge (Eng.)
Trinity (U.S.A.)
Ucayali (S. Am.)
Uruguay (S. Am.)
Vistula (Pol.)
Walkato (N.Z.)
Warrego (Austral.)
Washita (U.S.A.)
Waveney (Eng.)
Welland (Eng.)
Wichita (U.S.A.)
Yangtse (China)
Yarkand (Asia)
Yenesei (Sib.)
Ystwith (Wales)
Yuruari (S. Am.)
Zambezi (Af.)

8

Amu Darya (Asia)
Arkansas (U.S.A.)
Beaulieu (Eng.)
Beresina (U.S.S.R.)
Big Black R. (U.S.A.)
Blue Nile (Af.)
Brisbane R. (Austral.)
Campaspe (Austral.)
Cape Fear R. (U.S.A.)
Chambezi (Af.)
Cherwell (Eng.)
Chindwin (Burma)
Clarence (Austral.)
Colorado R. (U.S.A.)
Columbia (N. Am.)
Delaware (U.S.A.)
Demerara (S. Am.)
Dniester (U.S.S.R.)
Evenlode (Eng.)
Gallinas (W. Af.)
Gatineau (Can.)
Georgina (Austral.)
Godavari (Ind.)
Goulburn (Austral.)
Great Kei (S.A.)
Guadiana (Spain)
Hankiang (China)
Huallaga (S. Am.)
Humboldt (U.S.A.)
Itimbiri (Af.)
Kankakee (U.S.A.)
Kelantan (Malay.)
Kennebec (U.S.A.)
Klondyke R. (Can.)
Kootenay (N. Am.)
Mahanadi (Ind.)
Mazaruni (S. Am.)
Merrimac (U.S.A.)
Missouri (U.S.A.)
Mitchell (Austral.)
Nebraska (U.S.A.)
Ob Irtish (U.S.S.R.)
Paraguay (S. Am.)
Parahiba (S. Am.)
Putumayo (S. Am.)
Red River (U.S.A.)
Richmond (Austral.)
Rimouski (Can.)
Rio Negro (S. Am.)
Rio Tinto (Sp.)
Saguenay (Can.)
St. Claire (Can.)
Santiago (S. Am.)
Savannah (U.S.A.)
Syr Daria (U.S.S.R.)
Tunguska (Sib.)

Umvolosi (S.A.)
Wanganui (N.Z.)
Wansbeck (Eng.)
Windrush (Eng.)
Winnipeg (Can.)

9

Abbitibee (Can.)
Churchill (Can.)
Crocodile R. (S.A.)
East River (U.S.A.)
Esmeralda (S. Am.)
Essequibo (S. Am.)
Euphrates (Iraq., Turk., Syria)
Gala Water (Scot.)
Great Fish R. (S.A.)
Great Ouse (Eng.)
Guadalete (Spain)
Indigirka (U.S.S.R.)
Irrawaddy (Burma)
Kalamazoo (U.S.A.)
Kizil Uzen (Iran)
Mackenzie (Can.)
Mallagami (Can.)
Miramichi (Can.)
Mirimichi (Can.)
Missimabi (Can.)
Nipisquit (Can.)
Paranaíba (S. Am.)
Penobscot (U.S.A.)
Pilcomayo (S. Am.)
Rede River (Eng.)
Rio Branco (S. Am.)
Rio Grande (Braz.)
Rio Grande (U.S.A., Mex.)
Rio Grande (W. Af.)
Saint John (Can.)
Saint Paul (W. Af.)
Salt River (U.S.A.)
Tennessee (U.S.A.)
Tocantins (S. Am.)
Toombudra (Ind.)
Umsimvubu (S.A.)
Umsimkulu (S.A.)
White Nile (Af.)
Wisconsin (U.S.A.)
Zarafshan (Asia)

10

Allenwater (Scot.)
Black River (U.S.A.)
Blackwater (Eng.)

Blackwater (Ire.)
Blood River (S.A.)
Great Slave R. (Can.)
Green River (U.S.A.)
Hawkesbury (Austral.)
Kizil Irmak (Turk.)
Lackawanna (U.S.A.)
Macquarrie (Austral.)
Manzanares (Sp.)
Monagahela (U.S.A.)
Paranahiba (S. Am.)
Parramatta (Austral.)
Sacramento (U.S.A.)
San Joaquin (U.S.A.)
Saint John's (U.S.A.)
St. Lawrence (Can.)
Shat-el-Arab (Asia)
Shenandoah (U.S.A.)
Snake River (U.S.A.)
White River (U.S.A.)
Yarra Yarra (Austral.)

11 AND OVER

Big Black River (U.S.A.) (13)
Big Blue River (U.S.A.) (12)
Big Horn River (U.S.A.) (12)
Big Sandy River (U.S.A.) (13)
Big Sioux River (U.S.A.) (13)
Bonaventure (Can.) (11)
Brahmaputra (Ind.) (11)
Desaguadero (S. Am.) (11)
Ettrickwater (Scot.) (12)
Great Kanawka (U.S.A.) (12)
Guadalquivir (Sp.) (12)
Mississippi (U.S.A.) (11)
Modder River (S.A.) (11)
Murray-Darling (Austral.) (13)
Rappahannock (U.S.A.) (12)
Restigouche (Can.) (11)
Rio del Norte (Mex.) (11)
Saint Claire (Can.) (11)
Saint Lawrence (Can.) (13)
São Francisco (Braz.) (12)
Saskatchewan (Can.) (12)
Shubenacadia (Can.) (12)
Susquehanna (U.S.A.) (11)
Upper Paraná (S. Am.) (11)
Yangtse Kiang (China) (12)
Yarrowwater (Scot.) (11)
Yellow River (China) (11)

Towns and cities: United Kingdom

(E.) = England.   (N.I.) = Northern Ireland.   (S.) = Scotland.   (W.) = Wales

3 AND 4

Alva (S.)
Ayr (S.)
Bala (W.)
Barr (S.)
Bath (E.)
Bray (E.)
Bude (E.)
Bury (E.)
Clun (E.)
Deal (E.)

Diss (E.)
Duns (S.)
Elie (S.)
Ely (E.)
Eton (E.)
Eye (E.)
Holt (E.)
Holt (W.)
Hove (E.)
Hull (E.)
Hyde (E.)
Ince (E.)

Kirn (S.)
Leek (E.)
Looe (E.)
Luss (S.)
Lydd (E.)
Mold (W.)
Muff (N.I.)
Nigg (S.)
Oban (S.)
Pyle (W.)
Reay (S.)
Rhyl (W.)

Rona (S.)
Ross (E.)
Ryde (E.)
Rye (E.)
Shap (E.)
Stow (S.)
Uig (S.)
Usk (E.)
Ware (E.)
Wark (E.)
Wem (E.)
Wick (S.)

Yarm (E.)
York (E.)

5

Acton (E.)
Alloa (S.)
Alton (E.)
Annan (S.)
Appin (S.)
Avoch (S.)
Ayton (S.)
Bacup (E.)
Banff (S.)
Beith (S.)
Blyth (E.)
Bourn (E.)
Brora (S.)
Bunaw (S.)
Busby (S.)
Calne (E.)
Ceres (S.)
Chard (E.)
Cheam (E.)
Chirk (W.)
Clova (S.)
Clune (S.)
Colne (E.)
Cowes (E.)
Crail (S.)
Crewe (E.)
Cupar (S.)
Denny (S.)
Derby (E.)
Doagh (N.I.)
Downe (S.)
Dover (E.)
Egham (E.)
Elgin (S.)
Ellon (S.)
Epsom (E.)
Errol (S.)
Filey (E.)
Flint (W.)
Fowey (E.)
Frome (E.)
Fyvie (S.)
Glynn (N.I.)
Goole (E.)
Govan (S.)
Hawes (E.)
Hedon (E.)
Hurst (E.)
Hythe (E.)
Insch (S.)
Islay (S.)
Keady (N.I.)
Keiss (S.)
Keith (S.)
Kelso (S.)
Lairg (S.)
Largo (S.)
Larne (N.I.)
Leeds (E.)
Leigh (E.)
Leith (S.)
Lewes (E.)
Louth (E.)
Louth (N.I.)
Luton (E.)
March (E.)
Nairn (S.)
Neath (W.)
Nevin (W.)
Newry (N.I.)

Olney (E.)
Omagh (N.I.)
Otley (E.)
Perth (S.)
Poole (E.)
Reeth (E.)
Ripon (E.)
Risca (E.)
Rugby (E.)
Salen (S.)
Sarum (E.)
Selby (E.)
Stoke (E.)
Stone (E.)
Tebay (E.)
Tenby (W.)
Thame (E.)
Toome (N.I.)
Towyn (W.)
Tring (E.)
Troon (S.)
Truro (E.)
Wells (E.)
Wigan (E.)

6

Aboyne (S.)
Alford (E.)
Alford (S.)
Alston (E.)
Amlwch (W.)
Antrim (N.I.)
Ashton (E.)
Augher (N.I.)
Bangor (W.)
Barnet (E.)
Barrow (E.)
Barton (E.)
Barvas (S.)
Batley (E.)
Battle (E.)
Bawtry (E.)
Beauly (S.)
Bedale (E.)
Belcoo (N.I.)
Belper (E.)
Beragh (N.I.)
Bervie (S.)
Biggar (S.)
Bodmin (E.)
Bognor (E.)
Bolton (E.)
Bo'ness (S.)
Bootle (E.)
Boston (E.)
Brecon (W.)
Bruton (E.)
Buckie (S.)
Builth (W.)
Bungay (E.)
Burton (E.)
Buxton (E.)
Callar (N.I.)
Carney (N.I.)
Carron (S.)
Castor (E.)
Cawdor (S.)
Cobham (E.)
Comber (N.I.)
Comrie (S.)
Conway (W.)
Crieff (S.)
Cromer (E.)
Cullen (S.)

Culter (S.)
Darwen (E.)
Dollar (S.)
Drymen (S.)
Dudley (E.)
Dunbar (S.)
Dundee (S.)
Dunlop (S.)
Dunnet (S.)
Dunoon (S.)
Durham (E.)
Dysart (S.)
Ealing (E.)
Eccles (E.)
Edzell (S.)
Epping (E.)
Exeter (E.)
Findon (S.)
Forfar (S.)
Forres (S.)
Girvan (S.)
Glamis (S.)
Goring (E.)
Hanley (E.)
Harlow (E.)
Harrow (E.)
Havant (E.)
Hawick (S.)
Henley (E.)
Hexham (E.)
Howden (E.)
Huntly (S.)
Ilford (E.)
Ilkley (E.)
Ilsley (E.)
Irvine (S.)
Jarrow (E.)
Kendal (E.)
Killin (S.)
Kilmun (S.)
Lanark (S.)
Lauder (S.)
Leslie (S.)
Leyton (E.)
Linton (S.)
Lochee (S.)
London (E.)
Ludlow (E.)
Lurgan (N.I.)
Lynton (E.)
Lytham (E.)
Maldon (E.)
Malton (E.)
Marlow (E.)
Masham (E.)
Meigle (S.)
Moffat (S.)
Morley (E.)
Naseby (E.)
Nelson (E.)
Neston (E.)
Newark (E.)
Newent (E.)
Newlyn (E.)
Newton (E.)
Norham (E.)
Oakham (E.)
Oldham (E.)
Ormsby (E.)
Ossett (E.)
Oundle (E.)
Oxford (E.)
Penryn (E.)
Pewsey (E.)
Pinner (E.)
Pladda (S.)

Pudsey (E.)
Putney (E.)
Ramsey (E.)
Raphoe (N.I.)
Redcar (E.)
Reston (S.)
Rhynie (S.)
Ripley (E.)
Romney (E.)
Romsey (E.)
Rosyth (S.)
Rothes (S.)
Ruabon (W.)
Rugely (E.)
Ruthin (W.)
St. Ives (E.)
Seaham (E.)
Seaton (E.)
Selsey (E.)
Settle (E.)
Shotts (S.)
Shrule (N.I.)
Snaith (E.)
Strood (E.)
Stroud (E.)
Sutton (E.)
Thirsk (E.)
Thorne (E.)
Thurso (S.)
Tongue (S.)
Totnes (E.)
Walton (E.)
Watton (E.)
Weston (E.)
Whitby (E.)
Widnes (E.)
Wigton (E.)
Wilton (E.)
Wishaw (S.)
Witham (E.)
Witney (E.)
Wooler (E.)
Yarrow (S.)
Yeovil (E.)

7

Airdrie (S.)
Alnwick (E.)
Andover (E.)
Appleby (E.)
Arundel (E.)
Ashford (E.)
Aylsham (E.)
Balfron (S.)
Balloch (S.)
Bampton (E.)
Banavie (S.)
Banbury (E.)
Barking (E.)
Beccles (E.)
Bedford (E.)
Belfast (N.I.)
Belford (E.)
Belleek (N.I.)
Berwick (E.)
Bewdley (E.)
Bexhill (E.)
Bickley (E.)
Bilston (E.)
Bourton (E.)
Bowfell (E.)
Bowmore (S.)
Braemar (S.)
Brandon (E.)

Brechin (S.)
Bristol (E.)
Brixham (E.)
Brodick (S.)
Bromley (E.)
Burnham (E.)
Burnley (E.)
Burslem (E.)
Caistor (E.)
Caledon (N.I.)
Canobie (S.)
Cantyre (S.)
Carbost (S.)
Carbury (W.)
Cardiff (W.)
Cargill (S.)
Carluke (S.)
Carrick (N.I.)
Catford (E.)
Cawston (E.)
Charing (E.)
Chatham (E.)
Cheadle (E.)
Cheddar (E.)
Chesham (E.)
Chester (E.)
Chorley (E.)
Clacton (E.)
Clifton (E.)
Clogher (N.I.)
Crathie (S.)
Crawley (E.)
Croydon (E.)
Culross (S.)
Cumnock (S.)
Cwmbran (W.)
Darsley (E.)
Datchet (E.)
Dawlish (E.)
Denbigh (W.)
Denholm (S.)
Dervock (N.I.)
Devizes (E.)
Dorking (E.)
Douglas (E.)
Douglas (S.)
Dundrum (N.I.)
Dunkeld (S.)
Dunmore (N.I.)
Dunning (S.)
Dunster (E.)
Elstree (E.)
Enfield (E.)
Evanton (S.)
Everton (E.)
Evesham (E.)
Exmouth (E.)
Fairlie (S.)
Falkirk (S.)
Fareham (E.)
Farnham (E.)
Feltham (E.)
Fintona (N.I.)
Galston (S.)
Gifford (S.)
Gilford (N.I.)
Glasgow (S.)
Glenarm (N.I.)
Glencoe (S.)
Glossop (E.)
Golspie (S.)
Gosport (E.)
Gourock (S.)
Granton (S.)
Grimsby (E.)
Guthrie (S.)

Halifax (E.)
Halkirk (S.)
Hampton (E.)
Harwich (E.)
Haworth (E.)
Helston (E.)
Heywood (E.)
Hitchin (E.)
Honiton (E.)
Hornsea (E.)
Hornsey (E.)
Horsham (E.)
Ipswich (E.)
Ixworth (E.)
Kenmore (S.)
Kessock (S.)
Keswick (E.)
Kilmory (S.)
Kilmuir (S.)
Kilsyth (S.)
Kinross (S.)
Kington (E.)
Kintore (S.)
Lamlash (S.)
Lancing (E.)
Langton (E.)
Larbert (S.)
Ledbury (E.)
Leyburn (E.)
Lifford (N.I.)
Lincoln (E.)
Lisburn (N.I.)
Lybster (S.)
Macduff (S.)
Maesteg (W.)
Malvern (E.)
Margate (E.)
Matlock (E.)
Maybole (S.)
Meldrum (S.)
Melrose (S.)
Melvich (S.)
Methven (S.)
Molesey (E.)
Monikie (S.)
Moreton (E.)
Morpeth (E.)
Mossley (E.)
Muthill (S.)
Newbury (E.)
Newport (E.)
Newport (W.)
Newport (S.)
Newtown (W.)
Norwich (E.)
Oldbury (E.)
Overton (E.)
Padstow (E.)
Paisley (S.)
Peebles (S.)
Penrith (E.)
Polmont (S.)
Poolewe (S.)
Portree (S.)
Portsoy (S.)
Poulton (E.)
Prescot (E.)
Preston (E.)
Rainham (E.)
Reading (E.)
Redhill (E.)
Redruth (E.)
Reigate (E.)
Renfrew (S.)
Retford (E.)
Romford (E.)

Rossall (E.)
Royston (E.)
Runcorn (E.)
Saddell (S.)
St. Asaph (W.)
St. Neots (E.)
Salford (E.)
Saltash (E.)
Sandown (E.)
Sarclet (S.)
Saxelby (E.)
Scourie (S.)
Seaford (E.)
Selkirk (S.)
Shifnal (E.)
Shipley (E.)
Shipton (E.)
Silloth (E.)
Skipton (E.)
Spilsby (E.)
Staines (E.)
Stanley (E.)
Stilton (E.)
Strathy (S.)
Sudbury (E.)
Sunbury (E.)
Swanage (E.)
Swansea (W.)
Swindon (E.)
Swinton (E.)
Tarbert (S.)
Tarland (S.)
Taunton (E.)
Tayport (S.)
Telford (E.)
Tenbury (E.)
Tetbury (E.)
Thaxted (E.)
Tilbury (E.)
Torquay (E.)
Tranent (S.)
Turriff (S.)
Tundrum (S.)
Twyford (E.)
Ullster (S.)
Ventnor (E.)
Walsall (E.)
Waltham (E.)
Wantage (E.)
Wareham (E.)
Warwick (E.)
Watchet (E.)
Watford (E.)
Weobley (E.)
Wickwar (E.)
Windsor (E.)
Winslow (E.)
Winster (E.)
Wisbeck (E.)
Worksop (E.)
Wrexham (W.)
Yetholm (S.)

8

Aberavon (W.)
Aberdare (W.)
Aberdeen (S.)
Abergele (W.)
Aberlady (S.)
Abingdon (E.)
Abington (S.)
Ahoghill (N.I.)
Alfreton (E.)
Alnmouth (E.)

Amesbury (E.)
Ampthill (E.)
Arbroath (S.)
Armadale (S.)
Arrochar (S.)
Auldearn (S.)
Axbridge (E.)
Aycliffe (E.)
Bakewell (E.)
Ballater (S.)
Ballybay (N.I.)
Banchory (S.)
Barmouth (W.)
Barnsley (E.)
Barrhill (S.)
Beattock (S.)
Berkeley (E.)
Beverley (E.)
Bicester (E.)
Bideford (E.)
Blantyre (S.)
Bolsover (E.)
Brackley (E.)
Bradford (E.)
Brampton (E.)
Bridgend (W.)
Bridport (E.)
Brighton (E.)
Bromyard (E.)
Broseley (E.)
Burghead (S.)
Caerleon (E.)
Camborne (E.)
Canisbay (S.)
Cardigan (W.)
Carlisle (E.)
Carnwath (S.)
Caterham (E.)
Chepstow (E.)
Chertsey (E.)
Clevedon (E.)
Clovelly (E.)
Coventry (E.)
Crediton (E.)
Creetown (S.)
Cromarty (S.)
Dalkeith (S.)
Dalmally (S.)
Daventry (E.)
Debenham (E.)
Dedworth (E.)
Deptford (E.)
Dewsbury (E.)
Dingwall (S.)
Dirleton (S.)
Dolgelly (W.)
Dufftown (S.)
Dumfries (S.)
Dunbeath (S.)
Dunblane (S.)
Dungiven (N.I.)
Dunscore (S.)
Earlston (S.)
Egremont (E.)
Eversley (E.)
Eyemouth (S.)
Fakenham (E.)
Falmouth (E.)
Findhorn (S.)
Fortrose (S.)
Foulness (E.)
Glenluce (S.)
Grantham (E.)
Grantown (E.)
Greenlaw (S.)
Greenock (S.)

111

Hadleigh (E.)
Hailsham (E.)
Halstead (E.)
Hamilton (S.)
Hastings (E.)
Hatfield (E.)
Hawarden (W.)
Helmsley (E.)
Hereford (E.)
Herne Bay (E.)
Hertford (E.)
Hilltown (N.I.)
Hinckley (E.)
Holbeach (E.)
Holyhead (W.)
Holywell (W.)
Hunmanby (E.)
Ilkeston (E.)
Inverary (S.)
Inverury (S.)
Jeantown (S.)
Jedburgh (S.)
Keighley (E.)
Kidwelly (W.)
Kilbride (S.)
Kilniver S.)
Kilrenny (S.)
Kinghorn (S.)
Kingston (E.)
Kirkwall (S.)
Knighton (W.)
Lampeter (W.)
Langholm (S.)
Latheron (S.)
Lavenham (E.)
Lechlade (E.)
Leuchars (S.)
Liskeard (E.)
Llanelly (W.)
Llanrwst (W.)
Loanhead (S.)
Longtown (E.)
Lynmouth (E.)
Markinch (S.)
Marykirk (S.)
Maryport (E.)
Midhurst (E.)
Minehead (E.)
Moniaive (S.)
Monmouth (E.)
Montrose (S.)
Monymusk (S.)
Muirkirk (S.)
Nantwich (E.)
Neilston (S.)
Newburgh (S.)
Newhaven (E.)
Newmilns (S.)
Nuneaton (E.)
Ormskirk (E.)
Oswestry (E.)
Pembroke (W.)
Penicuik (S.)
Penzance (E.)
Pershore (E.)
Peterlee (E.)
Petworth (E.)
Pevensey (E.)
Pitsligo (S.)
Plaistow (E.)
Plymouth (E.)
Pooltiel (S.)
Portrush (N.I.)
Pwllheli (W.)
Quiraing (S.)
Ramsgate (E.)

Redditch (E.)
Rhayader (W.)
Richmond (E.)
Ringwood (E.)
Rochdale (E.)
Rothbury (E.)
Rothesay (S.)
St. Albans (E.)
St. Fergus (S.)
St. Helens (E.)
Saltburn (E.)
Sandgate (E.)
Sandwich (E.)
Sedbergh (E.)
Shanklin (E.)
Shelford (E.)
Shipston (E.)
Sidmouth (E.)
Skegness (E.)
Skerries (W.)
Skifness (W.)
Sleaford (E.)
Southend (E.)
Spalding (E.)
Stafford (E.)
Stamford (E.)
Stanhope (E.)
Stanwell (E.)
Stirling (S.)
Stockton (E.)
Strabane (N.I.)
Stratton (E.)
Strichen (S.)
Surbiton (E.)
Swaffham (E.)
Talgarth (W.)
Talisker (S.)
Tamworth (E.)
Taransay (S.)
Thetford (E.)
Thornaby (E.)
Tiverton (E.)
Traquair (S.)
Tredegar (W.)
Tregaron (W.)
Trillick (N.I.)
Tunstall (E.)
Uckfield (E.)
Ullapool (S.)
Uxbridge (E.)
Wallasey (E.)
Wallsend (E.)
Wanstead (E.)
Westbury (E.)
Wetheral (E.)
Wetherby (E.)
Weymouth (E.)
Whithorn (S.)
Woodford (E.)
Woodside (S.)
Woolwich (E.)
Worthing (E.)
Yarmouth (E.)

9

Aberaeron (W.)
Aberdovey (W.)
Aberfeldy (S.)
Aberffraw (W.)
Aberfoyle (S.)
Aldeburgh (E.)
Aldershot (E.)

Allendale (E.)
Alresford (E.)
Ambleside (E.)
Ardrossan (S.)
Ashbourne (E.)
Ashburton (E.)
Avonmouth (E.)
Aylesbury (E.)
Ballintra (N.I.)
Ballymena (N.I.)
Ballymore (N.I.)
Banbridge (N.I.)
Beaumaris (W.)
Belturbet (N.I.)
Berridale (S.)
Bettyhill (S.)
Blackburn (E.)
Blacklarg (S.)
Blackpool (E.)
Blandford (E.)
Blisworth (E.)
Bracadale (S.)
Bracknell (E.)
Braeriach (S.)
Braintree (E.)
Brentford (E.)
Brentwood (E.)
Brighouse (E.)
Broadford (S.)
Broughton (E.)
Broughton (S.)
Buckhaven (S.)
Bushmills (N.I.)
Cairntoul (S.)
Callander (S.)
Cambridge (E.)
Carstairs (S.)
Carnarvon (W.)
Carnforth (E.)
Castleton (E.)
Chesilton (E.)
Chingford (E.)
Clitheroe (E.)
Coleraine (N.I.)
Congleton (E.)
Cookstown (N.I.)
Cranborne (E.)
Cranbrook (E.)
Crewkerne (E.)
Criccieth (W.)
Cricklade (E.)
Cuckfield (E.)
Dartmouth (E.)
Devonport (E.)
Doncaster (E.)
Donington (E.)
Droitwich (E.)
Dronfield (E.)
Dumbarton (S.)
Dungannon (N.I.)
Dungeness (E.)
Dunstable (E.)
Edinburgh (S.)
Ellesmere (E.)
Faversham (E.)
Ferintosh (S.)
Festiniog (W.)
Fishguard (W.)
Fleetwood (E.)
Fochabers (S.)
Gateshead (E.)
Glaslough (N.I.)
Godalming (E.)
Gravesend (E.)
Greenwich (E.)
Grinstead (E.)

Guildford (E.)
Harrogate (E.)
Haslemere (E.)
Haverhill (E.)
Hawkhurst (E.)
Holmfirth (E.)
Ilchester (E.)
Immingham (E.)
Inchkeith (S.)
Inveraray (S.)
Inverness (S.)
Johnstone (S.)
Kettering (E.)
Kildrummy (S.)
Killybegs (N.I.)
King's Lynn (E.)
Kingswear (E.)
Kingussie (S.)
Kircubbin (N.I.)
Kirkcaldy (S.)
Lambourne (E.)
Lancaster (E.)
Leadhills (S.)
Leicester (E.)
Lichfield (E.)
Liverpool (E.)
Llanberis (W.)
Llandudno (W.)
Lochgelly (S.)
Lochinvar (S.)
Lochnagar (S.)
Lockerbie (S.)
Logierait (S.)
Longridge (E.)
Lowestoft (E.)
Lyme Regis (E.)
Lymington (E.)
Maidstone (E.)
Mansfield (E.)
Mauchline (S.)
Middleton (E.)
Milngavie (S.)
Moneymore (N.I.)
Newcastle (E.)
Newcastle (N.I.)
Newmarket (E.)
New Radnor (W.)
New Romney (E.)
Northwich (E.)
Otterburn (E.)
Pembridge (E.)
Penistone (E.)
Penkridge (E.)
Penyghent (E.)
Peterhead (S.)
Pickering (E.)
Pitlochry (S.)
Pontypool (E.)
Portadown (N.I.)
Port Ellen (S.)
Portcawl (W.)
Portmadoc (W.)
Prestwick (S.)
Rasharkin (N.I.)
Riccarton (S.)
Rochester (E.)
Rostrevor (N.I.)
Rotherham (E.)
Rothiemay (S.)
St. Andrews (S.)
St. Austell (E.)
St. Fillans (S.)
Salisbury (E.)
Saltcoats (S.)
Saltfleet (E.)
Sevenoaks (E.)

Sheerness (E.)
Sheffield (E.)
Sherborne (E.)
Shieldaig (S.)
Slamannan (S.)
Smethwick (E.)
Southgate (E.)
Southport (E.)
Southwell (E.)
Southwold (E.)
Starcross (E.)
Stevenage (E.)
Stewarton (S.)
Stockport (E.)
Stokesley (E.)
Stourport (E.)
Stranraer (S.)
Stratford (E.)
Strathdon (S.)
Strontian (S.)
Tarporley (E.)
Tavistock (E.)
Tenterden (E.)
Thornhill (S.)
Tobermory (S.)
Todmorden (E.)
Tomintoul (S.)
Tonbridge (E.)
Tobermore (N.I.)
Towcester (E.)
Tynemouth (E.)
Ulverston (E.)
Upminster (E.)
Uppingham (E.)
Uttoxeter (E.)
Wainfleet (E.)
Wakefield (E.)
Warkworth (E.)
Welshpool (W.)
Weybridge (E.)
Whernside (E.)
Wimbledon (E.)
Wincanton (E.)
Wokingham (E.)
Woodstock (E.)
Worcester (E.)
Wymondham (E.)

10

Abbotsford (S.)
Accrington (E.)
Achnasheen (S.)
Aldborough (E.)
Altrincham (E.)
Anstruther (S.)
Applecross (S.)
Ardrishaig (S.)
Auchinleck (S.)
Ballantrae (S.)
Ballybofir (N.I.)
Ballyclare (N.I.)
Ballyhaise (N.I.)
Ballymoney (N.I.)
Ballyroney (N.I.)
Barnstaple (E.)
Beaminster (E.)
Bedlington (E.)
Bellingham (E.)
Billericay (E.)
Birkenhead (E.)
Birmingham (E.)
Blackadder (S.)

Bridgnorth (E.)
Bridgwater (E.)
Bromsgrove (E.)
Broxbourne (E.)
Buckingham (E.)
Cader Idris (W.)
Caernarvon (W.)
Canterbury (E.)
Carmarthen (W.)
Carnoustie (S.)
Carshalton (E.)
Carsphairn (S.)
Castlederg (N.I.)
Castlefinn (N.I.)
Castletown (S.)
Chelmsford (E.)
Cheltenham (E.)
Chichester (E.)
Chippenham (E.)
Chulmleigh (E.)
Coatbridge (S.)
Coggeshall (E.)
Colchester (E.)
Coldingham (S.)
Coldstream (S.)
Crickhowel (W.)
Cullompton (E.)
Cushendall (N.I.)
Dalbeattie (S.)
Darlington (E.)
Donaghadee (N.I.)
Dorchester (E.)
Drumlithie (S.)
Dukinfield (E.)
Eastbourne (E.)
East Linton (S.)
Eccleshall (E.)
Farningham (E.)
Ffestiniog (W.)
Folkestone (E.)
Freshwater (E.)
Galashiels (S.)
Gillingham (E.)
Glengariff (N.I.)
Glenrothes (S.)
Gloucester (E.)
Halesworth (E.)
Hartlepool (E.)
Haslingdon (E.)
Heathfield (E.)
Horncastle (E.)
Hornchurch (E.)
Hungerford (E.)
Hunstanton (E.)
Huntingdon (E.)
Ilfracombe (E.)
Johnshaven (S.)
Kenilworth (E.)
Kilconnell (N.I.)
Kilcreggan (S.)
Killenaule (E.)
Kilmainham (S.)
Kilmalcolm (S.)
Kilmarnock (S.)
Kilwinning (S.)
Kincardine (S.)
Kingsbarns (S.)
Kingsclere (E.)
Kirkmaiden (S.)
Kirkoswald (E.)
Kirkoswald (S.)
Kirriemuir (S.)
Launceston (E.)
Leamington (E.)
Lennoxtown (S.)
Leominster (E.)

Lesmahagow (S.)
Linlithgow (S.)
Littleport (F.)
Livingston (S.)
Llandovery (W.)
Llanfyllin (W.)
Llangadock (W.)
Llangollen (W.)
Llanidloes (W.)
Maidenhead (E.)
Malmesbury (E.)
Manchester (E.)
Markethill (N.I.)
Mexborough (E.)
Micheldean (E.)
Middlewich (E.)
Mildenhall (E.)
Milnathort (S.)
Montgomery (W.)
Motherwell (S.)
Nailsworth (E.)
Nottingham (E.)
Okehampton (E.)
Orfordness (E.)
Pangbourne (E.)
Patrington (E.)
Peacehaven (E.)
Pittenweem (S.)
Plinlimmon (W.)
Pontefract (E.)
Portaferry (N.I.)
Porth Nigel (W.)
Portishead (E.)
Portobello (S.)
Portsmouth (E.)
Potter's Bar (E.)
Presteigne (W.)
Ravenglass (E.)
Rockingham (E.)
Ronaldsay (S.)
Rutherglen (S.)
Saintfield (N.I.)
St. Leonards (E.)
Saxmundham (E.)
Shepperton (E.)
Sheringham (E.)
Shrewsbury (E.)
Stalbridge (E.)
Stonehaven (S.)
Stonehouse (S.)
Stoneykirk (S.)
Stowmarket (E.)
Strangford (N.I.)
Stranorlar (N.I.)
Strathaven (S.)
Strathearn (S.)
Strathmore (S.)
Sunderland (E.)
Tanderagee (N.I.)
Teddington (E.)
Teignmouth (E.)
Tewkesbury (E.)
Thamesmead (E.)
Torrington (E.)
Trowbridge (E.)
Tweedmouth (S.)
Twickenham (E.)
Warminster (E.)
Warrington (E.)
Washington (E.)
Wednesbury (E.)
Wellington (E.)
West Calder (S.)
Westward Ho (E.)
Whitchurch (E.)
Whithaven (E.)

Whitstable (E.)
Whittlesey (E.)
Willenhall (E.)
Wilsontown (S.)
Winchelsea (E.)
Winchester (E.)
Windermere (E.)
Windlesham (E.)
Wirksworth (E.)
Withernsea (E.)
Wolsingham (E.)
Woodbridge (E.)
Workington (E.)

11

Aberchirder (S.)
Abergavenny (E.)
Aberystwyth (W.)
Ballycastle (N.I.)
Ballygawley (N.I.)
Balquhidder (S.)
Bannockburn (S.)
Basingstoke (E.)
Blairgowrie (S.)
Bognor Regis (E.)
Bournemouth (E.)
Braich-y-Pwll (W.)
Bridlington (E.)
Buntingford (E.)
Campbeltown (S.)
Carrickmore (N.I.)
Charlestown (S.)
Cleethorpes (E.)
Cockermouth (E.)
Crossmaglen (N.I.)
Cumbernauld (S.)
Downpatrick (N.I.)
Draperstown (N.I.)
Drummelzier (S.)
Dunfermline (S.)
East Retford (E.)
Ecclefechan (S.)
Enniskillen (N.I.)
Fettercairn (S.)
Fort William (S.)
Fraserburgh (S.)
Glastonbury (E.)
Great Marlow (E.)
Guisborough (E.)
Haltwhistle (E.)
Hampton Wick (E.)
Hatherleigh (E.)
Helensburgh (S.)
High Wycombe (E.)
Ingatestone (E.)
Invergordon (S.)
Kirkmichael (S.)
Letterkenny (N.I.)
Leytonstone (E.)
Littlestone (E.)
Londonderry (N.I.)
Lossiemouth (S.)
Lostwithiel (S.)
Ludgershall (E.)
Lutterworth (E.)
Mablethorpe (E.)
Machynlleth (W.)
Magherafelt (N.I.)
Manningtree (E.)
Market Rasen (E.)
Marlborough (E.)
Maxwelltown (S.)
Much Wenlock (E.) 113

Musselburgh (S.)
New Brighton (E.)
Newton Abbot (E.)
Northampton (E.)
Oystermouth (W.)
Petersfield (E.)
Pocklington (E.)
Port Glasgow (S.)
Portglenone (N.I.)
Port Patrick (S.)
Prestonpans (S.)
Pultneytown (S.)
Randalstown (N,I.)
Rathfriland (N.I.)
Rawtenstall (E.)
St. Margaret's (E.)
Scarborough (E.)
Shaftesbury (E.)
Southampton (E.)
South Molton (E.)
Stalybridge (E.)
Stourbridge (E.)
Strathblane (S.)
Tattershall (E.)
Wallingford (E.)
Walthamstow (E.)
Westminster (E.)
Whitechurch (E.)
Woodhall Spa (E.)

12

Attleborough (E.)
Auchterarder (S.)
Ballachulish (S.)
Bexhill-on-Sea (E.)
Castleblaney (N.I.)
Castle Dawson (N.I.)
Castle Rising (E.)
Castlewellan (N.I.)
Chesterfield (E.)
Christchurch (E.)
East Kilbride (S.)
Five Mile Town (N.I.)
Fort Augustus (S.)
Gainsborough (E.)
Garelochhead (S.)
Great Grimsby (E.)
Great Malvern (E.)
Hillsborough (N.I.)
Huddersfield (E.)
Ingleborough (E.)
Inishtrahull (N.I.)

Innerleithen (S.)
Lawrencekirk (S.)
Llandilofawr (W.)
Llantrissant (W.)
Long Stratton (E.)
Loughborough (E.)
Macclesfield (E.)
Milton Keynes (E.)
Morecambe Bay (E.)
North Berwick (S.)
North Shields (E.)
North Walsham (E.)
Peterborough (E.)
Portmahomack (S.)
Shoeburyness (E.)
Shottesbrook (E.)
South Shields (E.)
Stewartstown (N.I.)
Stoke-on-Trent (E.)
Strathpeffer (S.)
Tillicoultry (S.)

13

Auchtermuchty (S.)
Barnard Castle (E.)
Berkhampstead (E.)
Bishop's Castle (E.)
Boroughbridge (E.)
Brightlingsea (E.)
Brookeborough (N.I.)
Burton-on-Trent (E.)
Bury St. Edmunds (E.)
Carrickfergus (N.I.)
Castle Douglas (S.)
Chipping Ongar (E.)
Cockburnspath (S.)
Dalmellington (S.)
Derrygonnelly (N.I.)
Finchampstead (E.)
Godmanchester (E.)
Great Yarmouth (E.)
Haverfordwest (W.)
Higham Ferrers (E.)
Inverkeithing (S.)
Inverkeithnie (S.)
Kidderminster (E.)
Kirkby Stephen (E.)
Kirkcudbright (S.)
Kirkintilloch (S.)
Knaresborough (E.)
Littlehampton (E.)

Lytham St. Annes (E.)
Market Deeping (E.)
Market Drayton (E.)
Melcombe Regis (E.)
Melton Mowbray (E.)
Merthyr Tydfil (W.)
Middlesbrough (E.)
Newton Stewart (S.)
Northallerton (E.)
Rothiemurchus (S.)
Saffron Walden (E.)
Shepton Mallet (E.)
Wolverhampton (E.)

14

Berwick-on-Tweed (E.)
Bishop Auckland (E.)
Bishops Waltham (E.)
Chipping Barnet (E.)
Chipping Norton (E.)
Hemel Hempstead (E.)
Kirkby Lonsdale (E.)
Market Bosworth (E.)
Mortimer's Cross (E.)
Newtown Stewart (N.I.)
Stockton-on-Tees (E.)
Stony Stratford (E.)
Sutton Courtney (E.)
Tunbridge Wells (E.)
Wellingborough (E.)
West Hartlepool (E.)
Wootton Basset (E.)

15

Ashton-under-Lyne (E.)
Barrow-in-Furness (E.)
Burnham-on-Crouch (E.)
Castle Donington (E.)
Leighton Buzzard (E.)
Newcastle-on-Tyne (E.)
St. Leonards-on-Sea (E.)
Stratford-on-Avon (E.)
Sutton Coldfield (E.)
Weston-super-Mare (E.)

16

Bishop's Stortford (E.)
Welwyn Garden City (E.)

Towns and cities: United States

4

Gary
Lima
Reno
Troy
York
Waco

5

Akron
Boise
Bronx

Butte
Flint
Miami
Omaha
Ozark
Salem
Selma
Tulsa
Utica

6

Albany
Austin

Bangor
Biloxi
Boston
Camden
Canton
Dallas
Dayton
Denver
Duluth
El Paso
Eugene
Fresno
Lowell
Mobile
Nassau

Newark
Oxnard
Peoria
St. Paul
Tacoma
Toledo
Topeka
Tucson
Urbana

7

Abilene
Anaheim

Atlanta
Boulder
Brooklyn
Buffalo
Chicago
Columbus
Concord
Detroit
Hampton
Hoboken
Houston
Jackson
Lincoln
Madison
Memphis
Modesto
New York
Norfolk
Oakland
Orlando
Phoenix
Raleigh
Reading
Roanoke
St. Louis
Saginaw
San Jose
Seattle
Spokane
Wichita
Yonkers

Hartford
Honolulu
Lakeland
Las Vegas
New Haven
Oak Ridge
Palo Alto
Pasadena
Portland
Richmond
San Diego
Santa Ana
Savannah
Stamford
Stockton
Syracuse
Wheeling

Lexington
Long Beach
Manhattan
Milwaukee
Nashville
New London
Northeast
Princeton
Riverside
Rochester
Waterbury
Worcester
Ypsilanti

Sacramento
Saint Louis
San Antonio
Washington
Youngstown

11

Albuquerque
Cedar Rapids
Chattanooga
Grand Rapids
Minneapolis
Newport News
Palm Springs
Schenectady
Springfield

9

Anchorage
Annapolis
Arlington
Baltimore
Bethlehem
Cambridge
Champaign
Charlotte
Cleveland
Des Moines
Fairbanks
Fort Wayne
Fort Worth
Galveston
Hollywood
Johnstown
Kalamazoo
Lancaster

10

Atomic City
Baton Rouge
Birmingham
Charleston
Cincinatti
Evansville
Greensboro
Greenville
Harrisburg
Huntsville
Jersey City
Kansas City
Little Rock
Long Branch
Los Angeles
Louisville
Miami Beach
Montgomery
New Bedford
New Orleans
Pittsburgh
Providence

12 AND OVER

Atlantic City (12)
Beverly Hills (12)
Colorado Springs (15)
Corpus Christi (13)
Fayetteville (12)
Fort Lauderdale (14)
Independence (12)
Indianapolis (12)
Jacksonville (12)
New Brunswick (12)
Niagara Falls (12)
Oklahoma City (12)
Philadelphia (12)
Poughkeepsie (12)
St. Petersburg (12)
Salt Lake City (12)
San Francisco (12)
Santa Barbara (12)

8

Berkeley
Dearborn
Green Bay
Hannibal

Towns and cities: rest of the world

3 AND 4

Agra (Ind.)
Aix (Fr.)
Ava (Burma)
Baku (U.S.S.R.)
Bâle (Swit.)
Bari (It.)
Bray (Ire.)
Brno (Cze.)
Cali (Colombia)
Cobh (Ire.)
Cork (Ire.)
Fez (Moroc.)
Gaza (Isr.)
Gera (E. Ger.)
Giza (Egypt)
Homs (Syria and Libya)
Hue (Viet.)
Kano (Nig.)
Kiel (W. Ger.)
Kiev (U.S.S.R.)
Kobe (Jap.)
Köln (W. Ger.)
Lamu (Kenya)
Laon (Fr.)
Lodz (Pol.)
Luta (China)
Lvov (U.S.S.R.)
Lyon (Fr.)

Metz (Fr.)
Nice (Fr.)
Omsk (U.S.S.R.)
Oran (Alg.)
Pécs (Hung.)
Pisa (It.)
Riga (U.S.S.R.)
Sian (China)
Suez (Egypt)
Suhl (E. Ger.)
Tour (Fr.)
Troy (Asia M.)
Tyre (Lebanon)
Ufa (U.S.S.R.)
Vigo (Sp.)

5

Ajmer (Ind.)
Alwar (Ind.)
Arras (Fr.)
Aswan (Egypt)
Balla (Ire.)
Basel } (Swit.)
Basle }
Basra (Iraq)
Boyle (Ire.)
Beira (Moz.)
Brest (Fr. and U.S.S.R.)

Cadiz (Sp.)
Clare (Ire.)
Cuzco (Peru)
Delhi (Ind.)
Dijon (Fr.)
Essen (W. Ger.)
Galle (Sri)
Genoa (It.)
Ghent (Belg.)
Gorky (U.S.S.R.)
Hague (Neth.)
Haifa (Isr.)
Halle (E. Ger.)
Herat (Afghan.)
Izmir (Turk.)
Jaffa (Isr.)
Jidda (Saudi)
Kandy (Sri)
Kazan (U.S.S.R.)
Kells (Ire.)
Kotah (Ind.)
Kyoto (Jap.)
Liège (Belg.)
Lille (Fr.)
Lyons (Fr.)
Mainz (W. Ger.)
Malmö (Swed.)
Mecca (Saudi)
Memel (U.S.S.R.)
Milan (It.)

115

Minsk (U.S.S.R.)
Mosul (Iraq)
Namur (Belg.)
Nancy (Fr.)
Osaka (Jap.)
Ostia (It.)
Padua (It.)
Parma (It.)
Patna (Ind.)
Perth (Austral.)
Pinsk (U.S.S.R.)
Poona (Ind.)
Posen (Pol.)
Pskov (U.S.S.R.)
Pusan (S. Korea)
Rabat (Moroc.)
Reims (Fr.)
Rouen (Fr.)
Sidon (Lebanon)
Siena (It.)
Simla (Ind.)
Sligo (Ire.)
Trent (It.)
Trier (W. Ger.)
Turin (It.)
Varna (Bulg.)
Vilna (U.S.S.R.)
Wuhan (China)
Yalta (U.S.S.R.)
Ypres (Belg.)

6

Aachen (W. Ger.)
Abadan (Iran)
Aleppo (Syria)
Amiens (Fr.)
Anshan (China)
Arklow (Ire.)
Arnhem (Neth.)
Bantry (Ire.)
Baroda (Ind.)
Berber (Sudan)
Bergen (Nor.)
Bhopal (Ind.)
Bilbao (Sp.)
Bombay (Ind.)
Bochum (W. Ger.)
Bremen (W. Ger.)
Bruges (Belg.)
Calais (Fr.)
Canton (China)
Carlow (Ire.)
Cashel (Ire.)
Cassel (W. Ger.)
Dairen (China)
Danang (Viet.)
Danzig (Pol.)
Darwin (Austral.)
Dieppe (Fr.)
Dinant (Belg.)
Durban (S.A.)
Erfurt (E. Ger.)
Fushun (China)
Galway (Ire.)
Gdansk (Pol.)
Geneva (Swit.)
Harbin (China)
Hobart (Austral.)
Howrah (Ind.)
Ibadan (Nig.)
Imphal (Ind.)
Indore (Ind.)

Jaipur (Ind.)
Jhansi (Ind.)
Juarez (Mex.)
Kanpur (Ind.)
Kassel (W. Ger.)
Kaunas (U.S.S.R.)
Kohima (Ind.)
Krakow (Pol.)
Lahore (Pak.)
Leiden (Neth.)
Le Mans (Fr.)
Leyden (Neth.)
Lobito (Angola)
Lübeck (W. Ger.)
Lublin (Pol.)
Madras (Ind.)
Manila (Philip.)
Medina (Saudi)
Meerut (Ind.)
Mukden (China)
Munich (W. Ger.)
Mysore (Ind.)
Nagoya (Jap.)
Nagpur (Ind.)
Nantes (Fr.)
Napier (N.Z.)
Naples (It.)
Nelson (N.Z.)
Odessa (U.S.S.R.)
Oporto (Port.)
Ostend (Belg.)
Puebla (Mex.)
Quebec (Can.)
Quetta (Pak.)
Rampur (Ind.)
Recife (Braz.)
Reggio (It.)
Regina (Can.)
Rheims (Fr.)
Seville (Sp.)
Shiraz (Iran)
Smyrna (Turk.)
Soweto (S.A.)
Sparta (Gr.)
St. Malo (Fr.)
Sydney (Austral.)
Tabriz (Iran)
Thebes
 (Gr. and Egypt)
Tiflis (U.S.S.R.)
Tobruk (Libya)
Toulon (Fr.)
Trèves (W. Ger.)
Tsinan (China)
Venice (It.)
Verdun (Fr.)
Verona (It.)
Zagreb (Yug.)
Zurich (Swit.)

7

Ajaccio (Fr.)
Alençon (Fr.)
Alma-Ata (U.S.S.R.)
Antwerp (Belg.)
Athlone (Ire.)
Avignon (Fr.)
Babylon (Asia)
Badajoz (Sp.)
Bandung (Indo.)
Bayonne (Fr.)
Benares (Ind.)
Blarney (Ire.)
Bologna (It.)

Breslau (Pol.)
Calgary (Can.)
Clonmel (Ire.)
Coblenz (W. Ger.)
Cologne (W. Ger.)
Cordoba (Sp. and Arg.)
Corinth (Gr.)
Cottbus (E. Ger.)
Donetsk (U.S.S.R.)
Dongola (Sudan)
Dresden (E. Ger.)
Dundalk (Ire.)
Dunedin (N.Z.)
Dunkirk (Fr.)
Erzerum (Turk.)
Granada (Sp.)
Gwalior (Ind.)
Halifax (Can.)
Hamburg (W. Ger.)
Hanover (W. Ger.)
Homburg (W. Ger.)
Irkutsk (U.S.S.R.)
Isfahan (U.S.S.R.)
Jericho (Asia)
Jodhpur (Ind.)
Kalinin (U.S.S.R.)
Karachi (Pak.)
Kharkov (U.S.S.R.)
Kildare (Ire.)
Koblenz (W. Ger.)
Kunming (China)
Lanchow (China)
La Plata (Arg.)
Le Havre (Fr.)
Leipzig (E. Ger.)
Lemberg (U.S.S.R.)
Lourdes (Fr.)
Lucerne (Swit.)
Lucknow (Ind.)
Malines (Belg.)
Mansura (Egypt)
Mashhad (Iran)
Memphis (Egypt)
Messina (It.)
Mombasa (Kenya)
München (W. Ger.)
Mycenae (Gr.)
Nanking (China)
Orléans (Fr.)
Palermo (It.)
Palmyra (Syria)
Piraeus (Gr.)
Pompeii (It.)
Potsdam (E. Ger.)
Ravenna (It.)
Rostock (E. Ger.)
St. John's (Can.)
Salerno (It.)
San Remo (It.)
Sapporo (Jap.)
Tallinn (U.S.S.R.)
Tangier (Moroc.)
Tbilisi (U.S.S.R.)
Taiyuan (China)
Tel Aviv (Isr.)
Toronto (Can.)
Trieste (It.)
Uppsala (Swed.)
Utrecht (Neth.)
Vatican (It.)
Vilnius (U.S.S.R.)
Wexford (Ire.)
Wicklow (Ire.)
Yakutsk (U.S.S.R.)
Yerevan (U.S.S.R.)
Youghal (Ire.)

8

Acapulco (Mex.)
Adelaide (Austral.)
Agartala (Ind.)
Alicante (Sp.)
Amritsar (Ind.)
Auckland (N.Z.)
Augsburg (W. Ger.)
Besançon (Fr.)
Bordeaux (Fr.)
Boulogne (Fr.)
Brisbane (Austral.)
Bulawayo (Rhodesia)
Calcutta (Ind.)
Carthage (N. Af.)
Cawnpore (Ind.)
Clontarf (Ire.)
Dortmund (W. Ger.)
Drogheda (Ire.)
Edmonton (Can.)
Florence (It.)
Grenoble (Fr.)
Göteborg (Swed.)
Haiphong (Viet.)
Hamilton (Can.)
Hannover (W. Ger.)
Ismailia (Egypt)
Istanbul (Turk.)
Jamalpur (Ind.)
Kandahar (Afghan.)
Kilkenny (Ire.)
Kingston (Can.)
Lausanne (Swit.)
Limerick (Ire.)
Listowel (Ire.)
Mafeking (S.A.)
Mandalay (Burma)
Mannheim (W. Ger.)
Maynooth (Ire.)
Montreal (Can.)
Nagasaki (Jap.)
Novgorod (U.S.S.R.)
Nürnberg (W. Ger.)
Omdurman (Sudan)
Pamplona (Sp.)
Peshawar (Pak.)
Port Said (Egypt)
Przemysl (Pol.)
Rathdrum (Ire.)
Salonika (Gr.)
Salzburg (Aust.)
Sao Paulo (Braz.)
Sarajevo (Yug.)
Schwerin (E. Ger.)
Shanghai (China)
Shenyang (China)
Shillong (Ind.)
Soissons (Fr.)
Smolensk (U.S.S.R.)
Srinagar (Ind.)
Surabaja (Indo.)
Syracuse (It.)
Tangiers (Moroc.)
Tashkent (U.S.S.R.)
The Hague (Neth.)
Tientsin (China)
Timbuktu (Mali)
Toulouse (Fr.)
Valencia (Sp.)
Varanasi (Ind.)
Victoria (Can.)
Winnipeg (Can.)
Yokohama (Jap.)
Zanzibar (Tanz.)
Zaragoza (Sp.)

9

Abbeville (Fr.)
Agrigento (It.)
Ahmedabad (Ind.)
Allahabad (Ind.)
Astrakhan (U.S.S.R.)
Bangalore (Ind.)
Barcelona (Sp.)
Beersheba (Isr.)
Brunswick (W. Ger.)
Byzantium (Turk.)
Cartagena (Sp. and
  Colombia)
Changchun (China)
Cherbourg (Fr.)
Cherkessk (U.S.S.R.)
Chungking (China)
Connemara (Ire.)
Darmstadt (W. Ger.)
Dordrecht (Neth.)
Eindhoven (Neth.)
Frankfurt (E. Ger.)
Frankfurt (W. Ger.)
Gibraltar (Eur.)
Hiroshima (Jap.)
Hyderabad (Ind. and Pak.)
Innsbruck (Aust.)
Karaganda (U.S.S.R.)
Killarney (Ire.)
Kimberley (S.A.)
Krivoi Rog (U.S.S.R.)
Kuibyshev (U.S.S.R.)
Ladysmith (S.A.)
Las Palmas (Sp.)
Leningrad (U.S.S.R.)
Ljubljana (Yug.)
Magdeburg (E. Ger.)
Maracaibo (Venez.)
Marrakech ⎱ (Moroc.)
Marrakesh ⎰
Marseille (Fr.)
Melbourne (Austral.)
Monterrey (Mex.)

Newcastle (Austral.)
Nuremberg (W. Ger.)
Panmunjon (Korea)
Roscommon (Ire.)
Rotterdam (Neth.)
Samarkand (U.S.S.R.)
Santander (Sp.)
Saragossa (Sp.)
Stuttgart (W. Ger.)
Tipperary (Ire.)
Trondheim (Nor.)
Vancouver (Can.)
Volgograd (U.S.S.R.)
Waterford (Ire.)
Wiesbaden (W. Ger.)
Wuppertal (W. Ger.)

10

Alexandria (Egypt)
Baden Baden (W. Ger.)
Bad Homburg (W. Ger.)
Bratislava (Cze.)
Casablanca (Moroc.)
Chandigarh (Ind.)
Chittagong (Bangla.)
Darjeeling (Ind.)
Düsseldorf (W. Ger.)
Gothenburg (Swed.)
Heidelberg (W. Ger.)
Jamshedpur (Ind.)
Königsberg (U.S.S.R.)
Lubumbashi (Zaïre)
Marseilles (Fr.)
Port Arthur (China)
Sevastopol (U.S.S.R.)
Shillelagh (Ire.)
Simonstown (S.A.)
Stalingrad (U.S.S.R.)
Strasbourg (Fr.)
Sverdlovsk (U.S.S.R.)
Trivandrum (Ind.)

Valparaiso (Chile)
Versailles (Fr.)

11

Armentières (Fr.)
Bahia Blanca (Arg.)
Ballymurphy (Ire.)
Bhubaneswar (Ind.)
Fredericton (Can.)
Grahamstown (S.A.)
Guadalajara (Mex.)
Helsingborg (Swed.)
Kaliningrad (U.S.S.R.)
Novosibirsk (U.S.S.R.)
Saarbrücken (W. Ger.)
Sharpeville (S.A.)
Vladivostok (U.S.S.R.)

12

Bloemfontein (S.A.)
Christchurch (N.Z.)
Johannesburg (S.A.)
Niagara Falls (Can.)
Rio de Janeiro (Braz.)
San Sebastian (Sp.)

13 AND OVER

Aix-la-Chapelle (W. Ger.)
  (13)
Belo Horizonte (Braz.) (13)
Charlottetown (Can.) (13)
Clermont-Ferrand (Fr.) (15)
Constantinople (Turk.) (14)
Dnepropetrovsk (U.S.S.R.)
  (14)
Karl-Marx-Stadt (E. Ger.) (13)
Pietermaritzburg (S.A.) (16)
Port Elizabeth (S.A.) (13)

Waterfalls, the largest

Churchill (9) *Can.*
Gavarnie (8) *Fr.*
Giessbach (9) *Swit.*
Guaira (6) *Braz.*
Hamilton (8) *Can.*
Krimmler (8) *Aust.*

Multnomah (9) *U.S.A.*
Niagara (7) *Can.–U.S.A.*
Ribbon (6) *U.S.A.*
Roraima (7) *Guyana*
Salto Angel (10) *Venez.*
Sete Quedas (10) *Braz.*

Stanley (7) *Zaire*
Sutherland (10) *N.Z.*
Trümmelbach (11) *Swit.*
Vettisfos (9) *Nor.*
Victoria (8) *Zimbabwe/Zambia*
Yosemite, Upper (13) *U.S.A.*

Weather

3 AND 4

bise
calm
cold
cool
damp
dark
dry
dull
east
fog
föhn
gale

gust
hail
haze
hazy
heat
hot
icy
mild
mist
rain
smog
snow
tide
veer

warm
west
wet
wind

5

cirri
cloud
dusty
eurus
flood
foehn

foggy
frost
gusty
light
misty
muggy
north
rainy
sleet
snowy
south
storm
sunny
windy

117

6

arctic
auster
bright
chilly
cirrus
clouds
cloudy
colder
deluge
floods
freeze
frosty
hot day
lowery
meteor
mizzle
mizzly
nimbus
normal
samiel
shower
simoom
simoon
solano
squall
starry
stormy
sultry
torrid
trades
vortex
warmer
wet day
winter
wintry
zephyr

7

backing
blowing
climate
clouded
cold day
coldish
cumulus
cyclone
drizzle
drought
dry-bulb
fogbank
freshen
fresher
freshet
hailing
hottish
icy-cold
mistral
monsoon
muggish
pampero
rainbow

raining
set fair
showery
sirocco
snowing
squally
stratus
summery
sunspot
tempest
thunder
tornado
typhoon
veering
warm day
warmish
wintery

8

autumnal
blizzard
cold snap
cyclonic
dead-calm
doldrums
downpour
easterly
east wind
eddy wind
fireball
freezing
heatwave
hot night
hurlwind
landwind
levanter
lowering
meteoric
nubilous
overcast
rainfall
rainless
snowfall
sunlight
thundery
tropical
westerly
west wind
wet night
windless

9

cold night
drift wind
drizzling
dry season
hailstorm
hard frost
harmattan
hoarfrost
hurricane

lightning
moonlight
northeast
northerly
northwest
north wind
nor'-wester
raincloud
sea breeze
snow-storm
southeast
southerly
southwest
south wind
sou'-wester
starlight
tidal wave
trade wind
unclouded
unsettled
warm night
whirlwind
zephyrous

10

arctic cold
black frost
changeable
depression
euroclydon
freshening
frostbound
hot climate
hot weather
land breeze
March winds
monsoonish
pouring-wet
Scotch mist
storm-cloud
waterspout
wet weather
white frost

11

anticyclone
cats and dogs
cold climate
cold weather
dull weather
etesian wind
foul weather
hard weather
lowering sky
mackerel sky
meteorology
mild weather
rain or shine
rainy season
stiff breeze
storm signal

summer cloud
temperature
tempestuous
thunderbolt
thunderclap
warm weather
wind backing
wind veering

12

anticyclonic
April showers
atmospherics
cirrocumulus
cirrostratus
currocumulus
currostratus
easterly wind
equinoctials
freezing rain
mackerel gale
shooting star
storm brewing
thundercloud
thunderstorm
tropical heat
tropical rain
weather glass
westerly wind
windy weather

13 AND 14

aurora borealis (14)
autumn weather (13)
cumulostratus (13)
frosty weather (13)
meteorological (14)
moonlight night (14)
northeast wind (13)
northerly wind (13)
northwest wind (13)
sheet lightning (14)
southeast wind (13)
southerly wind (13)
southwest wind (13)
starlight night (14)
summer weather (13)
thunder-shower (13)
torrential rain (14)
weather report (13)
weather prophet (14)
wintry weather (13)

15

forked lightning
meteoric showers
prevailing winds
summer lightning
tropical climate

LAW AND GOVERNMENT
Legal terms

2

J.P.
K.C.
Q.C.

3 AND 4

abet
act
bail
bar
bars
case
dock
D.P.P.
fair
fee
fine
gaol
I.O.U.
jury
law
lien
m'lud
oath
plea
quit
rape
rent
riot
rob
seal
stay
sue
suit
tort
use
will
writ

5

alien
arson
award
bench
cause
clerk
costs
court
crime
false
forge
fraud
guilt
in rem
judge
juror
legal
libel
mulct
order
penal
plead
poach
police
prize
proof

quash
right
rules
steal
trial
trust
usher
usury
valid

6

access
action
affirm
appeal
arrest
attorn
bailee
bigamy
breach
charge
commit
deceit
de jure
disbar
duress
elegit
equity
escrow
estate
felony
fiscal
forger
guilty
Hilary
incest
injury
insult
junior
legacy
malice
master
motion
murder
pardon
parole
piracy
police
prison
puisne
remand
repeal
set-off
surety
surtax

7

accused
alimony
assault
assizes
bailiff
battery
bequest
borstal
bribery
capital

case law
caution
circuit
codicil
consent
control
convict
coroner
counsel
cruelty
custody
damages
de facto
defence
divorce
ex parte
faculty
forgery
garnish
hanging
harming
hearsay
illegal
impeach
inquest
justice
land tax
larceny
lawless
lawsuit
licence
neglect
non suit
offence
penalty
perjury
precept
probate
proving
querent
release
reserve
Riot Act
robbery
servant
service
sheriff
slander
statute
summary
summons
suspect
tel-quel
treason
trustee
verdict
warrant
witness

8

absolute
abstract
act of god
act of law
advocate
advowson
attorney
barratry
birching

bottomry
brawling
burglary
camera
canon law
chancery
civil law
coercion
contract
covenant
criminal
deed poll
disorder
distress
drafting
entailed
estoppel
eviction
evidence
executor
felo de se
fidelity
forensic
guardian
homicide
in camera
indecent
judgment
judicial
law agent
law lords
legal aid
licensee
litigant
majority
murderer
novation
nuisance
perjuror
petition
pleading
preamble
prisoner
receiver
recorder
reprieve
Salic law
sedition
sentence
Shops Act
stealing
subpoena
sui juris
testator
trespass
tribunal
Truck Act
true bill
unlawful
validity

9

abduction
accessory
acquittal
ademption
agreement
allotment
annulment

119

attainder
barrister
blackmail
bona fides
cestui que
champerty
code of law
collusion
common law
copyright
defendant
de son tort
deviation
discharge
dismissal
distraint
embracery
endowment
equitable
execution
executory
extortion
fee simple
feoffment
Gaming Act
good faith
grand jury
guarantee
guarantor
high court
income tax
indemnity
innocence
intestacy
intestate
judiciary
land court
licensing
endowment
litigious
loitering
mala fides
mandatory
murderous
not guilty
not proven
Old Bailey
plaintiff
precatory
precedent
privilege
probation
procedure
refresher
registrar
remission
restraint
servitude
solicitor
statutory
summing-up
surrender
testament
testimony

10

alienation
appearance
assessment
assignment
attachment
attornment
bankruptcy
common pleas

common riot
confession
connivance
conspiracy
corruption
decree nisi
deed of gift
defamation
disclaimer
enticement
estate duty
executrix
eye witness
finance act
forfeiture
fraudulent
gaming acts
government
gun licence
hard labour
high treason
illegality
impediment
in chambers
indictment
injunction
inter vivos
judicature
King's Bench
land tenure
law sitting
Law Society
legitimacy
limitation
liquor laws
litigation
magistrate
misconduct
misprision
negligence
next friend
parliament
Poor Law Act
post mortem
prize court
procurator
prosecutor
respondent
revocation
separation
settlement
trespasser
ultra vires

11

advancement
affiliation
appointment
arbitration
arrangement
assize court
association
attestation
civil wrongs
composition
concealment
condonation
congé d'élire
county court
criminal law
death duties
debtors' acts
deportation
dissolution

disturbance
enabling act
enforcement
engrossment
examination
extenuating
extradition
fair comment
fieri facias
foreclosure
impeachment
infanticide
issue of writ
king's pardon
maintenance
market overt
mayor's court
obstruction
prerogative
prosecution
Queen's Bench
regulations
requisition
restitution
root of title
royal assent
sheriff's act
stamp duties
stipendiary
subornation
suicide pact
third degree
trespassing
Vagrancy Act
vesting deed

12

adjudication
bona vacantia
case of thorns
causa proxima
caution money
caveat emptor
charter party
Companies Act
compensation
constabulary
conveyancing
co-respondent
crime and tort
cross-examine
crown witness
death penalty
disaffection
embezzlement
encroachment
express trust
ferae naturae
grand assizes
guardianship
Habeas Corpus
imprisonment
infringement
inherent vice
interpleader
intimidation
joint tenancy
king's proctor
land transfer
Lord Advocate
lord of appeal
manslaughter
mensa et thoro
misbehaviour

misdemeanour
misdirection
oral evidence
pendente lite
prescription
privy council
prostitution
Queen's Pardon
ratification
royal charter
royal warrant
sheriff clerk
supreme court
taxing master
testamentary

13

administrator
age of marriage
ancient lights
apportionment
appropriation
burden of proof
charging order
common assault
consideration
court of appeal
Court of Arches
criminal libel
damage feasant
ejection order
ejusdem generis
Ground Game Act
hereditaments
housebreaking
illegal action
interlocutory
judge advocate
justification
law of property
letters patent
lord president
parliamentary
petty sessions
public trustee
quantum meruit
recognisances
right of appeal
search warrant
simple larceny
statute barred
treasure trove
trial by combat
trial by ordeal
Witchcraft Act

14

act of indemnity
administration
Admiralty Court
choses in action
common nuisance
common sergeant
companies court
concealed fraud
conjugal rights
county judgment
court of justice
criminal appeal
default summons
false pretences
identification

identity parade
local authority
lord chancellor
naturalization
oyer and terminer
penal servitude
Queen's evidence
Queen's pleasure
second division

special licence
wrongful arrest

15

act of bankruptcy
act of parliament
Act of Settlement

attorney-general
autrefois acquit
benefit of clergy
charitable trust
commercial court
commissary court
compound a felony
compound larceny
consistory court

contempt of court
emergency powers
latent ambiguity
local government
marital coercion
marriage licence
official secrets
power of attorney
quarter sessions

Parliamentary and political

2

M.P.
P.M.
U.N.

3

act
bar
C.B.I.
C.I.A.
E.E.C.
gag
I.R.A.
K.G.B.
law
opt
P.L.O.
red
sit
tax
T.U.C.

4

ayes
bill
coup
Dail
D.O.R.A.
Duma
gain
left
lord
mace
N.A.T.O.
noes
oath
pact
pass
peer
poll
rump
seat
Tory
veto
'vide
vote
vuli
Whig
whip
writ

5

agent
amend

bylaw
chair
clerk
count
draft
edict
elect
enact
house
junta
legal
lobby
Nazis
order
paper
party
Provo
purge
rally
right
S.E.A.T.O.
sit-in
valid
voter

6

assent
backer
ballot
budget
caucus
clause
colony
commie
Cortes
decree
divide
enosis
Fabian
Führer
govern
heckle
Labour
leader
Maoism
member
motion
nation
picket
policy
putsch
quorum
recess
record
reform
report
ruling
secede
senate

sirkar
speech
strike
summon
swaraj
tariff
teller
tyrant

7

adjourn
Al Fatah
anarchy
barrack
borough
boycott
cabinet
canvass
censure
chamber
closure
cold war
Comecon
Commons
commune
council
deficit
détente
dissent
elector
embargo
fascism
fascist
federal
finance
gallery
Hansard
heckler
hot line
Knesset
lock out
liberal
mandate
Marxism
neutral
new left
opening
outvote
pairing
passage
politic
poor law
premier
primary
prolong
radical
reading
recount
re-elect

re-enact
Riksdag
senator
session
speaker
statute
toryism
tribune
tyranny
vacancy
Zionism
Zionist

8

apartheid
assembly
Black rod
blockade
caudillo
chairman
Chiltern (Hundreds)
commissar
commoner
Congress
democrat
dictator
dissolve
division
dominion
election
elective
feminism
free vote
Gerousia
home rule
hustings
left-wing
majority
minister
ministry
minority
national
official
politics
prorogue
republic
rollback
schedule
Sobranye
Storting
suffrage
Tanaiste
Treasury
triumvir
unionism
unionist
whiggery
woolsack

121

9

amendment
anarchism
ballot-box
Barebone's
bicameral
Bundestag
coalition
Cominform
Comintern
committee
communism
communist
democracy
deterrent
Eduskunta
exchequer
first lord
legislate
ombudsman
politburo
poujadist
president
red guards
Reichstag
right-wing
sanctions
secretary
shire-moot
show trial
socialism
socialist
Stalinism
Taoiseach
terrorism

10

block grant
by-election
capitalism
chancellor
collective

conference
devolution
government
guillotine
invalidate
monarchism
Monday Club
opposition
parliament
Plaid Cymru
plebiscite
psephology
radicalism
referendum
republican
resolution
revolution
scrutineer
sitting-day
Third Reich
Third World
trade union
Trotskyism
unicameral
Warsaw Pact
White House
white paper

11

adjournment
back-bencher
ballot-paper
bye-election
casting vote
coexistence
congressman
constituent
containment
co-operative
demarcation
dissolution
divine right
enfranchise

finance bill
imperialist
independent
legislation
legislative
legislature
McCarthyism
nationalist
package deal
party leader
prerogative
private bill
reactionary
revisionism
statute book
suffragette
syndicalism
syndicalist
Tammany Hall
Witenagemot
yeoman-usher

12

commissioner
Common Market
Commonwealth
conservatism
Conservative
constituency
constitution
dictatorship
division lobby
domino theory
federal union
House of Lords
house of peers
invalidation
lord advocate
lord chairman
privy council
reading clerk
snap division
ways and means
welfare state

13

demonstration
deputy-speaker
disengagement
free trade area
home secretary
international
lord president
lord privy seal
prime minister
shadow cabinet
single chamber
trade unionist
United Nations
vote of censure

14

constitutional
deputy chairman
deputy premier
deputy sergeant
gerrymandering
lord chancellor
representative
sergeant-at-arms
social democrat

15

attorney-general
cabinet minister
clerk of the house
general election
Marxist-Leninist
minister of state
people's republic
personality cult
totalitarianism

LITERATURE AND THE ARTS
Art

2 AND 3

air
art
bur
del.
exc.
fec.
hue
inc.
inv.
key
mat
oil
op
pop
sit

4

airy
arts
base
body
burr
bust
chic
dada
daub
draw
etch
flat
form
gild
halo
icon
ikon
limn
line
lipo
mass
nude
pinx.
pose
size

tone
wash

5

akkhr
batik
bloom
blush
board
brush
burin
cameo
chalk
couch
delin.
draft
easel
ember
Fauve
fecit
frame

genre
gesso
glaze
glory
gloss
grave
hatch
inert
japan
lay-in
lumia
magot
model
mount
mural
nabis
paint
pietà
prime
print
putto
rebus
salon

scene
sculp
secco
shade
Stijl
study
stump
tondo
torso
trace
vertu
virtu

6

action
artist
ashcan
cachet
canvas
colour
crayon
cubism
depict
design
doctor
ectype
emblem
emboss
enamel
engild
flambé
fresco
fylfot
gothic
ground
kitcat
kit-kat
limner
mastic
medium
mobile
mosaic
niello
nimbus
object
ormolu
ox-gall
pastel
patina
pencil
pinxit
plaque
plaster
purism
reflex
relief
rhythm
rococo
school
sculpt.
shadow
sitter
sketch
statue
studio
uncial

7

abbozzo
academy
acrylic
atelier

amorino
archaic
aureole
baroque
Bauhaus
bottega
bachiru
biscuit
camaieu
cartoon
carving
cissing
classic
collage
contour
Dadaism
daubing
De Stijl
diagram
diptych
draught
drawing
etching
excudit
faience
Fauvism
felt tip
gilding
glazing
gouache
graphic
hot tone
impaint
impasto
lacquer
lino-cut
lunette
montage
mordant
orphism
outline
painter
palette
picture
pigment
plastic
profile
realism
remodel
replica
reredos
rococo
scumble
shading
sketchy
stabile
stencil
stipple
support
surface
tableau
tempera
texture
tracery
T-square
varnish
vehicle
woodcut

8

abstract
academic
acid bath
acrolith

anaglyph
aquatint
armature
arriccio
artistic
blue four
charcoal
concours
cool tone
diaglyph
drypoint
engraver
figurine
fixative
freehand
frottage
Futurism
gargoyle
graffiti
grouping
hatching
half-tone
handling
idealism
intaglio
intonaco
luminist
majolica
makimono
monotype
mounting
negative
oil paint
ornament
painting
panorama
pastiche
penumbra
plein air
portrait
repoussé
romantic
seascape
seicento
statuary
symmetry
tachisme
tapestry
tectonic
tesserae
throwing
trecento
triglyph
triptych
vignette
warm tone

9

aggregate
alla prima
anti-cerne
appliqué
aquarelle
aquatinta
arabesque
asymmetry
ball-point
bas-relief
blockbook
bric-à-brac
cartridge
cartouche
cloisonné
colourist

crow quill
damascene
damaskeen
dichroism
distemper
emblemata
embossing
encaustic
engraving
facsimile
geometric
gradation
grisaille
grotesque
highlight
hot colour
indelible
indian ink
intimiste
japanning
landscape
lay figure
lithotint
mahlstick
mannerism
marquetry
maulstick
mezzotint
miniature
modelling
neo-gothic
oil colour
oleograph
painterly
phototype
polyptych
primitive
ready made
recession
sculpture
scumbling
serigraph
statuette
still-life
stippling
strapwork
stretcher
Symbolist
tailpiece
tattooing
tenebrism
Totentanz
Vorticism
woodblock
xylograph

10

accidental
achromatic
altogether
anaglyphic
anaglyptic
Art Nouveau
atmosphere
automatism
avant-garde
background
biomorphic
body colour
caricature
cartellino
cerography
classicism
cool colour

cornucopia	turpentine	lithography	daguerreotype
dead colour	warm colour	masterpiece	decorative art
embossment	xylography	neo-romantic	etching needle
embroidery		oil painting	expressionism
fitch brush		pavement art	glass painting
flat colour	**11**	perspective	Impressionism
foreground		photography	Neo-Classicism
full length	academician	pointillism	neoplasticism
hair pencil	alto-relievo	portraiture	Pre-Raphaelite
half-length	aquatinting	poster paint	primary colour
India paper	battle piece	primitivism	social realism
Jugendstil	calligraphy	renaissance	tactile values
kinetic art	chiaroscuro	restoration	underpainting
lithograph	chinoiserie	scenography	
mezzotinto	chromograph	stained glass	
monochrome	cinquecento	stereochromy	**14 AND OVER**
naturalism	colour print	tessellation	
night piece	composition	tracing linen	action painting (14)
organic art	concrete art	tracing paper	cabinet picture (14)
paint brush	connoisseur	watercolour	chromatography (14)
pen and wash	draughtsman		constructivism (14)
pencilling	eclecticism		conversation piece (17)
photograph	electrotype	**12**	draughtsmanship (15)
pietra dura	engravement		foreshortening (14)
plasticity	foreshorten	alkyd colours	Neo-Impressionism (16)
portcrayon	found object	bird's eye view	Neo-Romanticism (14)
Raphaelism	french chalk	illustration	pavement artist (14)
Raphaelite	ground plane	palette knife	picture gallery (14)
Romanesque	heliochrome	scraper board	plaster of paris (14)
serigraphy	heliochromy		portrait painter (15)
silhouette	iconography		Post-Impressionism (17)
silk screen	illusionism	**13**	representational (16)
Surrealism	imprimatura		socialist realism (16)
synthesism	life drawing	black and white	steel engraving (14)
terracotta		complementary	vanishing point (14)

Artists, architects, sculptors, cartoonists, etc.

3 AND 4		**5**

Adam	Gill	Marc	
Arp	Gogh	May	**5**
Bell	Good	Miró	
Bird	Gore	Mola	Aalto
Bone	Gow	Nash	Abbey
Both	Goya	Neer	Adams
Burn	Gris	Opie	Allan
Caro	Gros	Owen	Allen
Cima	Guys	Poy	Amiet
Cole	Hals	Puy	Appel
Cox	Hand	Pyne	Bacon
Cuyp	Hart	Reid	Baily
Dadd	Hemy	Reni	Balla
Dali	Herp	Rich	Banks
Dick	Holl	Rohe	Barry
Dine	Home	Ross	Barye
Dix	Hone	Ryn	Bates
Dodd	Hook	Sant	Beale
Doré	Hunt	Shaw	Bezzi
Dou	Jack	Sime	Blake
Dufy	John	Sims	Boehm
Dyce	Kane	Spee	Bosch
Dyck	Kerr	Swan	Bough
Egg	King	Todd	Brett
Etty	Klee	Toft	Brock
Eves	Lam	Tuke	Brown
Eyck	Lamb	Wade	Bundy
Faed	Lane	Wain	Burra
Fehr	Lear	Ward	Carra
Ford	Lee	Watt	Clark
Gabo	Lely	Webb	Clint
Gere	Lion	West	Cohen
	Low	Wood	Cooke
	Maes	Wren	Corot

Cross
Cossa
Costa
Cotes
Craig
Crane
Credi
Crome
Danby
David
Davie
Davis
Degas
Devis
Dixon
Drury
Durer
Ensor
Ernst
Foley
Frink
Frith
Furse
Gaddi
Gaudí
Gaunt
Gibbs
Giles
Gotch
Goyen
Grant
Grosz
Haden
Haghe
Hayes
Innes
Johns
Jones
Keene
Kelly
Klein
Klimt
Lance
Leech
Leger
Lemon
Le Vau
Lewis
Lippi
Lotto
Lowry
Lucas
Manet
Maris
Mason
Mauve
Moira
Monet
Moore
Munch
Nebot
Nervi
Nicol
Noble
Nolde
North
Orpen
Palma
Pater
Payne
Penny
Piper
Plaas
Platt
Ponte
Ponti

Poole
Prout
Pugin
Redon
Rodin
Rooke
Rossi
Sands
Scott
Segna
Short
Sleap
Small
Smith
Soane
Soest
Speed
Staël
Stark
Steen
Steer
Stone
Stott
Studd
Tobey
Tonks
Unwin
Uwins
Velde
Vonet
Watts
Wells
White
Wiens
Woods
Wyatt
Wyeth
Wylie
Yeats
Zoppo

6

Abbott
Albers
Allori
Archer
Arnold
Ashton
Barker
Barton
Baskin
Behnes
Benson
Benton
Berman
Bettes
Bewick
Birley
Bodley
Boxall
Braque
Briggs
Brough
Brunel
Buchel
Burnet
Burton
Butler
Calder
Callow
Campin
Carter
Casson
Claude

Clouet
Colton
Conder
Cooper
Copley
Corbet
Cotman
Cowper
Cozens
Currie
Dahmen
Dawson
Derain
De Wint
Dobson
Draper
Duccio
Dunbar
Elwell
Erlach
Ferber
Fildes
Fisher
Forbes
Foster
Fraser
Fuller
Fuseli
Geddes
Gellée
Gérard
Gibson
Gilman
Ginner
Giotto
Girtin
Glover
Gordon
Graham
Greuze
Guardi
Gulich
Hacker
Harral
Haydon
Heckel
Hilton
Holmes
Howard
Hudson
Hughes
Hunter
Ingres
Jagger
Joseph
Kaprow
Kettle
Keyser
Knight
Laroon
Laszlo
Lavery
Lawson
Leader
Lebrun
Ledoux
Legros
Le Nain
Leslie
Linton
Mabuse
McEvoy
Manson
Marini
Martin
Massys

Mesdac
Millet
Monaco
Morley
Morone
Morris
Müller
Murray
Newton
Nisbet
Noland
Oliver
Olsson
O'Neill
Palmer
Panini
Parker
Parton
Paxton
Pegram
Penley
Perret
Pettie
Piombo
Pisano
Potter
Ramsay
Renoir
Ribera
Ridley
Rivera
Rivers
Robbia
Robert
Romano
Romney
Rothko
Rubens
Ruskin
Sadler
Sandby
Sandys
Seddon
Serres
Seurat
Sisley
Smirke
Smythe
Spence
Stokes
Storck
Storey
Strang
Strube
Stuart
Stubbs
Tadema
Tanguy
Tayler
Taylor
Thomas
Titian
Turner
Vacher
Van Ryn
Varley
Vernet
Walker
Waller
Wallis
Walton
Wardle
Warhol
Watson
Weekes
Weenix

125

Weyden
Wilkie
Wilson
Windus
Wright
Wyllie
Yeames

7

Alberti
Aretino
Baldung
Barlach
Bassano
Bateman
Beechey
Belcher
Bellini
Bennett
Berchem
Bernini
Bomberg
Bonnard
Boucher
Bramley
Bridell
Brouwer
Calvert
Cameron
Campion
Cellini
Cézanne
Chagall
Chardin
Charles
Cheston
Chirico
Christo
Cimabue
Clausen
Cockram
Collier
Collins
Connard
Corinth
Cortona
Courbet
Cranach
Cundell
Dalziel
Daniell
Daumier
Da Vinci
De Hooch
De Lazlo
Dicksee
Dighton
Douglas
Downman
Duchamp
Edridge
Edwards
El Greco
Emanuel
Epstein
Flaxman
Fouquet
Fox-Pitt
Francia
Gabriel
Garstin
Gauguin
Gertlin
Gibbons

Gilbert
Gillray
Goodall
Goodwin
Greaves
Gregory
Gropius
Guarini
Guevara
Guthrie
Harding
Hartung
Hayward
Herbert
Herring
Hobbema
Hockney
Hofland
Hogarth
Hokusai
Holbein
Holland
Holroyd
Hoppner
Hopwood
Horsley
Housman
Indiana
Israels
Jackson
Jaggers
Johnson
Kneller
Knights
Kooning
Lambert
Lancret
Lanteri
Lessore
Linnell
Llander
Lucidel
Macbeth
Maccoll
Maclise
Maillol
Mansart
Maratti
Martini
Matisse
Memlinc
Merritt
Meunier
Michaux
Millais
Morandi
Morisot
Morland
Morrice
Murillo
Nasmith
Nattier
Neumann
Orcagna
Orchard
Osborne
Pacchia
Parrish
Parsons
Pasmore
Peacock
Peruzzi
Phidias
Philips
Phillip
Phil May

Philpot
Picabia
Picasso
Pickard
Pinwell
Pomeroy
Poussin
Poynter
Prinsep
Rackham
Raeburn
Raphael
Riviere
Roberts
Rouault
Roussel
Russell
Sargent
Schetky
Schiele
Shannon
Sickert
Siddall
Simpson
Smetham
Solomon
Spencer
Stanley
Stevens
Teniers
Tenniel
Thirtle
Thomson
Tiepolo
Uccello
Ugolino
Utrillo
Van Dyck
Van Eyck
Van Gogh
Vermeer
Watteau
Webster
Westall
Whiting
Woolner
Wynants
Zoffany

8

Allinson
Angelico
Armitage
Armstead
Aumonier
Beaumont
Beckmann
Beerbohm
Boccioni
Boffrand
Boughton
Brabazon
Bramante
Brancusi
Brangwyn
Brearley
Brooking
Brueghel
Calderon
Callcott
Calthorp
Carracci

Chambers
Chantrey
Crawhall
Creswick
Daubigny
De Keyser
De Laszlo
Delaunay
Del Prete
Deverell
Dietrich
Dressler
Dubuffet
Eastlake
Fielding
Fontaine
Frampton
Garofalo
Ghiberti
Giovanni
Gottlieb
Hartwell
Hepworth
Herkomer
Highmore
Hilliard
Hodgkins
Holloway
Houghton
Ibbetson
Inchbold
Jacobsen
Jan Steen
John Opie
Johnston
Jordaens
Kaufmann
Kirchner
Kokoshka
Kollwitz
Lambardo
Landseer
Lawrence
Leighton
Leonardo
Logsdail
Macallum
Macquoid
Magritte
Maitland
Mantegna
Marshall
Masaccio
Melville
Mondrian
Montalba
Montegna
Muirhead
Mulready
Munnings
Naviasky
Nevinson
Niemeyer
Palladio
Paolozzi
Paul Nash
Perugino
Phillips
Pissarro
Pontormo
Redgrave
Reynolds
Richmond
Ricketts
Robinson
Rossetti

Rousseau
Rugendas
Rushbury
Saarinen
Sassetta
Scamozzi
Schinkel
Segonzac
Severini
Simmonds
Solimena
Stanhope
Stothard
Stringer
Sullivan
Terbosch
Tinguely
Topolski
Vanbrugh
Van Goyen
Van Steen
Vasarely
Verbeeck
Veronese
Vlaminck
Waterlow
Wheatley
Whistler
Willcock
Williams
Woodward
Zakharov
Zurbarán

9

Ackermann
Alexander
Appleyard
Aston Webb
Bakhinzen
Beardsley
Biederman
Bonington
Botticini
Branwhite
Caldecot
Canaletto
Collinson
Constable
Correggio
Delacroix
d'Erlanger
Donaldson

Donatello
Farington
Feininger
Fragonard
Franz Hals
Friedrich
Gastineau
Géricault
Giorgione
Griffiths
Grünewald
Guido Reni
Halswelle
Hatherell
Hawksmoor
Henderson
Honthorst
Hurlstone
Jawlensky
Kandinsky
Kemp-Welch
Kokoschka
Lancaster
Lanfranco
La Thangue
Lee-Hankey
Lightfoot
Llewellyn
Louis Wain
MacGregor
MacKennal
McLachlan
McWhirter
Martineau
Maundrell
Mazzolino
Mestrovic
Mondriaan
Nicholson
Northcote
Pisanello
Rembrandt
Salisbury
Sansovino
Schalcken
Singleton
Stanfield
Steenwyck
Stevenson
Strudwick
Thornhill
Velasquez
Verrochio
Waterford
Whitcombe

10

Alma-Tadema
Archipenko
Botticelli
Breenbergh
Brockhurst
Burne-Jones
Caravaggio
Cattermole
Cruikshank
Del Pacchia
di Giovanni
Fiddes-Watt
Friedenson
Fulleylove
Giacometti
Glendening
Holman-Hunt
Jan van Eyck
Kennington
La Fresnaye
Lethbridge
Liebermann
Lorenzetti
Mackintosh
Meissonier
Michelozzo
Modigliani
Onslow Ford
Orchardson
Peppercorn
Pollaiuolo
Praxiteles
Richardson
Rowlandson
Saint-Aubin
Sanmicheli
Shackleton
Simon Vonet
Somerville
Sutherland
Swynnerton
Tintoretto
Van der Goes
Van der Meer
Van de Velde
Waterhouse
Winstanley

11

Apollodorus
Copley Heath

Della Robbia
Farquharson
Fra Angelico
Ghirlandaio
Hondecoeter
Le Corbusier
Lloyd Wright
Margaritone
Pickersgill
Poelenburgh
Polycleitus
Polykleitos
Rippingille
San Severino
Somerscales
Thornycroft
Van der Plaas
Van Ruisdael

12 AND OVER

Brunelleschi (12)
de Hondecoeter (13)
Della Francesca (14)
de Loutherbourg (14)
Fantin-Latour (12)
Ford Madox Brown (14)
Gainsborough (12)
Gaudier-Brzeska (14)
Grandma Moses (12)
Haynes-Williams (14)
Heath Robinson (13)
Huchtenburgh (12)
Hughes-Stanton (13)
Lawes Witteronge (15)
Leonardo da Vinci (15)
Lichtenstein (12)
Loutherbourg (12)
Michelangelo (12)
Middleton-Todd (13)
Muirhead-Bone (12)
Puvis de Chavannes (16)
Rauschenberg (12)
Rembrandt van Ryn (15)
Sassoferrato (12)
Sidney Cooper (12)
Spencer Pryse (12)
Toulouse-Lautrec (15)
Van der Weyden (12)
Van Huchtenburgh (15)
Van Ochtervelt (13)
Winterhalter (12)
Witherington (12)

Authors, poets, dramatists, etc.

3 AND 4

Amis
Ayer
Ball
Baum
Bede
Bell
Benn
Bolt
Buck
Cary
Coke
Cole

Dane
Day
Dell
Duse
Eden
Eyre
Ford
Fox
Fry
Fyfe
Gay
Gide
Glyn
Gray

Grey
Hall
Hart
Hay
Hine
Home
Hood
Hook
Hope
Hugo
Hume
Hunt
Hyne
Inge

Joad
Kant
King
Knox
Kyd
Lamb
Lang
Lear
Lee
Livy
Loos
Loti
Lyly
Lynd

Mais
Mann
Marx
Mill
More
Muir
Nash
Ovid
Owen
Poe
Pope
Pugh
Read
Reid
Rowe
Ruck
Sade
Sala
Shaw
Sims
Snow
Tate
Vane
Vega
Ward
West
Wood
Wren
Zola

5

Acton
Adams
Aesop
Agate
Aiken
Albee
Arden
Arlen
Auden
Ayres
Bacon
Barry
Barth
Bates
Behan
Betti
Beyle
Blake
Bloom
Blunt
Bowen
Bruce
Bunin
Burke
Burns
Byron
Cable
Caine
Camus
Capek
Clare
Colum
Couch
Croce
Dante
Dario
Defoe
Diver
Donne
Doyle
Dumas
Eliot
Ellis

Evans
Field
Freud
Frost
Gibbs
Gogol
Gorki
Gosse
Gower
Grimm
Hardy
Harte
Hegel
Heine
Henry
Henty
Homer
Hulme
Ibsen
Innes
Irwin
James
Jeans
Jones
Joyce
Kafka
Keats
Keith
Keyte
Lever
Lewis
Locke
Lodge
Logue
Lorca
Lucan
Lucas
Mason
Milne
Moore
Murry
Noyes
Ngugi
Odets
O'Dowd
Ogden
O'Hara
Orczy
Orton
Otway
Ouida
Paine
Pater
Peake
Peele
Pepys
Plato
Pliny
Pound
Praed
Prior
Raine
Reade
Ridge
Rilke
Rolle
Sagan
Scott
Shute
Smart
Smith
Spark
Stark
Staël
Stein
Stern

Stowe
Swift
Synge
Taine
Tasso
Twain
Tynan
Udall
Varro
Verne
Walsh
Waugh
Wells
Wilde
Woolf
Wyatt
Yeats
Yonge
Young
Zweig

6

Adcock
Aldiss
Anstey
Aragon
Archer
Arnold
Asimov
Austen
Bailey
Balzac
Barham
Barrie
Begbie
Belloc
Bellow
Benson
Besant
Besier
Binyon
Borrow
Brecht
Bridie
Brieux
Briggs
Brontë
Brooke
Brophy
Browne
Bryant
Buchan
Bunyan
Burgin
Burney
Butler
Caesar
Chekov
Church
Cicero
Clarke
Clough
Conrad
Cooper
Coward
Cowley
Cowper
Crabbe
Cronin
Curzon
Darwin
Daudet
Davies
Dekker

Dennis
Dobson
Dryden
Dunbar
Duncan
Empson
Ervine
Euclid
Ennius
Evelyn
Farnol
Fichte
Fonson
France
Frazer
Freund
Froude
Ganpat
George
Gibbon
Godwin
Goethe
Gordon
Graeme
Graham
Graves
Greene
Hallam
Hamsun
Harris
Hawkes
Haynes
Hemans
Henley
Hesiod
Hobbes
Holmes
Holtby
Horace
Howard
Howitt
Hughes
Huxley
Ian Hay
Ibañez
Irving
Jacobs
Jepson
Jerome
Jonson
Jowett
Junius
Keller
Kuprin
Landor
Lao-Tse
Larkin
Lawson
Le Sage
London
Lowell
Ludwig
Lytton
Mailer
Malory
Mannin
Marcel
Martyn
Miller
Milton
Morgan
Mörike
Morris
Munthe
Murray
Musset

128

Kingsley
Kingston
Knoblock
Koestler
Laforgue
Lagerlöf
Langland
Lawrence
Leibnitz
Leishman
Lonsdale
Leopardi
Lovelace
Ludovici
Macaulay
MacNeice
Mallarmé
Melville
Meredith
Merriman
Michelet
Mirabeau
Mitchell
Mortimer
Palgrave
Pattison
Perrault
Petrarch
Plutarch
Ponsonby
Quennell
Rabelais
Rattigan
Reynolds
Rossetti
Rousseau
Sabatini
Salinger
Sandburg
Schiller
Shadwell
Sheridan
Sidgwick
Sillitoe
Sinclair
Smollett
Stendhal
Stephens
Strachey
Sturgess
Suckling
Taffrail
Tennyson
Thompson
Thurston
Tibullus
Tourneur
Traherne
Trollope
Turgenev
Vanbrugh
Verlaine
Voltaire
Vonnegut
Walbrook
Wheatley
Whittier
Williams
Zane Grey
Zangwill

9

Adam Smith
Addinsell

Aeschylus
Ainsworth
Aldington
Alec Waugh
Anita Loos
Antoninus
Aristotle
Bartimeus
Ben Jonson
Berta Ruck
Blackmore
Blackwood
Boccaccio
Bottomley
Boyd Cable
Bret Harte
Burroughs
Cervantes
Corneille
Churchill
Coleridge
D'Annunzio
David Hume
Delafield
De la Roche
De Quincey
Descartes
Dickenson
Dos Passos
Dudintsev
Du Maurier
Eddington
Edgeworth
Etheridge
Ehrenburg
Euripides
Froissart
Giraudoux
Goldsmith
Goncharov
Gutenberg
Guy Thorne
Hall Caine
Hauptmann
Hawthorne
Heidegger
Hemingway
Herodotus
Heyerdahl
Hölderlin
Isherwood
Kaye-Smith
La Bruyère
La Fontaine
Lamartine
Leigh Hunt
Lermontov
Linklater
Lomonosov
Lord Byron
Lucretius
MacCarthy
Mackenzie
Macrobius
Madariaga
Mansfield
Mark Twain
Masefield
Massinger
Maud Diver
Middleton
Mitchison
Montaigne
Nietzsche
Oppenheim
Pasternak

Pemberton
Pett Ridge
Priestley
Radcliffe
Robertson
Rochester
Ruby Ayres
Sackville
Sax Rohmer
Schreiner
Shenstone
Sholokhov
Sophocles
Spielmann
Stacpoole
Steinbeck
Stevenson
Suetonius
Swinburne
Thackeray
Tomlinson
Trevelyan
Turgeniev
Van Druton
Wodehouse
Wycherley
Zuckmayer

10

Ballantyne
Barrington
Baudelaire
Birmingham
Boldrewood
Brett Young
Chatterton
Chesterton
Conan Doyle
don Marquis
Dostoevsky
Drinkwater
Dürrenmatt
Elinor Glyn
Emil Ludwig
Fitzgerald
Galsworthy
Hungerford
Hutchinson
Jack London
Jane Austen
John Buchan
Jules Verne
Longfellow
Lope de Vega
Lord Lytton
Maupassant
Mayakovsky
Mcgonagall
Mickiewicz
Mrs. Gaskell
Muriel Hine
Noel Coward
Oscar Wilde
Phillpotts
Pierre Loti
Pirandello
Propertius
Pryce-Jones
Quintilian
Richardson
Ronaldshay
Saintsbury
Saint-Simon
Sean O'Casey

Strindberg
Sutton Vane
Tarkington
Thucydides
Victor Hugo
Williamson
Wordsworth

11

Abercrombie
Apollinaire
Dostoievski
Garcia Lorca
Grillparzer
Kierkegaard
Maeterlinck
Montesquieu
Montherlant
Omar Khayyam
Ravenscroft
Sainte-Beuve
Shakespeare
Tocqueville
Watts-Dunton
Yevtushenko

12

Aristophanes
Beaumarchais
Bulwer Lytton
Chesterfield
De Selincourt
Fiona Macleod
Hans Andersen
Hergesheimer
Macchiavelli
Quiller-Couch
Rider Haggard
Robbe-Grillet
Rose Macaulay
Solzhensitsyn
Storm Jameson
Wittgenstein
Wyndham Lewis

13

Andrew Marvell
Arnold Bennett
Baroness Orczy
Cecil Day Lewis
Cosmo Hamilton
Edgar Allan Poe
Ford Madox Ford
Hilaire Belloc
Jeffrey Farnol
Jerome K. Jerome
Ohlenschlager
Rouget de Lisle
Sackville-West
Sinclair Lewis
Stacy Aumonier
Upton Sinclair
Wilkie Collins

14

Agatha Christie
Compton-Burnett
Eden Philpotts

Lecomte de Lisle	Warwick Deeping	Granville Barker
Marcus Aurelius		La Rochefoucauld
Middleton Murry		Millington Synge
Rafael Sabatini	**15**	Pierre de Ronsard
Rudyard Kipling		Somerset Maugham
Storer Clouston	Beverley Nichols	Valerius Flaccus
Temple Thurston	Booth Tarkington	Washington Irving (16)

Building and architecture

3

bar
bay
hip
hut
inn
mew
pub
spa
sty
won

4

apse
arch
area
bank
barn
bema
byre
café
cage
cell
cyma
club
cowl
crib
dado
dais
dike
dome
door
exit
fane
flag
flat
flue
gaol
gate
grot
hall
jail
jamb
keep
khan
kiln
kirk
lath
lift
lock
loft
mart
maze
mews
mill
mint
moat
mole
nave

nook
oast
ogee
oven
pale
pane
pave
pier
pile
plan
post
quay
rail
ramp
rink
roof
room
ruin
sash
seat
shed
shop
sill
sink
site
slat
stay
step
stud
tile
tomb
town
trap
vane
vill
vyse
wair
wall
wing
wood
xyst
yard
yate

5

abbey
abode
aisle
alley
ambry
annex
attic
bayed
block
booth
bower
brace
brest
brick
build

built
cabin
choir
coign
compo
court
crypt
dairy
depot
domed
Doric
drain
eaves
entry
erect
fence
flats
floor
forum
gable
glass
glaze
grate
grout
gully
harem
hotel
house
hovel
hydro
igloo
ionic
jetty
joint
joist
jutty
kiosk
kraal
latch
ledge
lobby
lodge
manse
mitre
newel
niche
order
oriel
paned
panel
patio
plank
pound
putty
quoin
rails
ranch
range
scape
serai
sewer
shaft

shelf
shell
slate
slatt
socle
solar
spire
stack
stage
stair
stake
stall
stand
steps
stile
stone
store
stove
strut
study
suite
tabby
thorp
tiled
tourn
tower
trone
truss
Tudor
vault
villa
wharf
works

6

access
adytum
alcove
alette
annexe
arbour
arcade
ashlar
ashler
asylum
atrium
aviary
bakery
batten
belfry
bourse
bricks
canopy
casino
castle
cellar
cement
châlet
chapel
chevet

131

chunam
church
cilery
cimbia
cinema
cintre
circus
closet
coffer
coigne
column
coping
corbel
corona
coving
crèche
cupola
dagoba
débris
design
dogana
donjon
drains
dug-out
ecurie
estate
exedra
façade
fascia
fillet
finial
fresco
friary
fylfot
gablet
garage
garret
girder
glazed
godown
Gothic
grange
grille
grotto
gutter
hangar
hearth
hog-pen
hog-sty
hostel
impost
inwall
Ionian
kennel
ladder
lanary
larder
lean-to
linhay
lintel
locker
lock-up
loggia
log-hut
louver
louvre
lyceum
mantel
market
mihrab
mitred
morgue
mortar
mosaic
mosque
mud hut

museum
mutule
niched
Norman
office
outlet
pagoda
palace
paling
pantry
parget
paving
perron
pharos
piazza
pigsty
pillar
pinery
plinth
poling
portal
priory
prison
purlin
putlog
quarry
rabbet
rafter
rancho
recess
refuge
rococo
ropery
rosery
rubble
rustic
saloon
saw-pit
school
scroll
shanty
smiddy
smithy
soffit
spence
square
stable
stairs
staith
stores
stucco
studio
subway
tarsia
tavern
temple
tender
thatch
thorpe
tilery
tiling
timber
tolsey
trench
trough
turret
unroof
untile
veneer
vestry
vihara
vinery
vintry
vivary
volute
wattle

wicket
wigwam
window
xystos
zaccho
zareba
zenana

7

academy
acroter
air duct
air flue
alcazar
almonry
ambitus
ancones
annulet
anticum
arcaded
archway
armoury
atelier
balcony
ballium
baroque
bastion
bedroom
bossage
boudoir
brewery
builder
butlery
butment
buttery
cabinet
cafenet
canteen
capitol
cassino
castlet
ceiling
chamber
chancel
chantry
château
chevron
chimney
choltry
cistern
cob-wall
college
compost
conduit
convent
cornice
cortile
cottage
crocket
cubicle
culvert
curtain
deanery
demesne
domical
dooring
doorway
doucine
dovecot
dungeon
edifice
embassy
entasis
eustyle

factory
farmery
fernery
fixture
fluting
foundry
fullery
gallery
gateway
granary
grapery
grating
groined
grounds
hay loft
herbary
hip roof
hogcote
hospice
hot-wall
hydrant
impasto
jib door
joinery
juffers
kennels
keyhole
kitchen
knocker
kremlin
landing
lantern
lattice
laundry
lazaret
library
lunette
mansard
mansion
masonry
megaron
mill dam
minaret
minster
moellon
mud wall
mullion
munnion
nailery
narthex
nogging
nunnery
nursery
obelisk
oratory
ossuary
out-gate
paddock
pantile
parapet
parlour
passage
pension
pentice
pentile
piggery
pillbox
plaster
portico
postern
pugging
pug mill
pyramid
quarrel
railing
rebuild

rectory
re-edify
reeding
rejoint
repairs
reredos
rockery
roofing
rostrum
rotunda
sanctum
sawmill
seabank
seawall
section
shebeen
shelves
shelter
shingle
shutter
slating
spicery
stadium
staging
station
steeple
storied
surgery
systyle
tambour
tannery
taproom
tegular
terrace
theatre
tie-beam
tracery
tracing
transom
trellis
turncap
unbuilt
unpaved
untiled
vachery
varnish
vaulted
veranda
viaduct
village
voluted

8

abat-jour
abattoir
abat-voix
abutment
air-drain
airtight
anteroom
apophyge
approach
aquarium
arboured
atheneum
backdoor
backroom
ballroom
baluster
banister
basement
basilica
bathroom
building

bungalow
buttress
caliduct
caryatid
casement
causeway
cavation
cenotaph
cesspool
chaptrel
chatelet
cincture
cloister
clubroom
cockloft
coliseum
comptoir
concrete
contract
corn loft
corridor
cow house
cradling
crescent
cromlech
cross-tie
cupboard
curb roof
cutchery
darkroom
dead wall
decorate
detached
doghouse
domicile
door case
door nail
doorpost
doorsill
doorstep
dovecote
dovetail
dowel pin
drainage
draughty
dry store
dry stove
dust stove
dust hole
dwelling
elevator
emporium
entrance
entresol
epistyle
erection
espalier
estimate
excavate
fanlight
fireclay
fish weir
flagging
flashing
flatting
flooring
freehold
fretwork
frontage
fusarole
gargoyle
geodesic
grillage
grouting
handrail
hen house

hoarding
hoistway
home farm
hospital
hostelry
hothouse
ice house
intrados
jalousie
keystone
kingpost
kingwood
lathwork
lavatory
legation
lichgate
lift well
log cabin
loghouse
lychgate
madhouse
magazine
memorial
mill pond
monolith
monument
mortuary
moulding
newsroom
openwork
orangery
outhouse
overhang
palisade
panelled
pantheon
pavement
pavilion
pedestal
pediment
pentroof
pilaster
pinnacle
plashing
platform
plumbing
pointing
pothouse
propylon
refinery
registry
rockwork
rood loft
roof tree
ropewalk
sacristy
sail-loft
sale room
scaffold
seminary
seraglio
showroom
skirting
skylight
slop-shop
smeltery
snuggery
soil pipe
solarium
spanroof
stabling
stuccoed
sudatory
sun-proof
taphouse
tectonic

tenement
terminus
toll-gate
townhall
transept
trapdoor
triglyph
tympanum
underpin
upstairs
vicarage
wainscot
wardroom
waxworks
well hole
well room
windmill
windowed
woodwork
workroom
workshop
ziggurat

9

acropolis
acroteria
aerodrome
alarm bell
alignment
almshouse
apartment
arabesque
arch-brick
architect
archivolt
archstone
aerostyle
art school
ashlaring
athenaeum
bakehouse
bay window
bede house
bell gable
bell tower
belvedere
bivaulted
boathouse
bow window
brick clay
brick kiln
brick dust
campanile
cartouche
cathedral
ceilinged
cellarage
centering
chop house
claustral
clay slate
clay stone
cloakroom
clubhouse
coalhouse
cocoonery
coffer dam
colonnade
colosseum
construct
consulate
cooperage
copestone
courtyard

133

cross-beam
crown-post
day school
decastyle
distemper
doorplate
doorstead
doorstone
dormitory
dowelling
drain trap
dripstone
earthbank
elevation
embrasure
episenium
eremitage
escalator
esplanade
estaminet
excavator
farmhouse
ferestral
firebrick
fireplace
fir-framed
fishgarth
flagstone
flashings
floriated
framework
frontdoor
frontroom
gallery
garreting
gatehouse
gravel pit
grotesque
guardroom
guestroom
guildhall
gullyhole
gymnasium
headstone
hermitage
hexastyle
homestall
homestead
hypocaust
hypostyle
infirmary
interaxal
interaxis
ironworks
jettyhead
jut-window
kalsomine
kerbstone
Kitchener
labyrinth
lazaretto
leasehold
letterbox
lift-shaft
linenfold
Lob's pound
mausoleum
metalling
mezzanine
modillion
monastery
music hall
music room
octastyle
octostyle
orphanage

oubliette
outer door
outer gate
palladian
pargeting
parquetry
parsonage
parthenon
partition
party-wall
pay office
penthouse
peristyle
pillarbox
playhouse
pleasance
pontifice
poorhouse
pressroom
prize ring
promenade
quicklime
race-stand
rail-fence
rainproof
raintight
refectory
rendering
reservoir
residence
residency
rest-house
ring-fence
sallyport
scagliola
scantling
sectional
spareroom
staircase
stillroom
stinktrap
stockroom
stonewall
stonework
storeroom
stretcher
structure
swinecote
synagogue
tablature
tenements
threshold
tile-drain
tollbooth
tollhouse
tower-room
townhouse
treillage
triforium
turf-house
turnstile
undermine
underprop
undrained
vestibule
wallpaper
wall-plate
warehouse
wastepipe
watertank
whitewash
windproof
windtight
winevault
wiregauze
workhouse

10

à la grecque
antechapel
antetemple
araeostyle
arc-boutant
architrave
archivault
backstairs
ball-flower
balustered
balustrade
bargeboard
bedchamber
bell-turret
brick-built
brick earth
cantilever
catafalque
chapellany
chimney cap
chimney pot
clerestory
clock tower
coachhouse
coalcellar
common room
conversion
Corinthian
court house
covered way
crenulated
cripplings
cross-aisle
crown glass
culver-tail
damp-course
decoration
decorative
depository
dining hall
dining room
dispensary
distillery
ditriglyph
dome-shaped
doorhandle
doricorder
double-hung
double lock
dowel joint
drawbridge
dryingroom
Dutch tiles
earth house
embankment
enrockment
engine-room
excavation
facia panel
fir-wrought
first floor
fives court
flint glass
flock paper
forcing-pit
foundation
garden city
glass-house
grandstand
Greek cross
greenhouse
grotto-work
ground-plan
ground-sill

guardhouse
habitation
hipped roof
hippodrome
hunting box
hypaethral
intramural
Ionic order
Ionic style
jerry-built
laboratory
lady chapel
lancet arch
Latin cross
lazar-house
lighthouse
lumber-room
maisonette
manor house
market town
monopteros
necropolis
Norman arch
overmantel
panopticon
persiennes
plastering
plate glass
portcullis
post office
powder-house
propylaeum
proscenium
pycnostyle
quadrangle
repointing
repository
robing-room
rock-temple
Romanesque
roof garden
rose garden
rose window
roundhouse
roundtower
rubblework
sanatorium
sanitarium
settlement
skew bridge
skyscraper
slaked lime
smokestack
space frame
state house
stillatory
storehouse
streetdoor
structural
tetrastyle
tiring-room
Tudor style
undercroft
university
unoccupied
untenanted
varnishing
ventilator
vestry room
watch-house
watch-tower
water-tower
way-station
white-limed
wicket gate
window sash

windscreen
wine-cellar

11

antechamber
barge-course
caravansary
castellated
cementation
cementatory
chain-bridge
columbarium
compartment
concert hall
contabulate
coping stone
corbel steps
cornerstone
counterfort
curtail step
distempered
door knocker
dovetailing
drawing room
dress circle
entablature
entablement
finger plate
florid style
foundations
frieze-panel
glass-mosaic
ground-floor
hearthstone
lattice work
load-bearing
louvre-board
luffer board
machicoulis
mantelpiece
manufactory
market-cross
morning room
observatory
oeil-de-boeuf
office block
oriel window
out-building
picture rail
plasterwork
postern gate
postscenium
public house
purpose-built
reading room
reconstruct
renaissance
reservatory
residential
Roman cement

rustication
sarcophagus
scaffolding
shooting box
staddle roof
stringboard
sub-contract
summer house
superstruct
tessellated
tiled hearth
trelliswork
Turkish bath
Tuscan order
undercoated
unfurnished
uninhabited
ventilation
wainscoting
war memorial
water supply
weathercock
whitewashed
window frame
window glass
window ledge
wire grating
wooden house
wrought iron

12

amphitheatre
araeosystyle
archbuttress
architecture
assembly room
auction rooms
building site
caravanserai
chapel of ease
chimneypiece
chimneyshaft
cockle stairs
conservatory
construction
constructure
country house
covered court
culver-tailed
dormer window
draught-proof
dressing-room
entrance hall
floor timbers
folding doors
garden suburb
geodesic dome
guest chamber
half-timbered
Ionian column

kitchen range
labour-saving
lake dwelling
lightning-rod
lock-up garage
louvre window
machicolated
mansion house
meeting house
mission house
outer gateway
pantechnicon
parquet floor
penitentiary
power station
purbeck stone
retiring-room
spiral stairs
sub-struction
sub-structure
subterranean
sweating room
three-ply wood
tower bastion
town planning
tracing cloth
tracing linen
tracing paper
unmodernized
unornamented
unornamented
untenantable
unventilated
urban renewal
valance board
venetian door
wainscotting
weatherproof
winter garden

13

amphiprostyle
ancient lights
architectonic
architectural
assembly rooms
back staircase
breakfast room
butler's pantry
chimney corner
compass window
contabulation
coursing joint
Dutch clinkers
dwelling house
dwelling place
encaustic tile
entrance lobby
establishment

ferro-concrete
Grecian temple
lattice window
machicolation
martello tower
master builder
Norman doorway
portland stone
satellite town
skirting board
specification
sub-contractor
sweating house
transom window
triumphal arch
uninhabitable
vaulting shaft
venetian blind
vinyl emulsion
wattle and daub

14

architectonics
catherine wheel
central heating
drying cupboard
filling station
flying buttress
lath and plaster
mezzanine floor
office building
picture gallery
portland cement
powder magazine
reconstruction
superstructure
threshing floor
venetian window
wayside station
whispering dome

15

air conditioning
dampproof course
discharging arch
electric heating
feather boarding
foundation stone
hydraulic cement
pleasure gardens
pleasure grounds
refreshment room
spiral staircase
vitruvian scroll
weather boarding
withdrawing room

Characters in literature

Some characters from **Ben Jonson, Charlotte Brontë, Lord Byron, Chaucer,** and **Congreve**

List of works from which the following characters are taken, with reference numbers.

Ben Jonson

Ref. No.	Title	
1.	Alchemist, The,	(12 letters)
2.	Bartholomew Fayre	(16 ,,)
3.	Cynthia's Revels	(14 ,,)
4.	Devil is an Ass, The	(15 ,,)
5.	Epicoene	(8 ,,)
6.	Every Man in his Humour	(19 ,,)
7.	Every Man out of his Humour	(22 ,,)
8.	Magnetick Lady, The	(16 ,,)
9.	New Inn, The	(9 ,,)
10.	Poetaster, The	(12 ,,)
11.	Sad Shepherd, The	(14 ,,)
12.	Sejanus	(7 ,,)
13.	Volpone	(7 ,,)
14.	(Various)	

Lord Byron

Ref. No.	Title	
15.	Don Juan	(7 letters)
16.	(Various)	

Charlotte Brontë

17.	Jane Eyre	(8 letters)
18.	Professor, The	(12 ,,)
19.	Shirley	(7 ,,)
20.	Villette	(8 ,,)

Chaucer (Geoffrey)

21.	Canterbury Tales	(15 letters)

Congreve (William)

22.	Double Dealer, The	(15 letters)
23.	Love for Love	(11 ,,)
24.	Mourning Bride, The	(16 ,,)
25.	Old Bachelor, The	(14 ,,)
26.	Way of the World, The	(16 ,,)

Note: The numbers in brackets indicate *the works* in which the characters appear.

3 AND 4

Alp (16)
Anah (16)
Azo (16)
Baba (15)
Beck (20)
Busy (2)
Cash (6)
Cave (19)
Cob (6)
Cos (3)
Daw (5)
Dent (17)
Dudu (15)
Echo (3)
Ella (21)
Eyre (17)
Face (1)
Fly (9)
Gale (19)
Hall (19)
Hogg (19)
Home (20)
Hugo (16)
Inez (15)
Lara (16)
Lucy (25)
May (21)
Nero (12)
Otho (16)
Paul (18, 20)
Prue (23)
Pug (4)
Raby (15)
Rud (17)
Seyd (16)
Wasp (1)
Whit (2)
Zara (24)

5

Abbot (17)
Aesop (10)
Alken (11)

Arete (3)
Asper (7)
Beppo (16)
Betty (25)
Brisk (7, 22)
Burns (17)
Celia (13)
Chloe (10)
Cotta (12)
Cupid (3)
Donne (19)
Frail (23)
Froth (22)
Gabor (16)
Hedon (3)
Jenny (23)
Julia (10)
Kaled (16)
Laura (16)
Leila (15, 16)
Lloyd (17)
Lolah (15)
Lorel (11)
Lovel (9)
Lupus (10)
Manly (4)
Mason (17)
Minos (10)
Mitis (7)
Moore (19)
Moria (3)
Morus (3)
Mosca (13)
Neuha (16)
Osman (24)
Poole (17)
Pryor (19)
Roger (21)
Rufus (12)
Scott (19)
Selim (16)
Shift (7)
Snowe (20)
Steno (16)
Surly (1)
Tipto (9)
Topas (21)

Varro (12)
Ulric (16)
Waspe (2)
Whipp (19)
Yorke (19)

6

Albius (10)
Alison (21)
Arcite (21)
Arnold (16)
Asotus (3)
Bessie (17)
Caesar (10)
Canace (21)
Common (1)
Conrad (16)
Crites (3)
Damian (21)
Dapper (1)
Deliro (7)
Drusus (12)
Earine (11)
Emilia (21)
Ferret (9)
Foible (9)
Formal (6)
Gallus (10)
Giaour (The) (16)
Gelaia (3)
Graham (20)
Haidee (15)
Harold (16)
Hassan (16)
Horace (10)
Jaques (14)
Jeremy (23)
Kitely (6)
Lambro (15)
Legend (23)
Luscus (10)
Malone (19)
Mammon (1)
Marina (16)
Marino (16)

Maxime (21)
Medora (16)
Morose (5)
Myrrha (16)
Opsius (16)
Overdo (2)
Pliant (1)
Plyant (22)
Polish (8)
Reuter (18)
Setter (25)
Silvia (25)
Simkin (21)
St. John (Mr.) (17)
Subtle (1)
Symkin (21)
Tartar (dog) (19)
Tattle (23)
Temple (17)
Thopas (21)
Virgil (10)
Walter (21)
Werner (16)
Wittol (25)

7

Abolson (21)
Almeria (24)
Anaides (3)
Apicata (12)
Arbaces (16)
Astarte (16)
Azaziel (16)
Baillie (21)
Beleses (16)
Belinda (25)
Belmour (25)
Bertram (16)
Bobadil (1)
Boultby (19)
Bretton (20)
Buckram (23)
Buffone (7)
Clement (6)
Corvino (13)

Ned Careless (22)
Nightingale (2)
Paulina Home (20)
Robert Moore (19)
Roger Formal (6)
Simon Simkin (21)
Stralenheim (16)
Tom Quarlous (2)
Tribulation (1)

12

Asinius Lupus (10)
Brocklehurst (17)
Captain Bluff (25)
Carlo Buffone (7)
Harold Childe (16)
Harry Baillie (21)
John Seacombe (18)
Joseph Wittol (25)
Lady Wishfort (26)
Lord Tynedale (18)
Margaret Hall (19)
Matthew Yorke (19)
Monsieur Paul (18, 20)
Poore Persoun (The) (21)
Rev. Cyril Hall (19)

Richard Mason (17)
Sardanapalus (16)
St. John Rivers (17)
Symond Symkyn (21)

13

Dr. John Bretton (20)
Edward Belmour (25)
Edward Kno'well (6)
Epicure Mammon (1)
Georgiana Reed (17)
Hortense Moore (19)
Hugh of Lincoln (21)
Humphrey Waspe (2)
James Helstone (19)
James Loredano (16)
John Littlewit (2)
Lady Loadstone (8)
Lady Pinchbeck (15)
Lady Touchwood (22)
Lord Touchwood (22)
Magnetick Lady (The) (8)
Marino Faliero (16)
Master Stephen (6)
Miss Marchmont (20)
Miss Scatcherd (17)
Mrs. Crimsworth (18)

Philip Nunnely (19)
Rev. Mr. Sweeting (19)
Sir Paul Plyant (22)

14

Augustus Caesar (10)
Augustus Malone (19)
Captain Bobadil (6)
Captain Keeldar (19)
Edward Mirabell (22)
Francis Foscari (16)
Justice Clement (6)
Rev. Peter Malone (19)
Shirley Keeldar (19)
Wilful Witwould (26)

15

Anthony Witwould (26)
Clerk of Oxenford (21)
Ezekiel Edgworth (2)
Fastidious Brisk (7)
George Downright (6)
Hon. John Seacombe (18)
Madame Eglantine (21)
Sir Joseph Wittol (25)

Some characters from **Charles Dickens**
List of works from which the following characters are taken, with reference numbers.

Ref. No.	Title			Ref. No.	Title		
1.	Barnaby Rudge	(12 letters)		14.	Martin Chuzzlewit	(16 letters)	
2.	Battle of Life, The	(15	,,)	15.	Master Humphrey's		
3.	Bleak House	(10	,,)		Clock	(20	,,)
4.	Chimes, The	(9	,,)	16.	Mudfog Papers, The	(15	,,)
5.	Christmas Carol, A	(15	,,)	17.	Nicholas Nickleby	(16	,,)
6.	Cricket on the Hearth,			18.	Old Curiosity Shop,		
	The	(21	,,)		The	(19	,,)
7.	David Copperfield	(16	,,)	19.	Oliver Twist	(11	,,)
8.	Dombey and Son	(12	,,)	20.	Our Mutual Friend	(15	,,)
9.	Edwin Drood	(10	,,)	21.	Pickwick, or The Pick-		
10.	Great Expectations	(17	,,)		wick Papers	(8 or 17 ,,)	
11.	Hard Times	(9	,,)	22.	Sketches by Boz	(13	,,)
12.	Haunted Man, The	(13	,,)	23.	Tale of Two Cities, A	(16	,,)
13.	Little Dorrit	(12	,,)				

Note: The numbers in brackets indicate *the works* in which the characters appear.

2 – 4

Aged (The) (10)
Bell (16)
Bet (19)
Bray (17)
Bung (22)
Cobb (1)
Cute (4)
Dick (19)
Fang (19)
Fern (4)
Fips (14)
Fogg (21)
Gamp (14)
Gay (8)
Grip (bird) (1)
Grub (21)
Hawk (17)
Heep (7)

Hugh (1)
Jane (22)
Jip (dog) (7)
Jo (3)
Joe (21)
Jupe (11)
Kit (18)
Knag (17)
Mary (21)
Meg (4)
Mell (7)
Muff (16)
'Nemo' (3)
Peel (21)
Pell (21)
Peps (8)
'Pip' (10)
Pott (21)
Prig (14)
Pyke (17)

Riah (20)
Rosa (3)
Rugg (13)
Slug (16)
Slum (18)
Tigg (14)
Tim (5)
Tox (8)
Veck (4)
Wade (13)
Wegg (20)

5

Agnes (7)
Alice (15)
Bates (19)
Betsy (19)
Bevan (14)

Biddy (10)
Bloss (22)
Boxer (6)
Brass (18)
Brick (14)
Brown (8, 22)
'Caddy' (3)
Casby (13)
Chick (8)
Choke (14)
Clare (3)
Crupp (7)
Daisy (1)
Diver (14)
Drood (9)
Dumps (22)
Emily (7)
Evans (22)
Fagin (19)
Filer (4)

Fixem (22)
Flite (3)
Giles (19)
Gills (8)
Gowan (13)
Grace (2)
Green (22)
Gride (17)
Grove (18)
Guppy (3)
Gwynn (21)
Hardy (22)
Hicks (22)
Janet (7)
Jerry (18)
Jones (2)
Kenge (3)
Krook (3)
Lobbs (21)
Lorry (23)
Lupin (14)
Maggy (13)
Marks (15)
Miggs (1)
Mills (7)
Minns (22)
Molly (10)
Monks (19)
Mould (14)
Nancy (19)
Neddy (21)
Noggs (17)
Perch (8)
Pinch (14)
Pluck (17)
Price (17)
Pross (23)
Quale (3)
Quilp (18)
Rudge (1)
Sarah (22)
Scott (18)
Sikes (19)
Slyme (14)
Smart (21)
Smike (17)
Sophy (7)
Squod (3)
Stagg (1)
Tibbs (22)
Toots (8)
Tozer (8)
Trabb (10)
Trent (18)
Trott (22)
Tuggs (22)
Twist (19)
Venus (20)
Wosky (22)

6

Alfred (2)
Babley (7)
Badger (3)
Bagman (The) (21)
Bailey (14)
Bamber (21)
Bantam (21)
Barker (22)
Barkis (7)
Barley (10)
Barney (19)
Barton (22)
Beadle (13)

Bedwin (19)
Benton (15)
Bertha (6)
Bitzer (11)
Boffin (20)
Bowley (4)
Briggs (8, 22)
Bucket (3)
Budden (22)
Budger (21)
Bumble (19)
Bumple (22)
Bunsby (8)
Butler (22)
Buzfuz (21)
Calton (22)
Carker (8)
Carton (23)
'Cherub' (The) (20)
Codlin (18)
Cooper (22)
Corney (19)
Cousin (8)
Craggs (2)
Cuttle (8)
Dadson (22)
Danton (22)
Darnay (23)
Dartle (7)
Denham (12)
Dennis (1)
Dodson (21)
Dombey (8)
Dorrit (13)
Dounce (22)
Dowler (21)
Dr. Peps (8)
Durden (3)
Edkins (22)
Endell (7)
Etella (10)
'Fat Boy' (The) (21)
Feeder (8)
Folair (17)
George (3)
Gordon (1)
Graham (14)
Grueby (1)
Guster (3)
Harmon (20)
Harris (14, 18, 22)
Hawdon (3)
Helves (22)
Hexham (20)
Hilton (22)
Hobler (22)
Hubble (10)
Hunter (21, 22)
Hutley (21)
Jarley (18)
Jingle (21)
Johnny (20)
Lammle (20)
Lumbey (17)
Magnus (21)
Marion (2)
Marley (5)
Martha (22)
Marton (18)
Maylie (19)
Merdle (13)
Milvey (20)
Mivins (21)
Moddle (14)
Morfin (8)
Mullet (14)

Muzzle (21)
Nathan (22)
Nipper (8)
Noakes (22)
Orlick (10)
Pancks (13)
Parker (22)
Pegler (11)
Peploe (22)
Perker (21)
Phunky (21)
Pipkin (21)
Pirrip (10)
Pocket (10)
Pogram (14)
Potter (22)
Purday (22)
Rachel (11)
Raddle (21)
Redlaw (12)
Rigaud (13)
Rogers (22)
Sapsea (9)
Sawyer (21)
Sleary (11)
Sloppy (20)
Strong (7)
Stubbs (22)
Tapley (14)
Timson (22)
Toodle (8)
Tottle (22)
Tupman (21)
Tupple (22)
Varden (1)
Walker (22)
Warden (2)
Wardle (21)
Waters (22)
Weller (21)
Wilfer (20)
Willet (1)
Wilson (22)
Winkle (21)

7

Barbara (18)
Bardell (21)
Bazzard (9)
Blimber (8)
Blotton (21)
Bobster (17)
Boldwig (21)
Britain (2)
Brooker (17)
Browdie (17)
Bullamy (14)
'Charley' (3)
Chester (1)
Chillip (7)
Chivery (13)
Chuffey (14)
Cleaver (20)
Clenham (11)
Crackit (19)
Creakle (7)
Crewler (7)
Dawkins (19)
Dedlock (3)
Defarge (23)
Drummle (10)
Dr. Wosky (22)
Edmunds (21)
Evenson (22)

139

Mrs. Dowler (21)
Mrs. Harris (14)
Mrs. Hubble (10)
Mrs. Hunter (21)
Mrs. Jarley (18)
Mrs. Lammle (20)
Mrs. Maylie (19)
Mrs. Merdle (13)
Mrs. Milvey (20)
Mrs. Parker (22)
Mrs. Pegler (11)
Mrs. Peploe (22)
Mrs. Raddle (21)
Mrs. Stubbs (22)
Mrs. Varden (1)
Mrs. Wilfer (20)
Murdstone (7)
Ned Dennis (1)
Nell Trent (18)
Old Orlick (10)
Pardiggle (3)
Pecksniff (14)
Phil Squod (3)
Potterson (20)
Riderhood (20)
Ruth Pinch (14)
Sam Weller (21)
Sarah Gamp (14)
Silas Wegg (20)
Sludberry (22)
Smallweed (3)
Snodgrass (21)
Spruggins (22)
Swiveller (18)
Tackleton (6)
Tappertit (1)
'The Bagman' (21)
'The Cherub' (20)
'The Fat Boy' (21)
Tom Codlin (18)
Towlinson (8)
Uncle Bill (22)
Uriah Heep (7)
Veneering (20)
Verisopht (17)
Walter Gay (8)
Wickfield (7)
Will Marks (15)
Wisbottle (22)
Witherden (18)
Woodcourt (3)
Wrayburne (20)

10

Alice Brown (8)
Aunt Martha (2)
Ayresleigh (21)
Betsy Clark (22)
Bill Barker (22)
Bill Barley (10)
Billsmethi (22)
Bitherston (8)
Chevy Slyme (14)
Chuzzlewit (14)
'Cymon' Tuggs (22)
Dame Durden (3)
Doctor Peps (8)
Edwin Drood (9)
Emma Porter (22)
Flintwinch (13)
Heathfield (2)
Henry Gowan (13)
'Honest John' (22)

Jack Bamber (21)
Jack Bunsby (8)
Jem Larkins (22)
Job Trotter (21)
Joe Gargery (10)
John Carker (8)
John Dounce (22)
John Grueby (8)
John Harman (20)
John Willet (1)
'Kit' Nubbles (18)
Kittlebell (22)
Knight Bell (16)
Little Dick (19)
Little Paul (8)
MacStinger (8)
Mark Tapley (14)
Mary Graham (14)
Miss Benton (15)
Mrs. Bardell (21)
Mrs. Clenham (13)
Mrs. Crewler (7)
Mrs. Gargery (10)
Mrs Garland (18)
Mrs. General (13)
Mrs. Grudden (17)
Mrs. Jellyby (3)
Mrs. Jiniwin (18)
Mrs. Kenwigs (17)
Mrs. Macklin (22)
Mrs. Meagles (13)
Mrs. Nubbles (18)
Mrs. Parsons (22)
Mrs. Pipchin (8)
Mrs. Skewton (8)
Mrs. Sparsit (11)
Mrs. Squeers (17)
Mrs. Swidger (12)
Mrs. Taunton (22)
Mrs. Todgers (14)
Mrs. Wackles (18)
Mrs. Whimple (10)
Mrs. Wickham (8)
Paul Dombey (8)
Rosa Dartle (7)
Rose Maylie (19)
Rouncewell (3)
Sally Brass (18)
Sempronius (22)
Signor Jupe (11)
Simon Tuggs (22)
Sliderskew (17)
Smallweed (3)
Sowerberry (19)
Stareleigh (21)
Steerforth (7)
Tony Weller (21)
Turveydrop (3)
Williamson (22)
Wititterly (17)

11

Abel Garland (18)
Arthur Gride (17)
Balderstone (22)
Bella Wilfer (20)
Betsey Quilp (18)
Betty Higden (20)
Bob Cratchit (5)
Cecilia Jupe (11)
Copperfield (7)
Daniel Quilp (18)
Doctor Wosky (22)

Dolge Orlick (10)
Dora Spenlow (7)
Edith Dombey (8)
Emily Wardle (21)
Emma Peecher (20)
Fanny Dombey (8)
Fanny Dorrit (13)
Frank Milvie (20)
Gabriel Grub (21)
'Game Chicken' (The) (8)
Ham Peggotty (7)
Harry Maylie (19)
Jack Hopkins (21)
Jack Redburn (15)
Jacob Barton (22)
James Carker (8)
Jarvis Lorry (23)
Jemima Evans (22)
Jesse Hexham (20)
John Browdie (17)
John Chivery (7)
John Dawkins (19)
John Edmunds (21)
John Evenson (22)
John Jobling (14)
John Podsnap (20)
John Smauker (21)
John Wemmock (10)
Joseph Tuggs (22)
Lady Dedlock (3)
Lady Tippins (20)
Linkinwater (17)
Little Emily (7)
Louisa Chick (8)
Lucretia Tox (8)
Misses Brown (22)
Miss Gazingi (17)
Miss Larkins (7)
Miss Mowcher (7)
Monflathers (18)
Mrs. Brandley (10)
Mrs. Clupping (21)
Mrs. Crummles (17)
Mrs. Dingwall (22)
Mrs. Fielding (6)
Mrs. Finching (13)
Mrs. Gummidge (7)
Mrs. Micawber (7)
Mrs. Nickleby (17)
Mrs. Plornish (13)
Mrs. Sparkler (13)
Mrs. Tetterby (12)
Newman Noggs (17)
Oliver Twist (19)
Perrybingle (6)
Percy Noakes (22)
Peter Magnus (21)
Polly Toodle (8)
Pumblechook (10)
Robin Toodle (8)
Slackbridge (11)
Snevellicci (17)
Solomon Peel (21)
Solomon Pell (21)
Susan Nipper (8)
Susan Weller (21)
Sweedlepipe (14)
'The Bachelor' (18)
Tim Cratchit (5)
Toby Crackit (19)
Tom Chitling (19)
Tony Jobling (3)
Tracy Tupman (21)
Tulkinghorn (3)
Uncle George (22)
Uncle Robert (22)

141

Thomas Traddles (7)
Tim Linkinwater (17)
William Swidger (12)

15

Alexander Briggs (22)
Alexander Budden (22)
Alfred Mantalini (17)
Benjamin Britain (2)
Caroline Jellyby (3)
'Cherry' Pecksniff (14)
Clarissa Spenlow (7)
Clemency Newcome (2)
Conkey Chickweed (19)
Cornelia Blimber (8)
'Dolphus Tetterby (12)
Dora Copperfield (7)
Ebenezer Scrooge (5)

Edward Murdstone (7)
Estella Havisham (10)
Eugene Wrayburne (20)
Ferdinand Barnacle (13)
Frederick Dorrit (13)
General Fladdock (14)
Georgina Podsnap (20)
Godfrey Nickleby (17)
Henrietta Boffin (20)
Henry Wititterly (17)
Hon. Elijah Pogram (14)
Horatio Sparkins (22)
'Horatio St. Julien' (22)
James Steerforth (7)
John Peerybingle (6)
Jonas Chuzzlewit (14)
Josephine Sleary (11)
Josiah Rounderby (11)
Julia Wititterly (17)
Lavinia Dingwall (22)

Louisa Gradgrind (11)
MacChoakumchild (11)
Madame Mantalini (17)
Mary Peerybingle (6)
Miss Snevellicci (17)
Monsieur Defarge (23)
Mrs. Joseph Porter (22)
Nathaniel Pipkin (21)
Nathaniel Winkle (21)
Nicodemus Boffin (20)
Ninetta Crummles (17)
Paul Sweedlepipe (14)
Professor Mullet (14)
Richard Carstone (3)
Serjeant Snubbin (21)
Sir Joseph Bowley (4)
Sir Mulberry Hawk (17)
Smallweed Family (3)
Teresa Malderton (22)
'The Artful Dodger' (17)

Some characters from **Dryden, George Eliot, Fielding**, and **Goldsmith**.
List of works from which the following characters are taken, with reference numbers.

Dryden

Ref. No.   Title
1. Absalom and Achitophel
                              (20 letters)
2. (Various)

George Eliot·
11. Adam Bede   (8 letters)
12. Clerical Life, Scenes
     from   (12 or 22 ,,)
13. Daniel Deronda   (13   ,,   )
14. Felix Holt   (9   ,,   )
15. Middlemarch   (11   ,,   )
16. Mill on the Floss, The   (17   ,,   )
17. Romola   (6   ,,   )
18. Silas Marner   (11   ,,   )
19. Spanish Gipsy, The   (15   ,,   )

Fielding (Henry)

Ref. No.   Title
3. Amelia   (6 letters)
4. Jonathan Wild   (12   ,,   )
5. Joseph Andrews   (13   ,,   )
6. Mock Doctor, The   (13   ,,   )
7. Pasquin   (7   ,,   )
8. Tom Jones   (8   ,,   )
9. Tom Thumb   (8   ,,   )
10. (Various)

Goldsmith (Oliver)
20. Citizen of the World, The (20 letters)
21. Good-Natured Man, The   (17   ,,   )
22. She Stoops to Conquer   (18   ,,   )
23. Vicar of Wakefield, The   (19   ,,   )
24. (Various)

Note: The numbers in brackets indicate *the works* in which the characters appear.

2 – 4

Agag (1)
Amri (1)
Arod (1)
Bath (3)
Bede (11)
Cass (18)
Cei (17)
Cora (1)
Dane (18)
Doeg (1)
Holt (14)
Iras (2)
Juan (19)
Juno (dog) (11)
Lisa (17)
Lyon (14)
Maso (11)
Moss (16)
Og (1)
Omri (1)
Rann (11)
Rock (20)
Saul (1)
Snap (4)
Tibs (20)

Wild (4)
Wyld (4)

5

Adams (5)
Amiel (1)
Balak (1)
Bardo (17)
Booby (5)
Booth (3)
Burge (11)
Caleb (1)
Calvo (17)
David (1)
Deane (16)
Dorax (2)
Edwin (24)
Eppic (18)
Fanny (5)
Garth (15)
Glegg (16)
Gomaz (2)
Guest (16)
Jakin (16)
Jonas (1)

Jones (8)
Kezia (16)
Lofty (21)
Macey (18)
Moody (2)
Nadab (1)
Nello (17)
Place (7)
Sagan (1)
Sheva (1)
Tessa (17)
Tibbs (20)
Vincy (15)
Wakem (16)
Whang (20)
Zadoc (1)
Zarca (19)
Zelis (20)
Zimri (1)

6

Abdael (1)
Adriel (1)
Alexas (2)
Amelia (3)

Antony (2)
Arnold (23)
Badger (10)
Barton (3)
Bennet (3)
Blaize (24)
Blifil (8)
Brooke (15)
Casson (11)
Crispe (23)
Dobson (16)
Dr. Rock (20)
Elvira (2)
Emilia (2)
Garnet (21)
Gilfil (12)
Hingpo (20)
Honour (8)
Irwine (11)
Jarvis (21)
Jasper (6)
Jerwyn (14)
La Ruse (4)
Marlow (22)
Marner (18)
Massey (11)
Melema (17)

143

Michal (1)
Morris (11)
Olivia (21)
Phaleg (1)
Pounce (5)
Poyser (11)
Pullet (16)
Quaver (10)
Romola (17)
Shimel (1)
Skeggo (23)
Sorrel (11)
Square (8)
Squint (20)
Supple (8)
Waters (8)
Wilmot (23)

7

Absalom (1)
Andrews (5)
Annabel (1)
Artemis (2)
Aurelia (2)
Bagshot (4)
Beatrix (2)
Bellamy (2)
Benaiah (1)
Blister (10)
Bridget (8)
Brigida (17)
Buzzard (3)
Camillo (2)
Chettam (15)
Celadin (2)
Cennini (17)
Croaker (21)
Davilow (13)
Debarry (14)
Deronda (13)
Diggory (22)
Dominic (2)
Fedalma (19)
Glasher (13)
Gregory (6)
Grizzle (9)
Honoria (2)
Jim Salt (11)
Leonora (2)
Lumpkin (22)
Lydgate (15)
Mariana (10)
Maximin (2)
Meyrick (13)
Mrs. Bede (11)
Neville (22)
Phaedra (2)
Spanker (23)
Spindle (24)
Squeeze (20)
Tancred (2)
Tankard (7)
Tempest (20)
Thimble (4)
Western (8)
Wilkins (8)

8

Adam Bede (11)
Almanzar (2)
Angelina (2, 24)
Atkinson (3)

Aunt Moss (16)
Blueskin (4)
Bob Jakin (16)
Burchell (23)
Casaubon (15)
Chererel (5)
Dempster (12)
Didapper (5)
Don Silva (19)
Dr. Blifil (8)
Foxchase (7)
Goodwill (10)
Harrison (3)
Hastings (22)
Ladislaw (15)
Leonidas (2)
Leontine (21)
Lovegold (10)
Melantha (2)
Mordecai (13)
Mrs. Glegg (16)
Mrs. Tabbs (20)
Primrose (23)
Rabsheka (1)
Richland (21)
'Sandy Jim' (11)
Ser Cioni (17)
Seth Bede (11)
Slipslop (5)
Soderini (17)
Straddle (4)
Syllabub (20)
Theodore (2)
Thwackum (8)
Tom Jones (8)
Transome (14)
Tulliver (16)
Violante (2)
Williams (23)
Winthrop (18)

9

Allworthy (8)
Aunt Glegg (16)
Beau Tibbs (20)
Bellaston (8)
Boabdelin (2)
Charlotte (6)
Cleanthes (2)
Constance (2)
Dolabella (2)
Dubardieu (21)
Felix Holt (14)
Glumdalca (9)
Guiscardo (2)
Heartfree (4)
Honeywood (21)
Jenkinson (23)
Lady Booby (5)
Limberham (2)
Lord Place (7)
Lucy Deane (16)
Major Bath (3)
Mary Garth (15)
Monna Lisa (17)
Mrs. Bennet (3)
Mrs. Blaize (24)
Mrs. Blifil (8)
Mrs. Honour (8)
Mrs. Irvine (11)
Mrs. Poyser (11)
Mrs. Pullet (16)
Mrs. Waters (8)
Nonentity (20)

Partridge (8)
Rufus Lyon (14)
Sir Jasper (6)
Thornhill (23)
Tinderbox (20)
Trulliber (5)
Ventidius (2)
Will Booth (3)
Woodville (21)

10

Achitophel (1)
Amos Barton (12)
Aunt Pullet (16)
Bellarmine (5)
Caleb Garth (15)
Dr. Harrison (3)
Dr. Primrose (23)
Esther Lyon (14)
Goody Brown (8)
Grandcourt (13)
Hardcastle (22)
Huncamunca (9)
Ishbosheth (1)
Jenny Jones (8)
Joshua Rann (11)
Mark Antony (2)
Mrs. Croaker (21)
Mrs. Davilow (13)
Mrs. Glasher (13)
Mrs. Symonds (22)
Mrs. Western (8)
Mrs. Wilkins (8)
Northerton (8)
Sigismunda (2)
Tito Melema (17)
Torrismond (2)
Whitefield (8)

11

Ben Jochanan (1)
Black George (8)
Cadwallader (15)
Celia Brooke (15)
Count La Ruse (4)
Dinah Morris (11)
Dollallolla (9)
Donnithorne (11)
Dr. Nonentity (20)
Farebrother (15)
Ferravecchi (17)
Fitzpatrick (8)
Flamborough (23)
Godfrey Cass (18)
Hetty Sorrel (11)
Jack Spindle (24)
King Tancred (2)
Lachtia Snap (4)
Lady Tempest (20)
Lord Grizzle (9)
MacFlecknoe (2)
Miss Bridget (8)
Miss Neville (2))
Mrs. Primrose (23)
Mrs. Slipslop (5)
Mrs. Transome (14)
Mrs. Tulliver (16)
Parson Adams (5)
Peter Pounce (5)
Philip Wakem (16)
Silas Marner (18)
Tim Syllabub (20)

Tom Tulliver (16)
Tony Lumpkin (22)
Totty Poyser (11)
William Dane (18)
Young Marlow (22)

12

Bardo di 'Bardi (17)
Bartle Massey (11)
Captain Booth (3)
Don Sebastian (2)
Featherstone (15)
Francesco Cei (17)
Friar Dominic (2)
Geoffrey Snap (4)
Hester Sorrel (11)
Jonathan Wild (4)
Jonathan Wyld (4)
Lady Chererel (12)
Lawyer Squint (20)
Lucy Goodwill (10)
Lydia Glasher (13)
Martin Poyser (11)
Miss Richland (21)
Monna Brigida (17)
Mrs. Allworthy (8)
Mrs. Heatfree (4)
Mrs. Partridge (8)

Squire Badger (10)
Stephen Guest (16)
Will Ladislaw (15)

13

Daniel Deronda (13)
Dolly Winthrop (18)
Harry Foxchase (7)
Janet Dempster (12)
Jonathan Burge (11)
Joseph Andrews (5)
Lady Bellaston (3)
Lady Thornhill (23)
Maynard Gilfil (12)
Matthew Jermyn (14)
Molly Straddle (4)
Moses Primrose (23)
Mrs. Hardcastle (22)
Mrs. Whitefield (8)
Nancy Lammeter (18)
Philip Debarry (14)
Pietro Cennini (17)
Romola di' Bardi (17)
Rosamond Vincy (15)
Sophia Western (8)
Squire Tankard (7)
Squire Western (8)
Theodosia Snap (4)
Thomas Thimble (4)

14

Adolphus Irwine (11)
Arabella Wilmot (23)
Carolina Skeggs (23)
Deborah Wilkins (8)
Dorothea Brooke (15)
Edward Casaubon (15)
Frederick Vincy (15)
George Primrose (23)
Harold Transome (14)
Jenny Tinderbox (20)
Kate Hardcastle (22)
Maggie Tulliver (16)
Maximus Debarry (14)
Miss Hardcastle (22)
Mrs. Cadwallader (15)
Mrs. Fitzpatrick (8)
Olivia Primrose (23)
Sophia Primrose (23)

15

Augustus Debarry (14)
Leontine Croaker (21)
Mrs. Lydia Glasher (13)
Olivia Woodville (21)
Parson Trulliber (5)
Sir James Chettam (15)
Squire Thornhill (23)
Thomas Heartfree (4)

Some characters from **Jane Austen, Charles Kingsley, Kipling,** and **Longfellow**
List of works from which the following characters are taken, with reference numbers.

Jane Austen
Ref. No.   Title
1. Emma   (4 letters)
2. Lady Susan   (9 ,,)
3. Mansfield Park   (13 ,,)
4. Northanger Abbey   (15 ,,)
5. Persuasion   (10 ,,)
6. Pride and Prejudice   (17 ,,)
7. Sense and Sensibility   (19 ,,)
8. Watsons, The   (10 ,,)

Charles Kingsley
16. Alton Locke   (10 letters)
17. Hereward the Wake   (15 ,,)
18. Two Years Ago   (11 ,,)
19. Westward Ho!   (10 ,,)
20. Yeast   (5 ,,)
21. (Various)

Rudyard Kipling
Ref. No.   Title
9. Captains Courageous   (18 letters)
10. Day's Work, The   (11 ,,)
11. Life's Handicap   (13 ,,)
12. Naulahka, The   (11 ,,)
13. Soldiers Three   (13 ,,)
14. Stalky and Co   (11 ,,)
15. (Various)

Longfellow
22. Evangeline   (10 letters)
23. Golden Legend, The   (15 ,,)
24. Hiawatha   (8 ,,)
25. Hyperion   (8 ,,)
26. Kavanagh   (8 ,,)
27. Miles Standish   (13 ,,)
28. (Various)

Note: The numbers in brackets indicate *the works* in which the characters appear.

3 – 5

Alden (27)
Algar (17)
Allen (4)
Basil (22)
Bates (1)
Brady (9)
Bukta (10)
Cary (19)
Chinn (10)
Croft (5)
Darcy (6)
Doone (13)
Drake (19)
Elsie (23)

Elton (1)
Emma (1)
Estes (12)
Fawne (10)
Felix (23)
Four (14)
'Foxy' (14)
Grant (3)
Hogan (13, 14)
Hurst (6)
Kamal (15)
Kim (15)
King (14)
Leigh (19)
Lewis (12, 21)
Locke (16)

Mason (14)
Maxim (12)
Mowis (22)
M'Turk (14)
Nixon (14)
Nolan (12)
O'Hara (13)
Osseo (24)
Penn (9)
Platt (9)
Price (3)
Prout (14)
Scott (10)
Shadd (13)
Slane (13)
Smith (4, 20)

Sneyd (3)
Titus (23)
Troop (9)
Tulke (14)
Uriel (4)
Ward (3)
White (14)
Yates (3)
Yeo (19)
Zouch (19)

6

Alfgar (17)
Ansell (14)

Disko Troop (9)
Dr. Thurnall (18)
Earl Godwin (17)
Emma Watson (8)
Evangeline (22)
Fanny Price (3)
Findlayson (10)
Godwinsson (17)
Jane Bennet (6)
John Briggs (18)
John Thorpe (4)
King Ranald (17)
Lady Godiva (17)
Lady Vernon (2)
Lajeunesse (22)
Lucy Steele (7)
Mainwaring (2)
Miss Kinzey (9)
Miss Martin (10)
Miss M'Kenna (13)
Miss Morton (7)
Mrs. De Sussa (13)
Mrs. Edwards (8)
Mrs. Holdock (10)
Mrs. Johnson (2)
Mrs. Mullins (13)
Prometheus (28)
Strickland (11)
Tom Bertram (3)
Willoughby (7)

11

Alfred Chinn (10)
Barraclough (11)
Bracebridge (2)
Count of Lara (28)
Count Robert (17)
Dundas Fawne (10)
Earl Leofric (17)
Fanny Norris (3)
Frances Ward (3)
Harry Verney (20)
Henry Tilney (4)
Hinchcliffe (15)
James Burton (21)
Jane Fairfax (1)
Jerry Blazes (13)
John Gillett (14)
John Learoyd (11)
John Oxenham (19)
Kate Sheriff (12)
Lady Bertram (3)
Lady Osborne (8)
Lionel Chinn (10)
Lord Osborne (8)
Lucy Ferrars (7)
Lydia Bennet (6)
Mary Edwards (8)
Megissogwon (24)
Mudjekeewis (24)
Mrs. Dashwood (7)
Mrs. Gardiner (6)
Mrs. Jennings (7)
Paul Fleming (25)
René Leblanc (22)

Rev. Mr. Howard (8)
Rev. Mr. Norris (3)
Shawondasee (24)
Susan Vernon (2)
Thomas Leigh (19)
Tom Musgrave (8)
Tom Thurnall (18)

12

Abbot Leofric (17)
Admiral Croft (5)
Brimblecombe (19)
Brugglesmith (10)
Captain Leigh (19)
Colonel Nolan (12)
Dick Grenvile (19)
Earl of Mercia (17)
Earl of Wessex (17)
Eustace Leigh (19)
Frank Headley (18)
Harriet Smith (4)
Harvey Cheyne (9)
Jack Thurnall (18)
Jasper Purvis (8)
John Dashwood (7)
Julia Bertram (3)
Lady de Bourgh (6)
Lady de Courcy (2)
Lady Grenville (19)
Lord Lynedale (16)
Lucy Passmore (19)
Maria Bertram (3)
Mary Crawford (3)
Miss Bingleys (The) (6)
Miss Newbroom (20)
Miss Standish (27)
Mrs. Rushworth (3)
Paul Tregarva (20)
Pau-Puk-Keewis (24)
Robert Martin (1)
Robert Watson (8)
Rose Salterne (19)
Salvation Yeo (19)
Samuel Burton (21)
Sandy Mackage (16)
Uncle Salters (9)
William Price (3)

13

Admiral Winter (19)
Ali Baba Mahbub (15)
Alicia Johnson (2)
Bellefontaine (22)
Captain Gadsby (13, 15)
Captain Hunter (8)
Captain Maffin (13)
Captain O'Brien (8)
Captain Willis (18)
Colonel Dabney (14)
Corporal Slane (13)
Edmund Bertram (3)
Edward Ferrars (7)
Eleanor Tilney (4)

Emma Deercourt (13)
Emma Woodhouse (1)
Fanny Dashwood (7)
Father Campian (19)
Father Parsons (19)
Henry Crawford (3)
Henry Dashwood (7)
Humphrey Chinn (10)
John Middleton (7)
Julia Crawford (3)
Lady Middleton (7)
Lancelot Smith (20)
Little Mildred (15)
Lord Vieuxbois (20)
Major Campbell (18)
Mark Armsworth (18)
Mary Armsworth (18)
Mary Ashburton (25)
Miles Standish (27)
Raymond Martin (14)
Robert Ferrars (7)
Simon Salterne (19)
Thomas Bertram (3)
William Martin (10)

14

Captain Raleigh (19)
Cecilia Vaughan (26)
Colonel Brandon (7)
Earl Godwinsson (17)
Edward Thurnall (18)
Elinor Dashwood (7)
Emanuel Pycroft (15)
Father Felicien (22)
Frank Churchill (1)
Isabella Thorpe (4)
Miss Mainwaring (2)
Nicholas Tarvin (12)
Oliver Basselin (22)
Penelope Watson (8)
Rev. John Gillett (14)
Robert of Sicily (28)
Sir James Martin (2)
Thomas Thurnall (18)
Walter of Varila (21)

15

Amos Barraclough (11)
Catherine Vernon (2)
Elizabeth Bennet (6)
Elizabeth Watson (8)
Hereward the Wake (17)
Humphrey Gilbert (28)
Lady Susan Vernon (2)
Martin Lightfoot (17)
Private Mulvaney (13)
Private Ortheris (13)
Raphael Aben-Ezra (21)
Richard Grenvile (19)
Sergeant Mullins (13)
Sir Francis Drake (19)
Squire Lavington (20)
Valentia Headley (18)

Some characters from **Lord Lytton**
List of works from which the following characters are taken, with reference numbers.

Ref. No.	Title			Ref. No.	Title		
1.	Alice	(5 letters)		11.	Money	(5 letters)	
2.	Caxtons, The	(10	,,)	12.	My Novel	(7	,,)
3.	Devereux	(8	,,)	13.	Night and Morning	(15	,,)
4.	Ernest Maltravers	(16	,,)	14.	Parisians, The	(12	,,)
5.	Eugene Aram	(10	,,)	15.	Pelham	(6	,,)
6.	Godolphin	(9	,,)	16.	Richelieu	(9	,,)
7.	Harold	(6	,,)	17.	Rienzi	(6	,,)
8.	Kenelm Chillingly	(16	,,)	18.	Sea Captain, The	(13	,,)
9.	Last Days of Pompeii, The	(20	,,)	19.	Strange Story, A	(13	,,)
10.	Last of the Barons, The	(18	,,)	20.	What will he do with it?	(18	,,)
				21.	Zanoni	(6	,,)

Note: The numbers in brackets indicate *the works* in which the character appear.

3 AND 4

Aram (5)
Bolt (2)
Butt (8)
Dale (12)
Haco (7)
Ione (9)
King (14)
Lee (10)
Love (13)
Moor (5)
Odo (7)
Pike (2)
Rolf (7)
Vane (14)
Wood (5)

5

Algar (7)
Alice (1)
Alred (7)
Alton (14)
Alwyn (10)
Babel (15)
Bedos (15)
Bevil (14)
Boxer (13)
Bruce (12)
Bruse (7)
Burbo (9)
Clare (6)
Clump (13)
Crane (20)
Cutts (20)
Digby (8, 12)
Donce (1)
Dumas (21)
Duval (14)
Edith (7)
Emlyn (8)
Faber (19)
Frost (20)
Gates (10)
Githa (7)
Gower (2)
Grant (15)
Graul (10)
Green (13, 15)
Grimm (14)
Gurth (7)
Hales (5)
Hobbs (4)
Hodge (4)
Jones (4, 13, 19)

Julia (9)
Lloyd (19)
Lucia (17)
Luigi (17)
Lydon (9)
Madge (10)
Medon (9)
Merle (20)
Mills (20)
Nicot (21)
Niger (9)
Nixon (5)
Nydia (9)
Olave (7)
Pansa (9)
Paolo (21)
Payan (21)
Poole (20)
Price (13)
Rugge (20)
Rymer (3)
Sharp (13)
Smith (13, 15)
Sosia (9)
Speck (2)
Steen (8)
Stirn (12)
Tiddy (1, 4)
Thyra (7)
Vance (20)
Vebba (7)
Vesey (11)
Waife (20)
Willy (20)

6

Aubrey (1)
Avenel (12)
Ayesha (19)
Barlow (13)
Beavor (13)
Beevor (18)
Belton (15)
Benson (6)
Benzoni (3)
Birnie (13)
Blount (11)
Bovill (8)
Bowles (8)
Briggs (15)
Bungey (10)
Burley (12)
Burton (20)
Butler (1, 4)
Calton (15)

Caxton (2, 12)
Cetoxa (21)
Cibber (3)
Clarke (5)
Conway (15)
Crampe (20)
Currie (12)
Darvil (1, 4)
Dawson (15)
Dawton (15)
Derval (19)
Diomed (9)
Dubois (3)
Dysart (5)
Elmore (5)
Evelyn (11)
Favant (13)
Fleuri (3)
Forman (19)
Fulvia (9)
Godwin (7)
Gordon (8, 15)
Grayle (19)
Greggs (20)
Harold (7)
Haroun (19)
Hébert (14)
Herman (2)
Howard (1)
Jarvis (12)
Jeeves (19)
Jonson (15)
Justis (1)
Lebeau (14)
Legard (1)
Leslie (Mr.) (1, 12)
Lester (5)
Locket (8)
Losely (20)
Lovell (10)
Lufton (15)
Lumley (1)
Malden (6)
Mallet (7)
Margot (15)
Merton (1)
Mivers (8)
Morcar (7)
Morgan (12)
Morley (14, 20)
Morton (13)
Nevile (10)
Newman (1)
Norman (18)
Onslow (1)
Orsini (17)
Oswald (3)

Pelham (15)
Pietro (19)
Pisani (21)
Poyntz (19)
Rameau (14)
Renard (14)
Rienzi (17)
Ritson (15)
Rivers (10)
Rodolf (17)
Scales (10)
Simcox (4)
Siward (7)
Sloman (19)
Smythe (19)
Somers (8, 10)
Sporus (9)
Sprott (12)
Spruce (20)
Square (2)
Steele (3)
St. John (3)
St. Just (21)
Sultan (dog) (1)
Sweyne (7)
Tibson (5)
Tostig (7)
Trevor (6)
Uberto (19)
Vernon (6)
Vertot (14)
Vigors (19)
Violet (18)
Vivian (2)
Vyvyan (20)
Warner (10)
Watson (13)
Welles (10)
Zanoni (21)

7

Aberton (15)
Addison (3)
Adeline (17)
Alljack (12)
Arbaces (9)
Arundel (18)
Bacourt (14)
Baldwin (7)
Baradas (16)
Barnard (3)
Bawtrey (8)
Belvoir (6, 8)
Bolding (2)
Bullion (2)

Bunting (5)
Calenus (9)
Callias (9)
Cameron (1, 8)
Campion (8)
Caradoc (7)
Catesby (10)
Cazotte (21)
Chapman (20)
Chester (15)
Cicogna (14)
Cleland (3)
Clinton (15)
Clodius (9)
Colonna (17)
Compass (2)
Compton (8)
Congrio (9)
Coniers (10)
Corinne (14)
Couthon (21)
Danvers (4, 8, 13)
Darrell (20)
Davison (15)
Dealtry (5)
de Bohun (7)
de Brézé (14)
de Fulke (10)
Delmour (6)
de Maury (13)
de Passy (14)
Douglas (11, 15)
Dr. Faber (19)
Dr. Jones (19)
Dr. Lloyd (19)
Dumdrum (12)
Egerton (12)
Eulalie (14)
Fenwick (19)
Ferrers (4)
Ferrier (14)
Fossett (20)
Fulvius (9)
Gandrin (14)
Garrett (15)
Gawtrey (12, 13)
Georges (14)
Glaucus (9)
Glosson (6)
Glyndon (21)
Godrith (7)
Gotobed (20)
Gubbins (1)
Hammond (20)
Hartopp (20)
Heyford (10)
Hilyard (10)
Holwell (5)
Joe Wood (5)
Kneller (3)
Latimer (10)
Laurent (15)
Leofric (7)
Lepidus (9)
Liehbur (6)
Louvier (14)
Lyndsay (20)
Maigrot (7)
Marsden (13)
Mascari (21)
Mervale (21)
Monnier (14)
Montagu (10)
Mrs. Dale (12)
Mrs. Mole (2)
Neville (10)

Norreys (12)
Oldtown (15)
Peacock (2)
Pompley (12)
Raimond (17)
Raselli (14)
Rollick (2)
Rumford (15)
Sallust (9)
Savarin (14)
Saville (6)
Sexwolf (7)
Sharpon (15)
Spencer (13)
Squills (2, 12)
Stigand (7)
Stokton (10)
Stowell (12)
Stracey (6)
Strahan (19)
St. Simon (3)
Summers (5)
Tibbets (2)
Tyrrell (15)
Venosta (14)
Vespius (9)
Villani (17)
Vincent (15)
Vivaldi (17)
Walters (4)
Winsley (1)
Withers (10)
Wolnoth (7)

8

Allerton (10)
Ashleigh (19)
Asterisk (14)
Astuccio (17)
Barnabas (12)
Beaufort (13)
Belgioso (21)
Bonville (10)
Bookworm (3)
Brabazon (19)
Brettone (17)
Bruttini (17)
Cesarini (1)
Crabtree (15)
Cromwell (3)
D'Alvarez (3)
d'Anville (15)
Dartmore (15)
Dashmore (12)
de Balzac (3)
de Caxton (2)
De Courcy (15)
Delville (6)
Devereux (3)
Dosewell (12)
Dr. Herman (2)
Dr. Morgan (12)
Eumolpus (9)
Falconer (6)
Fielding (3)
Fitzhugh (10)
Franklin (11)
Franzini (12)
Gionetta (21)
Giuseppe (17)
Goupille (13)
Gryffyth (7)
Hamilton (3)
Hastings (10)

Haughton (19, 20)
Hebraist (5)
Houseman (5)
Jackeymo (12)
Jacobina (cat) (5)
Lanfranc (7)
Leofwine (7)
Lilburne (13)
Loredano (21)
Luscombe (15)
Madeline (5)
Margrave (19)
Melville (8)
Meredydd (7)
Montfort (20)
Montreal (17)
Mordaunt (8)
Mrs. Boxer (13)
Mrs. Bruce (19)
Mrs. Crane (20)
Mrs. Green (15)
Mrs. Hobbs (4)
Mrs. Jones (4)
Mrs. Poole (4)
Mrs. Tiddy (1)
O'Carroll (3)
Olinthus (9)
Pandulfo (17)
Paulding (15)
Peterson (2)
Phillida (9)
Plimmins (13)
Plympton (6)
Primmins (2)
Prudence (18)
Sancroft (10)
Saunders (20)
Sinclair (15)
Sir Isaac (dog) (20)
Solomons (12)
Staunton (15)
Stubmore (13)
Tarleton (3)
Thetford (8)
Thornton (15)
Trafford (15)
Vargrave (1, 4)
Violante (12)
Volktman (6)
Williams (20)
Winstoun (6)
Wormwood (15)

9

Apaecides (9)
Aspindale (6)
Babbleton (15)
Benedetta (17)
Blackwell (13)
Braefield (8)
Brimstone (15)
Brown Bess (mare) (13)
Callaghan (20)
Castleton (2)
Cleveland (1, 4)
Condorcet (21)
Courtland (5)
De Chatran (3)
de Mauléon (14)
de Mauprat (16)
Dollimore (15)
Doltimore (1)
Dr. Fenwick (19)
Duplessis (14)

149

Earl Agar (7)
Erpingham (6)
Fairfield (12)
Fairthorn (20)
Fillgrave (5)
Giraumont (13)
Glanville (15)
Godolphin (6)
Guloseton (15)
Hasselton (3)
Hazeldean (12)
Hennequin (14)
Job Jonson (15)
Jockleton (3)
Joe Spruce (20)
John Clump (13)
John Green (13)
Johnstone (6)
John Vesey (11)
King Louis (XIV) (3)
Lady Frost (20)
Lady Janet (14)
Lascelles (4)
Lemercier (14)
L'Estrange (12)
Liancourt (13)
Loubinsky (14)
Macgregor (13)
Marmaduke (10)
M'Catchley (12)
Millinger (6)
Montreuil (3)
Mrs. Avenel (12)
Mrs. Bowles (8)
Mrs. Butler (1)
Mrs. Caxton (2, 12)
Mrs. Elmore (5)
Mrs. Leslie (1, 12)
Mrs. Merton (1)
Mrs. Morley (14)
Mrs. Morton (13)
Mrs. Poyntz (19)
Mrs. Somers (8)
Mrs. Trevor (6)
Nelthorpe (15)
Nick Alwyn (10)
Paul Grimm (14)
Plaskwith (13)
Radclyffe (6)
Réné Dumas (21)
Richelieu (16)
Roseville (15)
Russelton (15)
Saxingham (1, 4)
Stalworth (8)
Stollhead (20)
St. Quintin (15)
Taillefer (7)
Templeton (1, 4)
Tetraides (9)
Thornhill (12)
Tom Bowles (8)
Townshend (15)
Trevanion (2)
Uncle Jack (2)
Vaudemont (13)
Warburton (15)
Westbrook (1)
Woodstock (15)
Woodville (10)

10

Adam Warner (10)
Beaudesert (2)

Bennington (15)
Brotherton (8)
Caleb Price (13)
Castruccio (4)
Chillingly (8)
Dame Newman (1)
Dame Ursula (17)
Dartington (6)
de Vandemar (14)
Dick Avenel (12)
Dolly Poole (20)
Doningdale (4)
Don Saltero (3)
Dr. Dosewell (12)
Earl Godwin (7)
Eugene Aram (5)
Fra Moreale (17)
Frank Vance (20)
Glenmorris (15)
Graham Vane (14)
Guy Bolding (2)
Guy Darrell (20)
Hal Peacock (2)
Helen Digby (12)
Hildebrand (7)
Jane Poyntz (19)
John Avenel (12)
John Bovill (8)
John Burley (12)
John Vernon (6)
Kate Morton (13)
King Edward (IV) (10)
King Harold (7)
Lady Dawton (15)
Lady Pelham (15)
Lethbridge (8)
Lord Belton (15)
Lord Calton (15)
Lord Dorset (10)
Lord Rivers (10)
Lord Scales (10)
MacBlarney (2)
Maltravers (1, 4)
Mandeville (6)
Marc le Roux (14)
Midgecombe (6)
Millington (15)
Miss Lockit (8)
Miss Starke (12)
Mrs. Bawtrey (8)
Mrs. Bertram (12)
Mrs. Cameron (8)
Mrs. Campion (8)
Mrs. Compton (8)
Mrs. Darrell (20)
Mrs. Dealtry (5)
Mrs. Egerton (12)
Mrs. Holwell (5)
Mrs. Lyndsay (20)
Mrs. Mervale (21)
Mrs. Pompley (12)
Nora Avenel (12)
Peter Hales (5)
Porpustone (10)
Rainsforth (2)
Riccabocca (12)
Richard Lee (10)
Robert Butt (8)
Saunderson (8)
Shallowell (6)
Snivelship (3)
Sophy Waife (20)
Stefanello (17)
Stratonice (9)
Tom Stowell (12)
Toolington (15)

Ulverstone (2)
Will Somers (10)

11

Abbé Vertpré (14)
Alban Morley (20)
Alice Darval (1, 4)
Bolingbroke (3)
Carrucarius (9)
Clutterbuck (15)
Count Cetoxa (21)
Dame Dealtry (5)
de Maintenon (3)
de Malvoisin (10)
de Montaigne (1, 4)
de Ventadown (1, 4)
Duke of Alton (14)
Farmer Bruce (12)
Fitzosborne (7)
Flora Vyvyan (20)
Friar Bungey (10)
Henry Nevile (10)
Henry Pelham (15)
Henry St. John (3)
Hugh Withers (10)
Jessie Wiles (8)
John Stokton (10)
John Tibbets (2)
John Walters (4)
Jonas Elmore (5)
Julia Elmore (5)
Julius Faber (19)
Kenelm Digby (8)
Kitty Caxton (2)
Lady Arundel (18)
Lady Delmour (6)
Lady Oldtown (15)
Longueville (10)
Lord Belvoir (6)
Lord Chester (15)
Lord Clinton (15)
Lord Montagu (10)
Lord Taunton (4)
Lord Vincent (15)
Lord Warwick (10)
Louise Duval (14)
Louis Grayle (19)
Malesherbes (21)
Marie Oswald (3)
Meeing Willy (20)
Miles Square (2)
Miss Chapman (20)
Mrs. Ashleigh (19)
Mrs. Beaufort (13)
Mrs. Haughton (20)
Mrs. Plimmins (13)
Mrs. Primmins (13)
Mrs. Saunders (20)
Paul Louvier (14)
Percy Norman (18)
Printer Pike (2)
Proteus Bolt (2)
Rev. Mr. Aubrey (1)
Rev. Mr. Merton (1)
Richard King (14)
Robespierre (21)
Roger Morton (13)
'Sisty' Caxton (2)
Squire Nixon (5)
Uncle Roland (2, 12)
Viola Pisoli (21)

12

Alfred Evelyn (11)
Allen Fenwick (19)
Arthur Morton (13)
Austin Caxton (2)
Baron di Porto (17)
Beau Fielding (3)
Captain Smith (13)
Clara Douglas (11)
Cola di Rienzi (17)
Count Baldwin (7)
Count de Passy (14)
Count William (7)
Dame Darkmans (5)
Daniel Clarke (5)
De Finisterre (14)
Dr. Riccabocca (12)
Dr. Shallowell (6)
Duc de St. Simon (3)
Earl of Mercia (7)
Edgar Ferrier (14)
Father Uberto (17)
Francis Vance (20)
General Grant (15)
George Howard (1)
George Legard (1)
George Morley (20)
Giles Tibbets (2)
Jacob Bunting (5)
James Holwell (5)
Jane Houseman (5)
Jasper Losely (20)
Lady Bonville (10)
Lady Delville (6)
Lady Franklin (11)
Lady Haughton (19)
Lady Montfort (20)
Lily Mordaunt (8)
Lord Bonville (10)
Lord Dartmore (15)
Lord Falconer (6)
Lord Fitzhugh (10)
Lord Hastings (10)
Lord Lilburne (13)
Lord Luscombe (15)
Lord Montfort (20)
Lord Plympton (6)
Lord Thetford (8)
Lord Vargrave (1, 4)
Madame Beavor (13)
Madame Vertot (14)
Maéstro Páolo (21)
Miss Asterisk (14)
Miss Brabazon (19)
Misses Burton (20)
Miss Paulding (15)
Miss Trafford (15)
Mrs. Braefield (8)
Mrs. Brimstone (15)
Mrs. Dollimore (15)
Mrs. Fairfield (12)
Mrs. Hazeldean (12)
Mrs. M'Catchley (12)
Mrs. Plaskwith (13)
Mrs. Shinfield (4)
Mrs. St. Quintin (15)
Mrs. Templeton (4)
Parson Quinny (15)
Peter Dealtry (5)
Philip Morton (13)
Ralph Rumford (15)
Randal Leslie (12)
Raoul De Fulke (10)
Rev. Mr. Dumdrum (12)

Rev. Mr. Summers (5)
Robin Hilyard (10)
Sharpe Currie (12)
Sibyll Warner (10)
Simon Gawtrey (13)
Sir Guy Nevile (10)
Sir John Comers (10)
Sir John Vesey (11)
Squire Lester (5)
Squire Tibson (5)
Tirabaloschi (4)
Vipont Morley (20)
Von Schomberg (4)
Walter Lester (5)
William Waife (20)
Will Peterson (2)

13

Abbé Montreuil (3)
Adolphus Poole (20)
Adrian Colonna (17)
Angelo Villani (17)
Arabella Crane (20)
Armand Monnier (14)
Audley Egerton (12)
Blanche Caxton (2, 12)
Bob Saunderson (8)
Bridget Greggs (20)
Captain Norman (18)
Charles Merton (1)
Colonel Dysart (5)
Colonel Elmore (5)
Colonel Legard (1)
Colonel Morley (14, 20)
Colonel Poyntz (19)
Count Devereux (3)
Count Hamilton (3)
de Grantmesnil (14)
de Rochebriant (14)
Duke of Orleans (16)
Earl of Warwick (10)
Ellinor Lester (5)
Evelyn Cameron (1)
Francis Vivian (2)
Gaetano Pisani (21)
George Belvoir (8)
George Clinton (15)
Georgina Vesey (11)
Gerald Danvers (8)
Gianni Colonna (17)
Goody Darkmans (5)
Gustave Rameau (14)
Gustavus Donce (1)
Hugues Maigrot (7)
Isaura Cicogna (14)
Isora D'Alvarez (3)
Jeremiah Smith (13)
John Courtland (5)
John Russelton (15)
John Stalworth (8)
Joseph Hartopp (20)
Lady Babbleton (15)
Lady Delafield (19)
Lady Doltimore (1)
Lady Erpingham (6)
Lady Glenalvon (8)
Lady Hasselton (3)
Lady Jane Babel (15)
Lady Lascelles (4)
Lady Mary Babel (15)
Lady Nelthorpe (15)
Lady Roseville (15)
Lady Trevanion (2)
Leopold Lufton (15)

Leopold Smythe (19)
Lord Castleton (2)
Lord Doltimore (1)
Lord Erpingham (6)
Lord Guloseton (15)
Lord L'Estrange (12)
Lord Saxingham (1, 4)
Louise Corinne (14)
Lumley Ferrers (4)
Madame de Maury (14)
Madame Laurent (15)
Madame Liehbur (6)
Madge Darkmans (5)
Marion de Lorme (16)
Mark Fairfield (12)
Martino Orsini (17)
Mary Westbrook (1)
Mike Callaghan (20)
Ned Porpustone (10)
Nicholas Alwyn (10)
Nina di Raselli (17)
Prince Richard (10)
Rev. Caleb Price (13)
Richard Avenel (12)
Richard Nevile (10)
Rinaldo Orsini (17)
Robert Hilyard (10)
Rowland Lester (5)
Seymour Conway (15)
Sir John Merton (1)
Sir Peter Hales (5)
Squire Rollick (2)
Thomas Mervale (21)
William Losely (20)
William Mallet (7)

14

Aubrey Devereux (3)
Augustus Lufton (15)
Benjamin Lufton (15)
Bishop of Bayeux (7)
Caroline Merton (1)
Cecilia Travers (8)
Colonel Cleland (3)
Colonel Danvers (4)
Colonel Egerton (12)
Colonel Pompley (12)
Count de la Roche (10)
Dorothy Dealtry (5)
Duke of Clarence (10)
Earl of Hereford (7)
Fanny Millinger (6)
Fanny Trevanion (2)
Farmer Sinclair (15)
Frank Hazeldean (12)
Gaffer Solomons (12)
'Gentleman Waife' (20)
Geoffrey Lester (5)
Gerald Devereux (3)
Giovanni Orsini (17)
Giulio Franzini (12)
Henry Johnstone (6)
Howard de Howard (15)
Humfrey Heyford (10)
Irene di Gabrini (17)
John Chillingly (8)
Lady Bennington (15)
Leopold Travers (8)
Lilian Ashleigh (19)
Lionel Haughton (20)
Lord Bennington (15)
Lord Dartington (6)
Lord Doningdale (4)
Lord Glenmorris (15)

151

Lord Rainsforth (2)
Lord Ulverstone (2)
Madeline Lester (5)
Margaret Poyntz (19)
Martino di Porto (17)
Matilda Darrell (20)
Morton Devereux (3)
Mrs. Bracegirdle (3)
Percy Godolphin (6)
Queen Elizabeth (10)
Richard Strahan (19)
Robert Beaufort (13)
Rodolf of Saxony (17)
Roland de Caxton (2)
Rolf of Hereford (7)
Sidney Beaufort (13)
Sir Henry Nevile (10)
Sir Kenelm Digby (8)
Stephen Colonna (17)
Teresa Cesarini (4)
Timothy Alljack (12)
Walter Melville (8)

15

Adrien de Mauprat (16)
Albert Trevanion (2)

Anthony Hamilton (3)
Arabella Fossett (20)
Armand Richelieu (16)
Arthur Godolphin (6)
Augustine Caxton (2)
Augustus Saville (6)
Beatrice di Negra (12)
Boulainvilliers (3)
Captain Barnabas (12)
Captain Dashmore (12)
Captain de Caxton (2)
Captain Haughton (20)
Catherine Morton (13)
Cecco del Vecchio (17)
Charles Haughton (20)
Clarence Glyndon (21)
Constance Vernon (6)
Corporal Bunting (5)
David Mandeville (6)
Duke of Aspindale (6)
Earl of Erpingham (6)
Earl of Worcester (10)
Evelyn Templeton (1)
Francisco Pietro (17)
Frederick Blount (11)
George Blackwell (13)
Gertrude Douglas (15)
Gilbert Ashleigh (19)

Harley L'Estrange (12)
Haughton Darrell (20)
Jemima Hazeldean (12)
Jessica Haughton (20)
Julian Montreuil (3)
Julie de Mortemar (16)
Katherine Nevile (10)
Lady Longueville (10)
Lanfranc of Pavia (7)
Leonardo Raselli (14)
Lord Bolingbroke (3)
Lucien Duplessis (14)
Major MacBlarney (2)
Margaret of Anjou (10)
Marmaduke Nevile (10)
Pandulfo di Guido (17)
Peter Chillingly (8)
Raoul de Vandemar (14)
Rev. Mr. Lethbridge (8)
Richard Cromwell (3)
Richard Houseman (5)
Sally Chillingly (8)
Sarah Chillingly (8)
Sibyl Chillingly (8)
Sir Philip Derval (19)
Sir Ralph Rumford (15)
Sir Robert Welles (10)
Squire Hazeldean (12)

Some characters from **Meredith, Milton** and **Thomas Moore**
List of works from which the following characters are taken, with reference numbers.

George Meredith
Ref. No.   Title
1. Beauchamp's Career   (16 letters)
2. Egoist, The   (9 „)
3. Evan Harrington   (14 „)
4. Harry Richmond   (13 „)
5. Rhoda Fleming   (12 „)
6. Richard Feverel   (14 „)
7. One of our Conquerors   (18 „)
8. Sandra Belloni   (13 „)
9. Vittoria   (8 „)
10. (Various)

John Milton
Ref. No.   Title
11. Comus   (5 letters)
12. Paradise Lost   (12 „)
13. Paradise Regained   (16 „)
14. (Various)

Thomas Moore
15. Fudge Family in Paris, The (21 letters)
16. Irish Melodies   (13 „)
17. Lalla Rookh   (10 „)
18. (Various)

Note: The numbers in brackets indicate *the works* in which the characters appear.

3 – 5

Alvan (10)
Azim (17)
Beppo (9)
Berry (6)
Camph (10)
Chloe (10)
Chump (8)
Comus (11)
Corte (9)
Dagon (12)
Dale (2)
Diana (10)
Drew (1)
Ellen (16)
Forey (6)
Forth (3)
Fudge (15)
Goren (3)
Hafed (17)
Hinda (17)
Julia (18)
Kilne (3)
Kirby (10)
Lea (18)

Moody (5)
Mount (6)
Nama (18)
Ople (10)
Pole (8)
Powys (9)
Puff (18)
Rizzo (9)
Rosa (18)
Selim (17)
Uriel (12)

6

Abdiel (12)
Aliris (17)
Arioch (12)
Austin (1)
Azazel (12)
Azazil (12)
Barmby (7)
Barnes (3)
Belial (12)

Benson (6)
Blaize (6)
Boulby (5)
Burman (7)
Busshe (2)
Callet (7)
Connor (15)
Corney (2)
Dacier (10)
Dalila (14)
Daphne (13)
Denham (1)
Durham (2)
Eccles (5)
Eglett (10)
Farina (10)
Gammon (5)
Graves (7)
Harley (6)
Kionis (4)
Laxley (3)
Lespel (1)
Lovell (5)
Lowton (3)

Manoah (14)
Nereus (11)
Noorka (10)
Oggler (1)
O'Ruark (16)
Oxford (2)
Pompey (13)
Radnor (7)
Raikes (3)
Romara (9)
Samfit (5)
Scipio (13)
Sedley (9)
Semele (13)
Strike (3)
Summer (8)
Syrinx (13)
Tethys (11)
Tinman (10)
Turbot (1)
Uploft (3)
Waring (5)
Zaraph (18)
Zelica (17)

7

Ammiani (9)
Amymone (13)
Antiopa (13)
Asmadai (12)
Bagarag (10)
Barrett (8)
Beamish (10)
Belloni (8)
Beltham (4)
Billing (5)
Calisto (13)
Clymene (13)
Cougham (1)
Culling (1)
De Craye (2)
Durance (7)
Eveleen (16)
Farrell (10)
Feverel (6)
Fleming (5)
Gambier (8, 9)
Gosstre (8)
Grossby (3)
Hackbut (5)
Halkett (1)
Harapha (14)
Jocelyn (3)
Killick (1)
Latters (5)
Lycidas (14)
Lydiard (1)
Mohanna (17)
Namouna (17)
Ottilia (4)
Parsley (3)
Pelleas (13)
Pempton (7)
Peridon (7)
Perkins (3)
Phillis (18)
Piavens (9)
Pierson (9)
Raphael (12)
Romfrey (1)
Sabrina (11)
Saracco (9)
Sedgett (5)
Shagpat (10)
Skepsey (7)
Sowerby (7)
St. Kevin (16)
Thyrsis (14)
Tuckham (1)
Warwick (10)
Weyburn (10)
Wicklow (5)
Zophiel (12)

8

Al Hassan (17)
Bakewell (6)
Blancove (5)
Blandish (6)
Bob Fudge (15)
Braintop (8)
Crossjay (2)
De Saldar (3)
Dr. Corney (2)
Dunstane (10)
Fenellan (7)
Feramorz (17)
Ithuriel (12)

Lancelot (13)
Miss Dale (2)
Mortimer (6)
Mrs. Berry (6)
Mrs. Chump (8)
Mrs. Forey (6)
Mrs. Mount (6)
Patterne (2)
Pericles (8, 10)
Redworth (10)
Richmond (4)
Shrapnel (1)
Thompson (6)
Tim Fudge (15)
Ugo Corte (9)
Vittoria (9)
Whitford (2)
Woodseer (10)

9

Adela Pole (8)
Alciphron (18)
Anemolius (18)
Armstrong (5)
Balderini (9)
Baskelett (1)
Beauchamp (1)
Beelzebub (12)
Blathenoy (7)
Cogglesby (3)
de Pyrmont (9)
Fadladeen (17)
Fionnuala (15)
Fleetwood (10)
Ilchester (4)
Jenkinson (2)
Lady Camph (10)
Maccabeus (13)
Middleton (2)
Mrs. Boulby (5)
Mrs. Burman (7)
Mrs. Harley (6)
Mrs. Lovell (5)
Mrs. Samfit (5)
Mrs. Sedley (9)
Nourmahal (17)
O'Donoghue (16)
Pellemore (13)
Phil Fudge (15)
St. Senanus (18)
Todhunter (6)
Tom Blaize (6)
Wentworth (6)

10

Adramelech (12)
Barrington (3)
Barto Rizzo (9)
Biddy Fudge (15)
Danisburgh (10)
de Croisnel (1)
Desborough (6)
Dr. Shrapnel (1)
Harrington (3)
Lady Busshe (2)
Lady Eglett (10)
Lalla Rookh (17)
Lord Laxley (3)
Lord Ormont (10)
Mark Tinman (10)
Miss Denham (1)
Mrs. Culling (1)

Mrs. Fleming (5)
Mrs. Lydiard (1)
Mrs. Wicklow (5)
Orator Puff (18)
Von Rüdiger (10)

11

Beau Beamish (10)
Blackington (7)
Dr. Middleton (2)
General Ople (10)
Jenny Denham (1)
Lady Feverel (6)
Lady Gosstre (8)
Lady Jocelyn (3)
Lady Romfrey (1)
Lenkenstein (9)
Lord of Rosna (16)
Lord Romfrey (1)
Major Waring (5)
Mountfalcon (6)
Mountstuart (2)
Mrs. Mortimer (6)
Percy Dacier (10)
Percy Waring (5)
Quidascarpi (9)
Ralph Morton (6)
Rose Jocelyn (3)
Roy Richmond (4)
Tom Bakewell (6)
Tripehallow (1)
Weisspriess (9)
Wilfrid Pole (8)

12

Adrian Harley (6)
Arabella Pole (8)
Carlo Ammiani (9)
Colonel Corte (9)
Cornelia Pole (8)
Count Ammiani (9)
Countess Lena (9)
Diana Warwick (10)
Duchess Susan (10)
Emma Dunstane (10)
Farmer Blaize (6)
George Lowton (3)
George Uploft (3)
Harry Jocelyn (3)
Harry Latters (5)
Lady Blandish (6)
Lady Patterne (2)
Laetitia Dale (2)
Laura Piavens (9)
Luigi Saracco (9)
Madame Callet (7)
Master Gammon (5)
Merthyr Powys (9)
Mrs. Beauchamp (1)
Mrs. Blathenoy (7)
Mrs. Cogglesby (3)
Mrs. Jenkinson (2)
Mrs. Wentworth (6)
Nataly Radnor (7)
Phelim Connor (15)
Robert Eccles (5)
Runningbrook (8)
Saint Senanus (18)
Squire Uploft (3)
Tom Cogglesby (3)
Victor Radnor (7)
William Moody (5)   153

13

Aminta Farrell (10)
Austin Feverel (6)
Captain Oxford (2)
Colney Durance (7)
Dahlia Fleming (5)
Daniel Skepsey (7)
Drummond Forth (3)
Dudley Sowerby (7)
Emilia Belloni (8)
Farmer Fleming (5)
Gower Woodseer (10)
Grancey Lespel (1)
Harapha of Gath (14)
Harry Richmond (4)
Horace De Craye (2)
John Todhunter (6)
Justice Harley (6)
Lawyer Perkins (3)
Luciano Romara (9)
'Mel' Harrington (3)
Mrs. Doria Forey (6)
Mrs. Harrington (3)
Sandra Belloni (8)
Shibli Bagarag (10)
Squire Beltham (4)
Timothy Turbot (1)

14

Anthony Hackbut (5)
Butcher Billing (5)
Captain Gambier (8, 9)
Caroline Strike (3)
Cecilia Halkett (1)
Clara Middleton (2)
Colonel De Craye (2)
Colonel Halkett (1)
Doctor Shrapnel (1)
Edward Blancove (5)
Evan Harrington (3)
Everard Romfrey (1)
Hippias Feverel (6)
Janet Ilchester (4)
Jonathan Eccles (5)
Lord Danisburgh (10)
Lucy Desborough (6)
Major de Pyrmont (9)
Margaret Lovell (5)
Matthew Weyburn (10)
Mrs. Mountstuart (2)
Nevil Beauchamp (1)
Richard Feverel (6)
Ripton Thompson (6)
Septimus Barmby (7)
Simeon Fenellan (7)

Thomas Redworth (10)
Vernon Whitford (2)
William Fleming (5)

15

Algernon Feverel (6)
Anna Lenkenstein (9)
Antonio Pericles (10)
Austin Wentworth (6)
Captain Fenellan (7)
Charlotte Eglett (10)
Countess Ammiani (9)
Dartrey Fenellan (7)
Earl of Fleetwood (10)
Lady Blackington (7)
Lena Lenkenstein (9)
Lord Mountfalcon (6)
Noorna fin Noorka (10)
Princess Ottilia (4)
Priscilla Graves (7)
Renée de Croisnel (1)
Robert Armstrong (5)
Rosamund Culling (1)
Samson Agonistes (14)
Sir George Lowton (3)

Some characters from **Sir Walter Scott**
List of works from which the following characters are taken, with reference numbers.

Ref. No.	*Title*		
1.	Abbot, The	(8 letters)	
2.	Anne of Geierstein	(16 ,,)	
3.	Antiquary, The	(12 ,,)	
4.	Aunt Margaret's Mirror	(19 ,,)	
5.	Betrothed, The	(12 ,,)	
6.	Black Dwarf, The	(13 ,,)	
7.	Bridal of Triermain, The	(20 ,,)	
8.	Bride of Lammermoor, The	(20 ,,)	
9.	Castle Dangerous	(15 ,,)	
10.	Count Robert of Paris	(18 ,,)	
11.	Fair Maid Of Perth, The	(18 letters)	
12.	Fortunes of Nigel, The	(18 ,,)	
13.	Guy Mannering	(12 ,,)	
14.	Heart of Midlothian, The	(20 ,,)	
15.	Highland Widow, The	(16 ,,)	
16.	Ivanhoe	(7 ,,)	
17.	Kenilworth	(10 ,,)	
18.	Lady of the Lake, The	(16 ,,)	
19.	Laird's Jock, The	(13 letters)	
20.	Lay of the Last Minstrel, The	(23 ,,)	

Ref. No.	*Title*		
21.	Legend of Montrose, The	(19 ,,)	
22.	Marmion	(7 ,,)	
23.	Monastery, The	(12 ,,)	
24.	Old Mortality	(12 ,,)	
25.	Peveril of the Peak	(16 ,,)	
26.	Pirate, The	(9 ,,)	
27.	Quentin Durward	(14 ,,)	
28.	Redgauntlet	(11 ,,)	
29.	Rob Roy	(6 letters)	
30.	Rokeby	(6 ,,)	
31.	St. Ronan's Well	(12 ,,)	
32.	Surgeon's Daughter, The	(19 ,,)	
33.	Talisman, The	(11 ,,)	
34.	Tapestried Chamber, The	(20 ,,)	
35.	Two Drovers, The	(13 ,,)	
36.	Waverley	(8 ,,)	
37.	Woodstock	(9 ,,)	

Note: The numbers in brackets indicate *the works* in which the characters appear.

3 AND 4

Adie (23)
Anna (Princess) (10)
Anne (Princess) (27)
Bean (36)
Beg (11)
Dods (31)
Eva (11)
Faa (13)
Gow (11)
Gray (8, 32)
Lee (37)
Lyle (21)

René (King) (2)
Tuck (16)
Weir (28)

5

Abney (37)
Allan (13)
Allen (24)
André (27)
Aston (37)
Aymer (16)
Bevis (horse) (22)

Binks (31)
Blair (11)
Block (2)
Blood (25)
Boeuf (16)
Brand (18)
Brown (29)
Caxon (3)
Clegg (25)
Croye (Countess) (27)
Deans (14)
Edgar (8)
Edith (Lady) (16)
Eppie (31)

9

Baldrick (5)
Berenger (5)
Bohemond (Prince) (10)
Boniface (1, 23)
Bullsegg (36)
Burleigh (Lord) (21)
Campbell (14, 15, 21, 28)
Cantrips (28)
Carleton (25)
Christie (12, 23)
Clifford (33, 37)
Colkitto (21)
Conachar (11)
Dalgarno (Lord) (12)
Dalgetty (21)
Damiotti (4)
Debbitch (25)
de Multon (33)
Dennison (24)
de Wilton (22)
Engelred (16)
Evandale (Lord) (24)
Fairford (28)
Falconer (4, 36)
Fitzurse (Lord) (16)
Flammock (5)
Forester (4)
Geraldin (Lord) (3)
Guenevra (33)
Headrigg (24)
Henry Gow (11)
Henry Lee (37)
Hereward (10)
Hermione (12)
Ingelram (23)
Jamieson (32)
Jellicot (37)
King René (2)
Lapraick (28)
l'Hermite (2, 27)
Locksley (16)
Macaulay (21)
Macready (29)
Margaret (Ladye) (20)
Melville (1)
Menteith (Earl of) (21)
Meredith (28)
Misbegot (3)
Mrs. Allan (13)
Mrs. Glass (14)
Musgrave (20)
Nicholas (23)
Olifaunt (12)
O'Todshaw (13)
Pauletti (Lady) (12)
Pleydell (13)
Porteous (14)
Protocol (13)
Quodling (25)
Rentowel (36)
Ringwood (12)
Scriever (36)
Spitfire (37)
Staunton (14)
Steenson (28)
Swanston (28)
Texartis (10)
Trapbois (12)
Turnbull (28)
Waltheof (11)
Waverley (36)
Wetheral (16)
Wildfire (14)
Wildrake (37)
Woodcock (1)
156 Wycliffe (30)

9

Agelastes (10)
Albert Lee (37)
Aldovrand (5)
Alice Bean (36)
Alice Gray (8)
Annot Lyle (21)
Armstrong (6, 12, 19)
Bellenden (24)
Bickerton (14)
Biederman (2)
Bimbister (26)
Bindloose (31)
Blackless (33)
Brengwain (5)
Cadwallon (5)
Chiffinch (25)
Christian (25)
Cleveland (Duchess of)
  (25, 26)
Clippurse (36)
Constance (22)
Cranstoun (20)
Cresswell (25)
de la Marck (27)
de Moncada (32)
de Valence (9)
Dick Tinto (8, 31)
Elshender (6)
Friar Tuck (16)
Galbraith (29)
Gellatley (36)
Guendolen (7)
Howleglas (1)
Inglewood (29)
Jack Jabos (13)
Jock Penny (13)
John Mengs (2)
Johnstone (13)
Josceline (33)
Lady Binks (31)
Lady Edith (16)
Lochinvar (22)
Lord North (25)
MacAlpine (29)
MacGregor (29)
MacIntyre (3)
MacTavish (15)
Major Weir (28)
Malvoisin (16)
Mannering (13)
Maugrabin (27)
Mayflower (37)
Merrilies (13)
Middlemas (32)
Mortcloke (13)
Mrs. Aylmer (37)
Mrs. Baliol (15)
Mrs. Blower (31)
Mumblazen (17)
Ochiltree (3)
Poundtext (24)
Ratcliffe (6)
Rewcastle (6)
Risingham (30)
Sturmthal (2)
Thoulouse (10)
Touchwood (31)
Turnpenny (28)
Twigtythe (36)
Wackbairn (14)
Wakefield (35)
Woodville (34)
Yellowley (26)
Zimmerman (2)

10

Alice Brand (18)
Amy Robsart (16)
Anne Bulmer (23)
Athelstane (16)
Aunt Judith (12)
Beaumanoir (16)
Bingo Binks (Sir) (31)
Blind Harry (11)
Blinkinsop (28)
Bridgeward (1, 23)
Colonel Lee (37)
Cranbourne (25)
Croftangry (11)
Dame Martin (28)
Davie Deans (14)
Desborough (37)
Donald Bean (36)
Dr. Damiotti (4)
Dryfesdale (1)
Earnscliff (6)
Effie Deans (14)
Enguerraud (33)
Flockheart (36)
Gabriel Faa (13)
Geierstein (2)
Gideon Gray (32)
Glee-Maiden (The) (11)
Grinderson (3)
Hammerlein (27)
Hatteraick (13)
Holdenough (37)
Howlaglass (25)
Hugo de Lacy (5)
Humgudgeon (37)
Huntingdon (Earl of) (33)
Ian Vanwelt (5)
Jacob Aston (37)
Jacob Caxon (3)
Jamie Howie (36)
Jenny Caxon (3)
Jerningham (35)
Lucy Ashton (8)
Meiklewham (31)
Mrs. Crosbie (28)
Mrs. Nosebag (36)
Murdochson (14)
Nanty Ewart (28)
Ned Shafton (29)
Old Dorothy (11)
Old Elspeth (3)
Penfeather (31)
Phillipson (2)
Quackleben (31)
Ravenswood (8)
Rough Ralph (25)
Saddletree (14)
Scambister (26)
Sir Kenneth (33)
Stanchells (29)
Sweepclean (3)
Theodorick (33)
Tibb Tacket (23)
Tom Hillary (32)
Toschach Beg (11)
Tressilian (17)
Whitecraft (25)
Will Badger (17)

11

Abel Sampson (13)
Adam Hartley (32)
Annie Winnie (8)

Ringan Aikwood (3)
Robert of Paris (Count) (10)
Roger Wildrake (37)
Sir Bingo Binks (31)
Sir Hugo de Lacy (5)
Sir Jacob Aston (37)
Stephen Butler (14)
Thomas Ackland (36)
William Ashton (8)

14

Adonbec el Hakim (33)
Augusta Bidmore (31)
Baldwin de Oyley (16)
Blondel de Nesle (33)
Brother Ambrose (16)
Captain Hillary (32)
Captain MacTurk (31)
Clement Dubourg (29)
Colonel Grahame (24)
Corporal Inglis (24)
Cuddie Headrigg (24)
Dame Whitecraft (25)
Davie Gellatley (36)
de Bois Guilbert (16)
Dirk Hatteraick (13)
Dominie Sampson (13)
Duncan Campbell (21)
Earl of Menteith (21)
Earl of Seaforth (21)
Edith Bellenden (24)
Edward Waverley (36)
Elspeth Brydone (23)
Eric Scambister (26)
Father Boniface (1)
Father Waltheof (11)
Geoffrey Hudson (25)
George Staunton (14)
Gilbert Glossin (13)
Grace Armstrong (6)
Harry Wakefield (35)
Heatherblutter (36)
Helen MacGregor (29)
Henry Cranstoun (20)
Jabesh Rentowel (36)
Jemima Forester (4)
Jessie Cantrips (28)
John Phillipson (2)
John Whitecraft (25)
Julia Mannering (13)
Lady Penfeather (31)
Maggie Steenson (28)

Major Bellenden (24)
Major Galbraith (29)
Malcolm Fleming (9)
Margaret Blower (31)
Margaret Ramsay (12)
Maria MacIntyre (3)
Martha Trapbois (12)
Nicholas Blount (17)
Nicholas Faggot (28)
Paulus Pleydell (13)
Peter Proudtext (24)
Philip Forester (4)
Pierçie Shafton (23)
Prince Bohemond (10)
Quentin Durward (27)
Richard Grahame (24)
Robert Melville (1)
Runnion Rattray (12)
Sir Gibbs Amoury (33)
Sir John Ramorny (11)
Thomas de Multon (33)
Thomas Turnbull (28)
Wilkin Flammack (5)
William Crosbie (28)
William Maxwell (24)
Willie Steenson (28)
Zamet Maugrabin (27)
Zarah Christian (25)
Zilia de Moncada (32)

15

Abdallah el Hadgi (33)
Adam Craigdallie (11)
Adie of Aikenshaw (23)
Albert Malvoisin (16)
Archie Armstrong (12)
Arnold Biederman (2)
Augustus Bidmore (31)
Balfour of Burley (24)
Brother Nicholas (23)
Captain Campbell (15)
Captain Carleton (25)
Captain Porteous (24)
Captain Waverley (36)
Catherine Glover (11)
Catherine Seyton (1)
Claus Hammerlein (27)
Countess of Croye (27)
Count Geierstein (2)
Deborah Debbitch (25)
Duncan Galbraith (29)
Edgar Ravenswood (8)

Edward Christian (25)
Ephraim Macbriar (24)
Erminia Pauletti (12)
Eveline Berenger (5)
Father Howleglas (1)
Flibbertigibbet (17)
General Campbell (28)
Geraldin Neville (3)
Hamish MacGregor (29)
Hamish MacTavish (15)
Hector MacIntyre (3)
Hector of the Mist (21)
Hubert Ratcliffe (6)
Jeanie MacAlpine (29)
Joceline Joliffe (37)
Jonathan Oldbuck (3)
Lady Mary Fleming (1)
Lady Plantagenet (14)
Lady Rougedragon (28)
Lawrence Scholey (26)
Lawrence Staples (17)
Lawyer Clippurse (36)
Madame Cresswell (25)
Madge Murdochson (14)
Magdalene Graeme (1)
Malcolm Misbegot (3)
Miss Walkingshaw (28)
Monsieur Dubourg (29)
Mordaunt Mertoun (26)
Murdoch Campbell (21)
Peter Bridgeward (1, 23)
Philip Malvoisin (16)
Phoebe Mayflower (37)
Raymond Berenger (5)
Richard Musgrave (20)
Richard Waverley (36)
Robert MacGregor (29)
Rob-Roy MacGregor (29)
Rose Bradwardine (36)
Simon of Hackburn (6)
Sir Damian de Lacy (5)
Sir Randal de Lacy (5)
Sir Thomas Copley (17)
Squire Inglewood (29)
Stephen Wetheral (16)
The Dougal Cratur (29)
Thomas Chiffinch (25)
Torquil of the Oak (11)
Tristan l'Hermite (2, 27)
Valentine Bulmer (31)
Wandering Willie (28)
Widow Flockheart (36)
Wilfrid Wycliffe (30)
Willie Johnson (13)

Characters from **Shakespeare**
List of plays from which the following characters are taken, with reference numbers.

Ref. No.	Title			Ref. No.	Title		
1.	All's Well that Ends Well	(20 letters)		12.	King Henry VI, Part 1	(7 or 11	„ .
2.	Antony and Cleopatra	(18	„)	13.	King Henry VI, Part 2	(7 or 11	„)
3.	As You Like It	(11	„)	14.	King Henry VI, Part 3	(7 or 11	„)
4.	Comedy of Errors, A	(15	„)	15.	King Henry VIII	(9 or 13	„)
5.	Coriolanus	'10	„)	16.	King John	(8	„)
6.	Cymbeline	. 9	„)	17.	King Lear	(8	„)
7.	Hamlet (Prince of Denmark)	(6	„)	18.	King Richard II	(9 or 13	„)
8.	Julius Caesar	(12	„)	19.	King Richard III	(10 or 14	„)
9.	King Henry IV, Part 1	(7 or 11	„)	20.	Love's Labour's Lost	(16 letters)	
10.	King Henry IV, Part 2	(7 or 11	„)	21.	Macbeth	(7	„)
11.	King Henry V	(6 or 10	„)	22.	Measure for Measure	(17	„)
				23.	Merchant of Venice, The	(19·	„)

Ref. No.	Title				Ref. No.	Title			
24.	Merry Wives of Windsor	(19	,,	)	31.	Tempest, The	(10	,,	)
25.	Midsummer Night's				32.	Timon of Athens	(13	,,	)
	Dream, A	(21	,,	)	33.	Titus Andronicus	(15	,,	)
26.	Much Ado About				34.	Troilus and Cressida	(18	,,	)
	Nothing	(19	,,	)	35.	Twelfth Night; or,			
27.	Othello, The Moor of					What You Will	(12	,,	)
	Venice	(7	,,	)	36.	Two Gentlemen of			
28.	Pericles, Prince of Tyre	(8	,,	)		Verona	(20	,,	)
29.	Romeo and Juliet	(14	,,	)	37.	Winter's Tale, The	(14	,,	)
30.	Taming of the Shrew, The	(19	,,	)					

Note: The numbers in brackets indicate *the plays* in which the characters appear.

(A.-B. of) = Archbishop of.   (B. of) = Bishop of.   (Card.) = Cardinal.   (C. of) = Count of. (C'ess of) = Countess of.   (D. of) = Duke of.   (D'ess of) = Duchess of.   (E. of) = Earl of. (K. of) = King of.   (M. of) = Marquis of.   (P. of) = Prince of.   (P'ess of) = Princess of.   (Q. of) = Queen of.

3 AND 4

Adam (3)
Ajax (34)
Anne (Lady) (19)
Bona (14)
Cade (13)
Cato (8)
Davy (10)
Dick (13)
Dion (37)
Dull (20)
Eros (2)
Fang (10)
Ford (24)
Ford (Mrs.) (24)
Grey (11)
Grey (Lady) (14)
Grey (Lord) (19)
Hero (26)
Hume (13)
Iago (27)
Iden (13)
Iris (31)
Jamy (11)
John (10)
John (Don) (26)
John (K.) (16)
Juno (31)
Kent (E. of) (17)
Lear (K.) (17)
Lion (25)
Luce (4)
Lucy (12)
Moth (20, 25)
Nym (11, 24)
Page (24)
Page (Mrs.) (24)
Peto (9, 10)
Puck (25)
Ross (Lord) (18)
Ross (21)
Say (Lord) (13)
Snug (25)
Time (37)
Vaux (13, 15)
Wart (10)
York (A.-B. of) (9, 10, 19)
York (D'ess of) (18, 19)
York (D. of) (11, 18, 19)

5

Aaron (33)
Abram (29)

Alice (11)
Angus (21)
Ariel (31)
Bagot (18)
Bates (11)
Belch (35)
Bigot (16)
Biron (20)
Blunt (9, 10)
Boult (28)
Boyet (20)
Bushy (18)
Butts (15)
Caius (6, 24)
Casca (8)
Celia (3)
Ceres (31)
Cinna (8)
Cleon (28)
Clown (22, 35)
Corin (3)
Court (11)
Curan (17)
Curio (35)
Denny (15)
Diana (1, 28)
Edgar (17)
Egeus (25)
Elbow (22)
Essex (E. of) (16)
Evans (24)
Flute (25)
Froth (22)
Ghost (7)
Gobbo (23)
Gower (10, 11, 28)
Green (18)
Helen (6, 34)
Henry (19)
Henry (K.) (9, 10, 11, 12, 13, 15)
Henry (P.) (16)
Julia (36)
Lafeu (1)
Louis (Dauphin) (11, 16)
Louis (K.) (14)
Louis (Lord) (19)
Lucio (22)
March (E. of) (9)
Maria (20)
Melun (16)
Menas (2)
Milan (D. of) (36)
Mopsa (37)
Osric (7)
Paris (29, 34)

Pedro (Don) (26)
Percy (9, 10, 18)
Percy (Lady) (9)
Peter (13, 22)
Phebe (3)
Philo (2)
Pinch (4)
Poins (9, 10)
Priam (34)
Queen (6)
Regan (17)
Robin (24)
Romeo (29)
Rugby (24)
Sands (Lord) (15)
Snare (10)
Snout (25)
Speed (36)
Timon (32)
Tubal (23)
Varro (8)
Viola (35)
Wales (P. of) (9, 10, 19)

6

Adrian (31)
Aegeon (4)
Aeneas (34)
Albany (D. of) (17)
Alexas (2)
Alonso (31)
Amiens (3)
Angelo (4, 22)
Antony (2)
Armado (20)
Arthur (16)
Audrey (3)
Banquo (21)
Basset (12)
Bianca (27, 30)
Blanch (16)
Blount (19)
Bottom (25)
Brutus (5, 8)
Bullen (15)
Cadwal (6)
Caesar (2)
Caphis (32)
Cassio (27)
Chiron (33)
Cicero (8)
Clitus (8)
Cloten (22)
Cobweb (25)

Worcester (E. of) (9, 10)
Young Cato (8)

10

Alcibiades (32)
Andromache (34)
Andronicus (33)
Anne Bullen (15)
Antipholus (4)
Archidamus (37)
Barnardine (22)
Brakenbury (19)
Buckingham (D. of) (13, 15, 19)
Calphurnia (8)
Canterbury (A.-B. of) (11, 15, 19)
Coriolanus (5)
Duke of York (11, 18, 19)
Earl of Kent (17)
Earl Rivers (19)
Euphronius (2)
Fortinbras (7)
Henry Percy (9, 10, 18)
Holofernes (20)
Hortensius (32)
Jaquenetta (20)
John Talbot (12)
King Henry V (10)
Longaville (20)
Lord Rivers (14)
Lord Scales (13)
Lord Scroop (11)
Lord Talbot (12)
Lysimachus (28)
Marc Antony (2)
Margarelon (34)
Menecrates (2)
Montgomery (14)
Mrs. Quickly (9, 10, 11, 24)
Prince John (10)
Proculeius (2)
Richard III (K.) (19)
Saturninus (33)
Sempronius (32)
Sir Michael (9, 10)
Somerville (14)
Starveling (25)
Touchstone (3)
Willoughby (Lord) (18)
Winchester (B. of) (15)

11

Abergavenny (Lord) (15)
Artimidorus (8)
Bishop of Ely (11, 19)
Bolingbroke (13, 18)
Dame Quickly (9, 10)
Doctor Butts (15)
Doctor Caius (24)
Duke of Milan (36)
Earl Berkley (18)
Earl of Essex (16)
Earl of March (9, 14)
James Gurney (16)
John of Gaunt (18)
King Henry IV (9, 10)
King Henry VI (12, 13, 14)
Lady Capulet (29)
Lady Macbeth (21)
Lady Macduff (21)
Lord Mowbray (10)

Lord Stanley (19)
Mrs. Anne Page (24)
Mrs. Overdone (22)
Mustardseed (25)
Peasblossom (25)
Philostrate (25)
Plantagenet (12, 13, 14)
Prince Henry (16)
Robert Bigot (16)
Rosencrantz (7)
Westminster (A.-B. of) (18)
William Page (24)
Young Siward (21)

12

Decius Brutus (8)
Duke of Albany (17)
Duke of Exeter (11, 14)
Duke of Oxford (14)
Duke of Surrey (18)
Duke of Venice (23, 27)
Earl of Oxford (19)
Earl of Surrey (15, 19)
Falconbridge (16)
Falconbridge (Lady) (16)
Guildenstern (7)
Julius Caesar (8)
Junius Brutus (5)
King of France (1, 17)
Lady Montague (29)
Lady Mortimer (9)
Lord Bardolph (10)
Lord Clifford (13, 14)
Lord Hastings (10, 14, 19)
Lord Stafford (14)
Marcus Brutus (8)
Popilius Lena (8)
Sir Hugh Evans (24)
Sir Nathaniel (20)
Sir Toby Belch (35)
Thomas Horner (13)
Three Witches (21)
Titus Lartius (5)
Westmoreland (E. of) (9, 10, 11, 14)
Young Marcius (5)

13

Alexander Iden (13)
Doll Tearsheet (10)
Duchess of York (18, 19)
Duke of Alencon (12)
Duke of Aumerle (18)
Duke of Bedford (11, 12)
Duke of Bourbon (11)
Duke of Gloster (13, 14, 19)
Duke of Norfolk (14, 15, 18, 19)
Duke of Orleans (11)
Duke of Suffolk (13, 15)
Earl of Douglas (9)
Earl of Gloster (17)
Earl of Suffolk (12)
Earl of Warwick (10, 11, 12, 13, 14)
Friar Lawrence (29)
Hubert de Burgh (16)
Joan la Pucelle (12)
King Henry VIII (15)
King Richard II (18)
Lord Fitzwater (18)
Owen Glendower (9)

Prince of Wales (10, 19)
Queen Margaret (14)
Sir Thomas Grey (11)
Young Clifford (13)

14

Cardinal Wolsey (15)
Christopher Sly (30)
Duke of Burgundy (11, 12, 17)
Duke of Clarence (10, 19)
Duke of Cornwall (17)
Duke of Florence (1)
Duke of Somerset (13, 14)
Earl of Pembroke (14, 16)
Earl of Richmond (19)
Edmund Mortimer (9, 12)
Hostess Quickly (9, 10)
Justice Shallow (10)
King Richard III (19)
Launcelot Gobbo (23)
Lord Willoughby (18)
Marcus Antonius (8)
Metellus Cimber (8)
Northumberland (E. of) (9, 10, 14, 18)
Northumberland (Lady) (10)
Octavius Caesar (2, 8)
Peter of Pomfret (16)
Pompeius Sextus (2)
Prince Humphrey (10)
Queen Elizabeth (19)
Queen Katharine (15)
Sextus Pompeius (2)
Sir James Blount (19)
Sir James Tyrrel (19)
Sir John Stanley (13)
Sir Walter Blunt (9, 10)
Sir William Lucy (12)
Smith the Weaver (13)
Tullus Aufidius (5)
Walter Whilmore (13)

15

Aemilius Lepidus (8)
Bishop of Lincoln (15)
Dromio of Ephesus (4)
Duke of Lancaster (18)
Earl of Cambridge (11)
Earl of Salisbury (11, 12, 13, 16, 18)
Earl of Worcester (9, 10)
Edmund of Langley (18)
Lord Abergavenny (15)
Margery Jourdain (13)
Marquis of Dorset (19)
Menenius Agrippa (5)
Prince of Arragon (23)
Prince of Morocco (23)
Robin Goodfellow (25)
Sicinius Volutus (5)
Sir Anthony Denny (15)
Sir Hugh Mortimer (14)
Sir John Falstaff (9, 10, 24)
Sir John Fastolfe (12)
Sir John Mortimer (14)
Sir Nicholas Vaux (15)
Sir Thomas Lovell (15)
Titus Andronicus (33)

Some characters from **Shelley, Sheridan** and **Smollett**
List of works from which the following characters are taken, with reference numbers.

Percy Bysshe Shelley

Ref. No.	Title	
1. Cenci, The	(8 letters)	
2. Prometheus Unbound	(17 ,,)	
3. Swellfoot the Tyrant	(18 ,,)	
4. (Various)		

Richard Brinsley Sheridan

5. Critic, The	(9 letters)	
6. Duenna, The	(9 ,,)	
7. Pizarro	(7 ,,)	
8. Rivals, The	(9 ,,)	

Ref. No.	Title	
9. School for Scandal, The	(19 letters)	
10. St. Patrick's Day	(13 ,,)	
11. Trip to Scarborough, A	(18 ,,)	

Tobias Smollett

12. Count Fathom	(11 letters)	
13. Humphry Clinker	(14 ,,)	
14. Peregrine Pickle	(15 ,,)	
15. Roderick Random	(14 ,,)	
16. Sir Launcelot Greaves	(19 ,,)	

Note: The numbers in brackets indicate *the works* in which the characters appear.

3 AND 4

Asia (2)
Cora (7)
Crab (15)
Fag (8)
Ione (2)
Ivy (13)
Joey (15)
Lory (11)
Loyd (13)
Lucy (8)
Mab (4)
Puff (5)
Quin (13)
Rosy (10)
Trip (9)

5

Acres (8)
Cenci (1)
Clara (6)
Crowe (16)
Dakry (3)
Daood (4)
David (8)
Flint (10)
Frail (14)
Gawky (15)
Gomez (7)
Gwynn (13)
Jones (13)
Julia (8)
Lewis (13)
Lopez (6)
Maria (9)
Moses (3, 9)
Oakum (15)
Ocean (2)
Orano (7)
Pipes (14)
Probe (11)
Rifle (15)
Rolla (7)
Scrag (14)
Snake (9)
Sneer (5)
Strap (15)

6

Alonzo (7)
Amanda (11)
Andrea (1)

Apollo (2)
Banter (15)
Barton (13)
Bumper (9)
Clumsy (11)
Cythna (4)
Dangle (5)
Darnel (16)
Dr. Rosy (10)
Duenna (The) (6)
Elvira (7)
Emilia (14)
Fathom (12)
Ferret (16)
Gobble (16)
Hassan (4)
Hatton (5)
Hoyden (11)
Ianthe (4)
Jermyn (13)
Julian (4)
Louisa (6)
Mahmud (4)
Mammon (3)
Martin (13)
Marzio (1)
Morgan (15)
Murphy (13)
Norton (13)
Oregan (15)
Orsino (1)
Pallet (14)
Pickle (14)
Random (15)
Rattle (15)
Rowley (9)
Simper (15)
Teazle (9)
Thomas (8)
Townly (11)
Vandal (15)
Weazel (15)
Willis (13)
Zuluga (7)

7

Adonais (4)
Alastor (4)
Almagro (7)
Ataliba (7)
Baynard (13)
Bowling (15)
Bramble (13)
Bulford (13)
Buzzard (13)

Camillo (1)
Candour (9)
Celinda (12)
Clinker (13)
Coupler (11)
Cringer (15)
Davilla (7)
Dick Ivy (13)
Dr. Lewis (13)
Fashion (11)
Freeman (15)
Giacomo (1)
Gonzalo (7)
Greaves (16)
Griskin (13)
Gwyllim (13)
Hopkins (5)
Jackson (15)
Jenkins (13)
Macully (13)
Maddalo (4)
Melford (13)
Mendoza (6)
Mercury (2)
Milfart (13)
Mrs. Loyd (13)
O'Connor (10)
Olimpio (1)
Panthea (2)
Pizarro (7)
Raleigh (5)
Rattlin (15)
Savella (1)
Silenus (4)
Snapper (15)
Solomon (3)
Sparkle (15)
Surface (9)
Taurina (3)
Thicket (15)
Trounce (10)
Ulysses (4)
Wagtail (15)
Whiffle (15)

8

Absolute (8)
Backbite (9)
Bernardo (1)
Besselia (16)
Bob Acres (8)
Burleigh (5)
Campbell (13)
Careless (9)
Crabshaw (16)

Some characters from **Southey, Spenser** and **Tennyson**
List of works from which the following characters are taken, with reference numbers.

Robert Southey
Ref.
No.　　　*Title*
1. Curse of Kehama, The　(16 letters)
2. Madoc　　　　　　　　(5　,,　)
3. Roderick, the Last of
　　the Goths　　　　　(8　,,　)
4. Thalaba the Destroyer　(19　,,　)
5. (Various)

Edmund Spenser
Ref.
No.　　　*Title*
6. Colin Clout's Come
　　Home Again　　　　(24 letters)
7. Faerie Queene, The　(15　,,　)
8. Shephearde's Calender,
　　The　　　　　　　　(22　,,　)
9. (Various)

Lord Tennyson
10. Enoch Arden　　　　(10 letters)
11. Idylls of the King　　(15　,,　)

12. (Various)

Note: The numbers in brackets indicate *the works* in which the characters appear.

3 AND 4

Alma (7)
Ate (7)
Atin (7)
Azla (1)
Azub (3)
Baly (1)
Cid (The) (5)
Dony (7)
Dora (12)
Dove (5)
Ebba (3)
Enid (11)
Flur (11)
Hoel (2)
Ida (12)
Lee (10)
Lot (11)
Lucy (7)
Mary (5)
Maud (12)
Ray (10)
Rose (12)
Una (7)

5

Alice (12)
Amias (7)
Anton (11)
Arden (10)
Aswad (4)
Balan (11)
Balin (11)
Belge (7)
Bleys (11)
Brute (7)
Celia (7)
Clare (12)
Cleon (7)
Clout (6)
Cuddy (8)
David (King) (2)
Dolon (7)
Doorm (11)
Edyrn (11)
Error (7)
Eudon (3)
Furor (7)
Guyon (7)
Indra (1)
Isolt (11)
Isond (11)

Laila (4)
Madoc (2)
Moath (4)
Odoar (3)
Orpas (3)
Pedro (3)
Phaon (7)
Talus (7)
Torre (11)
Tyler (5)
Urban (3)
Urien (2)
Willy (8)
Yamen (1)
Yniol (11)
Ysolt (11)

6

Abessa (7)
Action (6)
Adicia (7)
Alcyon (9)
Amavia (7)
Amidas (7)
Amoret (7)
Astery (9)
Aullay (1)
Aylmer (12)
Briana (7)
Burbon (7)
Cavall (dog) (11)
Coatel (2)
Diggon (8)
Donica (5)
Dubrie (11)
Duessa (7)
Elaine (11)
Elissa (7)
Favila (3)
Gareth (11)
Gawain (11)
Glauce (7)
Godiva (12)
Godmer (7)
Guisla (3)
Guizor (7)
Harold (12)
Igerna (11)
Ignaro (7)
Iseult (11)
Isolde (11)
Jasper (5)
Julian (3)

Kehama (1)
Khawla (4)
Lilian (12)
Llaian (2)
Magued (3)
Mammon (7)
Medina (7)
Merlin (11)
Modred (11)
Moorna (5)
Munera (7)
Newman (5)
Oenone (12)
Oneiza (4)
Orelio (horse) (3)
Oriana (12)
Orraca (Queen) (5)
Paeana (7)
Pelago (3)
Quiara (5)
Romano (3)
Ronald (12)
Senena (2)
Serena (7)
Sergis (7)
Shedad (4)
Terpin (7)
The Cid (5)
Thenot (8)
Theron (dog) (3)
Timias (7)
Turpin (7)
Vivian (12)
Vivien (11)
Witiza (3)
Yeruti (5)
Ygerne (11)
Yseult (11)
Zeinab (4)

7

Acrasia (7)
Adeline (12)
Aemelia (7)
Aladine (7)
Aloadin (4)
Amphion (12)
Aragnol (9)
Argante (7)
Artegal (7)
Arvalan (1)
Aveugle (7)
Cambina (7)

13 AND OVER

Chindasuintho (3)
Emma Plantagenet (2)
Father Maccabee (3)

Lady of Shalott (12)
Marian Margaret (6)
Red-Cross Knight (7)
Richard Penlake (5)
Saint Gualberto (5)
Sir Aylmer Aylmer (12)

Sir Richard Grenville (12)
Sir Shan Sanglier (7)
Sir Walter Vivian (12)
Squire of Dames, The (7)
Will Waterproof (12)

Some characters from **Thackeray**
List of works from which the following characters are taken, with reference numbers.

Ref. No.	Title	
1.	Adventures of Philip, The	(21 letters)
2.	Barry Lyndon	(11 ,,)
3.	Book of Snobs, The	(14 ,,)
4.	Catherine	(9 ,,)
5.	Denis Duval	(10 ,,)
6.	Fatal Boots, The	(13 ,,)
7.	Great Hoggarty Diamond, The	(23 ,,)
8.	Henry Esmond	(11 ,,)
9.	Lovel the Widower	(15 ,,)
10.	Major Gahagan, The Adventures of	(27 letters)
11.	Newcomes, The	(11 ,,)
12.	Pendennis	(9 ,,)
13.	Rebecca and Rowena	(16 ,,)
14.	Shabby Genteel Story, A	(19 ,,)
15.	Vanity Fair	(10 ,,)
16.	Virginians, The	(13 ,,)
17.	Wolves and the Lamb, The	(19 ,,)

Note: The numbers in brackets indicate *the works* in which the characters appear.

3 AND 4

Bell (12)
Bond (1)
Bows (12)
Bull (3)
'Cat' (4)
Craw (6)
Cuff (15)
Drum (7)
Gann (14)
Gray (3)
Grig (3)
Hall (4)
Holt (8)
Huff (2)
Hunt (1)
Kew (11)
Laws (16)
Legg (3)
Levy (5)
Maw (3)
Moss (15)
Nabb (6)
Page (5, 17)
Pash (7)
Pump (3)
Quin (2)
Ruck (7)
Runt (1, 2)
Sago (3)
Tagg (3)
Tidd (7)
Veal (15)
Ward (16)
Wing (5)
Wirt (3)
Wood (4)

5

Amory (12)
Arbin (5)

Baker (9)
Barry (2)
Bates (6)
Becky (14, 15)
Bevil (5)
Biggs (10)
Bluck (15)
Boots (9)
Bowls (15)
Brady (2)
Brock (4)
Bulbo (15)
'Carry' (14)
Chuff (3)
Clap (15)
Clink (15)
Clump (15)
Crabb (14)
Crump (3)
Daisy (mare) (2)
Denis (5)
Dobbs (4)
Dr. Maw (3)
Duffy (19)
Dumps (3)
Duval (5)
Fagan (2)
Fitch (14)
Flint (5)
Foker (12, 16)
Freny (2)
Gates (7)
Gorer (dog) (15)
Gumbo (16)
Hagan (16)
Hayes (4)
Hicks (3)
Higgs (15)
Hobbs (4)
Hugby (3)
Jowls (2)
Ketch (4)
Kicks (6)
Lovel (9)
Macan (10)

Macer (3)
March (Lord) (16)
Mohun (8)
O'Dowd (3, 15)
Piper (9)
Pippi (2)
Ponto (3)
Prior (9, 17)
Query (7)
Rudge (5)
Sambo (15)
Score (4)
Screw (2)
Sharp (15)
Smith (7)
Straw (7)
Tiggs (3)
Tizzy (3)
Toole (2)
Trial (1, 16)
Tufto (3)
Walls (1)
Wamba (13)
Wolfe (16)

6

Bagwig (Lord) (2, 3)
Barker (5)
Barlow (17)
Bayham (12)
Baynes (1)
Beales (5)
Bidois (5)
Billee (12)
Binnie (11)
Blades (3)
Briggs (15)
Brough (7)
Bungay (12)
Caffin (5)
Cedric (13)
Corbet (8)

Crutty (6)
Curbyn (2)
Dobbin (15)
Dobble (6)
Doolan (12)
Dr. Huff (2)
Dr. Wing (5)
Esmond (8, 16)
Famish (16)
Fermin (1)
Fizgig (7)
Franks (16)
Glowry (12)
Gobble (4)
Gretch (4)
Holkar (10)
Hooker (5)
Howard (5)
Howell (17)
Jowler (10)
Jowler (dog) (6)
Kiljoy (2)
Lyndon (2)
Martha (5)
Measom (5)
Moffat (4)
Morgan (2, 12)
Morris (16)
Murphy (2)
O'Dwyer (2)
Parrot (5)
Perron (10)
Philip (1)
Pincot (9)
Punter (2)
Puppet (7)
Rawson (2)
Redcap (4)
Ridley (1)
Rowena (13)
Rummer (12)
Scales (5)
Sedley (15)
Sheeny (10)
Smirke (12)
Snobky (3)
Spavin (3, 12)
Splint (2)
Steele (8)
Steyne (15)
St. John (Mr.) (8)
Strong (12)
Stubbs (6)
Swigby (14)
Tatham (12)
Temple (3)
Thrupp (10)
Tusher (8)
Waggle (3)
Waters (6)
Wenham (15)
Weston (5)
Wiggle (3)

7

Barnard (5)
Bavieca (horse) (13)
Bedford (9)
Boswell (2)
Brandon (1, 14)
Brisket (6)
Brownie (dog) (1)
Buckram (3)
Bulcher (10)

Bullock (4, 15)
Bunting (6)
Cassidy (1)
Clopper (6)
Cramley (3)
Crawley (15)
Danvers (16)
Dolphin (9)
Dr. Bates (6)
Dr. Dobbs (4)
Dr. Piper (9)
Fantail (4)
Gahagan (10)
Glogger (10)
Gregson (5)
Hawbuck (3)
Hookham (5)
Hoskins (7)
Huckles (9)
Humbold (16)
Ivanhoe (13)
Jawkins (3)
Jim Ward (7)
Johnson (2, 16)
Lambert (16)
Macarty (14)
Mrs. Gann (14)
Mrs. Kirk (15)
Mrs. Laws (16)
Mrs. Pash (7)
Mrs. Sago (3)
Mrs. Todd (15)
Mugford (12)
Mulcahy (7)
Newcome (11)
Osborne (15)
Parkins (12)
Pearson (5)
Penfold (1)
Perreau (5)
Pincott (12)
Pinhorn (9)
Portman (12)
Preston (7)
Purcell (2)
Rebecca (13, 15)
Rebecca (mare) (12)
Saladin (14)
Sampson (8,16)
Sargent (9)
Scraper (3)
Sicklop (4)
Shandon (12)
Slumley (9)
Sniffle (3)
Snobley (3)
Snorter (6)
Sowerby (1)
Spiggot (3)
Stuffle (10)
Swinney (7)
Thunder (2)
Tickler (2)
Tiggins (7)
Tiptoff (7)
Touchit (17)
Trippet (4)
Twysden (1)
Wapshot (12)
Woolsey (1)
Worksop (8)

8

Abednego (7)

Billings (4)
Bill Tidd (7)
Bob Tizzy (3)
Braddock (16)
Bulkeley (9, 17)
Cinqbars (14)
Clarisse (5)
Clodpole (4)
Cockspur (3)
Costigan (12)
Delamere (9)
Dempster (16)
Drencher (9)
Dr. Fermin (1)
Dr. Tusher (8)
Dr. Waters (6)
Dubobwig (6)
Fakenham (2)
Franklin (16)
Goldmore (3)
Golloper (3)
Hawkshaw (8)
Highmore (7)
Hoggarty (7)
Honeyman (9, 11)
Horrocks (15)
Jellicoe (5)
Lady Drum (7)
Lady Sark (8)
Lavender (2)
Lockwood (8, 16)
Lord Lake (10)
Lorrimer (3)
Lovelace (3)
Macheath (5)
MacManus (7)
Macmurdo (15)
Malowney (6)
Manasseh (6)
Marchand (10)
Milliken (17)
Miss Bell (12)
Miss Runt (14)
Miss Wirt (3, 15)
Mountain (16)
Mrs. Amory (12)
Mrs. Barry (2)
Mrs. Brady (2)
Mrs. Chuff (3)
Mrs. Crabb (14)
Mrs. Dobbs (4)
Mrs. Duval (5)
Mrs. Foker (16)
Mrs. Hayes (4)
Mrs. Lovel (9)
Mrs. Macan (10)
Mrs. O'Dowd (15)
Mrs. Ponto (3)
Mrs. Prior (9, 17)
Mrs. Rowdy (15)
Mrs. Score (4)
M'Whirter (7)
Napoleon (10)
Plugwell (9)
Ribstone (12)
Ringwood (1)
Sherrick (9)
Smithers (7)
Sullivan (2)
Talmadge (16)
Titmarsh (7)
Tom Walls (1)
Trestles (5)
Tufthunt (14)
Westbury (8)
Woolcomb (1)

Thomas Clodpole (4)
von Galgenstein (4)
Wilfred Ivanhoe (13)

15

Arthur Pendennis (1, 12)
Captain Costigan (12)
Captain Macheath (5)
Captain Macmurdo (15)
Captain Westbury (8)

Captain Woolcomb (1)
Charles Honeyman (11)
Charlotte Baynes (1)
Dr. Tobias Tickler (2)
Flora Warrington (16)
General Braddock (16)
George Marrowfat (3)
Harry Warrington (16)
Henry Warrington (16)
Isabella Macarty (14)
Jemima Pinkerton (15)
Lady Jane Crawley (15)

Lady Jane Preston (7)
Marquis of Bagwig (3)
Marquis of Steyne (15)
Misses Pinkerton (The) (15)
Miss Fotheringay (12)
Miss Montanville (9)
Mrs. Cecilia Lovel (9)
Queen Berengaria (13)
Ringwood Twysden (1)
Rosalind Macarty (14)
Sir George Esmond (8)
Sir John Hawkshaw (8)

Some characters from **Anthony Trollope**
List of works from which the following characters are taken, with reference numbers.

Ref. No.	Title		
1.	Alice Dugdale	(12 letters)	
2.	American Senator, The	(18 ,,)	
3.	Barchester Towers	(16 ,,)	
4.	Dr. Thorne	(8 ,,)	
5.	Editor's Tales, An	(14 ,,)	
6.	Eustace Diamonds, The	(18 ,,)	
7.	Framley Parsonage	(16 ,,)	
8.	Frau Frohmann	(12 ,,)	
9.	Is He Popenjoy?	(12 ,,)	
10.	Lady of Launay, The	(15 letters)	
11.	Last Chronicle of Barset, The	(24 ,,)	
12.	La Vendée	(8 ,,)	
13.	Ralph the Heir	(12 ,,)	
14.	Small House at Allington, The	(24 ,,)	
15.	Tales of all Countries	(19 ,,)	
16.	Telegraph Girl, The	(16 ,,)	
17.	Three Clerks, The	(14 ,,)	
18.	Warden, The	(9 ,,)	

Note: The numbers in brackets indicate *the works* in which the characters appear.

3 AND 4

Bean (2)
Bell (18)
Bold (3, 7, 18)
Bolt (9)
Boom (17)
Bull (8)
Cann (6)
Cox (13)
Dale (11, 14)
Dove (6)
Dunn (11)
Erle (6)
Fawn (6)
Gazy (18)
Grey (6)
Hall (16)
Hoff (8)
Jack (horse) (2)
Knox (9)
Love (12)
Lund (15)
Nogo (17)
Pie (3, 4)
Pile (13)
Pole (7)
Ring (15)
Toff (9)
Trow (15)
Watt (5)

5

Anton (8)
Baker (4)
Boyce (11; 14)
Brown (5, 15, 16, 17)
Brush (17)
Bunce (18)
Carey (13)
Crump (11, 14)
Dandy (horse) (6, 7)

Davis (17)
Denot (12)
Dobbs (14)
Donne (5)
Eames (11, 14)
Fooks (13)
Foret (12)
Fritz (15)
Gager (6)
Glump (13)
Green (2, 4, 9, 11, 16)
Grice (2)
Handy (18)
Hearn (14)
Heine (15)
Hiram (18)
Janet (4)
Jones (7, 9, 15, 17)
Joram (13)
Knowl (10)
Krapp (8)
Lebas (12)
Lupex (14)
Mason (11)
Miles (10)
Moggs (13)
Moody (18)
M'Ruen (17)
Muntz (8)
Nobbs (2)
Oriel (4, 11)
Penge (2)
Plume (12)
Pratt (11, 14)
Price (9)
Pryor (10)
Regan (5)
Ribbs (2)
Robin (7)
Romer (4)
Runce (2)
Sally (16)
Scott (17)
Sharp (5)

Slope (3)
Smith (5, 9, 15)
Snape (9, 17)
Stein (12)
Stemm (13)
Tozer (7, 11)
Tudor (17)
Tweed (1)
Upton (15)
Vigil (17)
Wheal (17)

6

Apjohn (4)
Arabin (3, 7, 9, 14)
Athill (4)
Aunt Ju (9)
Austen (7)
Battle (9)
Bawwah (13)
Baxter (11)
Bergen (15)
Bonner (13)
Boodle (6)
Botsey (2)
Brumby (5)
Buffle (11, 14)
Bunfit (6)
'Caudle' (14)
Clarke (4)
Cobard (8)
Cobble (1)
Conner (14)
Cooper (2)
Croft (11, 14)
Currie (2)
D'Elbée (12)
Draper (11)
Dr. Bold (18)
Duplay (12)
Fiasco (14)
Finney (18)

Finnie (3, 4)
Fisher (14)
Flurry (11)
Garrow (15)
Giblet (9)
Glemax (2)
Goarly (2)
Gowran (6)
Graham (16)
Greene (15)
Griggs (6)
Grimes (5)
Gwynne (3)
Hallam (5)
Harter (6)
Holmes (15)
Hoppet (2)
Jemima (7)
Jemima (mare) (2)
Jerome (12)
Joseph (15)
Launay (10)
Lupton (7, 11)
Mewmew (3)
Moffat (4)
Molloy (5)
Morgan (6)
Morris (6, 11, 13)
Morton (2, 15)
'Mrs. Val' (17)
Murray (16)
Nappie (6)
Neefit (13)
Neroni (3)
Newton (13)
Nickem (2)
Norman (17)
Nupper (2)
O'Brien (15)
Onslow (15)
Pabsby (13)
Pepper (13)
Precis (17)
Puffle (5)
Sawyer (9)
Scruby (9)
Seppel (8)
Sludge (11)
Smiler (6)
Soames (11)
Spicer (13)
Spruce (14)
Staple (3)
Stiles (3)
Stokes (9)
Temple (11)
Tendel (8)
Tewett (6)
Thorne (3, 4, 7, 11)
Towers (3, 7, 18)
Trauss (8)
Ushant (2)
Waddle (13)
Walker (7, 9, 11, 13, 15)
Wallop (13)
Weston (15)
Wilson (6, 16)

7

Adolphe (13)
Bangles (11)
Barrère (12)
Bateson (4)
Baumann (9)

Berrier (12)
Bonteen (6)
Boullin (12)
Buggins (7)
Burnaby (13)
Cashett (9)
Century (4)
Chapeau (12)
Chilton (6)
Cloysey (15)
Cobbold (2)
Coelebs (9)
Collins (5)
Conolin (8)
Couthon (12)
Cradell (11, 14)
Crawley (7, 11)
Crosbie (11, 14)
Crumbie (13)
Crumple (18)
De Baron (9)
Debedin (12)
de Guest (11, 14)
de Salop (17)
Dingles (14)
Dugdale (1)
Eardham (13)
Easyman (7)
Emilius (6)
Eustace (6)
Gazebee (4, 11, 14)
Germain (9)
Glossop (2)
Goesler (6)
Gotobed (2)
Grantly (3, 4, 7, 11, 18)
Gregory (10)
Gresham (4, 6, 7)
Gresley (5)
Gruffen (14)
Gushing (4)
Hampton (2)
Harding (3, 7, 11, 14, 18)
Hoffman (2)
Hoggett (11)
Hopkins (2, 11, 14)
Jobbles (17)
Johnson (18)
Judkins (15)
Kissing (11, 14)
'Kit' Dale (14)
Masters (2)
M'Buffer (17)
Mealyer (14)
Mildmay (9)
Minusex (17)
Monsell (7)
Mrs. Bold (3)
Mrs. Dale (11, 14)
Mrs. Gamp (mare) (7)
Mrs. Grey (6)
Mrs. Pole (7)
Mrs. Toff (9)
Mutters (18)
Pawkins (14)
Plomacy (3)
Podgens (7)
Poojean (13)
Porlock (4, 14)
Poulter (15)
Protest (9)
Proudie (3, 4, 7, 11)
Pumpkin (17)
Purefoy (2)
Puttock (2)
Roanoke (6)

Robarts (7, 11)
Rufford (2)
Scalpen (3)
Scrobby (2)
Scuttle (11)
Simkins (1)
Skulpit (18)
Snapper (11)
Sowerby (7)
Spooner (13)
Spriggs (18)
Starbod (17)
Surtees (2)
Talboys (15)
Tankard (2)
Tempest (11)
Thumble (11)
Tickler (7)
Toogood (11)
Trefoil (2, 3)
Trigger (13)
Tuppett (2)
Umbleby (4)
Wanless (1)
Wilkins (11)

8

Abel Ring (15)
Allchops (17)
Anticant (18)
Aunt Jane (6)
Bell Dale (14)
Benjamin (6)
Brabazon (9)
Brownlow (13)
Bumpwell (3)
Caneback (2)
Chadwick (3, 7, 11, 18)
Champion (11)
Charette (12)
Chiltern (6)
Coldfoot (6)
De Courcy (4, 11, 14)
de Laroch (12)
Dr. Crofts (11, 14)
Dr. Gwynne (3)
Dr. Nupper (2)
Dr. Thorne (3, 4, 7, 11)
Drummond (2)
Dumbello (7, 11, 14)
Fanfaron (14)
Filgrave (11)
Fleabody (9)
Fletcher (11)
Fleurist (12)
Frohmann (8)
Frummage (14)
Geraghty (17)
Groschut (9)
Gumption (7)
Hittaway (6)
Horsball (13)
Houghton (9)
Isa Heine (15)
John Bold (3, 18)
Jolliffe (14)
Lady Dale (14)
Lady Fawn (6)
Lily Dale (11, 14)
Lovelace (9)
Macallum (6)
Mary Bold (3, 18)
Mary Jane (5)
Meredith (7)

Composers

3 – 5

Arne
Bach
Balfe
Bart
Bax
Berg
Berio
Bizet
Bliss
Bloch
Brian
Bruch
Byrd
Cage
Carse
Cowen
Cui
Dufay
Dukas
Elgar
Falla
Fauré
Finck
Friml
Gatty
Gaul
Gluck
Grieg
Haydn
Henze
Holst
Ibert
Ives
Jones
Kern
Lehar
Liszt
Lully
Marks
Nono
Orff
Parry
Ravel
Rosse
Satie
Shaw
Smyth
Sousa
Spohr
Suppé
Tosti
Verdi
Weber
Weill
Wolf
Ysaye

6

Ansell
Arnold
Barber
Bartok
Berlin
Bishop
Boulez
Brahms
Bridge
Busoni

Chopin
Clarke
Coates
Coward
Czerny
Delius
Demuth
Duparc
Dvořák
Enesco
Foster
Foulds
Franck
German
Gillet
Glinka
Gounod
Handel
Isolde
Kodály
Liadov
Mahler
Morley
Mozart
Norton
Parker
Philip
Piston
Pleyel
Quantz
Rameau
Ronald
Schütz
Searle
Seiber
Stuart
Tallis
Taylor
Viotti
Wagner
Waller
Walton
Webern
Wesley

7

Albeniz
Bantock
Bazzini
Bellini
Bennett
Berlioz
Blacher
Borodin
Britten
Cleaver
Copland
Corelli
Debussy
Delibes
Dowland
Dunhill
Frankel
Fricker
Galuppi
Gibbons
Godfrey
Hermann
Ireland
Janáček

Joachim
Ketelby
Lambert
Lutyens
Martinů
Menotti
Milhaud
Nicolai
Nielsen
Novello
Poulenc
Puccini
Purcell
Quilter
Rodgers
Rossini
Roussel
Smetana
Stainer
Strauss
Tartini
Tippett
Torelli
Vivaldi
Weelkes

8

Albinoni
Ancliffe
Boughton
Brockman
Bruckner
Chabrier
Cimarosa
Couperin
Dohnanyi
Fletcher
Gabrieli
Gershwin
Glazunov
Grainger
Granados
Holbrook
Honegger
Kreisler
Mascagni
Massenet
Messager
Messiaen
Monckton
Paganini
Palmgren
Panufnik
Petrassi
Pizzetti
Raybould
Respighi
Schnabel
Schubert
Schumann
Scriabin
Sibelius
Stanford
Sullivan
Svendsen
Telemann
Tosselli
Victoria
Vittoria
Wagenaar

9 AND 10

Addinsell (9)
Balakirev (9)
Beethoven (9)
Bernstein (9)
Boccherini (10)
Buxtehade (9)
Cherubini (9)
Cole Porter (10)
Donizetti (9)
Hindemith (9)
Kabalevsky (10)
Locatelli (9)
Macdowell (9)
Meyerbeer (9)
Miaskovsky (10)
Monteverdi (10)
Mussorgsky (10)
Offenbach (9)
Pachelbel (9)
Paisiello (9)
Palestrina (10)
Pergolesi (9)
Ponchielli (10)
Prokofiev (9)
Rawsthorne (10)
Rodriguez (10)
Rubinstein (10)
Saint Saëns (10)
Scarlatti (9)
Schoenberg (10)
Schönberg (9)
Skalkottas (10)
Stravinsky (10)
Vieuxtemps (10)
Villa-Lobos (10)
Waldteufel (10)

11

Dimitriesen
Dittersdorf
Humperdinck
Leoncavallo
Mendelssohn
Moussorgsky
Rachmaninov
Stockhausen
Tchaikovsky
Wolf-Ferrari

12 AND OVER

Coleridge Taylor (15)
Dallapiccola (12)
Josquin des Prés (14)
Khachaturian (12)
Maxwell Davies (13)
Lennox-Berkeley (14)
Rachmaninoff (12)
Racine Fricker (13)
Rimsky Korsakov (14)
Richard Strauss (14)
Shostakovich (12)
Sterndale Bennett (16)
Tschaikovsky (12)
Vaughan Williams (15)

Music, musical instruments and terms

1–3

air
alt
bar
bis
bow
cue
do
doh
duo
fa
fah
gue
hum
jig
key
kit
la
lah
lay
mi
P.
Piu
pop
Pp.
rag
ray
re
run
sax
si
soh
sol
tie
ut
va
vox
zel

4

alla
alto
arco
aria
ayre
band
bard
base
bass
beat
bell
brio
clef
coda
drum
duet
echo
fife
fine
flat
fret
glee
gong
harp
high
hold
horn
hymn
jazz

kent
koto
lead
Lied
lilt
lute
lyre
mass
mode
mood
mort
mute
neum
node
note
oboe
opus
part
peal
pean
pipe
poco
port
reed
reel
rest
root
sign
sing
slur
solo
song
stop
tace
time
toll
tone
trio
tuba
tune
turr
vamp
vina
viol
vivo
voce
vola
wind
wood

5

acuta
adapt
album
arsis
assai
atone
banjo
basso
basta
baton
bebop
bells
blare
blues
bones
brass
breve
bugle

canon
canto
carol
cello
cento
chant
cheng
chime
choir
chord
clang
clank
corno
croma
crook
croon
crwth
dance
dirge
ditty
dolce
drone
duple
etude
elegy
étude
flute
forte
fugal
fugue
galop
gamba
gamut
gigue
grace
grave
knell
kyrie
largo
lento
lyric
major
march
metre
mezzo
minim
minor
molto
motet
motif
naker
nebel
neume
nodal
nonet
notes
octet
opera
organ
paean
pause
pavan
pedal
piano
pieno
piper
pitch
polka
primo
quill
rebec
reeds

regal
resin
rondo
round
sansa
scale
scena
score
segno
segue
senza
shake
shalm
sharp
shawn
sitar
sixth
slide
snare
soave
sol-fa
sound
stave
strad
strum
suite
swell
swing
tabor
tacet
tardo
tempo
tenor
theme
third
thrum
tonic
triad
trill
trite
trope
tuner
tutti
twang
valse
vibes
viola
vocal
voice
volee
volta
volti
waits
waltz
wrest
yodel
zinke

6

accent
adagio
anthem
arioso
atabal
atonal
attune
aubade
ballad
ballet
beemol

177

bolero	scales	cadence	natural
bridge	sennet	cadency	ocarina
bugler	septet	cadenza	octette
cadent	serial	calando	offbeat
cantor	sestet	calypso	organum
catgut	sextet	cantata	pandora
chaunt	shanty	canzona	pan-pipe
chimes	shofar	canzone	phonica
choral	singer	caprice	pianino
choric	sonata	celesta	pianist
chorus	spinet	'cellist	pianola
citole	stanza	cembalo	pibroch
contra	string	chamade	piccolo
corona	subito	chanson	piffero
cornet	tabour	chanter	pomposo
crooks	tabret	chikara	posaune
cymbal	tam-tam	chorale	prelude
da capo	tenuto	cithara	ragtime
damper	tercet	cithern	quartet
design	tierce	clapper	quintet
diesis	timbal	clarion	recital
ditone	timbre	clavier	refrain
divoto	tirade	con brio	reprise
drones	tom-tom	concert	requiem
duetto	treble	conduct	rescore
dulcet	trigon	cornett	ripieno
eighth	tucket	counter	romance
encore	tune up	cremona	rondeau
euphon	tuning	crooner	rondino
fading	tymbal	crotalo	rosalia
fiddle	tzetze	cymbals	roulade
figure	unison	czardas	sackbut
finale	up-beat	descant	sambuca
follia	vamper	descend	sambuke
fugato	veloce	descent	saxhorn
gallop	ventil	diagram	scherzo
giusto	vielle	dichord	schisma
graces	violin	discord	sciolto
ground	vivace	distune	scoring
guitar	volata	dittied	secondo
hammer	volume	drummer	septole
intone	warble	epicede	serpent
Ionian	zambra	euphony	settina
jingle	zincke	eutonia	settino
kettle	zither	fagotto	seventh
legato		fanfare	singing
Lieder		fermata	sistrum
litany	**7**	fiddler	sithara
lutist		fistula	skiffle
lydian		flatten	slurred
lyrist	aeolian	flutina	soloist
manual	aeolist	flutist	soprano
medley	agitato	fuguist	sordine
melody	allegro	furioso	sordono
minuet	alt-horn	gavotte	sospiro
monody	amoroso	gittern	spinnet
motive	andante	gravita	stopped
nobile	angelot	gravity	stretto
oboist	animato	G-string	strophe
octave	apotome	harmony	sub-bass
off-key	apotomy	harpist	subject
pavane	arghool	hautboy	syncope
phrase	arietta	juke-box	taborer
plagal	ariette	keynote	taboret
player	ars nova	locrian	tambour
presto	attuned	lullaby	tambura
quaver	bagpipe	maestro	theorbo
rattle	ballade	marimba	tibicen
rebeck	bandore	mazurka	timbrel
record	baryton	measure	timpani
revert	bassist	mediant	timpano
rhythm	bassoon	melisma	tipping
rounds	bazooka	melodic	toccata
rubato	bellows	mistune	tone-row
sacbut	bitonal	musette	tremolo
sancho	bravura	musical	triplet

trumpet
tubicen
tuneful
ukelele
upright
vespers
vibrato
vihuela
violist
violone
warbler
whistle
zithern
zufflolo

8

absonant
absonous
addition
alto-clef
antiphon
arch-lute
arpeggio
autoharp
bagpipes
baritone
barytone
bassetto
bass-drum
bass-horn
bass note
bass oboe
bass-viol
beat-time
bell harp
berceuse
canticle
canzonet
carillon
castanet
castrato
cavatina
chaconne
cheville
clappers
clarinet
clavecin
claviary
composer
composto
con amore
con anima
concerto
confusco
conjusto
continuo
couranto
cromorna
crotchet
deep-tone
demi-tone
diapason
diatonic
diminish
ding-dong
distance
doloroso
dominant
down beat
drumbeat
drum-head
duettist
dulcimer
eleventh

energico
ensemble
entr'acte
euphonic
euphonon
exercise
falsetto
fandango
fantasia
fantasie
flautist
folk-song
forzando
galement
galliard
gemshorn
grazioso
half-note
harmonic
harp lute
hawk-bell
high note
hornpipe
infinito
interval
intonate
isotonic
Jew's-harp
jongleur
keyboard
key-bugle
knackers
lentando
libretto
ligature
lutanist
lutenist
madrigal
maestoso
major key
melodeon
melodics
melodist
melodize
minor key
minstrel
mirliton
miserere
moderato
modulate
monotone
monotony
movement
musicale
musician
nocturne
notation
notturno
obligato
operatic
operetta
oratorio
organist
ostinato
overture
pan-pipes
part-song
pastoral
phantasy
phrasing
Phrygian
pianette
plectrum
post horn
psaltery
quantity

recorder
reed pipe
register
resonant
response
rhapsody
rigadoon
saraband
semitone
septette
sequence
serenade
serenata
sestetto
sextette
sforzato
side drum
smorzato
sonatina
songster
spiccato
spinette
staccato
sticcado
subtonic
symmetry
symphony
syntonic
tabourer
tabouret
tamboura
tell-tale
terzetto
threnody
timoroso
tonalist
tonality
tone down
tone poem
trap-drum
tremando
triangle
trichord
trombone
tympanon
tympanum
vigoroso
virginal
virtuosi
virtuoso
vocalist
voce colo
warbling
wood-wind
zambomba

9

accordion
acoustics
all-breve
allemande
alto-viola
andamento
andantino
antiphony
arabesque
archilute
atonality
bagatelle
balalaika
banjoline
barcarole
bass-flute
bird-organ

bombardon
bow-string
brass-band
brillante
bugle-horn
cacophony
cantabile
capriccio
castanets
celestina
charivari
chromatic
clarionet
claviharp
coach-horn
conductor
consonate
contralto
cornopean
crescendo
dead-march
death-bell
decachord
deep-toned
dissonant
dithyramb
drone-pipe
drumstick
dulcitone
elbow-pipe
elevation
euphonism
euphonium
euphonize
extempore
fiddle-bow
flageolet
flute-stop
folk-music
furibondo
gallopade
generator
glissando
grace-note
gradation
grandioso
Gregorian
guitarist
half-shift
hand organ
harmonica
harmonics
harmonium
harmonize
hexachord
high-pitch
high-toned
homophony
imbroglio
immusical
impromptu
improvise
in harmony
interlude
intonation
inversion
irregular
jazz music
lagrimoso
languente
larghetto
leger-line
leitmotif
mandoline
mandolute
melodious

179

metronome
mezzo-voce
modulator
monochord
monophony
monotonic
mouth harp
music-book
obbligato
octachord
orchestra
part music
pastorale
phonetics
pianolist
pitch-pipe
pizzicato
plainsong
polonaise
polychord
polyphony
polytonal
pricksong
quadrille
quartette
quintette
recording
reed organ
rehearsal
resonance
rhythmics
ricercare
roundelay
saxophone
semibreve
semitonic
septimole
seraphine
sforzando
siciliana
siciliano
signature
slow march
soft pedal
solfeggio
sollecito
sopranist
sostenuto
sotto-voce
sound-post
spiritosa
spiritual
strascino
succentor
symphonic
syncopate
tablature
tabourine
tail-piece
tambourin
tenor bass
tenor clef
tenor horn
tenor tuba
tenor viol
tessitura
theorbist
time-table
timpanist
trillando
trumpeter
tubophone
tympanist
union-pipe
unmusical
untunable

variation
viola alto
violinist
voluntary
vox humana
whistling
xylophone

10

accidental
adaptation
affettuoso
allegretto
appoggiato
attunement
background
bandmaster
barcarolle
base-spring
basset-horn
bassoonist
binotonous
bull fiddle
cantillate
canzonetta
chiroplast
chitlarone
chorus girl
clarichord
clavichord
coloratura
concertina
con-spirito
continuato
contrabass
cor anglais
cornettist
dance-music
demiditone
diastaltic
diminuendo
discordant
disharmony
dissonance
dissonancy
dolcemente
double bass
double time
dulcet-tone
embouchure
enharmonic
Eolian harp
Eolian lyre
euphonicon
euphonious
extraneous
flügelhorn
folk-singer
fortissimo
French harp
French horn
gramophone
grand piano
grand opera
ground bass
harmonicon
harp-string
homophonic
hurdy-gurdy
incidental
instrument
intermezzo
intonation
kettle-drum

lentamente
light opera
major chord
major scale
minor chord
minor scale
minstrelsy
mixolydian
modulation
monotonous
mouth-organ
mouth-piece
musica viva
musicology
opera buffa
opera music
ophicleide
orchestral
pentachord
percussion
pianissimo
pianoforte
polyphonic
prima donna
recitative
recitativo
ritardando
ritornello
semiquaver
sourdeline
sousaphone
staphyline
Stradivari
Strathspey
strepitoso
string-band
stringendo
submediant
supertonic
suspension
symphonion
symphonist
syncopated
syncopator
tamboureen
tambourine
tarantella
tetrachord
tin whistle
tonic chord
tonic major
tonic minor
tonic-sol-fa
triple-time
trombonist
troubador
tuning fork
twelve-tone
undulation
variamento
vibraphone
vistomente
vocal music
zumpé piano

11

accelerando
Aeolian harp
Aeolian lyre
alla capella
alto-ripieno
arrangement
ballad opera
barrel-organ

bene-placito
broken chord
canned music
capriccioso
church music
clairschach
clarion note
composition
concertante
contra-basso
contrapunto
contra-tenor
counterpart
decrescendo
demi-cadence
diatessaron
discordance
discordancy
equisonance
extemporize
fiddlestick
figured-bass
finger-board
first violin
graphophone
Guido's scale
harmoniphon
harmonizing
harpsichord
high-pitched
hunting-horn
hydraulicon
incantation
madrigalist
mandolinist
minnesinger
music-master
natural note
nickelodeon
opera bouffe
orchestrate
passing-bell
passing-note
piano-violin
polyphonism
prestissimo
progression
quarter note
quarter-tone
rallentando
rock and roll
sacred music
saxophonist
senza rigore
solmization
string music
subsemitone
symphonious
syncopation
transposing
tridiapason
unaccordant
viola d'amore
viol da gamba
violoncello
vivacissimo
voce-di-petto
voce-di-testa
volti-subito

12

accordionist
acoustic bass
allegrissimo

appassionata
appoggiatura
assai-allegro
augmentation
bass baritone
boogie-woogie
cembal d'ambre
chamber music
chromaticism
clarinettist
comedy ballet
concert grand
concert-pitch
contrapuntal
cottage piano
counterpoint
counter-tenor
divertimento
double-octave
extravaganza
false cadence
fiddle-string
funeral march
glockenspiel
inharmonious
instrumental
mezzo-relievo
mezzo-soprano
military band
musicologist
opéra comique
orchestrator
organ-grinder
organ recital
pandean-pipes
passion music

penny whistle
philharmonic
philomusical
polytonality
repercussion
sesquialtera
sounding-post
spheremelody
Stradivarius
thorough-bass
tuning-hammer
ukulele-banjo
viola da gamba
vocalization

13

accompaniment
bagpipe player
choral singing
conservatoire
cornet-à-piston
disharmonious
harmonic chord
musical comedy
music festival
operatic music
orchestration
ranz-des-vaches
sacred concert
sol-fa notation
staff notation
string octette
string quartet
superdominant

swanee whistle
terpsichorean
tetradiapason
transposition
violoncellist

14 AND OVER

Ambrosian chant (14)
banjo-mandoline (14)
brass instrument(s) (15, 16)
chromatic scale (14)
demisemiquaver (14)
direct interval (14)
double-tongueing (15)
electronic music (15)
fife-and-drum band (15)
flute-flageolet (14)
Gregorian chant (14)
Highland bagpipe (15)
instrumentalist (15)
instrumentation (15)
Lowland bagpipe (14)
mandoline player (15)
musical director (15)
musical festival (15)
musique concrète (15)
regimental band (14)
string quartette (15)
symphony concert (15)
tintinnabulary (14)
tintinnabulate (14)
tintinnabulation (16)
triple-tongueing (15)
wind instrument(s) (14, 15)

Poetry, prose, and grammar

2 AND 3

do
ego
lay
ms.
nō
nōh
ode
pun
tag
wit

4

agon
bard
case
coda
copy
dual
duan
Edda
epic
epos
foot
form
gest
glee
hymn
lamb
idyl

mime
mood
myth
noun
past
pean
play
plot
poem
poet
quip
rime
root
rule
rune
saga
scan
song
tone
verb
weak
word

5

affix
blurb
canto
caret
carol
casal
codex

colon
comma
dirge
ditty
drama
elegy
elide
epode
essay
fable
farce
folio
geste
gloss
haiku
humor
ictus
idiom
idyll
Iliad
image
index
infix
irony
lyric
maxim
metre
motif
novel
paean
poesy
prose
psalm

quote
rhyme
rondo
runic
scald
scene
shift
slang
stich
style
sylva
tense
theme
tilde
triad
Vedas
verse
vowel

6

accent
active
adonic
adverb
Aeneid
alcaic
annals
anthem
aorist
aptote
ballad

181

bathos	**7**	Sapphic	language
chanty		sarcasm	laureate
chorus	adjunct	scaldic	libretto
clause	anagram	semiped	limerick
cliché	analogy	servile	logogram
climax	analyse	setting	lyricism
comedy	anapest	sextain	madrigal
crisis	antonym	spondee	metaphor
critic	apocope	stichic	metrical
dactyl	apology	strophe	mispoint
dative	article	subject	mock epic
define	ballade	syncope	morpheme
derive	berhyme	synonym	negative
digram	bucolic	systole	nonsense
dipody	cadence	tiercet	Ossianic
ending	caesura	tragedy	oxymoron
epodic	cantata	trilogy	paradigm
epopee	cedilla	triolet	particle
finite	chanson	triplet	partsong
future	choreus	trochee	pastoral
gender	collate	villain	personal
genius	content	virelay	phonetic
gerund	context	Vulgate	Pindaric
gnomic	couplet	war song	poetical
govern	decline	western	positive
heroic	descant		prologue
hiatus	diction		quantity
homily	digraph	**8**	quatrain
hubris	distich		relative
humour	eclogue	ablative	rhapsody
hybris	edition	absolute	rhetoric
hymnal	elegiac	acrostic	romantic
hyphen	elision	allusion	scanning
iambic	epicene	alphabet	scansion
iambus	epigram	amoebean	scenario
jargon	epistle	analysis	sentence
kabuki	epitaph	anapaest	singular
lacuna	fantasy	anaphora	solecism
legend	fiction	anti-hero	stanzaic
lyrist	Georgic	antiphon	suspense
macron	harmony	apodosis	swan song
mantra	Homeric	archaism	syntaxis
memoir	homonym	assonant	systolic
monody	idyllic	asterisk	temporal
neuter	imagery	balladry	threnody
number	inflect	caesural	thriller
object	introit	canticle	tribrach
parody	journal	chiasmus	trimeter
pathos	lampoon	choliamb	triptote
period	leonine	choriamb	unpoetic
person	lexicon	clerihew	versicle
phrase	litotes	contrast	vignette
pidgin	lyrical	critique	vocative
plural	meiosis	dactylic	whodunit
poetic	mimesis	definite	word play
poetry	nemesis	dieresis	
prefix	novella	dialogue	
review	Odyssey	discrete	**9**
rhythm	paradox	doggerel	
riddle	parsing	dramatic	accidence
rondle	passive	ellipsis	adjective
satire	peanism	enclitic	ampersand
simile	perfect	epic poem	anapestic
sketch	persona	epigraph	Anglicism
slogan	phoneme	epilogue	anonymous
sonnet	poetics	epitrite	anthology
stanza	polemic	euphuism	apocopate
stress	present	feminine	archetype
strong	pronoun	folktale	Asclepiad
suffix	prosaic	footnote	assonance
symbol	prosody	full-stop	biography
syntax	proverb	generate	birthsong
thesis	psalter	genitive	broadside
umlaut	refrain	glossary	burlesque
verbal	regular	guttural	cacophony
zeugma	requiem	horation	catharsis

182

Theatre, opera, ballet, cinema, television and radio

2 AND 3

act
arc
bit
bow
box
cue
dub
fan
gag
ham
hit
mug
nō
pan
pit
rag
rep
run
set
tag
TV
wig

4

bill
book
boom
busk
cast
clap
clip
crew
dais
diva
duet
Emmy
epic
exit
film
flop
foil
gala
gods
grid
hero
idol
joke
lead
line
live
mask
mike
mime
mute
part
play
prop
role
rush
shot
show
skit
solo
spot
star
take
team
turn
wing

5

actor
ad lib
agent
angel
apron
aside
baton
break
clown
comic
debut
decor
drama
dry up
enact
exode
extra
farce
flies
focus
foyer
heavy
hokum
house
lines
mimer
mimic
movie
on cue
opera
Oscar
piece
props
radio
revue
scene
stage
stall
stunt
telly
usher
wings

6

acting
action
appear
backer
ballet
barker
big top
boards
buskin
camera
chorus
cinema
circle
circus
claque
comedy
critic
dancer
direct
dubbed
effect
encore
finale
flyman
kabuki

lights
make-up
masque
method
motley
movies
mummer
nautch
number
on tour
one act
parody
patron
patter
player
podium
prompt
puppet
recite
repeat
ring up
rushes
satire
screen
script
season
serial
series
singer
sitcom
sketch
speech
stalls
stooge
studio
talent
talkie
ticket
tights
timing
tinsel
troupe
TV show
viewer
walk-on
warm-up
writer

7

acrobat
actress
all-star
amateur
balcony
benefit
bit part
booking
buffoon
cabaret
callboy
cartoon
casting
catcall
catwalk
channel
charade
chorine
circuit
clapper
close-up
commère

company
compère
concert
console
costume
curtain
dancing
danseur
deadpan
dress up
drive in
dubbing
fan club
farceur
fantasy
feature
film set
gallery
heroine
ingenue
juggler
leg show
leotard
long run
matinée
mimicry
mummery
musical
mystery
new wave
on stage
overact
pageant
perform
phone-in
Pierrot
players
playing
playlet
pop star
portray
prelude
present
preview
produce
program
recital
reciter
re-enact
resting
revival
rostrum
scenery
show biz
showman
sponsor
stadium
stagery
staging
stand-in
stardom
starlet
support
tableau
talkies
theatre
the gods
tragedy
trailer
trilogy
trouper
tumbler
upstage

variety
vehicle
viewing
western

8

applause
artistry
audience
audition
backdrop
bioscope
burletta
carnival
chat show
Cinerama
clapping
clowning
coliseum
comedian
conjurer
coryphée
costumer
coulisse
danseuse
dialogue
director
disguise
dramatic
dumb show
duologue
entr'acte
entrance
epilogue
exit line
farceuse
fauteuil
festival
figurant
film crew
film star
film unit
filmgoer
first act
funny man
ham actor
interval
juggling
libretto
live show
location
magician
male lead
morality
newsreel
offstage
operatic
operetta
overture
parterre
pastoral
peep show
pictures
pit stall
platform
playbill
playgoer
première
producer
prologue
prompter
protasis
quiz show
rehearse

ring down
scenario
set piece
showbill
side show
smash hit
stagebox
star turn
straight
stripper
subtitle
telecast
Thespian
third act
tragical
travesty
typecast
wardrobe
wigmaker

9

animation
announcer
arabesque
backcloth
backstage
ballerina
bandstand
barnstorm
bit player
box office
broadcast
burlesque
cameraman
character
chorus boy
cinematic
clip joint
cloakroom
Columbine
conjuring
costumier
coulisses
criticism
cyclorama
discovery
double act
down stage
dramatics
dramatist
dramatize
drop scene
entertain
entrechat
exhibiter
figurante
film actor
film extra
fimstrip
first lead
flashback
floorshow
folkdance
full house
gala night
guest star
Harlequin
impromptu
interlude
limelight
love scene
low comedy
major role
melodrama

minor role
monodrama
monologue
movie star
movie-goer
music hall
night club
orchestra
panel game
pantaloon
pantomime
pas de deux
performer
photoplay
Pierrette
pirouette
pit-stalls
play-actor
playhouse
portrayal
programme
prompt-box
publicity
punch-line
quartette
rehearsal
repertory
represent
second act
slapstick
soap opera
soliloquy
soubrette
spectacle
spectator
spotlight
stage door
stagehand
stage left
stage-name
stage play
take a part
tap dancer
the boards
title role
tragedian
usherette
wisecrack

10

afterpiece
appearance
auditorium
chorus girl
clapper-boy
comedienne
comedietta
comic opera
commercial
continuity
coryphaeus
crowd scene
denouement
disc jockey
drama group
dramaturge
dramaturgy
fantoccini
filmscript
film house
first night
footlights
get the bird
high comedy

hippodrome
histrionic
horse opera
horror film
impresario
in the round
in the wings
junior lead
intermezzo
leading man
legitimate
librettist
marionette
masquerade
microphone
movie actor
music drama
newscaster
on location
opera buffa
opera house
performing
play-acting
playwright
prima donna
production
prompt-book
properties
proscenium
Pulcinella
puppet-show
rave notice
rave review
recitation
repertoire
repetiteur
ringmaster
screenplay
silent film
sound track
stagecraft
stage fever
stage right
star player
striptease
substitute
sword-dance
tap dancing
tear-jerker
television
theatre box
theatrical
torchdance
travelogue
understudy
variety act
vaudeville
walk-on part
wide screen

11

accompanist
all-star cast
art director
balletomane
barnstormer
black comedy
broadcaster
cap and bells
Cinemascope
circus-rider
cliff-hanger
comedy drama
comic relief

commentator
concert hall
credit title
cutting room
dance troupe
documentary
drama critic
drama school
dramatic art
dress circle
electrician
entertainer
equilibrist
exeunt omnes
feature film
film theatre
fire curtain
folkdancing
funambulist
greasepaint
Greek chorus
histrionics
illusionist
impersonate
kitchen-sink
leading lady
legerdemain
light comedy
matinée idol
method actor
miracle play
opera bouffe
opera singer
pantomimist
Passion play
performance
picture show
problem play
protagonist
psychodrama
Punchinello
scene change
set designer
set the scene
showmanship
show-stopper
sound effect
spectacular
stage design
stage effect
stage fright
stage player
stage school
stage-struck
star billing
star quality
star-studded
talent scout
technicolor
terpsichore

thaumaturgy
theatregoer
theatreland
theatricals
Thespian art
tragedienne
tragicomedy
trick-riding
unrehearsed
upper circle
variety show
ventriloquy
word-perfect

12

academy award
actor-manager
amphitheatre
ballet-dancer
balletomania
choreography
cinema studio
clapperboard
concert party
credit titles
dramaturgist
dressing-room
exotic dancer
extravaganza
film director
film festival
film producer
first-nighter
Grand Guignol
harlequinade
impersonator
introduction
juvenile lead
make-up artist
melodramatic
method acting
minstrel show
modern ballet
morality play
name in lights
natural break
opera glasses
orchestra pit
principal boy
Punch and Judy
puppet-player
scene-painter
scene-shifter
scene-stealer
screenwriter
scriptwriter
show business
silver screen

song and dance
sound effects
stage manager
stage whisper
starring role
steal the show
stock company
straight part
top of the bill

13

ballet dancing
burlesque show
cinematograph
contortionist
curtain-raiser
dance festival
emergency exit
entertainment
musical comedy
projectionist
Russian ballet
safety curtain
sleight-of-hand
sound engineer
studio manager
thaumaturgics
theatre school
ventriloquist

14 AND 15

acrobatic troupe (15)
ballet-mistress (14)
classical ballet (15)
continuity girl (14)
dancing academy (14)
domestic comedy (14)
dramatic critic (14)
dramatic society (15)
prima ballerina (14)
property master (14)
school of acting (14)
school of dancing (15)
shooting script (14)
situation comedy (15)
slide projector (14)
smoking concert (14)
sound-projector (14)
stage carpenter (14)
stage properties (15)
strolling player (15)
tableaux-vivants (15)
talking pictures (15)
tightrope-walker (15)
touring company (14)
variety theatre (14)

MEASUREMENT
Coins and currency

2 AND 3

as
cob
dam
ecu
far

lat
leu
lev
mil
mna
pie
ree

rei
sen
sho
sol
sou
won
yen

4

anna
baht
beka
biga
buck

cash
cent
daum
dime
doit
joey
kran
lira
mail
mark
merk
mite
obol
para
peag
peso
pice
rand
real
rial
ryal
tael
unik
yuan

5

angel
asper
belga
betso
broad
colon
conto
copec
crown
daric
dinar
ducat
eagle
franc
groat
krona
krone
liard
libra
litas
livre
locho
louis
medio
mohar
mohur
noble
obang
paolo
pence
pengo
penny
plack
pound
rupee
sceat
scudi
scudo
semis
soldo
stica
styca
sucre
sycee
tical
toman
uncia
unite
zloty

6

amania
balboa
baubee
bawbee
bezart
condor
copang
copeck
décime
doblon
dollar
escudo
florin
forint
fuorte
gourde
guinea
gulden
heller
kopeck
lepton
markka
nickel
pagode
peseta
rouble
sceatt
sequin
shekel
stater
stiver
talari
talent
tanner
tester
teston
thaler
tomaun
zechin

7

angelot
bolívar
carolus
centava
centavo
centime
cordoba
crusado
denarii
drachma
guilder
jacobus
lempira
milreis
moidore
ngusang
piastre
pistole
quarter
sextans
stooter
testoon
unicorn

8

ambrosin
denarius
didrachm
doubloon

ducatoon
farthing
florence
groschen
half anna
half mark
johannes
kreutzer
louis d'or
maravedi
napoleon
new pence
new penny
picayune
quetzale
sesterce
shilling
sixpence
stotinka

9

boliviano
cuartillo
didrachma
dupondius
gold broad
gold noble
gold penny
half ackey
half angel
half broad
half crown
half groat
halfpenny
pistareen
rixdollar
rose-noble
schilling
sestertii
sovereign
spur royal
two mohars
two mohurs
yellow boy

10

broad piece
crown piece
double pice
easterling
first brass
gold stater
half florin
half guinea
half laurel
quadrussis
sestertium
silverling
stour-royal
threepence
threepenny
tripondius
venezolano

11

Briton crown
double crown
double eagle
george noble
guinea piece

half guilder
half thistle
silver penny
spade guinea
tetradrachm
twelvepenny
two guilders

12 AND 13

double sequin (12)
half farthing (12)
half rose-noble (13)
half sovereign (13)
mill sixpence (12)
quarter angel (12)
quarter dollar (13)
quarter florin (13)
quarter laurel (13)
quarter noble (12)
silver-stater (12)
sixpenny piece (13)
tribute penny (12)
twenty dollars (13)
twopenny piece (13)
two-pound piece (13)

14 AND OVER

barbadoes penny (14)
five-guinea piece (15)
five-pound piece (14)
Hong Kong dollar (14)
quarter guilder (14)
three farthings (14)
threepenny piece (15)
twenty shillings (15)
two-guilder piece (15)
two-guinea piece (14)

Time (including specific dates, periods, seasons, annual festivals, etc.)

(H.) = Hindu. (I) = Islam. (J.) = Jewish months (variously spelt). (R.) = Roman.

2 – 4

Ab (J.)
Abib (J.)
A.D.
Adar (j.)
aeon
age
ages
ago
A.M.
B.C.
B.S.T.
date
dawn
day
Elul (J.)
eon
era
ever
fast
G.M.T.
Holi (H.)
hour
Ides (R.)
Iyar (J.)
July
June
last
late
Lent
May
morn
noon
now
N.S.
oft
once
O.S.
P.M.
slow
soon
span
term
then
tick
time
week
when
Xmas
year
yore
Yuga (H.)
Yule

5

adays
after
again
alway
April
bells
clock
cycle
daily
dated
early

epact
epoch
Fasti (R.)
feast
first
flash
horal
jiffy
Kalpa (H.)
later
March
month
never
night
Nisan (J.)
nones
of old
often
quick
reign
Sivan (J.)
spell
Tebet (J.)
teens
times
Tisri (J.)
to-day
trice
until
watch
while

6

always
annual
August
autumn
before
betime
brumal
Cisleu
curfew
decade
Diwali (H.)
Easter
faster
feriae
ferial
Friday
future
heyday
hourly
hiemal
Julian
Kislev (J.)
Lammas
lately
latest
May day
memory
mensal
midday
minute
modern
moment
Monday
morrow

o'clock
off-day
pay-day
period
record
rhythm
season
second
seldom
Shebat (J.)
slower
slowly
spring
summer
sunset
Tammuz (J.)
Tebeth (J.)
termly
timely
timous
Tishri (J.)
ultimo
Veadar (J.)
Veader (J.)
vernal
vesper
weekly
whilom
whilst
winter
yearly

7

almanac
already
ancient
anights
antique
bedtime
betimes
by and by
Calends (R.)
century
chiliad
Chisleu (J.)
dawning
daytime
diurnal
dog days
earlier
epochal
equinox
estival
eternal
etesian
evening
fast day
fête day
half-day
harvest
Heshvan (J.)
high day
hock-day
holiday
holy day
instant

interim
January
jubilee
lady day
lay-days
lustrum
mail day
mid-Lent
midweek
monthly
morning
new moon
nightly
noonday
October
post-day
proximo
quartan
quarter
quicker
quickly
quintan
Ramadan (I.)
regency
rent day
sabbath
slowest
sundial
sundown
sunrise
tea time
tertian
Thammuz (J.)
timeful
time gun
timeous
tonight
triduan
Tuesday
undated
wartime
weekday
weekend
whilere
workday
Xmas day
yestern

8

aestival
annually
antecede
antedate
anterior
biennial
bimensal
birthday
biweekly
calendar
carnival
chiliasm
chiliast
day by day
daybreak
dead-slow
December
domesday

doomsday
duration
earliest
eggtimer
estivate
eternity
eventide
every day
February
festival
forenoon
formerly
futurist
futurity
gangweek
Georgian
gloaming
half-past
half-term
half-time
half-year
hibernal
high noon
Hock-tide
Hogmanay
holidays
holy week
interval
kalendar
latterly
leap year
Lord's day
mealtime
menology
midnight
minutely
natal day
new style
noontide
noon-time
November
nowadays
nundinal
oft-times
old style
overtime
past time
periodic
postpone
punctual
quickest
Ramadhan (I.)
right now
Saturday
seasonal
seed time
semester
se'nnight
sidereal
slow time
sometime
speedily
Stone Age
Thursday
time ball
time bill
timeless
tomorrow
twilight
untimely
up to date
vacation
whenever
Yuletide
zero hour

9

Adar Shani (J.)
aforetime
after ages
afternoon
afterward
All Hallow
anciently
antedated
antelucan
antiquity
bimonthly
Boxing Day
Candlemas
centenary
Christmas
civil year
close time
continual
decennary
decennial
diurnally
diuturnal
Easter Day
Edwardian
Ember days
Ember fast
Ember tide
Ember week
eternally
feast days
fortnight
fruit time
Gregorian
Halloween
hard times
hereafter
hodiernal
honeymoon
hourglass
immediate
indiction
instantly
lean years
Low Sunday
lunar year
lunch time
market day
Martinmas
matutinal
menstrual
midsummer
midwinter
nightfall
night-time
nightward
novitiate
octennial
overnight
past times
peace time
postponed
premature
presently
quarterly
quick time
quotidian
recurrent
return day
right away
September
sexennial
sometimes
speech day
sunrising

Thermidor
ticket.day
timepiece
timetable
triennial
trimester
Victorian
Wednesday
whole time
yesterday
yestereve

10

aftertimes
afterwards
All Hallows
antecedent
antemosaic
anteriorly
anticipate
beforehand
before time
behind time
biennially
bimestrial
centennial
chiliastic
chronogram
continuous
days of yore
dinner time
diuturnity
Easter term
Ember weeks
estivation
Father Time
fence month
Good Friday
half-yearly
hebdomadal
Hilary term
isochronal
lunar cycle
lunar month
Michaelmas
Middle Ages
millennium
natalitial
occasional
oftentimes
olden times
Palm Sunday
quarter day
record time
seasonable
septennial
sexagesima
Shrovetide
solar month
sowing-time
spring time
summer term
summertime
sunsetting
synchronal
Theban year
thereafter
tiffin time
time enough
timekeeper
time server
time signal
triverbial
twelfth day

unpunctual
vespertine
watch night
wedding day
Whit Sunday
winter time
working day

11

All Fools' Day
All Souls' Day
anniversary
antecedence
antemundane
antenuptial
antepaschal
anteriority
Bank Holiday
behindtimes
bicentenary
Black Monday
Chalk Sunday
chronograph
chronometer
closing time
continually
cosmic clock
discount day
Elizabethan
everlasting
fashionable
fortnightly
half holiday
harvest home
harvest time
hebdomadary
holiday time
immediately
interregnum
isochronism
isochronous
jubilee year
Judgment Day
leisure time
millenarian
New Year's Day
New Year's Eve
Passion Week
prehistoric
prematurely
present time
pudding time
punctuality
quadrennial
quartz clock
Rosh Hashonah (J.)
seeding time
settling day
synchronism
synchronize
synchronous
thenceforth
time bargain
Tudor period
twelvemonth
ultramodern
Whitsuntide
yesternight

12

afterthought
All Saints' Day   189

antediluvial
antediluvian
antemeridian
anticipation
Ash Wednesday
betrothal day
bicentennial
carbon dating
Christmas Day
Christmas Eve
continuously
duodecennial
early closing
Easter Sunday
Embering days
emergent year
hebdomatical
luncheon time
Midsummer Day
Midsummer Eve
occasionally
old-fashioned
platonic year
Plough Monday
post-diluvial
post-diluvian
post-meridian
postponement

postprandial
quadragesima
quinquennial
red-letter day
Rogation days
Rogation week
sidereal year
standard time
synchronized
tercentenary
time contract
tricentenary
tropical year
twelfth night

13

All Hallowmass
All Hallowtide
April Fools' Day
breakfast time
calendar month
Childermas day
Christmastide
Christmastime
Edwardian days
everlastingly

golden jubilee
golden wedding
Gregorian year
holiday season
lunisolar year
Michaelmas Day
once upon a time
Shrove Tuesday
silver wedding
thenceforward
Trinity Sunday
Valentine's Day

14 AND 15

behind the times (14)
biological clock (15)
day in and day out (14)
early closing day (15)
early Victorian (14)
Maundy Thursday (14)
Michaelmas term (14)
prehistoric age(s) (14–15)
sabbatical year (14)
synchronization (15)
synodical month (14)
Walpurgis night (14)

Weights and measures

(A.) = Argentina
(B.) = Brazil
(b.) = bread
(C.) = Canada
(c.) = coal
(Ch.) = China
(E.) = Egypt
(elec.) = electricity
(Eth.) = Ethiopia
(F.) = France
(f.) = fish
(G.) = Greece
(H.) = Hebrew
(Hon.) = Honduras

(I.) = India
(Ice.) = Iceland
(Indo.) = Indonesia
(Ire.) = Ireland
(It.) = Italy
(J.) = Japan
(liq.) = liquids
(M.) = Malta
(Malay.) = Malaysia
(min.) = mining
(Mor.) = Morocco
(N.) = Norway
(O.) = Oriental
(pap.) = paper

(print.) = printing
(R.) = Russia
(Rom.) = Roman
(S.) = Spain
(s.) = silk or cotton
(S.A.) = South Africa
(SI) = Système International:
        metric system
(T.) = Turkey
(Thai.) = Thailand
(U.S.) = United States
(v.) = various commodities
(w.) = wool
(w.y.) = worsted yarn

Note: Words with no references against them are British weights or measures not necessarily confined to particular commodities. Many of the units listed are no longer in use.

1 – 3

A4 (pap.)
amp (elec.)
are (SI)
as (Rom.)
A.S.A.
aum (S.A.)
B.S.I.
B.T.U.
cab (H.)
cho (J.)
cor (H.)
cm. (SI)
cwt.
day
D.I.N.
dwt.
el
em (print.)

en (print.)
erg
fen (Ch.)
g. (SI)
hin (H.)
kat (E.)
keg
ken (J.)
kg.
kin (J. and Ch.)
km.
kor (H.)
lac (I.)
lb.
lea (s.)
li (Ch.)
log (H.)
m.
mho (elec.)
mil

mow (Ch.)
mu
niu (Thai.)
ohm (elec.)
oka (E.)
oke (T.)
pic (E.)
piu (It.)
rai (Thai.)
ri (J.)
rod
sen (Thai.)
sho (J.)
SI
sun (J.)
tan (Ch.)
to (J.)
tod (w.)
ton
tot

tun (liq.)
vat (liq.)
wah (Thai.)
wey (w.)

4

acre
area
bale (v.)
bath (H.)
bind (f.)
boll
butt (liq.)
cade (f.)
case (v.)
cask (liq.)
ch'ih (Ch.)
chop (Ch.)

comb
cord
coss (I.)
cran (f.)
darg
demy (pap.)
drah (Mor.)
dram
drop
drum (v.)
dyne
epha (H.)
feet
foot
funt (R.)
gill
gram (SI)
half
hand (horses)
hank (w.y.)
hath (I.)
heml (E.)
hide
hour
inch
keel (c.)
kela (E.)
kilo (SI)
knot
koku (J.)
koss (I.)
kwan (J.)
lakh (I.)
last (f., w.)
link
load (min.)
maze (f.)
mile
mina (H.)
muid (S.A.)
nail
natr (Eth.)
oket (Eth.)
omer (H.)
onza (A.)
pace
pail (lard)
pair
palm
peck
pike (G.)
pint
pipe (liq.)
pole
pood (R.)
post (pap.)
pund (N.)
raik (I.)
ream (pap.)
reed (H.)
reel (s.)
rood
rope
rotl (E.)
sack (c. w.)
seam
seer (I.)
span
step
tael (Ch.)
tare
tola (I.)
tret
troy
ts'un (Ch.)
unit

vara (Hon.)
volt (elec.)
warp (f.)
watt (elec.)
week
wrap (w.y.)
yard
year

5

almud (T.)
anker (S.A.)
ardeb (E.)
bahar (I.)
barge (c.)
baril (G.)
barre (I.)
bekah (H.)
bidon (liq.)
bigha (I.)
brace
cable
candy (I.)
carat
catty (Ch.)
cawny (I.)
chain
cloff
clove
coomb
count (w.y.)
crore (I.)
crown (pap.)
cubic
cubit
cycle
danda (I.)
ephah (H.)
galon (A.)
gauge
gerah (H.)
grain
gross
hertz (elect.)
homer (H.)
kileh (T.)
leash
legua (A.)
liang (Ch.)
libra (B.)
litre (SI)
livre (F. and G.)
masha (I.)
maund (I.)
mease
meter   (SI)
metre
minim (liq.)
month
obole
ocque (G.)
okieh (E.)
ounce
pally (I.)
pearl
perch
picul (Ch.)
piede (M.)
plumb
point (print.)
pound
proof
pugil
purse (T.)

qirat (E.)
quart
quire (pap.)
quota
royal (pap.)
sajen (R.)
shaku (J.)
sheet (pap.)
shock (U.S.)
sicca (I.)
skein (s.)
stere (SI)
stone
stoup (liq.)
terce (liq.)
therm
tithe
toise (F.)
token (pap.)
tonne
trone
truss
tsubo (J.)
ungul (I.)
vedro (R.)
verst (R.)
yojan (I.)

6

ampère (elec.)
aroura (E. and G.)
arroba (A. and B.)
arshin (T.)
assize
bandle (Ire.)
barrel (v.)
batman (T.)
bundle (v.)
bushel
cantar (E. and T.)
casing (pap.)
cental (C. and U.S.)
cental (B. and G.)
chatak (I.)
chopin (liq.)
cottah (I.)
cuarta (A.)
djerib (T.)
double
drachm
endaze (T.)
fanega (S.)
fathom
feddan (E.)
firkin
firlot
fother
gallon (liq.)
gramme (SI)
kantar (Eth.)
kentle
league
libbra (M.)
megohm (elec.)
metric
micron (SI)
minute
modius
moiety
morgen (S.A.)
noggin
obolus (G.)
octant
octave

octavo
oxgang
parsec
pocket (hops)
pottle (liq.)
quarto (pap.)
rotolo (M.)
sajene (R.)
schene (E.)
second
shekel (H.)
shtoff (R.)
staten (G.)
suttle
talent (G.)
thrave (Ice.)
thread (s.)
tierce (liq.)
visham (I.)
weight

7

acreage
boiling
caldron (c.)
Celsius
centner
century
chalder
chittak (I.)
coulomb (elec.)
dangali (I.)
drachma (G.)
ellwand
furlong
half-aum (S.A.)
half-ton
hectare (SI)
koonkee (I.)
leaguer (S.A.)
maximum
measure
megaton
mileage
minimum
minimus
modicum
outsize
pailful
per cent.
quantar (E.)
quartan
quantum
quarter
quinary
quintal
röntgen
sarplar (w.)
scruple
seamile
spindle (s.)
stadium (G.)
stature
stremma (G.)
ternary
ternion
tonnage

8

alqueire (B.)
angstrom
caroteel (O.)

191

chaldron (c.)
chaudron (c.)
chetvert (R.)
cubic ton
distance
division
elephant (pap.)
foolscap (pap.)
freezing
half hour
half inch
half mile
hogshead (liq.)
imperial (pap.)
infinity
kassabah (E.)
kilogram
kilowatt (elec.)
kincatty (Ch.)
metrical
mutchkin (liq.)
parasang (Iran)
plateful
puncheon (liq.)
roentgen
quantity
quartern (b.)
ship-load (c.)
short ton (C. and U.S.)
spoonful
toll dish
tonelada (A.)
yardwand
zolotnik (R.)

9

altimetry
amplitude
areometry
bisegment
cubic foot
cubic inch
cubic yard
cuartilla (A.)
decalitre (SI)
decametre (SI)
decilitre (SI)
decimetre (SI)
decistere (F.)

dekalitre (SI)
dekametre (SI)
dimension
foot-pound
half ounce
half pound
hectogram (SI)
isometric
kilocycle
kilohertz (elec.)
kilolitre (SI)
kilometre (SI)
large sack (c.)
light year
long dozen
megacycle
megahertz (elec.)
metric ton
milestone
milligram (SI)
nanometre (SI)
net weight
quadruple
quarterly
quintuple
sea league
three-fold
yardstick

10

barleycorn
barrel-bulk
centesimal
centigrade
centilitre (SI)
centimetre (SI)
centistere (F.)
cubic metre (SI)
dead-weight
decagramme (SI)
decigramme (SI)
dessiatine (R.)
dessyatine (R.)
double-demy (pap.)
double-post (pap.)
dry measure
eighth-part
Fahrenheit
fifty-fifty

fluid ounce
hectolitre (SI)
hectometre (SI)
kilogramme (SI)
lunar month
microfarad (elec.)
millesimal
millilitre (SI)
millimetre (SI)
millionary
quadrantal (Rom.)
square foot
square inch
square mile
square yard
super-royal (pap.)
tripartite
tron weight
troy weight

11

avoirdupois
baker's dozen
centigramme (SI)
day's journey
double-crown (pap.)
double-royal (pap.)
equibalance
equidistant
fluid drachm
half and half
hand-breadth
heavyweight
hectogramme (SI)
imperial-cap (pap.)
long hundred
  (eggs and f.)
long measure
milligramme (SI)
pennyweight
shipping ton
short weight
square metre (SI)
tape-measure
thermal unit
thermometer
trone weight
two-foot rule
wine measure
yard measure

12

angström unit
areometrical
auncel weight
bantam-weight
boiling point
cable's length
cubic measure
eleventh part
equidistance
great hundred
hair's breadth
half-quartern
measured mile
metric system
printer's ream (pap.)
quantitative
quartern loaf (b.)
Réaumur scale
water measure

13

calendar month
decimal system
feather-weight
freezing point
hundredweight
hypermetrical
inside measure
linear measure
medicine glass
square measure
three-foot rule

14

cubic decimetre (SI)
double-foolscap (pap.)
double-imperial (pap.)
outside measure
zenith distance

15

centigrade scale
cubic centimetre (SI)
square decimetre (SI)

NATURAL HISTORY   (1) LIVING CREATURES
Animals

2 AND 3

ai
ape
ass
bat
bok
cat
cob
cow
cub
cur
dam
doe
dog
dso

dzo
elk
ewe
fox
gib
gnu
goa
hog
kid
kob
ky
man
nag
ox
pad
pig

ram
rat
roe
sai
seg
sow
tat
teg
tit
tod
tup
ure
wat
yak
zho
zo

4

alce
anoa
atoc
atok
barb
bear
boar
buck
bull
cain
calf
cavy
colt
cony

coon
dauw
deer
dieb
dood
douc
eyra
fawn
foal
gaur
girl
goat
gyal
hack
hare
hart
hind
ibex
jade
joey
jomo
kine
koba
kudu
lamb
lion
lynx
maki
mare
mice
mico
mink
moco
mohr
moke
mole
mule
mona
musk
napu
neat
nout
nowt
oryx
oxen
paca
paco
pala
pard
peba
pika
poka
pony
pudu
puma
quey
rane
reem
roan
runt
rusa
saki
seal
seeg
shou
skug
sore
stag
stot
suni
tahr
tegg
topi
unau
urus
urva

vari
vole
wolf
zebu
zobo
zuna

5

addax
aguti
alces
ammon
ariel
arnee
beast
bhyle
bidet
biped
bison
bitch
bongo
brach
brock
bruin
burro
camel
caple
capra
capul
chiru
civet
coati
coney
coypu
crone
cuddy
daman
dhole
dingo
dipus
drill
dsomo
eland
equus
fauna
felis
filly
fitch
gayal
genet
goral
grice
grise
gyall
harpy
hinny
horse
hound
hutia
hyena
hyrax
indri
inuus
izard
jocko
jumbo
kaama
kalan
kevel
koala
kyloe
lemur
llama

loris
magot
major
manis
manul
maral
meles
moose
morse
mouse
nandu
nyala
okapi
oribi
otary
otter
ounce
panda
pekan
phoca
pongo
potto
poyou
punch
puppy
ranny
rasse
ratel
royal
sable
saiga
sajou
sasin
screw
serow
sheep
shoat
shrew
simia
skunk
sloth
sorel
sorex
spade
spado
spitz
staig
steed
steer
stirk
stoat
swine
tabby
talpa
tapir
tatou
taxel
tayra
tiger
tucan
urial
urson
ursus
vison
vixen
waler
whale
whelp
yapok
zebra
zerda
zibet
zizel
zoril
zorra
zorro

6

agouti
aliped
alpaca
angola
angora
argali
aye-aye
baboon
badger
bandar
barrow
bawsin
bawson
bayard
beaver
beeves
bovine
bronco
brumby
burhel
cabiai
castor
cattle
cayman
cayuse
cervus
chacma
chetah
coaiti
cosset
cougar
coyote
craber
dassie
desman
dickey
dik-dik
dobbin
dog fox
donkey
dragon
dzeren
dzeron
ermine
farrow
fennec
ferret
fisher
fox bat
galago
garran
garron
gavial
gerbil
gibbon
ginnet
gopher
grison
grivet
guemal
guenon
hacker
halfer
hangul
heifer
hircus
hogget
howler
hybrid
impala
jackal
jaguar
jennet
jerboa

jument
kalong
kelpie
keltie
kitten
koodoo
kyloes
langur
lechwe
lionel
malkin
mammal
margay
marmot
marten
mawkin
merino
messin
monkey
morkin
musk ox
musmon
mustac
nahoor
nilgai
ocelet
onager
oorial
ovibos
pallah
panter
porker
possum
pygarg
python
quagga
quokka
rabbit
racoon
red fox
reebok
renard
rhebok
rhesus
roarer
rodent
ronion
sajoin
sambar
sambur
sarlac
sarlyk
sea-ape
sea cow
serval
shammy
shelty
sorrel
sponge
suslik
taguan
tajacu
talbot
taurec
tapeti
tarpan
teledu
tenrec
thamin
theave
tomeat
tupala
vermin
vervet
vicuna
walrus

wapiti
warine
weasel
weeper
wether
wivern
wombat
wow-wow
wyvern
yapock

7

acouchy
ant-bear
assapan
aurochs
banting
bettong
bighorn
blesbok
blue cat
bonasus
boshbop
Bovidae
brawner
brocket
broncho
bubalis
buffalo
bulchin
bullock
bushcat
bush pig
caracal
caribou
cervine
cetacea
chamois
cheetah
cheslip
cheviot
chikari
chimera
chincha
clumber
colobus
courser
dasypus
dasyure
dolphin
draft-ox
eanling
Echidna
echimyd
epizoan
epizoon
ermelin
fatling
finback
fitchet
fitchew
foumart
fur seal
galla ox
gazelle
gelding
gemsbok
genette
giraffe
glutton
gorilla
grampus
griffin
griffon

grizzly
guanaco
hackney
hamster
huanaco
hystrix
jacchus
jackass
jumbuck
karagan
keitloa
kidling
klipdas
lagomys
lambkin
lemming
leopard
leveret
libbard
linsang
lioness
macacus
macaque
madoqua
mammoth
manatee
mangaby
Manx cat
maracan
marikin
mariput
markhor
marmose
megamys
meerkat
minever
miniver
mole-rat
mongrel
monture
morling
mormops
moschus
mouflon
muntjak
musiman
musk rat
mustang
mustela
mycetes
mycetis
mylodon
narwhal
nasalis
noctule
nylghau
opossum
palfrey
panther
pardale
peccary
polecat
potoroo
pricket
primate
procyon
pterope
raccoon
red deer
reed rat
rietbok
rock doe
roe deer
rorqual
sagouin
saimiri

sambhur
sapajou
sapling
sassaby
sciurus
scorpio
sea-bear
sea-lion
serpent
sheltie
siamang
soliped
sondeli
sounder
souslik
spitter
sumpter
tadpole
tamanoa
tamarin
tarsier
tatouay
thiller
tigress
toxodon
twinter
unicorn
urocyon
vampire
vansire
vicuana
viverra
wallaby
wart-hog
wheeler
wild cat
wild dog
wistiti
zamouse
zorille

8

aardvark
aardwolf
anteater
antelope
babirusa
bathorse
behemoth
black fox
black rat
bontebok
brant fox
brown rat
bull-calf
bushbaby
bushbuck
cachalot
cacholot
capuchin
capucine
capybara
cavicorn
chimaera
chipmuck
chipmunk
civet-cat
colocola
cotswold
cricetus
demi-wolf
dinosaur
dormouse
duckbill

elephant
entellus
filander
galloway
gin-horse
grysbock
hedgehog
hedgepig
hoggerel
hog steer
hylobate
indigene
kangaroo
kinkajou
kolinsky
lamantin
lamentin
macropus
mammalia
mandrill
mangabey
mantiger
marmoset
mastodon
meriones
milch-cow
mongoose
moufflon
musk deer
musquash
packmule
pangolin
physeter
platypus
polliwig
pollywog
polo pony
porkling
porpoise
red panda
reedbuck
reindeer
Rodentia
ruminant
sea-otter
serotine
sewer-rat
shorling
sika deer
sirenian
springer
squirrel
staggard
stallion
stinkard
suilline
suricate
surmulot
tabby-cat
talapoin
tiger cat
tortoise
twinling
ungulata
viscacha
wallaroo
wanderoo
war-horse
warrigal
water-hog
water-rat
weanling
wild boar
wild goat
yeanling
yearling

9

adelopode
alligator
amphioxus
amphipoda
Angola cat
annellata
anthobian
arctic fox
armadillo
bandicoot
barbastel
batrachia
bay-duiker
bezantler
black bear
black buck
blue whale
brood-mare
brown bear
carnivore
carpincho
cart-horse
catamount
chameleon
chickadee
chickaree
coalmouse
colemouse
commensal
deermouse
delundung
dicotyles
didelphys
dinoceras
draught-ox
dray-horse
dromedary
dziggetai
eared seal
flying fox
glyptodon
grimalkin
ground-hog
gruntling
guineapig
honey-bear
ichneumon
lagomorph
leviathan
malt-horse
marsupial
megalonyx
monoceros
monotreme
mousedeer
orang-utan
pachyderm
pack-horse
pademelon
padymelon
percheron
petaurist
phalanger
pipistrel
polar bear
porcupine
post-horse
predacean
prong-buck
prong-horn
quadruman
quadruped
racehorse
rearmouse

reermouse
reremouse
rosmarine
shearling
shoreling
shrew-mole
silver fox
sitatunga
southdown
spatangus
springbok
steerling
stonebuck
stud-horse
tchneuman
thylacine
todlowrie
tree hyrax
tree shrew
trematode
trematoid
waterbuck
watervole
white bear
wild horse
wolverene
wolverine
woodchuck
woodshock
youngling
zoophagon

10

amorphozoa
amphibials
angora goat
angwantibo
animalcule
anthropoid
articulata
babiroussa
barasingha
Barbary ape
birch mouse
buckjumper
camelopard
cardophagi
catarrhine
chevrotain
chimpanzee
chinchilla
chiroptera
chousingha
coach-horse
cockatrice
cottontail
Diphyodont
dolichotis
draft-horse
fallow deer
fieldmouse
fistulidae
giant panda
halmaturus
hartebeest
hippogriff
hippogryff
housemouse
human-being
Kodiak bear
Malay tapir
marsupials
monotremes
muscardine

musk beaver
natterjack
paddymelon
Persian cat
pichiciago
pilot whale
pine marten
prairie dog
pygmy shrew
quadricorn
quadrumana
raccoon dog
rhinoceros
right whale
river horse
rock badger
rock rabbit
ruminantia
saki monkey
scavernick
shrew-mouse
starveling
Thecodonts
vampire bat
vespertilio
wildebeest
.. wishtonwish
woolly lemur

11

American elk
anoplothere
barbastelle
black cattle
blood-sucker
branchireme
brown hyena
chlamyphore
digitigrade
douroucouli
entomophaga
fistulidans
flying lemur
flying mouse
fox squirrel
Grevy's zebra
grizzly-bear
horned-horse
insectivora
jumping deer
kangaroo rat
killer whale
Megatherium
mountain cat
orang-outang
pipistrelle
prairie wolf
Pterodactyl
red kangaroo
red squirrel
rock wallaby
sea elephant
snow leopard

12

anthropoglot
Barbary sheep
Bengal monkey
catamountain
chlamyphorus
chrysochlore
draught-horse

195

elephant seal
ferae-naturae
flittermouse
grey squirrel
harvest mouse
hippopotamus
horseshoe bat
klipspringer
Megalosaurus
mountain hare
mountain lion
pachydermata
Paleotherium
pouched mouse
rhesus monkey
rock squirrel
scheltopusik
Shetland pony
spider monkey
spotted hyena
striped hyena

tree kangaroo
water opossum
woolly monkey

13

Abyssinian cat
Anoplotherium
Australian cat
Bactrian camel
bearded lizard
carriage horse
Chapman's zebra
Cheirotherium
chinchilla cat
European bison
galeopithecus
golden hamster
hermaphrodite
Indian buffalo

laughing hyena
mountain zebra
Parry's wallaby
polyprotodont
ring-tail coati
sable antelope
semnopithecus
shorthorn bull
solidungulate
spiny anteater
Tasmanian wolf
tree porcupine

14

Australian bear
bridled wallaby
Burchell's zebra
crab-eating seal
dormouse-possum

flying squirrel
Indian elephant
Indian pangolin
Isabelline bear
laughing hyaena
marmoset monkey
Patagonian cavy
snoeshoe rabbit
Tasmanian devil

15

African elephant
American buffalo
Bennett's wallaby
flying phalanger
rabbit bandicoot
sabretooth tiger
Tasmanian possum
Thomson's gazelle

Birds

2 AND 3

auk
cob
daw
emu
fum
hen
jay
ka
kae
kea
kia
mew
moa
owl
pen
pie
poe
roc
ruc
tit
tui

4

alca
anas
arco
aves
barb
baya
bird
bubo
chat
cock
coot
crax
crow
dodo
dove
duck
erne
eyas
fowl
gawk
gier

guan
gull
hawk
hern
huia
ibis
kaka
kite
kiwi
knot
koel
lark
loom
loon
lory
mina
myna
naff
nias
nyas
pauw
pavo
pern
pica
piet
pope
pout
rail
rhea
rixy
rock
rook
ruff
rukh
runt
rype
shag
skua
smee
smew
sora
sore
swan
taha
teal
tern
tody
wavy

wren
xema
yaup
yunx
zati

5

agami
ajuru
amsel
amzel
ardea
biddy
bongo
booby
bowet
brant
bucco
capon
chick
claik
colin
crake
crane
creak
daker
didus
diver
drake
dunny
eagle
egret
eider
finch
galah
ganza
glede
goose
grebe
harpy
heron
hobby
jager
junco
larus
lowan

lyrie
macaw
madge
mavis
merle
minah
miner
monal
murre
mynah
nandu
noddy
ornis
ortyx
ousel
ouzel
owlet
pewet
pewit
picus
pipit
pitta
poult
purre
quail
radge
raven
reeve
robin
rodge
sacre
saker
sally
sasia
saury
scape
scarf
scaup
scray
senex
serin
shama
sitta
skite
snipe
solan
soree
spink

stare
stilt
stint
stork
strix
swift
tarin
terek
topau
topet
twite
umbre
urubu
veery
virgo
wader
wagel
whaup
wonga

6

aiglet
aigret
alcedo
alcyon
avocet
avoset
babbler
bantam
barbet
bonxie
bowess
brolga
buffel
bulbul
cagmag
canary
chough
chukar
citril
condor
corbie
corvus
coucal
cuckoo
culver
curlew
cushat
cygnet
cygnus
darter
dipper
drongo
ducker
dunlin
eaglet
einack
elanet
falcon
fulmar
galeen
gambet
gander
gannet
garrot
gentoo
godurt
godwit
gorhen
grakle
grouse
hacket
hagden
hareld

hoazin
hoopoe
hoopoo
jabiru
jacana
jaeger
jerkin
kakapo
kiddow
lanner
leipoa
linnet
loriot
magpie
marrot
martin
menura
merlin
merops
merula
missel
monaul
mopoke
mot-mot
musket
nandow
nestor
oriole
osprey
oxbird
parrot
paster
pavone
peahen
pecker
peewit
pernis
petrel
pigeon
plover
poulet
pouter
powter
puffin
pullet
pygarg
queest
quelea
redcap
reeler
roberd
roller
rotche
ruddoc
scobby
scoter
sea-bar
sea-cob
sea-mew
sea-pie
shrike
shrite
sicsac
siskin
smeath
strich
strick
sultan
tarsel
tercel
thrush
tirwit
tomtit
toucan
towhee
tringa

turbit
Turdus
turkey
turner
turtle
waggel
weaver
wigeon
willet
witwal
yaffle
ynambu
zivola
zoozoo

7

apteryx
attagas
attagen
awl-bird
babbler
barn owl
bee-bird
bittern
blue-cap
bluetit
buceros
bull-bat
bummalo
bunting
buphaga
bustard
buzzard
cackler
caponet
cariama
carvist
cat-bird
cheeper
chewink
chicken
ciconia
coaltit
coarser
cobswan
colibri
columba
corella
cotinga
courlan
cow-bird
creeper
cropper
Cuculus
dorhawk
dorking
dottrel
doucher
dovekie
dovelet
dum-bird
dunnock
egg-bird
emu-wren
fantail
fen duck
fern owl
fig-bird
fin-foot
flusher
gadwell
gavilan
gobbler
gorcock

gorcrow
goshawk
gosling
grackle
grallae
greylag
hacket
halcyon
harfang
harrier
hawk owl
hen-harm
hickway
hoatzin
horn owl
ice-bird
impeyan
jacamar
jackass
jackdaw
jacksaw
jacobin
jashawk
jedcock
kamichi
kestrel
killdee
kinglet
lagopus
lapwing
lavrock
Leghorn
lentner
lich-owl
lorilet
mallard
manakin
manikin
marabou
maracan
martlet
megamys
migrant
modwall
moorhen
motacil
moth-owl
mudlark
muggent
ortolan
oscines
ostrich
oven-tit
pandion
partlet
peacock
peafowl
pelican
penguin
percher
peterel
phaeton
phoenix
pinnock
pintado
pintail
pochard
poe-bird
poultry
puttock
quabird
quetzel
raddock
rantock
redhead
redpoll

197

redwing
robinet
rooster
rosella
rotchie
ruddock
sakenet
sawbill
scammel
scooper
sea-crow
sea-fowl
seagull
sea-hawk
senegal
seriema
serinus
shirley
simargh
sirgang
skimmer
skylark
snow-owl
sparrow
squacco
staniel
stannel
stanyel
stumpie
sturnus
sunbird
swallow
swimmer
tadorna
tanager
tarrock
tiercel
tinamou
tinamus
titlark
titling
touraco
tree tit
trochil
tumbler
turakoo
vulture
vulturn
wagtail
wapacut
warbler
waxbill
waxwing
weebill
whooper
widgeon
wimbrel
witlock
witwall
wood owl
wrybill
wryneck
yeldrin

8

accentor
aigrette
alcatras
amadavat
arapunga
avadavit
beam-bird
becafico
bee-eater

bell-bird
blackcap
bluebird
blue-wren
boat-bill
boat-tail
bobolink
bob-white
bockelet
bockeret
brancher
brevipen
bush chat
bush lark
calandra
calangay
caneroma
caracara
cargoose
clot-bird
cockatoo
cockerel
coquimbo
corn bird
curassow
cursores
cutwater
dabchick
daker-hen
dandy-hen
didapper
dinornis
dipchick
dorr-hawk
dotterel
duck-hawk
duckling
dun-diver
eagle-owl
estridge
fauvette
fig-eater
finnikin
firetail
fish-hawk
flamingo
flycatcher
gairfowl
gamecock
gang-gang
garefowl
garganey
great tit
grey teal
grosbeak
guachero
hawfinch
hazel-hen
hemipode
hernshaw
hickwall
hornbill
hula-bird
keskidee
killdeer
kingbird
landrail
langshan
lanneret
laverock
lorikeet
love-bird
lyrebird
marabout
marsh tit
megapode

mina bird
mire crow
moorcock
moorfowl
moorgame
morillon
musk duck
mute swan
mynabird
nestling
nightjar
notornis
nuthatch
paitrick
parakeet
paroquet
peachick
petchary
pheasant
plungeon
popinjay
puff-bird
redshank
redstart
ring dove
ring-tail
rock dove
screamer
scrub-tit
sea-eagle
shelduck
shoebill
shoveler
sittella
snowy owl
songbird
songlark
songster
starling
struthio
swamphen
tanagers
tantalus
tawny owl
thrasher
thresher
throstle
titmouse
tomnoddy
tragopan
tuke-nose
umbrette
waterhen
wheatear
whimbrel
whinchat
whip-bird
whistler
white-ear
white-eye
wildfowl
woodchat
woodcock
wood duck
woodlark
xanthura
yeldring
yeldrock
yoldring
zopilote

9

accipiter
albatross

andorinha
ant-thrush
autophagi
bean goose
beccafico
bell-minah
bergander
birgander
blackbird
black cock
black duck
black swan
blacktail
black tern
blue crane
bower-bird
brambling
broadbill
brown hawk
bullfinch
buzzardet
campanero
cassowary
cereopsis
chaffinch
chatterer
chevalier
chickling
church owl
cockatiel
columbine
cormorant
corncrake
crossbill
dandy-cock
deinornis
dowitcher
eagle-hawk
eider duck
field-duck
fieldfare
field wren
fig parrot
figpecker
firecrest
francolin
French pie
friar-bird
fringilla
frogmouth
gallinule
gerfalcon
gier-eagle
glaucopis
goldcrest
golden-eye
goldfinch
goldspink
goosander
grassbird
grass wren
great skua
grey heron
grossbeak
guillemot
guinea-hen
gyrfalcon
heathbird
heathcock
heronshaw
horned owl
Jenny-wren
jerfalcon
kittiwake
lint-white
log-runner

lorrikeet
macartney
mallemuck
mango bird
marshbird
merganser
merulidan
mouse-hawk
mud-sucker
muscicapa
natatores
night hawk
ossifrage
paradisea
paraquito
pardalote
parrakeet
parroquet
partridge
peregrine
phalarope
pied-goose
ptarmigan
quachilto
razorbill
redbreast
red grouse
rhynchops
rifle-bird
ring-ousel
rosefinch
rossignol
sandpiper
scratcher
scrub-bird
scrub-fowl
scrub-wren
shearbill
sheldrake
shitepoke
shoveller
shrike-tit
silver-eye
skunk-bird
snake-bird
snow goose
sooty tern
spinebill
spoonbill
stick-bird
stilt-bird
stock-dove
stonechat
stone-hawk
storm-bird
strigidae
swamp-hawk
swine-pipe
talegalla
tetraonid
thickhead
thornbill
tiercelet
trochilus
trumpeter
turnstone
waterbird
waterfowl
water-rail
wedgebill
wheat-bird
whiteface
whitetail
widow-bird
wild goose
willow tit

windhover
woodspite
wyandotte

10

aberdevine
ant-catcher
Arctic skua
Arctic tern
bell-magpie
bird of prey
blight-bird
blue-bonnet
blue-breast
blue-throat
boobook owl
brent goose
budgerigar
budgerygah
burrow-duck
butter-bird
butterbump
canary bird
canvas-back
chiffchaff
coddy-moddy
cow-bunting
crested tit
crow-shrike
demoiselle
didunculus
dishwasher
dollar bird
dusky minah
dusky robin
ember goose
eurylaimus
eyas-musket
fledgeling
flycatcher
fratercula
goatmilker
goatsucker
goldhammer
grassfinch
greenfinch
greenshank
grey falcon
grey parrot
grey plover
ground dove
ground lark
ground robin
guinea-fowl
gymnocitta
hen-harrier
honeyeater
honey-guide
hooded crow
jungle-fowl
kingfisher
king parrot
kookaburra
love-parrot
magpie-lark
mallee-fowl
maned-goose
meadow-lark
mutton-bird
night heron
night raven
noisy-minah
nutcracker
parson-bird

peewee-lark
petty-chaps
pratincole
ramphastos
regent-bird
rock parrot
rock pigeon
salpinctes
sanderling
sandgrouse
sandmartin
sassorolla
screech-owl
sea-swallow
shearwater
silver-gull
solan goose
song shrike
song thrush
summer-duck
tailor-bird
talegallus
tit-warbler
tree-runner
tropic-bird
turkey-cock
turtle dove
water-ousel
wattle-bird
weasel-coat
whidah-bird
white brant
white egret
white stork
whydah-bird
willow wren
wonga-wonga
woodgrouse
woodpecker
wood-pigeon
wood-shrike
yaffingale
yellow-bird
yellowlegs
zebra finch

11

apostle-bird
banded stilt
black falcon
black martin
bonebreaker
bristle-bird
brush-turkey
bush-creeper
butcher-bird
Canada goose
carrion crow
cattle egret
chanticleer
cock-sparrow
conirostres
corn bunting
Dorking fowl
dragoon-bird
fairy martin
fallow finch
flock pigeon
frigate-bird
fruit-pigeon
gallows-bird
gnat-snapper
golden eagle
grallatores

grey wagtail
harrier-hawk
herring gull
hooded robin
house martin
humming-bird
insectivora
kestrel-hawk
king penguin
lammergeier
leatherhead
leptodactyl
lily-trotter
magpie-goose
meadow-pipit
mocking-bird
mulga parrot
Muscovy duck
nightingale
Pacific gull
plain-turkey
powerful-fowl
procellaria
pterodactyl
punchinello
quail-thrush
querguedule
rainbow-bird
reed bunting
reed warbler
rock warbler
scarlet ibis
scissor-bill
sea-pheasant
shell-parrot
shrike-robin
singing-bird
snow-bunting
soldier-bird
sparrowhawk
stone curlew
stone plover
storm petrel
tree-creeper
tree sparrow
tree swallow
wall-creeper
whitethroat
whooper swan
wood-swallow
yellow robin

12

Adele penguin
adjutant bird
burrowing-owl
capercaillie
cardinal-bird
crested grebe
cuckoo-shrike
curvirostral
dentirostres
falcon-gentle
fairy penguin
fissirostres
golden oriole
golden plover
grass warbler
ground thrush
hedge sparrow
honey-buzzard
house sparrow
marsh harrier
marsh warbler

199

missel-thrush
mistel-thrush
mourning-dove
musophagidae
nutmeg-pigeon
painted quail
pallid-cuckoo
peaceful dove
pink cockatoo
razor-grinder
red-head finch
sage-thrasher
sedge warbler
shrike-thrush
stone-chatter
stone's-mickle
stormy petrel
stubble-goose
stubble-quail
swamp-harrier

tachydromian
tenuirosters
tiger-bittern
turbit-pigeon
turner-pigeon
water-wagtail
white goshawk
yellowhammer

13

Baltimore bird
barnacle goose
black cockatoo
carrier pigeon
coachwhip-bird
crested pigeon
fantail pigeon

long-tailed tit
mistletoe-bird
musk parrakeet
owlet-nightjar
oystercatcher
plain-wanderer
recurviroster
red-wattle bird
rosella parrot
secretary bird
shining parrot
spider-catcher
stink-pheasant
swallow-shrike
tumbler-pigeon
turkey-buzzard
white cockatoo
willow warbler
yellow bunting
yellow wagtail

14

babbling thrush
bird of paradise
canvas-back duck
diamond sparrow
double-bar finch
golden pheasant
horned screamer
king-lory parrot
Manx shearwater
mountain thrush
nankeen kestrel
rhinoceros-bird
robin-redbreast
silver pheasant
spotted harrier
tawny frogmouth
welcome swallow
whistling eagle

Dogs

3 AND 4

chow
cur
lym
minx
peke
pom
pug
pup
rach
rug
tike
tyke

5

bitch
boxer
brach
cairn
corgi
dhole
dingo
hound
husky
laika
pi-dog
pooch
puppy
spitz
whelp

6

bandog
barbet
basset
beagle
borzoi
canine
cocker
collie
Eskimo
gun-dog
jowler
lap-dog
limmer

pariah
poodle
pug-dog
pye-dog
pyrame
ranger
ratter
saluki
setter
shough
talbot
toy dog

7

beardie
bird-dog
bulldog
clumber
deer-dog
dry-foot
griffon
harrier
lion-dog
lurcher
mastiff
mongrel
pointer
samoyed
spaniel
starter
tarrier
terrier
tumbler
whippet
wolf-dog

8

Airedale
Alsatian
Blenheim
chow-chow
coach-dog
demi-wolf
Derby dog
Doberman
elkhound

field-dog
foxhound
hound-dog
house dog
keeshond
Labrador
papillon
Pekinese
St. Hubert
sealyham
sheepdog
spitz dog
springer
turnspit
watchdog
water-dog

9

badger dog
boarhound
buckhound
chihuahua
dachshund
Dalmatian
deerhound
Eskimo dog
Great Dane
greyhound
harehound
Kerry blue
limehound
Llewellyn
Molossian
Pekingese
police dog
red setter
retriever
St. Bernard
Schnauzer
staghound
wolfhound
yellow dog

10

Bedlington
bloodhound

Clydesdale
dachshound
elterwater
fox terrier
Iceland dog
Maltese dog
otter hound
Pomeranian
prairie dog
schipperke
Welsh corgi
Welsh hound

11

Afghan hound
basset hound
Bruxelloise
bull mastiff
bull terrier
carriage dog
Irish setter
Kerry beagle
King Charles
Skye terrier

12

Belvoir hound
Cairn terrier
Dandy Dinmont
gazelle hound
German collie
Gordon setter
Irish spaniel
Irish terrier
Newfoundland
Saint Bernard
Saintongeois
shepherd's dog
water spaniel
Welsh terrier

13

Alpine spaniel
border terrier

Boston terrier	**14** AND **15**	Egyptian bassett (15)	Norfolk springer (15)
cocker spaniel		English springer (15)	porcelaine hound (15)
Dandie Dinmont	Aberdeen terrier (15)	golden retriever (15)	Pyrenean mastiff (15)
English setter	Airedale terrier (15)	Highland terrier (15)	Scottish terrier (15)
French bulldog	blue Gascon hound (15)	Irish wolfhound (14)	Siberian wolf-dog (15)
Scotch terrier	Brussels griffon (15)	Japanese spaniel (15)	springer spaniel (15)
southern hound	clumber spaniel (14)	Lakeland terrier (15)	Thibetan mastiff (15)
Sussex spaniel	Cuban bloodhound (15)	Norfolk spaniel (14)	Tibetan mastiff (14)

Fish, etc.

2–4

amia	quab	nurse	bowfin
bass	ray	perch	braise
bib	roe	phoca	buckie
blay	rudd	piper	burbot
bley	ruff	pogge	caplin
bret	sapo	porgy	caranx
brit	scad	poulp	cepola
burt	scar	powan	cheven
cale	scup	prawn	chevin
carp	shad	reeve	clupea
chad	snig	roach	cockle
char	sole	roker	comber
chub	tai	ruffe	conger
clam	tau	saith	cultch
cod	tope	salmo	cuttle
coho	tuna	saury	dagoba
crab	tusk	scrod	dentex
cusk	zant	scurf	diodon
dab		sepia	doctor
dace		sewin	dugong
dar	**5**	shark	dun-cow
dare		skate	ellops
dart	ablen	smelt	finnan
dorn	ablet	smolt	gadoid
dory	allis	smout	ganoid
eel	angel	smowt	gardon
eft	apode	snook	ginkin
elva	banny	solen	goramy
esox	beroe	sprag	grilse
fash	binny	sprat	groper
file	bleak	sprod	gunnel
fin	bleck	squid	gurnet
gar	bogue	sudak	hilsah
ged	boops	sweep	hussar
goby	bream	tench	isopod
grig	brill	toado	jerkin
hake	charr	togue	kipper
huck	cisco	torsk	launce
huso	cobia	troll	loligo
id	cuddy	trout	margot
ide	cudle	tunny	meagre
jack	doree	twait	medusa
kelt	dorse	whale	megrim
keta	elops	whelk	milter
ling	fleck	whiff	minnow
lipp	fusus	witch	morgay
lomp	gadus		mud-eel
luce	gibel		mullet
mago	gummy	**6**	mussel
mort	guppy		narwal
newt	julis	alburn	otaria
opah	loach	alevin	oyster
orc	loche	allice	partan
orca	maray	anabas	plaice
orfe	minim	barbel	pollan
parr	moray	beakie	porgie
peal	morse	belone	poulpe
pike	mugil	beluga	puffer
pope	muray	blenny	puller
pout	murry	blower	quahog
	mysis	bonito	redcap
	myxon	bounce	red-cod

red-eye
remora
robalo
rochet
romero
roughy
ruffin
runner
sabalo
sadina
saithe
salmon
samlet
sander
sardel
sauger
saurel
saynay
scarus
scurff
sea-ape
sea-bat
sea-cow
sea-dog
sea-egg
sea-fox
sea-hog
sea-owl
sea-pad
sea-pig
sephen
shanny
shiner
shrimp
snacol
soosoo
sucker
tailor
tarpon
tarpum
tautog
tawtog
tiburo
tomcord
trygon
turbit
turbot
twaite
ulican
urchin
vendis
wapper
weever
whaler
winkle
wirrah
wrasse
zander
zeidae
zingel

7

abalone
acaleph
actinia
ale-wife
anchovy
asterid
batfish
bergylt
bloater
blue-cap
blue-eye
bocking

bonetta
box-fish
brassie
bubbler
bummalo
calamar
capelin
cat-fish
catodon
cetacea
cichlid
cidaris
cod-fish
codling
cow-fish
crabite
croaker
crucian
crusien
cyprine
dog-fish
dolphin
drummer
dun-fish
echinus
eel-fare
eel-pout
escolar
fiddler
fin-back
fin-fish
garfish
garpike
garvock
girrock
gladius
goldney
gourami
gournet
grampus
grouper
grundel
grunter
gudgeon
gunard
gwiniad
gwyniad
haddock
halibut
herling
herring
homelyn
houting
jewfish
keeling
lampern
lamprey
latchet
lobster
long-tom
mahseer
manatee
manchet
merling
monodon
moon-egg
morwong
mud-fish
muraena
murexes
murices
narwhal
nautili
oar-fish
octopus
old-wife

pandore
pegasus
pen-fish
pig-fish
pointer
pollack
pollard
pollock
polypus
pomfret
quinnet
rat-tail
red-fish
reef-eel
ripsack
rock-cod
ronchil
ronquil
rorqual
sand-eel
sardine
sawfish
schelly
scomber
sea-bear
sea-calf
sea-fish
sea-lion
sea-pike
sea-wolf
shadine
silurus
skegger
smerlin
snapper
sock-eye
spawner
sphyrna
squalus
sterlet
stripey
sun-fish
thwaite
tiddler
top-knot
torgoch
torpedo
tub-fish
ulichon
umbrine
vendace
whiting
worm-eel
xippias

8

acalepha
albacore
albicore
ammodyte
anableps
anguilla
asterias
band-fish
barnacle
bill fish
blue fish
boarfish
bullhead
cachalot
cackerel
calamory
cetacean
coalfish

corystes
crawfish
crayfish
dapedium
dapedius
dragonet
drum-fish
eagle-ray
errantes
eulachon
exocetus
file-fish
fin-scale
fire-fish
flagtail
flatfish
flathead
flounder
forktail
fox-shark
frog-fish
gillaroo
gilt-head
glass-eel
goatfish
goldfish
graining
grayling
green eel
grub-fish
gymnotus
hair-tail
halicore
hand-fish
horn-beak
horn-fish
jentling
John Dory
jugulars
kelp-fish
king crab
king-fish
lady-fish
lancelet
land crab
lump-fish
lung-fish
mackerel
melanure
menhaden
moon-fish
moray eel
mormyrus
nannygai
numbfish
ophidion
pickerel
pigmy-eel
pilchard
pipe-fish
polyneme
Poor John
porpoise
raft-fish
red perch
rock-cale
rock-fish
rockling
sail-fish
salt-fish
sand-fish
sardelle
saw-shark
sea-devil
sea-horse
sea-perch

sea robin
shore-eel
siskiwit
snake-eel
sparling
spelding
speldrin
speldron
spirling
springer
spurling
starfish
sting-ray
sturgeon
sun-bream
surf-fish
tarwhine
teraglin
testacea
thornbut
thrasher
thresher
toad-fish
trevalla
troutlet
tusk-fish
water-fox
weed-fish
wolf-fish

9

acalephae
acipenser
angel-fish
Argentine
ascidians
asteroida
barracuda
blackfish
black sole
blue nurse
blue shark
blue sprat
bony bream
bulltrout
bummaloti
calamarys
chaetodon
cling-fish
cole-perch
conger eel
coral fish
coryphene
cover-clip
crampfish
crustacea
devil fish
dolphinet
echinidan
engraulis
finny-scad
fire-flair
fish-royal
fortesque
frost-fish
globe-fish
golomynka
grey nurse
hard-belly
hardyhead
hippodame
houndfish
hybodonts
jaculator

jellyfish
John Dorée
jollytail
kingstone
mango fish
menominee
murray cod
pilot fish
porbeagle
pyllopodo
razor fish
red mullet
river crab
roundhead
sand-lance
saury-pike
schnapper
sea-mullet
sea-needle
sea-nettle
sea-urchin
sheat-fish
silver-eel
spear-fish
stargazer
stingaree
sting-fish
stink-fish
stockfish
stomapoda
suctorian
surmullet
sweetlips
swordfish
thorn-back
threadfin
tittlebat
troutling
trumpeter
tunny fish
whitebait
whitefish
wobbegong

10

amblyopsis
amphytrite
angel-shark
angler fish
banstickle
barracoota
barracouta
basket fish
black bream
black whale
blind shark
blue groper
blue puller
bottle-nose
brown trout
butterfish
cestracion
clouded eel
clypeaster
cock-paddle
coelacanth
cowanyoung
ctenoidans
cuttlefish
demoiselle
dragon-fish
echinoderm
fiddle-fish
fingerling

fistularia
flute-mouth
flying fish
ganoidians
garter fish
ghost-shark
giant toado
goblin-fish
great skate
grey mullet
groundling
hammerhead
hermit crab
holothuria
knight-fish
loggerhead
lumpsucker
mirror dory
morris pike
Moses perch
parrot-fish
pearl perch
periwinkle
pigmy perch
pycnodonts
rapier fish
red gurnard
red morwong
red rockcod
ribbon-fish
rudder-fish
Samsonfish
sand-hopper
sand-mullet
sandy sprat
sea-garfish
sea-leopard
sea poacher
sea-unicorn
silver dory
silverfish
silverside
sperm whale
square-tail
sturionian
sucker-fish
tailor-fish
tassel-fish
tiger shark
tongue-sole
triple-tail
turret-fish
velvet-fish
weaver-fish
whale-shark
white shark
yellow-tail
zebra shark

11

balance-fish
banded toado
bellows-fish
black-angler
blue-pointer
bridled goby
brown-groper
brown-puller
carpet-shark
carp-gudgeon
chanda perch
common skate
common toado
crested goby

cycloidians
electric eel
electric ray
finner-whale
five-fingers
golden perch
green turtle
gurnet perch
herring-cale
hippocampus
jackass-fish
javelin-fish
Jumping-Joey
kingsnapper
leatherskin
leopard-fish
lepidosiren
little tunny
man-o'-war fish
Moorish idol
orange perch
peacock-fish
peacock-sole
pennant-fish
prickleback
pterichthys
rainbow-fish
red bullseye
red fire-fish
rock-whiting
salmon-trout
sand-whiting
school-shark
scleroderms
sea-elephant
sea-scorpion
silver-belly
silver perch
silver toado
smooth toado
soldier-crab
soldier-fish
starry toado
stickleback
stonelifter
surgeon-fish
swallow-fish
tallegalane
trumpet-fish
whistle-fish
wolf-herring

12

basking shark
black drummer
black rock-cod
blue trevally
coachwhip ray
cucumber-fish
dipterygians
dusky morwong
fan-tailed ray
fatherlasher
fighting-fish
forehead-fish
gargoyle-fish
giant herring
gray tusk-fish
oyster-blenny
painted saury
piked dog-fish
plectognathi
Plesiosaurus
rainbow-trout

rat-tailed ray
river garfish
rock flathead
scarlet bream
sentinel crab
silver mullet
smooth angler
Stout Long-Tom

13

allports perch
banded-pigfish
barred-garfish
Barred Long-Tom
black king-fish
black-trevally
branchiostoma
climbing perch
dactylopterus
dusky flathead
entomostracan
findon-haddock
finnan-haddock
flying gurnard
giant boar-fish
horse-mackerel

leafy seahorse
leatherjacket
long-finned eel
magpie-morwong
marbled angler
mountain-trout
ox-eyed herring
porcupine-fish
Red-Indian fish
salmon catfish
salt-water fish
sandpaper-fish
scarlet angler
Sergeant Baker
silver batfish
silver drummer
snub-nosed dart
southern tunny
spiny flathead
spiny seahorse
striped angler
thresher-shark
tiger-flathead

14

banded sea-perch

black stingaree
branchiostegan
brown-sweetlips
butterfly-bream
enaliosaurians
estuary cat-fish
Greenland-shark
Greenland-whale
king barracouta
king parrot-fish
little numbfish
Macquarie perch
many-banded sole
marine annelida
one-finned shark
painted gurnard
purple sea-perch
red gurnet-perch
river blackfish
short-finned eel
shovel-nosed ray
Slender Long-Tom
smooth flathead
spotted whiting
striped catfish
striped gudgeon
striped sea-pike
white horse-fish

15

acanthopterygii
Australian perch
Australian smelt
beaked coral-fish
bottle-nose shark
common stingaree
crusted flounder
crusted weed-fish
edriophthalmata
frigate mackerel
hairback herring
little cling-fish
little conger eel
long-finned perch
marbled flathead
painted dragonet
short sucker-fish
small-headed sole
smooth stingaree
spangled grunter
Spanish mackerel
spermaceti whale
spotted cat-shark
spotted eagle-ray
spotted pipe-fish
white-spotted ray

Fossils, shells, etc.

(f.s.) = fossil shell (s.) = shell

4 AND 5

amber
auger
baler
chama (s.)
chank (s.)
conch (s.)
cone (s.)
donax (s.)
drill (s.)
galea
gaper (s.)
murex (s.)
peuce
razor (s.)
snail (s.)
tooth (s.)
tulip (s.)
Venus (s.)
whelk (s.)

6

bonnet (s.)
buckie (s.)
chiton (s.)
cockle (s.)
cowrie
crinoid
fornix (s.)
helmet (s.)
jingle (s.)
limpet (s.)
macoma (s.)
matrix
mussel (s.)
natica (s.)
nerite (s.)

Ogygia
oyster (s.)
quahog (s.)
tellin (s.)
triton (s.)
trivea (s.)
turban (s.)
volute (s.)
winkle (s.)

7

abalone (s.)
artemis (s.)
astarte (s.)
Babylon
crabite
crinoid
discoid (s.)
fungite
muscite
neptune (s.)
ovulite
piddock (s.)
scallop (s.)
zoolite

8

ammonite (f.s.)
argonaut (s.)
ark shell (s.)
balanite
buccinum (s.)
capstone
ceratite
choanite
cololite

conchite (f.s.)
dendrite
dog whelk (s.)
ear shell (s.)
echinite
epiornis
escallop (s.)
favosite
fig shell (s.)
galerite
janthina (s.)
mangelia (s.)
muricite
mytilite
nautilus (s.)
penshell (s.)
phyllite
ram's horn (f.s.)
retinite
scaphite (f.s.)
sea snail
solenite (f.s.)
strombus (s.)
testacel (s.)
topshell (s.)
trochite
tunshell (s.)
volulite (f.s.)
volutite (f.s.)

9

aepiornis
alasmodon (s.)
alcyonite
belemnite
buccinite (f.s.)
cancerite
carpolite

clam shell (s.)
comb shell (s.)
cone shell (s.)
Conularia
copralite
corallite
crow stone
dicynodon
encrinite
fan mussel (s.)
file shell (s.)
foot shell (s.)
frog shell (s.)
giant clam (s.)
harp shell (s.)
hippurite
horn shell (s.)
lima shell (s.)
lithocarp
lithophyl
marsupite
miliolite (f.s.)
moon shell }
moon snail } (s.)
muscalite (f.s.)
nautilite
nummulite
ostracite (f.s.)
palmacite
patellite (f.s.)
polymorphe (s.)
reliquiae
rock-borer (s.)
serpulite (f.s.)
slip shell (s.)
star shell (s.)
stone lily
strombite (f.s.)
tellinite (f.s.)
trilobite

turbinite (f.s.)
turrilite (f.s.)
tusk shell (s.)

10

agate shell
batrachite
canoe shell (s.)
confervite
dendrolite
entomolite
entrochite
euomphalus (f.s.)
gyrogonite
odontolite
palmacites
periwinkle (s.)
razor shell (s.)
screw shell (s.)
snake stone (f.s.)
tiger shell (s.)
tubiporite
ulodendron
wentletrap (s.)
wing oyster (s.)
xanthidium

11

asterialite
asterolepis

basket shell (s.)
carpet shell (s.)
cetotolites
cheirolepis
dinotherium
fairy stones
finger shell (s.)
finger stone
furrowshell (s.)
gongiatites (f.s.)
helmet shell (s.)
ichthyolite
madreporite
margin shell
milleporite
mohair shell (s.)
needle shell ⎫
needle whelk ⎭ (s.)
ornitholite
oyster drill (s.)
rhyncholite
sting winkle (s.)
strobolites
sunset shell (s.)
tiger cowrie (s.)
trough shell (s.)
turtle shell (s.)

12

amphibiolite
brocade shell (s.)
Chinaman's hat (s.)

cornu-ammonis (f.s.)
deinotherium
figured stone
holoptychis
Hungarian cap (s.)
lantern shell (s.)
macrotherium
megalichthys
pandora shell (s.)
pelican's foot (s.)
pentacrinite
saddle oyster (s.)
slipper shell (s.)
spindle shell (s.)
sundial shell (s.)
trumpet shell (s.)
zamiostrobus

13 AND 14

bothrodendron (13)
carboniferous (13)
conchyliaceous (f.s.) (14)
dolichosaurus (13)
lepidodendron (13)
lithoglyphite (13)
nacreous shells (s.) (14)
necklace shell (s.) (13)
palaeontology (13)
porphyry shell (s.) (13)
staircase shell (s.) (14)
syringodendron (14)
woodcock shell (s.) (13)

Insects, etc.

3 AND 4

ant
bee
bot
boud
bug
cleg
cob
dart
dor
flea
fly
frit
gnat
goat
grig
grub
lema
lice
mida
mite
moth
nit
pug
pupa
puss
puxi
sow
tant
tau
tick
wasp
zimb

5

acera
aphid
aphis
atlas
borer
brize
cimex
comma
culex
drake
drone
egger
emmet
eruca
hawk
imago
julus
larva
louse
midge
musca
ox-fly
pulex
splex
tinea
vespa

6

acarus
ant cow

aphids
aptera
ash-fly
bedbug
bee fly
beetle
blatta
botfly
breese
breeze
burnet
buzzer
caddis
chafer
chegre
chigoe
chigre
chinch
cicada
cicala
cimbex
cimiss
coccus
cocoon
crabro
dayfly
diurna
dog-bee
dog-fly
dorfly
earwig
elater
epeira
eupoda

evania
gadfly
hop-fly
hopper
hornet
jigger
lappet
larvae
locust
maggot
mantis
maybug
may-fly
midget
mygale
saw-fly
scarab
sow-bug
sphinx
spider
squill
termes
Thecla
Thrips
tipula
tsetse
veneer
weevil

7

acerans
agrilus

antenna
ant-hill
ant-lion
aphides
athalia
bean fly
beehive
bee moth
blowfly
boat fly
bruchus
bull-bee
bull fly
cheslip
coronet
crambus
cricket
culicid
cyclica
daphnia
deer-fly
diopsis
diptera
duck-ant
epeirid
epizoon
fig gnat
firefly
fish fly
fulgora
gallfly
globard
grayfly
gum moth
hexapod
hine-bee
horn-bug
hornfly
June bug
katydid
lady-cow
lampfly
microbe
papilio
path fly
pismire
puceron
pug moth
rose-bug
rotifer
salamis
sand fly
sawback
shad fly
skipper
stylops
termite
tin-worm
tortrix
wasp-fly
wax-moth
wood-ant

8

acaridan
adder-fly
antennae
arachnid
black ant
black-fly
braconid
bullhead
206 calandra

calandre
calomela
case-moth
cerambyx
chelifer
cocktail
Colorado
corn-moth
crane-fly
dog-louse
drake-fly
drone-bee
drone-fly
dybiscus
ephemera
erotylus
erycinia
flesh-fly
fossores
fruit-fly
gall-gnat
gall-wasp
gammarus
glow worm
goat-moth
green-fly
hawk-moth
honey-bee
horse-fly
house-fly
Isoptera
lace-lerp
ladybird
leaf-moth
lecanium
longhorn
mealy-bug
milleped
mosquito
mucivora
multiped
myriapod
natantes
night-fly
nocturna
parasite
paropsis
pedipalp
phyllium
pupipara
puss moth
queen ant
queen-bee
rotifera
sand-flea
sand-wasp
scolytus
sparkler
stone-fly
tenebrio
tetrapod
tung-tung
water-bug
water-fly
wheat-fly
white ant
white fly
woodlice
wood-mite
wood-moth

9

Amazon act
anopheles

aphid pest
arachnida
brimstone
bumble-bee
burrel-fly
butterfly
buzzardet
caddis fly
canker-fly
cedar-moth
centipede
chrysalis
churrworm
cicindela
clavicorn
cochineal
cockroach
corn-aphis
corn borer
crab-louse
cynipides
dermestes
dipterans
dorbeetle
dragon-fly
driver-ant
dumbledor
eggar-moth
egger-moth
eumenidae
fig-psylla
flying-ant
forest-fly
forficula
gall-midge
ghost-moth
grain-moth
hemiptera
hornet fly
humble-bee
ichneumon
lac-insect
leaf-louse
longicorn
membracid
millepede
orange-bug
orange-tip
pine-aphis
plant-lice
rug-weevil
sheep-lice
sheep-tick
spider-fly
squash-bug
sugar-mite
tanystoma
tarantula
tarentula
thysamura
tiger moth
tree-louse
tsetse-fly
tumblebug
turnip-fly
warble-fly
water-flea
wax-insect
wax-worker
wheat-moth
whirlygig
wood-borer
wood-louse
worker ant
worker bee
xylophaga

10

acacia-moth
bark-weevil
bird-spider
blister-fly
bluebottle
boll-weevil
bombardier
burnet moth
cabbage-fly
carpet moth
cheese-mite
chrysomela
coccinella
cockchafer
coleoptera
corn-weevil
death-watch
digger wasp
dolphin-fly
dorr-beetle
dung beetle
dynastidan
entomolite
ephemerans
fan-cricket
fen-cricket
flea-beetle
fritillary
frog-hopper
goat-chafer
hairstreak
hessian-fly
horse-emmet
jigger flea
lantern-fly
lappet moth
leaf-insect
leaf-roller
looper-moth
musk beetle
neuroptera
orthoptera
phylloxera
pine-weevil
plant-louse
red admiral
rice-weevil
ring-barker
rosechafer
saltigrade
sand-hopper
scaraebeus
seed-weevil
sheep-louse
silver-fish
soldier ant
Spanish fly
stag beetle
star-psylla
stone-flies
timber-moth
twig-psylla
veneer moth
vorticella
willow-moth
winter-moth
wolf-spider
xylophagan

11

ametabolian
apple-sucker

arachnidans
auger beetle
balm-cricket
beehawk moth
black beetle
cabbage moth
cantharides
capharis bug
caterpillar
chalcia wasp
clothes moth
codling moth
coprophagan
cryptophago
drinker moth
Emperor moth
entomophaga
Ephemeridae
flour weevil
gallinipper
grain beetle
grasshopper
green-bottle
horse-marten
Hymenoptera
leaf-bag moth
Lepidoptera
mole-cricket
painted lady
pine-girdler
scorpion-fly

snout-beetle
sponge-flies
stick-insect
subulicorns
swallow-tail
terebrantia
tetrapteran
thysanurans
tiger-beetle
timber-borer
Trichoptera
tussock-moth
vine-fretter
water beetle
water-skater
wattle moths
wheel-animal
wood-fretter

12

bent-wing moth
buzzard-clock
cabbage white
carpenter ant
carpenter bee
cecropia moth
cinnabar moth
clerid-beetle
diadem spider

dimerosomata
flower-beetle
ground beetle
horned-clerid
horse-stinger
milk-white ant
money-spinner
pinhole-borer
red-cedar moth
Rhynchophera
saprophagans
scarab beetle
spruce sawfly
sycamore-moth
walking-stick
water-boatman
wattle-psylla
white admiral

13

black-lecanium
daddy-long-legs
diamond beetle
fig-leaf beetle
giant wood-moth
goliath-beetle
green wood-moth
ichneumon-wasp
jumping-spider

leather-jacket
lime-tree borer
mangold beetle
purple emperor
shot-hole borer
slender-weevil
tailed-emperor

14

bag-shelter moth
bimia-longicorn
cabbage-root fly
Colorado beetle
death's-head moth
elephant-beetle
fig-branch borer
Hercules beetle
ichneumon flies
ironbark saw-fly

15

furniture beetle
seedling-gum-moth
striped hawk-moth
thickset-chalcid
wheel-animalcule
yellow-longicorn

Marine growths, etc.

4 – 6

algae (5)
astrea (6)
coral (5)
dulse (5)
fungia (6)
kelp (4)
laver (5)
limpet (6)
mussel (6)
naiads (6)
polyp (5)
sponge (6)
tang (4)
tangle (6)
varec (5)
ware (4)
wrack (5)

7 AND 8

actinia (7)
agar agar (8)
alcyonic (8)
astraea (7)
badioga (7)
barnacle (8)
blubber (7)
calycle (7)
eschara (7)
fungite (7)
gulf weed (8)
polypary (8)
polypus (7)
porifera (8)
red algae (8)
red coral (8)
sea moss (7)

seaweed (7)
seawrack (8)
tubipore (8)
zoophyte (8)

9

alcyoneae
alcyonite
bathybius
blue algae
Irish moss
madrepore
millepore
nullipore
pink coral
sea nettle
zoophytes

10 AND OVER

abrotanoid (10)
acorn barnacle (13)
alva marina (10)
animal flower (12)
bladder kelp (11)
bladderwrack (12)
brown algae (10)
coral zoophytes (14)
goose barnacle (13)
lithodendron (12)
lithogenous (11)
lithophyte (10)
marine plants (12)
milliporite (11)
sea anemone (10)
tubiporite (10)

Molluscs

3 – 5

bulla
chank
clam
clio
ensis
gaper
helix
murex
mya
sepia
slug

snail
solen
spat
squid
unio
venus
whelk

6

buckie
chiton

cockle
cuttle
dodman
dolium
isopod
limpet
loligo
mantle
mussel
naiads
nerite
ostrea
oyster

pecten
quahog
sea ear
teredo
triton
voluta
winkle

7

acerans
actaeon

aplysia
ascidia
balanus
bivalve
diceras
eschera
etheria
glaucus
isopod
mollusc
mytilus
nauplii
octopod
octopus
patella
piddock
polyzoa
purpura
quahaug
scallop
scollop
sea hare
spirula
taccata
tellina

8

anodonta
argonaut
blue-nose
buccinum
decapoda
mollusca
nautilus
ostracea
pagurian
pedireme
sea lemon
spirifer
strombus
teredine
tridacna
tunicary

9

acephalan
clausilia
dentalium

dolabella
gastropod
giant clam
hodmandod
lithodome
ostracian
pteropods
scaphopod
shellfish

10

amphineura
amphitrite
brachiopod
cephalopod
conchifera
cuttlefish
date-mussel
haliotidae
heteropoda
periwinkle
razorshell

stone borer
stone eater

11

dragon shell
fasciolaria
gasteropoda
pearl oyster
river oyster
siphonifers
terebratula
trachelipod

12 AND OVER

boring mussel (12)
cyclobranchiata (15)
entomostomata (13)
lamellibranch (13)
tectibranchiata (15)

Reptiles and amphibians

3 – 5

aboma
adder
agama
anole
anura
asp
aspic
boa
bom
cobra
draco
eft
elaps
emys
frog
gecko
guana
hydra
jiboa
kaa
krait
kufi
mamba
newt
olm
pama
rana
skink
snake
toad
viper
waral
worm

6

anolis
caiman
cayman
daboia
dipsas
dragon

gavial
hydrus
iguana
karait
lizard
moloch
mugger
python
Sauria
taipan
triton
turtle
worrel

7

axolotl
chelone
coluber
gharial
ghavial
hicatee
labarri
lacerta
langaha
monitor
ophidia
paddock
rattler
saurian
scincus
serpent
snapper
tadpole
testudo
tuatara
urodela
varanus
zonurus

8

acontias
amphibia

anaconda
asp viper
basilisk
bull frog
cat snake
cerastes
chelonia
Congo eel
dinosaur
dragonet
fox snake
hiccatee
horn toad
jararaca
keelback
lachesis
matamata
moccasin
pit viper
rat snake
red snake
ringhals
sand fish
sand toad
sea snake
slow-worm
terrapin
tortoise
tree frog
typhlops

9

alligator
batrachia
blind-worm
blue krait
boomslang
chameleon
corn snake
crocodile
dart snake
eyed skink
galliwasp

giant frog
giant toad
green toad
hamadryad
horned asp
king cobra
king snake
marsh frog
Ophidians
pine snake
Pterosaur
puff adder
ring snake
terrapeen
tree snake
water newt
whip snake
wolf snake

10

amphibians
black mamba
black snake
bushmaster
clawed frog
cockatrice
copperhead
coral snake
Cotylosaur
dabb lizard
death adder
Diplodocus
edible frog
eyed lizard
false viper
fer-de-lance
glass snake
grass snake
green mamba
green racer
green snake
hellbender
horned frog

Mosasaurus
natterjack
night adder
Plesiosaur
river snake
rock python
salamander
sand lizard
sea serpent
smooth newt
tic polonga
tiger snake
wall lizard
water pilot
water snake

11

banded krait
black cayman
carpet viper
cottonmouth
crested newt

flying snake
Gaboon viper
gartersnake
gila monster
green lizard
green turtle
horned viper
Ichthyosaur
Indian cobra
lace monitor
leopard frog
midwife toad
Ophiosaurus
Pterodactyl
rattlesnake
royal python
smooth snake
Stegosaurus
Surinam toad
thorn lizard
thorny devil
Triceratops
water lizard
water python

12

Brontosaurus
chained snake
chicken snake
flying lizard
green tree boa
horned iguana
horned lizard
Hylaesaurus
Komodo dragon
leopard snake
pond tortoise

13 AND OVER

aquatic lizard (13)
boa constrictor (14)
brown tree snake (14)
coach-whip snake (14)
cobra de capello (14)
Dolichosaurus (13)
egg-eating snakes (15)

fire salamander (14)
four-lined snake (14)
frilled lizard (13)
giant tortoise (13)
golden tree frog (14)
golden tree snake (15)
green pit viper (13)
green tree frog (13)
Himalayan viper (14)
horn-nosed viper (14)
Ichthyosaurus (13)
long-nosed viper (14)
Nile crocodile (13)
painted terrapin (15)
rat-tailed snake (14)
Russell's viper (13)
saw-scaled viper (14)
schaapsticker (13)
snake-eyed skink (14)
snapping turtle (14)
spade-foot toad (13)
spotted lizard (13)
Tyrannosaurus (13)
water moccasin (13)

NATURAL HISTORY   (2) PLANTS
Cereals, etc.

3 AND **4**

bere
bigg
bran
corn
dari
dohl
dura
far
gram
malt
meal
oats
poar
rice
rye
sago
zea

5

brank
durra

emmer
ervum
fundi
grama
grist
grout
maize
mummy
paddy
panic
pulse
spelt
straw
typha
wheat

6 AND **7**

barley (6)
casava (6)
corncob (7)
darnel (6)
dhurra (6)

farina (6)
groats (6)
hominy (6)
mealie (6)
meslin (6)
millet (6)
nocake (6)
raggee (6)
rokeage (7)
shorts (6)
sorghum (7)
tapioca (7)
zea mays (7)

8 AND **9**

arrowroot (9)
buckwheat (9)
espiotte (8)
garavance (9)
mangcorn (8)
middlings (9)
pearl rice (9)

pot barley (9)
seed corn (8)
seed grain (9)
semolina (8)
sweet corn (9)

10 AND OVER

barleycorn (10)
barleymeal (10)
German millet (12)
Guinea corn (10)
Indian corn (10)
Indian millet (12)
mountain rice (12)
pearl barley (11)
pearl millet (11)
Scotch barley (12)
spring wheat (11)
summer wheat (11)
turkey wheat (11)
winter barley (11)
winter wheat (11)

Flowers

3 AND **4**

aloe
arum
balm
flag
geum
iris
ixia
lily
lote
may

musk
pink
rose
weld
whin
wold

5

agave
aspic

aster
avens
blite
briar
broom
canna
daisy
erica
faham
flora
gilia
gorse

henna
lilac
linum
lotus
lupin
orris
ox-eye
oxlip
padma
pagle
pansy
peony

petal
phlox
poker
poppy
sepal
stock
tansy
thyme
tulip
viola
yucca
yulan

6

acacia
acaena
alpine
arnica
azalea
balsam
bellis
bennet
borage
cactus
cistus
clover
coleus
cosmea
cosmos
crocus
dahlia
datura
fennel
iberis
kochia
lupine
madder
mallow
malope
mimosa
myrtle
nerine
nuphar
orchid
orchis
paigle
reseda
rocket
rosula
salvia
scilla
sesame
silene
sundew
thrift
violet
wattle
zinnia

7

aconite
alonsoa
aloysia
alyssum
anchusa
anemone
begonia
blawort
blewert
blossom
bouquet
bugloss

campion
candock
catmint
chaplet
chelone
chicory
clarkia
cowslip
cup rose
cytisus
day lily
deutzia
dittany
dog rose
festoon
freesia
fuchsia
gazania
genista
gentian
gerbera
godetia
heather
hyacine
jacinth
jasmine
jessamy
jonquil
kingcup
lantana
linaria
lobelia
lupinus
marybud
may-lily
melissa
milfoil
mimulus
nelumbo
nemesia
nigella
nosegay
opuntia
papaver
petunia
picotee
primula
rambler
sea-pink
seringa
spiraea
statice
succory
syringa
tagetes
tea rose
thistle
ursinia
verbena
vervain
witloof

8

abutilon
acanthus
achillia
ageratum
amaranth
angelica
arum lily
asphodel
aubretia
auricula
bartonia

bedstraw
bignonia
bluebell
buddleia
calamint
camellia
capsicum
catchfly
clematis
cockspur
cyclamen
daffodil
dianthus
dicentra
dropwort
erigeron
foxglove
gardenia
geranium
girasole
gladiola
gladiole
glaucium
gloriosa
gloxinia
harebell
helenium
hepatica
hibiscus
hottonia
hyacinth
japonica
laburnum
larkspur
lavatera
lavender
magnolia
marigold
martagon
moss rose
musk rose
myosotis
nenuphat
nymphaea
oleander
phacetia
phormium
plumbago
pond lily
primrose
rock-rose
scabious
skull-cap
snowdrop
stapelia
starwort
sweetpea
tigridia
toad-flax
tuberose
valerian
veronica
viscaria
wild rose
wisteria
woodbind
woodbine
xanthium

9

Aaron's-rod
achimines
amaryllis

anagallis
aquilegia
buttercup
calendula
campanula
candytuft
carnation
carthamus
celandine
cherry pie
China rose
cineraria
clove pink
cockscomb
colt's foot
columbine
coreopsis
corn-poppy
dandelion
digitalis
dog violet
dove's foot
edelweiss
eglantine
forsythia
gladiolus
golden rod
hollyhock
hydrangea
jessamine
kniphofia
lotus lily
mayflower
moon daisy
narcissus
nemophila
pimpernel
polygonum
pyrethrum
saxifrage
speedwell
spikenard
sunflower
tiger lily
twayblade
verbascum
water flag
waterlily
wolf's-bane

10

agapanthus
amaranthus
bell flower
caffre lilly
calliopsis
China aster
chionodoxa
cinquefoil
coquelicot
cornflower
corn violet
crane's-bill
crow flower
damask rose
delphinium
Easter lily
fritillary
gaillardia
gelder rose
golden drop
gypsophila
heart's-ease
helianthus

heliophila
heliotrope
immortelle
lady's-smock
limnanthes
marguerite
mignonette
nasturtium
nightshade
orange lily
ox-eye-daisy
penny-royal
pentstemon
periwinkle
poinsettia
polianthus
potentilla
ranunculus
snapdragon
sweet briar
wallflower
white poppy
wind flower

11

antirrhinum
blood flower
cabbage rose
calandrinia

calceolaria
cheiranthus
convallaria
convolvulus
cotoneaster
everlasting
fig marigold
forget-me-not
gillyflower
globeflower
guelder rose
helichrysum
honey-flower
honeysuckle
kidney-vetch
London pride
loosestrife
love-in-a-mist
meadowsweet
pelargonium
pepper elder
poppy mallow
ragged robin
rambler rose
red-hot poker
schizanthus
sea lavender
spear flower
sweet rocket
sweet sultan
tiger flower

wild flowers
wood anemone
xeranthemum

12

apple blossom
autumn crocus
cuckoo-flower
heather bells
horn-of-plenty
Iceland poppy
Jacob's ladder
lady's slipper
old man's-beard
pasque flower
rhododendron
salpiglossis
shirley poppy
Solomon's seal
sweet william
virgin's bower

13

alpine flowers
blanket flower

bleeding heart
bougainvillea
Bristol flower
cherry blossom
Christmas rose
chrysanthemum
creeping jenny
eschscholtzia
grape-hyacinth
huntsman's horn
marsh marigold
orange blossom
passion flower
sweet calabash
traveller's joy
trumpet flower
water hyacinth

14 AND 15

Canterbury bell (14)
cardinal flower (14)
Christmas flower (15)
lily of the valley (15)
lords and ladies (14)
love-in-idleness (14)
Michaelmas daisy (15)
shepherd's purse (14)
star of Bethlehem (15)

Fruit

3 AND 4

akee
Cox
crab
date
fig
gage
gean
haw
hep
hip
kaki
lime
mast
nut
ogen
pear
pepo
plum
pome
rasp
skeg
sloe
ugli
uva

5

abhal
agava
agave
apple
arnot
betel
cubeb
drupe
eleot
grape

grout
guava
lemon
lichi
mango
melon
merry
morel
morus
olive
papaw
peach
pecan
prune
whort
whurt

6

almond
ananas
banana
biffin
cedrat
cherry
citron
citrus
cobnut
colmar
damson
drupel
durian
egriot
elk nut
groser
lichee
longan
loquat

lychee
mammee
medlar
muscat
nutmeg
orange
papaya
pawpaw
peanut
pignut
pippin
pomelo
quince
raisin
rennet
russet
samara
walnut
zapote

7

apricot
avocado
buckeye
bullace
capulin
catawba
cedrate
cheston
coconut
corinth
costard
currant
deal-nut
dessert
dog-wood
filbert
genipap

golding
hog-plum
karatas
kumquat
litchee
mahaleb
malmsey
mayduke
morello
naartje
pompion
pumpkin
quashey
rhubarb
satsuma
tangelo
wilding

8

allspice
bayberry
beechnut
bergamot
betelnut
bilberry
buckmast
burgamot
calabash
cat's-head
chestnut
coquilla
cream-nut
date-plum
dogberry
earthnut
fenberry
fig-apple
fox grape

hastings
hazelnut
honeydew
ivory nut
japonica
jonathan
mandarin
may apple
mulberry
muscadel
muscatel
musk pear
oleaster
pearmain
plantain
prunello
quandong
queening
rambutan
spondias
sweeting
tamarind
Valencia
whitsour

9

alkekengi
apple-john
aubergine
beechmast
blueberry
brazilnut
buck's horn
butternut
canteloup
carmelite
cherimoya
chokepear
corozo nut
crab-apple

cranberry
damascene
drupaceae
elvas plum
greengage
groundnut
hindberry
king apple
love apple
melocoton
mirabelle
monkey pot
muscadine
musk-apple
musk-melon
nectarine
ortanique
oxycoccus
persimmon
pineapple
pistachio
rambootan
rambostan
raspberry
star apple
tamarinds
tangerine
victorine
Worcester

10

adam's apple
bird cherry
blackberry
blackheart
breadfruit
cantaloupe
charentais
clementine
clingstone
corozo nuts

cream-fruit
damask plum
dried fruit
elderberry
gooseberry
granadilla
grapefruit
Indian date
loganberry
Madeira nut
mangosteen
marking nut
melocotoon
orange musk
pome-citron
pompelmous
queen apple
redcurrant
stone fruit
strawberry
watermelon
wild cherry
winter pear

11

anchovy pear
bitter apple
blood orange
candleberry
China orange
chokecherry
coquilla nut
French berry
granny smith
huckleberry
hurtleberry
Jaffa orange
leathercoat
monkey bread
myrtle berry

navel orange
pomegranate
pompelmoose
russet apple
scuppernong
winter apple

12

bitter almond
blackcurrant
chaumontelle
Chester grape
chocolate nut
cochineal fig
cooking apple
custard apple
passionfruit
pistachio nut
Victoria plum
white currant
whortleberry
winter cherry
winter citron

13 AND OVER

alligator pear (13)
Barbados cherry (14)
Blenheim orange (14)
Cape gooseberry (14)
Catherine pear (13)
conference pear (14)
cornelian cherry (15)
golden delicious (15)
mandarin orange (14)
morello cherry (13)
preserved fruit (14)
Seville orange (13)

Herbs and spices

3 – 5

anise
balm
basil
bay
chive
clary
cress
cumin
dill
grass
mace
mint
myrrh
rape
rue
sage
senna
tansy
thyme
woad

6

bennet
betony

borage
capers
chilli
chives
cloves
endive
fennel
galega
garlic
ginger
hyssop
isatis
lovage
lunary
nutmeg
orpine
savory
sesame
simple
sorrel

7

aconite
burdock
caraway
catmint

cayenne
chervil
chicory
comfrey
dittany
frasera
gentian
henbane
juniper
lettuce
milfoil
mustard
oregano
panicum
paprika
parsley
pot herb
rampion
saffron
succory
vanilla

8

agrimony
angelica
camomile

cinnamon
hog's-bean
lavender
lungwort
marigold
marjoram
mouse ear
plantain
purslane
rosemary
samphire
spicknel
tarragon
turmeric
waybread
wormwood

9

baneberry
bear's foot
chickweed
coriander
coronopus
eyebright
fenugreek
finocchio

goose foot
groundsel
hellebore
horehound
liquorice
sea fennel
sweet herb
tormentil

10

hyoscyamus
lemon thyme
motherwort
penny royal

peppermint
watercress
willow herb

11

dog's cabbage
dragon's head
hedge hyssop
horseradish
pot marigold
pot marjoram
sweet rocket
swine's cress
winter green

12 AND OVER

adder's tongue (12)
Florence fennel (14)
medicinal herbs (14)
mournful widow (13)
mustard and cress (15)
southernwood (12)
summer savory (12)
sweet marjoram (13)
thoroughwort (12)
winter savory (12)

Plants

3

box
cos
ers
hop
ivy
nep
oat
pea
pia
poa
rue
rye
seg
tod
yam
zea

4

aira
akee
alfa
aloe
anil
arum
bean
beet
bent
bigg
bulb
cane
coca
coco
coix
cole
corn
crab
dill
diss
dock
doob
dorn
fern
flag
flax
gale
geum
goss
hemp
herb
holm
ilex

iris
jute
kail
kale
kali
kans
leek
ling
mint
moss
musa
nard
peat
pipi
race
rape
reed
rice
root
rush
ruta
sage
sago
sida
sium
sloe
sola
spud
tare
taro
thea
tree
tutu
ulex
vine
wald
weed
weld
whin
woad
wold
wort

5

agave
ajuga
algae
alpia
anise
apium
aster
brake
brank

briar
broom
bugle
cacao
canna
cicer
clary
clove
cress
cumin
daisy
dicot
dryas
dwale
erica
eruca
ficus
fitch
fungi
furze
glaux
goman
gorse
gourd
grass
grias
henna
holly
liana
liane
lotus
loufa
madia
maize
medic
morel
moril
mucor
mudar
musci
napal
olive
orach
orris
oryza
oshac
osier
oxlip
paddy
palas
panic
poker
radix
rheum
rubia

rubus
runch
savin
savoy
scrog
sedge
shrub
sison
solah
stole
sumac
swede
tacca
tamus
tansy
thorn
thyme
trapa
tucum
vetch
vicia
vinca
viola
vitis
wahoo
wapon
wheat
whort
withy
wrack
yucca
yupon
zamia

6

acorus
alisma
amomum
aninga
arbute
bamboo
barley
batata
bejuco
betony
biblus
borage
bryony
burnet
cactal
cactus
caltha
cassia

213

catnip
cicely
cicuta
cissus
cistus
clover
cockle
conium
conyza
croton
cynara
daphne
darnel
dodder
eddoes
elaeis
endive
eringo
eryngo
exogen
fennel
ferula
fescue
filago
fimble
fiorin
frutex
fungus
funkia
fustet
galium
garlic
garrya
gervan
gnetum
gromil
guills
henbit
hervea
hyssop
iberis
indigo
jujube
juncus
kalmia
kiekie
kousso
lichen
locust
loofah
lupine
madder
maguey
mallow
manioc
marram
matico
milium
millet
mimosa
myrica
myrtle
nardoo
nerium
nettle
nubbin
oilnut
orache
orchid
orchis
origan
osmund
oxalis
paigle
pampas
peanut

peplis
pepper
potato
privet
protea
quinoa
quitch
raggee
rattan
reseda
ruscus
sabine
savine
savory
scilla
secale
sesame
sesban
seseli
smilax
sorrel
spurge
squash
squill
stolon
styrax
sumach
sundew
teasel
teazel
tutsan
urtica
viscum
wicker
yamboo
yarrow

7

absinth
aconite
alcanna
alhenna
all-good
all-heal
althaea
aquatic
arabine
arbutus
awlwort
azarole
barilla
bartram
begonia
bistort
bogbean
bracken
bramble
bugwort
bulbule
bulrush
burdock
bur-reed
calamus
calypso
campion
caraway
carduus
cassada
cassado
cassava
catmint
chicory
clivers
clot-bur

columba
comfrey
cowbane
cowhage
cow-itch
cow-weed
creeper
cudbear
cudweed
cup moss
cytisus
dionaea
dittany
dogbane
dog's rue
ear-wort
ehretia
elatine
esparto
eugenia
euryale
euterpe
felwort
festuca
ficaria
figwort
fitweed
foggage
foxtail
frogbit
fumaria
funaria
genista
gentian
ginseng
gladwyn
gutwort
hardock
heather
hemlock
herbage
honesty
hop-bind
hop-bine
hop-vine
humulus
ipomaea
jasmine
Jew's ear
juniper
karatas
kedlack
lucerne
lychnis
madwort
melilot
monocot
munjeet
mustard
opuntia
panicum
papyrus
pareira
parella
parelle
primula
pumpion
pumpkin
quamash
quassia
ragwort
rambler
rampion
rhatany
rhubarb
robinia

saffron
saligot
salsify
sanicle
sarcina
saw-wort
sencion
senecio
seringa
solanum
sonchus
spiraea
statice
syringa
talipot
taliput
tannier
thistle
tobacco
trefoil
truffle
turpeth
uncaria
vanilla
verbena
vervain
waratah
zalacca
zanonia
zedoary
zizania

8

acanthus
agrimony
air plant
amphigen
anthemis
asphodel
banewort
barberry
barometz
bearbind
bear's ear
bellwort
berberis
berberry
bilberry
bindweed
bogberry
bogwhort
boxthorn
brassica
bullweed
bullwort
calamint
camomile
cannabis
capsicum
carraway
cassweed
catchfly
cat's tail
centaury
cerealia
cetraria
charlock
chayroot
choyroot
cinchona
cinnamon
cleavers
clematis
clubmoss

clubrush
cocculus
cockspur
cockweed
coleseed
cornflag
cornrose
costmary
cowberry
cowgrass
cow-wheat
crithmum
crow silk
damewort
danewort
dewberry
diandria
dog briar
dog grass
dog's bane
dolichos
downweed
dropwort
duckmeat
duckweed
dumb-cane
earth nut
earth-pea
echinops
eggplant
eglatere
eleusine
epiphyte
erigeron
erisimum
euonymus
feverfew
finochio
fireweed
flaxweed
fleabane
fleawort
flixweed
foxglove
fragaria
fumitory
galangal
garcinia
gillenia
girasole
gloxinia
glumales
glyceria
gratiola
gromwell
hare's ear
hartwort
hawkweed
hawthorn
hibiscus
hockherb
ice plant
isnardia
knapweed
lacebark
larkspur
lavender
lungwort
lustwort
male fern
mandrake
mangrove
marjoram
mat grass
may bloom
mezereon

milkweed
monocarp
moonseed
moonwort
mulewort
mushroom
myosotis
nut grass
oenanthe
oleander
oleaster
orchanet
peat moss
phormium
pilewort
pink root
plantlet
plantule
pond weed
prunella
puffball
purslane
putchock
red algae
rib grass
roccella
rock-rose
rosebush
rosemary
rye grass
sainfoin
saltwort
scammony
seedling
sengreen
septfoil
shamrock
simaruba
skull-cap
smallage
soapwort
sourdock
sow bread
starwort
strobile
sun-plant
sweetsop
tamarack
tamarisk
tara fern
tarragon
tea plant
tentwort
tickweed
toad-flax
tree-fern
tremella
triticum
tuberose
turk's cap
turmeric
turnsole
valerian
veratrum
veronica
viburnum
victoria
wall-moss
wall-wort
wartwort
water-poa
wild oats
wild rose
wind seed
with-wine
woodbine

woodroof
woodruff
woodsage
woodwart
wormwood
wrightia
xanthium
zingiber

9

abrotanum
aerophyte
amaryllis
ampelosis
arbor-vine
arsesmart
artemisia
artichoke
asclepias
balsamine
basil weed
bean caper
bearberry
bent grass
bird's foot
bloodroot
bloodwort
blue algae
briar-root
brooklime
brookmint
brookweed
broomcorn
broomrape
burstwort
candytuft
canebrake
caprifole
cardamine
cariopsis
carrageen
caryopsis
celandine
cetrarine
chamomile
chaparral
chaya root
cherry-bay
chickweed
china root
choke-weed
cineraria
club-grass
coal plant
cockscomb
cock's head
colchicum
colocynth
colt's foot
columbine
commensal
coniferae
coral wort
coriander
corn poppy
corn salad
cotyledon
cramp-bark
crataegus
crowberry
cuckoo bud
culver key
cyclamine
decagynia

decandria
desert rod
didynamia
digitalis
digitaria
dittander
dockcress
doob grass
duck's foot
duck's meat
dulcamara
dyer's weed
eglantine
elaeagnus
equisetum
euphorbia
euphrasia
evergreen
evolvulus
eyebright
fenugreek
fever root
feverwort
gamagrass
gelanthus
germander
glasswort
golden cup
golden rod
goose corn
grapewort
grasspoly
ground ivy
groundnut
groundsel
hair grass
hoarhound
honeywort
horehound
horsefoot
horsetail
hypericum
Indian fig
jessamine
Job's tears
kite's foot
knee holly
knot grass
lark's heel
laserwort
liquorice
liverwort
milk vetch
mistletoe
monk's hood
moschatel
mousetail
nepenthes
nicotiana
patchouli
pellitory
pilularia
pimpernel
planticle
poison ivy
poison oak
pyracanth
rafflesia
rocambole
rosmarine
safflower
saintfoin
saxifrage
smartweed
snakeroot
snakeweed

215

snowberry
soap plant
socotrine
spearmint
spearwort
speedwell
spikenard
spirogyra
spoonwort
stellaria
stonecrop
sugarbeet
sugar cane
sun spurge
sweet flag
sweet john
sweet root
sweet rush
sweet wood
sweet wort
taraxacum
thallogen
theobroma
thorn-bush
toadstool
tonka bean
toothwort
tormentil
trifolium
twayblade
umbilicus
villarsia
wakerobin
wall cress
waterlath
waterwort
wax myrtle
whitecrop
widow wail
wincopipe
wolf's bane
wolf's claw
wormgrass
woundwort
xanthosia

10

adam's apple
adder grass
agrostemma
alabastrus
amaranthus
angiosperm
arbor vitae
asarabacca
beccabunga
bitterwort
brome grass
brown algae
butterbush
butterweed
butterwood
butterwort
cascarilla
cassumunar
cellulares
cinquefoil
cloudberry
corn cockle
corn rocket
cotton rose
cottonweed
couch grass
cow parsley

crake berry
crotalaria
devil's club
diadelphia
dog's fennel
dog's poison
dog's tongue
dracontium
elacampane
elaeococca
entophytes
eriocaulon
eriophoron
escallonia
eupatorium
fimble-hemp
friar's cowl
fritillary
furrow weed
gaultheria
globe daisy
globularia
goldenhair
goldy locks
goose grass
grass-wrack
gymnosperm
helianthus
hemp neetle
herds grass
honey stalk
Indian corn
Indian reed
Indian shot
Jew's mallow
kidney-wort
king's spear
knapbottle
lycopodium
maidenhair
manila hemp
mock orange
mock privet
muscardine
nasturtium
nightshade
nipplewort
panic grass
passiflora
pennyroyal
peppermint
pepperwort
periwinkle
poker plant
potentilla
race ginger
ranunculus
rest harrow
rhein berry
rhinanthus
rose acacia
rose mallow
saprophyte
sarracenia
setterwort
shave grass
silver weed
sneezewort
sow thistle
Spanish nut
speargrass
spleenwort
stavesacre
stitchwort
stonebreak
stork's bill

sweet briar
sweet brier
swine bread
swinegrass
swordgrass
throatwort
tiger's foot
touch-me-not
tragacanth
tropaeolum
Venus's comb
wall pepper
water plant
way thistle
whitethorn
wild indigo
willow herb
willow weed
witch hazel
wolf's peach
wood sorrel
yellow-root
yellow-wort

11

bear's breech
bishop's weed
blackbonnet
bottle gourd
brank ursine
calceolaria
calcyanthus
canary grass
chanterelle
coffee plant
contrayerva
convolvulus
corn parsley
cotton grass
cotton plant
crest marine
cuckoo's meat
dame's violet
dog's cabbage
dog's mercury
dracunculus
dragon's head
Dragon's wort
Dutch clover
erythronium
everlasting
fescue grass
fig marigold
finger grass
fuller's weed
giant cactus
giant fennel
guelder rose
hart's tongue
holy thistle
honeysuckle
humble plant
Iceland moss
Indian berry
Indian cress
indigo plant
ipecacuanha
kidney vetch
laurustinus
London pride
marram grass
marsh mallow
meadow-sweet
milk thistle

millet grass
moon trefoil
moving plant
myoporaceae
oyster plant
pedicedaris
pelargonium
pepper grass
poison sumac
prickly pear
red-hot poker
ribbon grass
ripple grass
scurvy grass
sempervivum
serpentaria
snail clover
snail flower
sparrow wort
stagger bush
star thistle
sulphur-wort
swallow-wort
sweet cicely
sweet cistus
sweet potato
swine's cress
thorough wax
tinkar's root
tonquin bean
tussac grass
twitch grass
viper's grass
water radish
water violet
white clover
white darnel
winter berry
winter bloom
winter cress
wintergreen
wood anemone
xanthoxylum
zygophyllum

12

adderstoupie
aerial plants
bladderwrack
buffalo grass
Christ's thorn
coloquintida
compass plant
corn marigold
cow's lungwort
custard apple
deadly carrot
dragon's blood
echinocactus
erythroxylon
feather grass
fennel flower
fool's parsley
German millet
globe thistle
hound's tongue
Indian millet
Indian turnip
mangel wurzel
melon thistle
palma christi
pickerel weed
pitcher plant
quaking grass

reindeer moss
rhododendron
sarsaparilla
snail trefoil
Solomon's seal
southern wood
Spanish broom
Spanish grass
spear thistle
swine thistle
timothy grass
tobacco plant
torch thistle
Venus flytrap
Venus's sumack
vinegar plant
virgin's bower
water parsnip
water pitcher
water soldier
white campion
whitlow grass
whortleberry

winter cherry
xanthorrhiza
yellow rattle

13

chrysanthemum
crown imperial
dog's-tail grass
elephant grass
elephant's foot
eschscholtzia
flowering fern
flowering rush
globe amaranth
golden thistle
Indian tobacco
meadow saffron
raspberry bush
Scotch thistle
spike lavender
summer cypress

sweet marjoram
traveller's joy
Venus's fly trap
vervain mallow
viper's bugloss
wall pennywort
water calamint
water crowfoot
water hyacinth
wayfaring tree

14

blackberry bush
blue couch grass
carline thistle
distaff thistle
fuller's thistle
giant groundsel
golden lungwort
golden mouse-ear

gooseberry bush
mountain sorrel
prince's feather
sensitive plant
shepherd's pouch
shepherd's purse
shepherd's staff
snake's-head iris
Spanish bayonet
starch hyacinth
treacle mustard
wood nightshade

15

golden saxifrage
Italian rye grass
shepherd's needle
Venus's navelwort
virginia creeper
woody nightshade

Trees, shrubs, etc.

2 AND **3**

asa
ash
bay
bo
box
elm
fig
fir
gum
haw
hip
hop
ivy
may
nut
oak
sap
tea
tod
yew

4

acer
akee
aloe
arum
atap
balm
bark
bass
bead
beam
bole
cork
dali
dari
date
deal
holm
huon
hura
ilex
jaca

lana
leaf
lime
lote
milk
mowa
palm
pear
pine
pipe
plum
roan
root
rose
shea
sloe
sorb
teak
teil
twig
upas
vine

5

abele
Abies
acorn
agave
alder
almug
amber
anise
anona
apple
arbor
areca
Argan
aspen
balsa
Banga
beech
birch
cacao
carob
cedar

clove
copse
coral
durio
dwarf
ebony
elder
fagus
fruit
glade
glory
grass
grove
guava
hazel
holly
judas
karri
kauri
larch
lemon
lilac
macaw
mahwa
mango
maple
mulga
myall
nyssa
oaken
olive
osier
palay
papaw
peach
pecan
pipal
plane
plank
quina
roots
rowan
salix
sapan
smoke
sumac
taxus

thorn
tilia
tingi
trunk
tsuga
tuart
tulip
ulmus
walan
yulan
xamia

6

abroma
acacia
almond
aralia
arbute
balsam
bamboo
banana
banyan
baobab
bog-oak
bombax
bo-tree
bottle
branch
brazil
butter
button
carica
cashew
catkin
caudex
cedrat
cerris
cerrus
cherry
citron
coffee
cornel
daphne
deodar
fustic

217

gatten
ginkgo
illipe
jarrah
kittul
kumbuk
laurel
lignum
linden
locust
mallee
manuka
mastic
medlar
mimosa
nargil
nettle
orange
pawpaw
pepper
pinery
poplar
privet
quince
redbud
red fir
red gum
rubber
sallow
sappan
she-oak
sissoo
sorrel
souari
spruce
sumach
sylvan
tallow
timber
titoki
tupelo
veneer
vinery
walnut
wampee
wattle
wicken
willow

7

ailanto
amboyna
aniseed
Arbutus
ash tree
avocado
banksia
bay tree
blossom
blue gum
boxwood
buckeye
cabbage
camphor
cam-wood
canella
catalpa
champac
coconut
conifer
coquito
corylus
cowtree
cypress

daddock
dammara
determa
dogwood
dottard
duramen
elk-wood
elm tree
emblica
fan palm
fig tree
fir cone
fir tree
foliage
genipap
gum tree
hemlock
hickory
hog palm
holm oak
jasmine
jugians
juniper
king gum
kumquat
lentisk
logwood
margosa
mastich
moringa
nut pine
oakling
oak tree
oil palm
orchard
platane
pollard
quercus
red pine
redwood
sandbox
sanders
sapling
sapwood
Sequoia
service
shittah
shittim
silk oak
snow-gum
sour-sop
spindle
tanghin
varnish
wallaba
wax palm
wax tree
wych-elm

8

agalloch
agalwood
alburnum
allspice
arbuscle
ash grove
bass wood
beam tree
beachnut
benjamin
black gum
box elder
calabash
castanea

chestnut
cinchona
coco-palm
coco-tree
cork tree
crab-tree
date palm
date plum
doom-palm
eucalypt
fraxinus
gardenia
giant gum
guaiacum
hardbeam
hawthorn
holly-oak
hornbeam
ironbark
ironwood
jack tree
jack wood
kingwood
laburnum
lima wood
long jack
magnolia
mahogany
mangrove
manna-ash
milk tree
mulberry
musk wood
mustaiba
palmetto
palm tree
pandanus
pear tree
pinaster
pine cone
pine tree
pistacia
pockwood
raintree
red cedar
red maple
rosewood
royal oak
sago palm
sapindus
scrub-oak
searwood
seedling
silky oak
sugar gum
swamp oak
sweet-bay
sweet gum
sycamore
tamarind
tamarisk
taxodium
toon-wood
white ash
white fir
white gum
white oak
wistaria
witch-elm

9

adansonia
ailanthus
aloes wood

alpine fir
angophora
araucaria
balsam fir
blackwood
brown pine
buckthorn
bud-scale
butternut
calambour
china tree
chincapin
crab apple
Cupressus
deciduous
erythrine
evergreen
forest oak
fruit tree
grapevine
greenwood
ground ash
ground oak
hackberry
ivory palm
jacaranda
Judas tree
kokrawood
lance wood
lentiscus
maracauba
mustahiba
paper bark
plane tree
quickbeam
rowan tree
sandarach
sapan wood
sapodilla
saskatoon
sassafras
satinwood
Scotch elm
Scotch fir
Scotch pine
screw-pine
shade tree
shell-bark
silver fir
sloethorn
snake-wood
sour-gourd
spicewood
stone pine
suradanni
terebinth
thorn tree
tigerwood
toothache
touch-wood
tulip tree
whitebeam
white pine
whitewood
woodlayer
yacca wood
zebra wood

10

agallochum
almond tree
artocarpus
balaustine
blackthorn

blue spruce
brazilwood
breadfruit
bunji-bunji
bunya-bunya
burra-murra
butter tree
coastal-tea
coccomilia
coniferous
cotton tree
cottonwood
Douglas fir
eucalyptus
fiddle wood
flindersia
flooded gum
garlic-pear
green-heart
hackmatack
holly berry
Indian date
japati palm
letter wood
lilly-pilly
manchineel
mangosteen
orange-ball
orange wood
palisander
paper birch
pine needle
prickly ash
quercitron

sandalwood
sand-cherry
sand-myrtle
silk-cotton
silver-bell
sneeze-wood
Spanish fir
strawberry
sugar-maple
swamp maple
tall wattle
thyine wood
weeping ash
white cedar
white thorn
wild cherry
witch hazel
woolly butt
yellow-wood

11

Algerian fir
bean trefoil
black walnut
black wattle
black willow
bottle-brush
cedar wattle
chrysobalan
coconut palm
cootamundra

copper beech
cypress pine
elaeocarpus
eriodendron
golden chain
golden mohur
hoary poplar
honey locust
Japan laurel
leper-wattle
lignum vitae
mountain ash
phoenix-palm
pomegranate
quicken tree
red-iron bark
red mahogany
sideroxylon
silver birch
stringybark
white poplar
white spruce
white willow

12

almond willow
betel-nut palm
caryophyllus
crow's-foot elm
cucumber tree
custard apple

flowering ash
golden wattle
horse-chestnut
monkey-puzzle
Norway spruce
silver-wattle
Spanish cedar
tree of heaven
umbrella palm
virgin's-bower
weeping birch
wellingtonia
white cypress
winter cherry
xylobalsamum

13 AND OVER

bird's-eye maple (13)
campeachy wood (13)
Cedar of Lebanon (14)
Christmas tree (13)
cornus florida (13)
dog-wood wattle (13)
galactodendron (14)
horse-chestnut (13)
Japanese cedar (13)
partridge wood (13)
sunshine wattle (14)
toxicodendron (13)
trembling poplar (15)
weeping willow (13)

Vegetables

3 AND 4

bean
beet
cole
corn
faba
kale
leek
neep
okra
pea(s)
sage
soy(a)
yam

5

caper
chard
chick
chili
chive
cibol
colza
cress
fitch
gourd
maize
onion
orach
pease
pulse
savoy
swede

6

carrot
celery
daucus
endive
fennel
garlic
girkin
greens
lentil
marrow
nettle
orache
porret
potato
radish
sprout
tomato
turnip

7

batatas
cabbage
cardoon
chicory
gherkin
haricot
hotspur
lactuca
lettuce
mustard
parsley
parsnip

pea bean
peppers
pimento
pompion
pumpkin
salsify
seakale
shallot
skirret
spinach
sprouts
zanonia

8

beetrave
beetroot
borecole
broccoli
capsicum
celeriac
chickpea
colewort
cucumber
eggplant
eschalot
hastings
kohlrabi
lima bean
mushroom
plantain
scallion
soyabean
tickbean
zucchini

9

artichoke
asparagus
aubergine
broad bean
calabrese
courgette
curly kale
dandelion
green peas
horsebean
mangetout
marrowfat
red pepper
split peas
sweetcorn
turban-top
turnip top

10

adzuki bean
beet radish
cos lettuce
cow parsnip
French bean
kidney bean
King Edward
red cabbage
runner bean
scorzonera
turnip tops
watercress
Welsh onion

219

11

cauliflower
French beans
green pepper
haricot bean
horseradish
scarlet bean
spinach beet
sweet potato

water radish
water rocket

12

bamboo shoots
chat potatoes
corn on the cob
giant shallot

savoy cabbage
Spanish onion
spring onions
spring greens
white cabbage

13 AND OVER

broccoli sprouts (15)

Brussels sprouts (15)
globe artichoke (14)
horse cucumber (13)
ladies' fingers (13)
marrowfat peas (13)
purple broccoli (14)
scarlet runners (14)
spring cabbage (13)
tankard turnip (13)
vegetable marrow (15)

PEOPLES AND LANGUAGES
African tribes

3

Ewe
Fon
Ibo
Ijo
Iru
Suk
Tiv
Vai
Yao

4

Agni
Baga
Bena
Bete
Bini
Bisa
Bubi
Fang
Fula
Guro
Haya
Hehe
Hima
Hutu
Lala
Lozi
Mali
Meru
Nama
Nupe
Nyao
Teso
Yako
Zulu

5

Afars
Anuak
Bamum
Bantu
Bassa
Baule
Bemba
Chewa
Chopi
Dinka
Dogon
Galla
Ganda
Gissi
Grebo
Hausa
Iraqu
Kamba
Lulua
Lunda
Masai
Mende
Mossi
Nandi
Ngoni
Nguni
Nguru
Pygmy
Riffs
Rundi
Shona
Sotho
Swazi
Tonga
Tussi
Tutsi
Venda
Xhosa

6

Angoni
Bakota
Balega
Basuto
Bateke
Bayaka
Chagga
Fulani
Herero
Ibibio
Kikuyu
Kpwesi
Lumbwa
Luvale
Murozi
Ngwato
Rolong
Sambaa
Senufo
Somali
Sukuma
Thonga
Tlokwa
Tsonga
Tswana
Tuareg
Veddah
Warega
Yoruba

7

Ashanti
Baganda
Bakweii
Bambara
Bangala

Bapende
Barotse
Barundi
Basonge
Batonka
Batutsi
Berbers
Bunduka
Bushmen
Dagomba
Griquas
Mashona
Namaqua
Nilotes
Samburu
Shillak
Songhai
Turkana
Watutsi

8

Bergdama
Bushongo
Kipsigis
Mamprusi
Mandingo
Matabele
Tallensi

9 AND OVER

Bangarwanda (11)
Bathlaping (10)
Hottentots (10)
Karamojong (10)
Kgalagedi (9)
Lunda-Bajokwe (12)

American Indian peoples

3 AND 4

Cree
Crow
Fox
Hopi
Hupa
Iowa
Maya
Moki
Pima
Sauk

Ute
Yuma
Zuni

5

Blood
Caddo
Campa
Creek

Haida
Huron
Incas
Kansa
Kiowa
Lipan
Miami
Moqui
Nahua
Omaha
Osage
Sioux

Teton
Wappo
Yaqui
Yuchi
Yunca

6

Abnaki
Apache

Aymara
Aztecs
Biloxi
Caribs
Cayuga
Cocopa
Dakota
Dogrib
Kichai
Mandan
Micmac
Mixtec
Mohave
Mohawk
Navaho
Nootka
Ojibwa
Oneida
Ostiak
Ottawa
Paiute
Pawnee
Pequot
Pericu
Piegan
Pueblo
Quakaw
Salish
Santee
Sarcee

Seneca
Toltec
Warrau

7

Abenaki
Arapaho
Araucan
Arikara
Catawba
Chilcal
Chinook
Choctaw
Hidatsa
Mapuche
Mohegan
Mohican
Natchez
Ojibway
Orejone
Quechua
Shawnee
Stonies
Tlingit
Tonkawa
Wichita
Wyandot

8

Aguaruna
Cherokee
Cheyenne
Comanche
Delaware
Illinois
Iroquois
Kickapoo
Kootenay
Kwakiutl
Menomini
Muskogee
Nez Percé
Onondaga
Powhatan
Quichuan
Seminole
Shoshoni
Shushwap

9

Algonkian
Algonquin
Apalachee
Ashochimi
Blackfeet

Chickasaw
Chipewyan
Chippeway
Flatheads
Karankawa
Menominee
Penobscot
Tuscarora
Winnebago

10

Araucanian
Assiniboin
Athabascan
Bella Coola
Leni-Lenapé
Minnetaree
Montagnais
Shoshonean

11 AND 12

Narraganset (11)
Pasamaquoddy (12)
Root-diggers (11)
Susquehanna (11)

Languages, nationalities, and races

2 AND 3

Edo
Ewe
Fon
Fur
Ga
Gur
Hun
Ibo
Ido
Ila
Jew
Kru
Kui
Kwa
Lao
Luo
Mon
Shi
Tiv
Twi
Vai
Wa
Wu
Yao

4

Akan
Ambo
Arab
Avar
Bali
Beja
Bini
Bodo
Boer

Celt
Chad
Copt
Dane
Efik
Erse
Fang
Finn
Garo
Gaul
Ge'ez
Gogo
Gond
Grig
Igbo
Kelt
Kurd
Lala
Lapp
Lari
Lett
Loma
Lozi
Luba
Mano
Manx
Moor
Moxu
Naga
Nuba
Nuer
Nupe
Pali
Pedi
Pict
Pole
Russ
Scot
Sena

Serb
Shan
Sikh
Slav
Sobo
Susu
Teso
Thai
Tswa
Turk
Urdu
Wend
Zend
Zulu

5

Acoli
Aleut
Aryan
Asian
Attic
Bantu
Bassa
Batak
Bemba
Benga
Berta
Bhili
Bulom
Bussi
Carib
Chaga
Chopi
Croat
Cuban
Cymry
Czech

Dayak
Dinka
Doric
Dutch
Dyold
Dyula
Fante
Frank
Galla
Ganda
Gbari
Gipsy
Gondi
Greek
Gypsy
Hadza
Hausa
Hindi
Idoma
Indic
Ionic
Iraqi
Irish
Kadai
Kafir
Kamla
Karen
Kazak
Khasi
Khmer
Kissi
Kongo
Lamba
Lango
Latin
Lenge
Lomwe
Malay
Mande

221

Maori
Masai
Mossi
Munda
Nandi
Naron
Negro
Ngala
Nguni
Nkore
Norse
Nyong
Nyoro
Oriya
Oscan
Punic
Roman
Ronga
Rundi
Sango
Saudi
Saxon
Scots
Shilh
Shona
Sinic
Sotho
Swazi
Swede
Swiss
Tamil
Temne
Tigré
Tonga
Uzbeg
Venda
Welsh
Wolof
Xhosa
Yupik
Zande

6

Acholi
Aeolic
Afghan
Altaic
Arabic
Arawak
Argive
Aymara
Baltic
Baoule
Basque
Berber
Bokmal
Brahui
Breton
Briton
Bulgar
Celtic
Chokwe
Coptic
Creole
Cymric
Danish
Dorian
Eskimo
Fijian
French
Fulani
Gaelic
Gallic
Gascon

German
Gothic
Hebrew
Herero
Ibibio
Indian
Inupik
Ionian
Italic
Jewess
Jewish
Judaic
Kabyle
Kaffir
Kanuri
Kikuyu
Korean
Kpelle
Kpessi
Kurukh
Libyan
Luvale
Manchu
Mongol
Navaho
Ndonga
Nepali
Ngbaka
Ngombe
Norman
Nsenga
Nubian
Nyanja
Ostman
Papuan
Parian
Parsee
Patois
Polish
Pushto
Pushtu
Rajput
Romaic
Romany
Rwanda
Ryukyu
Sabine
Samoan
Sérère
Sindhi
Slavic
Slovak
Somali
Soviet
Sukuma
Syriac
Syrian
Telegu
Teuton
Theban
Thonga
Tongan
Trojan
Tsonga
Tswana
Tuareg
Tungus
Turkic
Tuscan
Viking
Votyak
Yankee
Yemeni
Yoruba
Zenaga

7

Acadian
African
Amharic
Angolan
Arabian
Aramaic
Aramean
Armoric
Asiatic
Avestan
Bagirmi
Balanta
Balochi
Bambara
Bedouin
Belgian
Bengali
Bisayan
British
Burmese
Bushmen
Catalan
Chechen
Chilean
Chinese
Cornish
Cypriot
Dagomba
Dalicad
Dialect
English
Finnish
Fleming
Flemish
Frisian
Gambian
Gaulish
Guarani
Haitian
Hamitic
Hebraic
Hessian
Hittite
Iberian
Ilocano
Iranian
Israeli
Italian
Karanga
Khoisan
Kirghiz
Kurdish
Kuwaiti
Laotian
Laotien
Lappish
Latvian
Lingala
Lombard
Lugbara
Maduran
Malinke
Maltese
Mandyak
Manxman
Marathi
Mexican
Moorish
Mordvin
Morisco
Mozareb
Mulatto
Nahuatl
Nauruan

Ndebele
Negress
Ngbandi
Nilotic
Nynorsk
Ottoman
Pahlavi
Palaung
Persian
Prakrit
Punjabi
Quechua
Romance
Romansh
Russian
Rwandan
Samiote
Samoyed
Sandawe
Santali
Semitic
Serbian
Shilluk
Siamese
Slovene
Songhai
Spanish
Spartan
Swahili
Swedish
Tagalog
Tibetan
Tigrina
Turkish
Ugandan
Umbrian
Umbundu
Venetic
Walloon
Yiddish
Zairese
Zambian

8

Abderite
Akkadian
Albanian
Algerian
American
Andorran
Antiguan
Armenian
Assamese
Assyrian
Austrian
Balinese
Bavarian
Bermudan
Bohemian
Bolivian
Cambrian
Canadian
Chaldaic
Chaldean
Chamorro
Cherokee
Corsican
Cushitic
Cyrenaic
Delphian
Dutchman
Egyptian
Estonian
Ethiopic

Etruscan
Eurasian
Frankish
Gallican
Georgian
Germanic
Ghanaian
Gujarati
Gujariti
Guyanese
Hawaiian
Hellenic
Helvetic
Honduran
Illyrian
Irishman
Japanese
Javanese
Kashmiri
Kimbundu
Kingwana
Kuki-Chin
Kukuruku
Kwanyama
Lebanese
Liberian
Makassar
Malagasy
Malawian
Mandarin
Mandingo
Mandinka
Memphian
Moroccan
Moru-Madi
Negritos
Nepalese
Nigerian
Nuba-Fula
Nyamwesi
Octoroon
Old Norse
Old Saxon
Parthian
Pelasgic
Peruvian
Phrygian
Prussian
Romanian
Romansch
Rumanian
Sanskrit
Scotsman
Scottish

Sicilian
Slavonic
Spaniard
Sudanese
Sumerian
Teutonic
Tunisian
Turanian
Turkomen
Vandalic
Visigoth
Welshman

9

Abkhasian
Afrikaans
Afrikaner
Anatolian
Armorican
Barbadian
Bengalese
Brazilian
Bulgarian
Byzantian
Byzantine
Cambodian
Cantonese
Caucasian
Ceylonese
Chari-Nile
Cheremiss
Cimmerian
Colombian
Congolese
Dravidian
Esperanto
Esquimaux
Ethiopian
Frenchman
Hanseatic
Hibernian
Hottentot
Hungarian
Icelander
Icelandic
Israelite
Jordanian
Kabardian
Kannarese
Low German
Malayalam
Malaysian

Mauritian
Mongolian
Negrillos
Nepaulese
Norwegian
Ostrogoth
Pakistani
Provencal
Red Indian
Rhodesian
Roumanian
Samaritan
Sardinian
Sere Mundu
Sinhalese
Sri Lankan
Sundanese
Taiwanese
Tanzanian
Tocharian
Ukrainian
Ulotrichi
Uruguayan

10

Abyssinian
Afrikander
Algonquian
Anglo-Saxon
Australian
Autochthon
Babylonian
Circassian
Costa Rican
Ecuadorian
Englishman
Finno-Ugric
Florentine
Guatemalan
High German
Hindustani
Indonesian
Israelitic
Lithuanian
Melanesian
Mingrelian
Monegasque
Neapolitan
Nicaraguan
Nicobarese
Niger-Congo
Panamanian

Paraguayan
Patagonian
Philippine
Philistine
Phoenician
Polynesian
Pomeranian
Portuguese
Rajasthani
Senegalese
Serbo-Croat
Singhalese
Venezuelan
Vernacular
Vietnamese

11

Afro-Asiatic
Argentinian
Azerbaijani
Bangladeshi
Greenlander
Indo-Hittite
Indo-Iranian
Mauretanian
Palestinian
Scots Gaelic
Sino-Tibetan
Trinidadian

12

Basic English
Byelorussian
Indo-European
King's English
Moru-Mangbetu
mother tongue
New Zealander
Plattdeutsch
Scandinavian
Tibeto-Burman

13

Pidgin English
Queen's English
Rhaeto-Romanic
Serbo-Croatian

RELIGION AND MYTHOLOGY
Biblical characters

3

Asa
Eve
God
Ham
Job
Lot

4

Abel
Adam

Ahab
Amos
Baal
Boaz
Cain
Esau
Jael
Joab
John
Jude
Leah
Levi
Luke
Magi (The)

Mark
Mary
Moab
Noah
Paul
Ruth
Saul
Shem

5

Aaron
Annas

Caleb
David
Demas
Devil (The)
Elihu
Enoch
Herod
Hiram
Hosea
Isaac
Jacob
James
Jesse
Jesus

Joash
Jonah
Judas
Laban
Linus
Lydia
Micah
Moses
Nahum
Naomi
Peter
Satan
Sihon
Silas
Simon
Titus
Uriah
Uriel
Zadok

6

Abijah
Andrew
Balaam
Christ
Daniel
Darius
Dorcas
Elijah
Elisha
Esther
Festus
Gehazi
Gideon
Haggai
Isaiah

Jairus
Joseph
Joshua
Judith
Kohath
Miriam
Naaman
Naboth
Nathan
Philip
Pilate
Rachel
Reuben
Samson
Samuel
Simeon
Sisera
Thomas
Uzziah
Yahweh

7

Abraham
Absalom
Ananias
Azariah
Clement
Delilah
Eleazar
Ephraim
Ezekiel
Gabriel
Japheth
Jehovah
Jezebel
Joiakim

Lazarus
Lucifer
Malachi
Matthew
Meshach
Michael
Obadiah
Pharaoh
Raphael
Shallum
Solomon
Stephen
Timothy
Zebulon

8

Abednego
Barnabas
Benjamin
Caiaphas
Gamaliel
Habakkuk
Hezekiah
Issachar
Jeremiah
Jeroboam
Jonathan
Maccabee
Matthias
Mordecai
Nehemiah
Philemon
Rehoboam
Sapphira
Shadrach
Zedekiah

9

Abimelech
Bathsheba
Jehoiakim
Nathanael
Nicodemus
Thaddaeus
Zacchaeus
Zachariah
Zacharias
Zechariah
Zephaniah

10

Bartimaeus
Belshazzar
Holofernes
Methuselah
Theophilus

11

Bartholomew
Jehoshaphat
Melchizedek
Sennacherib

13 AND 14

Mary Magdalene (13)
John the Baptist (14)
Nebuchadnezzar (14)
Pontius Pilate (13)

Mythology

2 AND 3

Aah
Aea
Ahi
Ali
Amt
Ana
Anu
Aon
Ate
Bel
Bes
Con
Cos
Dis
Ea
elf
Eos
Eru
fay
Fum
Ge
Gog
Heh
Hel
Ida
Ino
Io
Ira
Lar

Ler
Lif
Mab
Min
Neo
Nix
Nox
Nut
On
Ops
Pan
Pax
Ra
Ran
Roe
Set
Shu
Sol
Sua
Tiw
Tyr
Ule
Uma
Ve

4

Abae
Abas
Abia

Abii
Acis
Agni
Ajax
Amam
Amen
Amor
Amsi
Amsu
Anit
Ankh
Annu
Anpu
Apia
Apis
Area
Ares
Argo
Asia
Askr
Aten
Atys
Auge
Baal
Bakh
Bast
Beda
Beli
Bias
Bilé
Bran

Buto
Ceyx
Chac
Chin
Clio
Core
Danu
Deva
Dice
Dido
Dino
Donu
Duse
Dwyn
Echo
Eden
Elli
Enna
Enyo
Eris
Eros
Esus
Fama
Faun
Frig
Fury
Gaea
gods
gram
Gwyn
Gyes

Hapi
Hebe
Heno
Hera
hero
Hest
Idas
Ikto
Ilia
Ilus
Iole
Iris
Irus
Isis
Issa
Itys
Iynx
jinn
Jove
Juno
Kali
kama
Lear
Leda
Leto
Llyr
Lofn
Loki
Maia
Mara
Mark
Mars
Math
Moly
Mors
muse
Myth
Nabu
Naga
Nebu
Nick
Nike
Nila
Nubu
Nudd
Odin
ogre
Pasi
Peri
Pero
pixy
Ptah
Puck
Rahu
Raji
Rama
Rhea
Roma
saga
Selk
Shai
Sita
Siva
Soma
Styx
Susa
tabu
Tadg
Thia
Thor
Tros
Troy
Tupa
Tyro
Upis
Vata

Vayu
Wasi
Xulu
Yama
Yggr
Ymir
Yoga
Yuga
yule
Zeus
Zume

5

Abila
Acron
Actor
Aedon
Aegir
Aegis
Aegle
Aello
Aenea
Aesir
Aeson
Aesop
Aetna
Agave
Ahura
Alope
Amata
Ammon
Amset
Anava
angel
Anher
Anhur
Anius
Antea
Anxor
Anxur
Apepi
Arawn
Arete
Argos
Argus
Ariel
Arimi
Arion
Armes
Artio
Asius
Atlas
Attis
Aulis
Bacis
Barce
Belus
Bennu
Beroe
Bitol
Biton
Bogie
Borvo
Bragi
Butis
Byrsa
Cacus
Cales
Canis
Capra
Capys
Carna
Ceres
Chaos

Cilix
Circe
Coeus
Creon
Crete
Cupid
Cyane
Dagda
Dagon
Damon
Danaë
Dares
Delos
demon
Deuce
Deuse
devas
Diana
Dione
Dirce
djinn
Dolon
Donar
Doris
Dryad
Durga
dwarf
Dyaus
Dylan
Edoni
Egypt
elfin
elves
embla
Enlil
Epeus
Epona
Erato
Estas
Evius
faery
fairy
Fates
Fauna
Fides
Flora
Freya
Freyr
Fulla
Gades
Galar
Galli
Garme
genii
Getae
ghoul
giant
Gihil
gnome
Gorge
Grail
Gwyar
Gyges
Gymir
Hades
Harpy
Helen
Helle
Herse
Homer
Honor
Horae
Horta
Horus
houri
Hydra

Hylas
Hymen
Hymir
Iamus
Iapyx
Iason
Ichor
Idmon
Idyia
Ilama
Ilium
Indra
Ionia
Iphis
Irene
Istar
Iulus
Ixion
Janus
Jason
Jorth
Kaboi
Kabul
Ladon
Laius
Lamia
Lamus
lares
Lethe
Liber
Linus
Lludd
Lotis
Lugus
Lycus
Macar
Macha
Maera
Magog
Manes
Maron
Mazda
Medea
Medon
Melia
Metis
Midas
Mimas
Mimir
Minos
Mitra
Moira
Molus
Momus
Monan
Mothi
Mullo
Muses
naiad
Nanda
Nandi
Nemon
Niobe
Nisus
Nixie
Norna
norns
Nymph
Orcus
Oread
Orion
Paean
Pales
Panes
Paris
Pavan

225

Perse
Phaon
Phyto
Picus
pigmy
pisky
pixie
Pluto
Poeas
Priam
Pwyll
Remus
Rimac
Rudra
Sakra
Salus
santa
satyr
Sesha
Sibyl
Sinis
Sinon
Siren
Skuld
Sulis
Supay
sylph
Syren
taboo
Tages
Talos
Tanen
tarot
Ta-urt
Theia
Thoas
Thoth
Thule
Thyia
Titan
Tohil
Tonan
Troll
Uazit
Uller
Urien
Urthr
Ushas
Vanir
Venti
Venus
Vesta
Woden
Wotan
Xquiq
Zamna
Zelia
Zetes

6

Abaris
Abdera
Abeona
Abydos
Acamus
Achaei
Achaia
Actaea
Admeta
Adonis
Aeacus
Aeetes
Aegeus
Aegina

Aegypt
Aeneas
Aeneid
Aeolus
Aerope
Aethra
Africa
Agenor
Aglaia
Agrius
Alecto
Aletes
Aleuas
Aloeus
Althea
Amazon
Amen-Ra
Ampyse
Amycus
Amydon
Anapus
Andros
Angont
Antium
Anubis
Anukit
Aphaca
Apollo
Aquilo
Araxes
Arctos
Arthur
Asgard
Asopus
Athena
Athene
Athens
Atreus
Augeas
Aurora
Avatar
Avalon
Bacabs
Baldur
Balius
Battus
Baucis
Befana
Bendis
Benshi
Bestla
Bitias
Boreas
Brahma
Byblis
Byblus
Cabiri
Cadmus
Calais
Canens
Cardea
Caryae
Castor
Caurus
Celeus
Charis
Charon
cherub
Chione
Chiron
Chryse
Clotho
Clytie
Codrus
Comana
Consus

Cratos
Creios
Creusa
Crissa
Crocus
Cronus
Cybele
Cycnus
Cyrene
Damona
Danaus
Daphne
Daulis
Daunus
Delius
Delphi
Dictys
Dipsas
Dirona
Dodona
Dragon
Dryads
Dryope
Dumuzi
Durinn
Echion
Egeria
Egesta
Elatus
Elymus
Empusa
Eostre
Eponae
Erebus
Euneus
Europa
Evadne
Evenus
Faerie
Faunus
Febris
Fenrir
Fenris
fetish
Fidius
Fimila
Fjalar
Foliot
Fornax
Frigga
Furies
Furnia
Galeus
Ganesh
Gemini
Genius
Geryon
Ghanna
Glance
Goblin
Gorgon
Graces
Graeae
Haemon
Haemus
Hafgan
Hamhit
Haokah
Hather
Hecale
Hecate
Hector
Hecuba
Helice
Helios
Hellen

Hermes
Hesiod
Hestia
Heyoka
Hroptr
Huginn
Hyades
Hygeia
Hyllus
Ianthe
Iarbas
Iasion
Iasius
Icarus
Ilaira
Iliona
Inferi
Iolaus
Iphias
Ishtar
Iseult
Isolde
Ismene
Italus
Ithaca
Ithunn
Itonia
Kobold
Kraken
Kvasia
Latona
Lilith
Lucina
Lycaon
Lyceus
Maenad
Mamers
Mammon
Marica
Medusa
Megara
Memnon
Mentor
Merlin
Merman
Merops
Mestra
Mictla
Miming
Mintha
Minyas
Mithra
Moccos
Moirae
Moloch
Mopsus
Munnin
Mygdon
Mythic
naiads
Narada
Natose
Nectar
Neleus
Nereid
Nereus
Nergal
Nessus
Nestor
Ninlil
Nireus
Niskai
Nomius
Nornas
nymphs
Oberon

Oeneus
Oenone
Oeonus
Ogmios
ogress
Ogyges
Ogygia
Oileus
Olenus
Ophion
oracle
Ormuzd
orphic
Orthia
Orthus
Osiris
Palici
Pallas
Pallos
Panope
Paphus
Parcae
Peleus
Pelias
Pelion
Pelops
Peneus
Perdix
Peryda
Phenix
Pheres
Phoebe
Pholus
Phylas
Pirene
Pistor
Plutus
Polias
Pollux
Pomona
Prithi
Prithu
Pronax
Psyche
Pulaha
Pushan
Pyrrha
Python
Rhenea
Rhesus
Rhodes
Rhodos
Rumina
Safekh
Samana
Sancus
Sappho
Saturn
Satyrs
Scylla
Scyros
sea-god
Selene
Semele
Semnai
Sestus
Sethon
Sibyls
Sigeum
Simois
Sirens
Sirona
Somnus
Sothis
Sphinx
spirit

sprite
Sthanu
Syrinx
Talaus
Tammuz
Tarvos
Tereus
Tethys
Teucer
Thalia
Theano
Themis
Thetis
Thisbe
Thunor
Thyone
Tiamat
Titans
Tityus
Tlaloc
Tmolus
Triton
Typhon
Ulixes
Umbria
Undine
Urania
Uranus
Utgard
Utopia
Vacuna
Valkyr
Varuna
Vishnu
Vulcan
Xangti
Xelhua
Xolotl
Xuthus
Yaksha
Zancle
Zethus
zombie

7

Abderus
Acarnam
Acastus
Acerbas
Acestes
Achaeus
Achates
Acheron
Acoetes
Actaeon
Achtaeus
Admetus
Aegaeon
Aegiale
Aenaria
Aepytus
Aesacus
Aetolus
Agamede
Agyieus
Ahriman
Alastor
Alcides
Alcmene
Alcyone
Alpheus
Aluberi
Amathus
Amazons

Ampelus
Amphion
Ampycus
Amymone
Amyntor
Anaburn
Anagnia
Anaphae
Anaurus
Ancaeus
Angitia
Anigrus
Antaeus
Antenor
Anteros
Anthene
Antiope
Antissa
Aphetae
Aphytos
Arachne
Arcadia
Arestor
Ariadne
Arsinoë
Artemis
Asathor
Astarte
Asteria
Astraea
Ataguju
Athamas
Atropos
Autonoë
Auxesia
Avatars
Avernus
Bacchae
Bacchus
banshee
banshie
Belenos
Bellona
Beltane
Bifrost
bogyman
Bochica
Bona Dea
Brahman
Branwen
Brauron
Briseis
Bromius
Brontes
brownie
Busiris
Caeneus
Calchas
Calypso
Camelot
Camenae
Camilla
Canopus
Capella
Caranus
Carneus
Cecrops
Celaeno
centaur
Cepheus
Cercyon
Cessair
Chelone
Chimera
Chloris
Chryses

Cinyras
Cleobis
Clymene
Cocytus
Copreus
Coronis
Creteus
Curetes
Cyaneae
Cyclops
Cythera
Dactyls
Daphnis
Delphus
Demeter
demi-god
Diomede
Dwynwen
Echemus
Echidna
Ehecatl
Electra
Elicius
Elpenor
Elysian
Elysium
Epaphus
Epigoni
Erigone
Erinyes
erl-king
Eumaeus
Eumelus
Eunomia
Euryale
Eurybia
Euterpe
Evander
evil eye
Exadius
Februus
Feronia
Formiae
Fortuna
Fylgjur
Galatea
Galleus
Gargara
Gelanor
Glaucus
Gnossos
Goibniu
Gordius
Gorgons
Grannus
Gremlin
griffin
Grimnir
Gryphon
Gungnir
Halesus
Hamoneu
hanuman
Harpies
Helenus
Helicone
Hesione
Hilaira
Hor-Amen
Hun-Ahpu
Hunbatz
Hurakan
Hydriad
Hygeian
Hylaeus
Iacchus

Gigantes
Gilgames
good folk
Govannon
Gucumatz
Halcyone
Harmonia
Haroeris
Heliadae
Heracles
Hercules
Hermione
Hersilia
Hesperus
Hyperion
Iardanes
Ilithyia
Illatici
Iphicles
Jarnsaxa
Jurupari
Keridwen
Kukulcan
Labdacus
Lachesis
Lampetie
Lancelot
Laodamas
Laodamia
Laomedon
Lapithae
Libertas
Libitina
Lupercus
Maeander
Mama Nono
Marpessa
Megareus
Melampus
Meleager
Menelaus
Merodach
Minotaur
Morpheus
Mulciber
Myrtilus
Narayana
Nausicaa
Niflheim
Nin-Lilla
Oceanids
Odysseus
Oenomaus
Olympian
Orithyia
Othrerir
Pacarina
Palaemon
Pandarus
Panopeus
Panthous
paradise
Parjanya
Pasiphaë
Pasithea
Pelasgus
Penelope
Pentheus
Pephredo
Percival
Periphas
Pessinus
Phaethon
Philemon
Phintias
Phlegyas

Phoronis
Picumnus
Pierides
Pilumnus
Pisander
Pittheus
Pleiades
Podarces
Polyxena
Porthaon
Poseidon
Prithivi
Proximae
Psamathe
Pulastya
Quiateot
Quirinal
Quirinus
Ragnarok
Rakshasa
Rhodopis
Rosmerta
Rubezahl
Sahadeva
Sarawati
Sarpedon
Schedius
Sciathus
Seriphos
Silvanus
Sipontum
Sisyphus
Sparsana
Srikanta
succubus
Summanus
Talassio
talisman
Tantalus
Tartarus
Tecmessa
Telephus
Terminus
Thamyri
Thanatos
Theogony
Thyestes
Tiresias
Tithonus
Tonatiuh
Tristram
Ucalegon
Valhalla
Valkyrie
Vasudeva
Vesuvius
Victoria
Virginia
Visvampa
Wakinyan
water god
Waukkeon
werewolf
Xpiyacoc
Yadapati
Zalmoxis
Zephyrus

9

Acherusia
Achilleum
Acmonides
Adsullata
Aegialeus

Aegisthus
Aethiopia
Agamemnon
Agathyrsi
Alcathous
Alcyoneus
Amalivaca
Ambrosial
Amphrysus
Anaxarete
Andraemon
Androclus
Androgeus
Andromeda
Antandrus
Antevorta
Aphrodite
Areithous
Areopagus
Argonauts
Aristaeus
Ascalabus
Asclepius
Ashtoreth
Assoracus
Autolycus
Automeden
Aventinus
Bacchante
Bosphorus
Brunhilde
Bucentaur
Bzyantium
Cassandra
Cerberean
Chalcodon
Charybdis
Chthonius
Clitumnus
Coatlicue
Cockaigne
Concordia
Cytherean
Davy Jones
Deiphobus
Demophoon
Dervonnae
Deucalion
Diancecht
Diespiter
Dionysius
Domdaniel
Enceladus
Epidaurus
Eumenides
Euphorbus
Eurybates
Eurypylus
Eurysaces
Excalibur
Fabia Gens
Fairyland
fairy tale
Faustulus
Ferentina
Feretrius
Fjawrgynn
Friar Tuck
Gagurathe
Gargathon
Ghisdubar
Guinivere
Hamadryad
Harmakhis
Heimdallr
Hippolyte

hobgoblin
Holy Grail
Hypsipyle
Idacanzas
Idomeneus
Indigetes
Iphigenia
Iphimedia
Ixiomides
Jotunheim
Lyonesse
Melanthus
Melisande
Melpomene
Menoeceus
Menoetius
Metaneira
Missibizi
Mnemosyne
Mnestheus
Nanahuatl
Narcissus
Noncomala
Nyctimene
Oceanides
Orgiastic
Palamedes
Pandareos
Pandrosos
Parnassus
Patroclus
Pelopidae
Periander
Philammon
Philomela
Phoroneus
Pirithous
Polydamas
Polydorus
Polynices
Polyphron
Portumnus
Postvorta
Pudicitia
Pygmalion
Quahootze
Rakshasas
Rediculus
Rigasamos
Robin Hood
Sagittary
Salmoneus
Samavurti
Saturnius
Scamander
Scyllaeum
Sibylline
Siegfried
Sthenelus
Strophius
Taranucus
Tawiscara
Telchines
Telegonus
Thersites
Thymoetes
Tisamenus
Tisiphone
Toutiorix
Uxellimus
Valkyrean
Valkyries
Vasishtha
Vertumnus
Walpurgis
white lady

229

wood nymph
Xbakiyalo
Xbalanque
Yggdrasil
Zacynthus
Zerynthus

10

Abantiades
Achillides
Aetholides
Ahsonnutli
Ahura Mazda
Ambisagrus
Amisodarus
Amnisiades
Amphiaraus
Amphictyon
Amphitrite
Amphitryon
Andromache
Antilochus
Antitaurus
Arcesilaus
Archemoros
Berecyntia
Bussumarus
Callirrhoe
Cassiopeia
changeling
Cihuacoatl
cockatrice
compitalia
cornucopia
Corybantes
Cyparissus
Delphinium
Eileithyia
Eldhrimnir
Emathiades
Epimenides
Epimetheus
Erechtheum
Erechtheus
Erymanthus
Euphrosyne
fisher king
Galinthias
Gwenhwyvar
Hamadryads
Heliopolis
Hephaestus
Hesperides
Hippocrene
Hippodamia
Hippogriff

Hippolytus
Hippomedon
Hippothous
Horbehutet
Juggernaut
Kaneakeluh
King Arthur
leprechaun
Lifthrasir
little folk
Maid Marian
Mama Quilla
Melanippus
Melanthius
Menestheus
mundane egg
Nausithous
Necessitas
Nilmadhava
Onocentaur
Pachacamac
Palladinus
Pallantias
Parnassian
Persephone
Phlegethon
Phosphorus
Pigwidgeon
Plisthenes
Polydectes
Polydeuces
Polyhymnia
Polymestor
Polyphemus
Porphyrion
Prajapatis
Procrustes
Prometheus
Proserpina
Qebhsennuf
Rhea Silvia
Round Table
Sakambhari
Samothrace
Santa Claus
Saptajihiva
sea serpent
Strophades
Talthybius
Telemachus
Tlepolemus
Trophonius
Utgardloki
Visvakarma
Visvamitra
Vrihaspati
Vukub-Cakix
Wonderland
Yajneswara

Yoganindra

11

Aesculapius
Alaghom Naom
Alalcomenae
Amphilochus
Anna Perenna
Antaeopolis
Anthesteria
Aphrodisias
Apocatequil
Arimaspians
Atius Tirawa
Awonawilona
Bellerophon
Britomartis
Canopic jars
Cueravaperi
Dam Gal Nunna
Eileithyias
Enigohatgea
Erysichton
Eurysthenes
Ginnungagap
Gladsheimir
Harpocrates
Heracleidae
mythologist
mythologize
Nantosvelta
Neoptolemus
Pandora's box
Penthesilea
Philoctetes
Polyphontes
Protesilaus
Savitripati
Scamandrius
Sraddhadeva
Symplegades
Terpsichore
Thrasymedes
Triptolemus
troglodytes
Ultima Thule
Vishnamvara

12

Acca Larentia
Achaemenides
Acroceraunia
Agathodaemon
Aius Locutius

Ancus Martius
Belatucadrus
Chrysothemis
Clytemnestra
Erichthonius
Gigantomachy
Golden Fleece
Hippocentaur
Hyperboreans
Hypermnestra
Jormundgandr
Kittanitowit
Mount Olympus
mythographer
mythological
Pallas Athene
Purushattama
Quetzalcoatl
Rhadamanthus
Tezcatlipoca
Theoclymenus
Trismegistus
Wandering Jew
white goddess
Xochiquetzal
Yohualticitl
Yudhishthira

13 AND OVER

Achilleus Dromos (15)
Apochquiahuayan (15)
Apple of Discord (14)
Augean stables (13)
Calydonian Hunt (14)
Colonus Hippius (14)
Damocles' sword (13)
Elysian Fields (13)
Father Christmas (15)
Halirrhathius (13)
Hermaphroditus (14)
Huitzilopochtli (15)
Itsikamahidis (13)
Jupiter Elicius (14)
Jupiter Pluvius (14)
Laestrygonians (14)
Llew Llaw Gyffes (14)
Mayan Mythology (14)
Never Never Land (14)
Oonawieh Unggi (13)
Phoebus Apollo (13)
Quetzalcohuatl (14)
Tloque Nahuaque (14)
Tonacatecutli (13)
Tuatha de Danann (14)
Walpurgis night (14)
Yoalli Ehecatl (13)

Religion, ecclesiastical terms, etc.

2–4

abbé
alb
alms
amen
apse
ark
ave
Baal

bier
bon
chan
cope
cowl
curé
dana
dean
Ebor
Eden

Eve
evil
ewer
fane
fast
font
God
guni
hadj
hajj

hell
holy
host
hymn
icon
idol
I.H.S.
Imam
I.N.R.I.
jah

Jain
Jew
joss
ka'ba
lama
lay
Lent
mass
monk
nave
N. or M.
nun
obit
pall
pew
pica
pie
pome
pope
pray
pyx
R.I.P.
rite
rood
rupa
sect
see
sext
sin
Siva
soul
Sufi
text
Toc H
Veda
veil
vow
Xmas
yang
yin
yoga
Zen
Zion

5

abbey
abbot
abdal
agape
aisle
Allah
altar
amice
angel
Arian
banns
beads
Bible
bigot
bless
bodhi
burse
canon
carol
chant
chela
choir
credo
creed
cross
curia
Dagon
deify
deism

deist
deity
demon
devil
dirge
dogma
double
druid
elder
ephod
exeat
faith
fakir
friar
glory
godly
grace
Grail
guild
hades
hafiz
Hindu
image
imaum
Islam
Kaaba
karma
Koran
laity
lauds
logos
manse
matin
mitre
morse
myrrh
pagan
papal
pasch
paten
piety
pious
prior
psalm
purim
rabbi
relic
saint
Sarum
Satan
selah
stole
Sudra
Sunna
sutra
synod
taboo
terce
Torah
tract
vedic
vicar
vigil
zazen

6

abbacy
abbess
adamic
Advent
adytum
anoint
anthem
ashram

aumbry
banner
beadle
Belial
bikkhu
bikshu
bishop
Brahma
Buddha
burial
cantor
censer
chapel
cherub
chrism
Christ
church
cierge
clergy
cleric
corban
culdee
cruets
curacy
curate
deacon
decani
dervis
devout
dharma
divine
donary
dossal
dunker
Easter
Elohim
Exodus
ferial
flamen
friary
gloria
Gospel
hallow
heaven
Hebrew
Hegira
heresy
hermit
homily
housel
hymnal
I-ching
intone
Jesuit
Jewess
Jewish
Judaic
keblah
latria
lavabo
lector
legate
Levite
litany
living
mantra
martyr
matins
missal
Mormon
mosaic
Moslem
mosque
mullah
Muslim
mystic

novice
nuncio
oblate
octave
ordain
orders
orison
pagoda
painim
palmer
papacy
papism
papist
parish
Parsee
parson
pastor
popery
prayer
preach
priest
primus
proper
psalms
pulpit
purana
Quaker
rector
repent
ritual
rochet
rosary
rubric
sacred
Saddhu
sangha
santon
schism
scribe
seraph
sermon
server
Shaker
shaman
Shiite
Shinto
shrine
shrive
sinful
sinner
solemn
Sofism
spirit
Sunday
suttee
Talmud
tantra
te deum
temple
theism
trance
triune
tunker
verger
vestry
virgin
Vishnu
votive
Wahabi

7

Aaronic
Abaddon
abelian

acolyte
acolyth
Adamite
advowee
Alcoran
Alkoran
alms-bag
ampulla
angelic
angelus
animism
apostle
Arahant
atheism
atheist
baptism
baptist
baptize
beatify
Beghard
Beguard
Beguine
bigotry
biretta
Brahman
Brahmin
calvary
cassock
chalice
chancel
chaplet
chapter
charity
chrisom
Cluniac
collect
confirm
convent
convert
croslet
crozier
crusade
dataria
deanery
decanal
deified
dervise
dervish
devilet
diocese
diptych
diviner
docetae
Elohist
epistle
Essenes
eternal
evangel
exegete
faculty
fasting
frontal
Galilee
gaudete
Gehenna
Genesis
gentile
glorify
gnostic
goddess
godhead
godhood
godless
godlike
godling
godship

gradine
gradual
gremial
hassock
heathen
heretic
hexapla
holy day
hosanna
impiety
incense
infidel
introit
Jainism
Jehovah
Judaism
Judaize
Lady Day
lamaism
Lateran
lectern
lection
liturgy
Lollard
low mass
madonna
maniple
mattins
messiah
mid-Lent
minaret
minster
miracle
mission
muezzin
mystics
narthex
nirvana
nocturn
numbers
nunnery
oratory
ordinal
orphrey
Our Lady
penance
peshito
pietist
pilgrim
piscina
pontiff
popedom
prayers
prebend
prelate
prester
primacy
primate
profane
prophet
psalter
puritan
Quakery
Ramadan
rebirth
rectory
requiem
reredos
retable
retreat
Sabbath
sacring
sainted
saintly
sanctum
Saracen

satanic
saviour
sedilia
service
Shaster
Shastra
Sivaite
sontane
steeple
stipend
sub-dean
Sunnite
synodal
tantric
tempter
tonsure
trinity
tunicle
unblest
unction
unfrock
Vatican
Vedanta
vespers
Vulgate
worship
Xmas day

8

ablution
aceldama
acephali
advowson
agnostic
agnus dei
alleluia
almighty
altarage
anathema
anchoret
Anglican
anointed
antiphon
antipope
antistes
apostasy
apostate
apparels
Arianism
Arminian
atheneum
ave maria
beatific
benifice
bénitier
biblical
brethren
breviary
Buddhism
Buddhist
cantoris
capuchin
cardinal
carmelin
catacomb
canonize
cathedral
Catholic
cemetery
cenobite
cenotaph
chasuble
cherubim
chimere

chrismal
christen
ciborium
cincture
clerical
compline
conclave
confalon
corporal
covenant
creation
credence
crucifer
crucifix
dalmatic
deaconry
deifical
demoness
devilish
devilkin
devotion
diaconal
dies irae
diocesan
disciple
ditheism
ditheist
divinity
divinize
doctrine
Donatism
donatist
doxology
druidess
druidism
ebionite
elements
Ember Day
enthrone
epiphany
episcopy
epistler
Erastian
Essenism
Eternity
ethereal
Eusebian
evensong
evermore
evildoer
exegesis
exegetic
exorcist
faithful
feretory
foot-pace
frontlet
futurist
God's acre
Hail Mary
heavenly
hell fire
hierarch
high mass
hinayana
holy name
homilies
holy rood
Holy Week
Huguenot
hymn book
idolater
idolatry
immortal
indevout
infernal

Jesuitic
Jesuitry
Judaizer
lay-clerk
libation
literate
lord's day
Lutheran
lych-gate
mass-book
mahayana
minister
ministry
minorite
miserere
modalist
Mohammed
monachal
monastic
moravian
nativity
navicula
Nazarene
nethinim
novatian
obituary
oblation
offering
ordinary
orthodox
paganism
pantheon
papistry
pardoner
Passover
pharisee
pontifex
preacher
predella
priestly
prioress
prophecy
prophesy
Proverbs
psalmist
Puseyism
Puseyite
quietism
quietist
Ramadhan
recollet
redeemer
religion
response
reverend
reverent
rogation
Romanism
Romanist
Romanize
sacristy
Sadducee
sanctify
sanctity
satanism
sequence
seraphim
sidesman
skullcap
Sunnites
superior
surplice
swastika
tenebrae
thurible
thurifer

transept
trimurti
triptych
unbelief
unbishop
unchurch
venerate
versicle
vestment
viaticum
vicarage
zoolatry

9

ablutions
alleluiah
allelujah
All Hallow
All Saints
alms bason
altar tomb
anchorite
anointing
antipapal
apocrypha
apostolic
archangel
archfiend
archiarcy
Ascension
athenaeum
atonement
baptismal
beatitude
Beelzebub
beneficed
bishopric
bismillah
black mass
blasphemy
Calvinism
Candlemas
Carmelite
catechism
cathedral
celestial
cere-cloth
Christian
Christmas
churching
clergyman
co-eternal
communion
confessor
Cordelier
cremation
Dalai Lama
dalmatica
damnation
deaconess
dedicated
desecrate
diaconate
dissenter
dissident
dominical
eagle-wood
Easter day
Easter eve
Ember Days
Ember Fast
Ember Tide
episcopal
epistoler

eucharist
eutychian
evangelic
gospeller
Gregorian
Halloween
hierarchy
hierogram
hierology
high mass
holy ghost
holy water
incumbent
induction
interment
interdict
Islamitic
Jansenism
Jansenist
Jesuitism
joss-stick
Lammas Day
lay reader
Lazarists
Lazarites
Levitical
Leviticus
Low Church
Low Sunday
Mahomedan
Maronites
martyrdom
Methodism
Methodist
moderator
monachism
monastery
Mormonism
mundatory
Mussulman
Nestorian
obeisance
offertory
orthodoxy
ostensory
pantheism
pantheist
paraclete
Parseeism
patriarch
Pentecost
pharisaic
plainsong
prayer mat
prayer rug
preaching
precentor
presbyter
priestess
proselyte
prothesis
purgatory
pyrolatry
Quakerism
quasimodo
quicunque
reading-in
reconvert
red rubric
reliquary
religieux
religious
repentant
responses
reverence
ritualism

ritualist
rural dean
sabbatism
sabianism
sacrament
sacrifice
sacrilege
sacristan
salvation
sanctuary
Scripture
semi-Arian
sepulchre
shamanism
solemnity
solemnize
spiritual
sub-beadle
subdeacon
subrector
succentor
suffragan
suffrages
sutteeism
synagogue
synergism
synodical
teleology
Testament
theatines
theocracy
theomachy
theomancy
theopathy
theophany
theosophy
Theravada
tritheism
Vaishnava
Vajrayana
venerable
vestments
Waldenses

10

Abelonians
absolution
abstinence
aladinists
Albigenses
alkoranist
All Hallows
altar bread
altar cloth
altar cross
altar light
altar piece
altar steps
altar table
Anabaptism
Anabaptist
anointment
antichrist
apocalypse
apostolate
apotheosis
archbishop
archdeacon
archflamen
archimagus
archpriest
armageddon
assumption
Athanasian

baptistery
benedicite
Bernardine
Bethlemite
bible class
biblically
black friar
Brahminism
Buddhistic
Carthusian
catechumen
Celestines
ceremonial
cherubical
chronicles
church army
churchgoer
church work
churchyard
Cistercian
confessant
confession
conformist
consecrate
consistory
cosmolatry
devotional
ditheistic
divination
Dominicans
doxologize
dragonnade
Eastertide
ecumenical
Ember Weeks
episcopacy
episcopate
epistolary
evangelism
evangelist
evangelize
free chapel
Free Church
Genevanism
gnosticism
Good Friday
gospel side
gymnosophy
halleluiah
hallelujah
hallowmass
heathenism
heaven-born
heliolater
heliolatry
heptateuch
hierocracy
High Church
high priest
holy orders
holy spirit
hylotheism
hyperdulia
iconoclasm
iconoclast
iconolater
iconolatry
idolatress
impanation
indulgence
infallible
invocation
irreligion
irreverent
juggernaut
lady chapel

lay brother
lectionary
magnificat
mariolatry
meditation
ministrant
missionary
Mohammedan
monotheism
monotheist
monstrance
omnipotent
ophiolatry
ordination
Palm Sunday
Pentateuch
pentecost
pharisaism
pilgrimage
prayer book
prayer flag
prebendary
presbytery
priesthood
prophetess
Protestant
puritanism
rectorship
redemption
repentance
reproaches
revelation
rock temple
rood screen
sacerdotal
sacrosanct
sanctified
sanctifier
schismatic
scriptural
septuagint
sepulchral
Sexagesima
Shrovetide
subdeanery
syncretism
tabernacle
temptation
39 articles
Tridentine
unanointed
unbaptized
unbeliever
uncanonize
unclerical
unorthodox
veneration
white friar
Whit Sunday
worshipper
Zend-Avesta

11

acephalites
agnosticism
All Souls' Day
altar screen
antepaschal
antependium
antiphonary
apotheosize
archdiocese
arches court
Arminianism

aspersorium
baldeochino
Benedictine
benediction
benedictory
bibliolatry
bibliomancy
black rubric
blasphemous
Bodhisattva
Catabaptist
Catholicism
chalice veil
celebration
chrismation
chrismatory
Christendom
christening
church house
commination
communicant
consecrator
convocation
crematorium
crucifixion
deification
desecration
devotionist
divine light
doxological
ecclesiarch
episcopalia
epistle-side
Erastianism
eschatology
eternal life
evangelical
evening hymn
everlasting
exhortation
fire-worship
freethinker
Geneva Bible
genuflection
hagiography
Hare Krishna
hierarchism
hierography
humeral veil
immortality
incarnation
inquisition
intercessor
irreligious
irreverence
Karmathians
Latin Church
Lord's supper
Lutheranism
miracle play
mission room
Mohammedism
Nicene Creed
parishioner
œcumenical
passing bell
passionists
passion play
Passion Week
paternoster
patron saint
Pedobaptism
pharisaical
Plymouthism
pontificate
pontifician

prayer wheel
priestcraft
procession
proselytism
proselytize
protomartyr
purificator
Reformation
religionary
religionism
religionist
religiosity
reservation
ritualistic
Roman Church
sacramental
sacring-bell
Sadduceeism
sarcophagus
scientology
Socinianism
theosophist
trinitarian
unbeneficed
uncanonical
undedicated
unorthodoxy
unrighteous
Wesleyanism
Whitsuntide
Zoroastrian

12

All Saints' Day
annunciation
altar frontal
archdeaconry
Ascension Day
Ash Wednesday
Augustinians
Bible Society
chapel of ease
choir service
Christianity
Christmas Day
Christmas Eve
church living
church parade
churchwarden
confessional
confirmation
Confucianism
congregation
consecration
consistorial
devil worship
discipleship
disciplinant
disestablish
dispensation
ditheistical
Easter Sunday
Ecclesiastes
ecclesiastic
ecclesiology
enthronement
episcopalian
evangelicism
exomologesis
frankincense
hot gospeller
image worship
intercession
interdiction

Low Churchman
metropolitan
mission house
New Testament
nunc dimittis
Old Testament
omnipresent
postillation
Presbyterian
purification
Quadragesima
reconsecrate
reconversion
red letter day
religionless
residentiary
Resurrection
Rogation Days
Rogation Week
Salvationist
sanctus bell
spiritualism
Sunday school
superfrontal
thanksgiving
Unitarianism
universalism
unscriptural
vicar general

13

All Hallowmass
All Hallows Eve
All Hallowtide

Anglican music
Anglo-Catholic
antichristian
antiepiscopal
Apostles' Creed
archarchitect
archbishopric
archdeaconate
baptismal shell
beatification
bidding prayer
burial service
burnt offering
canonical hour
ceremoniarius
Christianlike
church service
confessionary
convocational
Corpus Christi
credence table
devotionalist
Eastern Church
excommunicate
glorification
High Churchman
holy innocents
incense burner
lord spiritual
miracle worker
mission church
Mohammedanism
Nonconformist
paschal candle
pastoral staff
pectoral cross

prayer-meeting
Protestantism
Quinquagesima
Roman Catholic
reincarnation
Sacerdotalism
Salvation Army
sanctuary-lamp
scripturalist
Shrove Tuesday
Swedenborgian
Tractarianism
Trinity Sunday
unconsecrated
unevangelical
way of the cross

14

antiscriptural
black letter day
burnt sacrifice
church assembly
communion table
crutched friars
Easter offering
ecclesiastical
Ecclesiasticus
ecclesiologist
evangelicalism
evangelization
extreme unction
fire-worshipper
fundamentalism
Gregorian chant

high priesthood
Maundy Thursday
Orthodox Church
Oxford Movement
psilanthropism
psilanthropist
reconsecration
redemptionists
Reformed Church
Rogation Sunday
sacramentarian
sanctification
sign of the cross
transmigration
trine immersion
Trinitarianism
vicar apostolic

15

antievangelical
antiministerial
antitrinitarian
Athanasian Creed
cardinal virtues
Episcopalianism
excommunication
harvest festival
infernal regions
Jehovah's Witness
metropolitanate
Mothering Sunday
Presbyterianism
suffragan bishop
transfiguration

Saints

Note.—The numbers of letters mentioned do not include "St" or "Saint," for which allowances should be made when necessary.

3 AND 4

Abb
Ann
Anne
Bee
Bede
Bega
Cyr
Ebba
Gall
Jean
Joan
John
Jude
Just
Loe
Luce
Lucy
Luke
Mark
Mary
Paul
Roch
Zeno

5

Agnes
Aidan

Alban
Amand
André
Asaph
Barbe
Basil
Bavon
Bride
Bruno
Clair
Clara
David
Denis
Elias
Genny
Giles
Hilda
James
Kilda
Louis
Lucia
Marie
Olave
Paola
Peter

6

Albert
Andrea

Andrew
Anselm
Ansgar
Bertin
Brieuc
Claire
Cosmas
Fabian
Fergus
Gallus
George
Helena
Heiler
Hilary
Hubert
Jerome
Joseph
Ludger
Magnus
Martha
Martin
Maurus
Michel
Monica
Philip
Pierre
Thomas
Ursane
Ursula
Valery
Xavier

7

Ambrose
Anschar
Anthony
Austell
Barbara
Bernard
Bridget
Cecilia
Charles
Clement
Crispin
Damascus
Dominic
Dorothy
Dunstan
Elsinus
Emidius
Etienne
Eustace
Francis
Germain
Gregory
Isodore
Joachim
Leonard
Matthew
Maurice
Michael
Nazaire

Nicolas
Pancras
Patrick
Raphael
Raymond
Romuald
Saviour
Stephen
Swithin
Swithun
Vincent
William

Eusebius
Ignatius
Lawrence
Longinus
Margaret
Nicholas
Placidus
Vericona
Walpurga
Waltheof
Winifred
Zenobius

Fredewith
Hyacinthe
Joan of Arc
Mamertius
Sebastian
Servatius
Sylvester
Valentine
Walpurgis

Hippolytus (10)
Jeanne d'Arc (10)
Mercuriale (10)
Peter Martyr (11)
Philip Neri (10)
Scholastica (11)
Symphorien (10)
Zaccharias (10)

8

Aloysius
Augustus
Barnabas
Benedict
Bernhard
Damianus
Denevick
Donatian

9

Apollonia
Augustine
Catherine
Christina
Demetrius
Eanswythe
Elizabeth
Exuperius

10 AND 11

Apollinaris (11)
Athanasius (10)
Bartholomew (11)
Bernardino (10)
Benhardino (11)
Bonaventura (11)
Christopher (11)
Ethelburga (10)
Eustochium (10)
Gallo Abbato (11)
Gaudentius (10)

12 AND OVER

Anthony of Padua (14)
Bridget of Sweden (15)
James the Great (13)
James the Less (12)
John the Baptist (14)
Louis of Toulouse (15)
Mary Magdalene (13)
Nicholas of Bari (14)
Nicholas of Myra (14)
Simon Stylites (13)
Thomas Aquinas (13)
Vincent Ferrer (13)

SCIENCE AND TECHNOLOGY
Agriculture

3

awn, bin, cob, cod, cow, cub, dig, ear, erf, ewe, far, feu, gid, hay, hep, hip, hoe, hog, ket, kex, kid, kip, lea, moo, mow, pig, pip, ram, ret, rye, sow, ted, teg, tup, vag, vat, zea

4

akee, aril, avel, bale, barn, bawn, beam, beef, bent, bere, bigg, boon, bran, bull, byre, calf, cart, clay, corn, cote, crop, culm, curb, drey, dung, farm, foal, gait, galt, gape, harl, haum, herd, hind, hink, holt, hops, hull, husk, kine, lamb, lime, loam, lyme, malm, mare, marl, meal, milk, neat, neep, nide, nout, nowt, oast, oats, odal, paco, peat, pest, pone, quey, rabi, rake, rape, resp, rime, root, roup, runn, rust, ryot, sand, scab, seed, sere, shaw, silo, skep, skug, slob, sock, soil, soya, span, stot, teff, toft, tope, tore, udal, vale, vega, weed, wold, yean, zebu

5

ammon, aphid, araba, baler, beans, bhyle, biddy, borax, bosky, bothy, braxy, briza, calve, carse, cavie, chaff, churn, clevy, closh, couch, croft, crone, crops, dairy, ditch, drill, drove, durra, ergot, ervum, farcy, fruit, fungi, gavel, gebur

glume
grain
grass
graze
guano
halfa
hards
haugh
haulm
hedge
hilum
hoove
horse
humus
kulak
lande
llano
lobby
maize
mower
mummy
ovine
plant
ranch
rumen
sewel
sheep
sheth
shoat
shuck
spelt
spuds
staig
stall
stich
stipa
stock
straw
swill
tilth
tiver
tuber
veldt
vimen
vives
vomer
wagon
wheat
withe
withy
worms
yield

6

angora
animal
arable
arista
barley
basset
beeves
binder
bosket
bottle
butter
carney
cattle
cereal
clover
colter
corral
cowman
cratch
cutter

digger
disbud
dobbin
drover
earing
eatage
écurie
enspan
fallow
farina
farmer
fodder
forage
furrow
gargol
garran
gaucho
gimmer
gluten
grains
grange
harrow
heifer
hogget
hogsty
hopper
huller
incult
inning
inspan
intine
jument
linhay
llanos
malkin
manger
manure
mealie
merino
milium
millet
milsey
mowing
nubbin
padnag
pampas
piglet
pigsty
plough
podzol
polder
porker
potato
punner
raggee
rancho
realty
reaper
roller
runrig
sheave
silage
socage
sowans
sowing
stable
steppe
stover
tanist
tomand
travis
trough
turnip
turves
warble
weevil

7

acidity
aerator
alfalfa
amidine
anthrax
avenage
binding
boscage
budding
bulchin
bullock
buttery
cabbage
calving
combine
compost
copland
cornage
coulter
cowherd
cowshed
demesne
digging
dipping
docking
drought
droving
eanling
erosion
farming
fee-tail
foaling
foldage
foot rot
forcing
fox trap
gadsman
granger
grazing
hallier
harvest
hay cart
hay rick
hedging
herding
hogcote
hop pole
hunkers
implant
infield
innings
kidling
lamb-ale
lambing
laniary
layland
leasowe
lucerne
maizena
marlite
milk can
milking
misyoke
morling
multure
murrain
novalia
nursery
pabular
paddock
panicum
pannage
pasture
peonage

piggery
pinetum
pinfold
polders
popcorn
poultry
prairie
praties
predial
provine
pruning
pulping
pummace
radicel
raking
rancher
reaping
rearing
retting
rhizome
rokeage
rundale
rustler
ryotwar
sickled
slanket
spancel
stacker
station
stooker
stubble
stuckle
subsoil
swinery
tantony
tascall
tax cart
threave
thwaite
tillage
tilling
tractor
trammel
trekker
trotter
udaller
vaquero
vitular
wagoner
windrow
yardman

8

agronomy
branding
breeding
clipping
cropping
ditching
drainage
elevator
ensilage
farmyard
forestry
gleaning
grafting
hayfield
haymaker
haystack
haywagon
hopfield
kohlrabi
landgirl
loosebox

milkcart
pedigree
pig-swill
plougher
rootcrop
rotation
shearing
sheep-dip
vineyard
watering
wireworm

grassland
harrowing
harvester
haymaking
hop-picker
horserake
husbandry
implement
incubator
livestock
pasturage
penthouse
phosphate
pig trough
ploughing
rice field
screening
separator
shorthorn
sugar beet
sugar cane
swineherd
thrashing
threshing
trenching
winnowing

10

agronomist
battery hen
cattle cake
cultivator
fertilizer
harvesting
husbandman
irrigation
mould-board
plantation
rounding-up
self-binder
transplant
weed killer
wheatfield

cultivation
fertilizing
germination
insecticide
motor plough
pastureland
poultry farm
reclamation
stock-taking
water-trough
weed control

9

agrimotor
agroville
allotment
cornfield
dairy-farm
dairymaid
disc drill
fertility
fungicide
gathering

11

agriculture
cake crusher
chaff cutter
chicken farm
crude plough

12

agricultural
feeding-stock
fermentation
horticulture
insemination
market garden
smallholding
swathe turner
turnip cutter

Astronomy

(a.) = asteroid.   (c.) = constellation.   (c.p.) = constellation (popular name).
(g.) = group of stars.   (p.) = planet.   (s.) = noted star.   (sa.) = large satellite.

2 – 4

Apus (c.)
Ara (c.)
Argo (c.)
belt
Bull (c.p.)
coma
Crab (c.p.)
Crow (c.p.)
Crux (c.)
Cup (c.p.)
Eros
Grus (c.)
halo
Hare (c.p.)
Hebe
Io
Juno
Leo (c.)
limb
Lion (c.p.)
Lynx (c.) (c.p.)
Lyra (c.)
Lyre (c.p.)
Mars (p.)
Mira (s.)
Moon
Net (c.p.)
Node
nova
orb
Pavo (c.)
pole
Ram (c.p.)
Rhea (sa.)
Star
Sun
Swan (c.p.)
Vega (s.)
Wolf (c.p.)

5

Algol (s.)
Altar (c.p.)
Apollo
Ariel (sa.)
Aries (c.)
Arrow (c.p.)
Ceres
Cetus (c.)
Clock (c.p.)
comet
Crane (c.p.)
Deneb (s.)
Digit
Dione (sa.)
Draco (c.)
Eagle (c.p.)
Earth (p.)
epact
epoch
error
flare
giant
Hamal (s.)
Hyads (g.)
Hydra (c.)
Indus (c.)
label
Lepus (c.)
Libra (c.)
lunar
Lupus (c.)
Mensa (c.)
Musca (c.)
nadir
Norma (c.)
orbit
Orion (c.)
phase
Pluto (p.)

Regel (s.)
Rigel (s.)
solar
space
Spica (s.)
stars
Titan (sa.)
Tucan (c.p.)
Twins (c.p.)
umbra
Venus (p.)
Vesta (a.)
Vrigo (c.)

6

albedo
Altair (s.)
Antlia (c.)
apogee
Aquila (c.)
Archer (c.p.)
astral
Auriga (c.)
aurora
binary
Boötes (c.)
Bolide
Caelum (c.)
Cancer (c.)
Castor (s.)
colure
Corona
corvus (c.)
crater
Crater (c.)
Cygnus (c.)
Dipper
domify
Dorado (c.)

Dragon (c.p.)
Europa (sa.)
Fishes (c.p.)
Fornax (c.)
galaxy
Gemini (c.)
gnomon
Hyades (g.)
Hydrus (c.)
Icarus (a.)
Indian (c.p.)
Lizard (c.p.)
lunary
meteor
moonet
nebula
Oberon (sa.)
Octans (c.)
Octant (c.p.)
octile
Pallas (a.)
parsec
Pictor (c.)
Pisces (c.)
planet
Plough (g.)
Pollux (s.)
pulsar
quasar
Radius
Saturn (p.)
Scales (c.p.)
Sirius (s.)
sphere
Square (c.p.)
sun-dog
syzygy
Taurus (c.)
Tethys (sa.)
triton (sa.)
Tucana (c.)

terrestrial
uranography
Water-bearer (c.p.)
Winged Horse (c.p.)

spectroscope
spiral galaxy
uranographic
Van Allen Belt
variable star

Bird of Paradise (c.p.)
Camelopardalis (c.)
Corona Borealis (c.)
interplanetary
Musca Australis (c.)
radio astronomy
radio telescope
right ascension
Sculptor's Tools (c.p.)
summer solstice
transit of Venus
vertical circle
winter solstice
Wolf-Rayet star
zenith distance

12

astronautics
astronomical
astrophysics
Charles's Wain (g.)
chromosphere
doppler shift
eccentricity
first quarter
Flying-dragon (c.p.)
Halley's comet
Horologium (c.)
intermundane
interstellar
lunar eclipse
lunar rainbow
Microscopium (c.)
Saturn's rings
shooting star
sidereal time
solar eclipse
Southern Fish (c.p.)

13

Alpha Centauri (s.)
Berenice's Hair (c.p.)
Canes Venatici (c.)
Coma Berenices (c.)
constellation
Crux Australis (c.)
meteorography
Northern Crown (c.p.)
Painter's Easel (c.p.)
River Eridanus (c.p.)
Serpent-bearer (c.p.)
sidereal clock
Southern Cross (c.p.)
Southern Crown (c.p.)
zodiacal light

14

annular eclipse
Aurora Borealis

15 AND 16

Alphonsine tables (16)
armillary sphere (15)
astronomical unit (16)
Aurora Australis (15)
celestial sphere (15)
Corona Australis (c.) (15)
Fraunhofer lines (15)
Magellanic Clouds (16)
meteoric showers (15)
Piscis Australis (c.) (15)
Sculptor's Chisel (c.) (15)

Biology, botany, and zoology

2 AND 3

ADH
ADP
ATP
bud
CNS
cud
DNA
ear
egg
ER
eye
FAD
fin
gel
gum
gut
IAA
jaw
lip
NAD
ova
pod
rib
RNA
rod
sap
sex

4

anal
anus
apex
axon
bark
bile
bird
body

bone
bulb
burr
cell
claw
cone
cork
corm
cyst
food
foot
gall
gene
germ
gill
haem
hair
hand
head
hoof
host
iris
leaf
lens
life
limb
lung
milk
NADH
NADP
neck
node
ovum
palp
pith
pome
pore
root
salt
seed
skin

stem
tail
urea
vein
wilt
wing
wood
yolk

5

actin
aorta
aster
auxin
berry
birth
blood
bract
brain
calyx
chyle
chyme
cilia
class
cline
clone
codon
colon
cutin
cycad
cycle
death
digit
drupe
druse
fauna
femur
fibre
flora

fruit
genus
gland
gonad
graft
heart
hilum
humus
hymen
ileum
imago
larva
latex
liver
lymph
molar
mouth
mucus
NADPH
nasal
nasty
nerve
order
organ
ovara
ovary
ovule
penis
petal
phage
plant
pubic
pubis
pupil
ramus
resin
scale
semen
sense
sepal
shell

shoot
sinus
skull
smell
sperm
spine
spore
stoma
style
sweat
taste
testa
thigh
tibia
touch
trunk
tuber
urine
vagus
villi
virus
whorl
wrist
xylem

6

achene
aerobe
albino
allele
amnion
animal
annual
anther
artery
atrium
biceps
biotic
botany
branch
bulbil
caecum
canine
carpal
carpel
caudal
chitin
climax
cloaca
coccyx
cocoon
coelum
cornea
cortex
dermis
dormin
embryo
enamel
energy
enzyme
facial
faeces
family
fibril
fibrin
fibula
floral
flower
foetus
forest
floral
fusion
gamete
gemmae

genome
girdle
growth
gullet
hybrid
hyphae
joints
labial
labium
labrum
lamina
larynx
leaves
lignin
mammal
mantle
marrow
mucous
muscle
mutant
nastic
nectar
neural
neuron
oocyte
oogamy
palate
pappus
pectin
pelvic
pelvis
phloem
phylum
pistil
plasma
pollen
purine
radius
rectum
retina
runner
sacrum
sexual
spinal
spleen
stamen
stigma
stolon
sucker
tactic
tannin
telome
tendon
tenson
testis
thorax
tissue
tongue
turgor
ureter
uterus
vagina
vessel
vision
zygote

7

abdomen
adenine
adipore
adrenal
aerobic
albumen
anatomy

annulus
antenna
antigen
asexual
atavism
auricle
biology
biotope
bipolar
bladder
bronchi
cambium
capsule
cardiac
carotid
cell sap
chaetae
chalaza
chiasma
chorion
cochlea
conifer
corolla
cranial
cranium
creeper
cristae
culture
cuticle
cutting
diploid
dormant
ecdysis
ecology
elastin
enteron
epiboly
epigeal
gastric
genital
gizzard
glottis
habitat
haploid
hearing
hepatic
histone
hormone
humerus
incisor
insulin
isogamy
jejunum
keratin
lacteal
linkage
mammary
medulla
meiosis
mitosis
myotome
nectary
nostril
nucleus
oogonia
organic
osmosis
oviduct
petiole
pharynx
pigment
pinnate
plastid
plumule
protein
pyloric

radicle
rhachis
rhizoid
rhizome
root cap
species
spindle
sternum
stomach
stomata
suberin
synapse
syngamy
systole
tapetum
tap root
teleost
tetanus
thallus
thyroid
trachea
triceps
trophic
tropism
urethra
vacuole
viscera
vitamin
zoology

8

abductor
abscisin
acoelous
acrosome
adductor
aeration
alkaloid
allogamy
alveolus
amoeboid
anaerobe
antibody
apospory
appendix
auditory
autogamy
bacteria
biennial
bile duct
bisexual
blastula
brachial
carapace
carotene
cellular
cell wall
cerebral
cerebrum
chordate
clavicle
cleavage
clitoris
coenzyme
collagen
cytology
dendrite
duodenum
ectoderm
efferent
egestion
endoderm
feedback
flagella

flatworm
follicle
ganglion
genetics
genitals
genotype
germ cell
holdfast
holozoic
homodont
hypogeal
inner ear
lamellae
lenticel
life span
ligament
mast cell
maxillae
membrane
meristem
mesoderm
midbrain
moulting
movement
muscular
mutation
mycelium
nerve net
nucellus
ontogeny
pancreas
papillae
parasite
pectoral
perianth
pericarp
perineum
placenta
plankton
polarity
polysome
pregnant
prop root
protozoa
receptor
ribosome
root hair
ruminant
sclereid
seedling
skeleton
spiracle
symbiont
syncarpy
taxonomy
tegument
tentacle
thalamus
tracheid
tympanum
vascular
vertebra
virology
zoospore

9

adrenalin
allantois
amino acid
anabolism
anaerobic
anisogamy
antennule

appendage
arteriole
autonomic
basal body
branchial
branching
capillary
carnivore
cartilage
cellulase
cellulose
centriole
chiasmata
chromatid
chromatin
chrysalis
commensal
community
corpuscle
cotyledon
cytoplasm
Darwinism
diaphragm
digestion
dominance
dura mater
dysploidy
ecosystem
ectoplasm
endocrine
endoplasm
endostyle
epidermis
eukaryote
evolution
excretion
excretory
exodermis
fertilize
forebrain
germinate
gestation
guttation
gynaecium
haemocoel
halophyte
herbivore
hindbrain
histology
homospory
hypocotyl
ingestion
inhibitor
internode
intestine
life cycle
life forms
megaspore
micropyle
middle ear
migration
mutagenic
nephridia
nerve cell
notochord
nucleolus
olfactory
oogenesis
operculum
optic lobe
organelle
organogeny
oxidation
pacemaker
perennial
pericycle

phagocyte
phellogen
phenotype
phylogeny
pituitary
proboscis
pulmonary
recessive
reflex arc
reticulum
retractor
sclerotic
sebaceous
secretion
secretory
selection
sieve cell
sieve tube
sporangia
Sporogony
sterility
stone cell
substrate
succulent
symbiosis
tricuspid
umbilical
unisexual
ventricle
xerophyte

10

acoelomate
actomyosin
alimentary
androecium
antheridia
anticlinal
aortic arch
apical cell
archegonia
autecology
biological
blastocoel
blastocyst
blastoderm
blastomere
blastopore
bronchiole
catabolism
centromere
centrosome
cerebellum
chemotaxis
chromomere
chromosome
coleoptile
copulation
dehiscence
dermatogen
entomology
epididymis
epiglottis
epithelium
fibrinogen
generation
geotropism
glomerulus
grey matter
guard cells
hemocyanin
hemoglobin
herbaceous
hereditary

heterodont
homocercal
homozygous
hygrophyte
hypophysis
incubation
inhibition
integument
interferon
Krebs cycle
Lamarckism
leaf sheath
leucoplast
locomotion
lymphocyte
mesenteron
metabolism
monoecious
morphology
mother cell
mycorrhiza
negentropy
nerve fibre
neural tube
nitrifying
nucleotide
oesophagus
omnivorous
osteoblast
osteoclast
parasitism
parenchyma
pathogenic
periosteum
phelloderm
photonasty
phototaxis
physiology
pineal body
polyploidy
population
prokaryote
prothallus
protoplasm
pyramidine
saprophyte
sarcolemma
schizogony
sieve plate
splanchnic
sporophyte
subspecies
succession
synecology
vegetation
vegetative
vertebrate
viviparity

11

aestivation
allelomorph
antibiotics
archenteron
autotrophic
autotropism
carbon cycle
carboxylase
carnivorous
chlorophyll
chloroplast
collenchyma
competition
conjugation

deamination
dessication
endothelium
environment
erythrocyte
exoskeleton
facultative
gall bladder
gametophyte
genetic code
germination
Golgi bodies
haemocyanin
haemoglobin
heterospory
hibernation
homeostatic
homeostatis
infundibulum
inheritance
loop of Henle
monoculture
muscle fibre
nematoblast
nucleic acid
orientation
parturition
pericardium
pinocytosis
plasmolysis
polar bodies
pollination
polypeptide
pseudopodia
respiration

somatic cell
spermatozoa
sub-cellular
tapetal cell
thermotaxis
triploblast
white matter
zooplankton

12

all-or-nothing
archesporium
back-crossing
bacteriology
biochemistry
buccal cavity
central canal
chondroblast
denitrifying
diploblastic
distribution
ectoparasite
endoparasite
endoskeleton
fermentation
flexor muscle
gastrulation
heliotropism
heterocercal
heterogamete
heterozygous
hypothalamus
invagination

invertebrate
mammary gland
medullary ray
microbiology
mitochondria
myelin sheath
nerve impulse
palaeobotany
phospholipid
phototropism
red blood cell
reductionism
reproduction
sclerenchyma
smooth muscle
spermatozoid
telolecithal

13

accommodation
bacteriophage
bicuspid valve
binary fission
cephalization
chemoreceptor
decomposition
dental formula
erector muscle
extracellular
Fallopian tube
fertilization
hermaphrodite
homoiothermic

insectivorous
intracellular
marine biology
mitochondrion
morphogenesis
multinucleate
ovoviviparity
palisade cells
parthenocarpy
photoreceptor
phytoplankton
plasmodesmata
proprioceptor
striped muscle
thermotropism
thigmotropism
translocation
transpiration

14 AND 15

Brunner's glands (14)
chemosynthesis (14)
extensor muscle (14)
Haversian canal (14)
multiple fission (15)
osmoregulation (14)
oxyhaemoglobin (14)
parthenogenesis (15)
photoperiodism (14)
photosynthesis (14)
poikilothermic (14)
polysaccharide (14)
vascular bundle (14)

Chemistry and metallurgy

2 AND 3

azo
DDT
DNA
E.M.F.
fat
gas
ion
oil
ore
pH
pKa
PVC
RNA
sol
TCP
tin
TNT

4

acid
acyl
alum
aryl
atom
base
bond
cell
clay
coal
coke
enol

gold
iron
keto
lead
lime
meta
mica
mole
neon
rust
salt
slag
soda
spin
zinc

5

aldol
alkyl
alloy
amide
amine
amino
anion
anode
arene
argon
basic
beryl
borax
boron
brass
chalk

ester
ether
ethyl
freon
glass
group
imine
invar
ionic
lipid
metal
model
molal
molar
monad
nylon
oxide
ozone
phase
radon
redox
resin
roast
smelt
solid
steel
sugar
vinyl
xenon

6

acetal
acetic

acetyl
acidic
adduct
aerate
alkali
alkane
alkene
alkyne
ammine
atomic
aufbau
barium
biuret
bleach
borane
borate
bronze
buffer
butane
carbon
cation
cerium
chrome
cobalt
copper
curium
dipole
dry ice
energy
enzyme
erbium
ethane
ferric
galena

243

gangue
gypsum
halide
helium
indium
iodate
iodide
iodine
iodite
iodize
isomer
ketone
ligand
liquid
litmus
methyl
nickel
octane
olefin
osmium
oxygen
period
phenol
phenyl
potash
proton
quartz
raceme
radium
reduce
refine
retort
ribose
rutile
silica
silver
sinter
sodium
solute
starch
sterol
sulfur
teepol
teflon
thymol

7

acetate
acetone
acidity
aerosol
alchemy
alcohol
alumina
amalgam
ammonia
analyse
aniline
anodize
antacid
arsenic
bauxite
benzene
bismuth
bonding
bromate
bromide
bromine
cadmium
caesium
calcium
carbide
cathode
chemist

chloric
cyanate
cyanide
diamond
dioxide
element
entropy
ferment
fermium
ferrate
ferrous
formate
gallium
gelatin
glucose
hafnium
halogen
holmium
hydrate
hydride
iridium
isotope
krypton
lithium
mercury
methane
mineral
monomer
naptha
neutral
neutron
niobium
nitrate
nitride
nitrite
nucleon
orbital
organic
osmosis
osmotic
oxidant
oxidize
oxyacid
pentane
peptide
pig iron
plastic
polymer
propane
protein
pyrites
quantum
quinine
reagent
rhenium
rhodium
silicon
soluble
solvent
spectra
spelter
sucrose
sulfate
sulfide
sulfite
sulphur
terbium
terpene
thorium
thulium
titrate
toluene
tritium
uranium
valence
valency

vitamin
vitriol
wolfram
yttrium

8

actinide
actinium
aldehyde
alkaline
aluminum
ammonium
analysis
antimony
aromatic
asbestos
astatine
Bakelite
Bessemer
caffeine
carbolic
carbonic
carbonyl
cast iron
catalyst
charcoal
chemical
chlorate
chloride
chlorine
chromate
chromite
chromium
cinnabar
corundum
covalent
cryolite
cyanogen
diatomic
diborane
didymium
disilane
dissolve
electron
europium
emission
enthalpy
ethylene
firedamp
fluoride
fluorine
francium
fructose
glycerol
graphite
gunmetal
half-life
haloform
hematite
hydrated
hydrogen
hydroxyl
ideal gas
inert gas
iodoform
kerosene
kinetics
litharge
lone pair
lutetium
magnesia
marsh gas
masurium
methanol

molecule
nichrome
nicotine
nitrogen
nobelium
noble gas
non-metal
oxyanion
paraffin
particle
peroxide
phosgene
platinum
polonium
pot metal
reactant
reaction
refining
rock salt
rubidium
samarium
saturate
scandium
selenium
silicate
solution
spectrum
suboxide
sulphate
sulphide
sulphite
tantalum
test tube
thallium
titanium
tungsten
unit cell
unstable
vanadium
water gas

9

acetylene
acylation
alchemist
alcoholic
aliphatic
allotropy
aluminate
aluminium
americium
amino acid
anhydrous
anti-knock
apparatus
aqua regia
bell metal
berkelium
beryllium
brimstone
carbonate
carbonium
catalysis
cellolose
chemistry
chokedamp
colombium
corrosion
deuterium
diazonium
duralumin
galvanize
germanium
haematite

histamine
homolysis
hydration
hydroxide
indicator
inorganic
insoluble
isomerism
lanthanum
limestone
limewater
magnesium
magnetite
manganese
metalloid
millerite
molecular
monatomic
neodymium
neptunium
nitration
nitronium
oxidation
palladium
periodic
permalloy
petroleum
phosphate
phosphide
plutonium
polar bond
polyester
polythene
polyvinyl
potassium
quicklime
rare gases
reductant
reduction
ruthenium
resonance
saltpetre
semi-metal
solvation
stability
strontium
sulphuric
synthesis
synthetic
tellurium
titration
vulcanite
ytterbium
zirconium

10

acetic acid
alkalinity

allotropes
amphoteric
analytical
bimetallic
bond energy
bond length
carnallite
catenation
chalybeate
chemically
chloroform
dative bond
double bond
dysprosium
electronic
enantiomer
exothermic
flotation
formic acid
free energy
gadolinium
heavy water
hydrolysis
isocyanide
laboratory
lactic acid
lanthanide
latent heat
lawrencium
mass number
metallurgy
mischmetal
molybdenum
Muntz metal
natural gas
neutralize
nitric acid
nucleotide
oxalic acid
phosphorus
polyatomic
polymerize
promethium
rare earths
saccharide
solubility
technetium
transition
whitemetal
zinc blende
zwitterion

11

acetylation
benzoic acid
bicarbonate
californium
cassiterite

cholesterol
crystallize
cyclohexane
dehydration
einsteinium
electrolyte
elimination
endothermic
equilibrium
free radical
German steel
ground state
hydrocarbon
hydrocyanic
hydroxonium
laughing gas
litmus paper
mendelevium
Muntz's metal
naphthalene
non-metallic
nucleophile
phosphorous
pitchblende
polystyrene
precipitate
prussic acid
quicksilver
radioactive
ribonucleic
sal ammoniac
Schiff's base
sublimation
substituent
tautomerism
transuranic
wrought iron

12

acetaldeyde
alkali metals
alkyl halides
atomic number
atomic weight
benzaldehyde
blast furnace
carbohydrate
carbonic acid
chlorination
condensation
covalent bond
deliquescent
diamagnetism
disaccharide
displacement
dissociation
distillation
electrolysis

electrophile
fermentation
formaldehyde
German silver
Haber process
halogenation
hydrochloric
hydrogen bond
permanganate
praseodymium
Prince's metal
protactinium
rate constant
sulphonamide
tartaric acid
zone refining

13

Bessemer steel
carbon dioxide
chain reaction
chromium steel
giant molecule
lattice energy
molecular mass
paramagnetism
periodic table
petrochemical
precipitation
radioactivity
reaction order
recrystallize
semiconductor
sulphuric acid
trisaccharide

14 AND OVER

Born-Haber cycle (14)
Britannia metal (14)
carbon monoxide (14)
carboxylic acid (14)
Chile saltpetre (14)
decarbonization (15)
deoxyribonucleic (16)
electrochemical (15)
esterification (14)
Grignard reagent (15)
monosaccharide (14)
organo-metallic (14)
oxidizing agent (14)
phosphor bronze (14)
photosynthesis (14)
polysaccharide (14)
reaction profile (15)
saponification (14)
trinitrotoluene (15)

Dyes, paints and colours

3

bay
dun
hue
jet
lac
red
tan
vat

4

acid
anil
ashy
bice
bise
blue
buff
cyan

dark
deep
drab
ebon
ecru
fast
fawn
food
gilt
gold

gray
grey
hoar
jade
kohl
lake
navy
pale
pink
puce

roan
room
rose
ruby
rust
sage
weld
woad
wold

5

amber
argal
argol
ashen
azoic
azure
basic
beige
black
brown
camel
chica
coral
cream
diazo
ebony
flame
grain
green
gules
hazel
henna
hoary
ivory
khaki
lemon
light
lilac
livid
mauve
murex
ocher
ochre
ochry
olive
orpin
paint
roset
rouge
ruddy
sable
sandy
sepia
snowy
sooty
stain
swart
tawny
ulmin
umber
white

6

anotta
anotto
archil
auburn
aureat
azured
bablah
bistre

bluish
cerise
cherry
chrome
claret
cobalt
copper
damask
direct
enamel
fallow
flaxen
fulvid
fustic
ginger
golden
greeny
indigo
isabel
kermes
lac dye
litmus
madder
marone
maroon
minium
modena
morone
murrey
orange
pastel
purple
reseda
roucou
rubian
rubied
rubric
rufous
russet
sallow
sanded
sienna
silver
sorrel
spotty
Tyrian
umbery
vermil
violet
virent
yellow

7

alkanet
almagra
annotta
annotto
apricot
arnotto
aureate
barwood
bezetta
camboge
camwood
carmine
carroty
cassius
catechu
cerulin
cesious
chermes
citrine
coupler
crimson

cudbear
cyanine
darkish
dracina
dracine
emerald
filemot
flavine
fulvous
fuscous
gamboge
grayish
greyish
grizzle
grizzly
hazelly
ingrain
logwood
magenta
mahaleb
minious
mordant
mottled
munjeet
nacarat
nankeen
natural
neutral
old gold
piebald
pigment
pinkish
plunket
reddish
red lead
rubican
ruby red
russety
saffron
scarlet
silvern
silvery
sinopia
sinopis
sky blue
solvent
spotted
stammel
streaky
striped
sulphur
swarthy
verdant
vermiel
watchet
whiting
whitish
xanthic
zaphara

8

alizarin
amaranth
amethyst
ashy pale
blood red
brownish
caesious
cardinal
carotene
cerulean
chay-root
chestnut
chromule

cinnabar
croceous
disperse
glaucous
greenish
gridelin
grizzled
iron grey
jet black
lavender
litharge
luteolin
mazarine
navy blue
nut brown
oak stain
ochreous
off-white
pea green
purplish
rose hued
rubrical
saffrony
sanguine
sap green
sapphire
saxe blue
sea green
speckled
streaked
titanium
verditer
viridian
xanthine
xanthium

9

alizarine
argentine
aubergine
azure tint
bone black
brilliant
carnation
chaya root
chocolate
coal black
cochineal
colour box
columbine
coralline
curcumine
developer
double dye
draconine
duck green
dun colour
Dutch pink
dyer's weed
dye stuffs
encrimson
envermeil
erythrean
ertythrine
euchloric
foliomort
Indian red
jade green
kalsomine
lampblack
leaf-green
lily white
lime green
myrobalan

oil colour
oxidation
pigmental
prasinous
puniceous
purpureal
purpurine
quercetin
royal blue
rufescent
safflower
sallowish
santaline
sapan wood
sap colour
sarcoline
Saxon blue
sky colour
silver grey
snow white
steel blue
turkey red
turquoise
verdigris
verditure
vermilion
vinaceous
virescent
white-lead
willowish
yellowish
zinc-white

10

alutaceous
apple green
aquamarine
atramental
aurigerous
Berlin blue
body colour
Brazil wood
Braziletto
burnt umber
carthamine
cobalt-blue

coquelicot
double-dyed
endochrome
erubescent
flavescent
florentine
French navy
giallolina
grass green
heliotrope
indigo blue
indigotine
ivory white
morbidezza
mosaic gold
ochraceous
olivaceous
olive green
powder blue
puce colour
quercitrin
roan colour
rose colour
ruby colour
salmon pink
smaragdine
snowy white
spadiceous
Spanish red
stone ochre
strawberry
swartiness
terra-cotta
terre verte
violaceous
whity-brown

11

aerial tints
anthocyanin
ash-coloured
atramentous
bombycinous
bottle green
burnt orange
burnt sienna

chlorophyll
chrome green
cineritious
cinnamon red
crimson lake
dun-coloured
ferruginous
feuillemort
fiesta pink
flame colour
flesh colour
fluorescent
incarnadine
king's yellow
lateritious
lemon yellow
liver colour
mandarining
neutral tint
orange tawny
peach colour
peacock blue
stone colour
straw colour
terra sienna
ultramarine
Venetian red
viridescent
water colour
yellow ochre

12

airforce blue
Avignon berry
cherry colour
chrome colour
claret colour
chrome yellow
copper colour
dragon's blood
Egyptian blue
electric blue
emerald green
ferruginated
feuillemorte
golden yellow

grain colours
Indian madder
Indian yellow
Lincoln green
midnight blue
Naples yellow
Persian berry
pillar-box red
Prussian blue
rose-coloured
sapphire blue
Spanish black
Spanish brown
Spanish white
thenard's blue
Tyrian purple

13

Adrianople red
auripigmentum
cadmium yellow
chestnut brown
couleur de rose
cream-coloured
fibre-reactive
flame-coloured
flesh-coloured
peach-coloured
rainbow-tinted
Scheele's green
straw-coloured
trout-coloured
versicoloured
yellow colours

14 – 15

atramentaceous (14)
Brunswick black (14)
Brunswick green (14)
chocolate colour (15)
copper-coloured (14)
divers-coloured (14)
Frankfort black (14)
highly coloured (14)
quercitron bark (14)

Engineering
See also **Instruments** and **Tools and simple machines**

2 AND 3

ace
amp
B.H.P.
cam
cog
dam
E.M.F.
erg
fan
fit
gab
hob
H.P.
hub
I.H.P.
ion
key

lag
nut
ohm
oil
ram
rig
R.P.M.
sag
tap
tew
tie
U.H.F.
V.H.F.

4

arch
axle

beam
belt
bolt
burr
cast
coak
cone
cowl
flaw
flux
fuel
fuse
gear
gibs
glue
hasp
hook
hose
jack

kiln
lens
lift
link
lock
loom
main
mill
mine
nail
nave
oily
pawl
pile
pipe
plan
plug
pump
rack

247

rail
reel
road
rope
rung
rust
shop
skid
slag
slue
stay
stop
stud
suck
sump
tamp
tank
test
tire
tool
tram
tube
turn
tyre
unit
vane
vent
void
volt
weir
weld
wire
work
worm

5

alloy
anode
binac
blast
braze
cable
chair
chase
civil
clamp
cleat
compo
crane
crank
crate
deuce
dowel
drill
drive
elbow
emery
felly
flawy
flows
flume
flush
force
gauge
girder
grace
H-beam
helix
hinge
hoist
ingot
input
jantu
jenny

jewel
joint
joist
keyed
laser
level
lever
lewis
maser
miner
model
motor
mould
oakum
oiler
pedal
pivot
plant
power
press
pylon
quern
radar
radio
ratch
relay
resin
rigid
rivet
rough
rusty
screw
shaft
short
shunt
slack
slide
sling
smelt
spoke
spool
spout
stamp
steam
still
strap
strut
stulm
swage
swape
taper
tewel
tommy
tools
tooth
T-rail
train
valve
video
waste
wedge
wharf
wheel
willy
wiper
works
X-rays

6

analog
aerial
anneal
axunge
barrel

bit-end
blower
bobbin
boiler
bridge
buffer
burner
camber
clutch
coppin
cotter
couple
cradle
cut-out
damper
derail
duplex
dynamo
energy
engine
fitter
flange
flashe
funnel
geyser
gutter
hinged
hooter
ingate
intake
jigger
kibble
lacing
ladder
lamina
latten
magnet
milled
mining
moment
monkey
nipple
nozzle
oil can
oil gas
output
petrol
pinion
piston
pulley
punkah
rarefy
repair
retard
rigger
rocket
roller
rotary
rundle
sagger
saw pit
sheave
siding
sleeve
sluice
smiddy
smithy
socket
solder
spigot
static
stoker
strain
stress
strike
sucker

switch
swivel
system
tackle
taglia
tappet
temper
tender
thrust
tie-bar
tie-rod
tinned
toggle
torque
tripod
trolly
tubing
tunnel
tuyere
uncoil
vacuum
washer
welded
welder
windle

7

adapter
air duct
airfoil
air pipe
air pump
air tube
air trap
artisan
autocar
autovac
battery
bearing
belting
booster
bracket
cab tyre
caisson
casting
cathode
chafery
chamfer
chimney
cistern
clacker
column
conduit
cutting
derrick
digital
drawbar
drawing
dry dock
dry pile
dynamic
exciter
exhaust
eyebolt
factory
ferrule
firebox
fitting
forging
founder
foundry
fulcrum
furnace
fuse box

gas trap
gearing
gimbals
gudgeon
hydrant
inertia
jointer
journal
lagging
lockage
lock-nut
machine
magneto
manhole
mill cog
mill dam
milling
monitor
moulded
moulder
mud hole
mud sill
nuclear
Ohm's law
oil fuel
oil lamp
oil pump
pattern
pig iron
pinhole
pontoon
program
pug mill
rag bolt
railway
ratchet
reactor
refract
rejoint
riveter
road bed
roadway
sawmill
scissel
seabank
seawall
shackle
shuttle
sleeper
smelter
soup pan
spindle
stamper
stand-by
statics
stopper
succula
suction
sump-pit
support
syringe
tamping
telefer
templet
tension
test bay
testing
thimble
tie-beam
tilting
tinfoil
tin mine
tinning
torsion
tracing
tramcar

tramway
treadle
trendle
trolley
turbine
turning
unrivet
unscrew
ventage
viaduct
voltage
voltaic
welding
wet dock
wringer
wrought

8

acentric
air brake
air valve
annealed
aqueduct
axletree
balancer
ball cock
bevelled
bridging
caliduct
camshaft
cam wheel
cassette
castings
cast iron
catenary
chainlet
chauffer
cog wheel
compound
computer
concrete
corn mill
coupling
cradling
cryotron
cylinder
Davy lamp
dead lift
declutch
draw gear
draw link
edge rail
electric
elevator
engineer
enginery
eolipile
fan blast
feed pipe
feed pump
fireclay
fireplug
flywheel
fracture
friction
fuse clip
galvanic
gas gauge
gas mains
gas works
gland nut
governor
gradient
hardware

hot blast
hot press
ignition
injecter
injector
ink stone
insulate
ironwork
irrigate
Jacquard
joint box
junk ring
klystron
laminate
land roll
leverage
limekiln
linch pin
linotype
lock gate
lock sill
lock weir
loop line
machinal
magnetic
main line
mechanic
mill pond
mill race
momentum
monorail
monotype
moulding
movement
mud valve
oilstone
oil store
oil stove
operator
ozonizer
pendulum
penstock
pile shoe
platform
polarity
pressure
puddling
pump gear
pump hood
purchase
radiator
rag wheel
railroad
recharge
refinery
register
repairer
repolish
rheostat
rigidity
ring bolt
rotatory
shearing
silk mill
skew arch
smeltery
smelting
soft iron
software
spinnery
split pin
stamping
standard
starling
stone pit
stopcock

strength
stuffing
tail race
tapering
telotype
tempered
template
terminal
textbook
throttle
tidegate
tide mill
tile kiln
time ball
tinplate
tractile
traction
tractive
train oil
tram rail
tramroad
turbojet
turnpike
tympanum
unclutch
uncoiled
unsolder
velocity
water gas
windmill
wind pump
wire-draw
wireless
wood mill
workable
workshop
wormgear

9

acoustics
air engine
air filter
air vessel
amplifier
artificer
bevel gear
brakedrum
brakepipe
brick kiln
blue light
blueprint
cast steel
chain belt
chain pump
clockwork
condenser
conductor
cotter pin
craftsman
crosshead
cyclotron
datum-line
dead level
diaphragm
disc brake
disk brake
dynamical
earthwork
eccentric
electrify
electrize
electrode
equirotal
escalator

female die
fire brick
fish joint
fishplate
floodgate
fog signal
foot valve
force pump
framework
funicular
galvanism
galvanist
galvanize
gas engine
gas fitter
gas geyser
gas holder
gasometer
gas retort
gearwheel
horse mill
hydraulic
hydrostat
idle wheel
induction
inductive
inertness
injection
insertion
insulated
insulator
ironsmith
ironworks
jet engine
knife edge
laminated
lewis bolt
Leyden jar
limelight
lubricant
lubricate
machinery
machinist
magnetist
magnetize
male screw
man engine
master key
mechanics
mechanism
mechanist
mechanize
mild steel
millstone
mine shaft
mud sluice
nodal line
nose piece
off-spring
oil engine
oil geyser
perforate
petrol can
piston rod
pneumatic
polarizer
porous pot
power loom
programme
propeller
prototype
pump break
pump spear
pump stock
radiation
rectifier

reflector
regulator
repairing
reparable
reservoir
resultant
rheomotor
rheophore
road metal
roughcast
sandpaper
scapement
shop board
shunt coil
sliderule
smack mill
soapworks
soldering
spring box
spur wheel
stanchion
steam pipe
stiffener
stock lock
stoke hole
structure
superheat
telephone
tempering
tin lining
tin mining
train road
transform
trunk line
tunnel pit
turntable
twin cable
unscrewed
vibration
voltatype
vulcanite
vulcanize
waste weir
watermark
water tank
well drain
wheelrace
whip graft
white heat
winepress
wire gauze
wire wheel
worm wheel
X-ray plant

10

accelerate
air machine
alarm gauge
alternator
anelectric
automation
automobile
bevel wheel
broad gauge
cantilever
caseharden
centigrade
clack valve
coach screw
combustion
crankshaft
crown wheel

dead weight
derailment
dielectric
discharger
disc wheels
dish wheels
diving bell
donkey pump
drawbridge
earth plate
economizer
efficiency
electrical
electronic
embankment
emery cloth
emery paper
emery wheel
engine room
escapement
fire escape
flange rail
fluid drive
footbridge
fuse holder
galvanized
gas turbine
glass paper
goods train
goods truck
grid system
gudgeon pin
guillotine
hair spring
heart wheel
hogger pump
horsepower
hydrophore
Indian fire
inertitude
inflexible
instrument
insulating
insulation
iron heater
irrigation
isodynamic
laboratory
lamination
leaf bridge
lewis joint
lock paddle
locomotive
lubricator
macadamize
magnetizer
male thread
mechanical
nodal point
paper cable
pentaspast
percolator
petrol tank
piledriver
pneumatics
powder mill
powerhouse
power-plant
programmer
pulverizer
pump-handle
recondense
refraction
rejointing
resistance
revolution

rubber-wire
safety-lamp
scoop-wheel
self-acting
skew bridge
smokestack
soap boiler
socket pipe
socket pole
solid state
spokeshave
stationary
steam gauge
stiffening
streamline
structural
swing wheel
swivel hook
telegraphy
telescopic
television
telpherage
temper heat
thermopile
thermostat
toll bridge
torque tube
transients
transistor
tunnelling
unclutched
unpatented
unsoldered
voltaic arc
voltaplast
water crane
water power
watertight
water tower
waterwheel
waterwings
waterworks
wave motion
well-boring
windtunnel
wiped joint

11

accelerator
accumulator
aerodynamics
air fountain
anelectrode
atomic clock
bell founder
bell foundry
block system
Bramah press
brush wheels
cable laying
candlepower
carburetter
carburettor
compression
computation
contrivance
coupling box
coupling pin
damask steel
diamagnetic
driving band
driving belt
dynamometer
edge railway

electrician
electricity
electric jar
electrolyze
electrolyte
electronics
endless belt
engineering
exhaust pipe
female screw
frame bridge
gas governor
graving dock
gutta percha
helical gear
incinerator
inking table
iron filings
iron founder
iron foundry
laminations
latten-brass
lock chamber
low pressure
lubrication
machine-tool
maintenance
manilla rope
manufactory
mechanician
mini-computer
mono-railway
narrow gauge
oil purifier
oil strainer
perforation
piledriving
pilot engine
power factor
rack-railway
rarefaction
reconstruct
retardation
revolutions
rolling mill
rubber cable
safety valve
searchlight
service pipe
skeleton key
socket joint
steam boiler
steam engine
steam hammer
stuffing box
suction pipe
suction pump
summit level
superheater
swing bridge
switchboard
synchronism
synchronize
synchrotron
tappet valve
toggle joint
transformer
transmitter
trundle head
tube railway
underground
uninsulated
voltaic pile
vulcanizing
warping bank
water cement

water engine
water furrow
water hammer
water supply
welding heat
wind furnace
wire drawing
wire grading
workmanship
wrought iron

12

acceleration
anti-friction
arterial road
artesian well
assembly line
balance wheel
belt fastener
blast furnace
block machine
block signals
canalization
chain reactor
coaxial cable
counterpoise
danger signal
diamagnetism
diesel engine
differential
disc coupling
disintegrate
donkey engine
double acting
driving shaft
driving wheel
dry-core cable
eccentric rod
eduction pipe
electric bulb
electric fire
electric fuse
electric iron
electric wire
electrolysis
electromotor
endless screw
engine driver
exhaust valve
female thread
flexible wire
floating dock
flying bridge
flying pinion
founder's dust
founder's sand
gas condenser
gas container
gas regulator
hanging valve
high pressure
hydraulic ram
hydrodynamic
inking roller
installation
jewel bearing
lubrifaction
machine tools
magnetomotor
make-and-break
manilla paper
marine boiler
marine engine
master spring

negative pole
non-conductor
nuclear power
oxy-acetylene
palification
paratonnerre
pattern maker
petrol engine
petrol filter
plummer block
polarization
pressure pump
pyro-electric
radiator muff
ratchet wheel
Réaumur scale
rolling press
rolling stock
service cable
short circuit
shunt winding
single acting
sleeve button
slitting mill
solar battery
specific heat
spinning mill
stamping mill
steam heating
steam turbine
steam whistle
suction valve
synchronized
terminal post
thermocouple
toothed wheel
transmission
unmechanical
unmechanized
vibratiuncle
water battery
water turbine
wheel-and-axle
wheel cutting
working model

13

buffing spring
civil engineer
compound-wound
contrate wheel
control theory
Cornish boiler
Cornish engine
counterweight
direct current
draught engine
drummond light
eccentric gear
electric cable
electric clock
electric fluid
electric light
electric motor
electric stove
electrifiable
electrization
electromagnet
engine-turning
expansion gear
ferrumination
flexible cable
floodlighting
fluid flywheel

friction balls
friction cones
inflexibility
injection cock
insulated wire
kinetic energy
lifting bridge
liquid starter
lubrication
magnetic fluid
magnetization
movement maker
non-conducting
overshot wheel
pneumatic tyre
pontoon bridge
pressure gauge
printing press
rack-and-pinion
roller bearing
series winding
shock absorber
snifting valve
standard gauge
telegraph line
telegraph pole
telegraph wire
telephone line
telephone wire
thermo-current
throttle valve
thrust bearing
water drainage
wave mechanics
whirling table
X-ray apparatus

14

analog computer
blowing machine
contra rotation
diesel-electric
discharge valve
discharging rod
disintegration
eccentric strap
eccentric wheel
electric cooker
electric cut-out
electric kettle
electrodynamic
electrostatics
electrothermic
explosive rivet
floating bridge
friction clutch
friction wheels
galvanized iron
hydraulic-press
insulated cable
lubricating oil
magnetic needle
multi-core cable
nuclear reactor
petrol strainer
plaster of paris
pneumatic drill
portable engine
reconstruction
resino-electric
resultant force
shellac-varnish
shunt regulator
thermo-electric

251

three-core cable
traction engine
universal joint
vitreo electric
voltaic battery
washing machine
wave telegraphy

15 AND 16

brake horsepower

block signalling
Centigrade scale
concentric cable
digital computer
electric battery
electric circuit
electric current
electric machine
electrification
electrochemical
electrodynamics
electrokinetics
electromagnetic

electronegative
electronic brain
electropositive
expansion engine
Fahrenheit scale
friction rollers
galvanic battery
hydraulic cement
insulating paper
irrigation canal
linotype machine
machine language
magnetic battery

magneto-electric
ohmic resistance
perpetual motion
pressure machine
railway engineer
smelting furnace
specific gravity
spigot-and-socket
synchrocyclotron (16)
tensile strength
water-tube boiler

Instruments

See also **Engineering** and **Tools and simple machines**

4 – 6

abacus
agate
camera
clock
dial
dynamo
filter
flange
fleam
flume
funnel
gauge
gasket
grid
gauge
lancet
laser
lens
lever
maser
megger
meter
nozzle
octant
octile
orrery
pole
probe
relay
rule
ruler
scale
square
style
tester
tool
trocar
toner
tube
U-tube
valve

7

aerator
ammeter
aneroid
balance
bearing
bellows
binocle
caltrop
compass

counter
divider
doubler
pH meter
quadrat
scriber
sextant
snubber
sundial
T-square
turbine
vernier
wet-bulb

8

analyser
biograph
bioscope
boot-jack
boot-last
boot-tree
calipers
computer
detector
diagraph
gasmeter
horologe
iriscope
manostat
odometer
ohm-meter
otoscope
quadrant
receiver
recorder
rheostat
solenoid
spy glass
udometer
waywiser
wireless
zootrope

9

acoumeter
aeolipile
aerometer
altimeter
altometer
ambulator
antimeter
apparatus

arcograph
areometer
astrolabe
atmometer
auriscalp
auxometer
backstaff
barograph
barometer
baroscope
clepsydra
compasses
condenser
cornmeter
cosmolabe
dynameter
dynometer
eidograph
engiscope
eriometer
excitator
flow meter
gasometer
garoscope
generator
graduator
gyroscope
heliostat
hodometer
holometer
hour glass
litholabe
lithotome
logometer
lucimeter
magnifier
manometer
marigraph
megaphone
megascope
metronome
microtome
microtron
nilometer
oleometer
optigraph
optometer
pedometer
periscope
polygraph
polyscope
pyrometer
pyroscope
rain gauge
rectifier
retractor

rheometer
rheoscope
rheotrope
rotameter
saccarium
scarifier
set-square
shot gauge
slide rule
sonometer
steelyard
tasimeter
taximeter
telegraph
telephone
telescope
televisor
tellurion
tide gauge
trebuchet
voltmeter
wattmeter
wind gauge
zoeotrope

10

acetimeter
acidimeter
altazimuth
anemograph
anemometer
anemoscope
angioscope
anglemeter
astrometer
astroscope
audiometer
audiophone
balling-gun
binoculars
calculator
calorifier
chiroplast
clinometer
collimator
cometarium
cross-staff
cryophorus
cyanometer
cyclograph
declinator
drosometer
duplicator
ear-trumpet

elaeometer
elaiometer
endiometer
field glass
goniometer
gravimeter
heliograph
heliometer
helioscope
heliotrope
hydrometer
hydrophore
hydroscope
hyetograph
hyetometer
hygrometer
hygroscope
lactometer
lactoscope
litrameter
macrometer
metrograph
micrometer
microphone
microscope
multimeter
multiplier
night glass
nitrometer
noctograph
ombrometer
operameter
ozonometer
pantagraph
pantograph
pantometer
pelvimeter
pentagraph
phonograph
phonoscope
photometer
photophone
piezometer
plane-table
planimeter
pleximeter
pole-finder
protractor
pulsimeter
radiometer
respirator
spirometer
steam-gauge
tachometer
teinoscope
theodolite
thermostat
transistor
tribometer
tuning-fork
typewriter

viscometer
voltameter
water-clock
water-gauge
water-meter
water-poise

11

actinograph
actinometer
aleurometer
alkalimeter
atmidometer
beam compass
calorimotor
cardiograph
chlorometer
chronograph
chronometer
chronoscope
clog almanac
comptometer
conchometer
cosmosphere
craniometer
dendrometer
depth-finder
diagnometer
dynamometer
eccaleobion
eclipsareon
elatrometer
graphometer
indigometer
locatograph
magnetophon
odontograph
optical lens
plantascope
pluviameter
pluviometer
poking stick
polarimeter
polariscope
polemoscope
pseudoscope
range-finder
salinometer
seismograph
seismometer
seismoscope
sideroscope
sliding-rule
spherograph
spherometer
stereometer
stereoscope
stethometer
stethoscope

teleprinter
thaumatrope
thermometer
thermoscope
torsiograph
transformer
transmitter
zymosimeter

12

aethrioscope
alcoholmeter
arithmometer
assay balance
averruncator
blanchimeter
bow compasses
burning glass
camera lucida
centrolinead
chondrometer
control valve
declinometer
ductilimeter
electrepeter
electrometer
electrophone
electroscope
ellipsograph
elliptograph
endosmometer
enorthotrope
evaporometer
field glasses
galactometer
galvanometer
galvanoscope
harmonometer
inclinometer
kaleidoscope
laryngoscope
machine ruler
magnetograph
magnetometer
measuregraph
microcoustic
night glasses
opera glasses
oscillograph
otacousticon
perambulator
psychrometer
reading glass
scarificator
sliding scale
spectrometer
spectroscope
speed-counter
sphygmometer

thermocouple
tuning hammer
weather glass
zenith sector

13

alcoholimeter
alcoholometer
bubble chamber
burning mirrow
camera obscura
chromatometer
diaphanometer
dipleidoscope
dipping needle
electric meter
electrophorus
esthesiometer
Geiger counter
parallel ruler
pneumatometer
potentiometer
pressure gauge
probe scissors
pyrheliometer
reflectometer
refractometer
saccharometer
sidereal clock
spring balance
sympiesometer
watt-hour meter

14

aesthesiometer
air thermometer
circumferentor
desk calculator
diffractometer
dinactinometer
geothermometer
hydrobarometer
interferometer
manifold writer
ophthalmoscope
radio telescope
sonic altimeter
wire micrometer

15

chemical balance
digital computer
magnifying glass
mariner's compass
solar microscope

Mathematics

2 AND 3

add
arc
cos
csc
Ln
log

p.c.
set
tan

4

area

axes
axis
base
cone
cube
edge
face
line

loci
math
mean
plus
ring
root
sine
term

unit
zero

5

acute
angle
chord
conic
cosec
cotan
cubic
curve
equal
focal
focus
force
graph
group
index
lemma
limit
locus
maths
minus
plane
point
power
probe
proof
radii
range
ratio
slope
solid

6

centre
choice
circle
conics
conoid
convex
cosine
cuboid
degree
divide
domain
equals
factor
height
matrix
maxima
median
minima
minute
modulo
moment
motion
normal
number
oblate
oblong
obtuse
period
radial
radian
radius
random
scalar
secant
sector
series

sphere
square
subset
vector
vertex
volume

7

algebra
average
cissoid
complex
concave
conical
cycloid
decagon
divisor
ellipse
evolute
hexagon
indices
inverse
mapping
maximum
minimum
modulus
nonzero
numeral
oblique
octagon
percent
polygon
produce
prolate
problem
pyramid
rhombic
rhombus
scalene
section
segment
subtend
surface
tangent
theorem
trapeze
unitary

8

abscissa
addition
analysis
binomial
bisector
calculus
centroid
circular
codomain
constant
converse
cosecant
cube root
cuboidal
cylinder
diagonal
diameter
dihedral
distance
division
elliptic
equation
friction

frustrum
function
geometer
geometry
gradient
helicoid
heptagon
identity
infinity
integers
integral
involute
matrices
meridian
momentum
multiply
negative
new maths
operator
ordinate
osculate
parabola
parallel
pentagon
positive
quadrant
quartile
quotient
rational
rhomboid
rotation
sequence
spheroid
subtract
symmetry
triangle
trigonal
variable
velocity

9

amplitude
asymptote
Cartesian
chi-square
corollary
cotangent
directrix
dodecagon
ellipsoid
expansion
factorize
frequency
geometric
half-angle
hexagonal
hyperbola
identical
imaginary
increment
induction
inflexion
intersect
isosceles
logarithm
Napierian
numerator
numerical
octagonal
parabolic
parameter
perimeter
polygonal
polyhedra

primitive
quadratic
rectangle
remainder
resultant
spherical
trapezium
trapezoid

10

arithmetic
concentric
continuity
decahedron
derivative
dimensions
eigenvalue
epicycloid
equivalent
expression
hyperbolic
hypotenuse
hypothesis
irrational
kinematics
multiplier
octahedron
orthogonal
osculation
paraboloid
percentage
polyhedral
polyhedron
polynomial
proportion
regression
right angle
semi-circle
square root
statistics
stochastic
tangential
unit vector

11

approximate
associative
coefficient
combination
commutative
coordinates
denominator
determinant
eigenvector
equiangular
equilateral
equilibrium
exponential
geometrical
hyperboloid
icosahedron
integration
isomorphism
orthocentre
permutation
probability
progression
real numbers
rectangular
rectilinear
right-angled
subtraction

symmetrical
tetrahedron
translation

semicircular
straight line
substitution
trigonometry

quadrilateral
right bisector
solid geometry

12

acceleration
conic section
differential
dodecahedron
eccentricity
harmonic mean
intersection
least squares
number theory

13

approximation
circumference
geometric mean
linear algebra
parallelogram
perpendicular
plane geometry
power function

14 AND 15

arithmetic mean (14)
binomial theorem (15)
complex numbers (14)
convexo-concave (14)
differentiation (15)
multiplication (14)
natural numbers (14)
rational numbers (15)
transformation (14)

Medicine

2 AND 3

ana
arm
ear
ECT
ENT
eye
fit
flu
hip
ill
jaw
leg
lip
LSD
pox
pus
rib
tic
toe
VD
wen

4

ache
acne
ACTH
ague
back
bile
bleb
boil
bone
burn
chin
clap
clot
cold
corn
cure
cyst
damp
derm
diet
disk
dope
dose
drug
face
falx
foot

gena
germ
gore
gout
hand
head
heal
heel
iris
knee
lame
limb
lint
lobe
lung
mole
nail
neck
nose
otic
ovum
pain
pang
pill
rale
rash
rete
scab
scar
shin
sick
skin
sore
stye
swab
tolu
ulna
vein
ward
wart
weal
womb
X-ray
yaws

5

achor
acute
agony
algid
algor
aloes

ancon
angst
aorta
ataxy
aural
belly
blend
blood
botch
bowel
brain
cheek
chest
chill
chyle
cilia
colio
colon
copos
cough
cramp
croup
dress
drops
elbow
ether
faint
femur
fever
gland
heart
joint
lance
leech
liver
lymph
M and B
mania
mouth
mucus
mumps
myopy
navel
nerve
nurse
opium
ovary
ozena
palsy
penis
phial
plica
polio
probe

pulse
reins
rheum
rigor
salts
salve
scald
scalp
scurf
semen
senna
serum
sinus
skull
sleep
sling
spasm
sperm
spine
sprue
stoma
stone
stool
stupe
swoon
tabes
teeth
thigh
thumb
tibia
tonic
torso
toxin
truss
ulcer
unfit
urine
uvula
virus
wound
wrist
X-rays

6

ailing
angina
anemia
antrum
apepsy
armpit
artery
asthma

ataxia
aurist
axilla
bellon
biceps
bruise
bulimy
bunion
cancer
canker
caries
clinic
cornea
coryza
deflux
dengue
doctor
dorsal
dosage
dropsy
earlap
eczema
elixir
emetic
fester
fibula
finger
flexor
foment
gargle
gather
goitre
gravel
gripes
grippe
growth
gullet
healer
health
heroin
herpes
idiocy
infect
infirm
insane
iodine
iritis
kidney
larynx
lesion
lotion
lunacy
maimed
malady
maniac
matron
matter
megrim
muscle
myopia
opiate
oxygen
pelvis
pepsin
phenol
phenyl
physic
pimple
plague
pleura
poison
potion
powder
quinsy
radium
ranula

remedy
renule
retina
saliva
scurvy
sepsis
spleen
splint
sprain
stitch
stupor
tablet
tannin
tartar
temple
tendon
tetany
thorax
throat
thrush
thymol
tissue
tongue
tonsil
torpor
trance
tremor
trepan
troche
tumour
typhus
unwell
uterus
vagina
vomica

7

abdomen
abscess
acidity
aconite
adenoid
adipose
ailment
albumen
aliment
allergy
alopecy
amnesia
anaemia
anatomy
anconal
anodyne
antacid
anthrax
antigen
apepsia
aphasia
arsenic
aseptic
aspirin
atrophy
autopsy
bandage
bilious
blister
boracic
bromide
bubonic
calomel
cardiac
cascara
catarrh
caustic

cautery
chafing
chloral
choking
cholera
chronic
cocaine
cranium
cupping
curable
culture
cuticle
deltoid
dentist
dietary
dieting
disease
dissect
draught
dresser
dysopsy
earache
eardrum
empyema
endemic
enteric
erosion
eupepsy
fasting
femoral
fistula
forceps
forearm
formula
gastric
glottis
gumboil
harelip
healing
healthy
hormone
humerus
hygiene
illness
insulin
invalid
knuckle
leprosy
leprous
linctus
lockjaw
lozenge
lumbago
luminal
lunatic
malaria
massage
measles
medical
menthol
microbe
mixture
morphia
myalgia
nervous
nostrum
occiput
oculist
operate
organic
otalgia
palsied
panacea
patella
patient
pharynx

pillbox
pink-eye
plaster
polypus
pustule
pyretic
quinine
recover
rickets
roseola
scabies
scalpel
seasick
sick-bay
stamina
starved
sterile
sternum
stertor
stomach
stunned
styptic
sunburn
surgeon
surgery
symptom
syncope
syringe
tetanus
therapy
thyroid
toxemia
trachea
triceps
tympana
typhoid
vaccine
veronal
vertigo
vitamin
wet-pack
whitlow
wry-neck

8

abortion
abrasion
acidity
acidosis
adenoids
adhesion
albumina
amputate
aneurysm
antibody
antidote
apoplexy
appendix
Asian flu
asphyxia
atropine
backache
bacteria
baldness
beri beri
blue pill
botulism
caffeine
cataract
club foot
collapse
compress
creosote
cystitis

dandruff
deafness
debility
deceased
deformed
delirious
delirium
delivery
demented
dementia
diabetes
diagnose
diseased
dressing
drop-foot
dropsied
dyslexia
emulsion
epidemic
epilepsy
excision
eyedrops
fainting
feverish
first aid
flat feet
forehead
formalin
fracture
freckles
fumigate
ganglion
gangrene
glaucoma
hay fever
headache
heat spot
hiccough
hip joint
hospital
hygienic
hypnotic
hysteria
impetigo
incision
infected
inflamed
insanity
iodoform
irritant
jaundice
lameness
laudanum
laxative
lethargy
ligament
ligature
liniment
magnesia
malarial
mal-de-mer
medicine
membrane
mescalin
migraine
morphine
narcosis
narcotic
neuritis
neurotic
ointment
otoscope
overdose
paranoia
paranoic
paranoid

paroxysm
pastille
phthisis
pleurisy
poisoned
poultice
ptomaine
pulmonic
recovery
Red Cross
remedial
rest cure
revivify
ringworm
sanitary
schizoid
sciatica
sedative
shingles
shoulder
sickness
sickroom
smallpox
sneezing
specific
surgical
swelling
syphilis
tapeworm
terminal
tincture
underfed
uric acid
varicose
vertebra
vomiting
wheezing
windpipe

9

adrenalin
alleviate
allopathy
ambulance
analgesic
antalkali
antitoxin
arthritis
asthmatic
bedridden
blindness
Caesarean
carbuncle
cartilage
castor oil
catalepsy
cauterize
chilblain
cirrhosis
cold cream
contagion
contusion
cortisone
curvature
deformity
delirious
dentistry
deodorant
diagnosis
diaphragm
diathermy
dietetics
dietetist
dietician

digestion
digestive
disinfect
dislocate
dissector
doctoring
dropsical
dysentery
dyspepsia
emaciated
emollient
epileptic
eye lotion
eyestrain
faintness
frost-bite
gastritis
gathering
germicide
giddiness
glycerine
hartshorn
healthful
heartburn
hepatitis
hunchback
hygienist
hypnotism
hypnotist
hysterics
impactation
infirmary
influenza
inoculate
invalided
isolation
isoniazid
leucaemia
leukaemia
liquorice
listerine
liver spot
long-sight
medicated
medicinal
menopause
monomania
nephritis
neuralgia
nightmare
nostalgia
novocaine
nux vomica
open-heart
operation
osteopath
paralysis
paralytic
phlebitis
physician
pneumonia
poisoning
poisonous
pregnancy
psychosis
psychotic
pulmonary
pulsation
pyorrhoea
radionics
rheumatic
rock-fever
sclerosis
silicosis
sinusitis
soporific

squinting
sterilize
stiff neck
stiffness
stimulant
stone dead
stone deaf
stretcher
sunstroke
toothache
treatment
umbilicus
underdose
unhealthy
vaccinate
vasectomy
water cure

10

albuminous
amputation
antibiotic
anti-poison
antiseptic
apoplectic
apothecary
aureomycin
blood count
brain fever
breastbone
bronchitis
chicken pox
chloroform
collar bone
concussion
congestion
contortion
convalesce
convulsion
cotton wool
depression
diphtheria
dipsomania
disability
dispensary
dispensing
dissecting
dissection
double bind
emaciation
enervation
epidemical
epiglottis
Epsom salts
erysipelas
eucalyptus
euthanasia
fibrositis
flatulence
fumigation
gingivitis
gonorrhoea
healthless
heat stroke
hemorrhage
homoeopath
hydropathy
hypodermic
incubation
indisposed
infectious
inhalation
insanitary

interferon
ionization
knock-kneed
laryngitis
lung cancer
medicament
meningitis
metabolism
nettle rash
ophthalmia
orthocaine
osteopathy
out-patient
oxygen tent
palliative
penicillin
pestilence
post mortem
psychiatry
quarantine
recuperate
relaxation
rheumatism
sanatorium
sanitarium
scarlatina
shell-shock
short sight
sickle-cell
specialist
spinal cord
stammering
starvation
stone blind
strengthen
strychnine
stuttering
tourniquet
tracheitis
transplant
unremedied
urethritis

11

acupuncture
albuminuria
aminobutene
anaesthetic
anti-pyretic
asthmatical
astigmatism
bandy-legged
barbiturate
biliousness
calabar bean
circulation
cod-liver oil
colour-blind
consumption
consumptive
corn plaster

dengue fever
disablement
dislocation
embrocation
epileptical
face-lifting
finger stall
fomentation
frostbitten
haemophilia
haemorrhage
homoeopathy
hydrophobia
hypothermia
inoculation
intercostal
intravenous
jungle fever
mustard bath
nursing home
palpitation
peritonitis
perspiration
prickly heat
psittacosis
radiography
restorative
sal volatile
seasickness
spina bifida
stethoscope
stomach-pump
suppuration
temperature
thalidomide
therapeutic
tonsillitis
tracheotomy
transfusion
trench fever
typhus fever
unconscious
vaccination
vivisection
yellow fever

12

appendicitis
carbolic acid
chemotherapy
convalescent
cough lozenge
cough mixture
court plaster
day blindness
degeneration
disinfectant
disinfection
Dover's powder
enteric fever
friar's balsam

gastric fever
group therapy
growing pains
heart disease
hospital case
homoeopathic
hysterectomy
immunization
inflammation
menstruation
neurasthenia
Politzer's bag
prescription
prophylactic
psychiatrist
radiotherapy
recuperation
recuperative
sarsaparilla
scarlet fever
skin-grafting
spinal column
streptococci
streptomycin
subcutaneous
taka diastase
talcum powder
tartar emetic
tertian fever
thyroid gland
tuberculosis
typhoid fever
unremediable
zinc ointment

13

adipose tissue
anti-spasmodic
bubonic plague
contraception
convalescence
duodenal ulcer
dusting powder
elephantiasis
eucalyptus oil
fever hospital
gamma globulin
German measles
hydrocephalus
indisposition
ipecacuanha
lead poisoning
malarial fever
materia medica
medical school
medicine glass
mononucleosis
mortification
non-contagious
osteomyelitis
pharmacopoeia

poliomyelitis
pyretic saline
radioactivity
St Vitus's-dance
schizophrenia
shooting pains
shoulder blade
smelling salts
social disease
sterilization
stretcher case
tranquillizer
varicose veins
whooping cough

14

Achilles tendon
angina pectoris
blood poisoning
Bright's disease
cascara segrada
conjunctivitis
corticosteroid
corticotrophin
floating kidney
Gregory's powder
hallucinations
hallucinogenic
housemaid's-knee
medical student
medicine bottle
mucous membrane
mustard plaster
night blindness
organic disease
pasteurization
patent medicine
plastic surgery
psychoanalysis
Seidlitz powder
smelling bottle

15

Addison's disease
adhesive plaster
alimentary canal
blackwater fever
counter-irritant
delirium tremens
endocrine glands
Eustachian tubes
linseed poultice
locomotor ataxia
manic depression
medicine dropper
radiation hazard
radium treatment
unconsciousness
water on the brain

Minerals (including metals, ores, precious stones, rocks, etc.)

3 AND **4**

bort
clay
coal

gold
iron
jade
jet
lead

mica
onyx
opal
rock
ruby

sard
spar
talc
tin
tufa

wad
wadd
zinc

5

agate
albin
argil
baria
beryl
chert
emery
flint
fluor
magma
ochre
prase
shale
slate
spalt
steel
topaz

6

albite
aplome
augite
basalt
blende
cobalt
copper
davina
dipyre
doggar
egeran
gabbro
galena
garnet
gneiss
gypsum
humite
indium
iolite
jargon
jasper
kaolin
kunkur
marble
mesole
mundic
nappal
nickel
ophite
ormolu
pewter
pinite
plasma
pumice
pyrope
quartz
radium
rutile
schorl
silica
silver
sinter
sodium
sphene
tombac
xylite
yenite
zircon

7

adamant
alumina
alunite
amianth
anatase
aphrite
arsenic
asphalt
axilite
azurite
barytes
bauxite
biotime
bismuth
bitumen
barnite
breccia
cadmium
calcite
calcium
calomel
cat's-eye
cuprite
cyprine
desmine
diamond
diorite
edelite
emerald
epidote
epigene
erinite
euclase
fahlerz
fahlore
felsite
felspar
fuscite
gassoul
glucina
granite
greisen
helvine
hessite
hyalite
ice spar
iridium
jargoon
kyanite
lignite
lithium
mengite
mercury
nacrite
olivine
peridot
petzite
pycnite
pyrites
realgar
romeine
sahlite
sinoper
sinople
syenite
talcite
thorite
thorium
thulite
tripoli
uranium
wolfram
yttrium
zeolite

zeuxite
zincite
zoisite
zurlite

8

achirite
adularia
amethyst
andesite
antimony
aphanite
asbestos
blue John
austerite
bronzite
calamine
calc-spar
cast iron
chabasie
chlorite
chromite
chromium
cinnabar
corundum
cryolite
dendrite
diallage
diopside
dioptase
dolerite
dolomite
embolite
epsomite
essonite
feldspar
felstone
fireclay
fluorite
graphite
hematite
hyacinth
idocrase
ilmenite
jasponyx
konilite
laterite
lazulite
ligurite
limonite
lirocone
lomonite
meionite
melanite
mesolite
mesotype
micanite
mimetene
monazite
napolite
nemalite
nephrite
obsidian
orpiment
pagodite
pea stone
petalite
platinum
plumbago
porphyry
prehnite
psammite
pyroxene
ragstone

reussite
rhyolite
rock cork
rock salt
rock soap
rock wood
sapphire
sardonyx
selenite
siberite
siderite
smaltine
sodalite
spinelle
stellite
stibnite
stilbite
thallium
tin stone
titanium
trachyte
trap-rock
triphane
tungsten
turmalin
vesuvian
voltzite
weissite
wood opal
wood rock
worthite
xanthite
xylonite
yanolite

9

alabaster
allophane
almandine
aluminium
alum shale
alum slate
amianthus
amphibole
anamesite
anglesite
anomalite
anorthite
aphrisite
argentite
argillite
aromatite
arquifoux
asphaltum
baikalite
basaltine
boltonite
brick-clay
brown-coal
brown-spur
byssolite
carbonado
carbuncle
carnelian
carnalite
cat-silver
cerussite
ceylanite
chabasite
chabazite
chalybite
cobaltine
cornelian
corn stone

259

earth flax
elaeolite
elaterite
erythrine
erythrite
eudyalite
eukairite
firestone
fluorspar
galactite
gmelinite
granilite
granulite
graystone
graywacke
grenatite
greystone
greywacke
haematite
heavy spar
horn slate
hornstone
indianite
ittnerite
johannite
killinite
latrobite
laumonite
lenzinite
limbilite
limestone
lodestone
magnesite
magnesium
magnetite
malachite
manganese
marcasite
margarite
marmatite
melaphyre
mellitite
meteorite
mica slate
mispickel
moonstone
moorstone
muscovite
nagyagite
natrolite
necrolite
necronite
nepheline
niccolite
noumeaite
omphacite
ozokerite
pargasite
pearl spar
pectolite
pegmatite
periclase
phenacite
phonolite
physalite
pleonaste
plinthite
potassium
proustite
pyrophane
quartzite
raphilite
rhodonite
rhombspar
rubellite
sandstone

satin spar
scapolite
scheelite
scolecite
soapstone
spinthere
spodumene
strontium
sylvanite
tantalite
tautalite
tellurium
torbanite
torrelite
tremolite
turnerite
turquoise
veinstone
vulcanite
wavellite
wernerite
willemite
withamite
witherite
woodstone
xanthocon
zinc bloom
zirconite

10

actinolite
amianthoid
amygdaloid
anthracite
aquamarine
aventurine
azure stone
batrachite
bergmanite
beudantite
bismuthite
bloodstone
calaverite
cannel coal
cervantite
chalcedony
chonikrite
chrysolite
clinkstone
cross-stone
diallogite
dyscrasite
eagle stone
false topaz
floatstone
gabbronite
glauberite
glaucolite
glottalite
greenstone
heterosite
heulandite
hornblende
hornsilver
hydrophane
hyperstene
indicolite
iridosmine
iron glance
karpholite
Kentish rag
koupholite
lead glance
lepidolite

malacolite
meerschaum
melaconite
mica schist
mocho stone
molybdenum
nussierite
nuttallite
orthoclase
osmiridium
paranthine
phosphorus
picrosmine
polyhalite
pyrochlore
pyrolusite
rathoffite
redruthite
retinalite
rock butter
rose quartz
sapphirine
sardachate
saussurite
serpentine
sismondine
smaragdite
sparry iron
sphalerite
stalactite
stalagmite
staurolite
stephanite
talc schist
thomsonite
topazolite
tourmaline
vanadinite
villarsite
websterite
zinc blende

11

alexandrite
amblygonite
amphibolite
amphiboloid
Babbit metal
black silver
brewsterite
cassiterite
chlorophane
chondrodite
chromic iron
chrysoberyl
cobalt bloom
crichtonite
crocidolite
dendrachate
diving stone
epistilbite
ferrachrome
figure stone
franklinite
hypersthene
Iceland spar
iron pyrites
lapis lazuli
libethenite
milky quartz
molybdenite
Muller glass
muschel kalk
napoleonite

needlestone
octahedrite
phillipsite
pitchblende
polymignite
psilomelane
pyrallolite
pyrargyrite
pyrosmalite
rock crystal
sillimanite
smithsonite
smoky quartz
sordavalite
sphaerulite
tetradymite
thumerstone
titanic iron
yttrocerite

12

cobalt glance
copper glance
forest marble
greyweathers
jeffersonite
kupfernickel
mineral black
mineral green
mineral resin
montmartrite
mountain cork
mountain milk
mountain soap
murchisonite
oriental ruby
puddingstone
pyrargillite
pyromorphite
quartz schist
somervillite
Spanish chalk
specular iron
sprig crystal
tetrahedrite
woolastonite

13

agaric mineral
anthophyllite
chlorophaeite
cinnamon stone
cleavelandite
copper pyrites
emerald copper
kerosene shale
needle zeolite

14 AND 15

antimony glance
arkose sandstone
bituminous coal
brown haematite
Cairngorm stone
chlorite schist
elastic bitumen
graphic granite
hydromica schist
mountain leather
quartz porphyry

Physics

2 AND 3

a.c.
bar
bel
e.m.f.
erg
gas
lux
mev
ohm
rpm
UHF
VHF

4

atom
cell
dyne
flux
foci
halo
heat
kaon
lens
mach
mass
muon
node
pile
pion
pole
rays
spin
tube
volt
watt
wave
work
X-ray

5

anode
curie
cycle
diode
earth
farad
field
fluid
focus
force
image
joule
laser
lever
light
lumen
maser
meson
motor
phase
pitch
power
prism
radar
radio
shell
solid
sonic
sound
speed
valve
weber

6

ampere
atomic
baryon
camera
charge
corona
dipole
energy
fusion
impact
isobar
kelvin
lepton
liquid
magnet
moment
motion
newton
optics
period
photon
plasma
proton
quanta
torque
triode
vacuum
vector
weight

7

ammeter
aneroid
battery
beta ray
calorie
candela
cathode
Celsius
circuit
coulomb
crystal
current
damping
decibel
density
dry cell
elastic
element
entropy
fission
gaseous
gravity
hyperon
impulse
inertia
machine
maxwell
neutron
nuclear
nucleon
nucleus
nuclide
optical
orbital
pi-meson
quantum
reactor
röntgen
spectra
statics
thermal
torsion
voltage
voltaic

8

adhesion
aerofoil
antinode
beat note
betatron
brownian
cohesion
duo-diode
dynamics
electric
electron
emission
free fall
friction
graviton
half-life
infra-red
isogonic
kilowatt
kinetics
klystron
magnetic
magneton
molecule
momentum
negative
negatron
neutrino
overtone
particle
pendulum
polaroid
positive
positron
pressure
rest mass
roentgen
solenoid
spectrum
subshell
velocity

9

acoustics
adiabatic
amplifier
amplitude
antimeson
barometer
black body
bolometer

261

capacitor
coherence
condenser
conductor
cyclotron
electrode
frequency
gamma rays
generator
gyroscope
harmonics
impedance
induction
insulator
isoclinic
Leyden jar
magnetism
magnetron
manometer
mechanics
plutonium
potential
radiation
radio wave
real image
rectifier
resonance
spark coil
vibration
viscosity
voltmeter

10

aberration
absorption
achromatic
antilepton
antimatter
antiproton
atomic bomb
atomic mass
ballistics
binoculars
cathode ray
Centigrade
conduction
convection
cosmic rays
dielectric
dispersion
electrical
Fahrenheit
heavy water
horsepower
inductance
ionization
kinematics
latent heat
microscope
omega meson
oscillator

precession
reflection
refraction
relativity
resistance
ripple tank
scattering
shunt-wound
supersonic
thermionic
thermopile
transistor
vacuum tube
wavelength

11

accelerator
band spectra
capacitance
capillarity
centrifugal
centripetal
compression
conductance
declination
diffraction
electricity
falling body
focal length
gravitation
hypercharge
newton-metre
oscillation
positronium
radioactive
resistivity
restitution
series-wound
solar energy
spectrogram
statcoulomb
synchrotron
temperature
transformer
transuranic

12

acceleration
angstrom unit
antiparticle
atomic number
atomic weight
beta particle
centre of mass
cloud chamber
conductivity
critical mass
diamagnetism
eccentricity

electrolysis
electroscope
interference
kilowatt-hour
oscilloscope
permittivity
polarization
specific heat
spectrograph
wave equation

13

alpha particle
bubble chamber
chain reaction
critical angle
discharge tube
elastic impact
electric field
electric motor
electric power
electromagnet
electromotive
electron shell
electrostatic
geiger counter
gravitational
induction coil
kinetic energy
magnetic field
magnetic poles
paramagnetism
photoelectric
quantum number
quantum theory
radioactivity
rectification
scintillation
semiconductor
standing waves
thermal capacity
transmutation

14 AND OVER

centre of gravity (15)
electric current (15)
electric energy (14)
electrification (15)
electromagnetic (15)
electrostatics (14)
ferromagnetism (14)
nuclear reactor (14)
Planck's constant (15)
potential energy (15)
specific gravity (15)
terminal velocity (16)
thermodynamics (14)
thermoelectric (14)
Wheatstone bridge (16)

Poisons

4 AND 5

acids
agene
bane
coca
drug

dwale
ergot
fungi
lysol
nitre
opium
toxin

upas
venom

6

alkali

brucia
cicuta
curare
heroin
iodine
ourali
phenol

7

aconite
alcohol
ammonia
aniline
arsenic
atropia
atropin
bromine
brucina
brucine
cadmium
calomel
caustic
chloral
coal gas
cocaine
gamboge
henbane
hyoscin
hypoxia
markuri
veronal
violine
vitriol
woorali
woorara
woralli
wourali

8

antidote
antimony
atropina
atropine
botulism
chlorine
chromium
ergotine
morphine
nicotine
oenanthe
paraquat
pearl ash
phosgene

ptomaine
ratsbane
selenium
soap lees
sulfonal
veratrum

9

amanitine
antiarine
baneberry
beryllium
chromates
colchicum
colocynth
croton oil
echidnine
grapewort
hellebore
herbicide
lead ethyl
mercurial
monkshood
nux vomica
potassium
rat poison
spit venom
strychnia
toadstool
white lead
wolf's bane
zinc ethyl

10

antiseptic
aqua fortis
belladonna
chloroform
cyanic acid
mustard gas
nightshade
nitric acid
oxalic acid
phosphorus

picric acid
salmonella
snake venom
strychnine
thorn apple
weed-killer

11

blue vitriol
boracic acid
caustic soda
dog's mercury
insecticide
lead acetate
luna caustic
prussic acid
snake poison
sugar of lead

12

barbiturates
bitter almond
carbonic acid
fool's parsley
pharmacolite
water hemlock
white arsenic

13 AND OVER

allantotoxicum (14)
carbonate of lead (15)
carbonic oxide (13)
carbon monoxide (14)
caustic alkali (13)
caustic potash (13)
deadly nightshade (16)
hydrocyanic acid (15)
irritant poisons (15)
meadow saffron (13)
narcotic poisons (15)
sulphuric acid (13)
yellow arsenic (13)

Sciences

5 AND 6

augury (6)
botany (6)
conics (6)
logic (5)
optics (6)

7

algebra
anatomy
biology
cookery
ecology
farming
finance
geodesy
geogony
geology
gunnery

history
hygiene
myology
orology
otology
pandect
phonics
physics
poetics
science
statics
surgery
tanning
trivium
weaving
zoology
zootomy

8

aerology

agronomy
analysis
atmology
barology
bio-assay
biometry
breeding
bryology
calculus
commerce
cytology
dairying
dosology
dynamics
ethology
etiology
eugenics
forestry
genetics
geometry
glyptics
horology

kinetics
medicine
mycology
nosology
ontology
penology
pharmacy
politics
pomology
posology
rheology
rhetoric
sinology
sitology
spherics
taxonomy
tidology
tocology
topology
typology
virology
zymology

263

9

acoustics
aerometry
aetiology
agriology
aitology
allopathy
altimetry
anemology
annealing
areometry
astronomy
barometry
biometrics
bleaching
cartology
chemistry
chiropody
chorology
cosmology
dentistry
dietetics
diplomacy
economics
embalming
emetology
engraving
ethnology
gardening
geography
gnomonics
harmonics
histology
horometry
husbandry
hydrology
hygrology
hymnology
ichnology
lithology
mammalogy
mechanics
micrology
neurology
ophiology
orography
osteology
otography
pathology
petrology
philology
phonetics
phonology
phytogeny
phytology
phytotomy
radiology
sitiology
sociology
surveying
taxidermy
telephony
uranology
zoography

10

actinology
aerography
aesthetics
apiculture
archaeology
arithmetic
ballistics

bathymetry
biophysics
cardiology
catoptrics
cell biology
chromatics
clinometry
conchology
craniology
demography
dendrology
docimology
Egyptology
embryology
energetics
entomology
entomotomy
enzymology
eudiometry
game theory
gastrology
geophysics
homeopathy
hydraulics
hydrometry
hydropathy
hygrometry
hypsometry
immunology
kinematics
lexicology
metallurgy
microscopy
morphology
nematology
nephrology
nosography
obstetrics
odontology
oneirology
organology
osteopathy
pedagogics
pediatrics
phlebology
photometry
phrenology
physiology
planimetry
pneumatics
potamology
psychiatry
psychology
relativity
seismology
selenology
semeiology
somatology
spasmology
spermology
splenology
splenotomy
statistics
technology
telegraphy
teratology
topography
toxicology
trepanning
typography

11

aeronautics
aerostatics

agriculture
anemography
arachnology
archaeology
arteriology
arteriotomy
campanology
carcinology
cartography
chondrology
chronometry
climatology
cosmography
craniometry
criminology
cupellation
cybernetics
dermatology
dermography
desmography
diacoustics
electricity
electronics
engineering
entozoology
ethnography
foundations
games theory
geomedicine
gynaecology
haematology
heliography
homoeopathy
hydrography
hyetography
ichthyology
ichthyotomy
lichenology
linguistics
mathematics
methodology
micrography
myodynamics
neurography
ornithology
osteography
paleography
petrography
photography
phytography
probability
prophylaxis
pteridology
radiography
sericulture
skeletology
spectrology
stereometry
stereoscopy
stethoscopy
stratigraphy
thanatology
uranography
ventilation
watch-making

12

aerodynamics
amphibiology
anthropology
architecture
astrophysics
atomic theory
auscultation

biochemistry
biogeography
brachygraphy
chronography
cometography
cytogenetics
econometrics
electropathy
epidemiology
epirrheology
floriculture
geochemistry
horticulture
hydrostatics
lexicography
lymphography
microbiology
nephrography
neuroanatomy
neurobiology
number theory
oceanography
opthalmology
organography
ornithoscopy
palaeography
pharmacology
physiography
pisciculture
pneumatology
protozoology
real analysis
seismography
silviculture
spectroscopy
spermatology
stratigraphy
sylviculture
syndesmology
synosteology
trigonometry
zoophytology

13

anthropometry
arboriculture
arteriography
bioenergetics
cephalography
chondrography
chrematistics
climatography
combinatorics
crustaceology
endocrinology
geochronology
geomorphology
helminthology
hydrodynamics
hydrokinetics
ichthyography
land measuring
land surveying
lichenography
linear algebra
marine biology
matrix algebra
meteorography
palaeontology
pharmaceutics
psychophysics
psychotherapy
quantum theory
saccharometry

264

sedimentology
splanchnology
stoichiometry
wave mechanics
zoophysiology

14

architectonics
bioclimatology
chromatography
cinematography
electrobiology

electrostatics
fluid mechanics
hippopathology
hydrophytology
macroeconomics
microeconomics
natural history
natural science
parapsychology
photogrammetry
phytopathology
psychonosology
radiochemistry
symptomatology

syndesmography
thermodynamics

15

computer science
crystallography
electrodynamics
electrokinetics
material science
neurophysiology
psychopathology
thermochemistry

Tools and simple machines
See also **Engineering** and **Instruments**.

3

adz
awl
axe
bit
die
dog
fan
gad
gin
hod
hoe
jig
loy
saw
zax

4

adze
bill
bore
brog
burr
cart
celt
crab
file
fork
frow
gage
hink
hook
jack
last
loom
mall
maul
mule
nail
pick
pike
plow
rake
rasp
rule
sock
spud
tool
trug
vice
whim

5

anvil
auger
basil
beele
bench
besom
betty
bevel
blade
borer
brace
burin
chuck
churn
clamp
clams
clasp
cleat
cramp
crane
croom
croze
cupel
dolly
drill
flail
flang
forge
gauge
gavel
gouge
hoist
incus
jacks
jemmy
jimmy
knife
lathe
level
lever
mower
parer
plane
plumb
preen
prise
prong
punch
quern
quoin
ratch
razor

sarse
screw
sieve
spade
spike
spile
spill
swage
temse
tommy
tongs
tromp
trone
wedge
winch

6

barrow
beetle
bender
blower
bodkin
borcer
bow-saw
brayer
broach
burton
chaser
chisel
colter
crevet
cruset
dibber
dibble
doffer
dredge
driver
fanner
faucet
ferret
folder
gimlet
graver
hackle
hammer
harrow
jagger
jigger
jig saw
ladder
mallet
mortar

muller
oliver
pallet
pencil
pestle
pitsaw
planer
pliers
plough
pontee
pooler
rammer
rasper
reaper
riddle
ripsaw
rubber
sander
saw-set
screen
scythe
segger
shears
shovel
sickle
sifter
skewer
sledge
slicer
square
stiddy
stithy
strike
tackle
tenter
trepan
trowel
tubber
turrel
wimble
wrench

7

boaster
bradawl
capstan
catling
cautery
chamfer
chip-axe
chopper
cleaver

265

couloir
coulter
crampon
crisper
crowbar
cuvette
derrick
diamond
dog-belt
drudger
fistuca
forceps
fretsaw
fruggin
gradine
grainer
grapnel
grub axe
hacksaw
handsaw
hatchel
hatchet
hay fork
jointer
mandrel
mattock
nippers
nut hook
pickaxe
piercer
pincers
plummet
pole axe
pounder
pricker
salt-pan
scalpel
scauper
scraper
screwer
scriber
seed lop
spaddle
spanner
spittle
sprayer
strocal
tenoner
thimble
trestle
triblet
T-square
twibill
twister
whip-saw
whittle
woolder

8

bark mill
bar shear
beakiron
bench peg
bill hook
bistoury
bloomary
blowlamp
blowpipe
boathook
bowdrill
bull nose
butteris
calender
calipers

canthook
centre bit
chopness
crow mill
crucible
die stock
dowel bit
drill bow
edge tool
filatory
fire kiln
flame gun
flax comb
gavelock
gee cramp
glass pot
handloom
handmill
hand vice
hay knife
horse hoe
lapstone
lead mill
mitre box
molegrip
muck rake
nut screw
oilstone
paint pad
panel saw
picklock
pinchers
plumb bob
polisher
power saw
prong-hoe
puncheon
reap hook
saw wrest
scissors
scuffler
shoehorn
slate axe
stiletto
strickle
tenon saw
throstle
tooth key
tweezers
twist bit
watercan
water ram
weed hook
windlass
windmill

9

belt punch
bench hook
bolt auger
boot crimp
canker bit
cannipers
can opener
centrebit
compasses
corkscrew
cotton gin
cramp iron
curry comb
cutter bar
dog clutch
draw knife

draw-plate
excavator
eyeleteer
fillister
fining pot
fork chuck
gas pliers
hammer axe
handbrace
handscrew
handspike
holing axe
hummeller
implement
jackknife
jackplane
jackscrew
lace frame
lawnmower
nail punch
nut wrench
pitch fork
plane iron
planisher
plumbline
plumbrule
screwjack
scribe awl
shearlegs
sheep hook
steelyard
sugar mill
tin opener
try square
turf spade
turn bench
turnscrew
watermill

10

bush harrow
churn staff
claspknife
clawhammer
cold chisel
crane's bill
cultivator
dray plough
drift bolts
drillpress
drillstock
emery wheel
fire engine
fire escape
firing iron
grindstone
instrument
masonry bit
masticator
mitre block
motor mower
mould board
nail drawer
paintbrush
perforator
pipe wrench
safety lamp
screw press
sleek stone
snowplough
spokeshave
steam press
stepladder
tenterhook

thumbscrew
thumbstall
tilt hammer
trip hammer
turf cutter
turnbuckle
watercrane
watergauge
waterlevel
wheel brace

11

breast drill
chaff cutter
chain blocks
chain wrench
cheese press
cigar cutter
countersink
crazing mill
crisping pin
crosscut saw
drill barrow
drill harrow
drill plough
fanning mill
grubbing hoe
helvehammer
jagging iron
machine tool
monkey block
paint roller
ploughshare
pointed awl
pruning hook
rabbet plane
reaping-hook
sawing stool
screwdriver
single-edged
skim coulter
snatch block
spirit level
squaring rod
steam hammer
stone hammer
straw cutter
strike block
stubble rake
sward cutter
swingplough
tapemeasure
turfing iron
two-foot rule
warping hook
warping post
weeding fork
weeding hook
weeding rhim
wheelbarrow

12

barking irons
belt adjuster
brace-and-bits
branding iron
breastplough
caulking tool
counter gauge
cradle scythe
cramping iron
crimping iron

crisping iron
curling tongs
drill grubber
driving shaft
driving wheel
emery grinder
flour dresser
glass furnace
hat stretcher
hydraulic ram
mandrel lathe
marline spike
monkey wrench
pruning knife
pulley blocks
running block
scribing iron
sledge hammer
sliding bevel
socket chisel
stone breaker
straightedge
straightener
swingle knife
touch needles
trench plough
turfing spade
turning lathe

water bellows
weeding tongs

13

butcher's broom
chopping block
chopping knife
cylinder press
electric drill
grappling-iron
hydraulic jack
mowing machine
packing needle
scribing block
sewing machine
soldering bolt
soldering iron
sowing machine
spinning jenny
spinning wheel
stocking frame
subsoil plough
three-foot rule
two-hole pliers
weeding chisel

14

blowing machine
carding machine
draining engine
draining plough
pneumatic drill
reaping machine
shepherd's crook
smoothing plane
swingling knife
three-metre rule
thrusting screw
weeding forceps

15

carpenter's bench
crimping machine
dredging machine
drilling machine
envelope machine
entrenching tool
pestle and mortar
pump screwdriver
weighing machine
whitworth thread

TRANSPORT
Aviation and space travel

3 AND 4

ace
air
bank
bay
bump
buzz
car
crew
dive
dope
drag
fin
flap
fly
fuel
gap
gas
hull
jet
kite
knot
land
lane
leg
lift
loop
mach
nose
prop
rev
rib
roll
slip
span
spar
spin
tail
taxi

trim
UFO
veer
wash
wind
wing
yaw
york
zoom

5

aloft
apron
bends
cabin
cargo
chock
chord
cleat
climb
craft
crash
crate
ditch
drift
flaps
flier
float
glide
pitch
plane
prang
pylon
radar
range
rev up
rigid
slots

stall
strut
stunt
valve

6

aerial
airbus
airman
airway
basket
beacon
bomber
camber
canard
cruise
cut out
drogue
fabric
flight
floats
flying
gas-bag
glider
hangar
intake
launch
module
nose-up
octane
piston
ram jet
refuel
rocket
rudder
runway
wash-in
yawing

7

aileron
air base
aircrew
airdrop
air flow
air foil
air lane
airlift
airline
airport
air-raid
airship
aviator
ballast
balloon
banking
biplane
birdman
bale out
bomb bay
capsule
ceiling
cellule
charter
chassis
chopper
clipper
cockpit
compass
contact
co-pilot
cowling
descent
ejector
fairing
fighter
flyover
flypast

gliding
gondola
helibus
inflate
landing
lift-off
Mae West
nacelle
nose-cap
on board
pancake
payload
re-entry
ripcord
rolling
sponson
sputnik
tail fin
take-off
taxiing
twin-jet
wingtip

8

aerodyne
aerofoil
aeronaut
aerostat
air brake
airborne
aircraft
airfield
air force
airframe
airliner
air route
air scoop
airscrew
airspace
airspeed
airstrip
airwoman
altitude
approach
anhedral
autogiro
aviation
aviatrix
ballonet
bomb-rack
buoyancy
corridor
cruising
decalage
dihedral
drip-flap
elevator
envelope
flat spin
fuel pipe
fuselage
grounded
gyrostat
heliport
in flight
intercom
jet pilot
jet plane
joystick
moonshot
non-rigid
nose-cone
nosedive
nose down

pitching
pulse-jet
radiator
seaplane
sideslip
spaceman
squadron
stopover
streamer
subsonic
tail-boom
tail-skid
tail unit
terminal
throttle
triplane
turbojet
twin-tail
volplane
warplane
wind cone
windsock
wing-flap
Zeppelin

9

aerodrome
aeroplane
air intake
air pocket
airworthy
altimeter
amphibian
astrodome
astronaut
autopilot
backplate
cabin crew
carlingue
cosmonaut
countdown
crash-land
crow's-foot
delta-wing
dirigible
empennage
fuel gauge
fuel intake
gyroplane
jet bomber
launch pad
launching
lift-wires
longerons
low-flying
monocoque
monoplane
navigator
overshoot
parachute
power dive
propeller
rudder bar
sailplane
satellite
semi-rigid
spacecrew
spaceship
spacesuit
spacewalk
stability
stratojet
sweepback
tailplane

test pilot
touch down
turboprop
twin-screw
wind gauge

10

aerobatics
aero-engine
aeronautic
aerostatic
air balloon
air control
air defence
air hostess
air service
air steward
air support
air traffic
anemometer
ballooning
balloonist
cantilever
cargo plane
dive bomber
flight deck
flight path
flight plan
flying boat
ground crew
helicopter
hydroplane
jet fighter
landing run
mach number
outer space
oxygen mask
pilot plane
robot plane
rudder-post
slipstream
solo flight
spacecraft
space probe
splashdown
stabilizer
stewardess
supersonic
test flight
V-formation

11

aeronautics
aerostatics
afterburner
air terminal
air umbrella
blind flying
combat plane
ejector-seat
flying speed
free balloon
ground speed
heat barrier
heavy bomber
kite-balloon
laminar flow
landing deck
landing gear
leading-edge
loop the loop
moon landing

mooring-mast
ornithopter
parachutist
retro-rocket
retractable
sesquiplane
slotted wing
soft landing
space centre
space flight
space rocket
space travel
stabilizers
stunt flying
vapour trail
weather-vane

12

aerodynamics
airfreighter
air-sea rescue
arrester gear
beacon lights
belly landing
control tower
crash landing
ejection seat
fighter pilot
flying circus
flying saucer
gliding-angle
jet-propelled
landing light
landing speed
landing wires
launching pad
maiden flight
manned rocket
night fighter
pilot balloon
pressure suit
pursuit plane
radar scanner
radial-engine
sound barrier
space capsule
space station
space vehicle
trailing-edge

13 AND OVER

aircraft-carrier (15)
airworthiness (13)
control-column (13)
cruising speed (13)
decompression (15)
engine-mounting (14)
escape-velocity (14)
forced landing (13)
ground control (13)
heavier-than-air (14)
in-line-engines (13)
lighter-than-air (14)
looping the loop (14)
radio-location (13)
semi-retractable (15)
shock-absorber (13)
space traveller (14)
stalling-speed (13)
troop-transport (14)
undercarriage (13)
weightlessness (14)

Boats and ships
See also **Nautical terms**

3 AND 4

ark
bac
bark
boat
brig
buss
caic
cog
cot
dhow
dory
four
gig
grab
hoy
hulk
junk
koff
pair
pram
proa
punt
raft
saic
scow
ship
snow
sub
T.B.D.
tub
tug
yawl

5

balsa
barge
batel
boyer
canoe
caper
casco
coble
craft
E-boat
eight
ferry
fifie
float
funny
hopper
kayak
ketch
kobil
liner
P-boat
praam
Q-ship
razee
R-boat
scull
shell
skiff
sloop
smack
tramp
U-boat
umiak

whiff
xebec
yacht

6

argosy
banker
barque
bateau
bawley
bireme
bug-eye
caique
carvel
coggle
cooper
cutter
decker
dinghy
dogger
droger
dugout
galeas
galiot
galley
hopper
hooker
launch
lorcha
lugger
packet
pirate
puffer
pulwar
puteli
PT boat
randan
sampan
sealer
settee
slaver
tanker
tartan
tender
tosher
trader
trough
vessel
wafter
whaler
wherry

7

airboat
almadie
budgero
bumboat
caravel
carrack
carrier
clinker
clipper
coaster
cockler
collier
coracle
corsair

cruiser
currach
dredger
drifter
drogher
dromond
eel punt
felucca
flyboat
four-oar
frigate
galleon
galliot
gondola
gunboat
hog-boat
ice-boat
lighter
man-o'-war
minisub
monitor
muletta
pair-oar
permagy
pinnace
piragua
pirogue
polacca
pontoon
rowboat
sea-sled
shallop
shoaler
spy boat
steamer
tonkong
tow boat
trawler
trireme
tugboat
warship

8

baghalak
bilander
car ferry
coalship
cockboat
corocole
corvette
dahabeah
dahabiya
derelict
eight-oar
fireboat
fireship
flagship
galleass
galliass
gallivat
hoogarts
hoveller
ice yacht
Indiaman
ironclad
keelboat
lifeboat
longboat
mailboat

man-of-war
netlayer
sailboat
schooner
showboat
smuggler
steam-tug
tilt-boat
trimaran
waterbus
well-boat
woodskin

9

bomb-ketch
bucentaur
cable ship
canal boat
cargo boat
catamaran
crocodile
depot ship
destroyer
ferryboat
fire-float
freighter
frigatoon
funny-boat
guard boat
guard ship
horse-boat
houseboat
hydrofoil
jollyboat
lightship
minelayer
motorboat
oil tanker
outrigger
peter-boat
pilot boat
pilot ship
powerboat
privateer
prize ship
river boat
rotor ship
sand yacht
sheer-hulk
slave dhow
speedboat
steamboat
steamship
storeship
submarine
swampboat
transport
troopship
tunny-boat
two-decker
whaleboat
wheelboat

10

advice boat
barge-yacht
barkentine

battleship
bomb vessel
brigantine
cattleboat
chain-ferry
cockleboat
Deal lugger
flying boat
four-master
hovercraft
hydroplane
icebreaker
monkey-boat
motor yacht
narrowboat
nuclear sub
ocean liner
ore-carrier
packet-boat
paddleboat
patrol boat
picket boat
pirate-ship
quadrireme
repair-ship
rescue boat
rivercraft
rowing boat
royal barge
sloop-of-war
small craft
submarine
supply ship
survey ship
target ship
tea-clipper
turret ship
victualler
Viking ship
windjammer
watercraft

11

barquentine
capital ship

chasse-marée
cockleshell
dreadnought
fishing boat
galley foist
hydroglider
merchantman
minesweeper
motor launch
motor vessel
mystery ship
naval vessel
pilot cutter
prize vessel
quinquereme
racing shell
Rob-Roy canoe
sailing boat
sailing ship
sardine boat
slavetrader
steam launch
steam vessel
submersible
three-decker
three-master
torpedo boat
victual ship

12

cabin cruiser
coasting boat
coasting ship
despatch boat
East Indiaman
ferry steamer
fishing smack
heavy cruiser
landing barge
landing craft
light cruiser
merchant ship
motor drifter
motor trawler
pirate cutter

pleasure boat
police launch
pontoon crane
river gunboat
sailing barge
sailing craft
sculling boat
square-rigger
steam gondola
survey vessel
Thames bawley
training ship

13

battlecruiser
Bermuda cutter
Canadian canoe
container ship
double-sculler
four-oared boat
hovelling-boat
motor lifeboat
paddle-steamer
passenger-boat
passenger-ship
sailing vessel
ship-of-the-line
trading vessel

14 AND **15**

aircraft-carrier (15)
cable-laying ship (15)
cable-repair ship (15)
coasting vessel (14)
despatch cutter (14)
eight-oared boat (14)
electric launch (14)
flotilla leader (14)
seaplane tender (14)
submarine chaser (15)
topsail schooner (15)
torpedo-gunboat (14)
Yorkshire coble (14)

Motoring

2 AND **3**

A.A.
c.c.
air
cam
can
cap
car
cog
fan
fit
gas
G.T.
hub
h.p.
jam
jet
key
lap
lug
map

M.O.T.
nut
oil
pin
pit
R.A.C.
rev
rim
rod
run
ton
top

4

axle
belt
body
bolt
boot
boss

bulb
bush
clip
coil
dash
disc
door
drum
flat
fuse
gear
hood
hoot
horn
idle
jack
lane
lock
nail
park
pink
plug

pump
road
roll
rope
seat
skid
sump
tail
tank
test
tire
tour
tube
tyre
veer
wing

5

apron
brake

cable	hooter	offside	manifold
chain	hot rod	oil-feed	missfire
chart	hubcap	parking	motoring
choke	idling	pillion	motorist
clamp	klaxon	pinking	motorway
coupé	lock-up	pull out	mudguard
cover	louvre	reverse	nearside
crank	mascot	roadhog	oil gauge
cut in	milage	roadmap	oncoming
drive	mirror	roadtax	open road
float	octane	rolling	overhaul
frame	oilcan	run into	overpass
gauge	one-way	seizing	overtake
joint	petrol	service	overturn
knock	pile up	skidpan	pavement
lay-by	pinion	spindle	prowl car
level	piston	springs	puncture
lever	saloon	starter	radiator
model	signal	test run	rattling
motor	spokes	toolkit	rear axle
on tow	spring	top gear	rear lamp
pedal	swerve	touring	ring road
rally	switch	towrope	roadside
rev up	tappet	traffic	road sign
rivet	timing	trailer	road test
rotor	torque	viaduct	roofrack
route		warning	rush hour
scale		wingnut	side road
screw	**7**		sideslip
sedan			silencer
shaft	air hose	**8**	skidding
shift	airlock		skid mark
spark	axle-box	air brake	slip road
speed	battery	air inlet	slow down
spoke	bearing	airtight	slow lane
squab	blowout	armature	speeding
stall	bollard	arterial	squad car
start	build-up	Autobahn	stock car
ton up	bus lane	backfire	tail skid
tools	bus stop	back seat	tail gate
tread	carpark	bodywork	taxi rank
U-turn	carport	brakerod	throttle
valve	cat's eye	camshaft	tire pump
wheel	chassis	cat's eyes	two-speed
wiper	contact	clearway	tyre pump
works	control	coasting	
	cooling	converge	
6	dipping	coupling	**9**
	drive-in	crankpin	
adjust	driving	cruising	air filter
big end	exhaust	cul-de-sac	alignment
bonnet	fanbelt	cylinder	anti-glare
bumper	flyover	declutch	autoroute
bypass	gearbox	delivery	back wheel
camber	give way	dipstick	ball-valve
car tax	goggles	driveway	batteries
charge	gudgeon	fastback	brakedrum
clutch	hardtop	fast lane	brakeshoe
cut out	highway	feed pipe	breakdown
dazzle	joyride	feed pump	bus driver
de-icer	L driver	flat tyre	cab driver
de luxe	L plates	flywheel	car driver
detour	licence	foglight	car polish
dickey	linkage	footpump	chain-link
divert	locknut	freezing	chauffeur
driver	log book	friction	clearance
dynamo	luggage	fuelpipe	coachwork
engine	magneto	fuel tank	concourse
fitter	map-case	garaging	condenser
flange	mileage	gasoline	cotter pin
funnel	misfire	gradient	crank axle
garage	missing	guide-rod	crankcase
gasket	mixture	handpump	crossroad
grease	muffler	ignition	cutting in
handle	no entry	inlet cam	dashboard
	non-skid	knocking	dashlight

271

defroster
dipswitch
direction
dirt track
diversion
estate car
filler cap
footbrake
framework
free-wheel
front axle
front seat
fuel gauge
gear lever
generator
Grand Prix
grease-box
grease-gun
guarantee
handbrake
headlight
hit-and-run
inner tube
insurance
limousine
lubricate
motorbike
motorcade
motor show
nipple key
oil filter
overdrive
passenger
patrol car
petrol can
piston rod
point duty
police car
racing car
rear light
reflector
revving up
road sense
road works
saloon car
spare tire
spare tyre
sports car
spotlight
switch off
taximeter
third gear
tire lever
T-junction
tramlines
trunk road
two-seater
tyre lever
underpass
underseal
wheel base
wheel spin
white line

10

access road
adjustment
amber light
anti-dazzle
antifreeze
bevelwheel
bottom gear
box-spanner
brakeblock

brake pedal
broken down
car licence
coachbuilt
combustion
commutator
crankshaft
crossroads
dickey seat
dry battery
four-seater
front wheel
gear casing
gear change
green light
gudgeon pin
headlights
horsepower
inlet valve
insulation
lighting up
low-tension
lubricator
motorcycle
overtaking
petrol pump
petrol tank
piston ring
private car
radial tire
radial tyre
rear mirror
rev counter
right of way
roadworthy
roundabout
safety belt
signalling
spare wheel
speed limit
streamline
suspension
tachometer
thermometer
third-party
three-speed
toll bridge
touring car
traffic cop
traffic jam
two-wheeler
upholstery
ventilator
wheelbrace
windscreen
wing mirror

11

accelerator
accessories
accumulator
blind corner
brake-lining
built-up area
carburetter
carburettor
carriageway
clutch pedal
compression
convertible
crash helmet
decarbonize
de-luxe model
distributor

driving test
exhaust pipe
exhaust port
feeler-gauge
front lights
highway code
ignition key
interrupter
lorry driver
lubrication
luggage rack
motor spirit
needle-valve
number plate
oil pressure
overhauling
overheating
over-revving
owner-driver
petrol gauge
pre-ignition
racing model
radiator cap
request stop
reverse gear
reverse turn
rotary valve
screen-wiper
self-starter
sliding roof
speedometer
sports model
streamlined
sunshine roof
synchromesh
tappet valve
through road
ticking over
trafficator
vacuum brake
valve-timing
wheel wobble

12

acceleration
approach road
arterial road
ball-bearings
breakdown van
clutch-spring
coachbuilder
contact-screw
countershaft
cylinder head
diesel engine
differential
double-decker
driving-chain
driving-shaft
exhaust valve
float-chamber
freewheeling
fuel injection
gear changing
lock-up garage
miles per hour
motor scooter
motor vehicle
motorcyclist
parking light
parking meter
parking place
petrol filter

pillion rider
racing driver
ratchet-wheel
registration
repair outfit
road junction
running-board
single-decker
sparking plug
steering gear
transmission
two-speed gear
warning light

13

admission-pipe
breakdown gang
chain-adjuster
connecting rod
cooling system
driving mirror
fluid flywheel
hydraulic jack
induction pipe
inspection pit
licence-holder
pillion-riding
pressure-gauge
rack-and-pinion
roller-bearing
servo-assisted
shock absorber
shooting brake
speed merchant
starting motor
steering wheel
traffic signal

14

adjusting-screw
circuit-breaker
compression tap
contact-breaker
double-declutch
driving licence
exhaust-cam axle
filling station
friction-clutch
grease-injector
lighting-up time
lubricating oil
luggage-carrier
miles per gallon
propeller shaft
reclining seats
reversing lights
service station
starting handle
steering column
third-party risk
three-speed gear
universal joint

15

carriage-builder
dual carriageway
instrument panel
insurance policy
seating capacity
windscreen wiper

Nautical terms
See also **Boats and ships**

2 AND 3

A.B.
aft
A1
bay
bow
box
cat
cay
C.I.F.
con
cox
ebb
fay
fid
F.O.B.
fog
guy
H.M.S.
hog
jaw
jib
lee
log
man
nut
oar
ply
ram
rig
R.M.
R.N.
rum
run
sag
sea
set
SOS
tar
top
tow
way
yaw

4

ahoy
alee
back
bale
beam
beat
bend
bitt
boom
bows
brig
bunk
bunt
buoy
calk
calm
coak
comb
cott
crew
deck
dive
dock

down
dune
east
eddy
fake
fend
flag
floe
flow
foam
fore
foul
frap
furl
gaff
gale
gang
gear
girt
grog
hank
hard
haul
haze
hazy
head
helm
hold
hove
hulk
hull
jack
junk
keel
knot
land
last
lead
leak
line
list
load
loof
luff
lute
mast
mess
mine
mist
mole
moor
navy
neap
oars
peak
pier
poop
port
prow
punt
quay
raft
rail
rake
rank
rate
rear
reef
ride
roll
rope

rove
rung
sail
scud
seam
ship
sink
skid
slip
slue
spar
stay
stem
step
surf
swab
swig
tack
taut
tend
tide
tilt
toss
trim
trip
vang
veer
voya
waft
wake
wapp
warp
wave
wear
west
whip
wind
wing
yard
yarn

5

aback
abaft
abeam
afore
afoul
after
ahead
ahull
aloft
apeak
aport
atrip
avast
awash
beach
belay
belee
below
berth
bibbs
bight
bilge
bilts
bitts
blirt
block
board

bosun
bower
bowse
brace
brail
bream
briny
cabin
cable
cadet
canal
cargo
caulk
chain
chart
check
chock
clamp
cleat
craft
crank
cuddy
davit
depth
diver
douse
downs
dowse
draft
drift
embay
entry
fanal
flake
fleet
float
fluke
foggy
gauge
grave
gusty
hands
hatch
haven
hawse
hitch
hoist
horse
jetty
jutty
kedge
kevel
lay-to
lay up
leach
leaky
leech
ligan
liner
lobby
lurch
metal
misty
naval
north
oakum
ocean
order
orlop
panch
pitch

273

prick
prize
prore
radar
radio
range
refit
rhumb
right
roads
ropes
route
rower
royal
sally
salve
salvo
sands
screw
sheer
sheet
shelf
shoal
shore
siren
skeet
sling
sound
spars
spoom
sprit
steer
stern
storm
surge
swell
swing
thole
tidal
trice
truck
truss
waist
watch
weigh
wharf
wheel
windy
woold
wreck

6

aboard
adrift
afloat
anchor
armada
ashore
astern
aweigh
awning
balker
batten
beacon
becket
billow
bonnet
bridge
bumkin
bunker
burton
cablet
canvas
careen

carina
comber
convoy
course
crotch
cruise
debark
diving
double
driver
earing
embark
engine
ensign
escort
fathom
fender
fo'c'sle
for'ard
fother
funnel
furled
galley
gasket
gromet
gunnel
halser
hawser
hounds
hove-to
inship
jetsam
jetson
jigger
kedger
lading
lateen
launch
lay-off
leeway
Lloyd's
locker
manned
marina
marine
marker
maroon
marque
masted
mayday
mid-sea
mizzen
moored
mutiny
nautic
neaped
needle
offing
on deck
outfit
paddle
patrol
pay off
pay out
pennon
Pharos
pillow
pintle
piracy
pirate
piston
pooped
poppet
raider
rating
ratlin

reefed
reefer
rigged
rigger
rocket
rudder
sailor
saloon
salute
salvor
sculls
sealer
seaman
seaway
sheets
shroud
signal
sinker
sinnet
splice
squall
square
stocks
stormy
strake
strand
stream
tackle
tender
thwart
tiller
timber
toggle
towage
unbend
unbitt
uncoil
undock
unfurl
unlade
unload
unmoor
unship
vessel
voyage

7

aground
athwart
backing
bale out
ballast
beached
bearing
beating
bilboes
blister
boarder
bobstay
bollard
boomkin
bowline
bow wave
boxhaul
bracing
breaker
bulwark
bunkage
buntine
bunting
buoyage
caboose
calking
can-buoy

capsize
capstan
captain
cast off
catfall
cathead
cat's-paw
channel
charter
claw off
coaling
coaming
cockpit
compass
conning
cordage
corsair
counter
cresset
cringle
cyclone
deadeye
deep-sea
degauss
dismast
dockage
dog-vane
dolphin
drabler
draught
dry-dock
dunnage
ease off
ebb-tide
embargo
eye-bolt
fairway
fishery
flotsam
flotson
fogbank
foghorn
foretop
forward
founder
freight
freshen
freshet
futtock
gangway
gimbals
go about
go below
grapnel
grating
graving
grommet
gudgeon
gun-deck
gunnage
gun-port
gun-room
gunwale
guy-rope
half pay
halyard
harbour
harpoon
haul off
head off
head sea
headway
heave to
horizon
iceberg
icefloe

inboard
inshore
Jack Tar
jib boom
jibstay
keelage
keelson
landing
laniard
lanyard
lashing
lastage
latches
leaking
lee-gage
lee side
lee tide
leeward
listing
loading
logbook
logline
logreel
lookout
luffing
lugsail
maintop
mariner
marines
marline
marling
matelot
mistral
monsoon
moorage
mooring
mudhook
oarsman
oceanic
offward
old salt
on board
outport
oversea
painter
pennant
pooping
port-bar
quayage
rafting
rations
ratline
reefing
reeming
ride out
rigging
rollers
rolling
rope-end
rostrum
rowlock
rundown
sailing
salvage
scupper
scuttle
seacard
seafolk
sea-lane
sea-legs
seamark
sea-ooze
sea-room
seasick
seaward
set sail

sextant
shallow
shelves
shipper
shipway
shrouds
sick-bay
sinking
skipper
skysail
slipway
spanker
spencer
squally
stand-by
steward
stopper
stowage
tacking
tackled
tackler
tactics
tempest
thimble
tonnage
top deck
top mast
topping
topsail
topside
tornado
torpedo
towline
towpath
towrope
transom
trysail
typhoon
unladen
unsling
unslung
veering
waftage
ward off
warping
wavelet
waveson
wet dock
whistle
wrecked
wrecker
yardarm

8

anchored
anteport
aplustre
approach
armament
at anchor
aweather
backstay
backwash
barbette
bargeman
barnacle
beam-ends
bearings
becalmed
berthage
berthing
binnacle
boat-deck
boathook

bolt-rope
bowsprit
broach to
bulkhead
bulwarks
buntline
castaway
caulking
claw away
club-haul
coasting
crossing
cruising
cutwater
dead slow
deadwood
deckhand
derelict
disembay
ditty-bag
ditty-box
dockyard
dogwatch
doldrums
doubling
downhaul
drifting
driftway
easterly
eastward
even keel
fife-rail
flag-rank
floating
flotilla
fogbound
foot-rope
forefoot
foremast
forepeak
foresail
foreship
forestay
forewind
free-port
gaffsail
go aboard
go ashore
halliard
hard-alee
hatchway
headfast
head into
headwind
helmless
helmsman
high seas
high tide
hornpipe
hull-down
icebound
icefield
iron-sick
jackstay
jettison
jury mast
keelhaul
keel over
land ahoy!
landfall
landmark
landsman
landward
land wind
larboard
lead-line

leeboard
lee shore
lifebelt
lifebuoy
lifeline
load-line
loblolly
logboard
long haul
low water
magazine
mainboom
main deck
mainmast
mainsail
mainstay
mainyard
make sail
maritime
martinet
masthead
mastless
messmate
midships
moorings
moulinet
mutineer
mutinous
nauscopy
nautical
navigate
neap tide
ordnance
outboard
overrake
overseas
paravane
periplus
picaroon
pierhead
pilotage
plimsoll
poop deck
porthole
portoise
portside
pratique
pumproom
put about
put to sea
quarters
reef-knot
re-embark
ride easy
ride hard
roadster
sail-loft
sail-room
sail-yard
salvable
salvager
sandbank
scudding
seaborne
sea-chest
seafarer
seagoing
sea-rover
shallows
shark-net
sheer off
ship ahoy
shipmate
shipment
ship oars
shipping

275

sounding
spy-glass
squadron
standard
stand off
staysail
steerage
sternage
sternway
stowaway
stranded
streamer
submerge
tackling
tafferel
taffrail
thole-pin
timoneer
tranship
traverse
unbuoyed
uncoiled
underset
under way
unfurled
vanguard
wall-knot
wardroom
waterman
water-rot
waterway
waveworm
westerly
westward
west wind
windlass
wind-rode
wind-sail
windward
woolding
wreckage
yachting

9

about-ship
admiralty
affreight
afterdeck
air-funnel
all aboard
alongside
amidships
anchorage
anchoring
back-stays
bargepole
barnacles
beaconage
below deck
bilge-keel
bilge-pump
blue peter
boardable
boat drill
broadside
bunkering
captaincy
careenage
chartered
chartroom
close haul
coastwise
companion
corposant

crossjack
crosstree
crosswind
crow's nest
Davy Jones
dead-water
deck cargo
demurrage
departure
disanchor
discharge
disembark
doggerman
dogshores
dress ship
drift-sail
driftwood
Elmo's-fire
false keel
firedrill
floodmark
flood-tide
flying jib
foreshore
foundered
gangboard
gangplank
gather way
groundage
half-hitch
hard aport
high water
hoist sail
holystone
house-flag
houseline
hurricane
jack-block
jack-staff
jack-stays
kentledge
land ahead
lobscouse
lower deck
maelstrom
mainbrace
mainsheet
manoeuvre
midstream
minefield
minute-gun
mizzentop
naumachia
navicular
navigable
navigator
neptunian
northerly
northward
north wind
ocean lane
orlop deck
outrigger
overboard
parbuckle
periscope
press-gang
privateer
prize-crew
promenade
quicksand
recharter
reckoning
red ensign
reef-point
refitment

revictual
rhumb-line
roadstead
rockbound
royal mast
Royal Navy
rum-runner
sailcloth
seafaring
sea-letter
sea-robber
seaworthy
semaphore
sheething
shipboard
shipowner
ship's crew
shipshape
shipwreck
shoreward
sick-berth
sidelight
sight land
southerly
southward
south wind
sou'wester
spindrift
spinnaker
spritsail
stanchion
starboard
stateroom
steersman
sternfast
sternmost
sternpost
stokehold
storm-beat
stormsail
stormstay
stretcher
tarpaulin
telescope
tide-table
tophamper
trade wind
twin-screw
two-decker
unballast
uncharted
unharbour
unlighted
unsounded
upper deck
water-line
water-sail
whirlwind
wind-bound
wring-bolt
yachtsman

10

A1 at Lloyd's
aboard ship
after-guard
after-hatch
after-sails
alongshore
anchorable
anchor buoy
anchor hold
astarboard
ballasting

batten down
Bermuda rig
bilgewater
blue ensign
bluejacket
breakwater
bootlegger
breastfast
bridge deck
cargo space
cast anchor
casting-net
catch a crab
chain-cable
chain-plate
charthouse
coal-bunker
cork-jacket
cross-piece
crosstrees
deadlights
degaussing
diving-bell
dockmaster
downstream
drop anchor
drop astern
embarkment
engine room
escutcheon
fathomless
fiddlehead
figurehead
fore-and-aft
forecastle
forge ahead
freightage
freshwater
frostbound
full-rigged
gaff rigged
harbourage
heavy-laden
high-and-dry
hollow-mast
jigger-mast
Jolly Roger
jury-rigged
jury rudder
landlocked
landlubber
lateen sail
lateen yard
lay a course
liberty-man
life-jacket
lighterage
lighthouse
lookout-man
loxodromic
manoeuvres
marine soap
marker buoy
martingale
middle deck
midshipman
mizzenmast
mizzensail
mizzenstay
navigating
navigation
night-watch
ocean-going
orthodromy
parcelling
pilothouse

pipe aboard
port of call
powder-room
prize-court
prize-money
quarantine
raking fire
reduce sail
rendezvous
reshipment
rope-ladder
round-house
rudderless
rudder post
Samson post
seamanlike
seamanship
ship-broker
shipmaster
shipwright
signalling
skyscraper
slack-water
spring-tide
square-sail
stanchions
stay-tackle
stern-board
stern-frame
sternsheet
submariner
supercargo
take in sail
tally-clerk
tidal basin
tidal river
tiller-rope
topgallant
unfathomed
unfordable
upperworks
water-borne
waterspout
watertight
wheel-house
wring-staff

11

abandon ship
beachcomber
belaying pin
captainship
centreboard
chafing-gear
close-hauled
compass card
compass rose
contact mine
debarkation
depth-charge
dismastment
diving bell
diving suit
dock charges
echo-sounder
embarcation
embarkation
escape hatch
foam-crested
fore-topmast
foul weather
gallows-tops
get under way
go alongside

graving-dock
ground-swell
harbour dues
harness-cask
hug the shore
innavigable
keelhauling
landing deck
lifeboatman
loblolly-boy
loxodromics
maintopmast
maintopsail
make headway
marine store
mess steward
middle watch
mizzen course
monkey-block
naval rating
orthodromic
overfreight
paddle wheel
port charges
port of entry
press-of-sail
quarterdeck
range-finder
reconnoitre
riding-light
sailing date
Samson's-post
searchlight
seasickness
sheet anchor
shipbreaker
ship's doctor
ship's papers
sliding-keel
snatch-block
sounding-rod
south-wester
spanking boom
spring a leak
standing off
station-bill
steerage-way
stern-chaser
sternsheets
storm signal
three-masted
thwartships
tidal waters
torpedo tube
unballasted
unchartered
under canvas
under-masted
unnavigable
unnavigated
unsheltered
unsoundable
waistcloths
waterlogged
weather-gage
weathermost
weather-roll
weather side
weigh anchor
white ensign

12

air-sea rescue
between-decks

bill of lading
breeches-buoy
cable's-length
canvas length
caulking iron
change course
collision-mat
companionway
conning tower
counter-brace
displacement
double-banked
double-braced
double-manned
equinoctials
fishing fleet
floating dock
futtock-plate
ground-tackle
hard-aweather
jack-o'-lantern
jacob's ladder
lateen-rigged
line of battle
longshoreman
magnetic mine
maiden voyage
man overboard
marine boiler
marine engine
marline-spike
measured mile
minesweeping
naval command
navigability
orthodromics
outmanoeuvre
outward-bound
Plimsoll line
Plimsoll mark
privateering
recommission
ride at anchor
ship-chandler
shipping line
ship's husband
slack in stays
square-rigged
starboard bow
stream anchor
studding sail
tourist class
training ship
transhipment
Trinity House
undercurrent
unfathomable
war-insurance
weatherboard
weatherbound
weather cloth
weatherglass
weatherproof
westerly wind
will-o'-the-wisp

13

affreightment
cat-o'-nine-tails
close quarters
compass signal
dead reckoning
deck passenger
fishing-tackle

floating light
grappling-iron
high-water mark
hurricane deck
life-preserver
mizzen rigging
naval dockyard
naval ordnance
navigableness
north-east wind
northerly wind
north-west wind
order-of-battle
re-embarkation
royal dockyard
ship-of-the-line
south-east wind
southerly wind
south-west wind

spilling-lines
starboard beam
starboard side
steering-wheel
weather report

14

circumnavigate
compass-bearing
disembarkation
futtock shrouds
hard-astarboard
letter-of-marque
Lloyd's Register
mushroom-anchor
naval architect
powder magazine

prevailing wind
running-rigging
schooner-rigged
screw-propeller
ship's-carpenter
swivel-rowlocks
topgallant mast

15

Admiralty Office
circumnavigable
command of the sea
companion ladder
marine insurance
mariner's compass
operation orders
victualling yard

Vehicles

3 AND 4

auto
bier
biga
bike
bus
cab
car
cart
dan
drag
dray
duck
fly
gig
jeep
loco
mini
pram
skis
sled
tank
taxi
tram
trap
tube
van
wain

5

bogey
bogie
brake
brett
buggy
chair
coach
coupé
cycle
dilly
float
lorry
moped
motor
pulka
sedan
sulky

tonga
train
truck
wagon

6

banger
barrow
Berlin
calash
chaise
dodgem
dennet
doolie
drosky
engine
fiacre
gingle
go-cart
hansom
hearse
jalopy
landau
limber
litter
oxcart
pulkha
saloon
sledge
sleigh
surrey
tandem
tender
tonga
tri-car
troika
waggon
whisky

7

amtrack
autobus
autocar
bicycle
britzka
caboose
cacolet

caravan
cariole
chariot
dogcart
droshky
flivver
fourgon
growler
gyrocar
hackery
hackney
haywain
helibus
kibitka
mail car
mail-van
minibus
minicab
minicar
omnibus
phaeton
pullman
railcar
railbus
scooter
sidecar
taxicab
tilbury
tonneau
tractor
trailer
tramcar
trolley
trundle
tumbrel
tumbril
turnout
vis-á-vis
voiture

8

barouche
brakevan
britzska
brougham
cablecar
carriage

clarence
curricle
cycle-car
dustcart
equipage
goods van
handcart
ice-yacht
jump-seat
mail-cart
milk-cart
motorbus
motorcar
old crock
pushcart
quadriga
rickshaw
roadster
rockaway
runabout
sociable
stanhope
steam-car
toboggan
tricycle
victoria

9

ambulance
amphibian
applecart
bandwagon
bath-chair
boat-train
bob-sleigh
box-wagon
bubblecar
bulldozer
cabriolet
charabanc
diligence
dining car
dodgem car
dormobile
guard's van
hansom cab
ice skates
landaulet

land rover
limousine
mail-coach
mail-train
milkfloat
motorbike
motorcade
muletrain
palanquin
prison van
saloon car
sand yacht
sportscar
streetcar
stretcher
wagonette
water-cart

post-chaise
pullman car
sedan chair
smoking car
snowplough
spring-cart
stagecoach
state coach
tip-up lorry
touring car
tramway-car
trolley-bus
trolley-car
velocipede
waggonette
war chariot
wheelchair

12

baby carriage
coach-and-four
coach-and-pair
furniture-van
hackney-coach
invalid chair
luggage train
magic carpet
motor scooter
pantechnicon
perambulator
railway train
three-wheeler
watering-cart

10

automobile
Black Maria
boneshaker
chapel cart
conveyance
donkey-cart
fire-engine
four-in-hand
glass coach
goods train
goods truck
hackney cab
invalid cab
hand-barrow
jinricksha
locomotive
motorcoach
motorcycle
motor lorry

11

armoured car
brewer's dray
bullock cart
caterpillar
delivery van
four-wheeler
goods waggon
gun-carriage
horse-litter
jaunting-car
landaulette
mail phaeton
sleeping car
state landau
steam engine
steamroller
three-in-hand
waggon train
wheelbarrow

13

ambulance cart
electric truck
governess cart
mourning-coach
penny-farthing
state carriage
steam-carriage
wheel-carriage

14 AND 15

ambulance wagon (14)
bathing-machine (14)
hackney carriage (15)
invalid carriage (15)
luggage trailer (14)
railway carriage (15)
traction-engine (14)

MISCELLANEOUS
Abbreviations

1 AND 2

A   ampere
A.A.   Automobile Association,
          Anti-aircraft, Alcoholics
          Anonymous
A.B.   ablebodied seaman
A.C.   alternating current
a/c   account
A.D.   Anno Domini (In the year of our
          Lord)
A.F.   Admiral of the Fleet
A.G.   Adjutant-General
a.m.   ante meridiem (before noon)
A1   First-class in Lloyd's Register
AS   Anglo-Saxon
A.V.   Authorised Version
Av.   avenue, average
b.   born, bowled
B.A.   Bachelor of Arts
B.C.   Before Christ, British Columbia
B.D.   Bachelor of Divinity
b.l.   bill of lading
B.M.   British Museum
B.P.   British Pharmacopœia
b.p.   boiling point
Bp.   Bishop

B.S.   Bachelor of Surgery, Bachelor of
          Science
Bt.   Baronet
C.   centigrade, Conservative
c.   caught, chapter, cents, circa
ca.   circa (around, about)
C.A.   chartered accountant
C.B.   Companion of the Bath, confined to
          barracks
C.C.   cricket club, county council
C.E.   Church of England, civil engineer
C.F.   Chaplain to the Forces
ch.   chapter
C.I.   Channel Islands
C.J.   Chief Justice
cl.   class, clause
cm.   centimetre
C.O.   commanding officer, Colonial Office
Co.   company, county
c/o   care of
Cr.   creditor
C.U.   Cambridge University
d.   daughter, old penny, old pence, died
D.C.   direct current, District of Columbia
          (U.S.)
D.D.   Doctor of Divinity
DM   Deutschemark

279

do.	ditto
D.P.	displaced person
D.R.	District Railway
Dr.	drachm, drachma, doctor, debtor
D.V.	deo volente (God willing)
E.	east
ea.	each
E.C.	east-central
Ed.	editor
E.E.	electrical engineer, errors excepted
e.g.	exempli gratia (for example)
E.I.	East Indies
eq.	equal
E.R.	Elizabeth Regina (Queen), East Riding (Yorkshire)
ex.	example, without, from
F.	Fahrenheit
f.	feminine, francs, forte
F.A.	Football Association
F.C.	football club
ff.	fortissimo
F.M.	field-marshal, frequency modulation
F.O.	Foreign Office
fo.	folio
Fr.	French, Friday
ft.	foot, feet
G.B.	Great Britain
G.C.	George Cross
G.I.	general issue (U.S.A.)
Gk.	Greek
gm.	gram(s)
G.M.	George Medal, Grand Master
G.P.	General Practitioner
G.R.	Georgius Rex (King George)
Gr.	Greek
gr.	grain(s), grammar, gross
gs.	guineas
Gt.	great
h.	hour(s)
H.C.	House of Commons
H.E.	high explosive, His (Her) Excellency
H.F.	high frequency
hf.	half
H.H.	His (Her) Highness
H.M.	His (Her) Majesty
H.O.	Home Office
h.p.	high pressure, horsepower
H.Q.	headquarters
hr.	hour
H.T.	high tension
HZ	Hertz
Ia.	Iowa
id.	idem (the same)
i.e.	id est (that is)
in.	inch(es)
Is.	island
I.W.	Isle of Wight
J.	Joule, judge
Jn.	junction
J.P.	Justice of the Peace
Jr.	junior
K	kelvin
K.C.	King's Counsel, Knight Commander
kc	kilocycle
K.G.	Knight of the Garter
kg.	kilogram(s)
km.	kilometre(s)
K.P.	Knight of St. Patrick
Ks.	Kansas
K.T.	Knight of the Thistle
Kt.	knight
L.	Latin, Liberal
l.	litre

lb.	libra (pound)
L.C.	Lord Chancellor
l.c.	lower case (printing)
Ld.	limited, lord
L.F.	low frequency
L.P.	low pressure
L.T.	low tension
Lt.	Lieutenant, light
M.	monsieur, member, thousand (mille)
m.	metre(s), mile(s), masculine, married
M.A.	Master of Arts
M.B.	Bachelor of Medicine
M.C.	Master of Ceremonies, Military Cross
M.D.	Doctor of Medicine
ME	Middle English
mf.	Mezzoforte
mg.	milligram
M.I.	mounted infantry
M.M.	Military Medal
MM.	Messieurs (Fr.)
mm.	millimetre(s)
M.O.	medical officer
Mo.	Missouri, month
M.P.	Member of Parliament
M.R.	Master of the Rolls
Mr.	mister
MS.	manuscript
Mt.	mount
M.T.	mechanical transport
N.	newton, north, nitrogen
n.	neuter, noun
N.B.	North Britain, nota bene (note well)
N.E.	north-east
N.F.	National Front
No.	number (numero)
N.P.	new paragraph
n.p.	new pence
nr.	near
N.S.	New style, Nova Scotia
N.T.	New Testament
N.W.	north-west
N.Y.	New York
N.Z.	New Zealand
O.	Ohio, oxygen
ob.	obiit (died)
O.C.	Officer Commanding
O.E.	Old English , Old Etonian(s)
O.M.	Order of Merit
Op.	opus (work)
o.p.	out of print
Or.	Oregon
O.S.	old style
O.T.	Old Testament
O.U.	Oxford University
oz.	ounce(s)
P.	Prince, President
p.	page, penny, pence, piano
P.C.	Police Constable, Privy Councillor
p.c.	per cent., post card
p.d.	per diem, potential difference
pd.	paid
pf.	pianoforte
pl.	plural, place
P.M.	Prime Minister, Provost Marshal, Past Master, Postmaster
p.m.	post meridiem, post mortem
P.O.	post office, postal order
pp.	pages, pianissimo
p.p.	Per procuration (by proxy)
P.S.	postscript
Pt.	part, port
pt.	pint, point
q.	query, question

Q.C.	Queen's Counsel
Q.M.	Quartermaster
qr.	quarter
qt.	quart
q.v.	quod vide (which see)
R.	Réaumur, Royal, Rex (King), Regina (Queen), right, rupee
R.A.	Royal Academician, Royal Artillery
R.C.	Roman Catholic
Rd.	road
R.E.	Royal Engineers
R.M.	Royal Mail, Royal Marines
R.N.	Royal Navy
Rs.	Rupees
R.U.	Rugby Union
ry.	railway
S.	Saint, second, singular, shilling, son, south
S.A.	South Africa
s.c.	small capitals (printing)
S.E.	south-east
s.g.	specific gravity
S.J.	Society of Jesus
S.M.	Sergeant-Major
sq.	square
sr.	senior
s.s.	same size, steamship
St.	Saint, street, stone (wt.), stumped
S.W.	south-west
T.B.	torpedo-boat, tuberculosis
T.D.	Territorial Decoration
TV	television
u.c.	upper case (printing)
U.K.	United Kingdom
U.N.	United Nations
U.S.	United States
V	volt
v.	verb, versus (against)
Va.	Virginia
V.C.	Victoria Cross
V.D.	Volunteer Decoration, Venereal Disease(s)
v.g.	very good
V.O.	Victorian Order
V.R.	Victoria Regina (Queen)
W.	watt, west
W.C.	water closet, West Central
W.D.	War Department
w.f.	wrong fount (printing)
W.O.	War Office, Warrant Officer
wt.	weight
yd.	yard
yr.	your

3

A.A.A.	Amateur Athletic Association, American Automobile Association
A.A.G.	Assistant Adjutant-General
ABC	alphabet
Abp.	archbishop
A.C.A.	Associate of the Institute of Chartered Accountants
A.C.F.	Army Cadet Force
A.C.W.	Aircraftwoman
A.D.C.	aide-de-camp, amateur dramatic club
adj.	adjective
Adm.	Admiral
adv.	adverb
A.E.U.	Amalgamated Engineering Union
A.O.C.	Army Ordnance Corps
A.O.D.	Army Ordnance Dept.
A.O.F.	Ancient Order of Foresters

A.P.M.	Assistant Provost Marshal
Apr.	April
A.R.A.	Associate of the Royal Academy
Ark.	Arkansas
A.R.P.	Air Raid Precautions
arr.	arrive(s, ed)
A.T.C.	Air Training Corps
A.T.S.	Auxiliary Territorial Service
Aug.	August
aux.	auxiliary
ave.	avenue
B.B.C.	British Broadcasting Corporation
B.C.L.	Bachelor of Civil Law
bde.	brigade
B.E.F.	British Expeditionary Force
b.h.p.	Brake horsepower
B.M.A	British Medical Association
B.M.J	British Medical Journal
B.O.T.	Board of Trade
Bro.	brother
B.Sc.	Bachelor of Science
B.T.U.	British Thermal Unit(s)
B.V.M.	Blessed Virgin Mary
B.W.G.	Birmingham Wire Gauge
cap.	capital
C.B.E.	Commander of the British Empire (Order)
C.B.I.	Confederation of British Industry
C.I.A.	Central Intelligence Agency
C.I.D.	Criminal Investigation Department
C.I.E.	Companion of the Indian Empire (Order)
c.i.f.	cost, insurance, freight
C.I.O.	Congress of Industrial Organizations (U.S.)
C.M.G.	Companion of St. Michael and St. George (Order)
co.	company
c.o.d.	cash on delivery
col.	Colonel, column
C.P.R.	Canadian Pacific Railway
C.S.M.	Company Sergeant-Major
C.V.O.	Commander of the Victorian Order
cwt.	hundredweight
D.A.G.	Deputy Adjutant-General
D.B.E.	Dame Commander of the British Empire (Order)
D.C.L.	Doctor of Civil Law
D.C.M.	Distinguished Conduct Medal
DDT	dichlorodiphenyl trichlorocethane
Dec.	December
deg.	degree(s)
D.E.S.	Department of Education and Science
D.F.C.	Distinguished Flying Cross
D.F.M.	Distinguished Flying Medal
div.	Dividend
D.L.O	Dead Letter Office
D.N.A.	deoxyribonucleic acid
D.O.E.	Department of the Environment
doz.	dozen
D.S.C.	Distinguished Service Cross
D.Sc.	Doctor of Science
D.S.M.	Distinguished Service Medal
D.S.O.	Distinguished Service Order
dwt.	pennyweight
E.E.C.	European Economic Community
e.m.e.	electro-motive force
E.N.E.	east-north-east
E.S.E.	east-south-east
Esq.	Esquire
Etc.	etcetera
f.a.s.	free alongside ship

F.A.A.	Fleet Air Arm
F.B.A.	Fellow of the British Academy
F.B.I.	Federal Bureau of Investigation
F.C.A.	Fellow of the Institute of Chartered Accountants
F.C.S.	Fellow of the Chemical Society
Feb.	February
fem.	feminine
F.G.S.	Fellow of the Geological Society
F.I.A.	Fellow of the Institute of Actuaries
Fig.	figure
F.L.A.	Fellow of the Library Association
f.o.b.	free on board
F.R.S.	Fellow of the Royal Society
fur.	furlong
F.Z.S.	Fellow of the Zoological Society
gal.	gallon(s)
G.B.E.	Knight Grand Cross of the British Empire
G.C.A.	Ground Control Approach (Aviation)
G.C.B.	Knight Grand Cross of the Bath
G.C.F.	greatest common factor
G.C.M.	greatest common measure
Gen.	General
G.H.Q.	General Headquarters
Gib.	Gibraltar
G.L.C.	Greater London Council
G.M.T.	Greenwich mean time
G.O.C.	General Officer Commanding
G.O.M.	grand old man
G.P.O.	General Post Office
G.T.C.	Girl's Training Corps
gym.	gymnasium
H.A.C.	Hon. Artillery Company
H.B.M.	His (Her) Britannic Majesty
h.c.f.	highest common factor
Heb.	Hebrew(s)
H.I.H.	His (Her) Imperial Highness
H.I.M.	His (Her) Imperial Majesty
H.L.I.	Highland Light Infantry
H.M.S.	His (Her) Majesty's ship or Service
Hon.	honorary, Honourable
H.R.H.	His (Her) Royal Highness
hrs.	hours
I.B.A.	Independent Broadcasting Authority
I.C.S.	Indian Civil Service
i.h.p.	indicated horsepower
I.H.S.	Jesus, Saviour of men (Iesus Hominum Salvator)
I.L.O	International Labour Organization
I.L.P.	Independent Labour Party
Inc.	incorporated
I.O.F.	Independent Order of Foresters
I.O.U.	(acknowledgment of debt)
I.O.W.	Isle of Wight
I.R.A.	Irish Republican Army
I.S.O	Imperial Service Order
I.T.V.	Independent Television
I.U.D.	intra-uterine device
Jan.	January
Jas.	James
Jos.	Joseph
jun.	junior
Kan.	Kansas
K.B.E.	Knight Commander of the British Empire (Order)
K.C.B.	Knight Commander of the Bath
K.G.B.	Komitet Gosudarstvennoi Bezopasnosti (Committee of State Security)
K.K.K.	Ku-Klux-Klan

K.L.I.	King's Light Infantry
Knt.	knight
Lab.	Labour
l.b.w.	leg before wicket
L.C.C.	London County Council
L.C.J.	Lord Chief Justice
l.c.m.	lowest common multiple
L.D.S.	Licentiate in Dental Surgery
LL.B.	Bachelor of Laws
LL.D.	Doctor of Laws
loq.	loquitur (speaks)
L.S.D.	lysergic acid diethylamide
L.s.d.	Libræ (pounds); solidi (shillings); denarii (pence)
L.S.E.	London School of Economics
Ltd.	Limited
Maj.	Major
Mar.	March
M.B.E.	Member of the British Empire (Order)
M.C.C.	Marylebone Cricket Club
M.F.B.	Metropolitan Fire Brigade
M.F.H.	Master of Foxhounds
mil.	military
min.	mineralogy
Mme.	Madame
M.O.D.	Ministry of Defence
M.O.T.	Ministry of Transport
m.p.h.	miles per hour
M.Sc.	Master of Science
MSS.	Manuscripts
M.T.B.	motor torpedo boat
M.V.O.	Member of the Royal Victorian Order
N.C.O.	non-commissioned officer
neg.	negative
N.F.S.	National Fire Service
n.h.p.	nominal horsepower
N.N.E.	north-north-east
N.N.W.	north-north-west
Nos.	numbers
N.P.G.	National Portrait Gallery
N.R.A.	National Rifle Association
N.S.W.	New South Wales
N.U.J.	National Union of Journalists
N.U.M.	National Union of Mineworkers
N.U.R.	National Union of Railwaymen
N.U.S.	National Union of Seamen, National Union of Students
N.U.T.	National Union of Teachers
O.B.E.	Officer of the British Empire (Order)
Obs.	obsolete
Oct.	October
Ont.	Ontario
Ord.	order, ordinary, ordnance, ordained
O.T.C.	Officers' Training Corps
Pan.	Panama
par.	paragraph, parish, parallel
P.G.M.	Past Grand Master
Ph. D.	Doctor of Philosophy
P.L.O.	Palestine Liberation Organization
P.M.G.	Postmaster-General
pop.	population
P.P.C.	Pour prendre congé (to take leave)
P.R.A.	President of the Royal Academy
P.R.O.	Public Relations Officer
pro.	professional
P.T.O.	please turn over
P.V.C.	polyvinyl chloride
P.W.D.	Public Works Department
q.e.d.	quod erat demonstrandum (which was to be demonstrated)

q.e.f.	quod erat faciendum (which was to be done)
Q.M.G.	Quartermaster-General
Q.M.S.	Quartermaster-Sergeant
Que.	Quebec
R.A.C.	Royal Armoured Corps, Royal Automobile Club
R.A.F.	Royal Air Force
R.A.M.	Royal Academy of Music
R.B.A.	Royal Society of British Artists
R.C.M.	Royal College of Music
R.C.P.	Royal College of Physicians
R.C.S.	Royal College of Surgeons
ref.	reference
Rev.	Reverend
R.F.A.	Royal Field Artillery
R.G.A.	Royal Garrison Artillery
R.H.A.	Royal Horse Artillery
R.I.P.	requiescat in pace (may he (or she) rest in peace)
R.M.A.	Royal Military Academy
R.M.C.	Royal Military College
R.M.S.	Royal Mail steamer
R.N.R.	Royal Naval Reserve
R.S.M.	Regimental Sergeant-Major
R.S.O.	Railway Sorting Office
R.T.C.	Royal Tank Corps
R.T.O.	Railway Transport Officer
R.U.C.	Royal Ulster Constabulary
R.Y.S.	Royal Yacht Squadron
S.C.C.	Sea Cadet Corps
Sec.	secretary
sen.	senior
seq.	sequens (the following)
Soc.	society
S.P.G.	Society for the Propagation of the Gospel
S.S.E.	south-south-east
S.S.W.	south-south-west
Stg.	sterling
str.	stroke (rowing)
S.W.G.	standard wire gauge
T.B.D.	torpedo-boat destroyer
T.N.T.	trinitrotoluene (explosive)
T.U.C.	Trades Union Congress
typ.	typography
U.D.A.	Ulster Defence Association
U.D.I.	unilateral declaration of independence
uhf	ultra-high frequency
ult.	ultimo (last month)
U.N.O.	United Nations Organisation
U.S.A.	United States of America
V.A.D.	Voluntary Aid Detachment
Ven.	The Venerable
vhf	very high frequency
Vet.	veterinary surgeon
V.I.P.	very important person
viz.	videlicet (namely)
Vol.	volunteer
vol.	volume
W.M.S.	Wesleyan Missionary Society
W.N.W.	west-north-west
W.P.C.	Woman Police Constable
W.S.W.	west-south-west

4

ACTH	adrenocorticotrophin
actg.	acting
Adjt.	adjutant
advt.	advertisement
anon.	anonymous
A.Q.M.G	Assistant Quartermaster-General
A.R.A.M.	Associate of the Royal Academy of Music
A.R.C.M.	Associate of the Royal College of Music
asst.	assistant
B.A.O.R.	British Army of the Rhine
Bart.	baronet
Beds.	Bedfordshire
Brit.	British
Bros.	brothers
B.Th.U.	British Thermal Unit
Capt.	Captain
Cent.	centigrade
C.E.R.N.	Conseil Européen pour la Recherche Nucléaire
C.E.T.S.	Church of England Temperance Society
C. of E.	Church of England
Coll.	college
Corp.	Corporal, corporation
C.U.A.C.	Cambridge University Athletic Club
C.U.B.C.	Cambridge University Boat Club
C.U.C.C.	Cambridge University Cricket Club
D.A.A.G.	Deputy Assistant Adjutant General
Dept.	department
D.H.S.S.	Department of Health and Social Security
D.Lit.	Doctor of Literature
D.O.R.A.	Defence of the Realm Act
E. & O.E.	errors and omissions excepted
Ebor.	Eboracum (York)
E.C.S.C.	European Coal and Steel Community
E.F.T.A.	European Free Trade Association
elec.	electrical, electricity
E.N.S.A.	Entertainments National Service Association
Epis.	Episcopal
exam.	examination
F.I.D.O.	Fog Investigation Dispersal Operation
F.R.A.M.	Fellow of the Royal Academy of Music
F.R.A.S.	Fellow of the Royal Astronomical Society
F.R.C.P.	Fellow of the Royal College of Physicians
F.R.C.S.	Fellow of the Royal College of Surgeons
F.R.G.S.	Fellow of the Royal Geographical Society
F.R.S.L.	Fellow of the Royal Society of Literature
G.A.T.T.	General Agreement on Tariffs and Trade
G.C.I.E.	Knight Grand Commander of the Indian Empire (Order)
G.C.M.G.	Knight Grand Cross of St. Michael and St. George (Order)
G.C.S.I.	Knight Grand Commander of the Star of India (Order)
G.V.C.O.	Knight Grand Cross of the Victorian Order
geog.	geography
geom.	geometry
gram.	grammar
inst.	instant (in the present month), institution, Institute
I. of W.	Isle of Wight

283

K.C.I.E.	Knight Commander of the Indian Empire (Order)
K.C.M.G.	Knight Commander (of the Order of) St. Michael and St. George
K.C.V.O.	Knight Commander of the Royal Victorian Order
L.R.A.M.	Licentiate of the Royal Academy of Music
L.R.C.M.	Licentiate of the Royal College of Music
L.R.C.P.	Licentiate of the Royal College of Physicians
masc.	masculine
math.	mathematics
mech.	mechanics
memo.	memorandum
M.I.E.E.	Member of the Institution of Electrical Engineers
M.I.M.E.	Member of the Institution of Mechanical Engineers
Mlle.	Mademoiselle
M.R.C.P.	Member of the Royal College of Physicians
M.R.C.S.	Member of the Royal College of Surgeons
Mus.B.	Bachelor of Music
Mus.D.	Doctor of Music
Myth.	mythology
N.A.T.O.	North Atlantic Treaty Organization
N.E.D.C.	National Economic Development Commission
O.E.C.D.	Organization for Economic Co-operation and Development
O.E.E.C.	Organization for European Economic Co-operation
O.H.M.S.	On His (Her) Majesty's Service
O.U.A.C.	Oxford University Athletic Club
O.U.B.C.	Oxford University Boat Club
O.U.C.C.	Oxford University Cricket Club
O.U.D.S.	Oxford University Dramatic Society
P.A.Y.E.	pay as you earn
pref.	preference
pres.	present
Prof.	professor
prox.	proximo (next month)
R.A.M.C.	Royal Army Medical Corps
R.A.O.B.	Royal Antediluvian Order of Buffaloes
R.A.O.C.	Royal Army Ordnance Corps
R.A.S.C.	Royal Army Service Corps
R.A.V.C.	Royal Army Veterinary Corps
R.C.M.P.	Royal Canadian Mounted Police
recd.	received
Regt.	regiment
R.E.M.E.	Royal Electrical and Mechanical Engineers
R.I.B.A.	Royal Institute of British Architects
R.N.V.R.	Royal Naval Volunteer Reserve
R.S.V.P.	Répondez s'il vous plaît (please reply)
R.W.G.M.	Right Worshipful Grand Master
Sept.	September
S.P.C.K.	Society for Promoting Christian Knowledge
sp. gr.	specific gravity

Supt.	superintendent
Surg.	surgeon
T.H.W.M.	Trinity High-water Mark
Toc H	Talbot House
T.G.W.U.	Transport and General Workers' Union
W.A.A.F.	Women's Auxiliary Air Force
W.Cdr.	Wing Commander
W.J.A.C.	Women's Junior Air Corps
W.R.N.S.	Women's Royal Naval Service
Xmas.	Christmas
Y.M.C.A.	Young Men's Christian Association
Y.W.C.A.	Young Women's Christian Association
zool.	zoology

5

A.A.Q.M.G.	Acting Assistant Quartermaster-General
ad lib.	ad libitum (as much as desired)
Anzac.	Australian and New Zealand Army Corps
A.R.I.B.A.	Associate of the Royal Institute of British Architects
Assoc.	associate, association
A.S.T.M.S.	Association of Scientific Technical and Managerial Staffs
Bart's.	St. Bartholomew's Hospital
Corpn.	corporation
D.A.D.O.S.	Deputy Assistant Director of Ordnance Services
D.A.Q.M.G.	Deputy Assistant Quartermaster-General
D. Litt.	Doctor of Letters
Elect.	electrical, electricity
et seq.	et sequens (and what follows)
ex div.	without dividend
F.R.I.B.A.	Fellow of the Royal Institute of British Architects
Hants.	Hampshire
ht. wkt.	hit wicket
incog.	incognito
Lieut.	Lieutenant
Litt.D.	Doctor of Letters
L.R.C.V.S.	Licentiate of the Royal College of Veterinary Surgeons
Lt.-Col.	Lieutenant-Colonel
Lt.-Com.	Lieutenant-Commander
Lt.-Gen.	Lieutenant-General
Lt.-Gov.	Lieutenant-Governor
Mlles.	Mesdemoiselles
M.R.C.V.S.	Member of the Royal College of Veterinary Surgeons
N.A.A.F.I.	Navy, Army and Air Force Institutes
N.S.P.C.C.	National Society for the Prevention of Cruelty to Children
P. and O.	Peninsular and Oriental
photo.	photograph
R.A.F.V.R.	Royal Air Force Volunteer Reserve
Recce.	reconnaissance
R.S.P.C.A.	Royal Society for the Prevention of Cruelty to Animals
Rt. Hon.	Right Honourable

Rt. Rev.	Right Reverend	Lit. Hum. (6)	Literæ Humaniores (classics)
Salop.	Shropshire		
S.E.A.T.O.	South-east Asia Treaty Organization	Maj.-Gen. (6)	Major General
		Matric. (6)	matriculation
Sergt.	Sergeant	Messrs. (6)	Messieurs
Suppl.	supplement(al, ary)	M. Inst. C.E. (7)	Member of the Institution of Civil Engineers
Treas.	treasurer		
U.N.R.R.A.	United Nations Relief and Rehabilitation Administration	nem. con. (6)	nemine contradicente (none objecting)
Xtian	Christian	Non-com. (6)	non-commissioned officer
		per pro. (6)	per procurationem (by proxy)

6 AND OVER

Cantab. (6)	of Cambridge	prelim. (6)	preliminary
Cantuar. (7)	of Canterbury	pro tem. (6)	pro tempore (for the time being)
Col.-Sergt. (8)	Colour-Sergeant	prox. acc. (7)	proxime accessit (a close second)
Dunelm. (6)	of Durham		
E. and O.E. (6)	Errors and omissions excepted	U.N.E.S.C.O. (6)	United Nations Educational Scientific and Cultural Organization
Lieut.-Col. (8)	Lieutenant-Colonel		
Lieut.-Gen. (8)	Lieutenant-General	verb. sap. (7)	verbum sapienti (a word to the wise)
Lieut.-Gov. (8)	Lieutenant-Governor		

French Revolutionary Calendar

Nivôse (6) *snow, Dec.*
Floréal (7) *blossom, April*
Ventôse (7) *wind, Feb.*
Brumaire (8) *fog, Oct.*
Fervidor (8) *heat, July*
Frimaire (8) *sleet, Nov.*
Germinal (8) *seed, March*

Messidor (8) *harvest, June*
Pluviôse (8) *rain, Jan.*
Prairial (8) *pasture, May*
Fructidor (9) *fruit, Aug.*
Thermidor (9) *heat, July*
Vendémiaire (11) *vintage, Sept.*

Group terms

3 AND 4

band (of musicians)
bevy (of larks, quails, roes, or women)
box (of cigars)
brew (of beer)
case (of whisky or wine)
cast (of hawks)
cete (of badgers)
clan (people)
club (people)
crew (oarsmen or sailors)
crop (of farm produce)
down (of hares)
dule (of doves)
fall (of woodcock)
form (at schools)
four (card-players, oarsmen, or polo team)
gang (of elk, hooligans, labourers, slaves, or thieves)
hand (at cards)
herd (of asses, buffalo, cattle, cranes, deer, giraffes, goats, or oxen)
host (of angels)
hunt (hounds and hunters)
husk (of hares)
knob (of pochards, teal, toads, or widgeon)
leap (of leopards)
lepe (of leopards)
lot (in auctioneering)
meet (of hounds and hunters)
mess (military and naval)

mute (of hounds)
nest (of machine-guns, mice, rabbits, or wasps)
nide (of pheasants)
nine (baseball team)
pace (of asses)
pack (of grouse, hounds, wolves, or cards)
pair (of oarsmen and various)
park (of guns or cars)
peal (of bells)
pile (of arms)
pod (of whiting or peas)
pony (betting; £25)
pool (various)
posy (of flowers)
rag (of colts)
rope (of onions or pearls)
rout (of wolves)
run (of poultry)
rush (of pochards)
sect (of religious people)
set (of various articles)
show (of agricultural products, dogs, horses, etc.)
side (of players)
six (of cub scouts, sportsmen)
sord (of mallards or wild-fowl)
stud (of horses and mares)
sute (of mallards or wild-fowl)
trio (of musicans)
team (of ducks, horses, oxen, or players)
tuft (of grass)

walk (of snipe)
wing (of plovers)
wisp (of snipe)
wood (trees)
yoke (of oxen)

5

batch (of bread and various)
bench (of bishops or magistrates)
blast (of hunters)
blush (of boys)
board (of directors)
brace (of bucks, partridges, etc.)
brood (of hens)
bunch (of flowers, grapes, teal, or widgeon)
caste (of bread)
charm (of goldfinches)
class (of children at schools)
clump (of trees)
copse (trees)
covey (of grouse, partridges, or other birds)
crowd (of people)
doylt (of tame swine)
draft (of police or soldiers)
drove (of cattle or kine)
eight (oarsmen)
field (hunters, race-horses, or runners)
fiver (money; £5)
fleet (of motor-cars or ships)
flock (of birds, pigeons, or sheep)
flush (at cards)
genus (of animals or plants)
grand (money; £1000 or $1000)
group (photographic and various)
guard (soldiers)
hoard (of gold, etc.)
horde (of savages)
leash (of bucks or hounds)
party (of people)
plump (of wildfowl)
posse (of police)
pride (of lions)
scrum (at rugby football)
sedge (of bitterns or herons)
sheaf (of corn)
shoal (of fish)
siege (of herons)
skein (of geese, silk, or wool)
skulk (of foxes)
sloth (of bears)
squad (of beaters or soldiers)
staff (of officials or servants)
stalk (of foresters)
stand (of arms)
state (of princes)
swarm (of bees and other insects)
table (of bridge or whist players)
tribe (of goats or people)
trick (at cards)
troop (of boy-scouts, brownies, cavalry,
   kangaroos, lions, or monkeys)
truss (of hay)
twins (people)
watch (of nightingales or sailors)

6

barren (of mules)
basket (of strawberries)
budget (of papers)
bundle (of asparagus, firewood, and
   various)
caucus (of politicians)

cellar (of wine)
clique (of people)
clutch (of eggs)
colony (of gulls or people)
covert (of coots)
desert (of lapwings)
double (in betting)
eleven (cricket and other teams)
faggot (of sticks)
family (of people or sardines)
flight (of aeroplanes, doves, dunlins, or
   pigeons)
gaggle (of geese)
galaxy (of beauties)
harras (of horses)
kennel (of dogs)
kindle (of kittens)
labour (of moles)
litter (of cubs, pigs, pups, or whelps)
melody (of harpers)
monkey (in betting; £500)
museum (of antiques, works of art, etc.)
muster (of peacocks or soldiers)
nation (of people)
outfit (of clothes or sails)
packet (of cigarettes)
parade (of soldiers)
punnet (of strawberries)
quorum (minimum number of people)
rayful (of knaves)
rubber (at cards)
school (of porpoises or whales)
sextet (of musicians)
sleuth (of bears)
spring (of teal)
stable (of horses)
string (of pearls or racehorses)
tenner (money; £10)
throng (of people)
trophy (of arms, etc.)
troupe (of actors, dancers, or minstrels)
twelve (lacrosse team)
vestry (parochial assembly)

7

battery (of guns)
bouquet (of flowers)
brigade (of troops)
clamour (of rooks)
clouder (of cats)
cluster (of grapes or stars)
company (of actors, capitalists, or widgeon)
council (advisers or local authorities)
dopping (of sheldrakes)
draught (of butlers)
fifteen (rugby football team)
gallery (of pictures)
library (of books or music)
nosegay (of flowers)
orchard (of fruit trees)
quartet (of musicians)
service (of china or crockery)
sounder (of boars or swine)
spinney (of trees)
thicket (of trees)
vintage (of wine)

8

assembly (of people)
audience (of people)
building (of rooks)
division (of troops)

flotilla (of boats)
jamboree (of boy-scouts)
paddling (of ducks)
partners (in business or games)
regiment (of soldiers)
richesse (of martens)
sequence (at cards)
squadron (of cavalry or ships)
triplets (people)

9

army corps (of troops)
badelynge (of ducks)
committee (people)
community (of people or saints)
cowardice (of curs)
gathering (of people and the clans)
morbidity (of majors)
orchestra (of musicians)
shrubbery (of shrubs)
subtiltie (of sergeants)
syndicate (of capitalists)

10

assemblage (of clergy and various)
buttonhole (of flowers)
chattering (of choughs)
collection (of stamps, works of art, etc.)
commission (committee of enquiry)
detachment (of police or soldiers)
exaltation (of larks)
exhibition (of commercial products,
    pictures, works of art, etc.)
observance (of hermits)
shrewdness (of apes)
simplicity (of subalterns)

11 AND OVER

confraternity (brotherhood, usually
    religious) (13)
congregation (of birds or worshippers) (12)
constellation (of stars) (13)
convocation (of clergy or university
    authorities) (11)
murmuration (of starlings) (11)

Heraldry

2 – 4

arms
band
bar
bend
boar
dawl
delf
enty
erne
fess
fret
garb
gore
gray
kite
lion
or
orle
pale
pall
paly
pean
pile
posé
rose
semé
vair
vert

5

alant
animé
armed
azure
badge
barry
baton
bendy
bouche
bowed

breys
cable
chief
crest
cross
eagle
erect
ermin
fesse
field
fusil
garbe
gorge
gules
gurge
gyron
label
motto
pheon
rebus
rompu
sable
scarp
torse
waved

6

aiglet
apaumy
argent
armory
at gaze
attire
baston
bazant
bendil
bevile
bezant
billet
blazon
border
buckle

canton
charge
checky
chequy
cleché
cotise
couché
coward
dexter
dragon
ermine
escrol
etoile
falcon
fillet
flanch
fleury
florid
fretty
fylfot
garter
ground
guttée
heater
herald
jessed
knight
manche
mascle
maunch
mullet
naiant
Norroy
pallet
rebate
rustre
sejant
shield
square
timbre
vairée
vested
voided
voider

volant
vorant
wivern
wyvern

7

adorsed
adossed
alberia
annulet
arrière
arrondi
attired
barruly
bearing
bendlet
bevilly
bordure
bottony
brisure
cadency
chapter
chevron
clarion
courant
croslet
dolphin
dormant
emblaze
embowed
embrued
enarmed
endorse
engoulé
engrail
ermelin
estoile
fretted
fructed
gardant
griffin
Ich Dien

leopard
lioncel
lozenge
lozengy
martlet
miniver
nombril
passant
potence
purpure
quarter
raguled
rampant
roundel
salient
saltire
sea-lion
sexfoil
shafted
sinople
statant
swallow
torqued
torteau
trefoil
unicorn

8

affronté
allerion
armorist
aversant
barrulet
bevilled
blazonry
caboched
caboshed
chaperon
couchant
crescent
dancetty
emblazon
englante
enmanché
erminois
escallop
gonfalon
haurient

heraldic
insignia
Lyon King
mantling
naissant
opinicus
ordinary
renverse
roundlet
sea-horse
sinister
standard
tincture
tressure

9

aquilated
arraswise
banderole
blazoning
carbuncle
cartouche
chevronel
combatant
diapering
displayed
embattled
enveloped
environed
erminites
estoillee
florettée
hatchment
lionceaux
lioncelle
Lyon-Court
regardant
scutcheon
spur-rowel
supporter

10

barrybendi
barry-bendy
bicorporal
cinquefoil

Clarenceux
coat-of-arms
cross-patée
difference
emblazoner
empalement
escalloped
escutcheon
fesse-point
fleur-de-lis
fleur-de-lys
king-at-arms
knighthood
pursuivant
quartering
quatrefoil
quintefoil
rebatement
surmounted

11 AND OVER

bend-sinister (12)
bendy-sinister (13)
bicapitated (11)
College of Arms (13)
counter-paled (12)
counter-passant (14)
countervair (11)
cross-crosslet (13)
cross-fleury (11)
cross-patencée (13)
Earl Marshal (11)
emblazonment (12)
engrailment (11)
escarbuncle (11)
escutcheoned (12)
garde-visure (11)
Garter King of Arms (16)
grant of arms (11)
heraldic emblem (14)
honour point (11)
inescutcheon (12)
Lyon King at Arms (14)
marshalling (11)
quarter arms (11)
Somerset herald (14)
transfluent (11)
unscutcheoned (13)

Law sittings

Hilary (6)   Easter (6)   Trinity (7)   Michaelmas (10)

Names: boys

Including abbreviations, nicknames, and some common foreign names.

3

Abe
Alf
Ali
Ben
Bob
Boy
Col
Dai

Dan
Dec
Don
Eli
Ely
Gus
Guy
Hal
Hay
Hew

Ian
Ira
Ivo
Jay
Jem
Jim
Job
Joe
Jon
Jos

Ken
Kid
Len
Leo
Mac
Mat
Max
Mee
Ned
Nye

Pan
Pat
Pip
Ray
Rea
Reg
Rex
Rod
Roy
Sam
Sid
Tam
Ted
Tim
Tom
Vic

4

Abel
Adam
Agar
Alan
Alec
Algy
Ally
Alma
Alva
Amos
Andy
Axel
Bald
Bart
Beau
Bede
Bell
Bert
Bill
Boyd
Buck
Bury
Cain
Carl
Cary
Cass
Ciro
Dahl
Deri
Dick
Dirk
Dion
Duff
Duke
Earl
Eddy
Eden
Edye
Elon
Emil
Eric
Eros
Esau
Esra
Euan
Evan
Ewen
Eyre
Ezra
Fitz
Flem
Fred
Fulk
Gary
Glen
Glyn

Goth
Gwyn
Hans
Hope
Hugh
Hugo
Hume
Hyam
Iain
Ifor
Ikey
Ioan
Iohn
Ivan
Ivor
Jack
Jake
Jean
Jess
Jock
Joel
Joey
John
Josh
Juan
Jude
Karl
Kaye
Keir
Kemp
Kent
King
Lacy
Leon
Leri
Lexy
Loel
Luke
Lyle
Lynd
Lyon
Marc
Mark
Matt
Mick
Mike
Muir
Neil
Nero
Nick
Noah
Noel
Ogie
Olaf
Orme
Otho
Otis
Otto
Owen
Page
Paul
Penn
Pery
Pete
Phil
Pung
René
Rhys
Riou
Rory
Ross
Saul
Sean
Seth
Stan
Theo

Toby
Tony
Vane
Vere
Walt
Will
Wing
Winn
Wray
Wynn
Yule

5

Aaron
Abdul
Abner
Abram
Airay
Alban
Albat
Algie
Allan
Alred
Alroy
Alves
Alwin
Alwyn
Amand
André
Angus
Anson
Anton
Archy
Ariel
Askew
Athol
Aubyn
Aurei
Aymar
Baden
Barry
Barty
Basil
Beaty
Bermy
Berty
Bevis
Billy
Bobby
Booth
Boris
Brian
Bruce
Bryan
Bunny
Cairn
Caius
Candy
Carew
Carne
Carol
Cecil
Clare
Claud
Clive
Clyde
Colet
Colin
Conan
Cosmo
Cyril
Cyrus
Dacre
Daddy

Dadoo
Damon
Darch
Darcy
D'arcy
David
Davie
Denis
Denny
Denys
Derby
Derek
Dicky
Drake
Drogo
Earle
Eddie
Edgar
Edwin
Edwyn
Eille
Eldon
Eliab
Ellis
Eliot
Elsye
Emery
Emile
Enoch
Ernie
Ernst
Evans
Ewart
Eyles
Felix
Franc
Frank
Franz
Frith
Fritz
Garth
Gavin
Geoff
Glyde
Glynn
Govan
Grant
Guido
Harry
Haydn
Hebel
Henri
Henry
Herne
Heron
Hiram
Hyman
Hymie
Iltyd
Inigo
Innes
Isaac
Jabez
Jacky
Jacob
Jaime
James
Jamie
Jason
Jemmy
Jerry
Jesse
Jevan
Jewel
Jimmy
Johan

Jonah	Speke	Crease	Hector
Jonas	Starr	Crusoe	Hedley
Jules	Steve	Curran	Henryk
Keith	Storm	Dallas	Henzel
Kenny	Tabor	Damian	Herman
Kevin	Taffy	Daniel	Hervey
Larry	Teddy	Dansil	Hilary
Leigh	Titus	Delves	Hilton
Lewin	Tommy	Declan	Hinton
Lewis	Trant	Demian	Hobart
Lexie	Tubby	Dennis	Holman
Lisle	Tudor	Dermot	Horace
Lloyd	Ulick	Derric	Howard
Louis	Usher	Dickie	Howell
Luigi	Wahab	Donald	Hubert
Lyall	Wally	Dougal	Hylton
Lynch	Willy	Dryden	Ignace
Major	Wolfe	Dudley	Inglis
Manly	Wyatt	Dugald	Irvine
Massy	Wylie	Duggie	Israel
Mavor	Wynne	Duncan	Jackey
Mayor	Wyvil	Dundas	Jackie
Meyer	Yorke	Dunlop	Jacomb
Micky		Earley	Jairus
Miles		Edmond	Janion
Monty	**6**	Edmund	Japhet
Moses		Eduard	Jasper
Moule	Adolph	Edward	Jerome
Myles	Adrian	Egbert	Jervis
Myrie	Aeneas	Eggert	Jeston
Neill	Albert	Eldred	Johann
Nigel	Albion	Elliot	Johnny
Odden	Alexis	Ernest	Joseph
Oprin	Alfred	Erroll	Joshua
Oriel	Alston	Ervine	Josiah
Orpen	Amilek	Esmond	Julian
Oscar	Andrew	Eugene	Julien
Osman	Angelo	Evelyn	Julius
Oswyn	Anselm	Fabian	Justin
Paddy	Anthon	Felton	Kersey
Paget	Antony	Fergus	Kirwan
Paton	Archer	Forbes	Laddie
Pedro	Archie	Franck	Lamley
Pelan	Armand	Freddy	Lawley
Percy	Arnold	Garnet	Leslie
Perry	Arthur	Gasper	Lionel
Peter	Aubrey	Gaston	Loftus
Phené	August	George	Lucien
Piers	Austin	Gerald	Ludwig
Power	Averil	Gerard	Lupton
Punch	Aylmer	Gideon	Luther
Ralph	Alywin	Gilbee	Magnus
Ramon	Balbus	Giulio	Mansel
Raoul	Baliol	Godwin	Marcel
Remus	Barney	Gonvil	Marcus
Renée	Baston	Gordon	Marten
Rider	Bedwyr	Graeme	Martin
Robin	Bennie	Graham	Mattos
Roden	Berend	Gregan	Mauris
Roger	Bertie	Gregor	Melvin
Rolfe	Blosse	Grizel	Merlin
Rollo	Braham	Grogan	Merrik
Romeo	Briton	Gunner	Mervyn
Romer	Brodie	Gunter	Mickie
Rowan	Brutus	Gustof	Millis
Royce	Bryden	Gwilym	Milton
Rufus	Bulwer	Hallam	Minden
Ryder	Caesar	Hamish	Montie
Sandy	Calvin	Hamlet	Moritz
Saxon	Carlos	Hamlyn	Morris
Scott	Caspar	Harold	Morvyn
Serge	Cedric	Harrel	Mostyn
Shane	Cicero	Harris	Murphy
Silas	Claude	Harrow	Murray
Simon	Conrad	Hayden	Nainby
Speed	Conway	Haydon	Nairne

Napier
Nathan
Nelson
Nevile
Nevill
Nickel
Nicols
Ninian
Norman
Norris
Norton
Nowell
Oliver
Onslow
Osbert
Osmond
Oswald
Pascoe
Pelham
Philip
Pierre
Powell
Prince
Rafael
Ramage
Ramsay
Randle
Ranson
Raphel
Ratsey
Rawden
Rayner
Reggie
Rendle
Reuben
Rhodes
Rippin
Robbie
Robert
Roddie
Rodger
Roland
Ronald
Rowley
Rowlie
Royden
Rudolf
Rupert
Samson
Samuel
Sander
Saurin
Sefton
Selwyn
Seumas
Shafto
Sidney
Simeon
Simons
Sinbad
Square
Squire
Steven
Stiven
St. John
Stuart
Sydney
Thomas
Tizard
Tobias
Trefor
Trevor
Vashon
Verney
Vernon
Vicary

Victor
Vivian
Vyvyan
Wallis
Walter
Warren
Watkin
Wesley
Willem
Willie
Wolsey
Yehudi
Xavier

7

Abraham
Ackroyd
Ainslie
Aladdin
Alfonso
Alister
Almeric
Alsager
Amadeus
Ambrose
Anatole
Andries
Aneurin
Anthony
Antoine
Antonio
Artemas
Artemus
Auguste
Baldwin
Balfour
Barclay
Barnaby
Barnard
Beaufoi
Bernard
Bertram
Berwald
Buckler
Burnard
Calvert
Cameron
Carlyon
Catesby
Charles
Charley
Chawner
Chester
Chewton
Clayton
Clement
Clinton
Compton
Connell
Crispin
Cyprian
Dalison
Dalziel
Dandini
Delancy
Denison
Derrick
Desmond
Dillwyn
Dominic
Donovan
Douglas
Downing
Duerdin

Eardley
Edouard
Emanuel
Emilius
Ephraim
Etienne
Eustace
Everard
Faraday
Faulder
Fielder
FitzRoy
Francis
Frankie
Freddie
Gabriel
Gaspard
Geoffry
Geraint
Gervais
Gervase
Gilbert
Gilmour
Gladwyn
Gloster
Godfrey
Goronwy
Grahame
Gregory
Gunther
Gustave
Hadrian
Herbert
Hermann
Hewlett
Hilaire
Hildred
Horatio
Humbert
Humphry
Ibrahim
Ingleby
Isidore
Jackson
Jacques
Jaffray
Jalland
Jeffrey
Jocelyn
Justice
Kenneth
Knyvett
Lachlan
Lambart
Lambert
Lennard
Leonard
Leopold
Lindsay
Lindsey
Lorimer
Lucifer
Ludovic
Madison
Malcolm
Matthew
Maurice
Maxwell
Maynard
Merrick
Michael
Montagu
Neville
Nicolas
Orlando
Orpheus

Orville
Osborne
Paladin
Patrick
Perseus
Pheroze
Phineas
Pierrot
Quentin
Quintin
Randall
Ranulph
Raphael
Raymond
Raymund
Redvers
Reynard
Richard
Roderic
Rodolph
Romulus
Ronayne
Rowland
Rudolph
Rudyard
Russell
Rutland
Sergius
Seymour
Shachel
Sheldon
Sigmund
Solomon
Spencer
Spenser
Stanley
St. Aubyn
St. Clair
Stenson
Stephen
Steuart
Stewart
St. Leger
Terence
Tertius
Timothy
Trenham
Ughtred
Ulysses
Umberto
Vaughan
Vauncey
Vincent
Wallace
Warwick
Westley
Wilfred
Wilfrid
Wilhelm
William
Winston
Wyndham
Ximenes
Zachary
Zebedee

8

Achilles
Adolphus
Alasdair
Alastair
Algernon
Alisdair
Alistair

Aloysius
Alphonse
Alphonso
Annesley
Antonius
Aristide
Augustus
Aurelius
Balliser
Bancroft
Banister
Barnabas
Bartlemy
Beaumont
Bedivere
Belgrave
Benjamin
Bernardi
Bertrand
Campbell
Carleton
Champion
Charnock
Clarence
Clementi
Clements
Clifford
Crauford
Crawford
Cuthbert
Diarmaid
Dominick
Ebenezer
Emmanuel
Ethelred
Faithful
FitzHugh
Florizel
François
Franklin
Frederic
Geoffrey
Geoffroy
Giovanni
Guiseppe
Greville
Gustavus
Hamilton
Harcourt
Harrison
Havelock
Herbrand

Hereward
Hezekiah
Horatius
Humphrey
Ignatius
Immanuel
Ironside
Jeremiah
Jonathan
Joscelyn
Josephus
Kingsley
Lancelot
Laurence
Lavallin
Lawrance
Lawrence
Leonhard
Leonidas
Llewelyn
Llywelyn
Lutwyche
Maddison
Maitland
Marshall
Martival
Meredith
Montague
Mortimer
Nicholas
Octavius
Oliphant
Ormiston
Oughtred
Paulinus
Perceval
Percival
Peregrin
Peterkin
Philemon
Randolph
Randulph
Reginald
Robinson
Roderick
Ruaraidh
Sandford
Scoltock
Secundus
Septimus
Sherlock
Siegmund

Sinclair
Spensley
Stafford
St. George
Sylvanus
Thaddeus
Theobald
Theodore
Trelawny
Valdimar
Vladimir
Wolseley

9

Abernethy
Abimeleck
Alaistair
Alexander
Allardyce
Almosnino
Alphonsus
Arbuthnot
Archibald
Aristotle
Armstrong
Athelstan
Augustine
Bartimeus
Beauchamp
Christian
Constable
Cornelius
Courtenay
Courteney
Creighton
Demetrius
Dionysius
Ethelbert
Ferdinand
Fortescue
Francisco
Frederick
Gascoigne
Glanville
Granville
Hazledine
Honoratus
Josceline
Llewellyn

Mackenzie
Marmaduke
Martineau
Nathaniel
Outhwaite
Peregrine
Rodriguez
Rupprecht
Sackville
Salvatore
Sebastian
Siegfried
Sigismund
Stanislas
Sylvester
Thaddeus
Theodoric
Valentine
Valentino
Wilbraham
Zachariah
Zechariah

10 AND OVER

Athanasius (10)
Athelstane (10)
Barrington (10)
Bartholomew (11)
Carmichael (10)
Chesterfield (12)
Christopher (11)
Constantine (11)
Cruickshank (11)
Fitzherbert (11)
Fitzpatrick (11)
Haliburton (10)
Hildebrand (10)
Llewhellin (10)
Maximilian (10)
Pierrepont (10)
Ravenscroft (11)
Sacheverel (10)
Skeffington (11)
Somerville (10)
Stanislaus (10)
Theodosius (10)
Theophilus (10)
Tyrrhenian (10)
Washington (10)
Willoughby (10)

Names: girls
Including abbreviations, nicknames, and some common foreign names.

3

Ada
Ame
Amy
Ann
Ave
Bee
Dot
Eda
Ena
Eva
Eve
Fay
Flo
Gay
Heë

Ida
Ina
Isa
Ivy
Iza
Jen
Joy
Kay
Kit
Liz
Lot
Mai
May
Meg
Nan
Pam
Pat

Peg
Pen
Ray
Rio
Sue
Una
Val
Viv
Yda
Zia
Zoë

4

Aase
Aimé

Alba
Alma
Alys
Anna
Anne
Anny
Avis
Baba
Babs
Bebe
Bess
Beth
Caré
Cely
Clea
Cleo
Cora

Dawn
Dido
Dodo
Dora
Edie
Edna
Edye
Ella
Elma
Elsa
Else
Emma
Emmy
Enid
Erna
Esmé
Etta
Etty
Evie
Fifi
Gaby
Gage
Gail
Gene
Gola
Gwen
Gwyn
Hebe
Hope
Ilse
Inez
Ioné
Iris
Irma
Isla
Isma
Ivey
Jane
Jean
Jess
Jill
Joan
Judy
June
Kate
Katy
Kaye
Lala
Leah
Lena
Lila
Lily
Lina
Lisa
Lita
Liza
Lois
Lola
Lucy
Lulu
Lynn
Maie
Mana
Mary
Maud
Meta
Mimi
Mina
Moll
Mona
Muff
Muir
Myra
Nell
Nena
Neva

Niki
Nina
Nino
Nita
Nora
Olga
Oona
Pola
Puss
Rena
Rita
Rosa
Rose
Rosy
Ruby
Ruth
Sara
Sita
Spry
Suky
Susy
Syme
Tess
Tina
Vera
Vida
Viki
Vita
Viva
Zena
Zita
Zooe

5

Abbie
Adela
Adele
Aggie
Agnes
Ailsa
Aimée
Alice
Aline
Altha
Angel
Anita
Annie
April
Arbel
Arden
Avice
Avril
Barbi
Becky
Bella
Belle
Berta
Beryl
Bessy
Betty
Biddy
Bobby
Budie
Buena
Bunty
Carol
Carré
Caryl
Cathy
Cecil
Celia
Chloe
Chune
Circe

Cissy
Clair
Clara
Clare
Coral
Daisy
Delia
Della
Denes
Diana
Diane
Dilys
Dinah
Dodie
Dolly
Donie
Donna
Dorah
Doris
Dreda
Dulce
Edith
Effie
Eilsa
Elena
Elfie
Elise
Eliza
Ellen
Ellie
Elsie
Emily
Emmie
Erica
Essie
Ethel
Ettie
Faith
Fanny
Feona
Filia
Fiona
Fleur
Flora
Freda
Gabie
Gemma
Gerty
Gipsy
Grace
Greer
Greta
Gussy
Hazel
Helen
Henny
Hetty
Hilda
Honor
Hulda
Hylda
Idina
Innes
Irene
Isold
Janet
Janey
Janie
Janny
Jenny
Jessy
Joann
Joyce
Julia
Julie
Karen

Karin
Katey
Katie
Kitty
Laila
Laura
Lelia
Letty
Lilia
Lilly
Lizzy
Lorna
Lotta
Lotty
Lucia
Lucie
Lydia
Lynne
Mabel
Madge
Maeve
Magda
Maggy
Mamie
Manie
Manon
Maria
Marie
Matty
Maude
Mavis
Meave
Megan
Mercy
Merry
Milly
Minna
Mitzi
Moira
Molly
Morag
Moyra
Myrle
Nancy
Nanny
Naomi
Nelly
Nessa
Nesta
Netta
Ninie
Ninny
Niobe
Norah
Norma
Olive
Pansy
Patsy
Patty
Paula
Pearl
Peggy
Penny
Phebe
Pippa
Pixie
Polly
Poppy
Queen
Renée
Rhoda
Rhona
Robin
Rosie
Sadie
Sally

Sarah
Sasie
Sonia
Susan
Susie
Sybil
Tania
Tanya
Tanis
Teify
Terka
Thora
Trudy
Urith
Venis
Venus
Vesta
Vicki
Viola
Vivie
Wanda
Wendy
Zeeta
Zelia

6

Agatha
Aileen
Airlie
Alicia
Alison
Almond
Althea
Amanda
Amelia
Amelie
Anabel
Angela
Anthea
Armyne
Astrid
Audrey
Aurora
Awdrey
Azelle
Babbie
Beatie
Benita
Bertha
Bessie
Bettie
Bibbie
Biddie
Billie
Binnie
Birdie
Blanch
Blonde
Bobbie
Brenda
Brigid
Carmen
Carrie
Cecile
Cecily
Celina
Cherry
Cicely
Cissie
Claire
Connie
Daphne
Davina
Debbie

Denise
Doreen
Dorice
Dulcie
Editha
Edwina
Edythe
Eileen
Elaine
Elinor
Emilie
Esther
Eunice
Evelyn
Eyleen
Fannie
Fatima
Felice
Galena
Gerrie
Gertie
Gleana
Gladys
Gloria
Godiva
Gracie
Greeba
Gretel
Gussie
Gwenda
Gwynne
Hattie
Hannah
Helena
Hester
Hilary
Honora
Honour
Ileana
Imelda
Imogen
Ingrid
Ioanna
Isabel
Ishbel
Isobel
Isolde
Jackie
Janice
Jeanie
Jeanne
Jemima
Jennie
Jessie
Joanne
Joanna
Judith
Juliet
Kirsty
Lalage
Lallie
Lassie
Leonie
Lesley
Leslie
Lettie
Levina
Lilian
Lilias
Lillah
Lillie
Lizzie
Lorina
Lottie
Louisa
Louise

Lucilla
Lucile
Maggie
Maidie
Maimie
Maisie
Marcia
Margot
Marian
Marion
Marnie
Martha
Marthe
Mattie
Maxine
Melita
Mercia
Meriel
Mignon
Millie
Mimosa
Minnie
Miriam
Mollie
Monica
Moulie
Muriel
Murtle
Myrtle
Nadine
Nancie
Nancye
Nellie
Nelsie
Nessie
Nettie
Nicole
Noreen
Odette
Olivia
Paddie
Pamela
Parnel
Pattie
Pegeen
Peggie
Pernel
Persis
Petula
Phoebe
Pinkie
Poppet
Poppie
Popsie
Portia
Psyche
Rachel
Ramona
Regina
Renira
Richie
Robina
Rosina
Rowena
Roxana
Sabina
Sabine
Salome
Sandra
Sappho
Seabel
Selina
Seonad
Sharon
Sheena
Sheila

Sicele
Simone
Sophia
Sophie
Stella
Sybell
Sylvia
Tamsin
Teresa
Tertia
Tessie
Thalia
Thecla
Thelma
Tootie
Trixie
Ulrica
Ursula
Verity
Verona
Violet
Vivian
Vivien
Vyvyen
Willow
Winnie
Yvette
Yvonne

7

Abigail
Adeline
Alberta
Alethea
Alfrida
Ameline
Ankaret
Annabel
Annette
Anstice
Antonia
Antonie
Ariadne
Asenath
Athenia
Augusta
Aurelia
Babette
Barbara
Barbary
Beatrix
Belinda
Bettina
Billy Jo
Blanche
Blodwen
Blossom
Bridget
Camilla
Cecilia
Cherrie
Clarice
Claudia
Colette
Colleen
Coralie
Cynthia
Damozel
Darling
Deborah
Deirdre
Delysia
Diamond
Dolores

294

Dorinda
Dorothe
Dorothy
Dorrice
Dulcima
Eleanor
Elfreda
Elfrida
Ellenor
Ellinor
Elspeth
Emerald
Emiline
Estelle
Etienne
Eudoxia
Eugenia
Eugenie
Evaline
Eveline
Fayette
Felicia
Fenella
Feodora
Florrie
Flossie
Frances
Georgia
Gertrud
Gillian
Gladden
Gwennie
Gwenyth
Gwladys
Gwyneth
Gwynnie
Harriet
Heather
Hellena
Horatia
Hypatia
Janette
Janitha
Jessica
Jocelyn
Johanna
Juliana
Lavinia
Leoline
Leonora
Letitia
Lettice
Lettuce
Lillian
Lillias
Lisbeth
Lucille
Mabelle
Mafalda
Margery
Marjery
Marjory
Matilda
Maureen
Melanie
Michèle
Mildred
Minerva
Miralda
Miranda
Myfanwy
Nanuoya
Natalie
Natasha
Nigella
Ninette

Octavia
Ophelia
Ottilie
Palmyra
Pandora
Paulina
Pauline
Perdita
Phillis
Phyllis
Queenie
Rebecca
Rhodena
Ricarda
Roberta
Rosalie
Rosella
Rosetta
Rosette
Shambra
Sidonia
Susanna
Susanne
Suzanne
Sybilla
Tabitha
Tatiana
Theresa
Therese
Titania
Tootles
Valerie
Valetta
Vanessa
Venetia
Winsome
Yolande
Zirphie

8

Adelaide
Adrienne
Albertha
Amabelle
Angelica
Angelina
Angeline
Angharad
Arabella
Araminta
Atalanta
Beatrice
Berenice
Cammilla
Carlotta
Carolina
Caroline
Cathleen
Catriona
Christie
Chrystal
Clemency
Clotilde
Consuelo
Cordelia
Cornelia
Dorothea
Dorothie
Drusilla
Dulcinia
Eleanora
Eleanore
Elfriede
Ellaline

Emmeline
Euphemia
Evelinda
Everalda
Felicity
Filomena
Florence
Francine
Georgina
Germaine
Gertrude
Gretchen
Grizelda
Grizelle
Harriett
Hermione
Hortense
Isabella
Jeanette
Jennifer
Jeromina
Julianna
Julietta
Juliette
Katharin
Kathleen
Laburnum
Laetitia
Lavender
Lorraine
Lucretia
Madeline
Magdalen
Marcella
Marcelle
Margaret
Marianne
Mariette
Marigold
Marjorie
Marvella
Michelle
Mireille
Morwenna
Murielle
Nathalie
Nathanie
Patience
Patricia
Penelope
Petronel
Philippa
Primrose
Prudence
Prunella
Raymonde
Rebeccah
Reinagle
Reinelde
Rosalind
Rosamond
Rosamund
Rosemary
Samantha
Sapphire
Seabelle
Sheelagh
Susannah
Tallulah
Theodora
Veronica
Victoria
Violetta
Virginia
Vivienne
Vourneen

Winifred

9

Albertine
Alexandra
Ambrosine
Anastasia
Annabelle
Britannia
Cassandra
Catherine
Celestine
Charlotte
Christian
Christina
Christine
Clarenore
Cleopatra
Clothilde
Columbine
Constance
Corisande
Desdemona
Eglantine
Elisabeth
Elizabeth
Ermengard
Ernestine
Esmeralda
Esperance
Francisca
Frederica
Gabrielle
Georgiana
Geraldine
Guglielma
Guinivere
Gwendolen
Gwenllian
Harriette
Henrietta
Henriette
Hortensia
Hyacinthe
Iphigenia
Josephine
Kathailin
Katharine
Katherine
Madeleine
Magdalena
Magdalene
Maraquita
Margarita
Melisande
Millicent
Pepronill
Pierrette
Priscilla
Rosabelle
Rosaritta
Stephanie
Theodosia
Thomasina
Valentine
Winefride

10 AND 11

Alexandrina (11)
Antoinette (10)
Bernadette (10)

Christabel (10)
Christiana (10)
Christobel (10)
Cinderella (10)
Clementina (10)
Clementine (10)
Constantia (10)
Desiderata (10)

Ermentrude (10)
Ethelwynne (10)
Evangelina (10)
Evangeline (10)
Fredericka (10)
Gwendolene (10)
Gwendoline (10)
Hildegarde (10)

Irmentrude (10)
Jacqueline (10)
Margaretta (10)
Margherita (10)
Marguerite (10)
Petronella (10)
Philippina (10)
Wilhelmina (10)

Nine Muses

Calliope (8) *epic*
Clio (4) *history*
Erato (5) *love songs*
Euterpe (7) *lyric poetry*
Melpomene (9) *tragedy*

Polyhymnia (10) *sacred poetry*
Terpsichore (11) *choral song and dance*
Thalia (6) *comedy and idyllic poetry*
Urania (6) *astronomy*

Palindromes

3

aba
aga
aha!
ala
ama
ana
asa
ava
bab
bib
bob
bub
dad
did
dod
dud
eke
ere
eve
ewe
eye
gag
gig

gog
hah!
huh!
mam
mim
mum
nan
non
nun
oho!
oxo
pap
pep
pip
pop
pup
s.o.s.
tat
tit
tot
tut!
wow
zuz

4

abba
anna
boob
deed
dood
ecce
keek
ma'am
noon
otto
peep
poop
sees
toot

5

alula
anana
civic
kayak
level

madam
minim
put-up
radar
refer
rotor
sagas
sexes
shahs
sohos
solos
tenet

6 AND OVER

Able was I ere I saw Elba (19)
marram (6)
pull-up (6)
redder (6)
repaper (7)
reviver (7)
rotator (7)
terret (6)

Seven Deadly Sins

accidie (7)
acedia (6) } *sloth*
anger (5)
covetousness (12)
envy (4)
gluttony (8)
lust (4)
pride (5)
sloth (5)
vainglory (9) *pride*

Seven Virtues

charity (7)
faith (5)
fortitude (9)
hope (4)
justice (7)
love (4) *charity*
prudence (8)
temperance (10)

Seven Wonders of the World

The Pyramids of Egypt
The Hanging Gardens of Babylon
The Tomb of Mausolus
The Temple of Diana at Ephesus
The Colossus of Rhodes
The Statue of Zeus by Phidias
The Pharos of Alexandria
          or
The Palace of Cyrus (cemented with gold)

Signs of the Zodiac

Aquarius (8), *Water-bearer*
Aries (5) *Ram*
Cancer (6) *Crab*
Capricorn (9), *Goat*
Capricornus (11), *Goat*
Gemini (6), *Twins*
Leo (3), *Lion*
Libra (5), *Balance*
Pisces (6), *Fishes*
Sagittarius (11), *Archer*
Scorpio (7), *Scorpion*
Taurus (6), *Bull*
Virgo (5), *Virgin*

Index